STUDY OF PALAEOART OF THE WORLD

A quest for understanding the evolution of human constructs of reality

STUDY OF PALAEOART OF THE WORLD

A Quest for Understanding the Evolution of Human Constructs of Reality

A volume in honour of

Professor Robert G. Bednarik

Convener, International Federation of Rock Art Organisations (IFRAO)

Editor

GIRIRAJ KUMAR

Prof. in Rock Art Science and Indian Culture

President, Rock Art Society of India (RASI)

PATHAK PUBLISHER AND DISTRIBUTORS

New Delhi (INDIA)

STUDY OF PALAEOART OF THE WORLD

A Quest for Understanding the Evolution of Human Constructs of Reality

Editor : Giriraj Kumar
Prof. in Rock Art Science and Indian Culture
President, Rock Art Society of India (RASI)

ISBN : 978-93-91952-70-9

Price : 6500/-

First Edition: 2024

Book cover photo: Prof. Robert G. Bednarik with Dr Ram Krishna, studying KEM in the early cupules in Daraki-Chattan Cave, Indragarh in Chambal basin, India.

Photo by Prof. Giriraj Kumar, 2016.

Book cover design: By Hridayshri, Artist and Communication Designer, India.

Published by :
PATHAK PUBLISHER AND DISTRIBUTORS
E-6/33c & 34, Ground Floor, Sangam Vihar
New Delhi-110080
E-mail: pathakppd@gmail.com
Mob 9818085794, 9667766461
In Association with :
RESEARCH INDIA PRESS

Typographic Design by: G. R. Sharma

Printed by Thomson India Ltd.

Robert G. Bednarik

Prof. Robert G. Bednarik, Australia, is the Convener and Editor-in-Chief of the International Federation of Rock Art Organisations and is affiliated with Hebei Normal University, China. His principal research interests are the origins of the human ability to create constructs of reality, the evolution of humans, and a variety of fields providing supplementary information in that quest, including the world's rock art. He has produced nearly 1500 academic publications.

CONTENTS

Part 1: Robert G. Bednarik and his Contribution to Rock Art Discipline

Part 2: Latest Research on Palaeoart of the World

20 August 2023

PREFACE

Study of palaeoart of the world: A quest for understanding the evolution of human constructs of reality, is a volume in honour of Professor Robert G. Bednarik, Convener, International Federation of Rock Art Organisations (IFRAO). It consists of 28 articles by 25 experienced scholars, which have been presented in two parts. Part I comprises 11 articles highlighting the personality, contributions, and achievements of Robert G. Bednarik in the field of palaeoart research and sweet memories of working with him by different scholars from all over the world. Part II contains 17 articles on study of Palaeoart of the world by veteran scholars who are highly knowledgeable and experts in their field of research. The areas covered are rock art research, the cognitive and cultural development of humans, the development of the brain, cognitive capabilities, language, different aspects of the cultures of humans and their reflections in rock art, Stone Age art and communication design, scientific dating and other areas of rock art science such as protection, conservation, and management of rock art heritage sites, etc. The articles echo the life-long experiences and in-depth study of the subjects in palaeoart by the scholars from different parts of the world.

The papers in this volume reflect the dedication and deep involvement of the scholars for understanding the development of cultural landscape and human behaviour as an integral part of the nature through palaeoart. The volume is like a nectar of the experiences and learnings of highly experienced scholars. Going through it takes the reader to different horizons of understanding the concepts of reality in the journey of human evolution. The volume highlights the expeditions of the scientific research and development made in the discipline of palaeoart research during the last four and half decades. The vision and mission presented in this volume are going to give a new direction and energy to palaeoart research in the world.

Prof. Robert G. Bednarik from Australia is an inspiration to many scholars working on the scientific study of palaeoart and allied disciplines in all the continents of the world except Antarctica. He is highly respected and loved by scholars of all ages, having immensely contributed to establishing the rock art discipline on a scientific footing and securing its steady growth. To disseminate rock art science globally, he founded Australian Rock Art Research Association (AURA) in 1983 and its international journal, *Rock Art Research,* in 1984. In order to provide a global platform to all the scholars in this field, he established the International Federation of Rock Art Organisations (IFRAO) at the first AURA Congress in Darwin, Australia, in 1988, which has over 60 members at present. *Rock Art Research* is a top-ranked peer-reviewed journal of IFRAO on the scientific study of rock art and allied disciplines worldwide.

Hence, it would be a fitting opportunity to present Prof. Bednarik a volume brought out in his honour and felicitate him on his birthday on 6th April 2024 when he is turning 80. I discussed this idea with my friends and the scholars who worked with Robert in all parts of the world. Almost all of them happily agreed to the proposal and contributed their valuable articles lovingly on time. I had the honour to edit and combine them in the form of the present volume.

Prof. Giriraj Kumar
Prof. in Rock Art Science and Indian Culture
President, Rock Art Society of India (RASI)
E-mail; girirajrasi.india@gmail.com

ACKNOWLEDGEMENT

Study of palaeoart of the world: A quest for understanding the evolution of human constructs of reality is a volume brought out in honour of Prof. Robert G. Bednarik, Convener, IFRAO. It is a result of the contributions and cooperation made by many scholars on my invitation; hence, it is my duty to acknowledge them. My foremost and heartfelt thanks go to Prof. Robert G. Bednarik himself who kindly accepted my proposal to bring out a felicitation volume in his honour. He also helped me to contact the right persons from all over the world who have been working in different fields of learning about understanding the evolution of human constructs of reality through rock art. Most of them worked with Robert and some of them were familiar with him through his scholarly work. All of them were very happy with the idea and most of them lovingly contributed their personal experiences of working with Robert and their scholarly articles to this volume. Some of the senior scholars faced difficulties in meeting the editorial norms. But, all of them cooperated affectionately. Hence, I express my deep gratitude to all of them. My apology to be strict to get them to follow the editorial norms. It was all because I wanted to see the wonderful results in the form of the present volume.

My special thanks are due to Hridayshri, Artist and Communication Designer, India, who beautifully designed the book cover reflecting the spirit of the book. I also want to thank shri Suman Kumar Pathak, CEO, Pathak Publisher and Distributors, New Delhi, who took pains to get the volume published in a lovely getup with global standards.

The Editor

Part 1

ROBERT G. BEDNARIK AND HIS CONTRIBUTION TO ROCK ART DISCIPLINE

Study of Palaeoart of the World, Giriraj Kumar, pp. 3-14

1

ROBERT G. BEDNARIK: CONTRIBUTIONS AND ACHIEVEMENTS

THE EDITOR

Prof. Robert G. Bednarik is a cool and calm person like a *rishi* (a person in search of truth of life), fully confident in himself and completely devoted to his mission to understand scientifically the evolution of human constructs of reality through rock art. He was born in Baden, Austria on 6 April in 1944, and has been an Australian citizen since 1970. He is the most-published archaeological-rock art author, currently 1480 publications (about half of them in refereed academic journals), which have appeared in 32 languages and include about 15 books. He has been the editor of several scientific journals and monograph series. Prof. Bednarik is a complete autodidact and regards Aboriginal elders as his only teachers.

His *principal interests* are in the origins of the human ability to create constructs of reality, in the evolution of humans, and in a variety of fields providing supplementary information in that quest. This includes the beginnings of art and language, and technological developments providing a measure of early human capacities, such as seafaring and the use of beads.

Current offices held

Convener and Editor, International Federation of Rock Art Organisations (IFRAO)

Secretary and Editor, Australian Rock Art Research Association (AURA)

Chair Professor, International Centre of Rock Art Dating (ICRAD), Hebei Normal University, Shijiazhuang, China

Managing Director, Archaeological Publications and Archaeological Soil Lab

National Coordinator of CAR (International Comité pour l'art Rupestre, ICOMOS)

Director, The First Mariners Expeditions

Bednarik has appeared in 19 film documentaries, presented about 240 papers at professional meetings and invited lectures, and has given about 545 interviews to the printed and electronic media, in many parts of the world.

Field research in various thematic and geographical areas: especially in central, northern, eastern, western and southern Europe; Siberia, India, China, Mongolia, Saudi Arabia, Indonesia, Canada, USA, Mexico, Caribbean, various South American countries, southern Africa, Morocco, all regions of Australia.

Innovations

First in the world to date rock art directly with radiometric methods (reprecipitated carbonates in Malangine Cave, Australia); developed first non-interfering rock art dating method (microerosion method, first applied at Lake Onega, Russia); introduced advanced statistics in Australian archaeology (Brainerd-Robinson method). Developed new techniques for assessing weathering of silica minerals, and for studying cave climate; invented an instrument to measure the porosity of rock; conducted first comprehensive study of wall markings in caves, first to investigate Pleistocene seafaring, established taphonomic logic in 1993, metamorphology in 1995, human auto-domestication hypothesis in 2008; discovered kinetic energy metamorphosis in 2015 and compressive-tensile rock markings in 2018; founded archaeo-tribology in 2019. Responsible for major scientific discoveries in various countries, including largest corpus of rock art (Dampier Archipelago, 1967-1970) and oldest known rock art sites in the world, first Palaeolithic art of China, first petroglyphs in central India, first Pleistocene rock art of central Europe, oldest Palaeolithic site of Austria (excavated and studied from 1962 to 2022) and much of the cave art of Australia. Founded Archaeological Soil Lab in 1980, Archaeological Publications and AURA in 1983, IFRAO in 1988. Campaigned actively for Aboriginal control of sites of Australian indigenous heritage.

Figure 1: As published by Time Magazine in 1989.

Figure 2: India in 1990, visiting the Maharajah of Kota. Rajasthan (photo: Giriraj Kumar).

Figure 3: Yinchuan, China, in 1991, with Tang Huisheng (centre) and Li Fushun (right).

Figure 4: India in 1994.

Figure 5: Discovering a stegodont tooth in West Timor in 1998 (photo: Peter Rogers).

Figure 6: Crossing the open sea on a Stone Age bamboo raft, 1998 (photo: Peter Rogers).

Figure 7: With Bedouin leader at Arabian rock art site, 2002 (photo: Majeed Khan).

Figure 8: At IFRAO Congress in Agra, India, 2004 (photo: Giriraj Kumar).

Figure 9: At rock art site in Utah, USA, 2013 (photo: Jean Clottes).

Figure 10: With Prof. Tang Huisheng, China (left) and Prof. Giriraj Kumar, India (in the centre), China, 2015.

Main publications of the past 20 years

2002. Paläolithische Felskunst in Deutschland? *Archäologische Informationen* 25(1-2): 107-117.

2003. Seafaring in the Pleistocene. *Cambridge Archaeological Journal* 13(1): 41-66.

2003. A figurine from the African Acheulian. *Current Anthropology* 44(3): 405-413.

2004. Interpretatsiya dannykh o proiskhozhdeii iskusstva (Interpreting the evidence for art crigins). *Arkheologiy, etnografiy i antropologiy Evraziy* (Ethnology and Anthropology of Eurasia) 20(4): 35-47.

2005. Middle Pleistocene beads and symbolism. *Anthropos* 100(2): 537-552.

2006. The Middle Palaeolithic engravings from Oldisleben, Germany. *Anthropologie* 44(2): 113-121.

2006. *Australian apocalypse*. The story of Australia's greatest cultural monument. Occasional AURA Publication 14, Australian Rock Art Research Association, Melbourne.

2007. The Late Pleistocene cultural shift in Europe. *Anthropos* 102(2): 347-370.

2008. Rock art. In D. M. Pearsall (ed.), *Encyclopedia of archaeology*, pp. 1940-1952. Academic Press, New York.

2008. The origins of symboling. *Signs* 2: 82-113,

2008. Cupules. *Rock Art Research* 25(1): 61-100.

2008. Pedogenetic dating of loess strata. *Journal of Archaeological Science* 35(12): 3124-3129.

2008. The mythical Moderns. *Journal of World Prehistory* 21(2): 85-102.

2008. The domestication of humans. *Anthropologie* 46(1): 1-17.

2008. Zur Seefahrt im Paläolithikum. *Ethnographisch-Archäologische Zeitschrift* 49(3): 257-270.

2009. Fluvial erosion of inscriptions and petroglyphs at Siega Verde, Spain. *Journal of Archaeological Science* 36: 2365–2373.

2010. Pleistocene rock art in Australia. *Anthropos* 105(1): 3-12.

2010 [Edited with R. Querejazu Lewis]. *Mysterious cup marks: proceedings of the First International Cupule Conference*. BAR International Series 2073, Archaeopress, Oxford

2010 [With A. Achrati, M. Consens, F. Coimbra, G. Dimitriadis, T. Huisheng, A. Muzzolini, D. Seglie and Y. A Sher]. *Rock art glossary: a multilingual dictionary*, second edition. Occasional AURA Publication 16, Australian Rock Art Research Association, Inc., Melbourne.

2011. Palaeoart of the Lower Palaeolithic. In Lybov Ermolenko (ed.), *Археология Южной Сибири. К 80-летию Я. А. Шера (Yakov Sher 80th Anniversary Volume)*, pp. 31-35. Kemerovo State University, Kemerovo.

2011. *The human condition*. Springer, New York. Hardcover, ISBN 978-1-4419-9352-6.

2011. The origins of human modernity. *Humanities* 1(1): 1-53; *http://www.mdpi.com/2076-0787/1/1/1/*

2012. The utility of schist in rock art studies. *Horizons in Earth Science Research* 8: 1-36.

2012. The Arabian horse in the context of world rock art. In M. Khan (ed.), *The Arabian horse: origin, development and history*, pp. 397-425. Layan Cultural Foundation, Riyadh.

2012. [With Patricia A. Helvenston] The nexus between neurodegeneration and advanced cognitive abilities *Anthropos* 107(2): 511-527.

2013. On the neuroscience of rock art interpretation. *Time and Mind: The Journal of Archaeology, Consciousness and Culture* 6(1): 37–40.

2013. Brain disorder and rock art. *Cambridge Archaeological Journal* 23(1): 69-81.

2013. *Creating the human past.* Archaeopress, Oxford. ISBN 978-1-905739-63-9.

2013. Myths about rock art. *Journal of Literature and Art Studies* 3(8): 482-500.

2013-14. Archaeology and rock art science. *Almogaren* 44-45: 57-72.

2014. Paleoart studies: scientific methods. In D. Fiore, I. Domingo and J. McDonald (eds), *Encyclopedia of global archaeology, Archaeology of Art Section*, pp. 5734-5740. Springer, New York.

2014. Australian paleoart. *Encyclopedia of global archaeology*, Geographical and Cultural Overview Essays, edited Marcel Otte and Rebecca Miller, pp. 677-686. Springer, New York.

2014. Exograms. *Rock Art Research* 31(1): 47-62.

2014. Doing with less: hominin brain atrophy. *HOMO — Journal of Comparative Human Biology* 65: 433-449; DOI: 10.1016/j.jchb.2014.06.001

2014. *The first mariners*, 1st edn. Research India Press, New Delhi, ISBN 978-93-5171-007-3.

2014. The beginnings of maritime travel. *Advances in Anthropology* 4: 209-221.

2014. *The first mariners*, 2nd edn. Lambert Academic Publishing, Saarbrücken, Germany, ISBN 978-3-659-63097-2.

2015. The tribology of cupules. *Geological Magazine* 152(4): 758-765; doi:10.1017/S0016756815000060.

2015. An etiology of Theory of Mind in deep time. In E. Sherwood (ed.), *Theory of Mind: development in children, brain mechanisms and social implications*, pp. 115-144. Nova Science Publishers, Inc., New York.

2015. Palaeoart of the Lower Palaeolithic. *Progress in Arts and Humanities* 1(1): 1-12.

2015. Prehistoria sin nacionalismo (Pre-History without nationalism). *ISTOR: Revista de Historia Internacional* 15(60): 13-36.

2015. Kinetic energy metamorphosis of rocks. In Benjamin Veress and Jozsi Szigethy (eds), *Horizons in Earth Science Research 13: 119-134. NOVA Science Publishers, New York.*

2015. Hominin mind and creativity. In Barbora Půtová and Václav Soukup (eds), *The genesis of creativity and the origin of the human mind*, pp. 35-44. Department of Culturology, The Faculty of Arts, Charles University. Karolinum Press, Prague.

2015. *The first mariners*, 3rd edn (e-book). Bentham Science Publishers, Oak Park, IL; eISBN: 978-1-68108-019-2, ISBN: 978-1-68108-020-8.

2016. Art in caves. *Zeitschrift für Geomorphologie* 60 (Suppl. 2): 139-152.

2016. *Understanding human behavior: theories, patterns and developments* (editor). Perspectives on Cognitive Psychology, Nova Biomedical, New York. ISBN 978-1-63485-174-9.

2016. [Edited with Danae Fiore, Mara Basile, Giriraj Kumar and Tang Huisheng] *Paleoart and materiality: the scientific study of rock art*. Archaeopress Publishing Ltd, Oxford, ISBN 978-1-78491-429-5.

2016. Rock art and pareidolia. *Rock Art Research* 33(2): 167-181.

2016. The science of cupules. *Archaeometry* 58(6): 899-911.

2016w. *Myths about rock art*. Archaeopress Publishing Ltd, Oxford. ISBN 978-1-78491-474-5.

2016. The earliest known logboats of China (with Tang Huisheng and Jin Anni). *International Journal of Nautical Archaeology* 45(2): 441-466.

2017. *Palaeoart of the Ice Age*. Éditions universitaires européennes, Saarbrücken. ISBN 978-3-639-56008-4.

2017. Equine petroglyphs in Europe. *Journal of Archaeological Science: Reports* 13: 222-228.

2017. Aniconism and the origins of palaeoart. *Religion* 47(3): 353-365; doi.org/10.1080/0048721X.2017.1288785.

2017. Pareidolia and rock art interpretation. *Anthropologie* 55(1–2): 101–117.

2017. Scientific investigations into Saudi Arabian rock art: a review. *Mediterranean Archaeology and Archaeometry* 17(4): 43-59.

2017 (1395 Shamsi). The human condition (2nd edn, in Persian: وضعیت انسان). Translated by Vahid Askerpour.

2017. Dating rock art via speleothems: a critical review of results. In Benjamin Veress and Jozsi Szigethy (eds), *Horizons in Earth Science Research, Volume 17, pp. 179-196. Nova Science Publishers, New York.* ISBN 978-1-53612-831-4.

2017. *Palaeoart of the Ice Age* (2nd edn). Cambridge Scholars Publishing, Newcastle upon Tyne.

2018. [With Tang H., G. Kumar, Jin A., Wu J. and Liu W.] The 2015 rock art missions in China. *Rock Art Research* 35(1): 25-34.

2018. [With V. Santos Junior, R. Valle, H. Lavalle and D. Lima de Oliveira] Direct dating of petroglyphs in Rio Grande Do Norte, Brazil. *Rock Art Research* 35(1): 85-97.

2018. About woolly rhinos in rock art. *International Newsletter on Rock Art* 82: 25-29.

2018. Characterization of petroglyphs. In Sandra L. López Varela (ed.), *The encyclopedia of archaeological sciences,* doi:10.1002/9781119188230.saseas0079. John Wiley & Sons, Inc., Hoboken.

2019. *Tribology in geology and archaeology*. Nova Science Publishers, New York. ISBN 978-1-53614-909-8.

2019. [With I. Liritzis, G. Kumar, G. Polymeris, I. Iliopoulos, V. Xanthopoulou, N. Zacharias, A. Vafiadou and M. Bratitsi] Daraki-Chattan rock art constrained OSL chronology and multianalytical techniques: a first pilot investigation. *Journal of Cultural Heritage* 37(May–June): 29-43; https://doi.org/10.1016/j.culher.2018.09.018.

2019. Rock metamorphosis by kinetic energy. *Emerging Science Journal* 3(5): 293-302. DOI: 10.28991/esj-2019-01192.

2019. Compressive-tensile rock markings. *Geological Magazine* 156(12): 2113-2116. DOI: 10.1017/S0016756819001079.

2019. The earliest petroglyphs in the world. In M. A. Devlet, G. G. Korol, O. S. Sovetova and E. A. Miklashevich (eds), *Изобразительные и технологические традиции ранних форм искусства. Памяти Е. Г. Дэвлет* (*Iconographic and technological traditions in early forms of art. In memory of E. G. Devlet*), pp. 85-100. Proceedings of the Siberian Association of Primitive Art Researchers, Vol. XII, ISBN 978-5-202-01433-8. Kuzbassvuzizdat, Kemerovo.

2020. *The domestication of humans*. Routledge, Abingdon and New York, ISBN: 978-0-367-89787-1 (hardback), ISBN: 978-1-003-02113-1 (ebook).

2020. [With Tang Huisheng, Jin Anni, Li Man, Fan Zhiyan, Liu Weipeng and Giriraj Kumar] The 2017 rock art mission in Hubei Province, China. *Rock Art Research* 37(1): 67–73.

2020. Archaeotribology: the interaction of surfaces in relative motion in archaeology. *Tribology International* 141: 106198; doi:10.1016/j.triboint.2020.106198.

2020. (With Tang Huisheng, Giriraj Kumar and Jin Anni) Rock art of Heilongjiang Province, China. *Journal of Archaeological Science: Reports* 31; doi:10.1016/j.jasrep.2020.102348.

2020. Petroglyphs of Victoria. *Proceedings of the Royal Society of Victoria* 131(1): 7–11; doi:10.1071/RS20001.

2020. 岩画科学—远古艺术的科学研究 (*Rock art science: the scientific study of palaeoart*, Chinese edition), transl. by Jin Anni. Shaanxi People's Education Press (Shaanxi Xinhua Publishing & Media Group), Xi'an.

2020. First Pleistocene rock art found in central Europe. *L'Anthropologie* 124(3): ; doi:10.1016/j.anthro.2020.102778.

2020. The roles of tribology in palaeoart study. *Rock Art Research* 37(2): 217-227.

2021. [With Tang Huisheng] Rock art dating by ^{230}Th/^{234}U analysis: an appraisal of Chinese case studies. *Archaeological and Anthropological Sciences* 13(1): 1-10; doi: 10.1007/s12520-020-01266-0.

2021. Ethnographic interpretation of rock art through rock inscriptions. *Rock Art Research* 38(1): 70-83.

2021. About the origins of the human ability to create constructs of reality. *Axiomathes* 31(5); doi:10.1007/s10516-021-09537-8.

2021. An etiology of human modernity. *Anthropological Review* 84(3): 337–357; doi:10.2478/anre-2021-0020.

2021. Direct dating of Chinese immovable cultural heritage. *Quaternary* 4: 42; doi:10.3390/quat4040042.

2022. Pleistocene rock art discovered in central Europe. *Rock Art Research* 39(1): 3-14.

2022. [With Arthur Saniotis and Maciej Henneberg] Auto-domestication hypothesis and the rise in mental disorders in modern humans. *Medical Hypotheses* 164: 110874; doi: 10.1016/j.mehy.2022.110874.

2022. [With Julien Benoit and Charles Helm] Manuports pre-date modern humans: a response to Wilkins et al. (2021). *South African Archaeological Bulletin* 77(216): 76-78.

2022. The 2019 survey of petroglyphs in the Qinghai-Tibet Plateau, western China. *Rock Art Research* 39(2): 143-154.

2022. The dating of rock art and bone by the uranium-thorium method. *Rock Art Research* 39(2): 195-204.

2022. [With Jin Anni and Chao Ge] The travertine hand and footprints at Qiusang, Tibet. *Rock Art Research* 39(2): 215-218.

The full list of Bednarik's publications 1962 to present can be accessed at http://www.ifrao.com/publications-by-r-g-bednarik/

It includes work in rock art science, archaeology, ethnography, anthropology, hominin evolution, speleology, geology, philosophy and neuroscience but his most-read work is in psychology.

Prof. Giriraj Kumar
The Editor
E-mail: girirajrasi.india@gmail.com

2

FOR MY HUSBAND

ELFRIEDE K. BEDNARIK

Figure 1: The happy couple, Elfriede and Robert G. Bednarik (March 2002)

Having been married to Robert for 53 years has been exciting for me. We have made hundreds of journeys crisscrossing Australia, literally to every part of the continent, since well before he founded AURA. We have checked out hundreds of caves and been to hundreds of open rock art sites. In the process I have seen so much of this great country, Australia. But we also travelled abroad on many occasions, to countries such as India, China, New Zealand, France, Austria, Italy,

Germany, and Bolivia. All our journeys were strictly dedicated to rock art and archaeology, but they also enabled me to see many wonderful places and meet many delightful and amazing people. Professor Kumar will recall when we lived with him for a week or two in a two-bedroom apartment right above that of Professor Roy Querejazu Lewis in Cochabamba. What a great time we had in the more remote parts of Bolivia, finding rock art sites and meeting Aymara people. One of Robert's achievements is that he turned the rock art researchers of the world into one great family through IFRAO which he founded in the first international AURA Conference, Darwin, 1988. And one of the highlights in my life has been that I met so many indigenous people, especially Aboriginal elders.

Now that Robert is turning 80 and I am becoming frail, he still cares for me and looks after me the best he can. I am no writer and cannot express all I wish to say but I can say one thing: I could not wish for a better husband. Thank you, Robert, for a beautiful life together!

Elfriede Kathe Bednarik
W/o Prof. Robert G. Bednarik
P.O. Box 216
Caulfied South, Vic. 3162
Australia
E-mail: robertbednarik@hotmail.com

(*Note:* After a long illeness, Elfriede K. Bednarik passed away on 3 September 2023, shortly after providing this, her last message to us. Ed.)

3

ROBERT G. BEDNARIK AS I KNOW HIM

GIRIRAJ KUMAR

Robert as a person

Prof. Robert G. Bednarik, henceforth simply Robert, is a well-built, straight-tall figure with a beard and looks a little like Karl Marx. Generally, he is very calm and composed; he speaks little but is very well focussed and can work for days together without bothering for food. He has dedicated his whole life to understanding the epistemology of the authors of rock art at a global level. I first met him in Darwin at the First AURA Congress in 1988, where he invited me as the leader of the team of seven Indian delegates. I discussed with him many aspects of the scientific study of rock art and what can be done in India. Then, I organised a national conference on rock art in Dayalbagh Educational Institute (Deemed to be University) at Agra from 22–24 February 1990 and invited him as the Chief Guest of the conference (Figure 1).

Figure 1: Prof. Robert G. Bednarik invited as the Chief guest of the rock art conference, Dayalbagh, Educational Institute, Agra, India, 1990. Dr S. P. Gupta is welcoming him.

I also organised his one-month post-conference tour of India, where he got an opportunity to visit many rock art sites and study the early portable art in different parts of the country and limestone caves in Andhra Pradesh. Besides, the tour was organised so that he could meet prominent and renowned Indian rock art scholars and archaeologists working on Stone Age cultures in the country. This trip helped both of us to learn a lot from each other. Robert became exposed to the wealth of Indian rock art and portable palaeoart and the Indian way and approach of working on it. He observed that the vitality and optimism characterising current Indian rock art studies, as well as the potential of the palaeoart itself to provide some surprises in the future, make India one of the regions to watch (Bednarik 1990). At the same time, I learned a lot about the latest trends and scientific study of rock art and how India and Australia can collaborate to work on it. It led to the foundation of Indo-Australian collaboration for working on the rock art of India, which is still ongoing, working on many scientific projects on early petroglyphs and rock paintings.

In the field, Robert becomes a workaholic, forgetting everything except the desired work. He used to take very little food. I had to ask him to take proper food during the fieldwork. In a light mood, he used to say that at home in Australia, his wife lovingly over-fed him, so for him, fieldwork used to be an opportunity to reduce his weight. Born and brought up in Austria in Europe in 1944, he shifted with his family to Australia in 1970 and made it his own country. He is against any form of discrimination based on colour or race and is a staunch supporter of Aborigines, not only in Australia but of indigenes in other parts of the world also.

Robert as a pioneering scholar in many fields of learning

The African Eve model of archaeology dominated the world in the twentieth century. It was a Eurocentric model of study, establishing the supremacy of Europe in the cultural development of the world. Initially, Robert deeply studied the work done on rock art and excavated material on palaeoart obtained from European archaeologists' excavations, silently observing the scholars' presentations and intentions in international events. Finally, he presented the alternative evolutionary model of the cultural development of the hominins. It shattered the very base of the Eve model and paved the way for finding evidence of the evolutionary model of cultural development in countries other than those of Europe. It laid the foundation of the concept of looking for evidence of the early cognitive and cultural developments especially in Asia, Africa and Australia. The result is evident.

Through the EIP Project's excavations, India produced authentic evidence of the Lower Palaeolithic petroglyphs and hammerstones used for their production from Daraki-Chattan Cave in the Chambal basin. The EIP Project had been a high-profile international project, a joint venture of the Rock Art Society of India (RASI) and the Australian Rock Art Research Association (AURA) under the aegis of the International Federation of Rock Art Organisations (IFRAO). Giriraj Kumar and Robert G. Bednarik are the Indian and Australian directors of the project, supported by the Archaeological Survey of India, Indian Council of Historical Research and Australia-India Council,

Canberra (Figure 2). The EIP project also endorsed the evidence of Lower Palaeolithic petroglyphs observed in Wakankar's trench in the Auditorium cave at Bhimbetka by Robert (Bednarik 1993). The Indian early evidence of human symbolism is not in isolation; rather, the tradition continues in other parts of the world. Linear arrangements of engraved lines on elephant bones belonging to Lower Palaeolithic cultural periods were obtained at Bilgingsleben in Germany. Similarly, petroglyphs belonging to Mode 2 and Mode 3 cultural phases from South Africa came to light. Most of the early rock art from Australia is associated with essentially Middle Palaeolithic tools. A prototype of human form enhanced by hominins was obtained from Berekhat Ram from the Late Acheulean of Golan Heights, Israel, dated to 280,000–250,000 BP (Bednarik et al. 2005; Kumar et al. 2005). Robert contributed another example, the proto-figurine of Tan-Tan in Morocco, which is older (Middle Acheulean).

Figure 2: From left, Prof. Robert G. Bednarik, Dr A. Pradhan, Prof. Giriraj Kumar and Dr Manoj Rathore waiting to fall night for collecting soil samples for OSL dating from the spill channel at Indragarh dam in Chambal basin, India, 2016.

Thus, recent research has shown that our understanding of art origins is rapidly changing. More than any other evidence during the last 100 years, the evidence produced by the EIP Project, especially from the excavations at Daraki-Chattan and Auditorium Caves, has shown that we have misjudged the time depth of palaeoart and human cognition, creative ability, and symbolism. Now the time has come to change our mindset. The evidence is so important that it is set to affect not only our concepts of Pleistocene hominin development in southern Asia but also influence how we view cognitive evolution. This is an important contribution of India to the Rock Art Discipline in the world (Bednarik et al. 2005; Kumar et al. 2005).

The evolutionary model of cultural development revolutionised palaeoart studies and understanding of the cognitive development of hominins in the last decade of the twentieth century and the first two decades of the twenty-first century. It motivated the scholars to change their mindset to look for evidence of early human symbolism beyond Upper Palaeolithic European cave art. It paved the way for observing the evidence of the early creative traditions and emphasised understanding the processes involved rather than the end products. It helped to change our way of looking towards rock art as a product of the entire process of the technological and cultural development of early humans and understanding its continuity in the present-day communities practising rock art or associated somehow with such sites (Kumar 2023).

KEM and Tribology

Robert and I were deeply observing the early cupules for their survival in the open. During replication of the early cupules of Daraki-Chattan, we observed that because of the striking of hammerstones, a hard layer is formed in some cupules, which is resistant to penetrating further. In the field, we also observed that the so-formed cream-coloured hard layer in the cupules is also resistant to weathering. This observation helped Robert to develop the idea of Kinetic Energy Metamorphosis in the cupules and write a book on *Tribology in geology and archaeology*. Generally, geological principles help the study of archaeology and rock art; however, here, it was the rock art discipline that helped to understand the principle of tribology in geology, and credit for it goes to Robert (Bednarik 2019).

Established IFRAO on a highly decentralised democratic foundation

Robert, along with his like-minded friends working on rock art throughout the world, established the International Federation of Rock Art Organisations (IFRAO) in the first AURA Congress at Darwin in 1988. Robert is also the founder of AURA and its international journal, *Rock Art Research (RAR)*. *RAR* also became the official journal of IFRAO in 1988. The constitution adopted for IFRAO is highly democratic, where the office of each participating member organisation is also the office of IFRAO, and the IFRAO meetings can be hosted by the IFRAO members only. The host of the IFRAO meeting automatically becomes the President of IFRAO till the next IFRAO meeting. It is a great honour to the IFRAO members. Because of this unique constitutional set-up, each IFRAO member tries its best to work for the benefit of the scientific development of the Rock Art Discipline in the world. For devising that system of governance, credit goes to Robert. All the IFRAO Members use the IFRAO Standard Scale, specially developed by Robert with the suggestions from the IFRAO members. It is an important tool to retrieve the original colour of rock art documented by using it even hundreds of years from now, as the colours used in it are coded in numerical values.

Saving the rock art of the Dampier Archipelago in Australia at the risk of his life

Dampier Archipelago in the Pilbara region of Western Australia has been full of petroglyphs (estimated to be at least a million petroglyphs). However, because of the activities of the resource industries, rock art was destroyed. Robert made it his mission to save the remainder. Though he received a threat to his life for that, nothing could distract him (Bednarik 2011a). Because of his sustained efforts, much of the rock art of Dampier Archipelago could be saved, and the entire site was added to Australia's National Heritage List of Natural and Cultural Places of Outstanding Heritage Value to the Nation in 2007. Six years later, the Murujuga National Park was created in response to his efforts, and the land was returned to the Aboriginal community.

His helping nature

Robert helped Indians, Saudi Arabians and Chinese to bring rock art site complexes under the UNESCO World Heritage List. His work in Saudi Arabia has become an inspiration to Muslim countries to work on and save the rock art heritage in their countries, which were otherwise predisposed against figurative forms. It shows Robert's vision to promote rock art, especially in the Muslim countries in western Asia. He also motivated Bolivians, Brazilians, Peruvians and many others to form rock art organisations and helped them to join IFRAO, promote their rock art heritage worldwide and make their best efforts to protect it. Robert inspired and extended his great support to Prof. Tang Huisheng to establish the International Centre of Rock Art Dating and Conservation (ICRAD) in China. It was established at Hebei Normal University in China, the first facility of its kind in Asia, with Tang as its Director. Robert obtained nearly 50 microerosion dates for the petroglyphs in China. Later, at the request of Tang Huisheng, he became the visiting professor of the ICRAD and not only provided all the basic data on the efforts made for dating rock art in the world but promoted it at global level.

His help comes selflessly to all the countries in the world that are interested in the scientific study and protection of rock art. Above all, as far as I know, he never accepted travel expenditure or remuneration for his services.

His work in Samson's Shaft in Brazil

His work in Samson's Shaft (Toca do Buraco do Sansao) in Brazil in 1987 is exemplary and a dare-devil act for the cause of research and humanity. Samson's Shaft is a huge vertical shaft cave located on the slope of a limestone hill near Barragem, a small town in the State of Piauí in the northeast of Brazil, where nearly one-thousand people live in very harsh conditions of a desert. The people living in the village were crippled and suffering from many diseases as they were using highly polluted water for drinking.

Prof. Niède Guidon, the renowned Brazilian rock art scholar and a prehistorian, was working on Samson's shaft, occupied by killer bees at its mouth. She is a brave lady who tried to enter the shaft, the depth of which was unknown. She was badly attacked by the killer bees and barely survived; however, her fingers are still crippled. She then invited Robert to help her explore Samson's Shaft. With all the precautions, Robert went into the shaft with two strong tribal men. The latter lost their courage at a depth of 30 m. So, Robert asked them to stay there, and he himself went down to the bottom of the shaft, nearly 100 m deep. There, he found very hard mineralised fossil bones of extinct megafauna and four crystal-clear freshwater lakes. He drew the map and location of the fossils on paper and put his observations as far as he could make, then came up.

As he emerged from Samson's Shaft after almost a day inside, a large crowd had gathered, sitting in silence, with the children in front. He remembered the moment vividly, he felt sorry for the little ones, they were visibly scared of the 'monster alien', emerging huffing and puffing from the massive cave. The shaft was spacious enough to fit a 30-storey skyscraper into it, so it had been a superhuman effort climbing up, under oppressive tropical heat and with hundreds of killer bees harassing him (Figure 3).

Figure 3: Prof. Robert G. Bednarik coming out of Samson's Shaft in Brazil in 1987. Courtesy R.G.B.

He requested Prof. Guidon to insert a pipe into the shaft down to the bottom of a lake and fill it with water by pump. The village people will then get fresh water through the siphon process without further effort, energy or expenditure. Since then, the villagers have gotten the best fresh potable water and become rid of their diseases. With that humanitarian work, Robert has become like an angel to them (Bednarik 1989, 1991).

His simplicity

As said earlier, I organised an all-India tour of Robert for the study of rock art sites and early mobiliary art objects in India in February-March 1990. At that time, I was in my early thirties, and that was my first experience working with any foreign scholar of the stature like Robert. At the same time, I was financially not able to afford rail journeys in an air-conditioned coach. So, I asked Robert to travel in an air-conditioned coach, and I would travel in sleeper class. He told me that I should travel with him in his coach and he would bear my expenses, which I denied. Then we both travelled in sleeper class on the train. Today, I realise how difficult it could have been for him to travel in the sleeper class coach on the train without any proper toilet facility and sleep and how foolish it was of me to take that decision. But he never complained about that.

Secondly, again in 2016, I organised nearly one-month-long fieldwork for dating of the early cupules of DC and study of the KEM in DC cupules and that in the paleochannel on Indragarh Hill near Bhanpura in district Mandsaur in Madhya Pradesh. The site is deep in the interior area. Any good hotel was available only at Jhalawar in Rajasthan, which was 50 km east of Bhanpura. I asked Robert if I should arrange his stay in a hotel in Jhalawar. To save the travel time, he denied that proposal; hence I organised our stay in the closer but simpler guest house of the electricity department of the Government of Madhya Pradesh at Gandhsagar No. 2. Though its location is very beautiful, being located on a hill and overlooking the Chambal Gorge full of water, its maintenance was very poor with no proper facility for preparation of food for a foreigner. Robert had to adjust somehow with a big rat in his room, and it was very difficult for him. He could not sleep for some days till he managed to eject the rat. He did the fieldwork with the minimum available facilities, he compromised with his food too. For many days he survived with soup. Probably no other foreigner could have worked in those conditions, but he completed the fieldwork. Such is his dedication to rock art and allied disciplines.

His dedication to work

Dr Jean Clottes, Robert and I organised the 10th IFRAO Congress in France in 2010. The international conference theme was 'Pleistocene art in the world'. The event was a great success, especially in establishing the creative abilities of the early humans in Lower and Middle Palaeolithic age in the Pleistocene period, instead of its beginning in the Upper Palaeolithic age in the terminal Pleistocene period. Robert attended all the meetings in the daytime and used to go for his research work in the caves at night. Later, he told me that at that time, his wife, Elfriede was seriously ill in Australia. Even in such a difficult situation, he remained composed and was able to concentrate not only on the IFRAO meetings but also on his research work.

He can change the difficulties into opportunities

The gradually deteriorating health of his wife, who was a great companion and strength to him, soon demanded more care and time from him. He cancelled many of his assignments to take care of her from 2010 onwards. However, he turned that difficult time into an opportunity to complete important books and had them published (Bednarik 2011b, 2013, 2014, 2019, 2020a, 2020b, 2022).

A loving husband

At present, when his wife needs complete care, Robert has devoted himself completely to taking care of her. Hence, he cancelled all his assignments and travel for the last few years. He is getting little sleep at night, but even in such difficult times, he brings out both the annual issues of *RAR* and other publications in time.

Concluding remarks

Robert is truly a global leader and an inspiring personality in Rock Art Discipline. Most of the scientific work in many fields of the discipline in different parts of the world is because of his far-sighted vision. Besides, he is a great human being who has set examples by his own work and life.

(Sorry, after a long illness his wife passed away on 3 September 2023)

Prof. Giriraj Kumar
President, Rock Art Society of India
Email: girirajrasi.india@gmail.com

References

Bednarik, R. G. 1989. On the Pleistocene settlement of South America. *Antiquity* 63 (238): 101–111.

Bednarik, R. G. 1990. Rock art tour of India - a report. *Purakala* 1(1): 16.

Bednarik, R. G. 1991. Purakala research in the service of humanity: adventures in the exploration of Samson's Shaft in Brazil. *Purakala* 2(2): 81–84.

Bednarik, R.G. 1993. Palaeolithic art in India. *Man and Environment* 18(2): 33–40.

Bednarik, R. G. 2011a. The Dampier Campaign. *Rock Art Research* 28(2): 27–34.

Bednarik, R. G. 2011b. *The human condition*. Springer, New York.

Bednarik, R. G. 2013: *Creating the human past: an epistemology of Pleistocene archaeology*. Archaeopress, Oxford.

Bednarik, R. G. 2014. *The first mariners*. Research India Press, New Delhi.

Bednarik, R. G. 2019. *Tribology in geology and archaeology*. Nova Science Publishers, New York.

Bednarik, R. G. 2020a. *The domestication of humans*. Routledge, Abingdon and New York.

Bednarik, R. G. 2020b. *Gudenus Cave: the earliest humans of Austria*. Archaeopress Archaeology, Oxford.

Kumar, G. 2023. Future direction of rock art research: a pursuit of the epistemology of rock art and the processes involved in it Rock Art Research 40(2): 205-2011.

Bednarik, R. G., G. Kumar, A. Watchman and R. G. Roberts 2005. Preliminary results of the EIP Project. *Rock Art Research* 22(2): 147–197.

Kumar, G., R. G. Bednarik, A. Watchman and R. G. Roberts 2005. The EIP Project in 2005: a progress report. *Purakala* 14–15: 13–68.

Kumar, G. and Krishna 2014. Understanding the technology of the Daraki-Chattan Cupules: The Cupule replication project. *Rock Art Research* 31(2): 177-186. Melbourne.

4

SPEAKING AFTER ROBERT G. BEDNARIK

KALYAN KUMAR CHAKRAVARTY

Abstract: This note is derived from Bednarik's observations, distilled, and synthesized from the record of his lifelong research all over the world, for working out scientifically falsifiable methods of recognition, dating, conservation and appreciation of the meaning and shape of rock art in India. He asks for locally evolved methods of combining and mutually validating scientific and ethnographic study of rock art, still preserved by hill and forest-based communities in India, away from postulates of priority and superiority of European rock art, developed in South Western Europe, and propagated as universally valid. He favours multi-linear evolution of human language, as it is implied by the global diversity in palaeoart, and does not see the Franco-Cantabrian or any other early tradition as evidence for a uni-linear evolution. He proposes greater human capacity for symbolling and abstraction in the prehistoric past, because of the growing atrophy of human brain, and emphasizes the feasibility of using bio neurological constants for understanding the similar human mind and condition, transcending phylogenetic diversity. The importance and methods of rock art study in India are explained in this note, after Bednarik's research and suggestions, for providing clues to the human language in the prehistoric past.

Despite lack of access to the global intellectual resource on rock art, the Indian rock art researchers, thanks to their exposure, through the Rock Art Society magazine, *Purakala*, are familiar with Bednarik's lifelong search for the cognitive beginnings of humanity, in a universal language and script of rock art. The edifying observations, distilled from his writings, about adapting replicable, falsifiable, and testable approaches to tool making and drawing, after the manner of the prehistoric artist and tool maker, recognition, dating, conservation, appreciation of meaning, international dialogue in Indian and global rock art study, have been harvested, in order to offer suggestions, in this regard, to Indian rock art researchers.

It has been pointed out by Bednarik that there is no priority for Europe for early hominin behavior or creative expressions because these were shared by human beings in Southeast and Eastern Asia between 800000 and 300000 years. He rejects the Eurocentric claim of cognitive priority, semiotic complexity, centrality, originality, rationality and superiority of figurative Franco-Cantabrian art in European caves, over non-figurative marking in Paleolithic Indian rock art in open rock shelters, as a phenomenon of taphonomic selection, according to geological situation. The great phylogenetic diversity described by him as characteristic of this period suggests the need for extensive research for fossil evidence and creative human activity, associated with rock art in India, to update the limited information available from India in this respect. Similar environmental requirements in different parts of the world would have demanded, according to his suggestion, similar phenotypic and archetypical inspiration. In India, such inspiration has to be searched out in similar forested and hilly habitats of tribal communities. The adaptive radiation of the divergence of related forms of rock art may not, however, be read as leading to adaption of similar meanings, as warned by Bednarik, because of differences in epistemology and tool behavior of communities in different parts of the world. The Freudian, Jungian, Marxist, Feminist, Structuralist, Semiotic or Arts for Art's sake theories of rock art meaning, born in the Western context and applied to Paleolithic rock art in India, as hunting magic, shamanic practice, fertility, matriarchal or totemistic cults have been shown by Bednarik as un falsifiable and un testable. He has, therefore, asked scholars to move beyond taxonomic pigeonholes rooted in tool typologies and inaccurate iconographic identifications, based on imagined scenes and motifs, derived from their predilections,leading to hasty conclusions about the sequence and nature of subsistence technologies and significance of various activities depicted in rock art. Such conclusions have to be moderated, on Bednarik's parameters, by diverse local eco and community-specific premises, without using Franco-Cantabrian terminology or associated western art theories, because South Western Europe was no more than a cultural and technological backwater of the Pleistocene world in non-European continents. He insists on a quest for multi-linear rather than unilinear developments from Middle to Upper Paleolithic times in rock art in Narmada, Betwa, Ganga, Yamuna, Godavari valleys of India, as well as in China, Europe or Africa.

Access to radio dosimetry, x-ray diffraction, infrared spectroscopy, proton-induced emission, and mass spectrometry, to analyze paint residues and organic inclusions, is difficult in India, Bednarik would agree, in the absence of adequate laboratory facilities. In view of this, the subjectivism of assessment of the intentions of human rock marking can be corrected in the Indian situation, to a certain extent, in places where hinterland communities have lived close to the rock art landscapes and nursed them with a continuing mindscape. Bednarik, who has worked extensively with Indian researchers in the wild glens, gullies, and flood plains, inhabited by tribal people in India, is sympathetic to the relevance of extensive Indian research on the ethnographic continuity between rock art shapes and current shapes of community art. He would agree that the search for manuports in bone, ivory, fiber, leather or wood, beads or pendants, cicatrices, or infibulations in lower or middle Paleolithic traditions in Europe or elsewhere in the world, can be usefully paralleled by a similar search in India, in view of their continuing use by Indian tribal groups. He would, however, like the Indian researcher to be careful before jumping to hasty conclusions with regard to the continuity in meaning, associated with such artifacts or practices. He would object, for example, to similarities drawn between Harappan script and the Odisha rock art, though he might agree to a search for patterns akin to writing in such rock art. His greatest sympathy would lie with lonely researchers who, without any backing of the state, or access to financial and academic resources, have tried to locate and seek protection for remote and isolated rock shelters. Their search for similar meaning across the world in terms of analogous mythology would be questioned by Bednarik, though he might uphold the validity of a quest for a universal language based on similar neurological responses to similar environment in rock art, the world over.

The rock art researchers in India have noticed many encrustations and cryptogamic growth, including lichen and wax, microorganisms and calcite skins, mud, and termite nests, forming around the rock art. Bednarik would ask them to look for the thalli or organic material in such encrustations for post quem dating in available labs, before destroying them, along with the rock art, in the name of conservation. The silicas, oxalates and carbonates that accumulate in the open rock shelters in India can serve as protective skins and can be analyzed for tentative dating, by combining the highly developed academic expertise of geology, forestry, anthropology, available in India, under the guidance of experts like Bednarik, instead of waiting for the development of fully equipped dating laboratories or for the gathering of International experts in India, which can be prohibitively expensive, and cannot be organized on a large scale to cover the extensive evidence of rock art in India. In such a dating exercise,Bednarik would suggest taking into account taphonomic distortion of evidence, geological, archaeological or biological, for avoiding the error of ignoring the taphonomic lag periods in open carbon systems of Indian rock art.

Bednarik's suggestion for correcting stylistic dating, in vogue in India, by direct dating, blind testing and meta-morphological resolution of probabilities, requires, in the absence of adequately equipped laboratories in India, a convergence of available academic and government resources, for arriving at an assessment of shape, meaning or conservation needs. In view of the lack of calibration curves for the Pleistocene rock art in India, his warning to distinguish biological from geological, and human from plant, kinetic, weathering, or petrographic markings, has to be taken into account by Indian rock art researchers. The use of micro erosion analysis, to study microscopic fracture of edges, has been difficult for yielding dates in India, in the absence of calibration and suitable lithologies. On Bednarik's premises, nano-stratigraphy can be feasibly done on Indian rock art, only when the direct relation of art with a rock has been preserved from impact scars and the process of examination can be done refutably. Bednarik would also object to scientistic conclusions of zoologists and geologists about rock art age on the basis of misidentification of extinct fauna or of so-called shamanic practices of ancient medicine men. No digital or finger flutings have been reported in Indian caves, thanks to the unstable speleo-climate, subject to diurnal and seasonal fluctuations.

Indian rock art is a non-renewable cultural resource. It has to be protected, in the light of Bednarik's campaigns the world over, including Dampier in Australia, against the environmental destruction wrought by mega-developmental assaults on the rock art and tribal habitats. His further suggestions would be to implement the environmental impact assessment procedures sincerely, under public scrutiny, to stop invasive construction of roads and introduction of mining activities, close to the rock shelters, which have been accelerating mass exfoliation of rock art by aggravating capillary and gravitational moisture, bush fires, insolation and solar radiation, thermal expansion, or contraction. The thoughtless ongoing tourist invasion, with use of fire for cooking, scratching of names and extraction of rock art slabs as mementos, has to be stopped by creating steel or timber board walks, artificial rock ledges, prickly bushes or steel cages around the rock shelters. Glass fiber brushes and alcohol swabs should be used with delicate care, to remove charcoal and lead pencil graffiti, without damaging the rock art. Most of the Indian rock shelters, being close to rivers and water streams, have to be guarded against moisture and interstitial, capillary seepage, with utmost care. Digital storage of rock art imagery, digital color management with high-fidelity records, using a universal device profile and color calibration, may be a substitute, Bednarik would agree, for invasive manual or mechanical examination of rock art. However, he would also add that lab research can hardly be used to dispense with field research using non-contact methods, respecting community customary laws. He would also insist that it is more important to move beyond reactive and minimal measures of rock art conservation, to create exclusion zones around rock art sites against construction, road building, mining and deforestation.

Far from agreeing to suggestions about immature or infantile perceptions of the world in Indian rock art, or rock art in prehistory by indigenous groups in different parts of the world, Bednarik suggests, on the basis of biological evidence, a greater capacity for symbolling, abstraction and pre-conceptual understanding in the prehistoric artist. He speaks of a decrease in brain size, growing brain atrophy and neotenization, reduction rather than expansion in cranial volume, i.e., reversal in encephalization, decrease in robusticity and increase in gracilization, in modern human being, as compared with the prehistoric human being. To him, Indian rock art would provide, in the background of such evidence of growing atrophy, a bank of human cultural memory and information, stored in exograms outside the brain, which may be harvested for their continuing value and relevance in contemporary contexts, instead of being dismissed as infantile responses to the world. Also of relevance in the Indian context is his warning against the tendency of inductive uniformitarianism in archaeology to treat past human societies as mechanistic entities with predictable behavior patterns reactive to environmental threats, devoid of pro-active creative experiments. He would thus demand caution in jumping to hasty conclusions about undeveloped and primitive perceptions of the surrounding environment in Indian rock art. He would, therefore, also not frown on the establishment of cognitive linkages between early symbolic and memory traces and contemporary Indian tribal manuports, both being probably a mature rather than puerile and magical response to the external world. The uncertainty about the change in the environmental radiation regime for determining the release of energy as a function of time will remain with rock art research in India in the absence of an adequate geological history, but the biggest strength of India will remain the survival of communities, who may offer a clue to phosphene universals or entoptic constants, substantiated by their continuing use of similar styles, materials, techniques, tools, motifs and patterns. This will be facilitated, Bednarik would suggest, by the standardization of rock art terminology, to enable easier communication among researchers, working with communities in different parts of the world. Bednarik would, however, insist that such ethno-archaeological research has to be corrected, through cognitive archaeology, by verifying the relationship and comparability between current and past behavioral patterns, lithic traditions and material conditions.

Bednarik's suggestion about the kinetic energy metamorphosis of sandstone, quartzite, and schistose facies in cupules, created by numerous hammer-stone blows, and checked by microerosion dating, reinforces his assessment of the great age of the Bhimbetka and Daraki Chattan cupules. Longevity being a taphonomic rather than a cultural accident, his assessment of the cupules at Auditorium rock in Bhimbetka or in Indragarh Hill in Mandsaur as being some of the oldest surviving rock art in erosion-resistant rocks, has been treated with respect. He provides similar examples from southern Africa. Bednarik's warning against pareidolia and apophenia or tendency of interpreters to impose symbolic value, derived from current experience, on ancient art, and, to confuse human with non-human, natural with artificial markings, is of relevance in the Indian context. His warning provides a strong reason for training Indian rock art researchers, with the help of zoologists, geologists and anthropologists,to recognize and differentiate anthropic from non-anthropic markings, and refrain from untested conclusions about continuing symbolism. He provides such examples of confusion from Inner Mongolia (China), Utah and Australia.

Bednarik's research on Indian and global rock art is of great help in abandoning a rational-intuitive, subject-object, conceptual-perceptual dichotomy, for arriving at neuropsychological processes of creating and understanding rock art, shared across the world among hinterland communities. He provides synaptic and cognitive pathways, rid of anthropocentric indices, for recovering an approximate understanding of ancient Indian rock art. Even if statistical probabilities rather than calendar dates are arrived at by using his suggestions, such an exercise will promote a meaningful global dialogue on Indian rock art. His work provides a road map for looking into Indian rock art as a representational as well as a significant cognitive mode. His warnings against scientistic as well as ethnocentric taxonomies emphasize the need of combining formal and epistemic studies, conceptual and pre-conceptual modes of investigation in Indian rock art.

Dr Kalyan Kumar Chakravarty, IAS (Rtd)
LX 2050, Utsa Luxury Condoville , Action Area 1 A
Beside Reliance Fresh and off New Town Bus stand
New Town, Rajarhaat , Kolkata , 700163. India
E-mail: msk4747@yahoo.in

References

Bednarik, R. G. 2020. *The domestication of humans*. Routledge, London & New York

Bednarik, R. G. 2019. *Tribology in geology and archaeology*. Nova Science Publishers, New York.

Bednarik, R. G. 2017. *Palaeoart of the Ice Age (2nd edn)*. Cambridge Scholars Publishing.

Bednarik, R. G. 2016. *Myths about rock art*. Archaeopress, Oxford.

Bednarik, R. G. 2014. *The first mariners*. Research India Press, New Delhi.

Bednarik, R. G. 2013. Creating the human past: an epistemology of Pleistocene archaeology. Archaeopress, Oxford.

Bednarik, R. G. 2011. *The human condition*. Springer, New York.

5

ROBERT G. BEDNARIK AS A GREAT TEACHER

Ram Krishna

In Indian cultural we highly venerate a teacher and consider his place even higher than the Almighty. Therefore, having a great teacher is the most fortunate thing to happen in a person's life because he is the force to transform one's life in a beautiful way.

Robert G. Bednarik is one of my great teachers. I was fortunate to work with him and got an opportunity to discuss various aspects of rock art, nature, and life. That uplifted benchmark of my thought process at an extraordinary level as a student of life. Following are some major events with him that played crucial role in my learning process.

1. I have known Prof. R. G. Bednarik through my father Prof. Giriraj Kumar since my childhood-stories of his adventure and scholarship. Kumar organized the 10th IFRAO International Conference in Jaypee Hotel Palace, Agra in 2004. Robert wanted to see the material obtained from the excavations of Daraki-Chattan Cave (DC) which was placed at our residence in Dayalbagh, Agra. As a young boy I got an opportunity to interact with him for the first time. Being with such a great personality was an amazing experience for me.
2. Robert again visited Kumar's studio at Agra to study the stone artefacts, cupules and hammerstones obtained from the excavations at DC in December 2012. He worked for 10 days in a stretch. I used to pick up him from his hotel at 7:30 am and leave him by 8 pm. The travel time (nearly 20 minutes) used to be an inspiring session of discussion on several aspects of rock art and life.

   During the day he used to study the excavated material from 8 am till evening at 7:30 pm. I observed that he was laser-sharp focused about his work, conducting it with complete dedication and involvement. He never took coffee, snacks, and lunch during the day. He never left his seat except for using washroom one or two times. He wanted to work with full capacity to increase the productivity. During that expedition

I also observed him to process the facts and data without being biased for preconceived notions including baseless interpretations.

3. He entrusted me the task to photograph the stone artefacts and other objects, though I was novice in photography. He told us that we must always have backup of the record of our research in the laboratory and in the field.
4. The major field experience came in 2016 when I was a part of the team to work on the EIP Project II led by Giriraj and Robert. During that expedition we studied Kinetic Energy Metamorphosis (KEM) and microerosion dating of the early petroglyphs. KEM is the phenonmenon when silica, the binding material of the constituent crystals of the rock, transforms in to hard quartz because of heat generated by continuous hammering during the process of cupule production on hard quartzite rock. KEM layer is highly resistant to weathering. Observation of its state of weathering on the cupules (and petroglyphs) in the field helps in understanding their antiquity (Figure 1).

Figure 1: Mud-coloured KEM inside the cupules on Chanchalamata Hill near DC Cave at Indragarh-Bhanpura. Photo courtesy Prof. Giriraj Kumar.

5. I used to accompany Robert throughout the field-work to help him in his work. I also use to observe him working in the field and learn a lot from him. He made us realize that only work is important, whatever the challenges might we face. He set example for me to see how he used to work all day in the field even when the challenges were immense, he being from a cold place in Australia he had to face different kind of climate, food, shelter,

cultural environment and even medical facilities. He used to become adjusted easily. A lot of challenges were faced at that time like to collect the soil sample for OSL dating in total darkness under the black plastic sheet in the night. In order to cut a sample of the petroglyph groove on a quartzite block we had to bring the electric power generator on top of the hill up to DC. It was a very difficult task, but we accomplished it. Study of the KEM in a cupule on the northern face of DC close to its mouth was another great challenge (Figure 2). But we did it successfully.

Figure 2: Robert G. Bednarik and Ram Krishna are working on the study of the Kinetic Energy Metamorphosis (KEM) on an early cupule at Daraki-Chattan (DC), 2016. Photo courtesy Prof. Giriraj Kumar.

6. While working in the field once I asked him that he was highly matured as compared to me, even then he used to discuss different issues with me. He told me that someone should be there to discuss in the field, the condition is that s/he must have rational thinking process. He embraced me as a companion to discuss in the field, so I was fortunate to learn a lot of scientific aspects of palaeoart study. That shows the respect he has for facts and science, and nothing else is important for him.

7. Once during the discussion he made me understand the value of scientific communication, when I used the word, 'air' in place of 'breeze'. He explained me the difference between them that air is a substance and breeze is a movement. Then he told me that use of proper words is must for proper and powerful communication.
8. He also taught us to use cactus fruits available in the wild as a source of nutrition in the field when needed.
9. The best time I had was in Italy in 2018 when we attended the international conference on Neanderthal man at Torino and IFRAO conference at Darfo Boario in Italy in 2018. I was the copilot of Robert while driving from Turin to Darfo Boario in his hired car. Prof. Kumar was also with us. That trip was the most amazing experience of my life as learning and fun were on their peak with extreme efficiency. In the way from Milano to Darfo we could not see even a single bird in the dense forest of the hill along the fresh water lake. We discussed this observation and reached the conclusion that it might be because of the pollution of strong electronic waves we have been using for communication. We visited Valcamonica and Valentina rock art sites, where I understood multiple technical aspects of scientific study of the petroglyphs. Robert explained me that we must observe the geological phenomenon for the scientific study of rock art. That was the time when I shared my understanding of sustainable development of rock art heritage with him. I imbibed all his inputs to make the best of my understandings. With his inspiration I could develop a dynamic model to quantify the sustainable development of rock art heritage sites and built up a scenario to minimize the damage and the cost of its conservation and management.
10. Robert always works with proper planning and precision. For an expedition from Torino to Darfo he along with his car was ready a day in advance just to perform faster and efficiently on time.

In the last I want to say that Robert G. Bednarik is one of the finest scholars and teachers and truly inspiring force for generations to come. He set high standards of working by his own example. As a student I learned from him the very high level of dedication, sincerity, integrity and focus with a strong determination like a steel to complete the research tasks. He has changed my way of thinking towards professional and personal life and he helped me to understand that how scientific study relates to environment and our life which are integral part of the nature's eco-system. He has set different level of benchmarks of scientific study of palaeoart in the process of learning and sharing. I find him as the most adventurous, hardworking, intelligent, and committed scholar and as a source of great inspiration.

Dr Ram Krishna
Joint Secretary, RASI; Assistant Professor in Business Management
Lovely Professional University, Phagwara, Jalandhar, Punjab, India
E-mail: ramkrishna.gem@gamil.com

6

THOUGHTS ON THE CONTRIBUTIONS OF ROBERT G. BEDNARIK TO BRAZILIAN ROCK ART RESEARCH

RAONI VALLE

Writing about the contributions of Robert G. Bednarik to rock art research in any corner of the planet, except in Antarctica (yet), is simultaneously a demanding and easy task. It is hard to describe due to the many things he did, like fieldwork and participation in scholarly key debates on almost every continent. He has produced an outstanding number of publications, rivalling in quality, addressing a wide range of topics from hominin cognitive and cultural evolution to kinetic energy metamorphosis of the rock surface inside cupules. His ingenious mind, painstaking work, and scientifically grounded assertions were cogent and influential enough to nurture and advance the field of rock art science. Not surprisingly, he became a well-known, rock-solid reference for global rock art research in the last 45 years.

On the other hand, it is easy to talk about his significance based on the same reasons mentioned above. His presence was influential on several rock art topics. Direct dating, taphonomy, technology, forensics, tribology, ethnography, and philosophy of knowledge, to mention a few. He indeed pioneered some of those areas. That is the case of direct dating approaches based on observing and measuring geological processes applied to rock art age estimation back in the late 70s (Bednarik, 1979). Therefore, it is relatively easy to perceive how Robert Bednarik became a go-to reference for those seriously aiming to study rock art. However, not always well-accepted, controversy also made its way along his trajectory, with some dissatisfied academic voices echoing over the decades.

During the 1980s, his main global-scale achievements took place: the foundation of the International Federation of Rock Art Organizations (IFRAO). He had already established the Australian Rock Art Research Association (AURA) and the most informative and peer-reviewed scientific journal, *Rock Art Research (RAR)*. These initiatives impacted the organization of rock art research worldwide. From that moment onward, the idea that rock art could have epistemological vitality and autonomy irrespective of archaeology, without falling into metaphysical interpretation or empty analogy, was slowly taking shape. The supportive role IFRAO had in the worldwide creation of specific organizations devoted to the research, management, and protection of petroglyphs, pictograms, and related phenomena, was critical to promoting rock art empowerment and its broad social acknowledgement as an invaluable, non-renewable, and endangered cultural resource besides a fundamental symbolic and artistic expression of humankind. IFRAO also sustained a crucial rock art activism fomenting protectionist global campaign to save the endangered rock art sites from developmental threats all around the planet. Summing up, his initiatives gave decisive steps to transcend the generally and traditionally attributed status to rock art as a poorly informative variable of the archaeological record towards the constitution of a rock art science.

In Brazilian rock art studies, however, the influence of Robert Bednarik was more indirect and sporadic. Therefore, it is a fair assumption that he is an author yet to be discovered by the specialized public in Brazil, mainly students. The first of his significant assertions regarding a Brazilian rock art context, with some internal and external repercussions, occurred in the late 80s (Bednarik, 1989). After visiting the Serra da Capivara National Park, invited by the most prestigious Brazilian archaeologist, Niède Guidon, he evaluated the case of the stratigraphically buried rock paintings of the Toca do Baixão do Perna I site as an exceptional context. Found below the sediment layers, radiocarbon dated between 9 500 and 10 530 years BP, those pictograms most likely had a final Pleistocene origin, thus situated among the oldest surviving rock art of the Americas (Bednarik, 2017). It is worth remembering that the Pleistocene age of the rock art sites discovered and researched by the Niède Guidon team in the Serra da Capivara National Park was under fierce contestation and dispute by then, especially by North American archaeologists. Only a few internationally renowned scientists, besides the French branch of her research team, were backing up the Brazilian discoveries. Bednarik was one of the first international rock art experts to support some of her claims based on his direct evaluation of the available evidence.

During the 1990s, Brazilian rock art research became more systematically internationalized. While the French structuralist school, mixed with a cultural-historical emphasis on the classification of traditions and chrono-styles, was still somewhat influential by the onset of the 90s, Brazilian rock art research was slowly diversifying its theoretical and methodological approaches over that decade. Along that process, how archaeologists perceived the articulations between rock art, the archaeological record and with living societies transformed considerably. Eventually, those slow-burning changes led to the creation of the Brazilian Rock Art Association (ABAR) under the *aegis* of IFRAO. Founded in 1997, almost a decade after IFRAO's foundation in Australia, ABAR has fueled some theoretical and methodological changes in the interactions between Brazilian archaeology and rock art.

Throughout its first two decades, ABAR has fostered the conditions for Brazilian researchers dedicated to the topic meet more often within increased numbers, deepening inter-regional exchanges. It also increased the participation of Brazilian scholars in the international meetings of IFRAO, potentiating information exchange on national and international levels, leading to an unprecedented maturation of that subfield in Brazilian archaeology. So, even indirectly, Bednarik influenced how Brazilian researchers got organized from the late 90s onward.

In 2009, Niède Guidon, herself president of ABAR, and her skilled team of collaborators hosted an International IFRAO meeting in São Raimundo Nonato, SE Piauí, in the deep hinterlands of Brazil. She managed to bring the eyes and minds of the entire rock art global community to the Serra da Capivara National Park once more. That event was a turning point in Brazilian rock art research, demarcating a paradox. While it displayed rock art research as deeply enrooted in Brazilian archaeology as never before, it also exhibited a lively epistemological autonomy as a scientific field of its own. In a sense, it demarcated the *end of the innocence* of rock art studies in Brazil. IFRAO acted closely with FUMHDAM, the foundation in charge of the archaeological and rock art research in the Serra da Capivara National Park coordinated by Guidon, to put forward the event. But her team did everything on the ground to organise a superb conference in an astonishing humanity heritage setting. That event reset the course of the discipline trajectory in Brazil, allowing for the first time the convergence of the worldwide practitioners of several strains of rock art investigation with Brazilian, yet somewhat provincial, though vibrating and effervescent, rock art archaeological academy.

So, the *aegis* of IFRAO towards ABAR was not an allegoric one. ABAR exists because of a provocation of the IFRAO. However, Bednarik alone could not have reached the Brazilian colleagues without the instrumental aid of the Portuguese Prof. Mila Simões de Abreu. Simões de Abreu bridged ABAR and IFRAO from the moment of the inception of the Brazilian association at the IFRAO meeting held in Portugal in 1997. Even if Bednarik and Guidon collaborated in the late 1980s, as stated before, only after the foundation of ABAR, Brazilian rock art research connected with the worldwide community and agenda of IFRAO. The 2009 international conference in the Serra da Capivara context and its aftermath helped crown ABAR as a national organization and paved the way for its definitive international acknowledgement. From 2010 onward, ABAR meetings started to receive more participants from regions of the country other than the northeast and even from abroad, which enriched further debates.

In 2014, the first Rock Art and Ethnography International Conference occurred in Cochabamba, Bolivia. The Rock Art Association of Cochabamba (AEARC) and the IFRAO hosted the event. Non-indigenous and indigenous, non-white and white researchers from Perú, Bolivia, Brazil, and elsewhere attended. Prof. Roy Querejazu Lewis (Universidad Mayor de San Simon/ AEARC) and Robert Bednarik (IFRAO) were the central figures of the event. As a result of that meeting, we joined a task force composed of representatives from APAR (Perú), AEARC (Bolivia), ABAR and IFRAO to rethink aspects of the decolonization of South American rock art research and management and taking a stand. Issues such as indigenous rights over rock art heritage, threats piling up against living indigenous traditions and sacred sites with rock art, and the participation of indigenous people in the construction of rock art knowledge were all tackled in that effort. Particularly alarming was the Munduruku Indigenous people's struggle against a complex of mega-dams planned to take place along the Tapajós River, Southern Amazonia.

The support of IFRAO was crucial to disperse that initiative throughout the rock art world, starting by gaining support from other South American organizations, like GIPRI from Colombia and CIARU from Uruguay. It consisted of a declaration signed by a pool of South American organizations, generally dedicated to rock art management, research, and conservation from a Western perspective. The statement, however, advocated that South American living Indigenous people, their territories, their epistemologies, their rights, and their well-being are complexly inter-connected with rock art heritage. It was named *The Cochabamba Manifest* and represented a modest but significant turning point in South American rock art research politics and ethics: the acknowledgement that rock art is also a matter of living indigenous well-beingness and rights. However, its acceptance was not immediate. In 2015, other IFRAO-affiliated organizations evaluated the manifest during the XIX IFRAO International conference in Cáceres, Spain. After a heated and polarized debate, a final decision was suspended and postponed. Notwithstanding, a later ballot on that petition resulted favourably and then, IFRAO assumed and released the Cochabamba Manifest on its front page. Robert Bednarik was pivotal in that articulation.

In 2016, Bednarik returned to Brazil for fieldwork in the Rio Grande do Norte state, Northeastern Brazil. The invitation came from professor Valdeci Júnior, from the Rio Grande do Norte State University, as part of his post-doc research on direct dating of petroglyphs in the central hinterland of that region. Bednarik came to gather microerosion data from the sites and estimate the age of their open-air petroglyphs. Prof. Júnior defined the sample based on criteria determined by the dating method. It was a 15-day intensive campaign where I had the opportunity to join the group and act as fieldwork assistant and translator between Bednarik and the Brazilian crew.

It was the first rock art direct dating expedition ever conducted in Brazil. It resulted in age estimations ranging from 5000 years ago to the early 17th century of our era. It allowed a more thorough understanding of a long-held assumption about rock art production in that region and elsewhere concerning long sequences of thousands of years of anthropogenic rock marking on the same rock surfaces and boulders. One of the sites, Papagaio III, the lithophone structure containing hundreds of cupules, yielded a sequencing of dates ranging as long as 2000 years of cupule making in the same spot, for instance. Another interesting result was the demonstration that rock art in that area was still being produced at the beginning of the European invasion, persisting at least one century after the onset of the colonial presence on the coast. Those later manifestations also showed marked stylistic and iconographic differences regarding earlier expressions. It was published in the May issue of the Rock Art Research journal in 2018, highlighting, besides these results, an overview of rock art dating attempts conducted in Brazil in the last 30 years (Santos Júnior et al., 2018).

In 2017, the Peruvian Rock Art Association (APAR) and IFRAO organized the Second Rock Art and Ethnography International Conference in Cusco. It was a productive event that amplified the aims of the first edition in Cochabamba. It received representatives and delegations from India, Saudi Arabia, the United States, Australia, Perú, Bolivia, and Brazil. Once more, Bednarik was one of the most enthusiastic about the articulation between rock art studies and ethnography in South America. The delegation from Brazil counted on the presence of Poani Higino Tenório Tuyuka, a renowned Indigenous scholar and professor from Northwest Amazonia. Prof. Tenório Tuyuka was also an Indigenous rock art expert and researcher in Brazil, the central figure of a decolonial wave in Brazilian rock art studies.

Particularly enlightening was the closing talk proffered by that indigenous professor. Following his thinking, the fundamental flaw in the theoretical matrix of South American rock art studies is the exclusion of indigenous knowledge. Ethnography as a western translation of indigenous thoughts may respond to one part of the problem, as it does not configure as indigenous knowledge itself. However, this has been slowly changing with the rise of Indigenous Anthropology in Brazil, giving birth to a third kind of knowledge since it is not traditionally indigenous (Shamans) nor traditionally ethnographic (Whites). Therefore, it was necessary to bring an indigenous philosopher from the Amazon to an international conference on rock art and ethnography to state that the issue is not about a poorly developed or missing rock art ethnography. The first issue is the epistemicising the Indigenous knowledge, the systematic extermination of the primary sources of the non-western knowledge. Secondly, the lack of epistemological acknowledgement that indigenous thinking consists of effective ways of researching and knowing rock art. The idea that indigenous knowledge about rock art consists of metaphysical interpretations of meaning is epistemologically detrimental. The same applies to valorizing indigenous knowledge based on its usefulness to the Western mindset, like counteracting the Anthropocene without getting insane, a tendency already perceived by others, as in the fascinating book *Ideas to Postpone the End of the World* (Krenak, 2019). In effect, indigenous knowledge does not depend on Western validation or translation.

Prof. Tenório Tuyuka introduced to the participants and the audience the basic concept of *culture of respect* (*Padeo Masirê*), i.e., epistemological alliances between different modes of being and knowing the cosmos, a pre-condition to well-being. In that sense, Indigenous knowledge is a bridge that can lead South American rock art studies towards its next evolutionary step, preventing it from becoming one more impoverished, disempowered, and outdated copycat version of Euromerican theories and methods. Bednarik was attentive in listening and was one of the few who understood the depth of that message. He immediately acknowledged the authority of Prof. Tenório Tuyuka and recorded that impression on his RAR report about that conference. The spirit of the Cochabamba Manifest was alive and deeply enrooted in us. Bednarik kept encouraging its message, reinforced in 2017 by a straightforward decolonial call to arms from Amazonian Indigenous Epistemologies.

In 2018, an interculturally authored paper (Valle et al., 2018) appeared in the second issue of RAR. It was the first time Native Amazonian intellectuals contributed as coauthors to a scientific paper published in an international peer-reviewed journal dedicated to rock art studies. Besides an academic article, it was also a direct decolonial action in South American rock art research, a modest step to better symmetrize indigenous authorial rights over native knowledge. When Prof. Poani Higino Tenório Tuyuka and Prof. Jairo Saw Munduruku signed that paper, they drew a line on the ground. Contemporary theorization on rock art in Amazonia and elsewhere can no longer proceed without listening to and engaging with Indigenous knowledge, keeping a symmetrical articulation, like those maintained with chemistry or geology. It was one more step towards the epistemological decolonization of Brazilian rock art studies. Robert Bednarik was very supportive of that endeavour over the whole process, knowing what was at stake in Amazonia. If part of the contemporary rock art world acknowledges the importance of these native Amazonian intellectuals as Indigenous rock art experts, Robert Bednarik played a relevant role in that process.

Then, the Pandemic came along with many life losses. Among those who died was Prof. Higino Tuyuka in June 2020. The ongoing epistemological decolonization of Brazilian rock art research received a hard blow. Perceiving that critical loss, Robert Bednarik has encouraged an initiative to honour his memory. I wrote an obituary and memorial of my indigenous professor, and Bednarik published it on RAR pages in 2021 (Valle, 2021). In this act of respectful and generous kindness of his sensibility, capable of broadly foreseeing, understanding, and supporting commitments and alliances among beings of different epistemic natures (i.e., *culture of respect*), Bednarik became half-responsible for the immortalization of the first Indigenous rock art researcher in Brazil.

So, these are exemplary contributions beyond those in the scientific realm, which Bednarik can engage with and promote. He has been doing similar things in other underdeveloped countries, supporting their rock art researchers committed to advancing local and regional scientific agendas, and helping protect global rock art heritage and its traditional knowledge sources. In this sense, a coherent way of emphasizing this core aspect of his character is calling it by its proper term: *Generosity* is his middle name.

Dr Raoni Valle
Associate professor and researcher
Visual Anthropology and Archaeology of Image Laboratory - LAVAI
Anthropology and Archaeology Program - PAA
Federal University of Western Pará – UFOPA
Santarém, Pará, Brazil, 11/11/2022.
E-mail: figueiradoinferno@hotmail.com

References

Bednarik, R. G. 1979. The potential of rock patination analysis in Australian archaeology (part 1*). The Artefact* 4 (3 & 4), 14-38.

Bednarik, R.G. 1989. On the Pleistocene Settlements of South America. *Antiquity* 63: 101-101.

Bednarik, R.G. 2017. *Palaeoart of the Ice Age.* Cambridge Scholars Publishing, UK. Pp: 87-87.

Krenak, A. 2019. *Ideias para Adiar o Fim do Mundo.* Editora Companhia das Letras, São Paulo, SP. 104 pp.

Santos J. V., Valle, R., Lavalle, H., Oliveira, D., & Bednarik, R. G. 2018. Direct dating of petroglyphs in Rio Grande do Norte, Brazil. *Rock Art Research,* 35(1), 85–97.

Valle, R., G.-T. Echevarría López, P. H. P. Tenório Tuyuka and J. S. Munduruku 2018. What is Anthropogenic? On the cultural aetiology of geo-situated visual imagery in Indigenous Amazonia. *Rock Art Research* 35 (2): 123–144.

Valle, R. 2021. An Obituary and Memorial of the first Indigenous rock art researcher in Brazil: Prof. Poani Higino Tuyuka, killed by Covid-19 and by the Brazilian government. *Rock Art Research* 38 (1): 08-11.

7

CONTRIBUTIONS OF ROBERT G. BEDNARIK TO PAMPACOLCA, PERU

JESUS E. CABRERA

The little known and studied painted stone tablets in a remote place in the Andes of Southern Peru aroused an interest in Prof. Robert G. Bednarik. Hence, he visited Pampacolca in 2017. His reaction was typical:

"We don't know who made them. We don't know how old they are. We don't know which culture they belong to. We don't know the purpose of these tablets. All we know is they are beautiful, and they are absolutely unique, and they don't occur anywhere else in the world; so, they are a real culture treasure" (personal communication 2017).

The painted rock is a shale, a sedimentary rock abundant in the Yato, Pampacolca area. The paintings are mostly polychrome, although some monochrome paintings are also present. The rock itself was used as a colour. In the painted stone tablet presented to Professor Robert Bednarik, the red, orange, and stone colour were used. The colour combination is astonishing because the coloures don't interfere to each other. The colours red, orange, white, green, blue, black, yellow, and natural colour of the stone were mostly used in the region.

To test the age of the Campanáyoc earth mound where several painted stone tablets can be found on its surface, a charcoal sample was taken from the south side, near the base of the mound where there were many more charcoal fragments in that lower stratum of the structure (R. G. Bednarik, pers. comm. 2017). Radiocarbon measurement from the Beta Analytic Radiocarbon Dating Facility is 2490 +/- 30 BP, conventional radiocarbon age. (Material analysed: Charred material. Report date: October 9, 2017).

The analytical lab test result corresponds to the Formative Period. Very little is known from this period, but the tablets, along with the monumental contexts associated with them in Antimpampa, demand further research. As Robert G. Bednarik notes (personal communication 2017), with these dates:

"We have a chronological anchor point. It doesn't provide a secure age for the painted tablets, but it does offer an initial framework. The first thing this evidence tells us is that 2500 years ago, there was a large population, large enough to provide the surplus-labour for creating such huge non-utilitarian structures. They were able to produce a food surplus; the irrigation system was then operational; therefore, Pampacolca has a long history, and since it is so deeply in the mountains, we can speculate that there must have been dense population elsewhere"

For all these feats in Pampacolca and throughout the world, he was subsequently presented by the people of Pampacolca, with a beautiful and artistic gold medal.

Figure 1: Painted stone tablet from Pampacolca Peru presented to Professor Robert Bednarik during his visit to Pampacolca, Peru.

'In recognition of outstanding accomplishments, contributions and distinguished services in the field of rock art research', the Editor of Rock Art Research, Robert G. Bednarik, has been awarded a gold medal at Pampacolca, Peru, on 22 August 2017. The 17 g, 38.1 mm medal was designed by Jesus E. Cabrera and made of 18-karats gold by Angeles Jeweller in Huaraz, Peru. It features a dedication to the recipient on one side and on the other an image of part of painted stone tablet 5026, one of the thousands recorded near Pampacolca and the Nevado Coropuna region. These fascinating finds, a mobiliar art unique in the world (Bednarik 2017) are the subject of an ongoing investigation, as their antiquity and purpose remain unknown (Cabrera 2012).

Figure 2: Pampacolca Gold Medal conferred on Prof. Robert G. Bednarik.

REFERENCS

CABRERA, J. E. 2012. *La cultura Antimpampa: Arqueología milenaria de Pampacolca en el sur Andino del Perú.* Signature Book Printing, Rockville, MD.

CABRERA, J. E. 2014. *Diseño gráfico arcaico. Testamento histórico de Antimpampa, Perú.* Signature Book Printing, Rockville, MD.

CABRERA, J. E. 2018. Pampacolca Gold Medal conferred on Prof. Robert G. Bednarik. *Rock Art Research 35(1)*: 117.

CABRERA, J. E. 2020. Mobiliary art of Pampacolca, Peru: a palaeoart unique in the world. *Rock Art Research* 37(1): 59-66.

8

WORKING WITH ROBERT G. BEDNARIK IN SAUDI ARABIA

MAJEED KHAN

Robert G. Bednarik, my co-worker and friend, is a world-renowned rock art specialist. We worked together on the rock art of Saudi Arabia, especially at the many sites of Jubbah and Shuwaymis in the north and Hima rock art area in the south of the country, which are now UNESCO World Heritage Sites. These were the first rock art monuments listed in the Middle East and in this part of the world. In addition to conducting extensive research at the sites, we had to prepare dossiers for submission to UNESCO. The Jubbah and Shuwaymis properties were submitted to UNESCO in 2014 and accepted for listing in 2015 ("Rock Art in the Hail Region of Saudi Arabia"). The huge rock art concentration at Hima, north of Najran, was submitted in 2018 and approved in 2021 ("Ḥimā Cultural Area"). Without his help it would not have been possible to do this. He also took part in the comprehensive rock art survey in the northern, central and southern region of the Kingdom.

Bednarik is a very active, highly devoted, and ambitious person. He is a reserved and hard person and it is not possible to make him one's friend easily, but he is my friend and I am proud of that. We have together conducted fieldwork in Saudi Arabia in 2001, 2004, 2013 (twice), 2015, 2017 and 2018. At Shuwaymis, Robert studied the rock art within a few months of the discovery of the monumental site complex, the most extensive Neolithic rock art in the world.

Besides working with him in Saudi Arabia ever since he was first invited there in 2001, I also met him at several rock art congresses and conferences in Australia, Italy, India, Saudi Arabia, China and other countries where he was involved intensively to make those conferences successful. He is the person who absolutely devoted himself to the rock art research, publications and taking care of "*Rock Art Research*", the outstanding journal on rock art of the world. Here are some pictures I am sure he will be happy to see, and that others shall know his devotion and services for Saudi Arabia.

Figure 1: Robert Bednarik Documenting a site near Riyadh, capital of Saudi Arabia.

Figure 2: Drinking camel milk in the desert (2004).

Figure 3: Bedouin rock art custodian (2004).

Figure 4: Negotiating with Bedouins in their living tent (2013).

Figure 5: Pit-stop in the desert (2017).

Dr. Majeed Khan
Consultant rock art
Ministry of Culture, Kingdom of Saudi Arabia
Email: Majeedkhan1942@yahoo.com

Study of Palaeoart of the World, *Tang Huisheng*, *pp. 48-58*

9

ROBERT G. BEDNARIK'S CONTRIBUTION TO THE DATING OF CHINESE ROCK ART

TANG HUISHENG

I have been in correspondence with Professor Robert G. Bednarik since 1987. He is an Australian rock art researcher and member of the Australian Rock Art Research Association (AURA) he founded in 1983. He is also a founder of the International Federation of Rock Art Organizations (IFRAO) and the editor-in-chief of *Rock Art Research*, the journal of these two associations. In September 1988, AURA held its first international congress in Darwin, Australia, and Bednarik strongly invited me to attend as a representative of China. But in those days, it was impossible to go to Australia to attend an international conference without funding. When he knew my situation, Bednarik immediately found financial support for me to attend the conference. Although I was unable to make the trip due to visa and other reasons, Bednarik's intentions in helping his students were evident.

The opportunity came to meet him for the first time at the International Petroglyph Conference held in Yinchuan in 1991. Bednarik was less than 50 years old at that time, with a big beard and dark hair, resembling Karl Marx. I remember very clearly that his presentation at the conference was "Direct dating of rock art". Later, this article was renamed "Developments in rock art dating" and published in *Acta Archaeologica* of the Hungarian Academy of Sciences in 1992. Although Bednarik's English with a strong German accent was difficult to follow for me, I was completely shocked by the huge modern scientific and technological information and the new concept of direct dating he presented. It turned out that rock art was a subject as old as archaeology, yet so profound and so high-tech! Since then, I have tried every means to search for his works, and once I found Bednarik's articles, I devoted myself to studying them.

It was in the process of reading a lot of Bednarik's writings that whenever there was something I didn't understand, I often asked him for advice by email. Bednarik always responded promptly and took the trouble to explain. I think he is an encyclopedic and learned professor, always so patient, gentle jade, and meticulous. By no means is it flippant rhetoric for me to say this, and Bednarik's more than 1,500 published professional articles and more than 20 monographs are worthy of the adjective "encyclopedic" I use. He advocates the use of scientific attitudes and methods to study rock art so that a unique scientific research paradigm is formed in the international rock art circle, which can be called "rock art science". That is the way he wrote his understanding into a book entitled *Rock Art Science.* By "scientific", we mean the research methods in the natural sciences as opposed to the humanities and arts. There is nothing wrong with the Chinese "Rock Art Science", but the English "Rock Art Science" sounds awkward. Is it "art" or "science"? But this is precisely the characteristic of Bednarik's research paradigm: the study of art as science. What is the scientific research paradigm? In short, humanities research is a set of inferences whose purpose is to "verify", while science is based on "falsification". Karl Popper's "falsificationism" holds that there is no such thing as scientific "verification" because interpreters can always choose "facts" to fit an existing theory, making it appear as if it has been "verified". But "falsification" is different. In *The Logic of Scientific Discovery*, Popper said that a theory must propose a conjecture that can be tested experimentally. The conjecture is tested experimentally, and whether the theory is falsified is determined by whether the result conforms to the prediction. A scientific theory must be falsifiable; otherwise, it is not part of science. For instance, Bednarik used experimental research methods when he studied prehistoric humans' maritime capabilities. He chopped bamboo with stone tools he made and then navigated from one Indonesian island to another in a raft, without any utensils, food, water, etc. He repeated such experiments several times, on one occasion travelling for two weeks from Timor to Australia. It is worth noting that he can't swim! This is to use life to practice his academic philosophy.

Taking the cupule petroglyphs as an example, let us look at how Bednarik carried out his scientific research around this phenomenon, that is, the process of falsification and verification, because it embodies his vast intellectual knowledge of rock art science: a small cupule contains a big theory.

The cupules refer to almost hemispherical shaped pits hammered into the rock surface. The diameter is generally between 5 and 20 cm, and the depth ranges from 2 to 10 cm. However, there are also larger and deeper pits. The cupules are like an immortal fairy. Their production began in the Lower Paleolithic and has continued to this day, and their distribution range includes all the world's continents. As early as 1993, Bednarik paid attention to the petroglyph phenomenon, and his research continues to this day. After nearly 30 years of research, Bednarik has published more than a dozen research articles on the subject of cupules, covering all aspects of rock art research, with titles such as "Cupules", "A short ethnography of cupules", "About lithophones", "Cupules: the oldest surviving rock art", "Discriminating between cupules and other rock markings", "Estimating the age of cupules", "Forensic Science of Cupules", "The First Cupule Conference introduction", "The interpretation of cupules", "The science of cupules", "The technology of cupule making", "The tribology of cupules", "About cupules", "The cupules on Chief's Rock,

Auditorium Cave, Bhimbetka", "The quartz cupules of Ajmer, Rajasthan", "Concerning a cupule sequence on the edge of the Kalahari Desert in South Africa" and more. In addition to ethnology, mythological interpretation, documentary records, type comparison, social meaning, functional speculation, cultural symbols, and historical evolution in humanistic research, it also focuses on the physical properties, production process and technology of the cupules, as well as the production process. The morphology involved, strike mechanics, energy investment, various quantitative and analyzable factors in the production process, including effects of kinetic energy metamorphism (KEM) phenomena and their consequences, tectonic bedding, and more. Scientific research is like solving a case, and it must be supported by a chain of evidence. Therefore, Bednarik has repeatedly asserted that in addition to logic, there must be sufficient scientific evidence, so the concept of forensics is often used. This is in line with the traditional Chinese to some extent, as the academic concept of "studying history being as rigorous as solving a case" (*zhi shi ru duan yu*) coincides.

These research articles on cupules provide a path into Bednarik's scientific research paradigm. Adapting to this scientific paradigm, he established a series of theories and methods to conduct rock art research, the most famous of which is the microerosion dating method of petroglyphs.

As we all know, the dating of petroglyphs is a difficult problem, even the more mature dating methods are often full of controversy. Cross dating traditionally used, comparative methods, comprehensive (documents, folklore, myths, and legends, etc.) analysis methods, logical positive methods, etc., are all "indirect dating" in Bednarik's view. The modern scientific and technological dating methods, such as the microerosion analysis he invented, are the direct determination of the age of petroglyphs, which is called "direct dating method". The principle of the microerosion dating method is very simple, that is, through the microscopic observation and measurement of the degree of micro-wane development after the rock crystal is fractured in the petroglyph production process. This is compared with a micro-wane of known age in the same area, and so the approximate petroglyph age is obtained. Compared with most other known direct dating methods, this dating method is scientifically clear in principle and simple in method. The standard of microerosion dating method refers to the actual age of the petroglyphs rather than the minimum or maximum age. And it is non-invasive, with neither contact with the petroglyphs nor contamination factors, and the method even allows the rock art to be dated on-site. However, it also has some limitations: so far, it is only suitable for observations of two minerals (quartz and feldspar); it requires a minimum grain size of about 1.5 mm and a cross-section angle of about 90° for credible measurements. The micro-wane must face the microscope, and since the petroglyphs were made, the rock surface must have been exposed to precipitation. Microerosion analysis provides very reliable but not particularly accurate age estimates for petroglyphs, with errors typically around 15%–20%. Significant differences in rainfall in different environments can be calibrated with microerosion curves of known age rock inscriptions. In recent years, a universal calibration has been created that will eventually eliminate the need for regional calibration curves. Secondly, the field operation of microerosion data requires a lot of practice to master its essence.

Modern research on Chinese rock paintings has developed for more than a hundred years if we start from 1915, when Professor Huang Zhongqin of Lingnan University investigated and researched the cliff stone carvings in Xianzitan, Fujian. In the past 100 years, the investigation, discovery, and preliminary classification of Chinese rock art have been completed. So, what kind of development will the research on Chinese rock art usher in the new century? Which direction should it go? Academic progress and development shall go in the direction of science. Just at this time, Bednarik's paradigm of "rock art science" and the needs of Chinese rock art study and development coincided by chance, forming a trend wave of science. For Chinese rock art study, the direction of rock art science is very clear: the scientific dating of rock art. The age of rock art has always been the weak underbelly of this discipline. If the Chinese rock art discipline is to move up a step towards science, then the first step is dating, which must be stepped over. Just as in the last century, by introducing stratigraphy into antiquities, modern archaeology emerged when science and typology solved the problem of the relative age of the antiquities. In other words, rock art is a labyrinth leading to the spiritual life, ideology, religious concept, aesthetic taste and artistic taste of the ancients, and this labyrinth has many entrances, but only one entrance can lead us to the center of the labyrinth. The key to find the correct entrance is dating.

Although the microerosion analysis method is still full of controversy and needs to be continuously improved patiently, it is the direction of science, after all. In 2014, I made an appointment with Bednarik. In the next few years, we would use the microerosion analysis method to date the relevant petroglyphs in China.

The first site for microerosion dating was Juci Mountain in Xinzheng, Henan Province. Juci Mountain is a newly discovered rock art site complex known for its cupules at the beginning of this century. It was an afternoon in June 2014. At the invitation of Henan Xinzheng Huangdi Hometown Culture Research Association, Professor Bednarik (representing the International Federation of Rock Art Organizations) and Professor Kumar Giriraj, representing the Rock Art Society of India, and I, representing Hebei Normal University, came to Xinzheng to form a joint rock art dating team to carry out microerosion dating of the cupules of Juci Mountain. At that time, Liu Wuyi, the deputy mayor of Xinzheng City, was the leader of the joint team. Although he was a government official, he was also a doctor of chemistry. He spoke fluent English, and the entire knowledge structure was sufficient to lead this professional team. Under the careful arrangement and full cooperation of Xinzheng Huangdi Hometown Culture Research Association, we carried out a carpet-like inspection of the entire cupules of Juci Mountain, and all petroglyphs suitable for microerosion analysis were subjected to detailed microscopic observation.

In the beginning, except for Bednarik, none of us could correctly find crystals and angles suitable for microscopic observation, so Bednarik, who was 70 years old at the time, was always in charge. In late June, the temperature in Henan was as high as nearly 40 degrees, while the temperature on the rock surface was as high as 50-60 degrees. When Bednarik had to lie on the hot rock surface for microscopic observation, it often took up to an hour! Every time he got up, there was a wet and clear human figure printed on the rock face, which reminded me of an ancient Chinese torture: gun baking, a person was tied up to a copper pillar which was heated. Although this association of ideas is not positive energy, it will help us to imagine how difficult the expedition was!

The subsequent discovery of a major rock art concentration in Henan Province prompted a very successful rock art dating expedition in that region and Ningxia and Jiangsu Provinces during June and July 2014. It utilised China's wealth of rock surfaces suitable for microerosion calibration, especially soundly dated rock inscriptions. Several calibration curves, as well as twenty-seven age estimates from petroglyphs, were secured. This work included testing previous archaeological age predictions for some of the best-known Chinese petroglyph complexes, such as those of Helanshan and Jiangjunya. For instance, there had been numerous age estimates for the famous Helanshan petroglyphs near Yinchuan, ranging from the Pleistocene to recent centuries, and based on various methods. The 2014 campaign furnished reliable estimates of E2000 to E2330 years BP.

On the other hand, the seven dates secured from the Jiangjunya site, 14 km west of Lianyungang, ranged widely, from about E369 to E5380 years BP, demonstrating the use of the site from Neolithic to recent historical times. At some of the site's, the petroglyphs have been demonstrated to have been retouched after their initial creation. For example, I made a petroglyph about 2210 years ago, but was retouched some 360 years ago. Such reworking of a petroglyph cannot be readily identified by any other dating method. All age estimates of this campaign were again obtained by microerosion analysis and are thus repeatable. Now or centuries afterwards in the future, any researcher can locate the dated motif and even the specific micro-wane and re-measure it. This adds the benefit that future erosion rates can be determined.

The microerosion dating missions of rock art in China started in 2014 and were all implemented in the summer. In June and October 2015, we successively carried out rock art dating work in Xinjiang, Inner Mongolia, Ningxia, Guangxi, Henan and other provinces. Although new age estimates were only secured from two of these regions, the expeditions provided an essential overview of the scale of Chinese rock art, the logistics of developing comprehensive approaches to its dating, and several other scientific data. More than any such work previously undertaken in China, these journeys impressed the need to develop flexible approaches utilizing multiple methods, with geomorphological procedures forming the most reliable core. Nevertheless, a series of five other microerosion estimates were secured from the Henan sites Xuanluoling, Taibailing and Paomaling, all forming part of the extensive Mt Juci complex.

In 2015, Xu Jialu, Vice-Chairman of the National People's Congress, wrote in *Guangming Daily*:

> "In recent years, with the high participation and support of various universities and research institutions, a lot of work has been carried out. In June 2014, the World Federation of Rock Art Organizations conducted the micro-erosion dating of the rock art of Juci Mountain in the Central Plains. The most representative result is E4520, +330/-580 years. In Mr. Sima Qian's account of the Yellow Emperor, recorded and passed down through oral traditions, did indeed once lived here for a

long time as a tribe or as a chief. We can basically confirm the legend that the Yellow Emperor was born here. " (Xu Jialu: "The Power of National Worship", *Guangming Daily*, November 09, 2015, 16th edition).

In 2015, the microerosion determination of the age of a human face petroglyph at the Xiaofengshan rock art site in Inner Mongolia, in particular, is consistent with the archaeological data on the human face in this area, and it could be considered as dual evidence. The petroglyph was hammered into rhyolite, and the dating results show that it belongs to the late Neolithic period, being about 4730 years old. This not only confirms the archaeological expectation that the rock art of human faces in this area belongs to that period but also serves as a scientific reference for understanding the age of rock art of human faces in other regions of China. When I inspected the petroglyph site of Xiaofeng Mountain in Inner Mongolia, it was already October, and the weather had turned cooler. We had to climb a hill to get to another site, and at the top, we encountered probably the biggest gusts of wind we had ever experienced in our lives. We stood on the top of the mountain, leaning at a 45-degree angle to the ground, and the wind blew our coats up like sacks full of grain. Watching the frost-haired Bednarik leaning against the wind, I suddenly remembered a poem: the hair is spread out like a sail in thousands of miles of autumn wind (*Wan Li Qiu Feng Liang Bin Peng*)! If a rope had been tied around our waists, we could have been flown as kites! The man who was 70 years old was enjoying the feeling of being weightless in the wind like a child. He opened his arms and stood against the wind for a long time, letting the strong wind hold up his body. At this time, he suddenly said a sentence to me, causing me to make a decision to dedicate myself to rock art study: it was so exhilarating to engage in rock art!

In June 2017, the joint team surveyed rock paintings in the Daxing'anling area of Heilongjiang Province, in the northernmost part of China. We obtained dating samples for $^{230}Th/^{234}U$ analysis, the first dating of Chinese rock paintings of the hunting-gathering people (or forest rock art). The dating results are significant and led to a fundamental reassessment of a method that has been scientifically controversial for years. Afterwards, the joint team moved to Tongbai Mountains in Yunxian County, Hubei Province, to conduct microerosion dating of the cupule petroglyphs. There are many petroglyphs in the Huaihe River Basin that are generally similar to those in the southern Henan region. We obtained dating data from eight petroglyph sites, all from cupule petroglyphs. The age of the rock paintings in the Tongbai Mountains is about 650-1270 years ago, indicating that the widely distributed cupules in this area are relatively young. The dating results of this work are interpreted according to a recently established universal calibration curve.

When we inspected the Cave of Northern Mountain in the Daxinganling Forest, we saw a stone path about 3 kilometers long, paved with square marbles, leading to the North Cave in the dense forest. Chinese creativity is infinite! Bednarik said, then looked at Professor Kumar with provocative eyes. Kumar shook his head and smiled graciously; Indians nodding their heads means no while shaking their heads means yes, thus expressing his approval. It was a way of harmony and friendship between Prof. Bednarik and Prof. Kumar. In fact, Bednarik is rather like an English gentleman, solemn, prudent, temperate, scientific, self-disciplined, polite, never excessive. Being with him often feels like a kind of historical travel, as if returning to the Victoria era. An English gentleman's lunch is always a sandwich, which is said to save time, and Bednarik is more diligent and industrious than an English gentleman. He never eats lunch. At noon there was a strange sight at our table: all the people were eating, only he, as if still sitting at his desk, kept busy writing, recording the morning's work. When we visited Tongbai Mountain, the weather was quite hot. After a whole day of observation and measurement during the day, we were very tired when we came back at night. After dinner, we were willing to take a walk by the river, chat and take a break. This is the most relaxing time of leisure moments. But Prof. Bednarik never joined us, and even though we invited him several times, he smiled, shook his head, and refused. Now it was time for Prof. Kumar's "pay back", saying that he is like a machine with no "humanity", no need for entertainment and relaxation, everything in life is designed according to drawings, and there are no accidents, no casual time, no entertainment, and no laziness.

When you first meet Bednarik, you will think that he is an unapproachable person, always so polite and well-behaved, but after getting to know him well, you will find that he is really a most approachable person. He never talks about himself or his family; he always talks about rock art. But another time, he told me that he had money and, therefore, he did not need to waste time trying to earn it. He said this not to arouse my coveting but to show a situation that he can use money to do something he likes. In addition to *Rock Art Research*, he is the editor of other archaeological journals and personally funded and edited some. Doing microerosion dating in China, including a training course on microerosion dating in Yinchuan, many companies wanted to pay him. Some of them were very generous, but he did not take a penny every time; sometimes, even the flight expenses from Melbourne to China were paid by himself. Hebei Normal University employs him as a chair professor, and he also lets the payment be put in the card, saying that in the future, he would spend it on the investigation, research, and protection of Chinese rock art. For religious people, living is to die; for non-religious people, living is to enjoy. And for Bednarik, living is for rock art. His situation reminds me of the European antiquarians in the 17th century or the epigraphists of the Qian-Jia school in China, who were sheltered by inheritance or ancestral resources, had no worries about food and clothing, were dedicated to learning, did what they liked, and produce the purest knowledge. It seems that my initial sense of historical travel was not groundless.

In 2017, I visited his house in Melbourne. His focus and expenses were obviously not on his house. Compared with his neighbors, his house was small and old, and the furnishings in the house were modest. He drove me around the South Pacific coast with a Chinese-made, Great Wall SUV truck, driving like a lad! This is a car that fully embodies his Chinese heart and simple life.

In 2019, the focus of rock art dating turned to the Qinghai-Tibet Plateau, especially the Garze Tibetan Autonomous Prefecture in Sichuan Province and the Yushu Tibetan Autonomous Prefecture in Qinghai Province. In August 2019, the joint team surveyed 12 petroglyph sites in the area, which contained many petroglyphs of animal forms and Buddhist engravings of the late period. Despite painstaking efforts, we were only able to extract one set of dating data from the petroglyphs. It comes from a geometric motif similar to a pagoda at the Kewa rock painting point in Chengduo County, Yushu, and is dated to about E2089+218/-295 years ago.

Professor Bednarik is a petrographer, prehistorian, and a lover of bear traces. When we inspected the Cave of Northern Mountain in the Daxinganling Forest, we found some traces at the top of the end of the cave, which Bednarik thought were bear claw marks. He has conducted extensive studies of the claw marks of the cave bear in European caves. At the time, Bednarik explained that this must be the trace of bears hibernating in the cave during the winter because the top of the cave is the warmest place in the whole cave. In August 2019, when we visited the Angsai National Geopark in the upper reaches of the Lancang River in Zaduo County, Yushu, it was said that there was a 12th-century pagoda called Ba Aixiong. Bednarik was not interested in the stupa, but when he heard that there were many bear claw marks on the stupa, he immediately became interested. The place where Ba Aixiong pagoda is a 12th-century monastery building located on the mountainside of a high mountain, without a road, and can only be accessed on foot or horseback. It was abandoned due to its remoteness and became a haunt of bears. There are some grains and butter as oblations in the pagoda, and the bears may want to open the pagoda to eat the oblations. Bednarik was as happy as he was seeing petroglyphs when we tried so hard to climb to Ba Aixiong Monastery and saw the bear's paw marks on the pagoda. Bear claw marks are a kind of bioglyph in Bednarik's eyes. When we rode through the woods, the guide whistled from time to time to avoid being attacked by bears. Bednarik complained a little: This would scare the bear away! There are not only petroglyphs of bears in European Paleolithic caves but also clay sculptures of bears, who were frequent visitors to prehistoric art sites. Like loving the branch as much as the tree, as a prehistorian or speleologist, Bednarik probably likes bears for this very reason.

In the summer of 2018, the International Rock Art Conference of the Camuno Center for Prehistoric Studies was held in the Camonica Valley, Italy. Professor Kumar and I arrived on the same day, and Bednarik also drove from Austria to Italy to attend the conference. After the meeting, he invited me to drive back to Austria with him to investigate some Paleolithic caves of the Alps in central Europe. The reason he invited me was to look for bear marks in the caves of the Alps. Sure enough, after Bednarik returned to Austria that year, he found bear claw marks. Still, he also unexpectedly discovered human finger markings of the Paleolithic in the Drachenhöhle, the largest cave bear cave in the Alps, thus ending the history of no rock art having been found in Central Europe. Later, Bednarik wrote the article "First Pleistocene rock art found in central Europe", published in the French archaeological journal *L'Anthropologie*. Although this is a Paleolithic rock art survey and research in central Europe, and although I regret not having been able to go to Austria with Bednarik for this historically well-known rock art survey, Bednarik's survey can be counted as work content of this joint team.

It is precisely because of the results of the microerosion dating expeditions in the first two years, and for the improvement and development of Chinese rock art research in a scientific direction, that I founded the International Center of Rock Art Dating (ICRAD). It was officially established at Hebei Normal University on May 16, 2016. The leading scientist of this center is Professor Bednarik.

The center will establish a comprehensive global information database that includes all the direct dating projects and results of petroglyphs and rock paintings in the world since the early 1980s and conduct rock art dating research in China. There is a simple ground rule for the International Center to rock art dating to ensure the scientific integrity of the record: investigative reports must be provided so that other researchers can attempt to replicate (or refute) the reported findings by the same or other methods. Therefore, the dating criterion must be described so that a second investigator can reliably relocate it. The International Center of Petroglyph Dating also stressed the need for a protocol that would stand the test of time and would not require major revisions in the future. To facilitate the implementation of this protocol, the Center established a system that attempts to number each petroglyph determination with a unique code, much like how radiocarbon dating results are identified. Without such a system, the growing amount of unorganized and incompatible data will eventually become unmanageable. The Center's direct dating database will eventually be made publicly available to facilitate its use worldwide.

Since the beginning of direct dating of Chinese rock art in this century, or since the establishment of the International Center of Rock Art Dating, China's efforts to directly date rock art have continued unabated. After 2019, due to the new corona-19 epidemic, the multinational joint expedition could not come to China and operations were suspended temporarily, but the work of rock art dating has never been interrupted. It is worth noting that in this direct dating project of rock art, in addition to microerosion analysis, methods such as carbon 14 and U-Th dating methods, etc. have also frequently entered the ranks of rock art dating.

In March 2019, a survey of parietal art in Guangxi discovered cat images in a cave, and members of the International Center for Rock Art Dating used the carbon-14 analysis method to determine the charcoal used to depict the paintings and superimposed on them. There is also a small residue of honeycomb wax on paint residues, which was also used to date. Charcoal particles in the white paint on the body parts of the cat-shaped image provided a dating result of about 250±30 years ago; the dating result of the honeycomb is about 80±30 years ago. With this relatively recent scientific dating of the rock paintings, combined with the use of ethnological materials, we are accurately able to explain the origin, popularity, and disappearance of cat-shaped rock art and the specific rituals of praying for rain related to Zhuang people in Guangxi, Thailand, and whole southeastern Asia.

In June 2020, the Center cooperated with Sichuan University of Science and Technology, Yibin Museum and other units to systematically survey and date the rock paintings and hanging coffins in Gongxian County, Sichuan. The U-Th dating result shows that rock painting occurred 388±158 years ago; that is, the works date from the time of Emperor Shizong of the Ming Dynasty during the Jiajing period. This provides a reliable basis for the age and interpretation of rock paintings in the historical period of the entire southwest China.

In November 2021, the Center, together with the Cultural Relics Administration of Diqing Tibetan Autonomous Prefecture in Yunnan Province, the Diqing Cultural Relics Protection Society in Yunnan Province, and the Xi'an Jiaotong University, conducted a joint rock art expedition to investigate 12 rock painting sites in the Jinsha River Basin of Shangri-La, Yunnan Province. The rock art sites were surveyed, and uranium-series dating samples were collected and age-analyzed at 10 of them. Although the article on the dating report has not yet been published, only from the current laboratory data, the age of the rock paintings in the Jinsha River Basin is undoubtedly in the late Paleolithic, and several of the data are between 10,000 and 30,000 years old, which is quite exciting. Upper Paleolithic art and rock art, although seemingly a forgotten academic field throughout the Far East, and China, in particular, is one of the archaeological subjects in the world which has been most talked about. The cave paintings in southwestern Europe are not only the earliest and largest collection of human artworks of the Upper Paleolithic in the world but also have always been regarded as the origin of human art and symbolic system. The belief that "this lamp has always been shining in the dazzling light of creativity in Europe" is also the root of Eurocentrism. However, the status of Eurocentrism has been challenged in recent years with the new discoveries of archaeological materials. In 2007, M. Aubert and others from Griffith University in Australia conducted uranium-series dating of animal rock paintings in East Timor, Indonesia, dating back more than 20,000 years ago; at the beginning of this century, Aubert *et al.* have performed uranium-series dating on the animals and handprint rock art in Leang Timpuseng, Sulawesi, Indonesia, and obtained 40,000-year-old data; in 2019, it was still Aubert *et al.* who did the uranium series dating of the earliest human hunting scene in the Leang Bulu 'Sipong 4 cave in Sulawesi. It obtained even more amazing ancient data dating back 43,900 years. It has been observed that the U/Th dates of rock art used to be 3-4 times higher than the actual dates throughout the world, hence need to be rechecked by other dating methods.

The significance of our joint team's survey and dating of the Paleolithic rock paintings on the Jinsha River from 2018 to 2020 is not only to confirm the antiquity of the Upper Paleolithic rock paintings in Asia but also to break the Eurocentrism on the origin of art and symbolic system. Although Professor Bednarik is of European (Austrian) origin, he is staunchly anti-Eurocentrism and anti-hegemonism. It was with his support that we carried out a persistent and systematic dating study of the Upper Paleolithic rock paintings in the Jinsha River Basin. Regarding the origin of Asian rock art, which rivals European counterparts, the recent dating data of Qiusang's feet in Tibet for 220,000 years has aroused strong attention from the world's art, rock art, and archaeological circles. Although there are different views on its age and whether it is rock art, it has added weight to Asia in the balance of the origin of art.

From July to August 2021, the Center and several units conducted direct dating of the rock paintings of Namtso Rim in Tibet by microerosion, uranium-thorium, carbon 14 and other methods, and for the first time, systematically obtained a large number of direct dating data of rock paintings in Tibet. This dating wave initiated by Professor Bednarik in China is still surging up at present. It is believed that driven by this powerful wave, Chinese rock art research is steadily moving in the direction of rock art science.

Acknowledgments

The work described here was sponsored by Guangxi Minzu University' talent introduction research project, 'The Collection and Arrangement of Rock Art Documents in Southeast Asia (Project Approval Number: 2020SKQD21); Guangxi Minzu University' research project, 'The Southwest Rock Art Symbols and the Construction of the Sense of Community for the Chinese Nation' (Project Approval Number: 2021GXMGY0306).

Prof. Tang Huisheng
Archaeological Dept, School of History and Culture
Hebei Normal University, 20 Naerhuandonglu,
Shijiazhuang, China
E-mail: tanghuisheng@163.com

10

MY PERSONAL FEELINGS ABOUT THE ACADEMIC COGNITION OF ROBERT G. BEDNARIK AND HIS METHODOLOGY

LI MAN

My initial encounter with Professor Robert G. Bednarik, an Australian rock art researcher, took place during our collaborative investigation in June 2017, exploring the Daxing'anling area in Heilongjiang Province and Suizhou, Hubei Province. Upon meeting Professor Bednarik for the first time, I was deeply impressed. He stood tall and robust, with white hair and a large beard, resembling Karl Marx. Despite learning about his age, it was difficult to believe that the strong and energetic figure before me was over 70 years old. This joint investigation marked my initial foray into the field of rock art dating as I entered my doctoral studies. At that time, my understanding of rock art and its research methods was still limited and vague. While I had encountered rock art in art history books, my knowledge was confined to the notion that "rock art is the oldest form of art," without any understanding of how to study it.Therefore, I consider myself fortunate to have been guided by Professor Bednarik and Professor Tang Huisheng, both esteemed figures in international rock art research. As a novice, their mentorship provided a guiding light in my journey, akin to walking through darkness with a beacon to illuminate the way.

In June 2017, the joint team led by Professor Bednarik, Professor Kumar Giriraj, an Indian rock art researcher, and Professor Tang Huisheng of the International Rock Art Dating Center of Hebei Normal University surveyed rock paintings in the Daxing'anling area of Heilongjiang Province, in the northernmost part of China. This expedition is of great significance. It is not

Manuscript received: 23 October 2022
Revised I: 26 May 2023
Revised II: 18 June 2023
Accepted: 18 June 2023

only the first dating of Chinese rock paintings of the hunting-gathering people (or forest rock art), but also to date the rock paintings in the area to about 2100 years ago. Importantly, this dating expedition has led to a fundamental reassessment of a method that has been scientifically controversial for years (Bednarik 2022; Tang 2021).

During the early summer, the heavily forested Greater Khingan Mountains posed a risk of tick bites for the joint investigation team as they ventured deep into the dense forest in search of rock paintings. From May to August each year, ticks in this area become active and reproductive. Ticks, belonging to the Parasitidae order and superfamily, are a prevalent poisonous bloodsucking insect in Northeast Heilongjiang Province. While they lack wings for flight, they navigate swiftly among plants and trees, earning them the local nickname "Cao pazi" or grass crawlers. Ticks typically target areas with relatively thin skin on their hosts, such as behind the ear, neck, and armpit, where scratching is less likely to occur. These bites often go unnoticed initially, as people generally don't feel pain due to the tick's secretion of a narcotic substance. However, once engorged with blood, a tick's body can swell to the size of a spider, tens or even hundreds of times its original size. During bloodsucking, the tick's chelicerae and suboral plate penetrate the host's skin, releasing substances that can harm the human body. Prompt removal of ticks is necessary once they penetrate the skin. Failure to do so can result in mild reactions, such as local congestion, edema, and acute inflammation. In the years following the bite, the affected area may become unbearably itchy during rainy weather. Severe cases can lead to high fever, deep coma, convulsions, and even forest encephalitis. Tick bites in China annually result in numerous serious consequences, including fatalities. To mitigate the risk, the team adhered to the guidance of local investigators, wearing long trousers and clothing made of smooth fabrics in the field. They ensured the collar, cuffs, and trouser legs were tightly secured to prevent ticks from attaching or penetrating the clothing. Despite their efforts, spending long hours in the field and remaining in the primary tick habitat of birch forests made it difficult to avoid becoming a victim. Fortunately, except for G. Kumar, none of the team members suffered tick bites over the course of several days.

After the expedition, the joint investigation team boarded a plane bound for Hubei to continue their rock art survey in the Suizhou area. However, just as the plane was about to take off, Robert noticed two blood-sucking ticks on Professor Kumar's neck, who was seated next to him. There were no medicines or tools available on the plane to deal with this situation, and we felt anxious and worried about how to resolve the issue. With a calm and composed demeanor, Professor Bednarik took out a mini handheld magnifying glass and a small pair of tweezers from his fanny pack of field tools to carefully inspect the tick bites. Subsequently, Robert explained that the oxygen supply to the ticks could be severed by applying any form of grease. Kumar then asked the flight attendant to provide vicks or any form of greasy material. The flight attendant kindly provided one that was used in cold. Robert applied a thick layer of it on the ticks to cut off their oxygen supply. Two hours later, when we arrived at Wuhan Tianhe International Airport and were waiting to collect our luggage, Robert inspected Kumar's neck and gently pulled out the ticks. He even drew a picture of it to explain the situation to the younger team members.

Although it was a small matter, I was deeply impressed by Robert's calm and composed demeanor in handling the entire incident. His approach of analyzing and solving problems in a scientific manner reflects his understanding and practice of the scientific spirit. Furthermore, his extensive expertise is truly admirable.

Afterward, the joint investigation team relocated to Tongbai Mountain in Yunxian County, Hubei Province, for the purpose of conducting microerosion dating on cupule petroglyphs. This marked the first direct dating project of rock art in Hubei Province. Unlike the rock paintings found in the Daxing'anling area of Heilongjiang Province, the cupule petroglyphs here exhibit a distinctively different style. Cupules are hemispherical concave patterns, ranging from 3 to 10 cm in diameter and 1 to 6 cm in depth, created by ancient people using stone or metal tools through direct or indirect percussion techniques. Occasionally, larger and deeper cupules can also be found.

In addition to the traditional "indirect dating methods" such as cross-dating, comparative analysis of cultural factors, comprehensive analysis methods (including historical documents, folklore, myths, and legends), and logical positive methods, the most reliable direct dating method for petroglyphs is microerosion dating, pioneered by Bednarik. This quantitative process at the microscopic level involves examining the micro-wane, which precisely reflects the time elapsed since the rock crystal fractures occurred during the creation of the petroglyphs. By comparing the micro-wane formation rate with the known age of the same area, an approximate age of the petroglyphs can be determined (Bednarik 1992; 1993). Unlike many other direct dating methods, microerosion dating provides the actual age of the petroglyphs rather than a minimum or maximum range. Moreover, it is a non-invasive technique that does not require direct contact with the rock art, eliminating the risk of contamination. This method even allows age determinations to be made on-site (Bednarik 2022). Dating data was obtained from eight cupule petroglyph sites, revealing that the petroglyphs in the Tongbai Mountains date back approximately 650-1270 years ago. This suggests that the widely distributed cupules in this area are relatively young, indicating a long-standing tradition of rock petroglyphs in the region.

Initially, I had limited knowledge about cupules and the principles and methods of microerosion dating. I found myself unsure of what to make of these neatly arranged small round cup marks on the rock, except for being intrigued by them. In comparison to the expertise displayed by the other members of the expedition, I felt more like a mere visitor. However, witnessing Professor Bednarik's enthusiastic, composed, precise, patient, and persistent approach to his work deeply touched and inspired me.

During mid-June, the temperature in Hubei Province soared above 30 degrees Celsius. Imagine spending an entire day lying on the scorching hot rock surface, as if being an ant on a sizzling pan, enduring every minute and second with great discomfort. Yet, Robert had to lie on the heated rock to carefully identify suitable crystals and angles for microscopic observation. This process often took tens of minutes, and sometimes even up to an hour! The fair-skinned Australian would quickly turn into a "red man" under the sun's relentless heat, and whenever he stood up, his sweat would leave a damp and distinct human figure imprinted on the rock face (Fig. 1). It is worth mentioning that even a young and robust individual would find it challenging to endure such intense "gun baking torture," which was a form of cruel punishment in ancient China. This experience made me truly appreciate Professor Bednarik's seriousness and unwavering dedication.

Figure 1: Professor Bednarik and his team are doing microerosion dating in Hubei Province, China.

In March 2019, the International Centre of Rock Art Dating (ICRAD) conducted a project investigating cave rock art in Guangxi Region that discovered a new type of cave rock paintings tradition rich in feline depictions. The investigators used 14C analysis to estimate the age of charcoal particles left in rock cracks applied in rock painting and the wax of a small beehive superimposed over paint residues, respectively. According to the dating results, the charcoal flakes in the white paint of a feline provided a date of 250±30 years BP, and the beehive yielded 80±30 years BP (Li 2022). This relatively recent tradition has been explained in terms of available ethnographic information provided by the Zhuang people of the region. For example, through the historical documents and ethnological materials about the ceremony of "做天" in Guangxi and the comparative study with the ceremony of "black south cat" praying for rain in Thailand. It is preliminarily believed that the cat-like rock paintings in Pingxiang area are the manifestation of the specific ritual of praying for rain and holding a memorial ceremony for the Zhuang people during the Kangxi period of the Qing Dynasty (Li in press)

After the investigation, encouraged by Professor Tang, I wrote the first-ever rock art research report in English titled "Discovery of new types of cave rock paintings in Guangxi Zhuang Autonomous Region of China" and submitted it to Rock Art Research, a prestigious journal in the field. Professor Robert G. Bednarik, the founder of the International Federation of Rock Art Organizations (IFRAO) and the editor-in-chief of *Rock Art Research*, played a pivotal role in this process. Initially, I had doubts about getting published in such a renowned journal. However, to my surprise, I received a letter from Robert, congratulating me on my work and commending the dating results of the rock paintings uncovered during the investigation of cave rock art in Guangxi Region.

Robert noted that our study represented the second case worldwide in which the age of a rock painting was estimated by determining the ^{14}C age of a beehive wax substance superimposed over paint residues. He provided me with insightful editorial opinions and revision suggestions, expressing his enthusiasm and encouragement. With his patient guidance, the article was ultimately published in Rock Art Research (Li 2020). Not only was the paper featured as the lead article in that issue, but the survey image was also used on the journal's cover. This recognition has undoubtedly bestowed upon me great honor and encouragement. Moreover, it has helped me discover and reinforce my direction and confidence in studying rock paintings in the future.

In August 2019, ICRAD shifted its focus of rock art dating to the Qinghai-Tibet Plateau in Western China, especially the Garze Tibetan Autonomous Prefecture in Sichuan Province and the Yushu Tibetan Autonomous Prefecture in Qinghai Province. The rock art on the Qinghai-Tibet Plateau is dominated by the "northern steppe style" characterized by directly striking or carving petroglyphs of animal form. The joint team conducted a week-long microerosion dating project on the Qinghai-Tibet Plateau, which surveyed 12 petroglyph sites in the area, which contained many petroglyphs of animal forms and Buddhist engravings of the late period. Despite painstaking efforts, we were only able to extract one set of dating data from the petroglyphs. It comes from a geometric motif similar to a pagoda at the Kewa rock painting point in Chengduo County, Yushu, and is dated to about E2089+218/-295 years ago. That is to say, some of the Kewa rock art was made in the Han Dynasty (Li 2022). This endeavour provides the first scientific rock art direct-dating result in Yushu and demonstrates the Early Metal Age of some petroglyphs in the Yushu area.

The Hengduan Mountains on the Qinghai-Tibet Plateau in China are renowned for their remarkable topographic diversity and complexity. This region is characterized by towering mountains, mighty rivers, expansive steppes, and abundant biodiversity. Situated at an average altitude of over 4200 meters, conducting field surveys in this high-altitude environment is extremely challenging, especially for individuals over 70 years old. Surprisingly, Robert remained unaffected by altitude sickness during various activities such as mountain climbing, horse riding, and river crossings. He moved with agility and vitality, refusing assistance from concerned young companions who worried about his physical endurance. Robert did not appreciate being treated differently due to his age and would often say, "Don't treat me like an old man" or "I'm not an old man."

During our investigation of the Gengzhuo Site Complex in Yushu Tibetan Autonomous Prefecture, we encountered scattered blocks with petroglyphs along a rural road at the base of mountains on the north bank of the Tongtian River, the primary source of the Yangtze River. The slope in this area was nearly vertical and covered with slippery gravel. The younger members of the expedition struggled to ascend the steep incline, but Robert effortlessly conquered it without much exertion or heavy breathing. It is important to note that he accomplished this feat at the age of 76! We couldn't help but admire his physical prowess and determination.

Figure 2: Professor Bednarik and his team were doing microerosion dating at Gengzhuo Site Complex in Yushu area, Qinghai Province.

While many view rock paintings as "art" or "culture," Robert perceives rock art as exograms and approaches its study with scientific and logical thinking, employing rigorous testing methods. He advocates for a scientific research paradigm in the study of rock art, utilizing the theories and methods of natural science. Unlike humanities research that relies on ethnology, myth interpretation, literature records, type comparison, social significance, functional speculation, and cultural symbols to "confirm" personal conjectures and inferences, scientific research should be verifiable and falsifiable. This means that proposed theories must withstand experimental testing and scientific theories must be capable of being disproven. Repetition is the foundation of science, as the verification of any hypothesis or inference requires logical rationality and a chain of supporting evidence.

In contrast to interpreting the content of rock art (the "what" and "why"), scientific research focuses more on determining the age, physical properties, production process, and production technology of rock art (the "when" and "how"). Robert emphasizes the use of scientific research methods to experimentally test theories and validate his conclusions. For example, in his book "The First Mariners," he explored the seafaring capabilities of prehistoric people by personally crafting stone tools to cut bamboo and construct a raft. Without any provisions, tools, or communication equipment, he successfully navigated from one Pacific Island to another, despite not knowing how to swim. This demonstrated Robert's commitment to scholarly rigor and his dedication to the principles of science.

As we are aware, dating petroglyphs is a challenging task, and even the more established dating methods often spark controversy. Microerosion analysis has emerged as the most reliable direct dating method, extensively utilized by researchers worldwide, including members of the International Federation of Rock Art Organizations (IFRAO). Direct dating of rock art involves determining its age based on the physical relationship between the petroglyph or pictogram and the dating criteria, which can be tested and falsified (Bednarik 2010). The claims of direct dating must adhere to the rigorous standards of scientific inquiry, distinguishing it epistemologically from traditional archaeological approaches used to establish the age of rock art. Traditional methods rely on deductive reasoning instead of untestable assumptions, such as archaeological excavation, style analysis, and iconography (Bednarik 2017). Scientific investigation demands precise predictions about measurable phenomena, describing regularities as consistent patterns explained by falsifiable theories that establish cause and effect relationships. Modern science adheres to a normative epistemic relativism, requiring concrete processes that can be falsified and experiments that can be repeated (Bednarik 2017). Robert consolidated this unique scientific research paradigm and theoretical methods in his book, "Rock Art Science," which encapsulates his comprehensive ideological and intellectual framework, as well as systematic research theories and methods in the field of paleoart science.

Looking back on the collaborative journey with Professor Bednarik over the past few years, I have been deeply influenced by his rigorous academic attitude, scientific research paradigm, and his enthusiastic and efficient work ethic. Professor Bednarik has not only provided valuable insights and guidance in the field of rock art, but more importantly, under his mentorship, I have come to realize the importance of applying scientific principles to rock art research. It has transformed my attitude towards rock paintings from mere curiosity to a genuine passion for the subject. In my opinion, Professor Bednarik embodies the spirit of "science as the sole pursuit." His unwavering commitment to academic rigor and pursuit of scientific knowledge is evident in his application of scientific methodology and critical thinking in rock art research. His enthusiasm and efficiency in his work have deeply resonated with scholars and continue to inspire the younger generation in the academic community. I firmly believe that under the guidance of Professor Bednarik, the study of Chinese rock art will further advance in a more scientific direction.

Dr. Li Man
School of Literature and History
Shijiazhuang University
No. 6 Changjiang Dadao, Yuhua District,
Shijiazhuang , Hebei Province, China
E-mail: liman223@163.com

References

Bednarik, R.G. 1992. A new method to date petroglyphs. *Archaeometry* 34: 279–291.

Bednarik, R.G. 1993. Geoarchaeological dating of petroglyphs at Lake Onega, Russia. *Geoarchaeology* 8(6): 443–463.

Bednarik, R. G., A. Achrati, M. Consens, F. Coimbra, G. Dimitriadis, T. Huisheng, A. Muzzolini, D. Seglies and Y. A Sher (eds) 2010. *Rock art glossary: a multilingual dictionary*, second edition. *Occasional AURA Publication* 16, Australian Rock Art Research Association Inc., Melbourne.

Bednarik R G. Developing ICRAD. 2017. *Rock Art Research* 34 (1):113-115.

Bednarik, R.G., translated by Li Man 2022. Direct Dating of China's Immovable Cultural Heritage", *Journal of Hebei Normal University* (Philosophy and Social Sciences Edition) Issue 6 (in press).

Li Man., Shi L., Wu X., Tang H. 2020. Discovery of new type of cave rock paintings in Guangxi Zhuang Autonomous Region, China. *Rock Art Research* 37(1): 5–18.

Li M., Lari J., Tang H., Li Y., Bednarik, R.G. 2022. The 2019 survey of petroglyphs in the Qinghai-Tibet Plateau, western China. *Rock Art Research* 39(2):143-154.

Li M., Shi L., Wu X., Tang H. Discovery and discuss of cat- like rock paintings in Pingxiang City, Chongzuo, Guangxi Province (*in press*).

Tang H., ednarik R G. 2021. Rock art dating by 230Th/234U analysis: an appraisal of Chinese case studies. *Archaeological and Anthropological Sciences* 13:19.

11

KEYWORDS: Robert G. Bednarik – Rock art – Rock art science – Scientometrics – Profile

ROBERT G. BEDNARIK : SCIENTOMETRIC PROFILE

GORI-TUMI ECHEVARRÍA-LÓPEZ AND RUBÉN URBIZAGÁSTEGUI-ALVARADO

Abstract: Using scientometric analysis techniques, the academic production of Australian researcher Robert G. Bednarik is evaluated. For this, 914 documents published by this author from 1968 to 2022, found through different digital databases and available online, were considered. Using statistical premises, the main academic interests of the author are examined, as topics such as productivity, co-authorships, and impact. It is concluded that Bednarik is one of the most productive and recognized individual researchers in the field of rock art science; whose themes maintain stable and scientific lines of research, and whose interests extend beyond this discipline, towards related topics such as hominization and neuroscience.

Keywords: *Robert G. Bednarik – Rock art – Rock art science – Scientometrics – Profile*

1. Introduction

The analysis of academic literature produced by a specific scientist was defined by Sen and Gan (1990) as "bio-bibliometric", sometimes referred to as "bibliometric biography" or also as a "scientometric portrait" of an academic (Bansal 2018, Jacso 2018). With this type of approach, the qualitative and quantitative aspects of the literature published by a scientist in his field of activity are analyzed, for which a complete collection of bibliographic data is needed with which it is possible to "...evaluate the productivity, diffusion, citation, interdisciplinarity, the formation of invisible schools, the versatility and the generation of various social and intellectual impact indices and the role of people in institutional construction, etc." (Sen and Gan 1990: 13).

The published literature using this biobibliometric technique is still scarce and even more so in the field of rock art research. Precisely, for this reason, the objective of this article is to analyze the academic literature produced by Robert G. Bednarik using various statistical techniques to

Article received: 20 December 2022
Revised I: 8 March 2023
Accepted: 10 March 2023

measure the productivity, collaboration, impact, growth, co-authorship networks, and keyword co-occurrence networks of this scientist. This analysis will make it possible to map the various aspects of the themes explored by this researcher and his contribution to the advancement of rock art science, a field in which he has left a great academic impact.

Bednarik is considered one of the world's foremost rock art scholars. Born on April 6, 1944, in Vienna, Austria, he moved to Australia in 1966 when he was 22 years old. He is an expert in the fields of palaeoart and human cognition. He has carried out investigations at rock art sites around the world, analysis of mobiliary art, and conducted studies of experimental archeology; he is a self-taught training scholar and editor of several scientific journals. He is a professor at the International Center for Rock Art Dating and Conservation (ICRAD) at Hebei Higher University in Shijiazhuang, China. Bednarik's main research interest, as he has pointed out on various occasions, is the origins of the human capacity to create constructs of reality; consequently, his research focuses on the origins of art, language, and the development of hominid technology. "His foremost interest lies with the minds of ancient people and how they became human or 'civilized'; the origins of the human ability, intellect, and imagination; and in a selection of fields that provide complementary information. This embraces the early stages of art and language and technological growth providing a gauge of early human faculties and capabilities, for example, seafaring, paleo-art of the Ice Age, stone tools, and the use of beads..." (Morey 2014: 834).

Despite these considerations, his publications have not yet been explored with the elements provided by scientometrics, therefore, it is a good opportunity to carry out this work with the assistance of this type of approach.

To achieve the proposed objectives, this article is organized as follows: after a brief introduction and establishment of the objectives of the article, the published literature that forms the theoretical framework of the investigation is reviewed. Then the material and methods used in the preparation of this work are described, with special care to offer the pertinent equations to the indicators that are to be built. Then the results are described trying to discuss the reasons for these findings. Finally, the conclusions are drawn up and the consulted literature is listed.

2. Theoretical framework

The first document that carried out a quantitative analysis of the bibliographic production of an individual author was by León (1983) who analyzed the bibliographic production of Honorio Delgado, a Peruvian psychologist. At a methodological level, León affirms that "for this purpose, we have used simple techniques typical of the so-called *quantitative history* which, despite their intrinsic limitations, allow a presentation objective of the results" (León, 1983: 107). This document was published seven years before Sen and Gan (1990) proposed the term "bio-bibliometrics" for the analysis of the bibliographic production of individual authors. Quantitative history is a branch of historiography, especially economic and social history, which is characterized by the use of statistical tools to explain historical phenomena; that is, "a method of economic history that integrates all the facts studied in a system of interdependent accounts and that draws its conclusions in the form of quantitative aggregates determined, entirely and solely, by the data of the system" (Marczewski 1973: 19, cited by Fernández Clemente 1995: 64).

An example of this type of work has been carried out by the second author of this article (Urbizagástegui -Alvarado 2020), who analyzed the demographic characteristics of the literature published by the historian Reiner Tom Zuidema, which included a determination of the indicators of productivity, collaboration, the impact of authors and journals; the growth of literature and the analysis of co-authorships and co-words. In this study, 190 documents were found, with a predominance of book chapters (44.7%) and articles (33.7%), with a preference for the English language (47.4% of the documents), and publications in 39 different journals; among other data of academic relevance.

Other investigations of this type have focused their objective on making a scientometric portrait of scientists operating in different disciplines, whether they are librarians, economists, chemists, or engineers, etc. (Ayala-Gascón, et. al. 2012; Bansal 2018; Bhattacharyya & Sahu 2020; Hussain 2020; Banerjee & Chakrabarti 2021; Gholampour & Noruzi 2021); which demonstrate the potential of this analytical approach. A work of this type has not yet been carried out in the field of rock research, and perhaps this is a good opportunity to examine the academic production of Robert G. Bednarik.

3. Material and methods

As units of analysis, the articles published by Robert G. Bednarik in academic journals, papers presented in congresses, round tables, books, and book chapters, that were accessible through the indexed sources, were taken. The data were collected through searches carried out by the name of the author in the bibliographic databases that appear mentioned in Annex A. The references found were exported to EndNote 8X, a bibliographic management software for the creation and organization of a specific bibliographic database on the academic production of the author.

Each of the works found was reviewed, to verify the subject dealt with and to build the corresponding keywords in cases that were not present in the retrieved document. The keywords were constructed from the title and complemented with readings of the identified texts. The bibliographic references of these publications were also reviewed to detect other possible documents published by the author, but not retrieved through the databases used for data collection. Duplicate references were eliminated, retaining only one mention. Keywords used in documents published in languages other than English were translated to normalize the data for the analysis.

To evaluate the demographic characteristics of the retrieved literature, as well as for the different analyzes of co-authorship networks and co-word networks, the igraph package (Csardi & Nepusz 2006) from Project R (R Core Team 2014) was used.

3.1. Publications demographics

As demography, we refer here to the size of the population analyzed, its composition, distribution, and unimodal descriptive statistical definition of its components. Information is provided on the types of publications identified and their respective volumes, their distribution according to the years of publication, fluctuations of the publications according to the grouping most appropriate to the data, and the languages in which they were published. To analyze the demographics of the publications, univariate descriptive statistics were used with the R Base package from RStudio.

3.2. Scientific productivity indicators

The number of publications is a useful index to assess the scientific productivity of an individual researcher. This indicator is just the logarithm of base 10, of the number of publications of the studied author. It is used to measure production in relation to time and obtain a rate of productivity of the author throughout his career. Therefore, it is possible to obtain a partial productivity index (by five-year periods) and a total productivity index in the life cycle of the studied scientist. The commonly used equation is:

$$\mathrm{IP} = \mathrm{Log}_{10}\, \mathrm{N}$$

where

IP = productivity index

N = number of documents published per five-year period

The rate of change of the author's productivity can also be used. The distribution of the rate of change shows the number of publications according to successive chronological years arranged in 5-year intervals. This way of organizing the data shows the fluctuations in the author's productivity, minimizing the years of lower productivity. This rate of change is estimated using the following equation:

$$\textit{Rate of change} = \frac{\Delta I}{\Delta t}$$

where:

ΔI = number of documents published

Δt = time interval in years (quinquenniums in this case)

3.3. Growth indicators of published literature

Price states that the number of scientific articles published each year can be taken as a rough indication of the activity displayed in any general or specialized field of research (Price 1951).

Three important conclusions can be drawn from these data: that almost all growth curves show the same trend; that growth is exponential; and that the constant of the exponential curve is capable of doubling the size in a period of 10 to 15 years. Apparently, the exponential law governs the growth in the size of science (Price 1956).

There are various forms of literature growth: linear, exponential, potential, logistic, etc. Exponential growth is the most common form of growth found in studies of literature spanning long periods, but other forms of literature growth can also be found. To assess model adjustment, a sparse "point cloud" plot is constructed that is based on cumulative observed data. This way of organizing the data makes it possible to assess whether there is regularity in the distribution of the observed frequencies, and when this regularity resembles the curve shown in the graph an attempt is made to adjust a statistical growth model suggested by the cloud of points, via linear or non-linear regression, depending on the case. To measure the growth rate of the literature published by Robert C. Bednarik, it was considered to explore the linear, polynomial, and exponential models with the following equations:

To measure the adjustment of linear growth, the following linear regression equation was used:

$$Y = \alpha + \beta X + \varepsilon$$

Polynomial growth, the following polynomial regression equation was used

$$Y = \beta_0 + \beta_1 X + \beta_2 X^2 + \varepsilon$$

To measure the adjustment to exponential growth, the following equation was used:

$$C(t) = c * g^t$$

3.4. Author impact indicators

Citation analysis is one of the most frequently used criteria for the evaluation of the "impact" of the producers of scientific literature, but it is one of the most controversial measures used for the evaluation of a scientific activity. It is assumed that the citations are indicators of the quality, influence, or impact produced by the contents of the documents on the academic community of the author's field of activity. Therefore, the number of citations made to the authors of published documents would indicate the impact of this author in a given scientific field. This means counting how many times an author is cited since apparently the most influential scientists are cited more frequently than others. Its use is based on the role that publications play in the dissemination of new knowledge. If this count were done manually, it would be almost impossible, which is why citation databases such as Science Citation Index (SCI) and the Social Sciences Citation Index (SSCI) were invented, nowadays consolidated in the Web of Science and from these databases, the h-index and its variants, such as the g-index and similar, can be calculated.

Hirsch (2005) proposed the h-index for the evaluation of citations by researchers in the area of physics, but this index has been expanded to all areas of human knowledge. This index is considered the safest way to measure the scientific quality of a researcher since it combines productivity with impact. An author has an h-index when h of his publications has received at least h citations. For example, when we say that a researcher's h-index is five, it means that they have at least five published articles, each of which has received at least five citations. The higher the number of articles published by the researcher, the higher the number of citations achieved and the higher the h-index will be. This index correlates well with citations in general and the mean ratio is

$$h_H = \sqrt{C/\alpha}$$

Several online resources can be used to directly estimate a scientist's impact. The most established are those offered by the Web of Science and Scopus, but two free options are Publish or Perish and Google Scholar. These sources were used to measure impact by researcher Robert G. Bednarik, and the h-index as well as the g-index were automatically provided by these sources. The g-index is a measure of the citations of an author and is calculated based on the distribution of citations received by the publications of a given researcher, so given a set of articles classified in decreasing order of the number of citations they received, the g-index is the largest number so the top g articles collectively received at least g^2 citations. Thus, a g-index of 10 indicates that an author's top 10 publications have been cited at least 100 times.

3.5. Impact indicators of dissemination journals

The number of citations that a published document receives and the impact factor of the journals where the document was published are used as indicators of the impact and visibility of the journals. The number of times a journal is cited is undoubtedly an indicator of the impact, whether positive or negative, that such a publication has on the scientific community. A high number of citations to a certain publication would reflect the fact that the publication communicates or disseminates new knowledge to the scientific community and that this community prefers this journal over others. For authors, the information on the impact factor (IF) can be used to decide whether to submit their manuscripts for evaluation by journals, since if you submit your manuscript to a journal with a higher IF, it may mean greater dissemination of your work, increasing its prestige and greater visibility in the academic community. In general, the journals with the highest IF are the most prestigious, with greater academic visibility and author recognition, but also with higher rejection rates. The minimum condition for selecting a journal to publish the research results must be that the chosen journal is indexed in a database that allows good visibility and information retrieval, although it does not guarantee a high impact factor.

This impact factor is calculated annually by the Institute for Scientific Information from Thompson Scientific Reuters for the journals indexed in its databases and is published by the Journal Citations Reports (JCR). To calculate the IF for a given year, the number of citations received by the journal in the two preceding years is considered, divided by the total number of articles published by the same journal in the same period. The equation used is the following:

$$FI = \frac{C_i}{A_r}$$

where

FI is the Impact Factor

C_i is the total number of citations received by articles published in a certain journal in the last two years;

A_r is the total number of articles that were published in the same journal in those two years.

3.6. Indicators of collaboration or co-authorship

If co-authorship and/or multiple authorship is becoming common in the field of social sciences, this co-authorship would also occur in the publication behavior of individual authors. Therefore, this co-authorship would also manifest itself in scientific collaboration networks, since one of the aspects studied in the publications is the formation of collaborative networks that exist between the different authors of research papers in a particular scientific field or discipline. In this way, two authors are considered connected if they have collaborated in the publication of the same article. From the collaboration between authors emerges a relational structure that can help to understand and evaluate the scientific production generated by groups of co-authors. The analysis of the co-authorship networks is based on the relationships between the actors that can be visualized, employing a connection graph. To achieve this visualization, the groups are formed based on patterns of relationships established between the actors. A strong direct relationship between the actors increases the probability that they can be grouped. In the case of authors, the more academic documents they produce in association, the relationships become more cohesive, forming identifiable groups of collaborators. To make Bednarik's co-authorship network visible, the igraph package (Csardi & Nepusz 2006) from Project R (R Core Team, 2014) was used.

3.7. Thematic indicators (analysis of co-words)

A shared paradigm in a scientific field designates and guides what the members of a given scientific community have in common. This paradigm refers to the entire set of problems, methods, theoretical principles, metaphysical assumptions, concepts, and evaluative standards that are present in concrete scientific achievement. This would be a kind of disciplinary matrix, a theoretical, methodological, and evaluative framework within which scientists carry out their research. This framework constitutes the discipline's basic assumptions about how to conduct research, what constitutes a good scientific explanation, and how it should be disseminated (Kuhn 1970, 1974). But the scientific practice also refers to the structures of consciousness at different times, to language, to the mode of knowledge, to cognitive maps, to reasoning structures, to agreements on procedures, symbolic technologies, and other similar aspects. According to actor-network theory, laboratories and literature are two powerful tools for scientists to transform societies. Scientists, then, build complex worlds in laboratories and print them on paper. This means that scientists attach particular importance to texts. Although science cannot be reduced to texts alone, texts remain a primary source for studies of how worlds are created and transformed in the laboratory. Therefore, instead of following the actors to see how they change the world, following the texts they publish is another way of mapping the dynamics of science. This dynamic is represented via maps of science, which are symbolic representations of scientific domains, in which the elements are distributed by their similarity in such a way that the most related actors are located closer and the less related ones are located further away (Noyons 2001). The analysis of the subjects studied is the space in which the maps of science have the greatest applications. It is a modality of analysis that allows discovering the evolution, continuity, changes, or extinction of lines of research over time, as well as indicating their development trends. In the processing and analysis of the data, specialized software and mathematical operations are used that apply algorithms that produce lists of frequencies of the use of words in the texts. To analyze the keywords of the documents published by Robert G. Bednarik, Bibexcel software (Persson, Danell and Schneider 2009) was used to build a matrix that could then be analyzed with the igraph package (Csardi and Nepusz 2006) from Project R (R Core Team 2014).

4. Results

4.1. Publication demographics

914 papers published from 1968 to 2022 by Robert G. Bednarik, which are the source for this analysis, could be identified and retrieved. Table 1 shows the types of publications of his authorship according to a five-year grouping from 1986 to 2022. What emerges from this way of grouping the data is a picture of constant academic production that becomes much more active from 1983 with the publication of articles in academic journals. The decade from 1988 to 1992 was the most productive in publications of this type. Bednarik was also an animator and organizer of symposiums and congresses of rock art specialists, so much so that his second form of contribution is papers presented at national and international congresses. Likewise, he is a sharp critic since his third form of publication is the type of critical review of books published by other authors mainly on the subject of rock art. Similarly, many of his scholarly outputs are published as book chapters and books.

A common procedure used by scientists to publicize advances in knowledge has been through the publication of articles in academic journals, which also serve as vehicles for the

Table 1. Types of publications grouped by five-year period

Quinquenios	*Books*	*Chapters of books*	*Confer*	*Journal papers*	*Newspapers articles*	*CR*	*Man*	***Total***
1968-1972				2				2
1973-1977				3				3
1978-1982				5	1		1	7
1983-1987		1	1	52		3		57
1988-1992	6	8	2	181	2	15	1	215
1993-1997	1	4	2	103				110
1998-2002	2	1	4	80		4	1	92
2003-2007	4		4	98		5	1	112
2008-2012	7	9	23	88		9	8	144
2013-2017	5	12	9	94		4		124
2018-2022	2	2	2	37		4		48
Total	27	37	47	743	3	44	12	914

RC = Critical Reviews Man = Manuscripts

communication of new ideas and discoveries. Repeatedly, through the publication of research results in academic journals, scientists have pointed out areas of study that require further investigation, as well as previous studies that need to be refuted; hence the publication of articles in academic journals is not far to Bednarik's interest and therefore the massive volume of publications of this type.

Figure 1 shows the flow of his publications from 1968 to 2022. Robert G. Bednarik published an average of 16.6 documents per year. His most productive period was between 1987 and 1992, which corresponds to the age he was between 42 and 48 years. It is assumed that at this age personal cultural capital is more consolidated and research and resources for the same also flow with greater advantages. Bourdieu (2004) highlights that scientific fields are places where two forms of power are exercised that correspond to two types of scientific capital: institutional or social capital, which is linked to holding important positions in scientific institutions; and specific cultural capital that is linked to the symbolic capital of acts of knowledge and recognition, almost exclusively by peers. Following Bourdieu (1986) it could be affirmed that cultural capital, symbolic capital, as well as social capital, are ensured by Bednarik at that age and these factors may have influenced the grander publication of documents in those years. At the end of the figure, the probable effects caused by the covid19 global pandemic can also be seen, with a drop in the volume of publications from 2019 onwards.

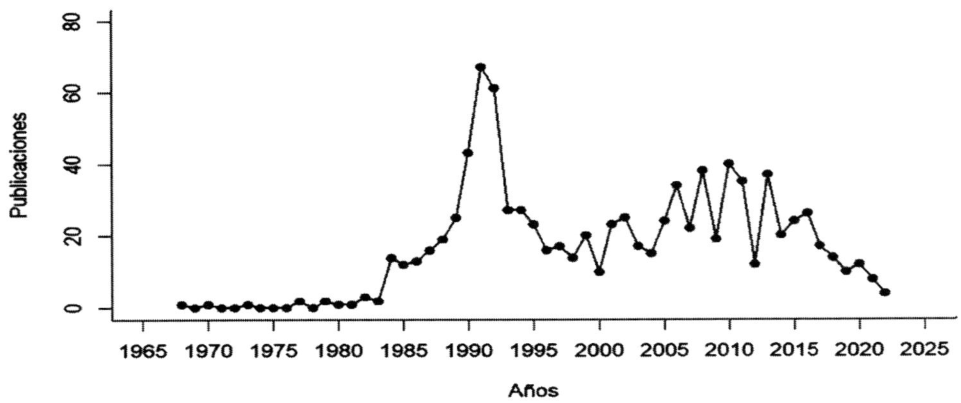

Figure 1: Distribution of publications according to years

To reaffirm this production of documents, Figure 2 exposes the fluctuations of the publications according to the grouping by five-year periods. It is observed how the fifth five-year period was its most productive stage.

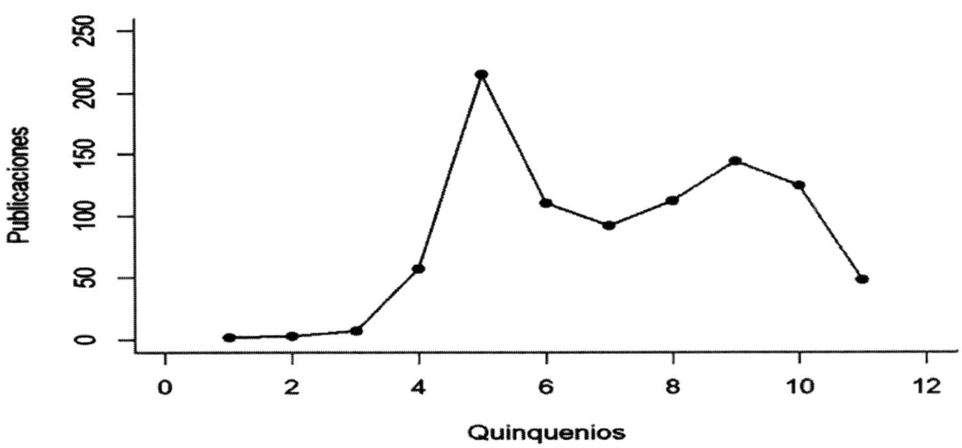

Figure 2: Fluctuation of publications according to the five-year periods

Table 2 presents the types of documents published grouped according to the languages of publication. The type of document that this author prefers are articles in academic journals (81.3%) disseminated mainly in English (88.8%), German (3.4%), and Spanish (2.7%). In this case, their publications in Spanish also contain some translations of their original articles published in English or French. Included here are the 21 articles (2.8%) published in both English and French at the same time. Of the papers presented in congresses, 47 (97.9%) are published in English. Then the critical reviews reach a total of 44 publications and 95.5% of which are also published in English.

Table 2: Types of publications grouped by five-year period according to language

	Tipo de publicaciones							
Languages	*Chap. Books*	*Articles books*	*journals*	*Conferences*	*Newspapers*	*Reviews*	*Manusc*	*Total*
English	26	34	660	46	3	42	12	823
French			10			1		11
German	1		25			1		27
Russian		2	1	1				4
Chinese			3					3
Spanish		1	20					21
Slovenian			1					1
Turkish			1					1
English /French			21					21
English /Italian			1					1
English /German			1					1
Total	27	37	743	47	3	44	12	914

Robert G. Bednarik's tendency to publish book chapters (4%) and books (3%) of his total publications respectively may be related to building his authority in the field of rock art. Possibly the types of documents best considered by competing peers in the field of paleoart are books, book chapters, and articles published in academic journals. Although we note that this is not the author's motivation; such weighting potentially means recognition possibilities to obtain the necessary grants to continue research, which results in recognition as an authority in the science of rock art.

Figure 3 shows the volume of publications according to a grouping by language. Please note that English is the preferred language; which is logical as English is the official language of Australia, besides that it is currently positioned as the fundamental language to disseminate knowledge. English is the dominant language most used as a supposed lingua franca of scientific communication. A possible response to explain this position is to consider the asymmetry of academic relations based on the opposition between center and periphery, since, in the current situation of globalization, there is a redefinition of the market for linguistic goods that promotes the emergence of a new hierarchy of the languages in which English acquires a central position to become the language of globalization. A harmful effect of this hierarchy is the abandonment and contempt of the publications produced in the periphery, as well as an uncritical acceptance of the "best" quality of the journals published in the countries of the center. As an example, the academic production of Australian intellectuals seems not to be adequately disseminated by the journals that are indexed and incorporated into the bibliographic databases that operate at the center of Anglo-Saxon academic power, and the publications of Robert G. Bednarik are no exception to this marginalization.

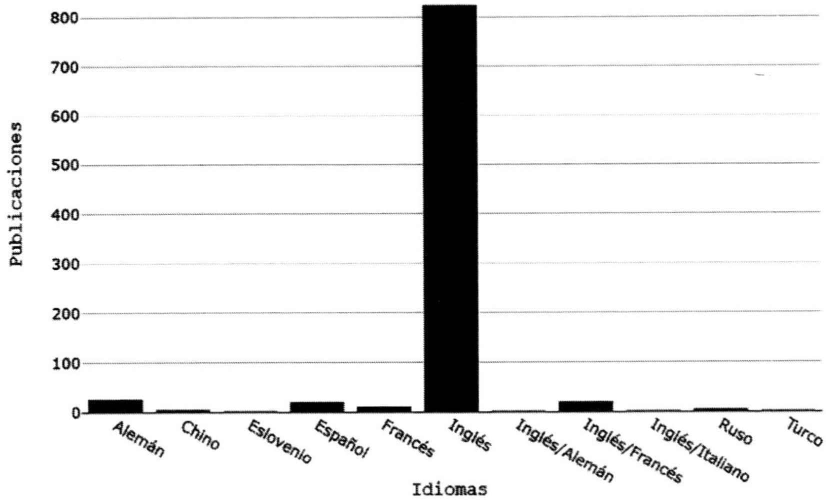

Figure 3: Bednarik publication languages

4.2. Scientific productivity indicators

Table 3 shows the productivity rate and the rate of change in the distribution of publications organized in five-year intervals. The productivity rate has a constant growth until the fifth five-year period (1988-1992), after which it begins to drop, but with very small oscillations. The largest oscillations are observed in the five-year periods 1987-1991 and 1982-1986, respectively, but it does not substantially alter the productivity rate. This is maintained at an average of 1.6 documents per five-year period. This means that the author produces an average of 39.8 ± 40 documents per

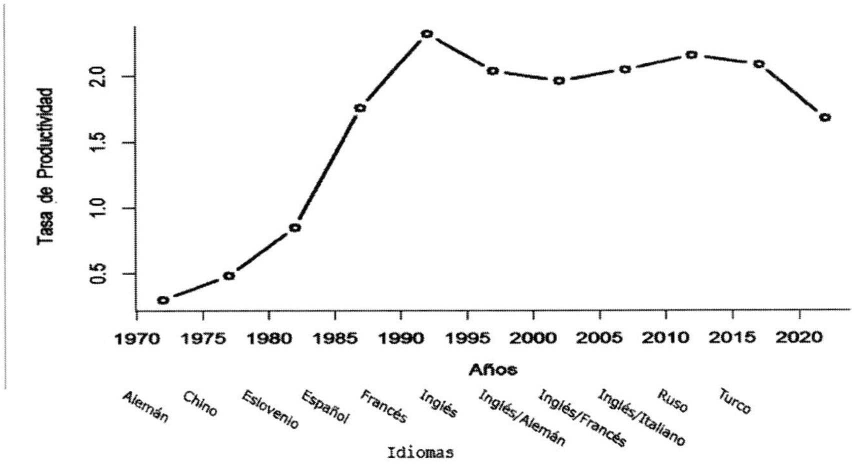

Figure 4: Robert G. Bednarik's Productivity Rate

five-year period. In general, this is a normal productivity rate for an academic, especially if is an individual or a lone researcher like Robert C. Bednarik.

Table 3: Productivity rate and rate of change

Periods	*Amount of publications*	*Rate of productivity*	*Rate of change*
1968-1972	2	0.30	0.4
1973-1977	3	0.48	0.6
1978-1982	7	0.85	1.4
1983-1987	57	1.76	11.4
1988-1992	215	2.33	43.0
1993-1997	110	2.04	22.0
1998-2002	92	1.96	18.4
2003-2007	112	2.05	22.4
2008-2012	144	2.16	28.8
2013-2017	124	2.09	24.8
2018-2022	48	1.68	9.6

Figure 4 shows the estimated productivity rate for Bednarik's publications and displays a constant growth until the fifth five-year period (1988-1992), after which it begins to drop, but with very small oscillations. The notorious reduction at the end of the last five years may be due to the effects of covid19; although it can also be due to other reasons as family issues or advance age.

The rate of change (Figure 5), related to the author's productivity, ranges from 0.6 documents in the five years referred to when he began as a researcher to 7.0 documents already in his consolidated stage. In general, his rate of change oscillates between two and three documents, but in his most productive stage as a consolidated researcher, it varies between five and seven documents produced.

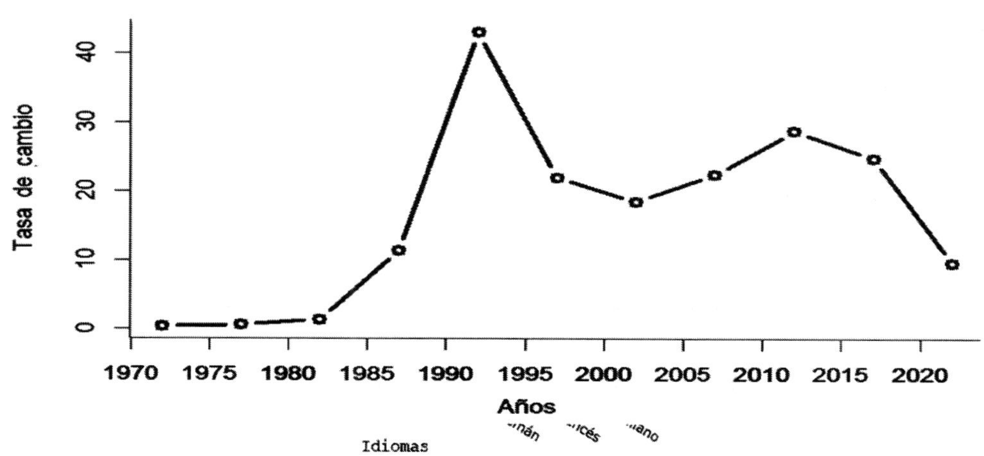

Figure 5: Rate of change of Robert G. Bednarik publications

4.3. Growth indicators of published literature

It was observed that the shape of the dispersion for the cloud of points in the documents published by Robert G. Bednarik had a strange profile of growth that looks like an almost straight initial line, which indicates that it follows a more or less homogeneous growth since it does not show evidence of having reached a saturation level. But it also has the shape of exponential growth with a concave start and then a straight line. It also shows a kind of linear variation called polynomial. Figure 6 shows the observed growth values for papers published by Robert G. Bednarik.

According to Price (1975), literature can be linear and then become exponential to reach a saturation point with a logistic form. This does not seem to be the case in Robert G. Bednarik's publications, as growth is more like a linear, polynomial, or exponential form. Using the statistical package R in RStudio, the values of the three statistical models mentioned were estimated. The correlation between both variables (years versus accumulated publications) was 0.9752, indicating a high correlation. Table 4 shows the estimated coefficients for the polynomial model, which was the model that best predicted the growth of the publications produced by Robert G. Bednarik.

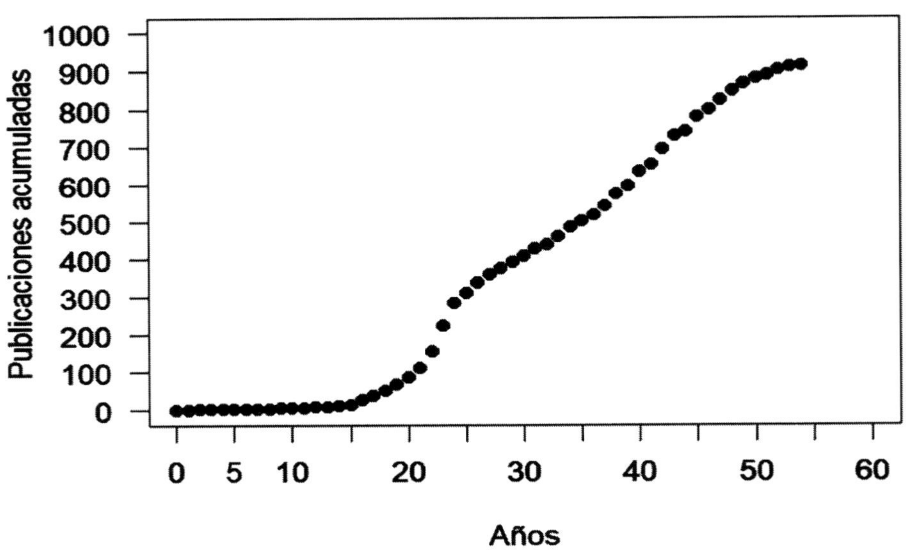

Figure 6: Form of growth of published documents

Table 4: Estimated coefficients of the polynomial model

Coefficients	*Estimated*	*Std. Error*	*t value*	*Pr(>|t|)*
Intercept	-68.77293	19.78578	-3.476	0.00104
Year	7.36858	1.69435	4.349	0.000063993297
Year 2	0.23692	0.03035	7.807	0.000000000257

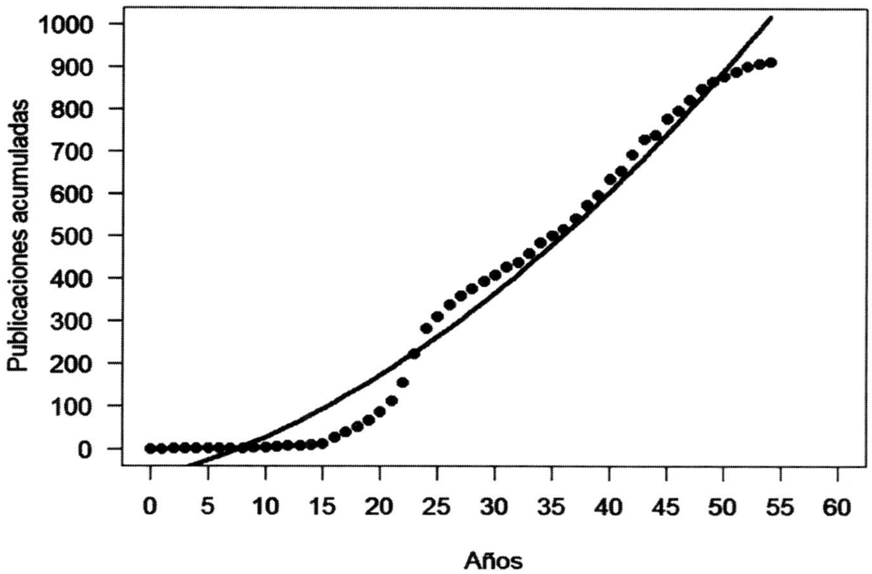

Figure 7: Observed and estimated values of document growth

The value of the intercept was equal to -68.77293, with a standard error of 19.78578. The value of the Year coefficient was equal to 7.36858, with a standard error of 1.69435 and the Year 2 coefficient was 0.23692, at a significance level of 0.001. The adjusted R^2 was equal to 0.9766, with 52 degrees of freedom and a significance level of 0.01 (p-value: < 0.00000000000000022). This indicates that the growth of the literature published by Robert G. Bednarik can be expressed by the following equation:

$$Y = -68.77293 + 7.36858\ X + 0.23692\ X^2 + \varepsilon$$

Figure 7 shows the observed values (in dots) and estimated values (in line) of polynomial growth for papers published by Robert G. Bednarik from 1968 to 2022.

4.4. Author impact indicators

Based on the citations that the authors of a certain scientific field have received, the visibility indices are calculated, which is defined as the number of citations that a document published by an author receives from the moment it is indexed in the Web of Science and Scopus databases. Table 5 shows the number of documents indexed in these databases, the number of citations, and the visibility indices corresponding to Bednarik's academic production. For comparison purposes, the search engines Publish or Perish and Google Scholar was added to these bibliographic databases.

Table 5: Visibility indices of Robert G. Bednarik

Source	*No. of Docs*	*No. of Citas*	*Index h*	*Index g*	*Index i-10*
Scopus	117	1269	20	-	-
Web of Science	134	642	15	-	-
Publish or Perish	556	9690	47	83	-
Google Scholar	672	11686	52	-	208

In Scopus, we found only 1269 citations with an h-index equal to 20. These documents represent only 12.8% of the total 914 documents identified in this research; this means that 87% of the documents produced by Bednarik are not indexed in this so-called "international" database. In Web of Science, when a search is done by author, the result is only 134 documents indexed between 2006 and 2022 and they represent only 14.7% of those identified in this research; this means that 85.3% of Bednarik's intellectual production is not indexed in this database of "international prestige". The h-index is equal to 15 with a mean of 4.82 citations per document. Not counting self-citations, his papers have been cited 642 times as of December 2022. Neither Scopus nor Web of Science offer the g-index.

In publish or Perish, 556 documents were found, which were published between 1988 and 2022, representing 60.8% of those identified in this research, and obtained a total of 9690 citations. These documents were cited on average 39 times a year, with an average of 179.44 a year and 17.43 citations per document. In Google Scholar, only 672 of his publications are listed (73.5% of those identified in this research). However, if only the citations from 2017 were counted, it accumulates a total of 3316 citations, it has an h-index equal to 25 and an i-10 index equal to 83. One of his articles has 948 citations and another 712 citations, and there are 21 documents with citations higher than 100. If the documents published by the author in Google Scholar are explored using "R.G. Bednarik or Robert G. Bednarik" as a search strategy, 1690 documents are retrieved. "The signs of all times: entoptic phenomena in Upper Palaeolithic art" has 948 citations; "Concept-mediated marking in the Lower Palaeolithic" has 256 citations; "A taphonomy of palaeoart" accumulates 222 citations and "Palaeoart and archaeological myths" has 201 citations; just to show some examples of the variations in the number of citations depending on the sources used to obtain the data+.

4.5. Impact of dissemination journals

When a journal is indexed in a bibliographic database, it means that it has been approved for indexing according to the evaluation criteria used by those databases. Many of these databases are maintained by national commercial organizations such as the Web of Science or Scopus, not necessarily meaning that the journals they index are the "best" journals in the world. Bednarik has communicated the results of his research in 134 different journals from various countries. The

Table 6: Dissemination journals

Journals	*No. of articles*	*Index h Index g*
Rock Art Research	265	16
AURA Newsletter	62	--
Purakala (India)	49	--
The Artefact (Melbourne, Australia)	43	--
International Newsletter on Rock Art	21	--
Pictogram Parkhurst (South Africa)	18	--
Australian Archaeology	17	21
Anthropos (Germany)	13	15
Anthropologie Brno (Czech Republic)	12	8
Préhistoire, art et sociétés	12	--
Cave Art Research	11	--
La Pintura (California)	11	--
Boletín de SIARB (Bolivia)	9	--
Boletín APAR (Perú)	7	--
Bulletin of the A A Society of Victoria	7	--
Acta Archaeologica	6	11
Almogaren	6	--
Arts Basel	6	--
Bollettino del Centro Camuno di Studi Preistorici	6	
Current Anthropology	6	144
Sahara	6	--
Survey: Bollettino del CSMAP di Pineloro (Italy)	6	--

22 journals in which he has published more than 6 articles in each of them are listed in Table 6. Apparently, the journal "Rock Art Research" began to be indexed in 2008 in the Web of Science and since then it has received 1305 citations, which means an average of 2.74 citations per item. This journal, directed by Bednarik himself, is unfortunately only accessible by subscription and is not available online. The Art & Architecture Source Publications Bibliographic database from EBSCO indexes this journal, but only volumes from 2003 onwards. In any case, Table 6 shows the number of articles published by Bednarik in these journals and the corresponding h-index and g-index, but only those identified in Web of Science and Scopus. Most of these journals are not indexed by these databases, indicating that Bednarik is not very interested in so-called high-impact journals to disseminate the results of his research.

4.5.1. Conferences for the dissemination of Research

Although Bednarik has participated in many academic events, the sources consulted show that he has presented papers at 14 different conferences. The most outstanding, in a volume of publications, have been the five congresses listed in Table 7. The author himself was involved in the organization, dissemination, and reception of most of these congresses, especially the congresses of the International Federation of Rock Art Organizations (IFRAO) and the Australian Rock Art Research Association (AURA). Attending a specialized conference is an important decision in the academic life of a professional, it is a way to get closer to the latest advances, studies, and ideas circulating in your field; an opportunity to interact with area leaders and perhaps inquire about potential peers for collaborative research or mentoring. For experienced researchers, it is the right occasion to expand their influence and disseminate recent findings in their research and perhaps the opportunity to get peers to help get funding for their future projects. These opportunities have not been outside the reach of Robert G. Bednarik.

Table 7: Dissemination conferences

Congresses	*Presentations*
IFRAO Congress	19
World Congress of the IUPP Sciences	8
International Cupule Conference	5
AURA Congress	4
Annual Chacmool Conference	3

4.6. Indicators of collaboration or co-authorship

Collaboration is defined as the joint co-occurrence of two or more academics in the authorship of a publication. Co-authorship is a phenomenon that has been growing rapidly, especially in the "mature" sciences, but it does not seem to be a common phenomenon in the social sciences where the productivity of authors is still an individual activity. Figure 8 shows the authors with whom Robert G. Bednarik collaborates in the production of articles. His collaboration is restricted mainly to five authors, therefore, it can be concluded that he is a solitary researcher with a low tendency to collaborate. Price (1963) argues that the proportion of multi-authored articles is growing so fast and continuously that single-authored articles would disappear. Greene (2007) also stated that the lone author had disappeared. However, Abt (2007) predicts that articles by individual authors will continue to be published. Bednarik seems to be the evidence for this prediction.

4.7. Thematic indicators (analysis of co-words)

To analyze the keywords used in the documents published by Robert G. Bednarik, his productive time was divided into three stages: from 1968 to 1986, from 1968 to 2004, and from 1968 to 2022, in cumulative periods to observe the variations in the thematic cores of his interest. Table 8 presents

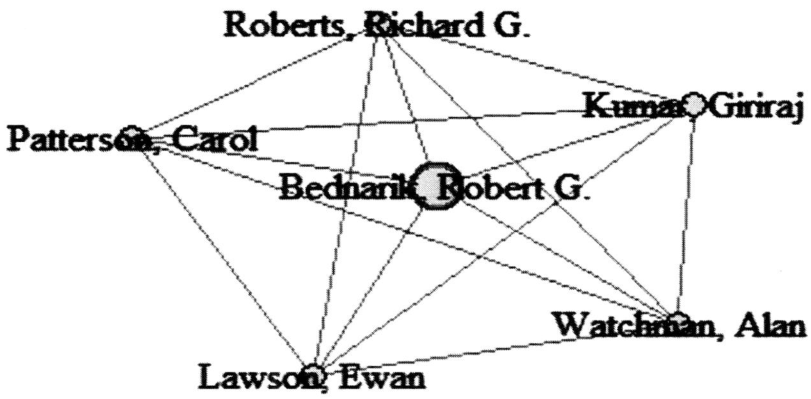

Figure 8: Bednarik co-authorship network

the values of the topographic measurements found in the co-words network of the documents. The most basic characteristic of a network is its size. The size is simply the number of members, usually called nodes, vertices, or actors, but in this case, keywords. In the period 1968-1986, the co-word network is composed of 139 keywords with 447 ties. These increase to 192 words with 501 ties for the second period from 1968 to 2004, remaining unchanged in the period 1968 to 2022.

The density is the proportion of ties observed in the network in relation to the maximum number of possible ties. It is a rate that can vary from 0 to 1. The closer the density is to 1, the more interconnected the network will be. The density shows the value (in percentages) of the network connectivity rate, that is if it has high or low density. It shows the potential of the network in terms of information flow, that is, the higher the density, the more intense the exchange of information will be in the network, and otherwise, the lower the density, the less intense the circulation of information will be. In this case, the proportion is really low, reaching 5% in the period 1968-1986, descending to 2.7% in the following period, and remaining stable at that level of 2.7% in the last period.

Table 8: Topographic characteristics of the network of co-words

	Periods		
Measures	*1968-1986*	*1968-2004*	*1968-2022*
Size	139, 447	192, 501	192, 501
Density	0.05	0.027	0.027
Components	5	4	3
Transitivity	0.432	0.255	0.181
Diameter	6	6	6
Average distance	2.79	3.02	2.86
Compactness	0.303	0.328	0.373
Reciprocity	1	1	1

In certain situations, a network is divided into distinct subgroups. A subgroup is a group of network actors in which all its members are directly or indirectly connected. In the period 1968 to 1986 there were 5 keyword components, which decreased to 4 keywords subgroups in the period 1968 to 2004, and again decreased to 3 subgroups in the latter period. In the three periods that were studied, the diameter of the network does not vary and is maintained at 6 steps. The diameter of the network is just the longest of the shortest paths that join all pairs of nodes and reflects the flow of resources that transit the network. This is a measure of network efficiency because the diameter reflects, in the worst-case scenario, the flow of resources through a network. Although social networks can be very large, they can still have small diameters due to their density and clustering. In this case, the longest of the shortest paths that cross all pairs of nodes is equal to 6 steps; that is, to get from keyword A to keyword B, the mediation of another 6 keywords is needed.

Transitivity refers to the proportion of closed triangles (triads in which three ties are observed). These closed triads are greater in the period 1968-1986 (43.2%), decrease in the period 1968-2004 (25.51%), and decreased again in the period 1968-2022 (18.1%). The average distance represents the average of the geodetic distance in the network. This means that resource flows were more expeditious and with fewer structural impediments in the period 1968-1986 (mean distance of 2.79), it becomes greater in the period 1968-2004 (3.02); and it is more expeditious in the period 1968-2022 (2.86). Compactness refers to the fact that a network can be quite concentrated or unconcentrated, that is, dispersed. The lower values indicate that on average the distances are shorter, in other words, the network is more compact. In the case of the network of co-words in Bednarik's documents in the period 1968-1986, this network is much more compact than in later periods. That is, as the network grows and diversifies, it becomes less compact.

Table 9 presents the characteristics of dominance and egalitarianism present in the co-word network. The degree of centralization indicates that this network is dominated by very few central

Table 9: Characteristics of dominance and egalitarianism

Centralization measures	*Periods*		
	1968-1986	*1968-2004*	*1968-2022*
Degree	0.276	0.308	0.376
Intermediation	0.232	0.383	0.338
Proximity	1.098	1.279	1.262
Eigenvector	0.854	0.903	0.896
Sd of degree	6.109	6.83	9.006
Sd of intermediation	311.87	712.65	740.45
Sd of proximity	0.092	0.0773	0.1429
Sd of eigenvector	0.184	0.131	0.138

keywords in the three study periods. This is confirmed by the standard deviation of the degree of network centralization. The degree of intermediations also indicates that few keywords operate as bridges in the co-word network. That is why the standardized deviation of intermediations is high. The degree of proximity evidences this extensive dispersion of the co-words in the network and for this reason, the standard deviation of proximity is also atypical and differentiated. The eigenvector indicates that the network is dominated by a few central nodes that control the flow of keywords in the network. This dominance has been more concentrated and greater between 1968-1986, gradually decreasing in recent periods.

4.7.1. Co-words network in the period 1968-1986

Figure 9 shows the components of the keywords network used in the documents published by Bednarik in the period from 1968 to 1986. It can be noted the existence of a giant cohesive subgroup made up of 119 different keywords, two groups of 6 keywords, and another two groups of 4 keywords not very extensive in functional relationships. In other words, the network is made up of 5 differentiated groups.

Figure 9: Components of the keywords network from 1968-1986.

To extract the core of this co-word network, the network of functional relations was sliced only to show those keywords with three and more relations. What emerges are the issues most explored by Bednarik up to 1986. Figure 10 shows these networks of central issues that bring together three different clusters that are focused on petroglyph research and rock art in Australia, where Bednarik began his specialization. The keyword *petroglyphs* are related to *archeology* and *dating systems* in Australia. On the other hand, *petroglyph* is also linked to research carried out in South Australia on *limestone caves, cave art,* and *finger flutings*. Keyword *rock art* links to the *international congresses* and the congresses organized by AURA, which reflect Bednarik's concerns for consolidating and reproducing the *doxa* of the discipline. These keywords coincide with the founding of AURA and IFRAO and the rise of their interest in international issues.

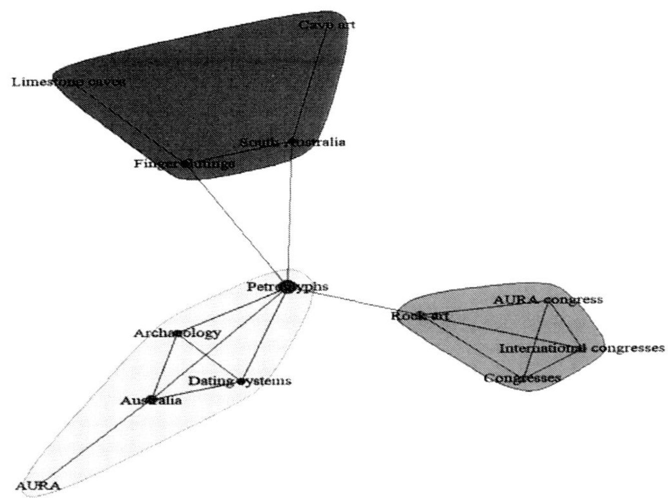

Figure 10: Central issues up to 1986

To understand the strength of the keywords that make up this network, their degrees of centrality were measured. Table 10 shows the results obtained. Centrality measures the extent to which the links in a keyword network are concentrated in a single word or group of words. The degree of centrality captures the number of relationships that a keyword has. High-centrality networks have keywords with many connections, low centrality networks have many keywords with low connections. The degree of centrality of a keyword measures its importance in the network since it counts the number of ties that each keyword has and where the most central keyword is the one with the most ties. Between 1968-1986, PC *Australia* is the most central followed by *petroglyphs, finger flutings, rock art,* etc. These keywords can be easily read from the table below.

Closeness measures how many steps it takes to access each keyword from a given other keyword. It gives points to each node based on its proximity to all other keywords on the network. This measure calculates the shortest paths between all nodes, then assigns each keyword a score based on the sum of the shortest paths. It is used to find the keywords that are best able to influence the entire network more quickly. The degree of closeness or proximity can help to find concentration on the issues explored by the authors and is useful to find the issues on which the analyzed author has focused his research; in this case: *Australia, petroglyphs, finger flutings, rock art, international congresses,* and so on.

Table 10: Degree of centrality up to 1986

Keywords	*degree*	*closeness*	*betweenness*	*eigenvector*
Australia	45	0.005	2267.396	1
Petroglyphs	34	0.005	1932.209	0.897
Finger flutings	29	0.004	686.297	0.915
Rock art	27	0.004	1300.603	0.648
International congresses	22	0.004	941.449	0.259
South Australia	21	0.004	458.153	0.513
Congresses	21	0.004	976.32	0.248
Limestone caves	20	0.004	239.705	0.658
Caves	20	0.004	690.843	0.480
Psychograms	17	0.004	462.785	0.493
France	14	0.004	384.428	0.532
Western Europe	13	0.004	456.000	0.442
Cave art	13	0.004	161.111	0.389
Mount Gambier	12	0.003	173.692	0.327
Tom Price Region	10	0.003	156.063	0.139

Betweenness is the number of shortest paths that pass through a particular keyword. It measures the potential for specialization in the subjects indicated by the keywords. It is based on the idea that a keyword is more important if it is more of an intermediary in the network. The concept of betweenness centrality is based on the geodesics between keywords since a keyword becomes more important if it lies within the geodesics of many pairs of keywords in the network; that is, the more intermediary a keyword is to other keywords, the more central its position in the network. This reflects the importance of being in the middle of network communications since it is needed in greater instances to achieve connection in network contact chains. For example, the keyword *Australia* has a high network betweenness, followed by *petroglyphs*, then *rock art, congresses,* and *international congresses.*

The centrality of the eigenvector is a measure of being well connected with those keywords that are also well connected. If a keyword is connected by many keywords that also have high eigenvector centrality, then this keyword will have high eigenvector centrality. The eigenvector centrality is a measure of the influence of a keyword on a network. The essence of eigenvector centrality is that it calculates the centrality of a keyword based on the centrality of its neighboring keywords. In this case, the keyword *Australia* is the best connected to its neighbors, so *finger flutings, petroglyphs, limestone caves, rock art,* and *France.*

4.7.2. Co-words network in the period 1968-2004

Figure 11 shows the components of the keyword network used in the documents published by Bednarik in the period from 1968 to 2004. The network is diversified into four components. The existence of a giant cohesive subgroup made up of 117 different keywords, two groups of four keywords and one group of three keywords with little extensive functional relationships can be seen.

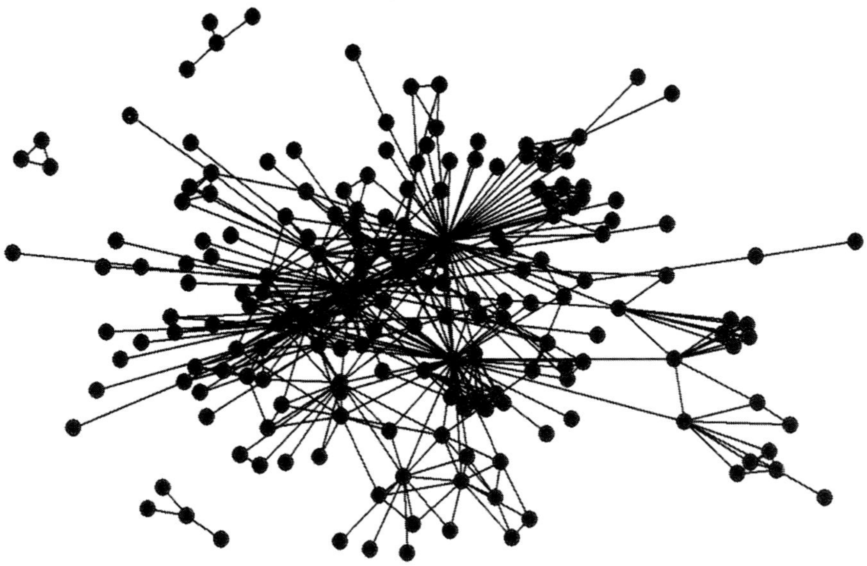

Figure 11: Network of co-words 1968-2004

To extract the central core of this co-word network, the network of functional relationships was sliced only to show those keywords with 6 and more relationships. What emerges are the issues most explored by Bednarik up to 2004. Figure 12 shows these core functional networks grouped into four different clusters. The issues investigated by Bednarik expand, but remain focused on rock art and petroglyphs.

Related to *rock art* are the issues *of dating methods, taphonomy*, and interest in rock art in *China*. On the other hand, the matter of *prehistoric art* appears related to *palaeoart* and *Paleolithic art*; but the interests in *Australia* and the organization and participation in international congresses on rock art remain. *Petroglyph* relationships extend to India and Portugal. In Australia the interest extends to *Western Australia*, to *Depuch Island*, the *Dampier Archipelago*, and the *Pilbara region*. Finally, the links of the investigations of the *petroglyphs* appear in relation to *professional ethics, methodology, dating in archeology* and *cave paintings*.

Table 11 shows the strength of the keywords that make up this network up to 2004. Once again, centrality measures to what extent the links of a keyword network are concentrated in a single word or group of words. The simplest measure is the degree of centrality, which counts the number of ties each keyword has and where the most central keyword is the one with the most ties. Between 1968 and 2004, the most central keyword is *Petroglyphs*,

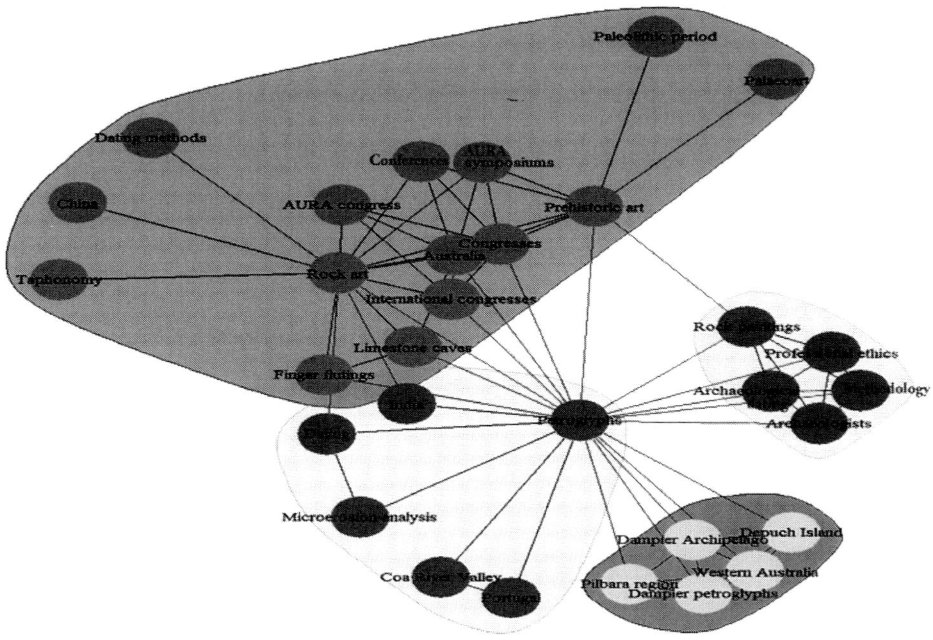

Figure 12: Central issues of interest up to 2004

followed by *Australia, Rock Art, Prehistoric Art,* and other keywords that can be read directly from this table.

Table 11: Degree of centrality up to 2004

Keywords	*degree*	*closeness*	*betweenness*	*eigenvector*
Petroglyphs	67	0.00325	6842.344	1
Australia	45	0.00307	5126.692	0.7578
Rock art	43	0.00295	3025.29	0.7733
Prehistoric art	32	0.00278	1608.268	0.6627
Lower paleolithic	18	0.00262	1323.233	0.3619
Rock paintings	17	0.00262	1037.056	0.4352
International congresses	15	0.00256	765.898	0.3628
Pleistocene	13	0.00254	490.085	0.3542
Archaeological dating	12	0.00225	375.928	0.2751
Indonesia	12	0.00213	786.177	0.121
Conferences	11	0.00251	89.655	0.3839
Congresses	11	0.00254	108.584	0.3915
Homo sapiens	11	0.00208	459.609	0.0955

contd. table 11

Keywords	*degree*	*closeness*	*betweenness*	*eigenvector*
Caves	10	0.00231	151.52	0.2368
Dating methods	10	0.00219	81.013	0.2178
Hominids	10	0.00215	216.393	0.1521
India	10	0.00237	430.764	0.2574
Limestone caves	10	0.00247	244.606	0.274
Photography	10	0.00213	122.759	0.1554
Chalking method	9	0.00228	706.65	0.1508
Cult. resource manag	9	0.00209	405.662	0.0837
Dating	9	0.00242	101.045	0.2864
Portugal	9	0.00227	49.603	0.2698

4.7.3. Network of co-words in the period 1968-2022

Figure 13 shows the components of the keyword network used in the documents published by Bednarik from 1968 to 2022. In the network, there are only three cohesive subgroups made up of 186 different keywords: one giant subgroup made up of 182 connected keywords and two subgroups of two keywords each, but little extensive in functional relationships.

To extract the core of this co-word network, the relationship network was sliced to show only those keywords with nine and more functional relationships. What emerges are the issues most explored by Bednarik up to 2022. Figure 14 shows these core functional networks grouped into four different clusters.

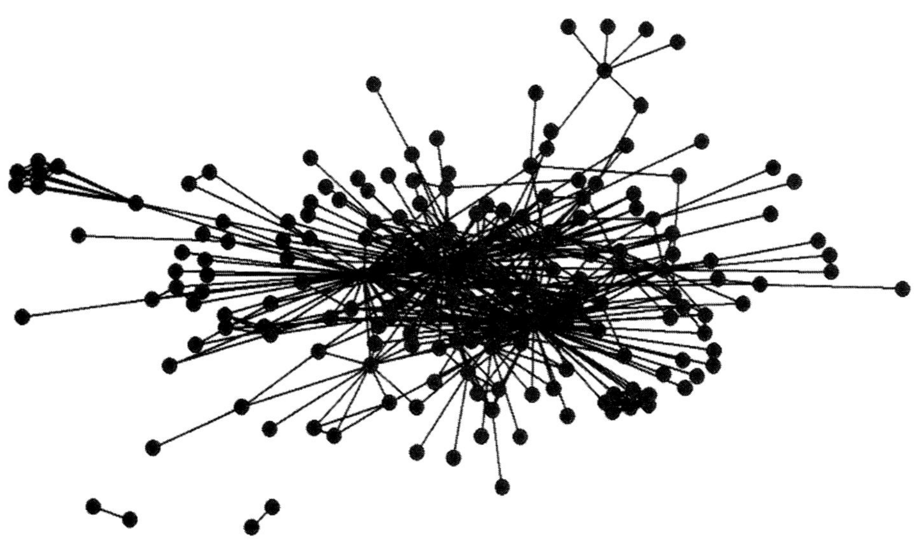

Figure 13: Network of co-words 1968-2022

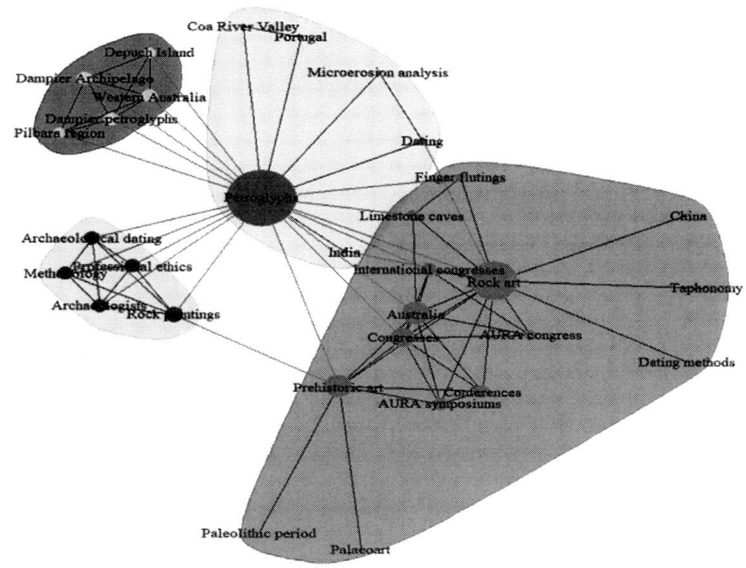

Figure 14: Central issues of interest until 2022

The matters investigated by Bednarik are not expanded or altered and remain focused on *rock art, petroglyphs*; *dating methods, taphonomy* and rock art in *China*. The same happens with the subject *prehistoric art,* related to *palaeoart and Paleolithic art. Petroglyph* relationships maintains its focus on India and Portugal (China also between 2014-2022); and this topic is also related to *professional ethics, methodology, dating in archeology,* and *cave paintings.* His interest is still concentrated in *Western Australia, Depuch Island,* the *Dampier Archipelago*, and the *Pilbara region.*

Table 12 shows the strength of the keywords that make up this network. Once again, centrality measures to what extent the links of a keyword network are concentrated in a single word or group of words. The simplest measure is the degree of centrality, which counts the number of ties each keyword has and where the most central keyword is the one with the most ties. Between 1968 and 2022, the most central keyword is *petroglyphs*, followed by *rock art, Australia, prehistoric art,* and so on. The other keywords can be read directly from the following table.

Table 12: Degree of centrality until 2022

Keywords	*degree*	*closeness*	*betweenness*	*eigenvector*
Petroglyphs	82	0.003	6690.941	0.975
Rock art	81	0.003	5187.900	1.000
Australia	52	0.003	4554.809	0.668
Prehistoric art	30	0.003	837.630	0.558
Lower paleolithic	21	0.003	854.994	0.388

contd. table 12

Keywords	*degree*	*closeness*	*betweenness*	*eigenvector*
Rock paintings	20	0.003	849.850	0.387
Congresses	15	0.003	125.159	0.349
Beads	14	0.002	754.962	0.247
Human evolution	14	0.002	1157.332	0.165
Pleistocene	14	0.003	193.839	0.344
India	13	0.002	67.902	0.297
International congresses	13	0.003	220.352	0.315
Archaeological dating	12	0.002	56.321	0.282
Engravings	12	0.002	332.947	0.281
Europe	11	0.003	312.338	0.291
Palaeoart	11	0.002	271.760	0.253
Dampier Archipelago	10	0.003	68.874	0.257
Western Australia	10	0.003	246.641	0.244
Conferences	9	0.002	28.533	0.216
Cupules	9	0.002	27.717	0.214
Asia	8	0.002	22.420	0.229
Cave art	8	0.002	220.575	0.212
Cultural resource management	8	0.002	1050.000	0.057
Dating	8	0.002	36.412	0.228
Methodology	8	0.002	64.470	0.174
Symbolism	8	0.002	28.474	0.137

5. Conclusions

As has been seen, scientometric analysis is a technical way of evaluating the performance and production of an intellectual in any branch of knowledge. Potentially, this analysis can reveal the academic interests, and the main tendencies or scientific orientation of these same intellectuals, which has been the central objective of this article. However, this technique depends entirely on the availability of access to the indexed digital resources; specially when examining data from international scholars. Since digital indexing is a recent development, it can be expected that there will be difficulties in the acquisition of the data, which can cause analytical discrepancies in the results. However, the volume of information handled by us to evaluate the trajectory of Robert G. Bednarik can be considered robust and highly indicative of his academic production.

In this text, the demography, growth, impact, diffusion, co-authorships, and relationships of the topics explored by Robert G. Bednarik were examined from a statistical perspective and the result of this must be pondered in quantitative terms of visibility. From this is evident that this academic prefers to disseminate his research in the form of articles published in academic and/ or similar journals and there is no doubt that he is not concerned if these journals are of high impact or are indexed in the Web of Science or Scopus, so much so that these databases index an insignificant part of his academic production. The low rate of Bednarik's mentions in this two major databases goes beyond the development of the digital indexing and could be seen as an effect of academic marginalization, a contemporary phenomenon in the production and diffusion of knowledge. Despise this situation, the documents published by Bednarik are highly cited as attested by the indices found in alternative search engines to these Anglo-Saxon databases.

Bednarik is a good example of differentiated indexing, which is part of what we could describe as a phenomenon of intellectual oppression exercised by the main world academic powers. This could affect the view of Bednarik's productivity, but it is not very noticeable mostly because of his strong scientific and prolific production, but it is affecting the scholars of underdeveloped countries, whose academic progress has been increasingly controlled by the hegemonic centers of intellectual knowledge. His strong position as a thinker and scientific, despise the marginalization, is also part of the image that Bednarik projects into his work and academic activities.

The data obtained on the growth of Bednarik's intellectual production show that it is stable, as well as his thematic interests, which progressively are expanding to other countries. The coherence of the issues that he investigates is notorious, which are disseminated to a large extent through the journals he edits and the congresses he organizes. In his work there is a clear orientation towards the establishment of scientific consensus; and the organization and participation in international congresses have allowed the creation of the International Federations of Rock Art Organizations (IFRAO), and the dissemination of scientific standards. An example of this is the publication of the Rock Art Glossary (Bednarik et al. 2010), the IFRAO Color Scale (Bednarik 1994), and the communication of technical parameters in the treatment and recording of rock evidence in the world.

Besides his clear interest in spreading scientific standards, and to promote a solid scientific community around the world, Bednarik's attention also addresses thematic not clearly noted in the indexing sources, such as ethnographic topics, which he has been able to observe in Australia, India, Bolivia or Peru; and these aspects of academic interest in non-hegemonic subjects are redounding in decolonial proposals, which do not stray from the scientific paradigms that dominate Bednarik's actions and influence in these countries.

On other side, because the level of quantitative visibility, some of his most recent work and collaborations are not so evident, especially those with South Africa or Saudi Arabia researchers; the last one with implications in the World Heritage List of UNESCO. For South America it is important to point out his collaborative work in Bolivia, Brazil or Peru, and the repercussions of this work is still very difficult to notice from a statistical level. Unlike other continents, with a large presence in Europe and Asia, Bednarik's influence in South America's rock art research is still low, largely due to the lack of dissemination of the articles and books he produces and publishes since most of these documents are not available online (open access) and are not indexed by misnamed "international" databases.

Beyond these aspects, the thematic axes noticed in the evaluation do not exhaust the creative vein of Robert G. Bednarik, which continues to grow. After a clear focus on the formalization of rock art science (*Rock Art Science* is his most complete work in this sense) and his interest in strengthening organizations such as AURA and IFRAO, Bednarik has expanded his range of interest with advanced proposals in topics such as neuroscience, cognitive development, and hominization; and indigenous intellectuals see his advance as an anti-hegemonic stance as well.

We agree with Dr. Chakravarty (2006), as we can see Bednarik´s work as:

> "...an attempt at negotiating the intellectual itinerary of the human mind through caves, seas, and continents and through millions of years of its history on earth planet. Rock art is a code word, a key to unlock [...] the mind of ancient human being. It is therefore, an epistemological venture to harness the rigorous and punishing discipline, imposed by Bednarik on himself and on others, to repossess, within the limited intellectual access of the modern interpreter, the cognitive approach of his ancestors to the world, as it shaped itself around them" (p. ix).

Whatever he explores, Robert G. Bednarik scientific logic is very dominant, as is his committed to humanity. This scientometric approach is just an essay, one limited by available digital media, which it would be nice to complete with an analysis of citations and the impact of these citations by alternative means to those offered by the Web of Science and Scopus.

Dr Gori-Tumi Echevarría-López
Professor. Universidad Nacional San Luis Gonzaga de Ica.
President. Peruvian Rock Art Association (APAR)
Email: goritumi@gmail.com

and

Dr Rubén Urbizagástegui-Alvarado (Ph. D. in Information Science)
University of California at Riverside, **University Library, Metada Department**
Riverside, Califfornia
E-mail: ruben@ucr.edu

References

Abt, H. 2007. The Future of Single-Authored Papers. *Scientometrics* 73(3): 353-358.

Ayala-Gascón, M., R. Aleixandre-Benavent and A. Gandía-Balaguer. 2012. Indicadores de actividad científica en investigadores singulares: perfil bibliométrico de Eduardo Primo Yúfera, expresidente del CSIC. *Revista Española de Documentación Científica* 35(2): 209-237.

Banerjee, S. and K. Chakrabarti. 2021. Scientometric Portrait of Joan C. Durrance, a Respected Researcher in the Community Focused Library Services. *Library Philosophy and Practice* (ejournal). 6603. https://digitalcommons.unl.edu/libphilprac/6603

Bansal, S. 2018. Scientometric Portrait of Nobel Laureate Arieh Warshel. *Journal of Advancements in Library Sciences* 5(2): 63-67.

Bednarik, R. G. 1994. Introducing the IFRAO Standard Scale. *Rock Art Research* 11: 74-75.

Bednarik, R. G., A. Achrati, M. Consens, F. Coimbra, G. Dimitriadis, T. Huisheng, A. Muzzolini, D. Seglie and Y. A. Sher. 2010. *Rock Art Glossary, a Multilingual Dictionary*. Ocacional AURA Publication 16, Melbourne.

Bhattacharyya, P. K. and N. B. Sahu. 2020. Informetric Portrait of Elinor Ostrom, the Nobel Laureate in the Field of Economic Sciences. *Journal of Scientometric Research* 9(2): 204-213.

Bourdieu, P. 1986. The Forms of Capital. In John G. Richardson (ed.), *Handbook of theory and research for the sociology of education*, pp. 241-258. Greenwood Press, New York.

Bourdieu, P. 2004. *Os Usos sociais da ciência: por uma sociologia clínica do campo científico*. Unesp, São Paulo.

Chakravarty, K. K. 2007. Foreword. In Reddy, P. C. (ed.), *Exploring the Mind of Ancient Man: Festschrift to Robert G. Bednarik*, pp. vii-xi. Research India Press, New Delhi, India.

Csardi, G. and T. Nepusz. 2006. The igraph software package for complex network research, *International Journal of Complex Systems* 1695(5): 1-9.

Fernández Clemente, E. 1995. La historia económica de España en los últimos veinte años (1975-1995): crónica de una escisión anunciada. *Revista de Historia Jerónimo Zurita*, 71: 59-94.

Gholampour, B. and A. Noruzi. 2021. Scientometric portrait of Professor Wolfgang Glanzel, an expert in the field of scientometrics. *Annals of Library and Information Studies* 68(2): 198-207.

Greene, M. 2007. The demise of the lone author. *Nature* 450(7173): 1165.

Hirsch, J. E. 2005. An index to quantify an individual's scientific research output. *Proceedings of the National Academy of Sciences of the United States of America* 102(46): 16569-16572.

Hussain, A. 2020. Trend setters in library and information studies in Pakistan: A Bio-bibliometric study of professor Hamid Rahman's contribution to LIS literature. *Library Philosophy and Practice* (e-journal). 4635. https://digitalcommons.unl.edu/libphilprac/4635

Jacso, P. 2018. The scientometric portrait of Eugene Garfield through the free ResearcherID service from the Web of Science Core Collection of 67 million master records and 1.3 billion references. *Scientometrics*, 114(2): 545-555.

Kuhn, T. S. 1970. *The Structure of Scientific Revolutions*. University of Chicago Press, Chicago.

Kuhn, T. S. 1974. Second Thoughts on Paradigms. In. Frederick Suppe (ed.), *The Structure of Scientific Theories*, pp. 459-482. University of Illinois Press, Urbana.

León, R. 1983. Honorio Delgado y el psicoanálisis, 1915-1930: un análisis cuantitativo. *Revista de Psicología Peruana 1(2): 107-128.*

Marczewski, J. 1973. *¿Qué es la historia cuantitativa?* Nueva Visión, Buenos Aires.

Morey, K. 2014. Bednarik, Robert G. In: C. Smith, (eds), *Encyclopedia of Global Archaeology*. pp. 834-836. Springer, New York. https://doi.org/10.1007/978-1-4419-0465-2_2395

Noyons, E. C. M. 2001. Bibliometric mapping of science in a policy context. *Scientometrics* 50(1): 83-89.

Persson, O., R. Danell and J. Wiborg Schneider. 2009. How to use Bibexcel for various types of bibliometric analysis. In F. Åström, R. Danell, B. Larsen and J. Schneider (eds.), *Celebrating scholarly communication studies: A Festschrift for Olle Persson at his 60th Birthday*, pp 9–24. International Society for Scientometrics and Informetrics, Leuven, Belgium.

Price, J. D. de S. 1951. Quantitative measures of the development of science. *Archives Internationales d'Histoire des Sciences* 14: 86-93.

Price, J. D. de S. 1956. The exponential curve of science, *Discovery*, 17: 240-243. Reprinted in: *The sociology of science*. Edited by Berbard Barber and Walter Hirsch. The Free Press of Glencoe, New York. 1962, pp. 516-524.

Price, J. D. de S. 1963. *Little Science, Big Science*. Columbia University, New York.

Price, J. D. de S. 1975. Diseases of science. In Price, J. D. de S. (author), *Science since Babylon*, pp. 161-195. Enlarged edition. Yale University Press, New Haven and London.

R Core Team. 2014. R: *A language and environment for statistical computing*. R Foundation for Statistical Computing, Vienna, Austria.

Sen, S. K. and K. S. Gan. 1990. Biobibliometrics: concept and application in the study of productivity of scientists. *International Forum on Information and Documentation* 15(3): 13-21.

Urbizagástegui-Alvarado, R. 2020. Reiner Tom Zuidema: un perfil bio-bibliométrico. *Ciência da Informação* 49(1): 124-148.

Annex A: Consulted bibliographic databases

Academic Search Complete
Anthropology Online
Anthropology Plus
AnthroSource
Archaeological Bibliography (Archäologische Bibliographie)
ArticleFirst
Arts and Humanities Citation Index (Web of Science)
JSTOR: The Scholarly Journal Archive
Scopus
Web of Science
WorldCat
Pascal and Francis Bibliographic Databases

Online resources and catalogs

AURANET Library
Melvyl Catalog
google scholar
National Library of Australia
National Library of South Africa

Personal sites on the internet

https://www.ifrao.com/robert-g-bednarik/
https://www.ifrao.com/robert-g-bednarik/rg-bednarik-library/
https://scholar.google.com/citations?user=Hunnq7oAAAAJ&hl=en

Part 2

LATEST RESEARCH ON PALAEOART OF THE WORLD

12

KEYWORDS: Children's art – Evo-devo (evolutionary developmental biology) – Geometric enigma – Phosphenes – Primary visual cortex (VI) – Woven world hypothesis

EVOLUTION OF THE MIND'S EYE: A POSSIBLE EXPLANATION FOR WHY EARLY HOMININS PRODUCED GEOMETRIC FIGURES BEFORE REPRESENTATIONAL ONES

DEAN FALK

Abstract: Hominins' earliest renderings of visual images in both Old and New Worlds were geometric rather than representational figures. Because the reasons for this are mysterious, some have referred to the priority of geometric figures as the "geometric enigma." Here, evo-devo comparative studies of chimpanzees, humans, and the development of drawing and painting in the youngsters of both are discussed to explore the emergence and development of artistic skills during the earliest part of the hominin record. Topics include the nature of early hominins' visual habitats and the changes that likely occurred in the neurological underpinnings of their visual cortices as they shifted from arboreal to diurnal terrestrial habitats. Hominins inherited the derived behavior of weaving arboreal sleeping nests each day from plant matter from their apelike ancestors, and eventually used weaving skills to make baby slings, which were likely the first portable tools and textiles invented. Patterns inherent in simple woven textiles appear in some of the oldest paleoart, are among the earliest geometric images produced by young children and are perceived when the visual cortices of people are stimulated electrically, pharmaceutically, or during migraine auras. These data are synthesized, and a testable "woven world" hypothesis is proposed as one possible explanation for the geometric enigma.

Introduction

An ability to infer what other individuals are thinking and how they are likely to behave is especially well-honed in contemporary humans. This capacity, 'Theory of Mind' (ToM), begins to develop shortly after birth as infants observe the behaviors of others and unconsciously compare them with their own experiences (Meltzoff 2007). Unlike inferring the thoughts and feelings of

Article received: 4 December 2022
Revised I: 9 December 2022
Revised II: 01 February 2023
Revised III: 30 June 2023
Accepted: 30 June 2023

contemporary people, and for obvious reasons, attribution of mental states to our ancestors lacks grounding in ToM developed from experiences within corresponding cultures. Such attributions must, therefore, be viewed cautiously.

When scholars interpret Paleolithic art, including rock art, they attempt to apply ToM that derives from the present to the past. However, "to just report discoveries of rock art sites, subjectively describing the motifs depicted in them and proceeding straight to their interpretation by imposing our conditioned mind has been standard practice throughout the world. After so many decades of applying this traditional archaeological approach, it has helped us little to answer significant research questions" (Kumar 2021:25). As with discussions about manufactured lithic tools, Paleolithic art has frequently been attributed anonymously to presumed males (Fritz et al. 2016), although the contributions of women and children have become a recent focus of discussion (Goldhahn et al. 2020; Janik and Williams 2018; Langley and Lister 2018; Snow 2013). Fortunately, rock art studies are beginning to adopt scientific approaches based on understanding "the lithology, taphonomy, topography, sedimentology, palaeoclimate of the sites and the epistemology of our ideas about rock art" (Kumar 2021:23).

Although determining the ages of rock art remains for the most part extremely difficult (Kumar 2021), humans are estimated to have produced it in the form of hand stencils and naturalistic depictions of animals "by ~40 kyr ago at opposite ends of the Pleistocene Eurasian world" (Aubert el al. 2014:223; Aubert et al. 2018; Tacon et al. 2018), while systematic processing and use of pigments, art (e.g. in the form of beads), and decoration occurred considerably earlier in Africa (Henshilwood et al. 2011; McBrearty and Brooks 2000). Notably, a cross-hatched pattern was applied with red ochre onto a 73,000-year-old flake from Bombos Cave, South Africa, which "predates the earliest previously known abstract figurative drawings by at least 30,000 years" (Henshilwood et al. 2018). Clearly, the Eurocentric idea of a relatively sudden cognitive revolution having occurred in association with Upper Paleolithic art in Western European *Homo sapiens* has been put to rest (Mc Brearty and Brooks 2000).

Despite this welcome development, very few researchers have sought evidence regarding the origins of artistic impulses in the earliest hominins that evolved after their lineage diverged from that of chimpanzees ~6.5 million years ago (mya, Kumar et al. 2022)—impulses that long preceded the emergence of rock art (and other creative forms). Even fewer have explored the possible biological bases for visually perceiving and producing art (but see Hodgson 2019). Robert Bednarik has done both (Bednarik 1984, 1987, 1998, 2006, 2020, 2021). After reviewing relevant background information, this paper picks up and expands on these two facets of Bednarik's research.

Visual perceptions are assembled from features that are extracted separately in the primary visual cortex

Although it may seem counterintuitive, visual perception does not happen in the eyes. When light from an object enters the eyes and stimulates the retina, the latter projects information to the lateral geniculate nucleus of the thalamus that, in turn, stimulates the primary visual cortex (V1, Brodmann area [BA] 17) at the back of the brain. It is here where the initial stages of visual processing take place. In V1, individual neurons respond selectively to specific orientations of lines/edges that contribute to the perception of shape in localized parts of the visual field (e.g., some neurons respond to vertical lines in a particular part of the visual field; others fire selectively for lines at other orientations, e.g. at a particular angle or horizontal) or contours (Hubel and Wiesel 1959). Other neurons in VI respond to specific colors at certain locations (Garg et al. 2019) or motion in a particular direction. After preliminary processing, neurons in V1 project discrete bits of information forward to higher visual areas in the occipital and temporal lobes, which process the stimuli further. Although V1 is particularly adept at detecting edges because of its many neurons that are selective for orientations, "for the visual system to extract a specific piece of information about a feature, such as the orientation and length, shape, color, and movement ... require[s] a comparison of the outputs of may cells" (Podoll and Robinson 2008: 246-247). The forward flowing accretionary processing that begins with VI results, eventually, in assembled unified visual perceptions.

Seminal experiments on animals demonstrate that the orientations of VI neurons are programmed during a critical period of postnatal development in response to environmental factors that help shape the physiological underpinnings of visual perceptions. In a classic example, recordings were made from single neurons in VI of kittens that were raised in two cohorts that lived in different environments in which high-contrast black-and-white stripes were oriented exclusively in either vertical or horizontal directions. Results showed that the distributions of the preferred orientations of VI neurons that were programmed during the kittens' critical period were completely abnormal and highly skewed toward the particular orientation of the stripes to which each cohort had been exposed (Blakemore and Cooper 1970).

Although one cannot, of course, perform such experiments on humans, it is interesting that people who were raised in so-called carpentered worlds that have lots of sharply defined edges at different orientations (e.g., in industrialized societies) are more susceptible to optical illusions that entail expectations about edges, lines and orientations (e.g., the famous Ponzo and Müller-Lyer illusions) than people who live in more rounded natural environments that lack these features (Phillips 2019; Segall et al. 1963). Similarly, people raised in different environments respond differently to depth cues in two-dimensional pictures. Whether or not the effects that the physical world has on visual perception in different cultures is associated with significantly different distributions of preferred orientations in VI neurons has not, to my not knowledge, been determined. It may, in fact, be that susceptibility to optical illusions depends on higher level visual processing than that which takes place in VI (BA 17) as suggested, for example, by a functional magnetic resonance imaging (fMRI) study that found that visual perceptions of everyday items by East Asian and American participants were associated with different activation patterns in visual areas BA 18 and 19 (Ksander et al. 2018).

That said, humans universally share certain evolved features of VI that differ from those of nonhuman primates. VI has migrated caudally and medially along the outside surface of the occipital lobes so that most of it is not visible on the external surface of the brain, as it is for other primates. Presumably in conjunction with this process, the proportion of VI that represents peripheral vision became significantly larger in the human lineage: "The difference between these two species appears to be that the function of the peripheral cortex has been strengthened in humans, most likely because the observation of the surroundings and objects is more complicated in humans compared to macaques," and may reflect differences between "arboreal primates vs. bipedal ground-dwellers" (Wu et al. 2012:1739). When it comes to the sensitivity of individual neurons in VI to lines with particular orientations, however, humans and macaques map similarly: "Despite 25 million years of evolutionary separation between humans and macaques, the monkeys showed essentially the same orientation-retinotopy relationship as the humans" (Sasaki et al. 2006:662.) Although the organization/location of VI in humans including its relatively large representation of peripheral vision distinguishes them from monkeys, and despite the fact that culture and environment impact the ways in which people process visual stimuli, the neurons in VI that respond selectively to orientations of lines and edges appear to be fundamentally similar across primates.

As we will see, the basic perceptions that arise when VI neurons are stimulated contribute not only to the assemblage of unified visual perceptions as signals move forward in the brain (i.e., sensory processing), they also play a role in the development of artistic skills in youngsters. More to the point, and as Bednarik hypothesized (1984, 1987), neurons in VI were also likely crucial for the perception and production of proto-artistic expressions in early hominins, as suggested by the kinds of visual experiences that are produced—patterns known as phosphenes—when the visual cortex is stimulated mechanically (e.g., by pressing on the eyelids), electrically (Penfield and Rasmussen 1968: Knoll and Kugler 1959), pharmaceutically (Lewis-Williams et al. 1988; Siegal 1977) or spontaneously (e.g., as part of migraine auras, Charles and Baca 2013).

Perception and production of phosphenes in humans

The anatomical substrates for processing vision are extremely complex, which makes them subject to possible disruption. Indeed, for this reason some visual perceptions do not have actual referents out there in the "real world." Phosphenes (meaning "light show"), for example, are imaginary shapes, lights, colors and movements such as "shooting stars" or geometric patterns (Savigny 1838) that may be experienced when individuals rub their eyes, stand up too quickly, or receive pressure or electrical stimulation anywhere along the optic pathway, including in the primary visual cortex. Although phosphenes occur in a huge variety of geometrical forms, analysis of 520 that were experienced from electrical stimulations by 313 adults yielded an illustrated taxonomy of 15 typical phosphene form groups (a so-called "phosphene-Linnaeus) (Fig. 1), which the authors compared to 300,000 drawings and paintings made by pre-school children from diverse ethnic backgrounds ("scribblings-Linnaeus," Kellogg et al. 1965).

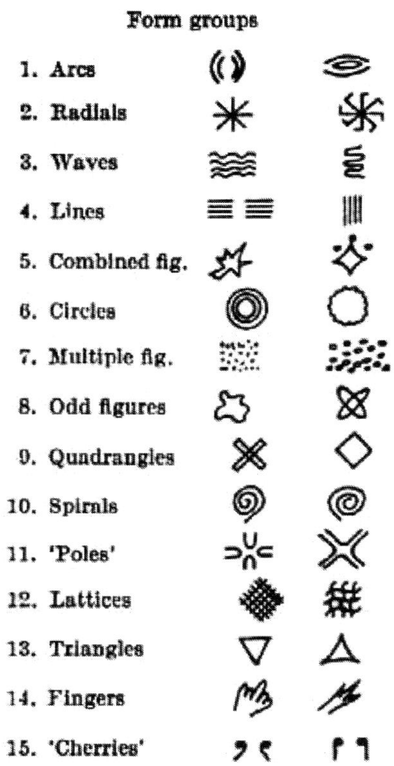

Figure 1: Fifteen typical phosphene form groups obtained by electrically stimulating the brains of 313 adults, which comprise the "phosphene-Linnaeus" of Kellogg et al. (1965: extracted from Table 1).

Nearly 90% of the phosphene forms stimulated electrically in adults appeared in the children's artwork, leading the authors to conclude that "such 'outlinings in geometrical style' play an important part in the development of a child's expression in drawing or painting." Thus, infants typically practice motor skills by scribbling, which will eventually be used to draw or paint images by the time they are two, similar to infants' prelinguistic babbles that precede their acquisition of speech (Falk 2009). As young children mature, so do their scribbles. They can, thus, typically scribble simple "geometric patterns" by the time they are three and are able to use them to produce elementary renderings of objects such as people, animals, houses, and the sun by around age four (Kellogg et al. 1965:1130). Phosphenes and children's early art both contain arcs, waves, lines, circles, dots, and triangles, etc. (Fig. 1). What's especially relevant for the present discussion is that infants' artistic skills develop through a predictable series of stages and entail production of images like the phosphenes that are experienced by adults when their primary visual cortices are stimulated. Clearly, there is something very fundamental about children's use of basic geometric patterns to depict objects in their visual worlds.

There is also something fundamental about the adult facility for subjectively perceiving images (with or without the eyes closed) of phantom geometric forms—i.e., forms that have no correspondents in the real world. Although, as noted, this experience can happen in response to mechanical, pharmaceutical, or externally applied electrical stimulation, perception of geometric (and other) forms can also occur spontaneously in association with (usually harmless) visual auras that precede migraine headaches in about 10-15% of the people that have them (Grüsser 1995), which is estimated to be about 6-8% of men and 15-25% of women in Western countries (Dreier 2011). Such auras "typically develop in a creeping fashion—a typical migraine aura might start as a scintillation-scotoma (spot of flickering light) in the visual field center and propagate to the field periphery of one visual hemifield of both eyes within about fifteen minutes, corresponding to a spreading depression of brain electrical activity that propagates in the primary visual cortex from the occipital pole forward" (Dreier 2011:443). Although visual auras may entail any of the geometric patterns discussed above as well as many other images (see Podoll and Robinson 2008 for hundreds of illustrations and Viana et al. 2019 for review), the archetype of visual aura, known as a "fortification" spectra (Hadjikhani and Vincent 2021), usually begins centrally as a small flickering zigzag and consists of a grayish C-shaped region that expands as it drifts laterally to one side or the other. (The propagation can also be from the outside to the center of the visual field, Queiroz et al. 2011.) The shifting crescentic region is a traveling blind spot, or scotoma, which has a visible leading edge that appears to be a bright zigzag line. The line and its trailing blind spot eventually drift off into the periphery and disappear.

The physiological events that underpin the fortification (and myriad other) visual auras appear to entail propagating waves in VI that sequentially excite, depolarize and depress columns of neurons with specific orientations (Hubel and Wiesel 1959). In the case of the classic fortification phosphene pattern, zigzags probably appear at the leading edge because excitatory transmitters simultaneously activate distinct groups of neurons that have different preferred orientations, i.e., that subserve extraction of specific information about the orientations of objects' various definitive lines and, thus, their shape (Grüsser 1995 for details). (Much more information about the neurological underpinnings of phosphenes is available in Podoll and Robinson 2008: 239-251). What is important for the present discussion is that the geometric forms of phosphenes appear to be intrinsically constrained/shaped by the properties of VI neurons, especially the orientations they respond to.

Although, as mentioned, VI also contains neurons that respond to color (clusters of which are called blobs) and studies frequently note in passing that phosphenes may appear in bright shimmering colors, not much attention has been paid to specific details about the colors. Brighter colors have been reported for auras in about 20% of the individuals who had them preceding migraines and "this sensation was sometimes very marked ('colours get so bright that I feel they will attack me')" (Vincent and Hadjikhani 2007:1369). Elsewhere, colors were reported to occur in about 40% of the migraineurs (with or without accompanying black, white and/or silver shades) who experienced visual auras, as compared to 50% whose phosphenes always appeared in black-and-white or black-and-silver (Queiroz et al. 2011). Another study found that, with respect to zigzags of fortification phosphenes, "the colours are seen as very pure; red and green are reported more frequently than the other colours of the spectrum. Some of the flickering particles are of a deep, 'brilliant' black" (Grüsser 1995: 1130). On the other hand, a survey of the non-black-and-white colors in 397 pictures that migraineurs produced to illustrate visual hallucinations reported the colors used from most to least often were yellow, red, blue, green, orange, purple, and brown (Podoll and Robinson 2008: Table 7.11). (Around 20% of the pictures were only in black-and-white.)

Phosphenes in early and recent art

It has long been recognized that geometric images like phosphenes are abundant in the textiles and art of nonindustrialized cultures (Blackburn 1977; Oster 1970; Siegal 1977) and that the earliest images depicted in the Paleolithic record of the Old World were geometric rather than iconic (Lewis-Williams et al. 1988), as was also true for the earliest human-made depictions in the (much more recently settled) Americas (Malotki and Dissanayake 2018; Dissanayake et al. 2019) during a time recognized as equivalent to the Upper Paleolithic elsewhere (Williams and Madsen 2020):

> "Since the Late Pleistocene, combinations of straight lines are commonly found, for instance in the engraved ochre plaquettes from Blombos cave, South Africa (about 75,000 years old), as are dots on Franco-Cantabrian cave walls (e.g., the spotted horses from Pech Merle, France, 16,000 years old). Such designs are also observed on artifacts from diverse periods (e.g., decorative lines and dots on earthenware from the Linear Pottery culture from the European Neolithic, 5500-4500 BC) and in the artistic production of many nonwestern cultures (e.g., geometric patterns on basketry or cloth). The pervasiveness of geometric designs across widely divergent cultures and periods may be explained by the fact that they are appealing to the early human visual system (De Smedt and De Cruz 2010: 699)".

It almost goes without saying that some forms of modern art also incorporate phosphene-like geometric images that may derive from or appeal to the physiological underpinnings of the human visual system. Thus, "abstract art often appeals strongly to early perceptual systems, by using vivid colors, straight lines, or sharp contrasts.... In the work of well-known artists like Klee, Mondriaan and Matisse.... 'to abstract' means 'going back to the essentials,' abstract art has indeed succeeded in stripping away cultural conventions by reverting to elementary responses of the human perceptual systems" (De Smedt and De Cruz 2010:702).

As we have seen, geometric images are not only the first hominin-made engravings/paintings in the archaeological record of people everywhere, they are also the first visual perceptions stimulated by the primary visual cortex and the first images that children produce once they are able to control scribbling. Although this remarkable confluence calls for investigation of the emergence and development of hominin's sensitivity to and production of geometrical images in the deep past, few researchers have taken such an evo-devo (evolutionary developmental biology) approach. Robert Bednarik (1984, 1987), however, not only observed that nearly all the phosphenes shown in Figure 1 (i.e., from Kellog et al. 1965's "phosphene- Linnaeus") appear among the non-figurative petroglyphs found across Australia, he also compared phosphene types from different sites and hypothesized that "the more frequently phosphene types occur in rock art, the more archaic it is. In the oldest traditions they may dominate to the point of exclusiveness. This suggests that the ability to externalize concepts of reality (i.e. art) was derived from phosphenes" (Bednarik 1984: 30). The hypothesis that phosphenes themselves may have developed over time is an important one that sets Bednarik's analyses apart from those of others, as does his appreciation of some of the earliest paleoart on record, including beads, pendants, portable plaques, figurines, use of pigments, australopithecine manuports (Bednarik 1998), and petroglyphs (Bednarik 2021).

Some time ago, Bednarik suggested that hominins may have begun externalizing certain geometric patterns beginning with parallel lines (1984:29), which appears to have been prophetic given that Wonderwerk Cave in South Africa has yielded around 20 incised slabs (mobiliary art) "that often feature well-spaced parallel curved lines ... from stratified cave contexts extending back to ~ 0.5 Myr ago" (Beaumont and Vogel 2006: 222). Around the same time, but far away in Java, a *Homo erectus* individual engraved a shell from a mussel that "was considerably older than the oldest geometric engravings described so far" with a simple pattern that included parallel lines and zigzags (Joordens et al. 2015: 228). The fact that these earliest known engraved geometric patterns preceded the later production of iconic petroglyphs as, indeed, seems to have been the case worldwide raises the question of what accounts for this so-called "geometric enigma" (Malotki and Dissanayake 2018). As Bednarik recently put it, "Malotki and Dissanayake have most competently identified the 'geometric enigma.' Let us see if archaeometry can rise to the challenge of undoing this veritable Gordian knot" (Bednarik 2020:114). As discussed below, an evo-devo approach may be helpful for exploring the mysterious reasons for the priority of geometric over representational images in the oldest known prehistoric art.

Woven world hypothesis

If one compares artistic development of young children and captive juvenile chimpanzees, gorillas, and orangutans, the scribbles of great apes and humans appear similar (Vancatova 2008). Like children, apes seem to enjoy making drawings and paintings, although they are often less engaged with the process than children and, at times, ignore or attempt to eat the art supplies (Pelé et al. 2021; Saito et al. 2014). One comparative study observed that, despite the non-figurative nature of ape art, "there is a choice in the use of colour, the type of strokes, and the use of space ... drawings from great apes do not result from totally random scribbles" (Pelé et al. 2021). Apes sometimes produce fans, loops and occasional shapes that appear somewhat geometrical (Pelé et al. 2021) and experiments suggest their art reveals a remarkable sense of composition and balance (Vancatova 2008), which is perhaps not surprising since great apes have a good grasp of 'folk physics and balance' when navigating their arboreal habitats (Falk 2024).

Nonetheless, apes never develop an ability to produce the six well-formed typical diagrams (Greek cross, square, circle, triangle, odd-shaped area and diagonal cross) that follow the emergence of 20 basic scribbles in children from diverse backgrounds (Kellogg 1955), let alone the elementary pictorial figures that children eventually make (see Kellogg et al. 1965 for illustrations of children's developing artistic output). Consistent with this, a study that compared artistic development in human toddlers and chimpanzees, found that the children, on average, could imitate humans' horizontal and vertical lines by around age 2&1/2 years, circles by about age 3, crosses by 3&1/2, and squares by age 4, but the chimpanzees were unable to imitate the images freely, although they developed the motoric skills to trace them (Saito et al. 2014). Unlike the children, chimpanzees were never able to fill in missing parts on images of faces, despite having good motor control. Significantly, the authors attributed these results to cognitive differences between the species that might be related to the development of global processing abilities in children compared to chimpanzees. In this context, it is interesting that children frequently comment on the scribbles they are producing, but apes make pictures without vocalizing (Vancatova 2008), and that by the time children begin producing well-formed geometric figures they are also in the process of acquiring grammatical language (Falk 2009).

The above comparative studies of artistic abilities are consistent with other data that support the idea that hominins may have evolved global neurological processing that became important for the evolution of visual perception and production. Recall, for example, that people utilize relatively more visual cortex to process objects in peripheral surroundings compared to other primates, likely due to humans' habitually terrestrial lifestyle (Wu et al. 2012). We should also remember that the lines and shapes that dominate individual's visual environments during critical stages of development influence how they, and the populations to which they belong, eventually process visual information, be they cats or people (Hubel and Wiesel 1959, Phillips 2019). Indeed, the carpentered world hypothesis that attributes susceptibility to certain optical illusions to formative experiences with parallel lines and sharp angles in manmade as opposed to natural environments (Segall et al. 1963) may be relevant when considering the geometric enigma.

The hominin and chimpanzee lineages are widely believed to have diverged from an apelike common ancestor (CA) around 6.5 mya (Kumar et al. 2022), after which hominins became increasingly adapted for, and committed to, terrestrial bipedalism. After they split, both groups shared a legacy from their arboreal ancestors, however, namely the visuospatial and motor skills for weaving and bending branches, twigs, and leaves together to make new sleeping nests in trees every evening. (Long after they had shifted to diurnal life on the ground, hominins continued sleeping in trees for safety's sake.) The great apes, in fact, invented tree nests among higher primates—i.e., making them is a derived and rather complex ability that eludes the 200 or so species of monkeys. Further, it is likely that arboreal sleeping nests were the first "tools" that apes invented after they separated long ago from monkeys (Fruth and Hohmann 1996). We humans have retained the great ape habit of sleeping in nests, although we've brought them to the ground.

Sleeping nests are constructed from plant matter including wood and, in a sense, the ancestors of chimpanzees and humans who invented them were, if not the first carpenters, at least the first proto-carpenters:

> Nests of all great apes are similarly constructed, despite interspecies differences in habitat and social organization...Nest-builders usually select horizontal side branches for the foundation, over which they bend and break adjacent branches. The rim of these platforms is formed by bending, breaking and occasionally interweaving additional smaller branches from the outer to the inner surfaces, resulting in a circular or oval, bowl-shaped structure. The center of this 'bowl' is often lined with detached leafy twigs .... construction types range from sturdy nests on side branches or in single treetops to nests integrating several adjacent trees, sometimes so flexible that the 'bowl' resembles a hammock. (Fruth et al. 2018:501).

Because apes typically build a new nest each day, they are likely to build many thousands of them during their lives. The arboreal habitats of apes are filled not only with vertical vines and tree trunks, but also with horizontal branches and other variously angled tree limbs. When bending and weaving branches into bowl-shaped nests (some chimps build triangular nests), apes see (and feel) branches crossing each other at different angles as well as coursing approximately in parallel with each other. Thus, although the visual worlds of apes are not carpentered like the industrialized environments of many humans, they contain an abundance of lines, angles, and shapes.

After hominins shifted to ground living, physical changes in the feet associated with bipedalism prevented infants from developing an apelike ability to cling independently to their traveling mothers (Falk 2009). This potentially disastrous situation for hominin survival was averted, I believe, because mothers used their innate nest weaving skills to invent little portable botanical nests with which to attach and carry their helpless infants—the first baby slings, which were likely hominins' first portable tools (Falk 2024). Ethnographic evidence suggests the first slings would have been extremely simple straps made of pliable plant matter, loosely woven baskets, or net bags. If so, natural textiles were invented very early in prehistory and so, too, was the routine manufacture of geometrical cross-hatching and other designs similar to some of the phosphenes that appear in paleoart.

Although the archaeological record of baby carrying devices is extremely recent, other evidence indicates that textiles were being made from botanic matter much earlier. Take, for instance, the cross-hatched patterns that are the oldest abstract representations in the archaeological record. These patterns were incised on pieces of ochre and engraved on stones from 100,000-60,000 years ago and somewhat more recently on ostrich eggshell containers in South Africa. As Helen Anderson of the British Museum in London observes, however, by the time these artifacts show up in the archaeological record, they do so fully formed. "What we may regard as abstract patterns may be, in fact, representational. Cross-hatch designs on stone, ochre, and ostrich eggshell ... dating to the Middle Stone Age...may indicate the transference of patterns and designs emanating from cordage, thread, nets, traps, and woven containers" (Anderson 2013:27). Anderson, like Bednarik and others, is keenly aware of the 5.0 mya engraved *Homo erectus* shell mentioned above. Significantly, when interpreting early engravings, she focuses on the possible role that weaving may have had in terms of stimulating the emergence of such apparently neurocognitively-based patterns.

> "Basketry, in all its various forms, is characteristic of our species and is ubiquitous. There are few cultures who have not used basket-weaving skills for fundamental purposes related to shelter, protection, harvesting food, storage etc. I think in evolutionary terms, the capacity to weave developed our cognitive abilities related to numbers, patterns and structures. Basketry may, indeed, have had a longer and more meaningful place in human culture than previously considered and may have played a role in the evolution of wider patterns of cognition and understanding (Falk 2024)".

Bednarik's suggestion that some phosphenes such as parallel lines may have appeared before others is consistent with the hypothesis that the earliest geometric engravings seen in paleoart might be derived from even earlier patterns related to the emergence of ubiquitous activities such as the weaving of pliable plant materials into slings, nets, and baskets (which I call the woven world [WW] hypothesis). As discussed, the WW hypothesis is compatible with the fact that hominin visual systems likely evolved, at least in part, in response to the lines, angles, etc. that predominated in their prehistorically earliest arboreal and terrestrial environments. The implication that phosphene images in paleoart may have become more derived over time is also consistent with the likelihood that, after hominins shifted to ground living, their visual systems adapted to incorporate greater attention to the peripheral world through which they routinely walked to obtain resources. In other words, becoming fully terrestrial may have contributed to the development of global visual processing abilities like those discussed above that separate the art of young children from the renderings of chimpanzees.

The WW hypothesis is compatible with the prediction that of the 15 typical phosphene form groups in the "phosphene-Linnaeus" of Kellogg et al. (1965), the relative frequencies of those that most closely resemble patterns associated with weaving (e.g., the ones labeled arcs, waves, lines, and lattices above in Fig. 1) will be higher than the others as one goes further back in the archaeological record of graphic/pictorial expressions of extant and extinct hominins. On the other hand, the typical forms that do not seem to be geometrical shapes associated with weaving (e.g., combined figs., fingers, 'cherries,' and perhaps triangles in Fig. 1) probably would not have appeared until more recently, just as the appearance of iconic/representational images in rock art and other paleoart postdate the emergence of purely geometrical patterns.

In sum, consideration of the earliest ecological and behavioral factors that may have contributed to the eventual emergence and evolution of artistic expression in hominins incorporates an evo-devo and phylogenetically dynamic approach that might, hopefully, generate testable hypotheses that explore the geometric enigma.

Conclusion

Although the archaeological record of hominin material culture is virtually empty during the first several million years following the divergence of chimpanzees and hominins, one can use comparative evo-devo analyses to begin to explore the likely events that sparked the eventual emergence of advanced hominin cognition, including the ability to conceptualize and make art. I have been reluctant to speculate about the intended meanings of paleoart, however, not because the topic isn't fascinating (it is), but for reasons discussed in the introduction, i.e., I don't have an adequate theory of mind for intuiting the thoughts of paleoartists. Not to mention, rock art and indeed most paleoart, is so recent with respect to the hominin timespan, and probably so relatively developed, that it casts little light that might help elucidate what Bednarik (2020) refers to as the "veritable Gordian knot" of the geometric enigma.

Ethnographic accounts are, of course, potentially relevant, although I have not focused much on them here. But who can fail to see the significance of ethnographic data that strongly suggest that artifacts associated with children's play may, at times, have been/be misinterpreted by archaeologists as evidence of adult ritual behavior (Langley and Lister 2018)? Or fail to consider the insights into the social and cultural context of rock art suggested by one woman's account as a child witness and participant in many rock art paintings during the 1950s and 1960s in the Northern Territory of Australia (Goldhahn et al. 2020)? However, it is important to keep in mind that such reports involve completely modern *Homo sapiens*.

I have long believed that the thing that drove the evolution of advanced cognition in hominins was the emergence and refinement of language and, further, that the distributed neurological networks associated with its emergence were exapted more recently for the invention of other advanced cognitive abilities such as mathematics, musical arts, and reading. I also think the neurological underpinnings that eventually supported language evolution began in conjunction with selection for bipedalism very soon after the divergence between chimpanzees and hominins (Larsson and Falk 2024). However, it is exceedingly difficult to identify criteria that can help pinpoint times by which humanlike (i.e., grammatical) language might have "arrived." The evo-devo comparison of art production in chimpanzee and human youngsters, discussed above, suggests that by the time early hominins were able to produce well-formed geometric patterns, they were likely developing grammatical language. Although others may disagree, for me the 500,000-year-old mussel shell engraved by *Homo erectus* in Java and the equally old engraved slabs from Wonderwerk Cave, South Africa, suggest a most recent date by which hominins in Asia and Africa were at least in the process of refining grammatical language. This estimate will become even earlier, of course, with the next discovery of an older artifact that was deliberately engraved with lines, zigzags, or perhaps other geometric patterns that appear in simple textiles.

Prof. Dean Falk
Department of Anthropology
Florida State University
Tallahassee, Florida 32306, USA
Email: dfalk@fsu.edu

References

Anderson, H. 2013. A Distinguishing Skill Art, Language, and Complex Cognition. *Journal of Consciousness Studies* 20(3-4): 6-32.

Aubert, M., A. Brumm, M. Ramli, T. Sutikkna, E. W. Saptomo, B. Hakim, M. J. Morwood, G. D. van den Bergh, L. Kinsley and A. dosseto 2014. Pleistocene cave art from Sulawesi, Indonesia. *Nature* 514(7521): 223-7.

Aubert, M., P. Setiawan, A. A. oktavoiana, A. Brumm, P. H. Suiiilistyarto, E. W. Saptomo, B. Istiawan, T. A. Ma'rifat, V. N. Wahyuono, F. T. Atmoko, J.-X. Zhao, J. Huntley, P. S. C. Taçon, D. L. Howard and H. E. A. Brand, 2018. Palaeolithic cave art in Borneo. *Nature* 564(7735): 254-257.

Beaumont, P. B. and J. C. Vogel 2006. On a timescale for the past million years of human history in central South Africa. *South African Journal of Science* 102: 217-228.

Bednarik, R. G. 1984. On the nature of psychograms. *The Artefact* 8: 27-32.

Bednarik, R. G. 1987. Engramme und Phosphene. *Zeitschrift für Ethnologie* 112(2): 223-235.

Bednarik, R. G. 1998. The 'australopithecine' cobble from Makapansgat. *South African Archaeological Bulletin* 53:4-8.

Bednarik, R. G. 2006. Neurophysiology and paleoart, Lecture No. 6, Semiotics Course 2006, Cognition and symbolism in human evolution. Unpublished.

Bednarik, R. G. 2020. Early rock art of the American West: the geometric enigma. *Rock Art Research* 37(1): 113-114.

Bednarik, R. G. 2021. About the Origins of the Human Ability to Create Constructs of Reality. *Axiomathes*: 1-20.

Blackburn, T. 1977. Biopsychological aspects of Chumash rock art. *The Journal of California Anthropology* 4(1): 88-94.

Blakemore, C. and G. F. Cooper 1970. Development of the Brain depends on the Visual Environment. *Nature* 228(5270): 477-478.

Charles, A. C. and S. M. Baca 2013. Cortical spreading depression and migraine. *Nature Reviews Neurology* 9(11): 637-644.

De Smedt, J. and H. De Cruz 2010. Toward an integrative approach of cognitive neuroscientific and evolutionary psychological studies of art. *Evolutionary Psychology* 8(4): 695-719.

Dissanayake, E., D. Falk and F. Martini 2019. The Geometric Enigma. A Book Symposium. *Aisthesis. Pratiche, linguaggi e saperi dell'estetico* 12(1): 85-98.

Dreier, J. P. 2011. The role of spreading depression, spreading depolarization and spreading ischemia in neurological disease. *Nature Medicine* 17(4): 439-447.

Falk, D. 2009. *Finding our tongues: Mothers, infants & the origins of language*. Pertheus (Basic Books), New York.

Falk, D. 2024. *The Botanic Age* (tentative title). In progress.

Fritz, C., G. Tosello and M. W. Conkey 2016. Reflections on the identities and roles of the artists in European Paleolithic societies. *Journal of Archaeological Method and Theory* 23(4): 1307-1332.

Fruth, B. and G. Hohmann 1996. Nest building behavior in the great apes: The great leap forward? *Great ape societies*: 225-240.

Fruth, B., N. Tagg and F. Stewart 2018. Sleep and nesting behavior in primates: A review. *Am J Phys Anthropol* 166(3): 499-509.

Garg, A. K., P. Li, M. S. Rashid and E. M. Callaway 2019. Color and orientation are jointly coded and spatially organized in primate primary visual cortex. *Science* 364(6447): 1275-1279.

Goldhahn, J., S. K. May, J. Maralngurra, Gumbuwa and J. Lee 2020. Children and rock art: a case study from western Arnhem Land, Australia. *Norwegian Archaeological Review 53(1): 59-82.*

Grüsser, O.-J. 1995. Migraine phosphenes and the retino-cortical magnification factor. *Vision Research* 35(8): 1125-1134.

Hadjikhani, N. and M. Vincent 2021. Visual Perception in Migraine: A Narrative Review. *Vision* 5(2): 20.

Henshilwood, C. S., F. D'errico, K. L. Van Niekerk, Y. Coquinot, Z. Jacobs, S-E Lauritzen, M. Menu and R. Garcia-Moreno 2011. A 100,000-year-old ochre-processing workshop at Blombos Cave, South Africa. *Science* 334(6053): 219-222.

Henshilwood, C. S., F. D'errico, K. L. Van Niekerk, L. Dayet, A. Queffelec and L. Pollarolo 2018. An abstract drawing from the 73,000-year-old levels at Blombos Cave, South Africa. *Nature* 562(7725): 115-118.

Hodgson, D. 2019 The origin, significance, and development of the earliest geometric patterns in the archaeological record. *Journal of Archaeological Science: Reports* 24: 588-592.

Hubel, D. H. and T. N. Wiesel 1959. Receptive fields of single neurons in the cat's striate cortex. *The Journal of physiology* 148(3): 574.

Janik, L. and J. C. Williams 2018. Community Art: Communities of Practice, Situated Learning, Adults and Children as Creators of Cave Art in Upper Palaeolithic France and Northern Spain. *Open Archaeology* 4(1): 217-238.

Joordens, J. C. A., F. D'errico, F. P. Wesselingh, S. Munro, J. De Vos, J. Wallinga, C. Ankjaergaard, T. Reimann, J. R. Wijbrans, and K. F. Kuiper 2015. *Homo erectus* at Trinil on Java used shells for tool production and engraving. *Nature* 518(7538): 228-231.

Kellogg, R. 1955. *What children scribble and why.* University of Illinois, Urbana-Champagne.

Kellogg, R., M. Knoll and J. Kugler 1965. Form-similarity between Phosphenes of Adults and pre-School Children's Scribblings. *Nature* 208(5015): 1129-1130.

Knoll, M. and J. Kugler 1959. Subjective light pattern spectroscopy in the encephalographic frequency range. *Nature* 184(4701): 1823-1824.

Ksander, J. C., L.E. Paige, H. A. Johndro and A. H. Gutchess 2018. Cultural specialization of visual cortex. *Social cognitive and affective neuroscience* 13(7): 709-718.

Kumar, G. 2021. Change of mindset: The need for developing scientific approaches to rock art studies. *Rock Art Research* 38(1): 23-30.

Kumar, S., M. Suleski, J.M. Craig, A. E. Kasprovicz, M. Sanderford, M. Li, G. Stecher and S. B. Hedges 2022. Time Tree 5: An Expanded Resource for Species Divergence Times. *Molecular Biology and Evolution* 39(8), msac 174 (https://academic.oup.com/mbe/article/39/8/msac174/6657692).

Langley, M. C. and M. Litster 2018. Is it ritual? Or is it children? Distinguishing consequences of play from ritual actions in the prehistoric archaeological record. *Current Anthropology* 59(5): 616-643.

Larsson, M. and D. Falk. 2024. Direct effects of bipedalism on early hominin fetuses stimulated later musical and linguistic evolution. *Current-Anthropology* in press.

Lewis-Williams, J. D., T. A. Dowson, P. G. Bahn, H.-G. Bandi, R. G. Bednarik, J. Clegg, M. Consens, W. Davis, B. Delluc and G. Delluc 1988. The signs of all times: Entoptic phenomena in Upper Palaeolithic art [and comments and reply]. *Current Anthropology* 29(2): 201-245.

Malotki, E. and E. Dissanayake. 2018. *Early rock art of the American west: the geometric enigma*. University of Washington Press, Seattle.

Mcbrearty, S. and A. S. Brooks 2000. The revolution that wasn't: a new interpretation of the origin of modern human behavior. *Journal of Human Evolution* 39(5): 453-563.

Meltzoff, A. N. 2007. 'Like me': a foundation for social cognition. *Developmental Science 10(1): 126-34.*

Oster, G. 1970. Phosphenes. *Scientific American* 222(2): 82-87.

Pelé, M., G. Thomas, A. Lienard, N. Eguchi, M. Shimada and C. Sueur 2021. I wanna draw like you: Inter-and intra-individual differences in orang-utan drawings. *Animals* 11(11): 3202.

Penfield, W. and T. Rasmussen 1968. *The cerebral cortex of man; A clinical study of localization of function.* Hafner Publishing Company, New York.

Phillips, W. L. 2019. Cross-cultural differences in visual perception of color, illusions, depth, and pictures. *Cross-Cultural Psychology: Contemporary Themes and Perspectives*: 287-308.

Podoll, K. and D. Robinson. 2008. *Migraine art: The experience from within (Foreward by Oliver Sacks).* North Atlantic Books, Berkely.

Queiroz, L. P., D. I. Friedman, A. M. Rapoport and R. A. Purdy 2011. Characteristics of migraine visual aura in Southern Brazil and Northern USA. *Cephalalgia* 31(16): 1652-1658.

Saito, A., M. Hayashi, H. Takeshita and T. Matsuzawa 2014. The origin of representational drawing: A comparison of human children and chimpanzees. *Child Development* 85(6): 2232-2246.

Sasaki, Y., R. Rajimehr, B. W. Kim, L. B. Ekstrom, W. Vanduffel and R. B. H. Tootell 2006. The Radial Bias: A Different Slant on Visual Orientation Sensitivity in Human and Nonhuman Primates. *Neuron* 51(5): 661-670.

Savigny, J. B. H. 1838. Phosphenes ou sensations loumineuses. *Archives Générale de Médecine* 3(2): 495-7.

Segall, M. H., D. T. Campbell and M. J. Herskovits 1963. Cultural differences in the perception of geometric illusions. *Science* 139(3556): 769-771.

Siegel, R. K. 1977. Hallucinations. *Scientific American* 237(4): 132-141.

Snow, D. R. 2013. Sexual dimorphism in European Upper Paleolithic cave art. *American Antiquity* 78(4): 746-761.

Taçon, P. S. C., M. Ramli, B. Hakim, A. Brumm and M. Aubert 2018. The contemporary importance and future of Sulawesi's ancient rock art. *Terra Australis* 48: 31-42.

Vancatova, M. 2008. Creativity and innovative behaviour in primates on the example of picture-making activity of apes: *https://nsu.ru/xmlui/bitstream/handle/nsu/3372/05.pdf;sequence=1* Accessed December 4, 2022.

Viana, M., E. A. Tronvik, T. P. Do, C. Zecca and A. Hougaard 2019. Clinical features of visual migraine aura: a systematic review. *Journal of Headache and Pain* 20(1): 64.

Vincent, M. B. and N. Hadjikhani 2007. Migraine aura and related phenomena: beyond scotomata and scintillations. *Cephalalgia* 27(12): 1368-1377.

Williams, T. J. and D. B. Madsen 2020. The Upper Paleolithic of the Americas. *PaleoAmerica* 6(1): 4-22.

Wu, J., T. Yan, Z. Zhang, F. Jin and Q. Guo 2012. Retinotopic mapping of the peripheral visual field to human visual cortex by functional magnetic resonance imaging. *Human Brain Mapping* 33(7): 1727-40.

13

KEYWORDS: Sensory consciousness – Body self-recognition – Self-awareness – Autopraxis – Cognitive behavioral hybridization

THE EVOLUTION OF HOMININ AUTOPRAXIS: ORIGINS AND EFFECTS

ROBERT ALEXANDER DIELENBERG

Abstract: Speculations on the evolution of hominin cognitive abilities draws on archaeological evidence, comparative psychological studies, and neuroscience. Here, I take this speculation further and examine one specific facet of its evolution, namely the origin and effects of *autopraxis*. A three-tiered model is adopted to explain the relationship of autopraxis with the brain and behavior over hominin evolutionary history. The first tier is *sensory consciousness*, which is based on cortical maps. The second is *body self-recognition* which is based on one part of the body instantiating itself as a controller over the rest of the body. The third tier is autopraxis which is based on one part of the brain dissociating itself into an independent stream of consciousness that is able to monitor and control other parts of the brain in limited fashion to modify future behavior. It is argued that hominins diverged from animals at the level of autopraxis which led them to develop the ability to codify their internal cognitions thus allowing them to manipulate them for individual and collective benefit. It is speculated that autopraxis originated out of an increase in *cognitive behavioral hybridization* (CBH). This began with the Acheulean circa 1.7 mya and indicates the acquisition of increased sequencing ability, one of the by-products of CBH. Sequencing ability and CBH then formed a synergistic relationship, leading to a strengthening of autopraxis and the advent of symbolic behavior.

Introduction

As the title suggests, I would like to trace the evolution of hominin autopraxis and its effect on our species. It is a broad subject and for the current paper I will focus on the period from when hominins first diverged cognitively from their non-human primate cousins and arrived at what would be regarded today as essentially fully formed symbolic ability, as exemplified by figurative cave art. This period, by my estimation, covers a span from approximately 1.8 mya to about 50

Article received: 29 November 2022
Revised I: 15 March 2023
Revised II: 29 May 2023
Revised III: 21 June 2023
Accepted: 21 June 2023

kya. To unpack the key milestones over this period, we will need to address what might appear to be a bewildering number of concepts. To manage these, we will again narrow down our focus to only a special mode of consciousness, namely self-awareness; by doing so we will automatically cut out the "hard problem of consciousness" (Chalmers, 1995) and we will limit ourselves mainly to non-human primates, although we will refer to other species on occasion where relevant.

The paper will be organized into two sections: a theoretical and an applied. In the theoretical section, I will attempt to define the key concepts that I believe are critical for understanding the evolution of autopraxis as best as I am able. In the applied section, I will then take those concepts and apply them to the case of hominin evolution. When complete, I hope that the reader will be able to get a deeper and more integrated idea of how the enigmatic process of autopraxis evolved in humans and what effect it had on our species, particular with respect to symbolic activity.

What are we talking about when we say "autopraxis"?

The term autopraxis – a term I have appropriated for its usefulness for the current topic – broadly comes under the rubic of *self-awareness* in the literature on consciousness studies. But self-awareness by itself is insufficient. The gist that I want to get across is insightful self-awareness, which means coming to awareness of oneself then acting on it for change. The "auto" refers to "self" and the "praxis" refers to turning *cognition* into action. When a writer uses the term self-awareness, most readers automatically understand that the author is talking about human beings and a special type of consciousness that we have that allows us to not only be cognitively aware, but *know* that we are cognitively aware. Cognition is usually defined as acquiring knowledge of ourselves and the world through *thinking* and *sentience*. Unfortunately, problems arise as soon as we try to nail down a specific definition of thinking. Even today, no philosopher or scientist has yet adequately provided a good explanation of what it is. Accordingly, I cannot claim that I know any better. As a neuroscientist, however, what I can do is define thinking as an activity that our brain performs inside our heads that backwardly refers to the more basic activities it performs such as sensing, emoting, feeling, propriocepting and kinesthetics. Which is to say that thinking is a derivative activity that represents lower level brain operations in some sort of propositional or symbolic way that lends itself to conscious description. I say conscious description, because it is generally recognized that the vast majority of brain activity remains unconscious to us. We are only able to consciously access the proverbial tip of the iceberg so to speak.

Nevertheless, in humans at least, it appears that the basic brain operations that are represented by thinking come in two dominant explicit forms: internal speech (Alderson-Day & Fernyhough, 2015; Morin, 2009; Scott, 2013), and internal imagery (Ganis et al., 2004; Kosslyn et al., 2006; Richardson, 1969), and one sub-dominant implicit form, feeling (Damasio, 1999; Panksepp, 2004). While it is assumed that all normal humans possess the ability to consciously access thinking, it is instructive to know that there is a percentage of humans that cannot access some sub-categories of thinking. For example, some humans do not experience mental imagery during waking consciousness (recently coined as "aphantasia") (Dance et al., 2022; Zeman et al., 2015), while others may not experience inner speech or audition or other forms of internal auditory "imagery" (recently coined as "anauralia") (Hinwar & Lambert, 2021). The other type of absence is through trauma or disease, in which case it is referred to as visual agnosia when there is loss or partial loss of visual perception, and auditory agnosia, when there is loss or partial loss of perception of language and sound (note: there are many types of agnosias). There are even cases of proprioceptive impairment (Chesler et al., 2016; Masingue et al., 2019). Despite lacking some channels of lower-level brain information, most of people living with these "deficits" conduct normal lives. However, when there is a maladaptive interpretation of inner speech and mental imagery it is generally recognized that it is indicative of a mental health disorder; e.g., schizophrenia (Cho & Wu, 2014; Oertel et al., 2009), obsessive compulsive disorder (Lavallé et al., 2020; Speckens et al., 2007), anxiety disorder (Hirsch & Holmes, 2007; Ratcliffe & Wilkinson, 2016), bipolar disorder (Di Simplicio et al., 2016; Toh et al., 2015), autism (Petrolini et al., 2020), Asperger's syndrome (Conson et al., 2013; Saalasti et al., 2008), borderline personality disorder (Schmidt & Fuchs, 2021; Schultebraucks et al., 2020), depression (Görgen et al., 2015; Tsuchiyagaito et al., 2022), to name a few. Lastly, on the opposite side of aphantasias, anauralias and agnosias is the phenomenon of synaesthesia. Synaesthesia refers to the cross-modal transformation of internal sensory experiences (Baron-Cohen & Harrison, 1997) so for example, a sound is perceived as an odor, or word or number is perceived as an image or a shape. Because of its cross-modal nature, and because language can be seen as a system of converting multi-modal sensory information into sound, it has been proposed that synaesthesia may have played a role in language evolution (Cuskley & Kirby, 2013).

Because we are talking about the inception of autopraxis in hominins, we cannot avoid referring to the time when hominins were for all intents and purposes cognitively similar to their animal cousins, the non-human primates. Our goal is to unveil the hallmarks of hominin cognition that are indicative of a divergence from non-human primates that ultimately led to our capacity for symbolic thinking. This means that something came before autopraxis. What was it?

Scholars of the evolution of consciousness typically rely on a three-tiered structure of consciousness to explain the progression from an animal that is sentient to a fully self-reflective human being (see Table 1). All these models share similarities and differences, but if reviewed here would take up an entire paper. Instead, I will begin with a common factor they all share, that is, in order to have consciousness, an organism must have a brain. The first tier of consciousness, therefore, is often attributed to the most essential feature of the brain-body relationship, sensation, so a number of scholars have taken to calling it *sensory consciousness* (Feinberg & Mallatt, 2016; Jerath et al., 2017; Seth et al., 2004). Not all scholars agree on their definition of what sensory consciousness is. I will use Feinberg & Mallat's definition as they have comprehensively reviewed it and honed it down to its essential feature, namely that it is based on cortical maps. These maps provide a dynamic link between the brain and the world. Thus, there are visual maps, auditory maps, olfactory maps and so forth. These maps have been validated by numerous studies (Doeller et al., 2010; Hafting et al., 2005; Huber et al., 2009; Lacalli, 2018; Mok & Love, 2019; O'Keefe & Dostrovsky, 1971; Schuck et al., 2016; Tolman, 1948) and have been theoretically extended to emotion (Nummenmaa et al., 2014), social (Tavares et al., 2015), and abstract cognitive maps (Constantinescu et al., 2016; Kriegeskorte & Storrs, 2016; Park et al., 2020). It is important to recognize that not all species may rely on cortical maps to experience sensory consciousness (Nieder, 2021; Nieder et al., 2020). In this case they may do it using an analogous structure. Also, sensory consciousness has been differentiated from *affective consciousness*, which is typically related to wakefulness and emotional responses in the organism (Panksepp, 2005; Van Honk et al., 2007) and is founded on deep structures in the brain such as the brainstem (Parvizi & Damasio, 2001). It is not necessary for us to discuss affective consciousness beyond the token recognition that one of its roles is in pain reception, which most organisms down to the most primitive are capable of experiencing if they have the rudiments of these structures in place (Allen, 2004).

Table 1: Examples of the three-tiered model of consciousness in evolution

Author	*Model*	*Reference*
Tulving	Anoetic Noetic Autonoetic	(Tulving, 1985)
Peñauzmán	Subjective Affective Metacognitive	(Peña-Guzmán, 2022)
Bekoff & Sherman	Phenotypic recognition Self-awareness Self-consciousness	(Bekoff & Sherman, 2004)
Cicogna & Bosinelli	Awareness as the phenomenal experiences of objects and events Awareness of being oneself Awareness of mental life itself	(Cicogna & Bosinelli, 2001)
Levine	Awareness of the experience that seems inseparable from any experience Representation of the world outside Representation of the experience when it is made the object of explicit introspective attention	(Levine, 2006)
Shipton	Normativity Recursion Abstraction	(Shipton, 2020)
Schooler	Non-conscious Conscious Meta-consciousness	(Schooler, 2002)

It is easy to talk about sensory consciousness in animals, but in humans, it is much harder because of our endless chattering and self-reflecting brains. These processes tend to get in the way of pure sensory experience. Nonetheless, philosophers of consciousness have traditionally called this state "phenomenological consciousness". Recently, one philosopher, Zahavi, has taken to calling it "pre-reflective self-consciousness" (Zahavi, 2020), and defines it as the feeling of being conscious without any self-reflectivity intervening at all. Obviously, this is an idealistic notion, and Zahavi therefore acknowledges that in humans, at least, a "thin form of self-awareness" is always present in this state. But if we were to idealize it, then it could be aligned with what has been described as the experience of "flow " (Csikszentmihalyi & Csikzentmihaly, 1990). This is when a person is fully living in the moment, such as when a sports person performs a "perfect" action, or when a meditator succeeds in "emptying" their brain. In this state, the person experiences their existence without thinking about this experience.

In the everyday world, however, we regularly attend to our bodies with a degree of conscious awareness, and this brings us to the second tier, *body self-recognition*. The classic test for this ability in both animals and humans is the Mirror Self-Recognition test (MSR). I have reviewed this elsewhere (Dielenberg, 2013), so I will only discuss those aspects of the test that are relevant for this paper. Initially, when it was first reported that chimpanzees could recognize themselves in mirrors, it was speculated that this may constitute evidence of a self-concept in these animals, however, because monkeys did not pass the test, it was thought that "the capacity for self-reflection may not extend below man and the great apes" (Gallup, 1970). Since then numerous other species have "passed" the MSR test, and include, but are not limited to, cetaceans (Delfour & Marten, 2001), other species of great apes (Allen & Schwartz, 2007; Westergaard & Hyatt, 1994), elephants (Plotnik et al., 2006), possibly corvids (Prior et al., 2008), some species of fish (Ari & D'Agostino, 2016; Kohda et al., 2019; Kohda et al., 2022), and, if it is to be believed, ants (Cammaerts Tricot & Cammaerts, 2015). Based on these findings, we could speculate that animals that pass the MSR, as well as animals that use tools and other affordances (such as decorations), all seem to share a common ability for body self-recognition in that they are able to use one body system to flexibly interact with another body system or object/s. Objects such as mirrors, tools, and decorations in this scheme are all affordances. If this theory is correct, then we should continue to find other instances of body self-recognition behaviors in the animal kingdom. Based on this line of reasoning, nest and trap building should be viewed as an affordance expressed along the same dimension as body self-recognition. After all, a bird that positions a twig in its nest is already displaying the necessary motor coordination and flexibility that could in theory be re-purposed to fish a grub out of a crack in tree bark with the same twig. In other words, the mirror in the MSR test is just another tool that the animal uses. It says nothing about self-awareness in the sense of being aware of internally generated cognitive content. Which brings us to the third tier in our discussion and the focus of this paper: self-aware cognition.

When I said, "use one body system to flexibly interact with another body system" I implied a form of parallel processing. Parallel processing is a well-accepted concept in the neurosciences.

When it is applied to the body it is uncontroversial (for example, we can tap our foot while rubbing our stomach). When it is applied to the cognition, however, the story becomes a little murky. We know from visual system research that there appears to be a dorsal and ventral stream of visual processing (Mishkin et al., 1983; Schneider, 1969). This is known as a functional dissociation, because it is possible for one stream to become defunct while the other still operates normally, as in the case of blindsight (Cattaneo et al., 2008; Zeman et al., 2010). The idea that self-awareness might also be a form of functional dissociation, however, is less well accepted. It is only recently that a name has been given to it: The Default Mode Network (DMN) (Mason et al., 2007; Raichle et al., 2001; Raichle & Snyder, 2007). This network is active when we day-dream or engage in mind-wandering. In other words, it appears to be gaining acceptance that it is principally associated with anything that has to do with self-referential thought; i.e., self-awareness (Davey et al., 2016). Put simply, we regularly switch from an outward-focussed consciousness to an inner-focussed consciousness and this switching (i.e., dissociation) is supported by dynamic modularity (Ferrarini et al., 2009) and is what underlies self-awareness (Johnson et al., 2006). It is important to note here that this switching is almost certainly not unique to humans. Which is to say dissociable neural mechanisms must have deep phylogenetic roots. Animals have limited concentration, just like humans. The switching from a sensory focused or body focussed pattern to an idle processing pattern probably evolved in the brain to conserve overall energy. The difference is that in humans, an additional function evolved that allowed us to consciously eavesdrop on the contents of idle neural operations. Carruthers, for example has proposed that it evolved when the ability to mind read others was turned on ourselves (Carruthers et al., 2012).

Whichever the case may be, in humans, the target of autopraxis is thinking, which is to say consciously focussing attention on brain operations that produce sensations, emotions, proprioceptions, kinesthetics, internal dialogue, internal imagery and feeling. It is reasonable to think that animals produce these same brain operations (give or take their specializations), but what is less certain, and almost doubtful, is that they think about these operations consciously in a long-term strategic way. Thus, at some point in evolutionary history, hominins, when they diverged from their animal cousins, underwent a brain transformation that gave rise to a newly dissociated stream of consciousness that allowed them to consciously eavesdrop on their brain operations and then manipulate the results of that act to modify future behavior; aka autopraxis. Later, in the applied section, we will examine some of the contributing factors that may have endowed hominins with the types of brains that allowed for the development of dissociable streams of consciousness.

In the meantime, I would like to focus on the mechanics of autopraxis itself. When I say "autopraxis", I imply a *self* that is doing the act of cognition. In humans, this self appears to be both a repository of contents derived from brain operations and an actor, a proactive agent that guides the body towards goals near and far both in time and space. The self is such a nebulous concept that any attempts to define it results in circularity. For the purpose of this paper, I will circumscribe it and define it as the "interpreter function". Gazzaniga has proposed that the left hemisphere is the locus of this function (Gazzaniga, 2015). Other research has honed in on the prefrontal cortex as the locus of self-awareness (Denny et al., 2012; Jenkins & Mitchell, 2011), and the anterior cingulate cortex as a salience and conflict evaluator (Bush et al., 2000; Van Veen et al., 2001). Naturally, there are a lot more brain areas involved, but for the purpose of this paper this toy model outlines the core system that produces self-awareness (Lou et al., 2017).

So far, so good. The problem, however, arises when we start to think about autopraxis in more detail. If we have a sensation, say an itch on our leg, we naturally reach down to scratch it. Animals do it, we do it. The difference with self-awareness in humans, however, is apart from merely being conscious of the itch, we *know* we are conscious of the itch. What is this knowing? Traditionally, it has simply been called self-awareness. This reduces the question to how can the brain both think and know that it is thinking? If knowing is also thinking, then this relationship simplifies to "thinking about thinking". The astute reader will immediately recognize that this is the official definition of *metacognition* (Kornell, 2009). From a straight forward definitional point of view, therefore, autopraxis could be replaced with metacognition. However, for reasons that will soon become apparent, the two terms cannot be so easily interchanged.

Let me use a more dramatic example to illustrate: hitting my thumb with a hammer. As if often the case with our modern brains, we can do one thing while thinking about something else (i.e., dissociate). In this case, while hammering a nail I am thinking about a conversation I had with my wife two hours earlier. This train of thought distracts me and causes me to lose focus on the hammer and nail and – bang! I cry out in pain. In that instant, my "mind" literally leaps into my thumb. My whole world is pain. I no longer think about the conversation I had with my wife. But now something special happens. As I cradle my thumb and moan, I begin to think about other things (i.e., I dissociate again). What an idiot! Why didn't I watch out? In those brief thoughts, I temporarily forget the pain, or at the very least it recedes so far back into my field of experience that I lose awareness of it ... but then my thumb throbs, and I am back in my thumb and pain again. This pattern repeats over and over until the pain subsides; I finally start forgetting about it all and get back to work whereupon I begin thinking about another conversation I had with someone else while hammering more nails. What appears to be going on here is a dissociable switching process. I switch from a body sensation stream of consciousness, to an internal, fantasy stream of consciousness that makes me forget I have a body.

Now comes the interesting part (if the previous part wasn't interesting enough). Several days pass and I reflect on the incident with the hammer (because I see my thumbnail has turned blue) and I remember that this was not the first time I had done that. I realize there is a pattern. I have done it least five times! I really am an idiot! This "interpretation" is derived from accumulated experiences. It would appear, therefore, that there are two versions of self-awareness. A short and a long version. The short version is awareness during the incident that I have awareness of specific brain operations (such as the sensation of pain). It is not just experiencing a sensation, but knowing I am experiencing a sensation. The long version kicks in when I look back on this knowing, and store an interpretation of it in my long-term memory. Importantly, I don't remember the pain. I only remember knowing I had the pain. This makes perfect sense from a biological point of view because if I re-experienced the actual pain I had each time I recalled it I would literally cease to function from all the pain I had accumulated during my life.

From the foregoing, therefore, I propose we divide self-awareness into a short and long version. It is the long version, therefore, when I use the term autopraxis. The usefulness of this division becomes apparent when you apply it to research into animal metacognition. It tells us that what researchers of animal metacognition have actually been studying is short metacognition. Moreover, in animals, it may not even be metacognition. It may be unconscious interferences drawn from sensory evaluations. Whether this is a fair interpretation is for another paper, but one thing is certain: researchers of animal metacognition have not found any evidence of autopraxis in animals, because no animal possesses it, or if they did, they never shared it with other animals and developed *cumulative culture*. (Note: I have defined cumulative culture elsewhere as *the cumulative social transmission of renewed hybridization of form and function* (Dielenberg, 2013)). Therefore, the crucial event in the evolution of hominin self-awareness is how and when did hominins acquire the capacity for autopraxis? It would appear that it must have evolved out of a synergistic process of production and sharing. In keeping with the structure of this paper, I will present a theoretical sketch of how I think autopraxis evolved, then in the applied section I will present evidence for when it happened, as well as elaborate on its effects.

How did autopraxis arise in the brain?

Forming a basis for any claims in evolutionary psychology is the underlying expectation that all organisms are subject to Darwinian evolution, where natural selection produces the best available fit to the environment. From the self-aware cognitive perspective this does not mean the fittest organism is the one whose behavior correlates most accurately with "reality". Reality here is defined as the *consequences of behavior*. If you mistake the tiger for rustling in the grass, you'll get eaten. Contrary to popular belief, however, Nature has been most lenient on the human species. Humans largely operate at the level of fantasy and Nature rarely punishes us for it (i.e., many of our cause and effect assumptions are false). It is for this reason that the majority of the humans still believe in supernatural entities and govern their lives by these beliefs despite there being no basis in fact for them. Thus, Darwinian evolution is not a mechanism of perfection, rather, it is *a mechanism of opportunity in a field of local and global resources*. The upshot of this view is that while autopraxis afforded those who had it with more efficient and adaptive cognitive abilities and behavior (Carruthers et al., 2012), it does not follow from this that it arose out of necessity. Many more animals would have developed it if that was the case. On the contrary, the evolution of self-awareness and subsequent autopraxis in hominins as early as 1.8 mya, was not demanded by Nature. It arose merely out of opportunity in an organism that had a fortuitous combination of traits.

Accordingly, when we look at the evolution of hominin autopraxis and ask how did it come into being, my answer is that it began with dextrous hands (Hashimoto et al., 2013; Kivell, 2015) and bipedalism (Crompton et al., 2010; Lieberman, 2022). These two fortuitous traits prepared hominins so that when the right opportunity arose, they naturally took advantage of it. The progression to higher cognitive functions therefore may have occurred for no other reason than the "butterfly effect" (Lorenz, 1972). Small changes in one variable of a large parameter set on initial conditions can lead to a large covariance of the parameter set on final conditions given enough time and complexity of interacting conditions.

As we shall see, the fortuitous trait of dextrous hands and bipedalism allowed hominins to opportunistically discover the application of stone to meat and bone, which in turn provided them with protein and fat that helped expand their brains. Their expanded brains in turn provided the cerebral volume (including anatomy and organization) for increased capacity for *working memory* (Nowell, 2010; Putt et al., 2019; Read et al., 2021). But this is not the whole story. The ability to perform autopraxis also requires an ordering or sequencing capacity. Not just the ability to perceive sequences, but variously compare them and make use of those comparisons. For this, an additional brain subsystem is required: the cerebellum. The cerebellum plays an important role as a predictive sequencer for fine motor control (Morton & Bastian, 2006), and this extends to any planned action or cognitive process (Sokolov et al., 2017). Vandervert has even suggested that the cerebellum not only played an important role in the evolution of fine motor control, but also the emergence of awareness of internal cognitions itself (Vandervert, 2018). Based on Leiner's suggestion that the cerebellum makes important contributions to prefrontal as well as other brain areas by refining their function (Leiner et al., 1989), Vandervert points out that experimental archaeologists (e.g., (Stout & Hecht, 2017)) have focussed too heavily on neocortical functions as the sole locus of action. Meanwhile, the cerebellum has been shown to process important cognitive functions related to working memory, sequencing, attention and control, that are equally, if not more important (Barton, 2012). Sequence detection and pattern recognition, in particular appears to be foundational in hominin cognitive evolution (Ghirlanda et al., 2017). Our ability to engage with extended sequences and patterns, whether motorically, or conceptually, is unparalleled in the animal kingdom, and has led one researcher to claim that it is the fundamental basis of most, if not all unique features of the human brain including intelligence, language, imagination, invention, and the belief in imaginary entities such as ghosts and gods (Mattson, 2014). If this is even partially true, then the cerebellum may indeed be much more important for the evolution of hominin cognition than we have hitherto conceived.

Mechanistically, what appears to happen is that contents derived from self-awareness are projected into a "mental space" where they are worked on by a cognitive sequencer that stores them in a registry from where it can later pull them out and compare them with other contents in sequential fashion until a desirable match or contrast is found. The result of this operation is often a hybridization of two or more items leading to the creation of a new "composite" item. I have taken to calling this process *cognitive behavioral hybridization* (CBH). CBH refers to the combining, joining, mixing of ideas and objects to form new ideas/objects in a lived space. CBH can be seen as a combination of the extended mind thesis (Clark & Chalmers, 1998) and niche construction theory (Laland et al., 2000). The extended mind thesis states that cognitive processes are *scaffolded* by the products and effects of behavior in the environment in a feedback loop (Barnard et al., 2016). Memory, for example, can be stored outside the brain in objects (as well as symbols), thereby boosting brain performance without utilizing additional memory space. Niche construction says that organisms modify sources of natural selection in their environment through activities such a nest building, seed dispersal, use of controlled fire, etc. CBH allows us to state that when ideas and objects in a lived space are sparse, then the frequency of CBH will be low. Conversely, when a lived space is densely filled with ideas and objects, the frequency of CBH will be high. CBH tells us that when action sequences are consistently and proactively shared between conspecifics, this creates a scaffold upon which cumulative culture can evolve, which in turn can foster more awareness of cognitive products. This makes autopraxis not so much a saltational event, but a learned one. It didn't appear in hominins fully formed and ready to go in one single event, but started as a glimmer and gradually grew in strength until it became a fixed feature of our brains, all the while aided by the increasing density of CBH.

This completes our theoretical excursion (a graphical representation of which is presented in Figure 1.) and we can now turn our attention to the milestones that accompanied the evolution of autopraxis in hominins.

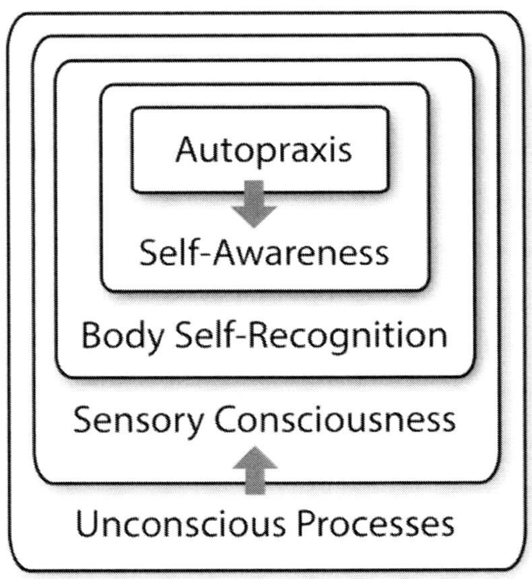

Figure 1: A hypothetical model of consciousness. Sensory consciousness, body self-recognition and self-awareness correspond to the three-tiered model depicted in Table 1. Unconscious (i.e., lower-level brain) processes filter up into self-awareness, and autopraxis influences downward into unconscious processes.

Milestone 1: Stone to meat and bone

A common and plausible assumption that many comparative cognitive scientists employ is the mapping of foraging-related behaviors of chimpanzees onto hominin evolutionary models. This includes using stones to crack nuts (Hannah & McGrew, 1987; Marshall-Pescini & Whiten, 2008), digging for underground storage organs (e.g., tubers) (Hernandez-Aguilar et al., 2007; McGrew, 2007), using sticks or other tools to fish for termites (Hicks et al., 2019), and algae-scooping (Bandini & Tennie, 2017), among others. At some point around 3.3 mya, hominins began making stone tools (Harmand et al., 2015). Found in West Turkana, Kenya, these tools predate the previously oldest "Oldowan" style tools (simple choppers) found at Gona, Ethiopia (Semaw et al., 2003), by some 700,000 years. It is not known what the West Turkana tools were used for, but the assumption is they were used for butchering. By 2.6 mya, this evidence is secure (Domínguez-Rodrigo et al., 2005; Semaw et al., 2003). Thus, sometime between 3.3-2.6 mya, hominins began applying stone to meat and bone, a behavior that is not too far removed from chimpanzees applying stone to nuts, except for perhaps the addition of cutting behavior which requires understanding the sharpness properties of a flaked stone. We don't know why hominins first began applying stone to meat and bone, but a parsimonious explanation could be that it came about serendipitously due to hunger and the inferior chewing apparatus of hominins compared to great apes (Raia et al., 2018), coupled with the opportunistic discovery of a large animal carcass near their home range offered up to them courtesy of the increased bovine traffic brought about by climate change (DiMaggio et al., 2015; Robinson et al., 2017). Hominins, because of their incipient bipedalism, may have also been less capable at catching monkeys in trees to eat, something chimpanzees are very good at with their four hands. In any case, what is significant is not that hominins used stone tools to unlock a new food source, but the consequences of this action. For chimpanzees, the consequences of nut-cracking was (and is) mundane. For hominins, the consequences of stone to meat and bone were momentous, for animals do not just provide meat, but fat, hides, bones, teeth, and hair; any of which could be used for energetic, utilitarian, or symbolic purposes (Daujeard & Prat, 2022). Thus, we find Dmanisi hominins reaching what is today modern Georgia by 1.85 mya with a brain size of around 600 cc (approximately half of *Homo sapiens*) using just Oldowan tools (Ferring et al., 2011), the Lantian *Homo erectus* with a brain size of around 780 cc reached Central China by 1.65 mya also using mostly Oldowan-style tools (Pan et al., 2022), and the Sangirin *erectus* (brain size unknown) reached Central Java by 1.6 mya (tools unknown) (Zaim et al., 2011), showing just how advantageous the discovery of stone to meat and bone was. The emigration may have started with an early variant of *H. erectus* and could have happened for no other reason than to simply follow the meat (Antón & Swisher, 2004; Ben-Dor & Barkai, 2021). Note: this does not necessarily imply a radical increase in meat consumption, rather, just a reliance on meat consumption (Barr et al., 2022).

Following the meat may have laid the foundations for generalized flexible behavior (Kalan et al., 2020). Generalized flexible behavior stands in contrast to mere flexible behavior because it can undergo analogous transfer to new domains of expression. For example, not just use a stick to make a nest then pick a grub out of tree bark, but use multiple sticks to weave a basket to carry food. It is not the same as migration, since birds, whales and other animals disperse widely into different habitats in cyclic fashion. They do not have to invent new behaviors to successfully migrate, as their routes and destinations are well-trodden paths. In comparison, when hominins followed the meat, it may have forced them to establish new home ranges, learn new foraging methods, develop new methods of in situ resource utilization, and learn new anti-predator defence strategies, and so forth. Those who could not transfer what they learned in the old environment to the new one would have gradually been culled by natural selection, leaving those who could to progenitor our ancestors. This is to say, following the meat was not responsible for the origin of generalized flexible behavior, rather, it scaffolded biological changes in hominins that then allowed them to flexibly take advantage of the new opportunities that were offered.

Milestone 2: The Acheulean

Studies investigating the neural correlates of simple stone flaking indicative of Oldowan technology have demonstrated that explicit prediction and evaluation of action outcomes may be unnecessary for this type of toolmaking (Stout et al., 2015; Stout et al., 2008). In other words, Oldowan toolmaking requires little more than smashing two rocks together. Sometime around 1.7 mya, however, a new lithic technology emerged, the Acheulean (Diez-Martín et al., 2015). Unlike its Oldowan precursor, Acheulean requires a long-term relationship with stone and a detailed understanding of fracture mechanics. The key innovation of the Acheulean is the teardrop shaped hand axe that has been symmetrically worked on both sides. While there is variation in the archaeological record (Gowlett, 2015; Lycett & von Cramon-Taubadel, 2008), in many assemblages there can be found some exemplars that have been made with great care; we can therefore assume that if someone can make a high-quality hand axe, they can also make a low-quality one. Due to the enigmatic nature of these artefacts, they have been studied extensively, and many detailed features about them have been quantified: their shape, size, symmetry, material used, lithic reduction sequence, etc. (Sánchez-Yustos et al., 2017; Sharon, 2007; Shipton, 2018). Roughly speaking, to produce an Acheulean hand axe one must first prepare a "core", essentially a large stone that has been knocked into a block-like shape (Sharon et al., 2009). From this, smaller flakes are sequentially knocked off going around the edge on both sides, including thinning, until the characteristic teardrop shape emerges. The finishing touches are often added using a bone billet, which allows for soft percussion, and is a new technique that is not used in Oldowan tool making. It takes a lot of practice to make an Acheulean hand axe, and this has led some researchers to conclude that it could only be achieved through an "apprenticeship" like process (Shipton, 2010; Stout & Hecht, 2017).

The emergence of the Acheulean as a technocomplex has been secularly linked to the appearance of African *Homo erectus* (Semaw et al., 2020; Suwa et al., 2007; Yravedra et al., 2020). This prompts us to examine what sort of cognitive abilities *H. erectus* might have had. It has often been suggested that making an Acheulean hand axe requires some sort of preconceived idea (Gowlett et al., 2014). If true, it does not explain how knappers managed to get from A to B: "A" being some sort of "idea and "B", the material outcome. Putting aside the thorny question of what is an "idea" for a moment, it would appear that getting from A to B requires a set of learned skills. Specifically, an ability to perform an extended sequence of operations. Concentration and focus to be sure. How *H. erectus* arrived at having such good sequencing ability is unclear. Cortical expansion of attentional networks is central to the story, of that there is no doubt (Patel et al., 2015), but as we have pointed out in our theoretical section, the evolution of the cerebellum was also critical in providing the capacity for improved fine motor control and sequential thinking that is necessary to produce an Acheulean hand axe. As a result, the "idea" of the form came after, not before its invention. This line of reasoning follows from evidence of animals and hominins being attracted to salient features in natural "extraordinary" objects; e.g., Tinbergen's concept of a "super-stimulus" (Niko, 1951). An intriguing example of this is the Makapansgat cobble (Bednarik, 1998). There is a distinct suggestion of symmetry in its features, and is all the more remarkable for its association with hominins circa 3 mya. This brings to mind the nature of walking on two legs, which unlike chimpanzee locomotion, specifically reduces to the symmetrical operation of two legs, and may have unconsciously heighted *H.* erectus' perception of balance, which through increased repetition of use made it a salient cognitive feature. Symmetry in stone may therefore have come about as a consequence of this heightened sensitivity to balance. All speculation of course.

The Makapansgat cobble suggests the Australopiths who curated it possessed a capability for recognition. They were attracted to the cobble for reasons they were wholly unaware of, but reacted to it at an emotional level nonetheless, which probably motivated them to carry it the fairly lengthy distance from where they found it to their cave. The Acheulean represents a development that lies further along this trajectory. Even though the status of *H. erectus* as a single or branched species is still hotly debated (Bruner et al., 2015), the archaeological evidence for the African variant shows a brain size approximately twice that of the Australopithecines, which is to say at least twice that of chimpanzees. This would have intrinsically given them more working memory capacity, which in turn would have improved their pattern recognition abilities. In making the Acheulean hand axe I used the word "idea", but this does not mean they were consciously aware of such. More likely they "saw" a shape floating before their eyes, in the external world, an image superimposed on reality that appeared to them while they were day-dreaming. In other words, they dissociated without realizing it. When we day dream, we know the images we see floating before our "inner eye" exists solely in our heads. This would not have been the case for *H. erectus*. But they had sufficient working memory to apprehend it and recognize it, and furthermore, act on it. It may have seized them, become a fascination, turning into a psychological fixation. Certainly, the longevity of the form suggests as much. Also, some of the hand axes are enormous in size, beyond what is feasibly practical to use. Whether these were practise articles, or had some other purpose, we do not know.

Archaeologists have struggled to explain the long "stasis" in lithic technology once the Acheulean was invented (Finkel & Barkai, 2018; Lycett & Gowlett, 2008). The form lasted from around 1.7 mya – 500 kya with relatively little change, a span of about 1.2 million years. If the Acheulean knappers were so smart, why didn't they progress to even better things sooner? One explanation for this is that it simply worked ("if it ain't broke why fix it?"). Alternatively, Shipton et al has argued that the Acheulean stasis derived from the enforcement of normativity (Shipton et al., 2021). As to the origin of normativity, they argue that its developmental foundation is to be found in the uniquely human trait of overimitation (Nielsen, 2012; Shipton, 2019) (but see (Evans et al., 2018) for a counter-argument). Given the brain size increase in *H. Erectus*, and the evidence for its incredible dispersion from Africa all the way to Europe, Central Asian and southeast Asia, I think it we can assume that it had a reasonably effective culture, and therefore, factors such as overimitation (or optimal imitation) probably played a determining role. However, I also think that we cannot ignore the curious and persistent effects of brain modularization in behavior. This deserves to be emphasized. Just because *H. erectus* was able to invent Acheulean technology, does not mean that it can suddenly go on to do other new things. The classic example of this is the Mayan wheel. Archaeologists have not found any evidence that the Maya used wheels for transport. Are we to conclude, therefore, that they did not have the ability to conceive of the wheel? Their brains, for-all-intents-and-purposes, were modern. They made children's toys and effigies that had wheels (Diehl & Mandeville, 1987). There were domesticated llamas in the Andes that could have pulled carts (Diamond, 1997). Yet, according to Diamond, the reason why the Mayans never evolved wheeled transport was because they never had contact (or need for contact) with the Andeans. More broadly speaking, the Mayans had ample numbers of slaves and peasants to carry things for them (Foster, 2002). This brings to mind the concept of *functional fixedness.* Duncker defined it as a mental block against using an object in a new way that is required to solve a problem (Duncker & Lees, 1945). By this argument, the Mayans were functionally fixed on human transport because it worked and was culturally sanctioned. This does not explain the cause of such functional fixedness however. They used logs to roll large stone blocks, and they had the aforementioned toy wheels, but they never generalized these concepts to wheeled transport. Other factors must have been at play.

To me it seems CBH is the more parsimonious explanation for the Mayan wheel and the long stasis of the Acheulean form. In the case of the Mayans, it would appear that they lacked sufficient CBH in one department: a wheel production industry. This would include axels, lubricants, fixings, reinforcings, as well as design ideas and trial and error. None of this was in place so any mental extrapolations of toy wheels etc would have ended in a cul-de-sac. It may have come down to the lack of a metallurgy industry to produce fixings and reinforcings, which in turn may have had its roots in insufficient quantities of iron ore and the lack of a large-scaled smelting industry. With respect to the Aucheulean industry, CBH extended to the use of a bone billet for soft percussion, the first application of *bone to stone* which had the potential to facilitate the arrival of the Acheulean, but may not have extrapolated to additional new technologies because the CBH density was still relatively low after its inception. Thus, while the hand axe could be hafted to a wooden handle, this required the use of glues and bindings which had not yet developed.

Milestone 3: Seafaring and early language – first increase of CBH

It is now well-established that *H. erectus* crossed the Wallace line and arrived on the island of Flores by no later than 800 kya (Brumm et al., 2006). Earlier, Bednarik's seafaring project demonstrated that Lower Pleistocene hominins were capable of this feat (Bednarik, 2001). This, then, definitively marks a point in time when language must have already been well in use (at least in this part of the world). We can assert this for the simple reason that to transport a viable breeding group of people across such a dangerous and deep-water channel requires, by necessity, a good group plan and group technological prowess. But what kind of language would be sufficient? It would appear, based on the available archaeological evidence, that the density of CBH is still rather low around 800 kya, but significantly increased since the advent of the Acheulean. This is reflected in the list of tasks required to make a raft and effect a successful crossing. To name a few: selection of the right materials, fibers for bindings, containers for water storage, oars and rudders for propulsion and steering, knowledge of currents, knowledge of weather and open sea conditions, navigation ability, seasonal knowledge. A pidgin-type language might be sufficient to get the job done. That is, have enough vocabulary combined with body language to pass on ideas, instructions, goals, etc. It may be that the level of self-awareness in these early seafarers did not progress to full autopraxis. There is no figurative expression. The culture is very concrete and practical. This is exemplified by the fact that the stone tools associated with these first seafarers lies somewhere along the dimension between the Oldowan style and the Acheulean.

Milestone 4: A fascination with sequential behavior – second increase of CBH

It appears that the brain had to enlarge again and reorganize before the next great leap could occur (Neubauer et al., 2018; Rightmire, 2004; Sherwood et al., 2008). Starting around 500 kya (the early Middle Stone Age) we find the first strong signatures of concrete and symbolic products of CBH in the archaeological record: geometric markings on objects (Bednarik, 2003; Mania & Mania, 1988), the use of shells to make necklaces (Bar-Yosef Mayer et al., 2020), the use of ochre (Brooks et al., 2018; McBrearty & Tryon, 2006), spear making (Milks et al., 2019), the hafting of stone points on spears (Wilkins & Chazan, 2012), and the consistent and widespread use of fire (MacDonald et al., 2021). This period seems to represent a strengthening of and an increase in confidence of hominins' self-aware abilities. Autopraxis has not evolved yet, but the foundations for it are being laid.

Robust evidence for geometric markings during this phase on a variety of media suggests an elaboration of the aforementioned adeptness at sequential behavior. The earliest such examples of these may be cupules (Bednarik, 2008), concave depressions made on rock surfaces by repetitive pounding. The oldest of these, found in India, date back to at least the start of the Middle Paleolithic (i.e., 330 kya), but in all likelihood are much older (Bednarik, 1996). Cupules are found wherever *H. Erectus* went, suggesting an association. Linear engravings on stone or bone are also prevalent, the oldest on bone of which can be found at Bilzingsleben, Germany, and date to about 300 kya. A similar time horizon for engraving on stone occurs for Wonderwerk Cave, South Africa (Bednarik & Beaumont, 2010). These engravings are made by repetitive gouging with a sharp tool. The geometric motifs becomes more elaborate by the Middle Stone age (circa 100 kya), and are attributed to *Homo sapiens*, as demonstrated by the Blombos Cave ochre artifact and the Diepkloof Rock Shelter ostrich shell engravings (Henshilwood et al., 2009; Tylén et al., 2020). But again, the repetitious nature of these engravings follows the same trajectory of earlier sequential behaviors. Almost all are comprised of straight lines which start to criss-cross as time evolves. It would appear then, that this may be indicative of an increased fascination with sequential control.

At the same time that fascination for geometric sequential control emerges, we find other fossilizable artefacts that also display a concomitant increase in sequential control. The drilling of holes in shells to make necklaces (again, a repetitious motif), the use of ochre (which requires repetitious abrasion to form powder), and the control of fire, which requires repetitious actions to create heat friction, and the emergence of the Levallois technique circa 300 kya (Schlanger, 1996). While not an explicit repetitious behavior, the hafting of stone points onto spears suggests the reuse of tools, which denotes an implicit repetition. We can surmise, therefore, that an overall mastery of repetitious actions applied to tools gradually transferred to other areas of life. We could extrapolate this to language and speculate that the kind of language that was used may have been based on repetitious utterances, such as strings of identical sounds. Onomatopoeia which occurs in many languages might represent an archaic hold-over of this development. The use of ochre pigment as body paint may have also been dominated by repetitious patterns, many of which we can still find in primitive cultures today.

Milestone 5: The emergence of exogrammatic control – third increase of CBH

The earliest deliberate figurative "art" known is from Sulawesi, Indonesia (Aubert et al., 2019; Brumm et al., 2021) and is dated to about 44 kya. Much older manuport proto-figurines have been found (e.g., the Berekhat Ram and Tan-Tan artefacts), but these demonstrate no evidence of deliberate sculpting apart from some enhancement of pre-existing features. Nevertheless, the increasing confidence of sequential behavior now made it possible for the emergence of more complex imprinting of cognitive contents into matter. While the term "paleoart" has been unofficially appropriated for such behavioral expression, I prefer the neutral term *exogrammatic expression* after Bednarik's use of the word "exogram" (Bednarik, 2014), which he derived from the concept of the "engram" first proposed by Semon (Semon, 1904, 1921). An engram is a hypothetical memory trace stored somewhere in neural tissue. These days, neuroscientists believe memories are not stored in any one specific location but are distributed throughout the brain, yet can be invoked at nodal junctions, as Penfield did in the 1930s, with his electrically stimulated cortices of awake epileptic patients (Curot et al., 2017). An exogram, by analogy, is an externally stored memory trace (or complex, in the case of sophisticated expressions). What we can say with surety about exogrammatic expressions is that they afforded their makers a permanent (or semi-permanent) storage of culturally constrained memory. But without knowledge of the culture, we cannot say anything specific about the exogram's purpose. All we can say is that it contributed to the "extended mind" of its makers, creating as it were, a cognitive niche, which afforded its makers a more secure way of transferring tradition, as well as reinforcing the cultural milieu they were in.

One of the most celebrated artefacts, and one of the oldest from this period, is the Löwenmensch (Lion Man), a sculpted ivory figurine half man/woman, half-lion dated to circa 40 kya (Kind et al., 2014). This artefact is clearly symbolic, in that its subject matter is exclusively derived from the inner psychological realm of its maker. We can say this because other figurines from this culture (the Aurignacians of Swabian Jura, Germany), were carved realistically, (i.e., in correct proportion and posture), whereas the Lion Man, even though it is more lion than human, has an upright posture suggestive of human traits. Thus, it is a hybrid creature, or as it is technically known, a therianthrope (half animal, half human). From 40 kya onward, therianthropes become more frequent in the archaeological record all the way from Africa to Indonesia and so it is not an isolated phenomenon. Locally even, a smaller Löwenmensch (dated circa 32 kya) was found at Hohle Fels some 50 km away from Hohlenstein-Stadel where the original Löwenmensch was found. However, rather than rushing to the typical (and stereotypical) religious interpretations of this mode of expression, I will instead explore its cognitive-behavioral aspects. And in order to do that, we need to get a better understanding of the ecological setting in which it was created, and the relationship that humans had with the mammoth (*Mammuthus primigenius*) and the cave lion (*Panthera spelaea*), since these comprise its media and subject matter.

The skeletal summary that follows is derived from the research of Hussain & Floss (Hussain & Floss, 2015). They determined that the mammoth was ever present in the Aurignacian Swabian environment, moving through it, changing it, which afforded humans the opportunity to co-adapt. The mammoth was also a social species and, probably like modern elephants, displayed a complex set of behaviors with individual personalities. Interestingly, the mammoth ivory used in Aurignacian carved artefacts and tools appears to be predominantly collected from carcasses rather than hunts (Niven, 2007). Mammoth ivory was found to have the highest frequency of use in the Swabian Aurignacian culture relative to all other animals (Wolf, 2015). In comparison to this, the cave lion was mostly hidden in the landscape – it hunted at night and operated as a competitor for animal protein. They were also deemed to be solitary predators. Alongside the mammoth, the cave lion is the most frequently depicted animal in the figurine sample from the Swabian Aurignacian (Conard et al., 2015; Floss, 2007).

Even though the mammoth was a potentially dangerous animal, so long as one stayed out of its way, life could go on peacefully. It could even be seen as a friend and provider (e.g., firewood from broken trees, hide and fur for shelters and warmth, ivory for carving). Not so with the cave lion. It may have competed for cave lodgings, and if one was not careful going to the toilet at night, one could easily be snatched away. The prowess of the cave lion as a hunter was almost certainly feared and revered. As hunters themselves, there is the possibility that the Aurignacians may have identified with some of its cognitive strengths. The need to have control over this marauding threat would have been a nightly concern. It is at this juncture that we could launch into all sorts of colorful explanations as to why it was carved. We shall leave that to the reader. More important here is that this dualistic relationship between a useful animal and predator is not new. It is a long-standing theme right through hominin evolution. Yet only now, around 50 kya in different parts of the world, do we see it depicted graphically for the first time. Why? The logical explanation, based on the foregoing, is the progressive densification of CBH throughout the Middle Stone Age. Its consequence would have been the emergence of specialist roles. The person who carved the Lion Man figurine evidently spent long hours at the task, so the artefact is as much a product of CBH as it is of one person's imagination. Which is to say that earlier hominins might have had glimmers of autopraxis, but the lack of CBH density stymied their outward expression of it. From this perspective, the emergence of autopraxis on top of self-awareness would seem to be as much a function of CBH density as it is of brain and cultural evolution. The advent of specialization allowed some individuals the time, space, and security to dream out loud. Once this happened, societies began to be populated by individuals who had the potential to become vanguards of visionary thinking. These individuals had the capacity to reflect on their self-awareness and thereby leverage it for bigger and better things. Once this phenomenon became widespread, the rest, as they say, is history.

Discussion

From the foregoing, it is proposed that the progression of hominins from a mostly sensory conscious state to a robust insightful cognitive state occurred over a long-time span and came about not through necessity, but opportunity (a representation of this progression is presented in Figure 2). The first autopraxis were fleeting. Gradually, as working memory evolved a larger capacity, the shifts to autopraxis grew in length, allowing hominins to take in larger "chunks" of data. These larger chunks eventually allowed hominins to form "ideas" and "structured intentions" as evidenced in the refinement of stone tool production. Prior to this ability, hominins were largely victims of their sensory environment. Their behavior was more or less animal-like in that they were constantly stimulus-bound. As the separate stream of consciousness grew stronger in them, they gradually emancipated themselves from this moment-to-moment binding. They evolved the ability to intervene over their instinctive response patterns to neutral stimuli and introduce alternate response strategies that were not immediately reactive. For example, not immediately running away upon hearing a rustle in the grass. It was at this point that hominins truly diverged from their chimpanzee cousins who, by remaining stimulus-bound to their environment, never evolved a cognitive capacity beyond body self-recognition. It needs to be said, many things can be done

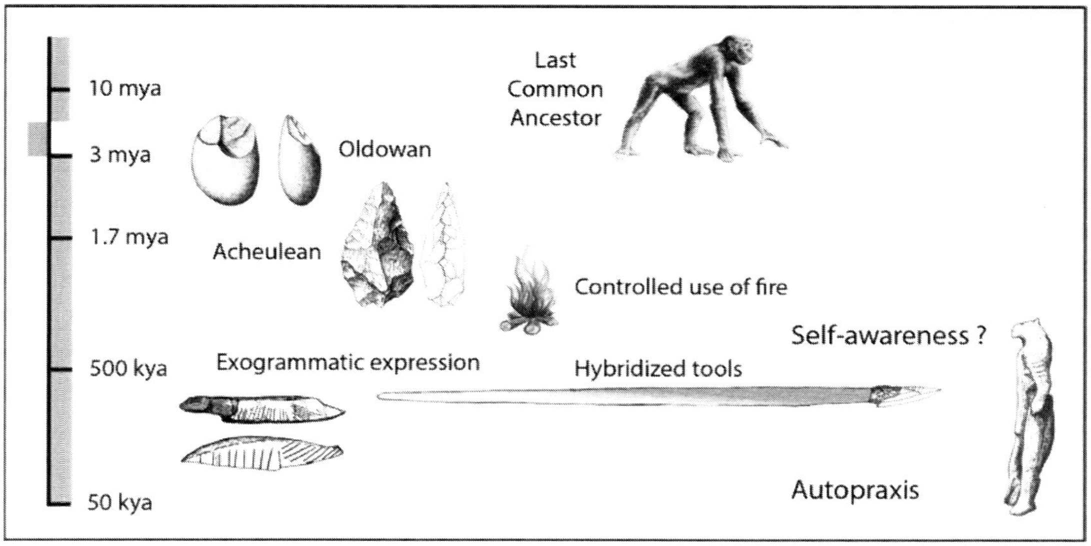

Figure 2: A speculative timeline for the evolution of autopraxis.

with body self-recognition, all the way up to knowing what others can and cannot see (Bräuer et al., 2007; Call, 2010; Call & Carpenter, 2001; Hare et al., 2000; Hare et al., 2006; Kaminski et al., 2008). In contrast to this, chimpanzees fall short on tests of causal reasoning about the *unseen* world (Penn et al., 2008; Derek C. Penn & Daniel J. Povinelli, 2007; Derek C Penn & Daniel J Povinelli, 2007; Penn & Povinelli, 2013; Povinelli, 2000; Povinelli, 2012; Povinelli et al., 2019), something humans excel at, for better or worse.

Probably one of the key steps in fostering a strengthened separate stream of conscious awareness in hominins was control over their environment, which afforded them more security and safety. The development of weapons, use of fire, and group cooperation are some of the behaviors that conceivably contributed to this. Meanwhile, the consistently higher levels of protein and fat intake (as compared to chimpanzees), contributed to changes in their bodies and brains. Fat in particular may have been pivotal. It has been suggested that it supported higher daily energy expenditure, and contributed to increased body fat levels and brain growth (Leonard et al., 2007). If true, then this must have become a catch-22 situation. Larger brains required more energy, which resulted in more behavior directed at obtaining fat. This may have been an impetus for hominins to hunt large animals as they have a much higher fat content compared to small animals. The lure of meat and fat on its own may have even spurred cooperative hunting (Tennie et al., 2009). By the time we reach the early Paleolithic, coordinated hunting became an established behavior, and with it, all the flow-on effects: cooperative-culture (Boyd & Richerson, 1982), advancement in tool manufacture (Faisal et al., 2010), slower brain growth, particularly in neonates (Cofran & DeSilva, 2015), self-domestication (Hare et al., 2012; Theofanopoulou et al., 2017), loss of body hair (Dror & Hopp,

2014; Rogers et al., 2004), use of controlled fire (James et al., 1989), and much more, all of which have contributed to the human condition. At the expense of sounding like an "externalist" model of hominin cognitive evolution, I want to emphasize that choice and chance also had a role to play. By choice or forced choice, hominins moved into new locations which then "released" the changes that followed. Chance, such as climate, volcanism, floods, disease, and so on, also acted on the system, so that the end result was a complex interplay of all these factors, which is why there is still no absolute consensus on the narrative of our evolution.

With respect to the Acheulean hand axe, there is no doubt that it was at least partly under genetic control (Corbey et al., 2016), in that the hominins who made it were driven by unconscious motivations. But once the artefact was made, like the stone tools that preceded it, its impact became the more important factor as it is likely that only a few specialists made the tool, while some who didn't make it also used it, and many more who didn't use it saw it and experienced its benefits (Hopkinson et al., 2013). Working memory, understandably, has been attractive in explaining the advent of abilities such as enhanced sequential behavior (Coolidge & Wynn, 2020; Nowell, 2010; Wynn & Coolidge, 2011; Zhang et al., 2022). But working memory is only the vehicle, not the engine of autopraxis. It explains the increased capacity to perform operations, but it tells us nothing about the motivation behind them, or how goal-directed behavior drives them. Without knowing the details of hominin culture, we cannot say what these were. We can only say that they were initially driven by instinctual needs, but as time went on and as hominins became more emancipated from stimulus-bound situations, cultural conventions probably began to take over as the dominant force.

Enhanced sequential control goes hand-in-hand with repetitious actions. A hominin that made stone tools on a regular basis stood a good chance of dreaming about it, since we know that repetitive activities, we focus on during the day can sometimes appear in our dreams at night (Eichenlaub et al., 2017). This, then, could provide another source of attraction to internal cognitive content in the hominin mind. The dreamer wakes up and connects their dream to the memory of stone tool production. At first, the hominin might find the dream an oddity, but over time it may grow accustomed to it, and may even incorporate it in their work flow. We simply don't know. But this progression is not implausible. Perhaps more importantly, if the hominin then found a way to communicate what it experienced in its dream, this then becomes a much more significant act, not just from the point of view of language, but from the point of view of the consequence of the dream itself. This brings to mind Blagrove's interpretation of dreams: it matters little what we think the neurological or psychological function of dreams are for (although this is obviously still important); what matters is its impact on the community through sharing (Blagrove & Lockheart, 2022; Blagrove et al., 2021). The sharing of dreams, therefore, could have become another source of motivated attraction to autopraxis and helped spread the skill through the community.

The same, therefore, applies to later hominins who shared other internal cognitive content in addition to dreams. This would have sped up the rate of cognitive behavioral hybridization and shifted hominins even further away from their animal ancestry. In essence, cognitive behavioral hybridization can be seen as the main driver of cumulative culture, which through its specializations has become the grandest experiment of all in exogrammatic expression. We can do so much more now because a large proportion of our internal cognitive content is off-loaded into codified systems. Who knows, this techno-behavior may even be behind the cause of our shrinking brains over the last 50 thousand years (Stibel, 2021). From this perspective, the first expressions of internal cognitive content were quite special in our evolutionary history. Once we figured out a way to codify them we were off and running. The first geometric scratchings some 500 kya seems like a long way off in the past. A thousand years is a long time, let alone one hundred years. This attests to the difficultly of learning about the internal world which, as a species, we still have a long way to go. It seems that we are extremely adept at shaping the external world to our intentions, but our ability to shape our internal world is a challenge that still largely perplexes us. If, as the evolutionary evidence suggests, that what we create outside of our bodies has a strong influence on what goes on inside our heads (over evolutionary time), then much work still needs to be done to find better ways of manipulating the world to gain a better understanding of how we work as biological creatures, and ultimately where we came from and who we are.

Conclusion

I would like to finish with a quote from *Animals and Men*, first published in 1937 and translated into English in 1953:

> The animal remains confined to the lower realms of insightful thought. Man, on the other hand, is, at least in principle, able to make use of the highest levels. On what is this difference based? First, only man is cable of emotional detachment from events, though emotional life as such does not divide man from the animals. Secondly, not only can man see, hear, and so on, but he can be aware both of what he sees and hears, and of the fact that he does so. Man not only has awareness; he can also appreciate that he has it. We may call this awareness of awareness. It even applies to the self, and we speak of self-awareness. In a curious way man can stand back from himself and inspect himself. Nothing in the behavior of animals suggests that they are able to do anything of this kind. Some animals almost seem to have some kind of self-awareness. Their exhibitionist behavior, e.g., the self-display of some birds, tends to make one think so. But this is really very different from reflective self-awareness. Certainly, man does not contemplate himself all day long. But self-awareness is as fundamental to his make-up as it is not to the animal's. It may well be said that the act of self-objectification was the start of man's 'fall from grace'. Once he had taken this step, he ceased to be merely part of nature. He gained access to a new reality, the world of ideas (Katz, 1937, pp. 177-178).

Apart from the antiquated language, it would appear that for all we have learned, little has changed.

Prof. Robert Alexander Dielenberg, (PhD Neuroscience)
15 Parry Street, Cooks Hill, NSW, 2300, Australia
dielenator@gmail.com

References

Alderson-Day, B., & C. Fernyhough 2015. Inner speech: Development, cognitive functions, phenomenology, and neurobiology. *Psychological Bulletin 141*(5): 931.

Allen, C. 2004. Animal pain. *Nous 38*: 617-643.

Allen, M. R., & B. L. Schwartz 2007. Mirror self-recognition in a gorilla (*Gorilla gorilla gorilla*). *Electronic Journal of Integrative Biosciences 5*(1): 19-24.

Antón, S. C., & I. Swisher, Carl C 2004. Early dispersals of *Homo* from Africa. *Annu. Rev. Anthropol. 33*: 271-296.

Ari, C., & D. P. D'Agostino 2016. Contingency checking and self-directed behaviors in giant manta rays: Do elasmobranchs have self-awareness? *Journal of Ethology 34*(2): 167-174.

Aubert, M., R. Lebe, A. A. Oktaviana, M. Tang, B. Burhan, A. Jusdi, B. Hakim, J.-x. Zhao, I. Geria, & P. H. Sulistyarto 2019. Earliest hunting scene in prehistoric art. *Nature 576*(7787): 442-445.

Bandini, E., & C. Tennie 2017. Spontaneous reoccurrence of "scooping", a wild tool-use behaviour, in naïve chimpanzees. *PeerJ 5*: e3814.

Bar-Yosef Mayer, D. E., I. Groman-Yaroslavski, O. Bar-Yosef, I. Hershkovitz, A. Kampen-Hasday, B. Vandermeersch, Y. Zaidner, & M. Weinstein-Evron 2020. On holes and strings: Earliest displays of human adornment in the Middle Palaeolithic. *Plos One 15*(7): e0234924.

Barnard, P., I. Davidson, & R. W. Byrne 2016. Toward a richer theoretical scaffolding for interpreting archaeological evidence concerning cognitive evolution. *Cognitive models in Palaeolithic archaeology*: 45-67.

Baron-Cohen, S., & J. Harrison 1997. Synaesthesia: A review of psychological theories. In John E. Harrison & Simon Baron-Cohen (Eds.), *Synaesthesia: Classic and Contemporary Readings* (pp. 109-122). Blackwell.

Barr, W. A., B. Pobiner, J. Rowan, A. Du, & J. T. Faith 2022. No sustained increase in zooarchaeological evidence for carnivory after the appearance of *Homo erectus*. *Proceedings of the National Academy of Sciences 119*(5): e2115540119.

Barton, R. A. 2012. Embodied cognitive evolution and the cerebellum. *Philosophical Transactions of the Royal Society B: Biological Sciences 367*(1599): 2097-2107.

Bednarik, R. G. 1996. The cupules on Chief's Rock, Auditorium Cave, Bhimbetka. *Artefact 19*(1996): 63-72.

Bednarik, R. G. 1998. The 'Australopithecine' Cobble from Makapansgat, South Africa. *South African Archaeological Bulletin 53*: 4-8.

Bednarik, R. G. 2001. Replicating the first known sea travel by humans: The Lower Pleistocene crossing of Lombok Strait. *Human Evolution 16*(3): 229-242.

Bednarik, R. G. 2003. The earliest evidence of palaeoart. *Rock Art Research 20*(2): 89-136.

Bednarik, R. G. 2008. Cupules. *Rock Art Research 25*(1): 61-100.

Bednarik, R. G. 2014. Exograms. *Rock Art Research 31*(1): 47-62.

Bednarik, R. G., & P. B. Beaumont 2010. Pleistocene engravings from Wonderwerk Cave, South Africa. *L'art pléistocène dans de monde, Actes du Congrès IFRAO, Tarasconsur-Ariège*: 96-97.

Bekoff, M., & P. W. Sherman 2004. Reflections on animal selves. *Trends in Ecology & Evolution 19*(4): 176-180.

Ben-Dor, M., & R. Barkai 2021. Prey size decline as a unifying ecological selecting agent in pleistocene human evolution. *Quaternary 4*(1): 7.

Blagrove, M., & J. Lockheart 2022. Dream-sharing and human self-domestication. *International Journal of Dream Research 15*(1): 86.

Blagrove, M., J. Lockheart, M. Carr, S. Basra, H. Graham, H. Lewis, E. Murphy, A. Sakalauskaite, C. Trotman, & K. Valli 2021. Dream sharing and the enhancement of empathy: Theoretical and applied implications. *Dreaming 31*(2): 128.

Boyd, R., & P. J. Richerson 1982. Cultural transmission and the evolution of cooperative behavior. *Human Ecology 10*(3): 325-351.

Bräuer, J., J. Call, & M. Tomasello 2007. Chimpanzees really know what others can see in a competitive situation. *Animal Cognition 10*(4): 439-448.

Brooks, A. S., J. E. Yellen, R. Potts, A. K. Behrensmeyer, A. L. Deino, D. E. Leslie, S. H. Ambrose, J. R. Ferguson, F. d'Errico, & A. M. Zipkin 2018. Long-distance stone transport and pigment use in the earliest Middle Stone Age. *Science 360*(6384): 90-94.

Brumm, A., F. Aziz, G. D. Van Den Bergh, M. J. Morwood, M. W. Moore, I. Kurniawan, D. R. Hobbs, & R. Fullagar 2006. Early stone technology on Flores and its implications for *Homo floresiensis*. *Nature 441*(7093): 624-628.

Brumm, A., A. A. Oktaviana, B. Burhan, B. Hakim, R. Lebe, J.-x. Zhao, P. H. Sulistyarto, M. Ririmasse, S. Adhityatama, & I. Sumantri 2021. Oldest cave art found in Sulawesi. *Science Advances 7*(3): eabd4648.

Bruner, E., D. Grimaud-Hervé, X. Wu, J. M. de la Cuétara, & R. Holloway 2015. A paleoneurological survey of *Homo erectus* endocranial metrics. *Quaternary International 368*: 80-87.

Bush, G., P. Luu, & M. I. Posner 2000. Cognitive and emotional influences in anterior cingulate cortex. *Trends in Cognitive Sciences 4*(6): 215-222.

Call, J. 2010. Do apes know that they could be wrong? *Animal Cognition 13*(5): 689–700.

Call, J., & M. Carpenter 2001. Do chimpanzees and children know what they have seen? *Animimal Cognition 3*(4): 207–220.

Cammaerts Tricot, M.-C., & R. Cammaerts 2015. Are ants (Hymenoptera, Formicidae) capable of self recognition? *Journal of Science 5*(7): 521-532.

Carruthers, P., L. Fletcher, & J. B. Ritchie 2012. The evolution of self-knowledge. *Philosophical Topics*: 13-37.

Cattaneo, Z., T. Vecchi, C. Cornoldi, I. Mammarella, D. Bonino, E. Ricciardi, & P. Pietrini 2008. Imagery and spatial processes in blindness and visual impairment. *Neuroscience & Biobehavioral Reviews 32*(8): 1346-1360.

Chalmers, D. J. 1995. Facing up to the problem of consciousness. *Journal of Consciousness Studies 2*(3): 200-219.

Chesler, A. T., M. Szczot, D. Bharucha-Goebel, M. Čeko, S. Donkervoort, C. Laubacher, L. H. Hayes, K. Alter, C. Zampieri, & C. Stanley 2016. The role of PIEZO2 in human mechanosensation. *New England Journal of Medicine 375*(14): 1355-1364.

Cho, R., & W. Wu 2014. Is inner speech the basis of auditory verbal hallucination in schizophrenia? *Frontiers in Psychiatry 5*: 75.

Cicogna, P., & M. Bosinelli 2001. Consciousness during dreams. *Consciousness and Cognition 10*(1): 26-41.

Clark, A., & D. Chalmers 1998. The extended mind. *Analysis 58*(1): 7-19.

Cofran, Z., & J. M. DeSilva 2015. A neonatal perspective on *Homo erectus* brain growth. *Journal of Human Evolution 81*: 41-47.

Conard, N. J., M. Bolus, E. Dutkiewicz, & S. Wolf 2015. *Eiszeitarchäologie auf der Schwäbischen Alb: Die Fundstellen im Ach- und Lonetal und in ihrer Umgebung*. Kerns Verlag.

Conson, M., E. Mazzarella, A. Frolli, D. Esposito, N. Marino, L. Trojano, A. Massagli, G. Gison, N. Aprea, & D. Grossi 2013. Motor imagery in Asperger syndrome: Testing action simulation by the hand laterality task. *Plos One 8*(7): e70734.

Constantinescu, A. O., J. X. O'Reilly, & T. E. Behrens 2016. Organizing conceptual knowledge in humans with a gridlike code. *Science 352*(6292): 1464-1468.

Coolidge, F. L., & T. Wynn 2020. The evolution of working memory. *L'Année psychologique 120*(2): 103-134.

Crompton, R. H., W. I. Sellers, & S. K. Thorpe 2010. Arboreality, terrestriality and bipedalism. *Philosophical Transactions of the Royal Society B: Biological Sciences 365*(1556): 3301-3314.

Csikszentmihalyi, M., & M. Csikzentmihaly 1990. *Flow: The Psychology of Optimal Experience* (Vol. 1990). Harper & Row.

Curot, J., T. Busigny, L. Valton, M. Denuelle, J.-P. Vignal, L. Maillard, P. Chauvel, J. Pariente, A. Trebuchon, & F. Bartolomei 2017. Memory scrutinized through electrical brain stimulation: A review of 80 years of experiential phenomena. *Neuroscience & Biobehavioral Reviews 78*: 161-177.

Cuskley, C., & S. Kirby 2013. Synesthesia, cross-modality, and language evolution. In Julia Simner & Edward Hubbard (Eds.), *Oxford Handbook of Synesthesia* (Vol. 20, pp. 869-907). Oxford University Press.

Damasio, A. R. 1999. *The Feeling of What Happens: Body and Emotion in the Making of Consciousness.* Mariner Books.

Dance, C., A. Ipser, & J. Simner 2022. The prevalence of aphantasia (imagery weakness) in the general population. *Consciousness and Cognition 97*: 103243.

Daujeard, C., & S. Prat 2022. What are the "costs and benefits" of meat-eating in human evolution? The challenging contribution of behavioral ecology to archeology. *Frontiers in Ecology and Evolution 10.*

Davey, C. G., J. Pujol, & B. J. Harrison 2016. Mapping the self in the brain's default mode network. *Neuroimage 132*: 390-397.

Delfour, F., & K. Marten 2001. Mirror image processing in three marine mammal species: killer whales (*Orcinus orca*), false killer whales (*Pseudorca crassidens*) and California sea lions (*Zalophus californianus*). *Behavioural Processes 53*(3): 181–190.

Denny, B. T., H. Kober, T. D. Wager, & K. N. Ochsner 2012. A meta-analysis of functional neuroimaging studies of self-and other judgments reveals a spatial gradient for mentalizing in medial prefrontal cortex. *Journal of cognitive Neuroscience 24*(8): 1742-1752.

Di Simplicio, M., F. Renner, S. E. Blackwell, H. Mitchell, H. J. Stratford, P. Watson, N. Myers, A. C. Nobre, A. Lau-Zhu, & E. A. Holmes 2016. An investigation of mental imagery in bipolar disorder: Exploring "the mind's eye". *Bipolar Disorders 18*(8): 669-683.

Diamond, J. M. 1997. *Guns, Germs, and Steel: The Fates of Human Societies*. W. W. Norton.

Diehl, R. A., & M. D. Mandeville 1987. Tula, and wheeled animal effigies in Mesoamerica. *Antiquity 61*(232): 239-246.

Dielenberg, R. A. 2013. The comparative psychology of human uniqueness: A cognitive behavioral review. In R. G. Bednarik (Ed.), *The Psychology of Human behavior* (pp. 111–182). Nova Science Publishers.

Diez-Martín, F., P. Sánchez Yustos, D. Uribelarrea, E. Baquedano, D. F. Mark, A. Mabulla, C. Fraile, J. Duque, I. Díaz, A. Pérez-González, J. Yravedra, C. P. Egeland, E. Organista, & M. Domínguez-Rodrigo 2015. The origin of the Acheulean: The 1.7 million-year-old site of FLK West, Olduvai Gorge (Tanzania). *Scientific Reports 5*(17839): 1-9.

DiMaggio, E. N., C. J. Campisano, J. Rowan, G. Dupont-Nivet, A. L. Deino, F. Bibi, M. E. Lewis, A. Souron, D. Garello, & L. Werdelin 2015. Late Pliocene fossiliferous sedimentary record and the environmental context of early *Homo* from Afar, Ethiopia. *Science 347*(6228): 1355-1359.

Doeller, C. F., C. Barry, & N. Burgess 2010. Evidence for grid cells in a human memory network. *Nature 463*(7281): 657-661.

Domínguez-Rodrigo, M., T. R. Pickering, S. Semaw, & M. J. Rogers 2005. Cutmarked bones from Pliocene archaeological sites at Gona, Afar, Ethiopia: Implications for the function of the world's oldest stone tools. *Journal of Human Evolution 48*(2): 109-121.

Dror, Y., & M. Hopp 2014. Hair for brain trade-off, a metabolic bypass for encephalization. *Springerplus 3*(1): 1-10.

Duncker, K., & L. S. Lees 1945. On problem-solving. *Psychological Monographs 58*(5): i.

Eichenlaub, J.-B., S. S. Cash, & M. Blagrove 2017. Daily life experiences in dreams and sleep-dependent memory consolidation. In *Cognitive Neuroscience of Memory Consolidation* (pp. 161-172). Springer.

Evans, C. L., K. N. Laland, M. Carpenter, & R. L. Kendal 2018. Selective copying of the majority suggests children are broadly "optimal-" rather than "over-" imitators. *Developmental Science 21*(5): e12637.

Faisal, A., D. Stout, J. Apel, & B. Bradley 2010. The manipulative complexity of Lower Paleolithic stone toolmaking. *Plos One 5*(11): e13718.

Feinberg, T. E., & J. M. Mallatt 2016. *The Ancient Origins of Consciousness: How the Brain Created Experience*. MIT Press.

Ferrarini, L., I. M. Veer, E. Baerends, M. J. van Tol, R. J. Renken, N. J. van der Wee, D. Veltman, A. Aleman, F. G. Zitman, & B. W. Penninx 2009. Hierarchical functional modularity in the resting-state human brain. *Human Brain Mapping 30*(7): 2220-2231.

Ferring, R., O. Oms, J. Agustí, F. Berna, M. Nioradze, T. Shelia, M. Tappen, A. Vekua, D. Zhvania, & D. Lordkipanidze 2011. Earliest human occupations at Dmanisi (Georgian Caucasus) dated to 1.85–1.78 Ma. *Proceedings of the National Academy of Sciences 108*(26): 10432-10436.

Finkel, M., & R. Barkai. 2018. The Acheulean handaxe technological persistence: A case of preferred cultural conservatism? *Proceedings of the Prehistoric Society.*

Floss, H. 2007, 16-18 septembre 2005. *Die Kleinkunst des Aurignacien auf der Schwäbischen Alb und ihre Stellung in der paläolithischen Kunst* Les Chemins de l'Art aurignacien en Europe – Das Aurignacien und die Anfänge der Kunst in Europa, Aurignac.

Foster, L. V. 2002. *Handbook to life in the ancient Maya world.* Oxford University Press.

Gallup, G. G. J. 1970. Chimpanzees: Self recognition. *Science 167* (3914): 86–87.

Ganis, G., W. L. Thompson, & S. M. Kosslyn 2004. Brain areas underlying visual mental imagery and visual perception: An fMRI study. *Cognitive Brain Research 20*(2): 226-241.

Gazzaniga, M. S. 2015. Tales from *Both Sides of the Brain: A Life in Neuroscience.* Harper-Collins.

Ghirlanda, S., J. Lind, & M. Enquist 2017. Memory for stimulus sequences: A divide between humans and other animals? *Royal Society Open Science 4*(6): 161011.

Görgen, S. M., J. Joormann, W. Hiller, & M. Witthöft 2015. The role of mental imagery in depression: Negative mental imagery induces strong implicit and explicit affect in depression. *Frontiers in Psychiatry 6*: 94.

Gowlett, J. 2015. Variability in an early hominin percussive tradition: The Acheulean versus cultural variation in modern chimpanzee artefacts. *Philosophical Transactions of the Royal Society B: Biological Sciences 370*(1682): 20140358.

Gowlett, J. A., N. Goren-Inbar, G. Sharon, & L. Equinox 2014. The elements of design form in Acheulean bifaces: Modes, modalities, rules, and language. In N. Goren-Inbar & G. Sharon (Eds.), *Axe Age: Acheulian Tool-making from Quarry to Discard* (pp. 1-20). Equinox.

Hafting, T., M. Fyhn, S. Molden, M.-B. Moser, & E. I. Moser 2005. Microstructure of a spatial map in the entorhinal cortex. *Nature 436*(7052): 801-806.

Hannah, A. C., & W. McGrew 1987. Chimpanzees using stones to crack open oil palm nuts in Liberia. *Primates 28*(1): 31-46.

Hare, B., J. Call, B. Agnetta, & M. Tomasello 2000. Chimpanzees know what conspecifics do and do not see. *Animal Behaviour 59*(4): 771–785.

Hare, B., J. Call, & M. Tomasello 2006. Chimpanzees deceive a human competitor by hiding. *Cognition 101*(3): 495–514.

Hare, B., V. Wobber, & R. Wrangham 2012. The self-domestication hypothesis: Evolution of bonobo psychology is due to selection against aggression. *Animal Behaviour 83*(3): 573-585.

Harmand, S., J. E. Lewis, C. S. Feibel, C. J. Lepre, S. Prat, A. Lenoble, X. Boës, R. L. Quinn, M. Brenet, & A. Arroyo 2015. 3.3-million-year-old stone tools from Lomekwi 3, West Turkana, Kenya. *Nature 521*(7552): 310-315.

Hashimoto, T., K. Ueno, A. Ogawa, T. Asamizuya, C. Suzuki, K. Cheng, M. Tanaka, M. Taoka, Y. Iwamura, & G. Suwa 2013. Hand before foot? Cortical somatotopy suggests manual dexterity is primitive and evolved independently of bipedalism. *Philosophical Transactions of the Royal Society B: Biological Sciences 368*(1630): 20120417.

Henshilwood, C. S., F. d'Errico, & I. Watts 2009. Engraved ochres from the middle stone age levels at Blombos Cave, South Africa. *Journal of Human Evolution 57*(1): 27-47.

Hernandez-Aguilar, R. A., J. Moore, & T. R. Pickering 2007. Savanna chimpanzees use tools to harvest the underground storage organs of plants. *Proceedings of the National Academy of Sciences 104*(49): 19210-19213.

Hicks, T. C., H. S. Kühl, C. Boesch, P. Dieguez, A. E. Ayimisin, R. M. Fernandez, D. B. Zungawa, M. Kambere, J. Swinkels, & S. B. Menken 2019. Bili-Uéré: A chimpanzee behavioural realm in northern Democratic Republic of Congo. *Folia Primatologica 90*(1): 3-64.

Hinwar, R. P., & A. J. Lambert 2021. Anauralia: The silent mind and its association with aphantasia. *Frontiers in Psychology*: 4620.

Hirsch, C. R., & E. A. Holmes 2007. Mental imagery in anxiety disorders. *Psychiatry 6*(4): 161-165.

Hopkinson, T., A. Nowell, & M. White 2013. Life histories, metapopulation ecology, and innovation in the Acheulian. *PaleoAnthropology 2013*: 61-76.

Huber, D. J., D. Khosla, & P. A. Dow. (2009). Fusion of multi-sensory saliency maps for automated perception and control. Signal Processing, Sensor Fusion, and Target Recognition XVIII,

Hussain, S. T., & H. Floss 2015. Regional ontologies in the Early Upper Palaeolithic: The place of mammoth and cave lion in the 'belief world'(Glaubenswelt) of the Swabian Aurignacian. In Primitiva Bueno-Ramírez & Paul G. Bahn (Eds.), *Prehistoric Art as Prehistoric Culture. Studies in Honour of Professor Rodrigo de Balbín-Behrmann* (pp. 45-58). Archaeopress Publishing.

James, S. R., R. Dennell, A. S. Gilbert, H. T. Lewis, J. Gowlett, T. F. Lynch, W. McGrew, C. R. Peters, G. G. Pope, & A. B. Stahl 1989. Hominid use of fire in the Lower and Middle Pleistocene: A review of the evidence [and comments and replies]. *Current Anthropology 30*(1): 1-26.

Jenkins, A. C., & J. P. Mitchell 2011. Medial prefrontal cortex subserves diverse forms of self-reflection. *Social neuroscience 6*(3): 211-218.

Jerath, R., S. M. Cearley, R. Paladiya, & V. A. Barnes 2017. Sensory consciousness is experienced through amplification of sensory stimuli via lateral inhibition. *World Journal of Neuroscience 7*(3): 244-256.

Johnson, M. K., C. L. Raye, K. J. Mitchell, S. R. Touryan, E. J. Greene, & S. Nolen-Hoeksema 2006. Dissociating medial frontal and posterior cingulate activity during self-reflection. *Social Cognitive and Affective Neuroscience 1*(1): 56-64.

Kalan, A. K., L. Kulik, M. Arandjelovic, C. Boesch, F. Haas, P. Dieguez, C. D. Barratt, E. E. Abwe, A. Agbor, & S. Angedakin 2020. Environmental variability supports chimpanzee behavioural diversity. *Nature Communications 11*(1): 1-10.

Kaminski, J., J. Call, & M. Tomasello 2008. Chimpanzees know what others know, but not what they believe. *Cognition 109*(2): 224–234.

Katz, D. 1937. *Animals and Men* (Hannah Steinberg & Arthur Summerfield, Trans.). Pelican.

Kind, C.-J., N. Ebinger-Rist, S. Wolf, T. Beutelspacher, & K. Wehrberger 2014. The smile of the Lion Man. Recent excavations in Stadel Cave (Baden-Württemberg, southwestern Germany) and the restoration of the famous Upper Palaeolithic figurine. *Quartär 61*: 129-145.

Kivell, T. L. 2015. Evidence in hand: Recent discoveries and the early evolution of human manual manipulation. *Philosophical Transactions of the Royal Society B: Biological Sciences 370*(1682): 20150105.

Kohda, M., T. Hotta, T. Takeyama, S. Awata, H. Tanaka, J.-y. Asai, & A. L. Jordan 2019. If a fish can pass the mark test, what are the implications for consciousness and self-awareness testing in animals? *PLoS Biology 17*(2): e3000021.

Kohda, M., S. Sogawa, A. L. Jordan, N. Kubo, S. Awata, S. Satoh, T. Kobayashi, A. Fujita, & R. Bshary 2022. Further evidence for the capacity of mirror self-recognition in cleaner fish and the significance of ecologically relevant marks. *PLoS Biology 20*(2): e3001529.

Kornell, N. 2009. Metacognition in humans and animals. *Current Directions in Psychological Science 18*(1): 11-15.

Kosslyn, S. M., W. L. Thompson, & G. Ganis 2006. *The Case for Mental Imagery.* Oxford University Press.

Kriegeskorte, N., & K. R. Storrs 2016. Grid cells for conceptual spaces? *Neuron 92*(2): 280–284.

Lacalli, T. 2018. Amphioxus, motion detection, and the evolutionary origin of the vertebrate retinotectal map. *EvoDevo 9*(1): 1–5.

Laland, K. N., J. Odling-Smee, & M. W. Feldman 2000. Niche construction, biological evolution, and cultural change. *Behavioral and Brain Sciences 23*(1): 131-146.

Lavallé, L., J. Brunelin, R. Bation, & M. Mondino 2020. Review of source-monitoring processes in obsessive-compulsive disorder. *World Journal of Psychiatry 10*(2): 12.

Leiner, H. C., A. L. Leiner, & R. S. Dow 1989. Reappraising the cerebellum: What does the hindbrain contribute to the forebrain? *Behavioral Neuroscience 103*(5): 998.

Leonard, W. R., M. L. Robertson, & J. J. Snodgrass 2007. Energetics and the evolution of brain size in early *Homo*. In W. Roebroeks (Ed.), *Guts and Brains: An Integrative Approach to the Hominin Record* (pp. 29-46). Leiden University Press.

Levine, J. 2006. Conscious awareness and (self-) representation. In Kenneth Williford & Uriah Kriegel (Eds.), *Self-Representational Approaches to Consciousness* (pp. 173-198). MIT Press.

Lieberman, D. E. 2022. Standing up for the earliest bipedal hominins. *Nature 609*(7925): 33-35.

Lorenz, E. 1972, December 29, 1972. *Predictability: Does the flap of a butterfly's wing in Brazil set off a tornado in Texas?* American Association for the Advancement of Science, Washington, DC.

Lou, H. C., J.-P. Changeux, & A. Rosenstand 2017. Towards a cognitive neuroscience of self-awareness. *Neuroscience & Biobehavioral Reviews 83*: 765-773.

Lycett, S. J., & J. A. Gowlett 2008. On questions surrounding the Acheulean 'tradition'. *World Archaeology 40*(3): 295-315.

Lycett, S. J., & N. von Cramon-Taubadel 2008. Acheulean variability and hominin dispersals: A model-bound approach. *Journal of Archaeological Science 35*(3): 553-562.

MacDonald, K., F. Scherjon, E. van Veen, K. Vaesen, & W. Roebroeks 2021. Middle Pleistocene fire use: The first signal of widespread cultural diffusion in human evolution. *Proceedings of the National Academy of Sciences 118*(31): e2101108118.

Mania, D., & U. Mania 1988. Deliberate engravings on bone artefacts of *Homo Erectus. Rock Art Research 5*: 91-97.

Marshall-Pescini, S., & A. Whiten 2008. Social learning of nut-cracking behavior in East African sanctuary-living chimpanzees (*Pan troglodytes schweinfurthii*). *Journal of Comparative Psychology 122*(2): 186–194.

Masingue, M., J. Fauré, G. Solé, T. Stojkovic, & S. Léonard-Louis 2019. A novel nonsense PIEZO2 mutation in a family with scoliosis and proprioceptive defect. *Neuromuscular Disorders 29*(1): 75-79.

Mason, M. F., M. I. Norton, J. D. Van Horn, D. M. Wegner, S. T. Grafton, & C. N. Macrae 2007. Wandering minds: The default network and stimulus-independent thought. *Science 315*(5810): 393-395.

Mattson, M. P. 2014. Superior pattern processing is the essence of the evolved human brain. *Frontiers in Neuroscience*: 265.

McBrearty, S., & C. Tryon 2006. From Acheulean to middle stone age in the Kapthurin formation, Kenya. In *Transitions before the Transition* (pp. 257-277). Springer.

McGrew, W. 2007. Savanna chimpanzees dig for food. *Proceedings of the National Academy of Sciences 104*(49): 19167-19168.

Milks, A., D. Parker, & M. Pope 2019. External ballistics of Pleistocene hand-thrown spears: Experimental performance data and implications for human evolution. *Scientific Reports 9*(1): 1-11.

Mishkin, M., L. G. Ungerleider, & K. A. Macko 1983. Object vision and spatial vision: Two cortical pathways. *Trends in Neurosciences 6*: 414-417.

Mok, R. M., & B. C. Love 2019. A non-spatial account of place and grid cells based on clustering models of concept learning. *Nature Communications 10*(1): 1–9.

Morin, A. 2009. Self-awareness deficits following loss of inner speech: Dr. Jill Bolte Taylor's case study. *Consciousness and Cognition 18*(2): 524-529.

Morton, S. M., & A. J. Bastian 2006. Cerebellar contributions to locomotor adaptations during splitbelt treadmill walking. *Journal of Neuroscience 26*(36): 9107-9116.

Neubauer, S., J.-J. Hublin, & P. Gunz 2018. The evolution of modern human brain shape. *Science Advances 4*(1): eaao5961.

Nieder, A. 2021. Consciousness without cortex. *Current Opinion in Neurobiology 71*: 69-76.

Nieder, A., L. Wagener, & P. Rinnert 2020. A neural correlate of sensory consciousness in a corvid bird. *Science 369*(6511): 1626-1629.

Nielsen, M. 2012. Imitation, pretend play, and childhood: Essential elements in the evolution of human culture? *Journal of Comparative Psychology 126*(2): 170.

Niko, T. 1951. *The Study of Instinct*. Clarendon Press.

Niven, L. 2007. From carcass to cave: Large mammal exploitation during the Aurignacian at Vogelherd, Germany. *Journal of Human Evolution 53*(4): 362-382.

Nowell, A. 2010. Working memory and the speed of life. *Current Anthropology 51*(S1): S121-S133.

Nummenmaa, L., E. Glerean, R. Hari, & J. K. Hietanen 2014. Bodily maps of emotions. *Proceedings of the National Academy of Sciences 111*(2): 646-651.

O'Keefe, J., & J. Dostrovsky 1971. The hippocampus as a spatial map: Preliminary evidence from unit activity in the freely-moving rat. *Brain Research 34*: 171-175.

Oertel, V., A. Rotarska-Jagiela, V. van de Ven, C. Haenschel, M. Grube, U. Stangier, K. Maurer, & D. E. Linden 2009. Mental imagery vividness as a trait marker across the schizophrenia spectrum. *Psychiatry Research 167*(1-2): 1-11.

Pan, L., C. Zanolli, M. Martinón-Torres, J. M. B. de Castro, L. Martín-Francés, S. Xing, & W. Liu 2022. Early Pleistocene hominin teeth from Gongwangling of Lantian, Central China. *Journal of Human Evolution 168*: 103212.

Panksepp, J. 2004. *Affective Neuroscience: The Foundations of Human and Animal Emotions*. Oxford University Press.

Panksepp, J. 2005. Affective consciousness: Core emotional feelings in animals and humans. *Consciousness and Cognition 14*(1): 30-80.

Park, S. A., D. S. Miller, H. Nili, C. Ranganath, & E. D. Boorman 2020. Map making: Constructing, combining, and inferring on abstract cognitive maps. *Neuron 107*(6): 1226-1238.E1228.

Parvizi, J., & A. Damasio 2001. Consciousness and the brainstem. *Cognition 79*(1-2): 135-160.

Patel, G. H., D. Yang, E. C. Jamerson, L. H. Snyder, M. Corbetta, & V. P. Ferrera 2015. Functional evolution of new and expanded attention networks in humans. *Proceedings of the National Academy of Sciences 112*(30): 9454-9459.

Peña-Guzmán, D. M. 2022. *When Animals Dream: The Hidden World of Animal Consciousness*. Princeton University Press.

Penn, D. C., K. J. Holyoak, & D. J. Povinelli 2008. Darwin's mistake: Explaining the discontinuity between human and nonhuman minds. *Behavioral and Brain Sciences 31*(2): 109-130.

Penn, D. C., & D. J. Povinelli 2007. Causal cognition in humans and nonhuman animals: A comparative, critical review. *Annual Review of Psychology 58*: 97–118.

Penn, D. C., & D. J. Povinelli 2007. On the lack of evidence that non-human animals possess anything remotely resembling a 'theory of mind'. *Philosophical Transactions of the Royal Society B: Biological Sciences 362*(1480): 731-744.

Penn, D. C., & D. J. Povinelli 2013. The comparative delusion. In Janet Metcalfe & Herbert S. Terrace (Eds.), *Agency and Joint Attention* (pp. 62–81). Oxford University Press.

Petrolini, V., M. Jorba, & A. Vicente 2020. The role of inner speech in executive functioning tasks: Schizophrenia with auditory verbal hallucinations and autistic spectrum conditions as case studies. *Frontiers in Psychology*: 2452.

Plotnik, J. M., F. B. De Waal, & D. Reiss 2006. Self-recognition in an Asian elephant. *Proceedings of the National Academy of Sciences 103*(45): 17053–17057.

Povinelli, D. J. 2000. *Folk Physics for Apes: The Chimpanzee's Theory of How the World Works.* Oxford University Press.

Povinelli, D. J. 2012. *World Without Weight: Perspectives on an Alien Mind.* Oxford University Press.

Povinelli, D. J., G. C. Glorioso, S. L. Kuznar, & M. Pavlic 2019. Dual systems for all: Higher-order, role-based relational reasoning as a uniquely derived feature of human cognition. *Behavioral and Brain Sciences 42*(E271): 44-45.

Prior, H., A. Schwarz, & O. Güntürkün 2008. Mirror-induced behavior in the magpie (*Pica pica*): Evidence of self-recognition. *PLoS Biology (Public Library of Science) 6*(8): e202.

Putt, S. S., S. Wijeakumar, & J. P. Spencer 2019. Prefrontal cortex activation supports the emergence of early stone age toolmaking skill. *Neuroimage 199*: 57-69.

Raia, P., M. Boggioni, F. Carotenuto, S. Castiglione, M. Di Febbraro, F. Di Vincenzo, M. Melchionna, A. Mondanaro, A. Papini, & A. Profico 2018. Unexpectedly rapid evolution of mandibular shape in hominins. *Scientific Reports 8*(1): 1-8.

Raichle, M. E., A. M. MacLeod, A. Z. Snyder, W. J. Powers, D. A. Gusnard, & G. L. Shulman 2001. A default mode of brain function. *Proceedings of the National Academy of Sciences 98*(2): 676-682.

Raichle, M. E., & A. Z. Snyder 2007. A default mode of brain function: a brief history of an evolving idea. *Neuroimage 37*(4): 1083-1090.

Ratcliffe, M., & S. Wilkinson 2016. How anxiety induces verbal hallucinations. *Consciousness and Cognition 39*: 48-58.

Read, D. W., H. M. Manrique, & M. J. Walker 2021. On the working memory of humans and great apes: Strikingly similar or remarkably different? *Neuroscience & Biobehavioral Reviews.*

Richardson, A. 1969. *Mental Imagery.* Springer.

Rightmire, G. P. 2004. Brain size and encephalization in early to Mid-Pleistocene *Homo. American Journal of Physical Anthropology 124*(2): 109-123.

Robinson, J. R., J. Rowan, C. J. Campisano, J. G. Wynn, & K. E. Reed 2017. Late Pliocene environmental change during the transition from *Australopithecus* to *Homo. Nature Ecology & Evolution 1*(6): 1-7.

Rogers, A., D. Iltis, & S. Wooding 2004. Genetic variation at the MC1R locus and the time since loss of human body hair. *Current Anthropology 45*(1): 105-108.

Saalasti, S., T. Lepistö, E. Toppila, T. Kujala, M. Laakso, T. Nieminen-von Wendt, L. von Wendt, & E. Jansson-Verkasalo 2008. Language abilities of children with Asperger syndrome. *Journal of Autism and Developmental Disorders 38*(8): 1574-1580.

Sánchez-Yustos, P., F. Diez-Martín, M. Domínguez-Rodrigo, J. Duque, C. Fraile, I. Díaz, S. de Francisco, E. Baquedano, & A. Mabulla 2017. The origin of the Acheulean. Techno-functional study of the FLK W lithic record (Olduvai, Tanzania). *Plos One 12*(8): e0179212.

Schlanger, N. 1996. Understanding Levallois: Lithic technology and cognitive archaeology. *Cambridge Archaeological Journal 6*(2): 231-254.

Schmidt, P., & T. Fuchs 2021. The unbearable dispersal of being: Narrativity and personal identity in borderline personality disorder. *Phenomenology and the Cognitive Sciences 20*(2): 321-340.

Schneider, G. E. 1969. Two visual systems: Brain mechanisms for localization and discrimination are dissociated by tectal and cortical lesions. *Science 163*(3870): 895-902.

Schooler, J. W. 2002. Re-representing consciousness: Dissociations between experience and meta-consciousness. *Trends in Cognitive Sciences 6*(8): 339-344.

Schuck, N. W., M. B. Cai, R. C. Wilson, & Y. Niv 2016. Human orbitofrontal cortex represents a cognitive map of state space. *Neuron 91*(6): 1402-1412.

Schultebraucks, K., M. Duesenberg, M. Di Simplicio, E. A. Holmes, & S. Roepke 2020. Suicidal imagery in borderline personality disorder and major depressive disorder. *Journal of Personality Disorders 34*(4): 546-564.

Scott, M. 2013. Corollary discharge provides the sensory content of inner speech. *Psychological Science 24*(9): 1824-1830.

Semaw, S., M. J. Rogers, J. Quade, P. R. Renne, R. F. Butler, M. Dominguez-Rodrigo, D. Stout, W. S. Hart, T. Pickering, & S. W. Simpson 2003. 2.6-Million-year-old stone tools and associated bones from OGS-6 and OGS-7, Gona, Afar, Ethiopia. *Journal of Human Evolution 45*(2): 169-177.

Semaw, S., M. J. Rogers, S. W. Simpson, N. E. Levin, J. Quade, N. Dunbar, W. C. McIntosh, I. Cáceres, G. E. Stinchcomb, & R. L. Holloway 2020. Co-occurrence of Acheulian and Oldowan artifacts with *Homo erectus* cranial fossils from Gona, Afar, Ethiopia. *Science Advances 6*(10): eaaw4694.

Semon, R. W. 1904, 1921. *The Mneme*. George Allen & Unwin Ltd.

Seth, A. K., D. B. Edelman, & B. J. Baars 2004. Let's not forget about sensory consciousness. *Behavioral and Brain Sciences 27*(4): 601-602.

Sharon, G. 2007. *Acheulian Large Flake Industries: Technology, Chronology, and Significance*. Archaeopress. https://books.google.com.au/books?id=1jRmAAAAMAAJ

Sharon, G., R. Barkai, J. Gowlett, D. Hodgson, K. Kuman, M. D. Petraglia, I. de la Torre, & G. Sharon 2009. Acheulian giant-core technology: A worldwide perspective. *Current Anthropology 50*(3): 335-367.

Sherwood, C. C., F. Subiaul, & T. W. Zawidzki 2008. A natural history of the human mind: Tracing evolutionary changes in brain and cognition. *Journal of Anatomy 212*(4): 426-454.

Shipton, C. 2010. Imitation and shared intentionality in the Acheulean. *Cambridge Archaeological Journal 20*(2): 197-210.

SHIPTON, C. 2018. Biface knapping skill in the East African Acheulean: Progressive trends and random walks. *African Archaeological Review 35*(1): 107-131.

SHIPTON, C. 2019. The evolution of social transmission in the Acheulean. In K. Overmann & F. L. Coolidge (Eds.), *Squeezing Minds from Stones* (pp. 332-354). Oxford University Press.

SHIPTON, C. 2020. Three stages in the evolution of human cognition: Normativity, recursion, abstraction. In Tracy B. Henley, Matt J. Rossano, & Edward P. Kardas (Eds.), *Handbook of Cognitive Archaeology: Psychology in Prehistory* (pp. 153-173). Routledge.

SHIPTON, C., M. NIELSEN, & F. D. VINCENZO 2021. The Acheulean origins of normativity. In Anton Killin & Sean Allen_Hermanson (Eds.), *Explorations in Archaeology and Philosophy* (pp. 197-212). Springer.

SOKOLOV, A. A., R. C. MIALL, & R. B. IVRY 2017. The cerebellum: Adaptive prediction for movement and cognition. *Trends in Cognitive Sciences 21*(5): 313-332.

SPECKENS, A. E., A. HACKMANN, A. EHLERS, & B. CUTHBERT 2007. Imagery special issue: Intrusive images and memories of earlier adverse events in patients with obsessive compulsive disorder. *Journal of Behavior Therapy and Experimental Psychiatry 38*(4): 411-422.

STIBEL, J. M. 2021. Decreases in brain size and encephalization in anatomically modern humans. *Brain, Behavior and Evolution 96*(2): 64-77.

STOUT, D., E. HECHT, N. KHREISHEH, B. BRADLEY, & T. CHAMINADE 2015. Cognitive demands of Lower Paleolithic toolmaking. *Plos One 10*(4): e0121804.

STOUT, D., & E. E. HECHT 2017. Evolutionary neuroscience of cumulative culture. *Proceedings of the National Academy of Sciences 114*(30): 7861-7868.

STOUT, D., N. TOTH, K. SCHICK, & T. CHAMINADE 2008. Neural correlates of Early Stone Age toolmaking: Technology, language and cognition in human evolution. *Philosophical Transactions of the Royal Society B: Biological Sciences 363*(1499): 1939-1949.

SUWA, G., B. ASFAW, Y. HAILE-SELASSIE, T. WHITE, S. KATOH, G. WOLDEGABRIEL, W. K. HART, H. NAKAYA, & Y. BEYENE 2007. Early pleistocene *Homo erectus* fossils from konso, southern Ethiopia. *Anthropological Science*: 0705240005-0705240005.

TAVARES, R. M., A. MENDELSOHN, Y. GROSSMAN, C. H. WILLIAMS, M. SHAPIRO, Y. TROPE, & D. SCHILLER 2015. A map for social navigation in the human brain. *Neuron 87*(1): 231-243.

TENNIE, C., I. C. GILBY, & R. MUNDRY 2009. The meat-scrap hypothesis: Small quantities of meat may promote cooperative hunting in wild chimpanzees (*Pan troglodytes*). *Behavioral Ecology and Sociobiology 63*(3): 421-431.

THEOFANOPOULOU, C., S. GASTALDON, T. O'ROURKE, B. D. SAMUELS, A. MESSNER, P. T. MARTINS, F. DELOGU, S. ALAMRI, & C. BOECKX 2017. Self-domestication in *Homo sapiens*: Insights from comparative genomics. *Plos One 12*(10): e0185306.

TOH, W. L., N. THOMAS, & S. L. ROSSELL 2015. Auditory verbal hallucinations in bipolar disorder (BD) and major depressive disorder (MDD): A systematic review. *Journal of Affective Disorders 184*: 18-28.

TOLMAN, E. C. 1948. Cognitive maps in rats and men. *Psychological Review 55*(4): 189–208.

TSUCHIYAGAITO, A., S. M. SÁNCHEZ, M. MISAKI, R. KUPLICKI, H. PARK, M. P. PAULUS, & S. M. GUINJOAN 2022. Intensity of repetitive negative thinking in depression is associated with greater functional connectivity between semantic processing and emotion regulation areas. *Psychological Medicine*: 1-12.

TULVING, E. 1985. Memory and consciousness. *Canadian Psychology/Psychologie canadienne 26*(1): 1-12.

TYLÉN, K., R. FUSAROLI, S. ROJO, K. HEIMANN, N. FAY, N. N. JOHANNSEN, F. RIEDE, & M. LOMBARD 2020. The evolution of early symbolic behavior in *Homo sapiens*. *Proceedings of the National Academy of Sciences 117*(9): 4578-4584.

VAN HONK, J., B. E. MORGAN, & D. J. SCHUTTER 2007. Raw feeling: A model for affective consciousness. *Behavioral and Brain Sciences 30*(1): 107-108.

VAN VEEN, V., J. D. COHEN, M. M. BOTVINICK, V. A. STENGER, & C. S. CARTER 2001. Anterior cingulate cortex, conflict monitoring, and levels of processing. *Neuroimage 14*(6): 1302-1308.

VANDERVERT, L. 2018. How prediction based on sequence detection in the cerebellum led to the origins of stone tools, language, and culture and, thereby, to the rise of *Homo sapiens*. *Frontiers in Cellular Neuroscience 12*: 408.

WESTERGAARD, G. C., & C. W. HYATT 1994. The responses of bonobos (Pan paniscus) to their mirror images: Evidence of self-recognition. *Human Evolution 9*(4): 273–279.

WILKINS, J., & M. CHAZAN 2012. Blade production 500 thousand years ago at Kathu Pan 1, South Africa: Support for a multiple origins hypothesis for early Middle Pleistocene blade technologies. *Journal of Archaeological Science 39*(6): 1883-1900.

WOLF, S. (2015). *Schmuckstücke: Die Elfenbeinbearbeitung im Schwäbischen Aurignacien* Kerns Verlag]. Tübingen.

WYNN, T., & F. L. COOLIDGE 2011. The implications of the working memory model for the evolution of modern cognition. *International Journal of Evolutionary Biology 2011*(741357): 1-12.

YRAVEDRA, J., S. RUBIO-JARA, L. A. COURTENAY, & J. A. MARTOS 2020. Mammal butchery by *Homo erectus* at the Lower Pleistocene acheulean site of Juma's korongo 2 (JK2), bed III, Olduvai Gorge, Tanzania. *Quaternary Science Reviews 249*: 106612.

ZAHAVI, D. 2020. Consciousness and (minimal) selfhood: Getting clearer on for-me-ness and mineness. In Uriah Kriegel (Ed.), *The Oxford Handbook of the Philosophy of Consciousness* (pp. 1-19). Oxford University Press.

ZAIM, Y., R. L. CIOCHON, J. M. POLANSKI, F. E. GRINE, E. A. BETTIS III, Y. RIZAL, R. G. FRANCISCUS, R. R. LARICK, M. HEIZLER, & K. L. EAVES 2011. New 1.5 million-year-old Homo erectus maxilla from Sangiran (Central Java, Indonesia). *Journal of Human Evolution 61*(4): 363-376.

ZEMAN, A. Z., S. DELLA SALA, L. A. TORRENS, V.-E. GOUNTOUNA, D. J. MCGONIGLE, & R. H. LOGIE 2010. Loss of imagery phenomenology with intact visuo-spatial task performance: A case of 'blind imagination'. *Neuropsychologia 48*(1): 145-155.

ZEMAN, A. Z., M. DEWAR, & S. DELLA SALA 2015. Lives without imagery - Congenital aphantasia. *Cortex 73*: 378-380.

ZHANG, H., Y. ZHEN, S. YU, T. LONG, B. ZHANG, X. JIANG, J. LI, W. FANG, M. SIGMAN, & S. DEHAENE 2022. Working memory for spatial sequences: Developmental and evolutionary factors in encoding ordinal and relational structures. *Journal of Neuroscience 42*(5): 850-864.

14

KEYWORDS: Rock Art – Hieroglyphs – Neuroimaging – Cuneiform – Visual Cortex – Visual Word Form Area – Writing.

NEUROSCIENCE, VISUAL IMAGERY, ROCK ART AND THE ORIGINS OF WRITING

DEREK HODGSON

Abstract: There has been much debate as to how writing first came about in several locations throughout the world. The means by which writing evolved is considered to be a product of cultural variables that provided the context from which different writing systems emerged. Recent neuroimaging research, however, has found correspondences that pertain to all writing systems. Such findings suggest that the inception of writing developed out of the way objects are perceived that demonstrates a surprising link between visual imagery and writing. In this paper, the relevance of such precursors will be explored, particularly with regard to the visual cortex, early rock art, and the emergence of writing systems. This paper will therefore demonstrate how recent research in neuroscience from the perspective of the visual brain can be applied to archaeology in a way that provides new insights into the underlying heuristics of the first writing systems.

Introduction

Various neuroimaging techniques of individuals engaged in reading and writing have provided novel insights into how the brain encodes such skills. Yet, how writing first developed as a unique system around 5,500 years ago is referred to briefly, if at all, by neuroscientists (for exceptions see Dehaene 2009; Ardila 2012). Similarly, except for Adam Smith (2013), few philologists give much credence to recent insights from neuroscience regarding how words are processed in the brain. Likewise, except for Overmann (2016, 2017), archaeologists generally remain unfamiliar with the neuroscientific research. This is unfortunate because many of the neuroscientific findings have important implications for understanding the origins of reading and writing. Thus, despite the copious amount of neuroscientific research, there continues to be a lack of understanding how such research may be informative of the archaeology of writing. In order to address that shortfall, Damerow (2006) suggested that the cooperation of specialists from several different fields is necessary. In response to that plea, the following

Article received: 17 July 2022
Revised I: 21 July 2022
Revised II: 22 July 2022
Revised III: 23 May 2023

will attempt to deal with that shortfall by demonstrating how a multidisciplinary approach can help clarify some of the main factors that led to the first writing systems.

The importance of applying the insights of neuroscience to the origins of writing is all the more pertinent now that recent archaeological discoveries are highlighting the possible precursors. In order to investigate the importance of neuroscientific research in the present context, it is necessary to set out the most significant findings from the field. Despite certain caveats to be explored, an approach from this standpoint is feasible as the modern human brain is basically the same as the brains of those who first invented writing.

Precursors to Writing: The Neuroscience of Depicting Objects

Houston (2004, p.234) once asked 'Why did humans devise strikingly similar ways of recording sound and meaning? Is there a cognitive rationale that emanates from the innate features of the human brain?' In this section, we will demonstrate that there are indeed certain 'innate' features related to the perception of objects that are highly relevant to understanding the rudiments of different writing systems. In fact, recent research and archaeological evidence into the origins of the alphabet converge on the distinct possibility that writing evolved directly from the depiction of objects (Houston 2004, p.236). As Houston states, 'This initial pictography is logical given that transient sounds are being described in terms of a solid, visual world.'

Fortunately, neuro-scans of individuals viewing photographs and drawings of objects are beginning to elucidate some of the cognitive precursors relating to object perception that underpin literacy. In that regard, one of the interesting observations gleaned from neuroimaging is that when a person views, for example, an animal, the same area of the brain becomes active when a representation of the animal is viewed. Even when a drawing of an animal containing only the outline is presented—an extremely abbreviated format—the same area of the visual cortex becomes active as if one were witnessing a real animal (Walther et al. 2011); an effect that occurs especially when the outline is in typical viewing perspective, that is, sideways-on with the most salient features prominent.

The sideways canonical view of depicted animals in early rock art can potentially be explained by perceptual factors relating to the visual brain in that the maximum amount of information is extracted in a way that requires the least cognitive effort (thereby conserving neural resources). The almost universal utilisation of the contour outline for depicting objects in prehistoric art can be similarly explained (Kennedy and Silver 1974). Those responsible for producing such representations seem to have benefited from an implicit awareness that the drawn line economically delineates objects in the same way as occurs in the visual cortex (Sayim and Cavanagh 2011), a finding confirmed by neuroscience (Kourtzi and Kanwisher 2000; Walther et al. 2011; Lowe et al. 2018). In short, the neural activity of the visual system in response to viewing line drawings is virtually the same as when coloured photographs are viewed, which indicates that line drawings capture the most important elements of a scene. Interestingly, internal colour and texture appear to be incidental for the purpose of recognition. In addition, when 75% of the outline is removed from a line drawing, the depicted object can still be reliably identified. Recovering the outline of a three-dimensional natural form is held to be the one of the main ways the visual system is able to detect animals, especially when camouflaged (Pizlo 2008), which suggests this is one of the foremost reasons outlines are so widespread in prehistoric art. That ability may derive from the need to detect animals in camouflaged situations where parts of an animal's anatomy often remain concealed in a way that requires the visual cortex to 'fill in' the missing parts (Hodgson 2013). Resolving the missing features of a camouflaged animal leads to a sense of achievement, which can explain why many early depictions of animals remain 'unfinished'. It seems that the authors were deliberately leaving parts of an animal's contour blank in order to provide the opportunity for the visual brain to complete the missing features –an example of the global precedence effect, an ability in which humans are particularly adept (Hodgson 2019).

An interesting outcome derived from producing animal outlines during the Upper Palaeolithic was that perceptual abilities were sharpened to the extent that sensitivity to outlines underwent enhancement (Hodgson 2008, 2013, 2019). The hand-eye coordination required to produce animal contours thereby led to the neural networks in the visual cortex becoming more efficient at making and perceiving lines. That feedback mechanism, as well as the heightened sensitivity, meant pleasure was experienced in producing simple patterns, whether animals were depicted or not. In fact, geometric motifs outnumber the depiction of animals during the UP and, moreover, predate the Upper Palaeolithic by tens of thousands of years (Henshilwood et al. 2018; Joordens et al. 2014). Individuals gain satisfaction from making geometric patterns because they stimulate the fundamental attributes the early visual cortex employs in order to discriminate objects (Hodgson 2000, 2006). This is related to ease of processing that gives rise to positive effect through what is termed 'neural fluency' (Chenier and Winkielman 2009); a phenomenon that can explain why many geometric marks are associated with animals (though some may have been co-opted to make tally marks [d'Errico et al. 2003]) in that they lend a sense of visual intensity to the depictions.

Links with Writing

Daniels (1996, p.3) states that writing did not develop from pictographs because writing involves functions that cannot be represented in pictures. Defrancis (1989) agrees by stating that none of the major writing systems developed from pictographs. That view stems from the abstract nature of 'true writing' which, unlike pictographs, is closely aligned to phonetics ('true writing' refers to when the written sign attempts to represent the spoken sign either directly or indirectly [Robertson 2004]). This, however, does not take into account the visual nature of writing systems or its relatively gradual development from the iconic through to the indexical to the fully symbolic as outlined by Peirce (1974) and Deacon (1997). In other words, language arises from lower-order attributes that is reflected in how writing developed from being more iconic to become increasingly symbolic and phonetic (Robertson 2004). Once having achieved symbolic expertise, the lower-order platform can, for the most part, be discarded (see Pulvermüller 2013 for how this process occurs in the neural structures of the cortex). In that way, the depictions of animals and other objects served as a necessary precursor to later iconic pictographs. Interestingly, drawing and writing have been found to recruit similar neural networks, except that writing is more left lateralised and finely targeted, which demonstrates the close affinity of the two procedures (Yuan and Brown 2014; Potgieser et al. 2015; Planton et al. 2017), as Figure 1 illustrates.

The incremental development from drawing to abstract schema and ultimately writing appears to have been a necessary outcome of societies that were becoming larger and structurally more complex, where information needed to be exploited for various functions from the economic to the religious in order to maintain the social hierarchy (Schmandt-Besserat 1992a, 1992b; Houston 2004). Such an external memory system was essential in this context as the average human working memory is restricted to four to seven items (Cowan 2001; Miller 1994). An efficient means of encoding information in a stable, enduring, abstract script provided a means of transcending such limitations by providing many important functional advantages to communities. However, this was not a straightforward unilineal process as it involved a mosaic of factors including stasis, regression, standardisation, reinforcement, consolidation, saltation, etc. As Houston (2004) reminds us, the developments leading up to writing can be haphazard because that process depends on a variety of factors but, when eventually conceived, writing can advance rapidly.

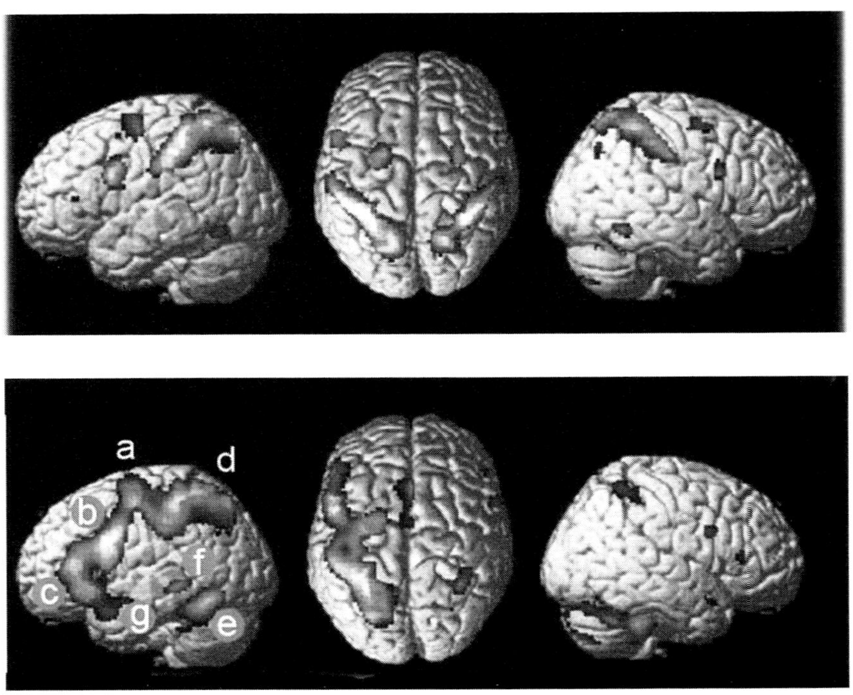

Figure 1. Areas of cortex active when drawing (top) and writing (bottom). (From Figure 2. Potgieser et al. 2015). (CC BY 4.0).

Visual Cortex and Schematics

The transition from naturalistic outline figures to abstract configurations is reflected in the way the visual cortex perceives, constructs and repurposes images of objects, mainly along the ventral visual pathway (see Figure 2). In order for this to occur there needed to be a recalibration of the neural substrates, which involves refining the neural circuits at earlier levels through a feedback loop assisted by eye-hand coordination carried out by the dorsal stream (see Figure 2). Neuroimaging of the neural substrates in modern participants indicates that this leads to the establishment of the Visual Word Form Area (VWFA) in the early to mid-levels of the occipito-temporal ventral visual cortex (Dehaene 2009; Dehaene et al. 2010). In short, those areas of the ventral cortex devoted to the recognition of objects, such as tools and faces, underwent appropriation for the purpose of reading and writing. Even the earliest parts of the visual cortex, such as V1, which deal with the most basic line configurations at high acuity, are co-opted into the procedure (Chang et al. 2015). This also involves a 'backward' tracing of the information flow from mid-cortical levels to earlier visual areas along the ventral stream where basic forms are processed.

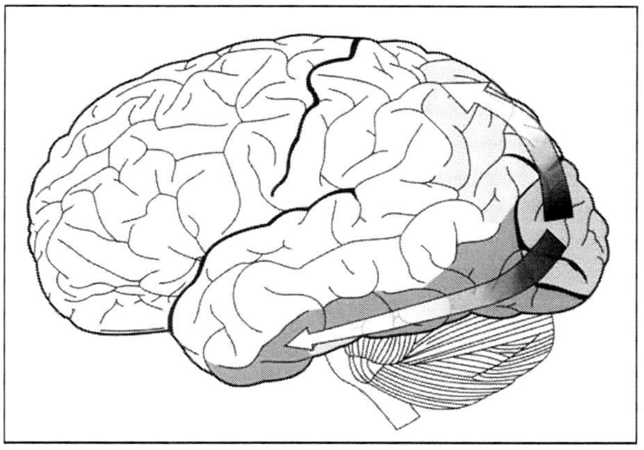

Figure 2: The ventral 'what' vision for perception (lower arrow) and dorsal 'where/how' vision for action (upper arrow) pathways in human cortex. The Visual Word Form Area is located in the ventral 'what' pathway (see below). CC BY-SA 3.0 (Author: Selket).

The paring down of information in depictions towards simpler configurations in the way described is pushed even further by the visual system in that neurons in the early to mid-level visual cortex respond with greater alacrity to semi-abstract schematic features compared to veridical images (Tanaka 2003; Lehky and Tanaka 2016). As stated by Tanaka 'The magnitude of responses [in visual cortex] often increased as the complexity of an image was reduced'. In effect, the visual cortex contains an 'alphabet' of pared down basic forms that preferentially trigger recognition (Ungerleider and Bell 2012), as shown in Figure 3. Such features provide an inventory of simplified motifs that cause neurons to fire when an object matching its profile is perceived. In a similar way

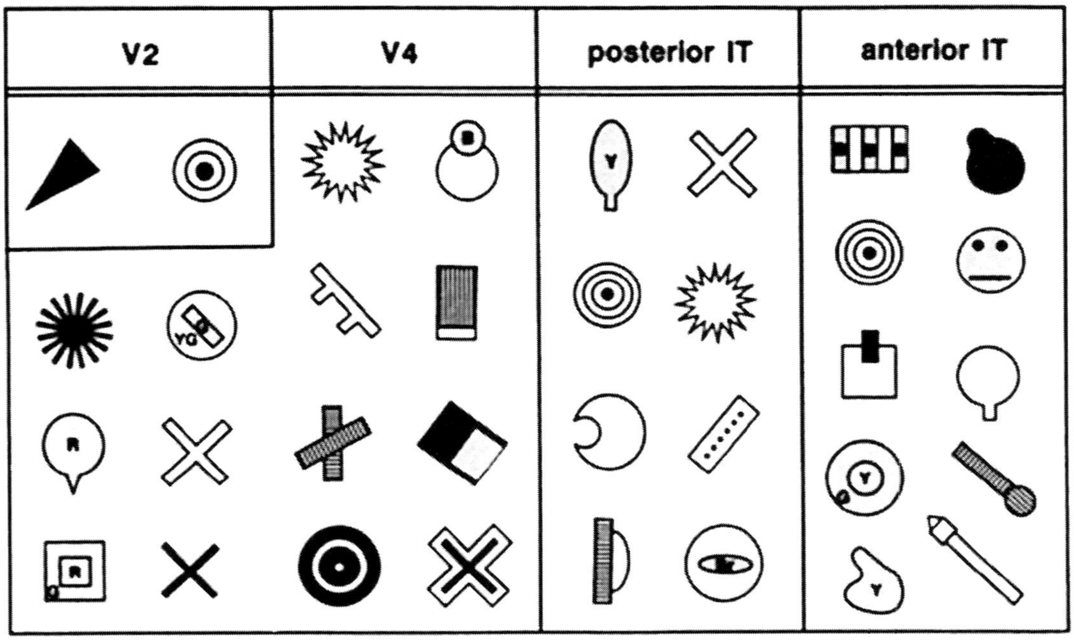

Figure 3: Critical stimuli that evoke the greatest response in neurons in areas V2, V4, and IT. (Original image from Kobatake and Tanaka 1994). CC BY-SA 3.0.

to alphabets, a limited set of basic features in the early to mid-level visual cortex is sufficient to encode an infinite number of consciously perceived objects.

Universal Topographies

Pared down attributes are not the only factors that link the transition from figurative depictions towards more abstract schematic forms that eventually gave rise to fully abstract writing systems. Research has found that a distinct similarity links different writing topographies, where the same basic graphic features, namely an interest in lines that form 'T' junctions, angles or 'L' motifs and cross hatches or 'X' features underlie all writing systems both ancient and modern (Changizi et al. 2006). 'T' tends to be the most common, then 'L', followed by 'X'. Moreover, topological features containing no more than three strokes incorporating such topologies form the basis of all writing systems (Changizi and Shimojo 2005). That universality stems from the fact that such configurations need to be easy to recognise and effortlessly accommodated by the visuo-motor system (Chang et al. 2015). Ultimately, however, ease of reading—as processed by the ventral stream—appears to take precedence over visuo-motor functions (though reading was dependent initially on the invention of writing [Overmann 2016]). That is because text may only be written once after which it is viewed by many different individuals over time, including those unable to write. Again, those preferences may be because the early visual system displays a distinct bias for certain motifs, namely lines, angles and intersections, which are a common attribute of the natural visual world (Roelfsema and de Lange 2016), that provide an efficacious means to quickly encode objects (Figure 4).

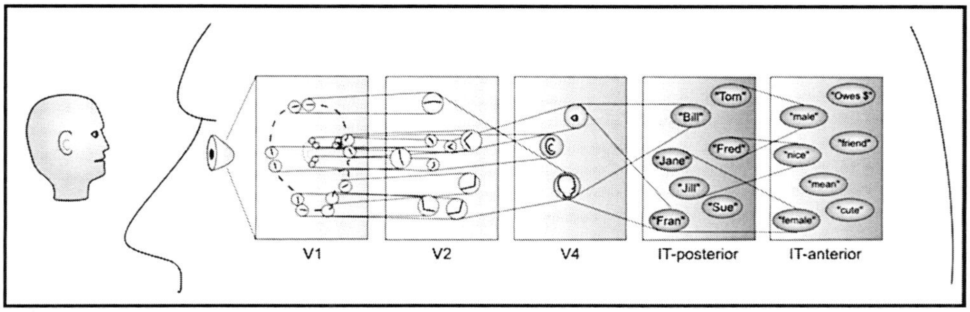

Figure 4: The hierarchy of increasing feature complexity arising along the ventral visual pathways. V1 contains elementary feature detectors (oriented edges), which are combined to make line junctions in V2, and so on up to IT where objects are conceived and where the Visual Word Form Area is located. (Image by Chatterjee 2019). CC BY-SA 3.0.

Biederman (1987) for example, showed that when the outline contours of objects at the corner intersections and junctions are preserved, objects are identified more rapidly than when only the mid segments are evident (Figure 5).

Figure 5: Recognition is superior for the abbreviated objects in the central column, which preserve vertices and junctions, compared to the right column where most of the vertices are omitted. (Figure by author based on Biederman 1987).

Because such contours are fundamental to recognising objects, they seem to have been co-opted to create graphically defined abstract writing systems. That finding is confirmed by Szwed et al. (2011) who also established that vertices (a point where two or more curves, lines, or edges meet)—as in Biederman's degraded objects—that are crucial; an approach also supported by Changizi as stipulated above (see also Dragoi et al. 2001).

For example, an L configuration signals an object's corner whereas a T junction indicates where one object stands in front of another. Thus, configurations commonly found in natural scenes are the same as those most often found in writing systems, including Egyptian hieroglyphics, cuneiform, and later orthographies. Those observations suggest that an intimate relationship exists between 'images' in the visual cortex and abstract geometric features of graphic systems.

Early Geometric Patterns and Visual Cortex

Basic engraved patterns have been found in the archaeological record, which predate the first figurative depictions of 40,000 BP by a considerable period (Henshilwood 2018; Joordens et al. 2014). The similarity of such early patterns over vast distances of space and time suggest the influence of long-standing constraints. Hodgson (2000, 2019) suggests that those constraints are based on perceptual criteria linked to how the early visual cortex encodes visual information as dictated by Gestalt principles, which gave rise to a proto-aesthetic sense. Although remote from early writing cultures, such marks, nevertheless, have implications for understanding how reading and writing evolved, as both rely on and exploit the biologically-based scene statistics implicit in the visual cortex (Chang et al. 2015). In essence, letter shapes were culturally selected to match the statistical properties of the natural environment that were integrated into the neural networks of the visual cortex; a scenario which has been simulated computationally by deep neural networks (Testolin et al. 2017). But as well as predating and prevailing into the Upper Palaeolithic, the same patterns are equally prevalent during the Mesolithic and Neolithic. Their similarity throughout space and time suggest they are not symbolic in the conventional sense, as proposed by von Petzinger (2017)—a fact confirmed by Malotki and Dissanayake (2018)—but stem from an 'intensification' (Smith 2013) of the above feedback system where the visual cortex increasingly becomes sensitised to such motifs. This is supported by the fact that false fonts, at first glance, look like true writing as illustrated here:

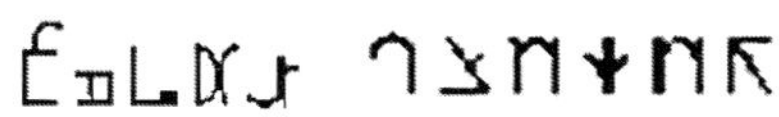

However, due to their saliency mediated by an implicit aesthetic appeal in the way described, they came to be valued as configurations in themselves and, as a result, were liable to become fetishized. Although Petrie (1912) discounted that writing originally developed from 'pictures', he nevertheless believed that a large number of 'signs', possibly as individual property marks, predated the first writing systems. As Petrie also pointed out, such signs seem to conform to the law of economy through refinement due to cultural diffusion and repeated use. In effect, not only does this suggest the influence of aesthetic criteria but also how, through successive approximation, 'signs' were undergoing refinement in order to conform more closely to how the visual cortex functions. Eventually, such signs would have been exploited for the purpose of creating property marks and writing systems etc.

False fonts activate the early visual cortex bilaterally as they are devoid of lexical or semantic input (Vinckier et al. 2007; Szwed et al. 2011). This suggests a trajectory of broad to more precise tuning as information passes from early visual cortex through to the higher levels of the visual hierarchy where neural networks are tuned to encode the precise visual coordinates of letters and words in the left hemisphere (Boring et al.2018; see also Glezer et al. 2015). Even baboons (Grainger et al. 2012) and macaques (Srihasam et al. 2012) have been trained to distinguish the difference between non-words and true words based solely on visual characteristics, which, again, derives from the basic features required to encode real objects. In humans, however, sensitivity to letter and word profiles leads to the appearance and tuning of the VWFA, as illustrated in Figure 6. Interestingly, in the same way that faces are recognised, Glezer et al. (2015) found that word recognition is based on its global character rather than specific letters. This is consistent with the midlevel visual cortex encoding words and their invariances within the VWFA (Dehaene and Cohen 2011), whereas earlier areas deal with individual letters and letter fragments. In short, reading seems to depend on an interaction of the local to global features of words (Overmann 2016).

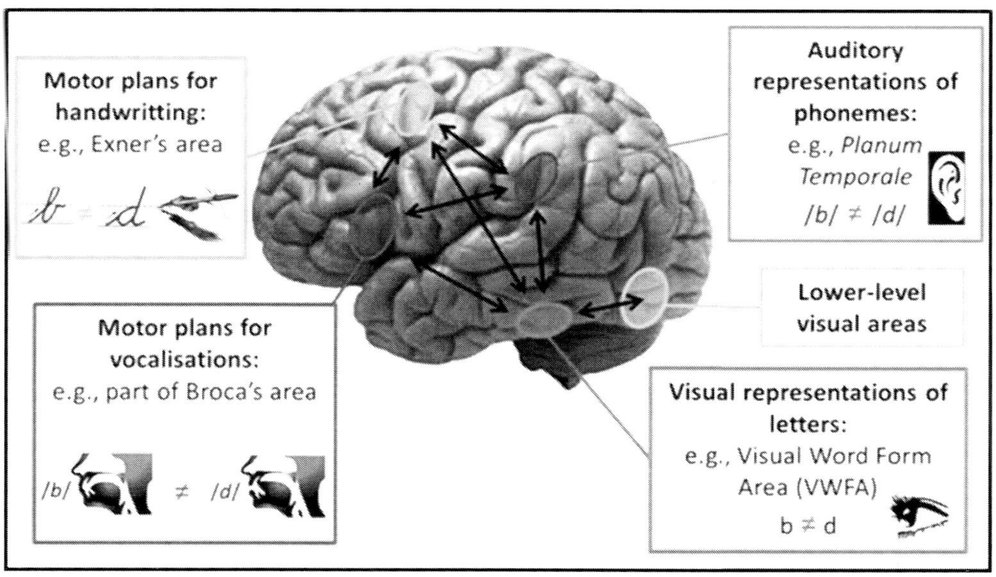

Figure 6: The Visual Word Form Area in the ventral pathway and its associated speech and writing networks in motor areas. (Adapted from: Pegado et al. 2014a) CC BY-SA 3.0

In order that abstract writing systems could develop, not only did naturalistic representation of animals, and to lesser extent humans, need to become increasingly schematic, but also required the recruitment of the early visual cortex, which is particularly proficient at perceiving fine detail. This means that the earliest areas of the visual cortex, including V1, needed to undergo 'training' via the above-mentioned feedback loop. The interaction of the occipitotemporal (middle) visual cortex with early areas, namely V1, V2 and V4 as well as LOC—by way of the same feedback system—led to the ability to decipher hieroglyphs and later alphabetic scripts (discussed in detail in the next two sections) at a fast rate by hyper-sensitising the visual pathway to the essential heuristics. The interest in producing geometric patterns in various scenarios before the onset of reading can therefore be regarded as stemming from a proto-aesthetic interest that was exploited to make signs for emblematic or ritualistic purposes rather than writing as such, especially as many of the patterns resemble false fonts. This can account for the numerous examples where signs are prevalent in Mesolithic and early Neolithic cultures (d'Errico 1992; Harmman 2005), which are, in fact, not true writing systems as some claim (Starović 2005). Note, many of those signs are similar to the false fonts and may have arisen because they copiously arouse the early visual cortex. Moreover, because they resonate so readily with the visual cortex and, as a result became fetishized, they were ideally suited to be employed in rituals and similar contexts, as proposed by Stordeur et al. (1997), Costello (2011), and Houston (2018). The numerous examples from the Neolithic illustrated by Haarmann (2005) and Forbes and Crowder (1979) are probably of this genre e.g., the Vinča Danube script. Appositely, such signs are often accompanied by iconic images and may, therefore, have originated from an aesthetic preference of the visual system for geometric configurations.

The Development of Egyptian Hieroglyphs: A Case Study

Having set out the neuronal substrates that underpin the ability to create outlines of objects and how this is associated with writing systems, we can now go on to explore how those insights can be applied to, and help understand, the emergence of particular scripts. We begin with a consideration of the emergence of Egyptian hieroglyphs.

Once natural figurative depictions had become normalised in Europe and elsewhere, such as in North Africa and Egypt, they could then undergo increasing formalisation and abbreviation. Indeed, at least 160 naturalistic animal outlines can be found in the Egyptian desert engraved on rock surfaces in proximity to the Nile dating up to 15,000 years ago (Huyge et al. 2007; Huyge 2008). See Figure 7 for typical examples that display a surprising similarity to the animal depictions of Upper Palaeolithic European caves.

The influence of such early naturalistic engravings can be observed in the depictions of animals and humans in the rock art of the Egyptian Western and Eastern Desert (Darnell 2009; Judd 2011), which mainly display the salient sideways features of animals in outline. The evolution from those depictions to increasingly schematic formats to the first hieroglyphs and related signs

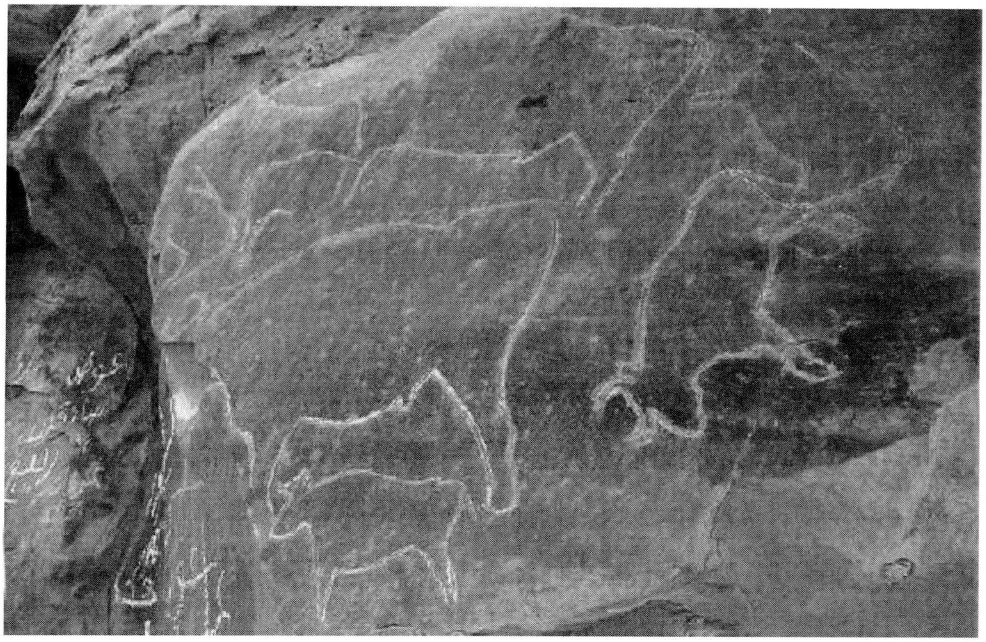

Figure 7: Sideways contour outlines of eight bovids on an outdoor rock surface at Qurta I, Egypt, eastern side of the Nile valley (Image from Huyge et al. 2007, reproduced with permission of the Antiquity journal. © Royal Museums of Art and History - Belgian Archaeological Mission to Qurta).

can be observed from more than 3,500 BCE up until the beginning of dynastic Egypt (Darnell 2009; Görsdorf et al. 1998; Dreyer 2011). Darnell's findings, as well of those of Dreyer (2011) and Najovits (2004, 55–56), provide support for the proposition that, rather than being influenced by Mesopotamia, Egyptian hieroglyphs evolved independently of the cuneiform system.

Thus, the trajectory involved in producing the first hieroglyphs seems to have begun with the depictions in the desert regions surrounding the Nile valley (Darnell 2009), where engravings of animals in outline profile occur. Darnell (Egyptian Ministry of Antiquities, 2018), states that the engravings of animals (including bulls, giraffe, sheep and donkeys) on rock outcrops at Bir Umm Tineidba in the Eastern Desert demonstrate how ancient Egyptians invented their unique writing system with a history extending to the beginning of the pre-dynastic era (from around 4000 - 3500 BCE) until the end of the ancient state (about 2350 BCE). Darnell emphasises that the engravings served as precursors to the later hieroglyphic writing and possible represent the oldest 'primitive' stages. Similarly, in the Eastern Desert at El-Khawy, engravings of storks, an ibis, a bull's head on a pole and an elephant, indicate a direct link between the Nile valley and later pharaonic culture. As further emphasised by Darnell 'This newly discovered rock art site of El-Khawy preserves some of the earliest—and largest—signs from the formative stages of the hieroglyphic script and provides evidence as to how the ancient Egyptians invented their unique writing system' (Connolly, 2017).

Those observations raise the possibility of a link between the rock art of hunter-gatherers, early nomadic herders (Hodgson 2013; Hodgson and Watson 2015; Hodgson 2019; Kennedy and Silver 1974), and the animals depicted in the rock art of the Eastern Desert. In fact, Kuper and Kröpelin (2006) suggest that the desert areas to the east of the Nile once benefited from substantial rainfall that provided pasture for animals. As a result of a drop in rainfall, desertification took place so, by around 3,500 BCE, herders had retreated to the remaining fertile areas nearer to the Nile. It is striking that, between 5,300 to 3,500 BCE at sites in the Eastern Sahara, rock art can be found at Jebel Ouenat and Gilf Kebir, which reflects the cultural priorities of herders living in the region at the time.

As stipulated, during the Upper Palaeolithic the portrayal of animals already displayed a tendency for schematisation. It was as if, through a feedback loop between the visual cortex and depictive outcomes, the brain was training itself to become increasingly sensitive to fewer cues for the purpose of recognition. Creating rock art in the challenging environmental conditions of the desert will have encouraged even more abbreviation in that the minimum amount of information could be deployed to maximum effect, which corresponds with the principle of least effort suggested by Pitt-Rivers (1875), Balfour's (1893) idea of 'unconscious variation', and Smith's (2013) notion of 'intensification'.

In order for that process to develop, the 'natural' tendency of the visual cortex for perceiving animals and humans needed to be recalibrated. That process began in the deserts of Upper Egypt with the carving of animal and human outlines on hard rock surfaces, which required considerable effort, which meant only the most salient parts of animals were depicted. The paring down of information in this way probably led to the realisation that it was possible to communicate information in an even more abbreviated form. A stage, however, must have been reached whereby foreknowledge was required before such representations could be decoded. Paring down images to their essential ingredients nevertheless meant that they could be produced more quickly, efficiently and economically—a factor that eventually took precedence over the obvious iconicity. As a result, making signs increasingly became the preserve of specialist scribes who—probably by way of cultural evolution—further refined and schematised the depictions to the extent that scholarship became a prerequisite (Smith's [2013] 'intensification'). This is corroborated by research showing that familiarity, rather than pictoriality or concreteness, takes precedence in such circumstances, which engenders specialised but easy-to-decipher iconic signs (McDougall et al. 2016). In effect, a 'biologically-based' tendency was eventually superseded by cultural evolution that eventually gave rise to the first hieroglyphs—a quintessential pictographic system (Graff 2018). From the naturalistic realism of the first European and North African rock art to the increasingly abstract contours of the Mesolithic Spanish Levant and predynastic Egyptian rock engravings, we see a development from naturalism towards essential schematic features that culminated in the first hieroglyphs. That trajectory follows the 'natural' course as to how abstraction and schematisation occurs in the visual cortex.

In order for that development to proceed, however, the imagery processed by the ventral pathway needed to undergo neural-recycling, thereby facilitating the development of the VWFA. In other words, writing could only gain traction within the ventral cortex by recourse to a visual image stage involving the essential vertices required to perceive objects as well as the outline of objects themselves. The more fundamental and significant route to the mechanics of writing involving letters, words, semantics, phonology, and syntax therefore took place through engagement of the occipitotemporal cortical region, initially through pictographs, and incrementally through repurposing that pathway through neuronal recycling. That is to say, the heavy lifting for the ability to create hieroglyphs relied on engaging and reassigning the ventral stream in order that the VWFA and associated semantic, phonological and lexical imperatives of the left fronto-parietal cortical areas could interconnect (López-Barroso et al. 2020).

Cuneiform and Iconicity

A similar trajectory seems to have occurred in the case of cuneiform as Figure 8 illustrates, where an obvious iconic feature became increasingly schematised and abstract.

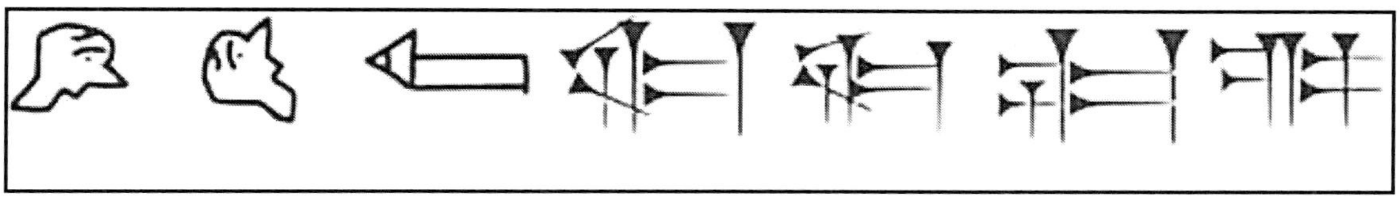

Figure 8: 'Natural' route to the invention of cuneiform as a continuation of schematisation of the Upper Palaeolithic through to the Neolithi (development of the sign SAG 'head'). CC BY-SA 3.0

Similarly, Dehaene (2009) views the depiction of naturalistic objects and pictographs as influential in that pictographs, in becoming more schematic, eventually culminated in cuneiform script (see also Diringer 1968; Overmann 2020, 2021). Only by activating the ventral stream could abstract writing systems, including cuneiform, hieroglyphs and alphabetic systems, arise. That process transpired by way of the VWFA within the fusiform gyrus, which formed reciprocal links with language areas in the left cortical hemisphere (Dehaene 2009; Dehaene et al. 2010) including the premotor regions (Longcamp et al. 2003) involving grapheme-phoneme correspondences (Brem et al. 2010) and semantics (Dehaene et al. 2005), as illustrated in Figure 6. That conclusion is bolstered by the fact that non-literate people who invent their own writing system known as 'emergent scripts' *tend* to begin with iconic representations that incrementally undergo compression and simplification by way of logograms that culminate in abstract graphic syllabaries (Kelly et al. 2021). In addition, the Chinese and Mayan writing systems seem to be similarly disposed in developing from iconicity towards schematic forms to eventually realise more abstract graphic features, where the emphasis gravitates from graphic essentials involving less complex phonological labelling towards greater stress on phonology (Smith 2013; Houston 2004).

Interestingly, individuals literate in simplified Chinese writing, tend to display enhanced visual skills related to a more accomplished intermediate visual cortex; a tendency accentuated further when comparing European with Chinese literates (Zhou et al. 2014). Except for certain regions of the visuo-system, however, the location of the VWFA is shared by all groups.

From that perspective, Schmandt-Besserat's proposal that counting served as the substantive precursor to cuneiform is challenged by neuroscience, which demonstrates that the cortical network for numbers (the Number Form Area or NFA) is located, and interfaces with, a different cortical region to the reading/writing areas (Brannon, 2005; Starrfelt 2007; Dehaene 2011; Shum et al. 2013; Hannagan et al. 2015; Dehaene and Dehaene-Lambertz 2016; Nemmi et al. 2018), as indicated in Figure 9.

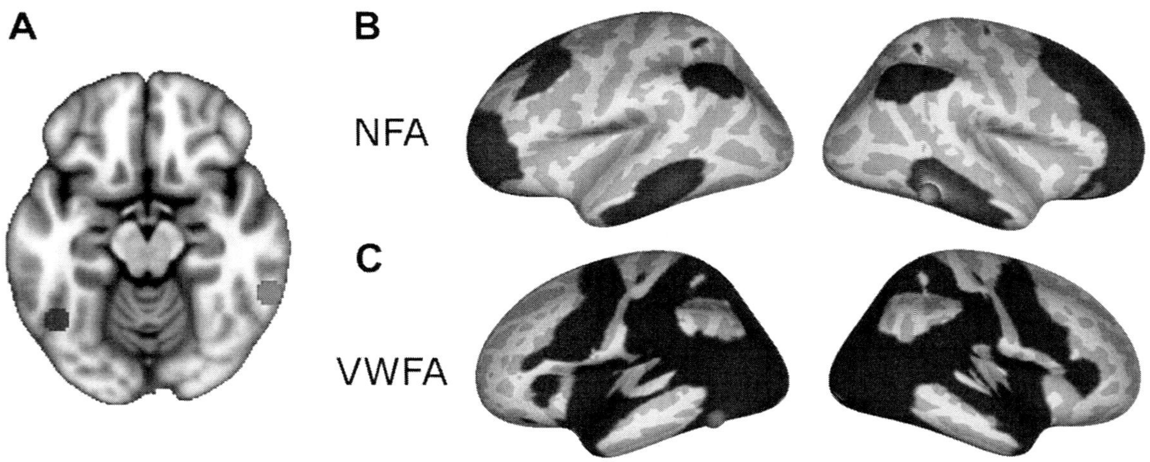

Figure 9: Cortical networks for numeracy and reading with associated networks. A. Location of NFA in right hemisphere and VWFA in left hemisphere. B. NFA indicated by small circle in right hemisphere. C. VWFA indicated by small circle in left hemisphere. (Reproduced from Nemmi et al. 2018. Permission of Frontiers in Human Neuroscience, CCBY).

Overmann (2020, 2021) makes a similar point with regard to the development of cuneiform, where writing and numeracy are shown to constitute different types of semiotic information that are processed separately in the brain.

A further demonstration of the independence of the reading/writing and number pathways derives from damage to specific areas of the cortex. For example, individuals with lesions to areas specialising in letters are unable to write or perceive letters, leading to aphasic agraphia and pure alexia, whereas, conversely, individuals who suffer from dyscalculia are unable to perceive numbers yet the ability to read is spared (Anderson et al. 1990; Delazer et al. 2002; Dehaene 2009). In short, numeracy recruits a different form system to language as revealed in the separate neural circuits (Brannon 2005).

In addition, the cortical network that encodes geometric forms (see Figure 10), which would have been engaged in making the clay geometric tokens—and purportedly gave rise to the cuneiform system—recruits a separate network to that of natural objects and speech/language (Amalric and Dehaene 2016) (see Figures 6 and 9 above). Moreover, in contrast to the VWFA and associated language areas located in the left hemisphere, the number network and NFA—though spanning both hemispheres—displays a bias towards the right cerebral hemisphere, with a similar tendency occurring for geometry. This makes the crossover from learning numbers and the use of geometric shapes to the invention of reading/writing problematic (see also Overmann 2016), precisely because the VWFA and the language network needed to be recruited before writing could develop.

The transformation observed in the Egyptian analysis from iconicity to hieroglyphs set out above, demonstrates the 'natural' route in the way that the cortex is able to exploit graphic correlates through cortical recycling to incrementally instantiate the VWFA and appropriate links to the language areas. That procedure is absent in the way cuneiform is supposed to have developed from counting and geometric attributes. Counting and the use of geometric tokens, it should be emphasised, would not have mapped onto the letter to word processing route in the occipitotemporal cortex in order to attain the 'abstracted immaterial sounds of speech' alluded to by Schmandt-Besserat, a point also made by Overmann (2020, 2021). Coincidentally, d'Errico and Colagè, (2018) make a similar misapplication with regard to the relevance of the neuroscience of numeracy to writing (they suggest counting existed in the Upper Palaeolithic) by claiming that repetitive marks were a form of preserved notation that eventually led directly to the ability to write (cuneiform in their example).

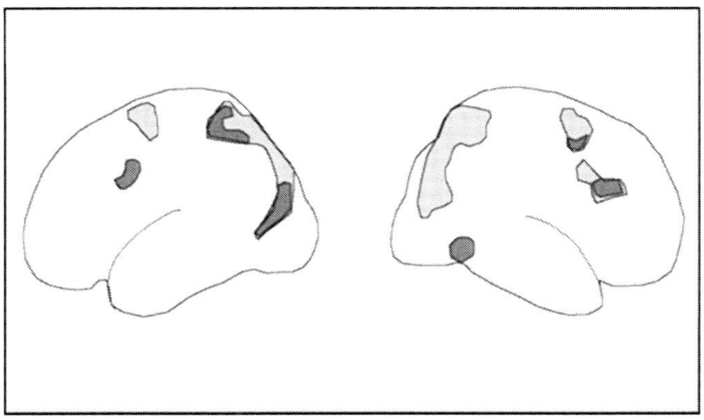

Figure 10: Cortical network for geometry in left and right hemispheres. Note the areas in each hemisphere interface at higher levels with the dorsal stream (figure by author based on Wang et al. 2019).

A further corollary of the above findings is that Sumerian and Egyptian scribes were adults who needed to expend considerable effort to learn the conventions of their scripts. However, learning to read and write in adults is more difficult than for children because the underlying neural structures and interconnections are already in place in the former, which makes neural recycling more challenging for adults. In fact, changes to the microstructure of the interconnecting white matter tracts in the arcuate fasciculus, which link the grapho-phonological decoding stream, has been observed in illiterates as they learn to read (de Schotten et al., 2014. As a result, early scribes needed to exploit existing marks or drawings as a means of scaffolding new writing systems as a way of counteracting such deficiencies. In a way, externally realised marks acted as a surrogate learning device that supplemented or scaffolded adult cortical limitations. Thus, figurative depictions served as an essential starting point for that procedure to develop. Though, as Ferrara (2014) points out, we cannot be sure of the ancient precursors of writing as they often remain opaque due to issues of preservation.

In effect, the invention of cuneiform must have involved a coming together of schematic iconicity, the ability to make marks, and speech networks. The cross-over seems to have occurred using the Rebus principle, (Schmandt-Besserat 2009 acknowledges this), where objects or people were signified by schematic representations. In fact, Valério and Ferrara (2020) suggest that the first writing systems derived from iconicity and the Rebus principle, and, perhaps also through acrophony, paved the way for the first abstract phonetic scripts to emerge (see also Goldwasser 2015). This raises the possibility of a much closer link between early naturalistic drawings, iconic representations and the invention of cuneiform than otherwise suggested. This involved a long tradition of schematic representations and pictographs dating to the early Neolithic which, through a feedback loop, reformatted the requisite neural networks in the ventral stream, which culminated in the appearance of the VWFA and associated direct connections to the speech areas in the way described.

Should there be any doubt as to the intimate association of writing systems—such as the Latin alphabet—with iconicity, one only has to look at the role of mirror invariance (Pegado et al. 2014a). This concerns the fact that those learning to read often confuse the letters'b' and 'd' or 'p' and 'q'. That confusion stems from the exploitation of redundancy in the visual cortex where, for example, in order to recognise an animal, it is unnecessary to encode both profile views as they display identical perceptual coordinates (Hodgson 2013). In that way, neural resources are economically allotted by employing the same neural contingencies to encode both side views thereby providing a rapid means to identify potentially threatening objects (Pegoda et al 2014b). That mechanism, however, causes confusion with certain letters in those learning to write. With repeated training in literacy that problem is eventually rectified, though some groups—such as dyslexics—may continue to experience difficulties. Pertinently, as Pegoda et al. (2014b) state, the redundancy associated with object reversals also exists in non-human primates in that it is a particular phenomenon related to perceiving predators and prey. In that sense, it has an obvious correspondence to the earlier observation regarding the perception and depiction of animals outlines in early rock art.

Conclusion

As stipulated, naturalistic and abbreviated iconicity might have played a greater role in the invention of writing than previously suggested. In the case of Egypt, hieroglyphs were presaged by a long development of naturalistic images of animals in the desert regions that gradually transformed into pictographs and hieroglyphs. The development of cuneiform script is complicated by the early advent of counting. The neuroscience of reading and numeracy suggests that reading/writing could not have emerged solely from numeracy, rather iconicity must also have played a significant if not defining role. In effect, the pictograph approach to understanding the invention of writing may need to be greater prominence given the recent insights of both neuroscience and archaeology.

Dr Derek Hodgson
Belle Vue Street, York
UK. YO10 5AY
Email: dehogson@googlemail.com

References

Amalric, M. and S. Dehaene. 2016. Origins of the brain networks for advanced mathematics in expert mathematicians. *Proceedings of the National Academy of Sciences of the United States of America.* 113 (18): 4909-4917.

Anderson, S. W., A. R. Damasio, and H. Damasio. 1990. Troubled letters but not numbers: domain specific cognitive impairments following focal damage to frontal cortex. *Brain.* 113: 749–766.

Ardila, A. 2012. Neuropsychology of writing. In E. Grigorenko, E. Mambrino and D. Preiss (eds), *Handbook of writing: A mosaic of perspectives and views,* pp. 309–321. Psychology Press, London.

Biederman, I. 1987. Recognition-by-Components: A Theory of Human Image Understanding. *Psychological Review.* 1917 (2): 115-147.

Boring, M. J., E. A. Hirshorn, Y. Li, M. J. Ward, R. M. Richardson, J. A. Fiez and A. S. Ghuman. 2018. Left mid-ventral temporal cortex interacts with early visual cortex and the anterior temporal lobe to support word individuation. *bioRxiv.* 411579; doi: https://doi.org/10.1101/411579

Brannon, E. M. 2005.The independence of language and mathematical reasoning. *Proceedings of the National Academy of Sciences of the United States of America.* 102 (9): 3177–3178.

Brem, S., S. Bach, K. Kucian, J.V. Kujala, T.K. Guttorm, E. Martin, H. Lyytinen, D. Brandeis and U. Richardson. 2010. Brain sensitivity to print emerges when children learn letter–speech sound correspondences. *Proceedings of the National Academy of Sciences of the United States of America.* 107 (17):7939-7944.

Chang, C. H. C., C. Pallier, D.H. Wu, K. Nakamura, A. Jobert, W-J. Kuo and S. Dehaene. 2015. Adaptation of the human visual system to the statistics of letters and line configurations. *Neuroimage.* 415. http://dx.doi.org/10.1016/j.neuroimage.2015.07.028

Changizi, M.A. and S. Shimojo. S. 2005. Character complexity and redundancy in writing systems over human history. *Proceedings of the Royal Society of London* B. 272: 267-275.

Changizi., M. A., Q. Zhang, H. Ye, and S. Shimojo. 2006. The Structures of Letters and Symbols throughout Human History are Selected to Match Those Found in Objects in Natural Scenes. *The American Naturalist.* 167(5): E117-E139

Chatterjee, H. S. 2019. A Basic Introduction to Convolutional Neural Network. https://medium.com/@himadrisankarchatterjee/a-basic-introduction-to-convolutional-neural-network-8e39019b27c4

Chenier, T. and P. Winkielman. 2009. The origins of aesthetic pleasure: Processing fluency and affect in judgment, body, and the brain. In N.M. Skov and O.Vartanian (eds). *Foundations and frontiers in aesthetic:Neuroaesthetic,* pp. 275-289. Baywood Publishing Co, Amityville, NY.

Connoly, B. 2017. Yale archaeologists discover earliest monumental Egyptian hieroglyphs. Yale News (June 20th). https://news.yale.edu/2017/06/20/yale-archaeologists-discover-earliest-monumental-egyptian-hieroglyphs

Costello, S. K. 2011. Image, Memory and Ritual: Re-viewing the Antecedents of Writing. *Cambridge Archaeological Journal.* 21:247-262.

Cowan, N. 2001. The magical number 4 in short-term memory: A reconsideration of mental storage capacity. *Behavioral and Brain Sciences.* Vol. 24 (1): 87–185.

Damerow, P. 2006.The Origins of Writing as a Problem of Historical Epistemology. *Cuneiform Digital Library Journal.* 1: 1-10.

Daniels, P.T. 1996. The study of writing systems. In P.T. Daniels and W. Bright (eds). *The World's Writing Systems,* pp. 3–17. Oxford University Press, New York.

Darnell, J. C. 2009. Iconographic Attraction, Iconographic Syntax, and Tableaux of Royal Ritual Power in the Pre- and Proto-Dynastic Rock Inscriptions of the Theban Western Desert. *Archéo-Nil.* 19: 83-107.

Deacon, T. 1997. *The Symbolic Species.* New York, Norton.

DeFrancis, J. 1989. *Visible speech, the diverse oneness of writing systems.* University of Hawaii Press, Honolulu.

Dehaene, S. 2009. *Reading in the Brain: The New Science of How We Read.* Penguin, New York.

Dehaene, S. 2011. *The Number Sense.* Oxford University Press, New York.

Dehaene, S. and L. Cohen 2011.The unique role of the visual word form area in reading. *Trends in Cognitive Sciences.* 15: 54–262.

Dehaene, S., L. Cohen, M. Sigman and F. Vinckier. 2005. The neural code of written words: a proposal. *Trends in Cognitive Sciences.* 9 (7): 335-341.

Dehaene, S. and G. Dehaene-Lambertz. 2016. Is the brain prewired for letters? *Nature Neuroscience.* 19(9):1192-1193.

Delazer, M., A. Lochy, C. Jenner, F. Domahs and T. Benke. 2002. When writing 0 (zero) is easier than writing O (o): a neuropsychological case study of. *Neuropsychologia,* 40: 2167–2177.

Dehaene, S., F. Pegado, L. W. Braga, P. Ventura, G.N. Filho, A. Jobert et al. 2010. How Learning to Read Changes the Cortical Networks for Vision and Language. *Science.* 330: 1359-1364.

D'errico, F. 1992. Technology, Motion, and the Meaning of Epipaleolithic Art. *Current Anthropology.* 33 (1): 94-108.

D'Errico, F. and I. Colagè. 2018. Cultural Exaptation and Cultural Neural Reuse: A Mechanism for the Emergence of Modern Culture and Behaviour. *Biological Theory.* 13:213–227.

D'Errico, F., C. Henshilwood, G. Lawson, M. Vanhaeren, A-M. Tillier, M. Soressi et al. 2003. Archaeological evidence for the

emergence of language, symbolism, and music–an alternative multidisciplinary perspective. *Journal of World Prehistory.* 17(1):1–70.

De Schotten, M. T., L. Cohen, E. Amemiya, L.W. Braga and S. Dehaene. 2014. Learning to Read Improves the Structure of the Arcuate Fasciculus. *Cerebral Cortex*. 24: 989–995.

Diringer, D. 1968. *The Alphabet.* Vol. 1. Hutchinson, London.

Draggi, V., C. M. Turcu and S. Mriganika. 2001. Stability of Cortical Responses and the Statistics of Natural Scenes. *Neuron*. 32: 1181–1192.

Dreyer, G. 2011. Tomb U-j:A Royal Burial of Dynasty 0 at Abydos. In E. Tweeter (ed.), *Before the Pyramids: The Origins of Egyptian Civilization,* pp.127-136. University of Chicago. Oriental Institute Museums Publication, 33: The Oriental Institute of Chicago. 1181–1192.

Egyptian Ministry of Antiquities. 2018 (14 June). https://www.facebook.com/moantiquities/posts/1811340648911577

Ferrara, S. 2014. Desecrating signs: 'hieroglyphic' writing systems and secondary script inventions. In Y.Galanakis, T. Wilkinson, and J. Bennet (eds). *AΘYPMATA: Critical essays on the archaeology of the Eastern Mediterranean in honour of E. Susan Sherratt*, pp. 73-79. Archaeopress, Oxford.

Forbes, A. and T. R. Crowder 1979. The problem of Franco-Cantabrian abstract signs: agenda for a new approach. *World Archaeology.* 10 (3): 350-366..

Glezer, L. S., J. Kim, J. Rule, X. Jiang and M. Riesenhuber 2015. Adding Words to the Brain's Visual Dictionary: Novel Word Learning Selectively Sharpens Orthographic Representations in the VWFA. *The Journal of Neuroscience.* 35(12): 4965– 4972.

Goldwasser, O. 2015. The Invention of the Alphabet: On 'Lost Papyri' and the Egyptian Alphabet. In C. Rico and C. Attucci. (eds), *Origins of the Alphabet: Proceedings of the First Polis Institute Interdisciplinary Conference*, pp.124–140.: Cambridge Scholars,Newcastle-upon-Tyne.

Görsdorf, J., G. Dreyer, and U. Hartung. 1998. New 14c Dating of the Archaic Royal Necropolis Umm el-Qaab at Abydos (Egypt). Proceedings of the 16th International 14C Conference W. G. Mook and J. van der Plicht (eds). *Radiocarbon.* 40(2): 641-647.

Graff, G. 2018. Predynastic Egyptian iconography: Contributions and relations with the hieroglyphic system's origin. In A. M. Jasink, J. Weingarten and S.Ferrara (eds), *Non-scribal Communication Media in the Bronze Age Aegean and Surrounding Areas: The semantics of a-literate and proto-literate media (seals, potmarks, mason's marks, seal-impressed pottery, ideograms and logograms, and related systems),* pp. 221-231. Firenze University Press, Firenze.

Grainger, J., S. Dufau, M. Montant, C. Ziegler and J. Fagot. 2012. Orthographic Processing in Baboons (*Papio papio*). *Science.* 336: 245-248.

HAARMANN, H. 2005. The challenge of the abstract mind: symbols, signs, and notational systems in European prehistory. *Documenta Praehistorica.* 32: 221-232. https://doi.org/10.4312/dp.32.17

HANNAGAN, T., A. AMEDI, L. COHEN, G. DEHAENE-LAMBERTZ and S. DEHAENE. 2015. Origins of the specialization for letters and numbers in ventral occipitotemporal cortex. *Trends in Cognitive Sciences.* 19 (7): 374-382.

HENSHILWOOD, C. S., F. D'ERRICO, K. L. VAN NIEKERK, L. DAYET, A. QUEFFELEC and L. POLLAROLO. 2018. An abstract drawing from the 73,000-year-old levels at Blombos Cave, South Africa. *Nature.* 562:115–118.

HODGSON. D. 2000. Art, Perception and Information Processing: An Evolutionary Perspective. *Rock Art Research.* Vol. 17 (1): 3-34.

HODGSON, D. 2006. Understanding the Origins of Palaeoart: The Neurovisual Resonance Theory and Brain Functioning. *Paleoanthropology.* http://paleoanthro.org/journal/2006/

HODGSON, D. 2008.The Visual Dynamics of Upper Palaeolithic Cave Art. *Cambridge Archaeological Journal.* 18(03):341–353. doi:10.1017/S0959774308000401

HODGSON, D. 2013. The Visual Brain, Perception, and the Depiction of Animals in Rock Art. *The Journal of Archaeology.* Article ID 342801. http://dx.doi.org/10.1155/2013/342801

HODGSON, D. 2019. *The Roots of Visual Depiction in Art: Neuroarchaeology, Neuroscience and Evolution.* Newcastle-upon-Tyne, Cambridge Scholars.

HODGSON, D. and B. WATSON. 2015. The visual brain and the early depiction of animals in Europe and Southeast Asia. *World Archaeology.* 47(5): 776-791.

HOUSTON, S. D. 2004. The Archaeology of Communication Technologies. *Annual Review of. Anthropology.* 33:223–250

HOUSTON, S. D. 2018. Writing that Isn't: Pseudo-Scripts in Comparative View. *L'Homme.* 227-228: 21-48. https://doi.org/10.4000/lhomme.32974

HUYGE, D. 2008. Côa in Africa: Late Pleistocene Rock Art along the Egyptian Nile. *International Newsletter on Rock Art* (INORA). 51: 1-7. http://www.bradshawfoundation.com/inora/ pdf/51.pd

HUYGE D. M., M. AUBERT, H. BARNARD. W. CLAES, J.C. DARNELL, M. DE DAPPER et al. 2007. Lascaux along the Nile: late Pleistocene rock art in Egypt. *Antiquity.* 81: 313.

JOORDENS, J.C.A., F. D'ERRICO, F. P. WESSELINGH, S. MUNRO, J. DE VOS, J. WALLINGA et al. 2014. *Homo erectus* at Trinil on Java used shells for tool production and engraving. *Nature.* 518: 228–231.

JUDD, T. 2011. What the 'animal' rock art images of the eastern desert of Egypt tell us about the people who drew them. *Rock Art Research. 28*(2): 187-195.

KELLY, P., J. WINTERS, H. MITON and O. MORIN. 2021. The predictable evolution of letter shapes: An emergent script of West Africa recapitulates historical change in writing systems. *Current Anthropology.* 62(6): 669–691.

KENNEDY, J. M. and J. SILVER. 1974. The surrogate functions of lines in visual perception: evidence from antipodal rock and cave artwork sources. *Perception.* 3(3): 313–322.

KOBATAKE, E. and K. TANAKA. 1994. Neuronal Selectivities to Complex Object Features in the Ventral Visual Pathway of the Macaque Cerebral Cortex. *Journal of Neurophysiology.* 71(3): 856-867.

KOURTZI, Z., and N. KANWISHER. 2000. Cortical Regions Involved in Perceiving Object Shape. *The Journal of Neuroscience.* 20(9): 3310–3318.

KUPER, R. and S. KRÖPELIN, 2006.Climate-Controlled Holocene Occupation in the Sahara: Motor of Africa's Evolution. *Science.* 313(5788): 803-807.

LEHKY, S. R., and K. TANAKA. 2016. Neural representation for object recognition in inferotemporal cortex. *Current Opinion in Neurobiology.* 37: 23-35.

LONGCAMP, M., J-L. ANTON, M. ROTH and J-L.VELA. 2003. Visual presentation of single letters activates a premotor area involved in writing. *Neuroimage.* 19:1492–1500.

LÓPEZ-BARROSO, D., M .THIEBAUT DE SCHOTTEN, J. MORAIS, R. KOLINSKY, L. W. BRAGA, A. GUERREIRO-TAUIL et al. 2020. Impact of Literacy on the Functional Connectivity of Vision and Language Related Networks. *NeuroImage.* 213:116722. doi:10.1016/j.neuroimage.2020.116722

LOWE, M. X., J. RAJSIC, S. FERBER and D. B. WALTHER. 2018. Discriminating scene categories from brain activity within 100 milliseconds. *Cortex.* 106: 275-287.

MALOTKI, E. and E. DISSANAYAKE. 2018. *Early Rock Art of the American West: The Geometric Enigma.* University of Washington Press, Seattle.

MCDOUGALL, S., I. REPPA, J. KULIK, and A. TAYLOR. 2016. What makes icons appealing? The role of processing fluency in predicting icon appeal in different task contexts. *Applied Ergonomics.* 55: 156-172.

MILLER, G. A. 1994. The magical number seven, plus or minus two: some limits on our capacity for processing information. *Psychological Review.* 101 (2): 343–52.

NAJOVITS, S. 2004. *Egypt, Trunk of the Tree: A Modern Survey of an Ancient Land.* New York: Algora Publishing.

NEMMI, F., M. A. SCHEL and T. KLINGBERG. 2018.Connectivity of the Human Number Form Area Reveals Development of a Cortical Network for Mathematics. *Frontiers in Human Neuroscience.* doi.org/10.3389/fnhum.2018.00465

OVERMANN, K. A. 2016. Beyond writing: The development of literacy in the Ancient Near East. *Cambridge Archaeological Journal.* 26(2): 285–303.

OVERMANN, K. A. 2017. Thinking Materially: Cognition as Extended and Enacted. *Journal of Cognition and Culture.* 17: 354–373.

OVERMANN, K. A. 2020. Writing System Transmission and Change: A Neurofunctional Perspective. In G. Gabriel, K. A. Overmann and A. Payne (eds). *Signs – Sounds – Semantics: Nature and Transformation of Writing Systems in the Ancient Near East.* Papers presented at the 64th Rencontre Assyriologique Internationale, University of Innsbruck, *16–20 July 2018*, LIT Verlag,Berlin.

OVERMANN, K. A. 2021. A Cognitive Archaeology of Writing: Concepts, Models, Goals. In P. Boyes, P. Steele and N. E. Astoreca (eds). *The social and cultural contexts of historic writing practices,* pp . 55-72. Oxbow Books, Oxford.

PEGADO, F., K. NAKAMURA and T. HANNAGAN. 2014a. How does literacy break mirror invariance in the visual system? *Frontiers in Psychology.* 5 (703): doi:10.3389/fpsyg.2014.00703

PEGADO, F., K. NAKAMURA, L. W. BRAGA, P. VENTURA, G. NUNES FILHO, C. PALLIER et al. 2014b. Literacy breaks mirror invariance for visual stimuli: A behavioral study with adult illiterates. *Journal of Experimental Psychology: General.* 143(2): 887–894.

PEIRCE, C. S. 1974. *Collected Writings.* Harvard University Press, Cambridge, MA.

PETRIE, F. 1912. *The Formation of the Alphabet.* Macmillan, London.

PITT-RIVERS, A. L-F. 1906 [1875]. On the evolution of culture. In J. L. Myres (ed). *The evolution of culture and other essays,* pp. 20-44. Clarendon Press, Oxford.

PIZLO, Z. 2008. *3D Shape: Its Unique Place in Visual Perception.* MIT Press, Cambridge.

PLANTON, S., M. LONGCAMP, P. PÉRANA, J-F. DÉMONETE and M. JUCLA. 2017. How specialized are writing-specific brain regions? An fMRI study of writing, drawing and oral spelling. *Cortex.* 88: 66-80.

POTGIESER, A.R.E., A. VAN DER HOORN and B.M. DE JONG. 2015. Cerebral Activations Related to Writing and Drawing with Each Hand. *PlosOne.* 10(5): e0126723. doi:10.1371/journal.pone.0126723

PULVERMÜLLER, F. 2013. How neurons make meaning: brain mechanism for embodied and abstract symbolic-semantics. *Trends in Cognitive Sciences.* 17(9): 458-70. http://dx.doi.org/10.1016/j.tics.2013.06.004

ROBERTSON, J. S. 2004. The possibility and actuality of writing. In S. D. Houston (Ed.), *The First Writing,* (pp.16-38). Cambridge University Press, Cambridge.

ROELFSEMA, P. R. and F. P. DE LANGE. 2016. Early Visual Cortex as a Multiscale Cognitive Blackboard. *Annual Review of Vision Science.* 2: 131-151.

SAYIM, B. and P. CAVANAGH. 2011. What line drawing reveal about the visual brain. *Frontiers in Human Neuroscience.* 5(118): https://doi.org/10.3389/fnhum.2011.00118

SCHMANDT-BESSERAT, D. 1992a. *Before Writing, Vol. I: From Counting to Cuneiform.* University of Texas Press, Austin.

SCHMANDT-BESSERAT, D. 1992b. *How Writing Came About.* University of Texas Press, Austin

SCHMANDT-BESSERAT, D. 2009. Tokens and Writing: The Cognitive Development. *Scripta.* 145-154.

SHUM, J., D. HERMES, B. L. FOSTER, M. DASTJERDI, V. RANGARAJAN and J. WINAWER. 2013. A Brain Area for Visual Numerals. *Journal of Neuroscience.* 33 (16): 6709-6715.

SMITH, A. 2013. Are Writing Systems Intelligently Designed? In Joshua Engelhardt (ed). *Early Writing and Agency in Archaeology,* pp. 75-94. University Press of Colorado, Boulder

SRIHASAM, K., J. B. MANDEVILLE, I. A. MOROCZ, K. J. SULLIVAN and M.S. LIVINGSTONE. 2012. Behavioural and anatomical consequences of early versus late symbol training in macaques. *Neuron.* Vol. 73(3): 608–619. doi:10.1016/j.neuron.2011.12.022

STAROVIĆ, A. 2005. If the Vinča script once really existed who could have written or read it? *Documenta Praehistorica.* 32: 253-260. https://doi.org/10.4312/dp.32.19

STARRFELT, R. 2007. Selective alexia and agraphia sparing numbers: A case study. *Brain and Language.* 102: 52–63.

STORDEUR, D., D. HELMER, and G. WILLCOX. 1997. Jerf el Ahmar: un nouveau site de l'horizon PPNA sur le moyen Euphrate syrien. *Bulletin de la Société préhistorique française.* 94(2): 282-285.

SZWED, M., S. DEHAENE, A. KLEINSCHMIDT, E. EGER, R. VALABRÈGUE, A. AMADON et al. 2011. Specialization for written words over objects in the visual cortex. *Neuroimage.* 1:56(1): 330-344.

TANAKA, K. 2003. Columns for Complex Visual Object Features in the Inferotemporal Cortex: Clustering of Cells with Similar but Slightly Different Stimulus Selectivities. *Cerebral Cortex.* 13:90–99.

TESTOLIN, A., I. STOIANOV, and M. ZORZ. 2017. Letter perception emerges from unsupervised deep learning and recycling of natural image features. *Nature Human Behaviour.* 1: 657–664.

UNGERLEIDER, L. G. and A. H. BELL. 2012. Uncovering the Visual 'Alphabet': Advances in our understanding of object perception. *Vision Research.* V51(7): 782–799.

VALÉRIO, M. and S. FERRARA. 2020. Rebus and acrophony in invented writing, *Writing Systems Research.* 11(1): 66-93. doi:10.1080/17586801.2020.1724239

VINCKIER, F., S. DEHAENE, A. JOBERT, J. P. DUBUS, M. SIGMAN and L. COHEN. 2007.Hierarchical Coding of Letter Strings in the Ventral Stream: Dissecting the Inner Organization of the Visual Word-Form System. *Neuron.* 55 (1): 143-156.

VON PETZINGER, G. 2017. *The First Signs: Unlocking the Mysteries of the World's Oldest Symbols.*: Simon and Schuster, Atria, NY.

WALTHER, D.B., B. CHAI, E. CADDIGAN, D.M. BECK, and L. FEI-FEI. 2011. Simple line drawings suffice for functional MRI decoding of natural scene categories. *Proceedings of the National Academy of Sciences of the United States of America.* 108(23): 9661–9666.

WANG, L., M. AMALRIC, W. FANG, X. JIANG, C. PALLIER, and S. FIGUEIRA. 2019. Representation of spatial sequences using nested rules in human prefrontal cortex. *NeuroImage.* 186: 245-255.

YUAN, Y. and S. BROWN. 2014. The Neural Basis of Mark Making: A Functional MRI Study of Drawing. *PlosOne.* 9(10): e108628

ZHOU, Y., C. MCBRIDE-CHANG, and N. WONG. 2014. What is the role of visual skills in learning to read? *Frontiers in Psychology (Developmental Psychology).* https://doi.org/10.3389/fpsyg.2014.00776

15

KEYWORDS: Palaeoart – Natural patterns – Semiotic affordances – Origin of graphic Signs

PERCEPTION, COGNITION, AND THE SEMIOTIC AFFORDANCE OF PATTERNS

PAUL BOUISSAC

Abstract. This paper advocates a reconsideration of rock art focusing on the numerous geometric signs that appear in great number in Palaeoart. It elaborates an evolutionary perspective on the adaptive perceptual and cognitive processing of natural patterns that provide a plausible semiotic affordance for the emergence of symbolic communication. The type-tokens relationship and the functionality of consistent differences form a potentially robust ground for encoding vital information when the need for this arises. AI technology can now parse large quantities of data and demonstrate whether clusters of signs within some bounded cultural areas display mere randomness or show significant degrees of systematic organization. The latter case would be a first necessary step toward a tentative decoding of the potential messages these graphic signs may convey and make an important contribution to the archaeology of writing.

Introduction

One of the main enigmas of the prehistoric archaeological record is the presence of geometric signs engraved and painted on the surface of cave walls, boulders, stones, pebbles, and bones. Early recordings of palaeolithic parietal art have focused on easily recognizable animal representations and have given rise to a variety of interpretations regarding their meaning for the humans who carved or painted them. Geometric signs which greatly outnumber "figurative" signs, have attracted less attention and have usually been explained as representations of artifacts (traps, weapons, ornaments) or sexual symbols (schematic vulvae, pubic triangles, erect penises) which are assumed to relate to fertility rituals or erotic visual stimulations. Until recently, there has been precious little attempts to study their mutual positions and combinations beyond the early observation that they are usually collocated in a rather consistent manner with figurative drawings (e.g., Sauvet & Sauvet 1988; Leroi-Gourhan 1992). A few inconclusive attempts have construed some geometric sign clusters as entoptic

Article received: 12 December 2022
Revised I: 30 June 2023
Revised II: 1 July 2023
Accepted: 2 July 2023

(hallucinatory) phenomena (e.g., Lewis-Williams 2002), calendar notations (e.g., Marshack 1972, 1988, 1991), artificial memory systems (e.g., D'Errico 1994), ideogrammatic or magic symbols (e.g., Anati 1994). Mainstream prehistorians have discussed at length the artistic and symbolic aspects of figurative panels and their potential narratives and visionary values, but have, until recently, excluded a priori the possibility that both geometric signs and figurative representations could constitute early forms of scripts, that is, visual signs encoding the meanings articulated in spoken languages or otherwise formalized knowledge that needed to be preserved in a non-perishable form for the purpose of cross-generational transmission or for keeping records of events. If this was indeed the case, it can be assumed that vital information was preserved for the exclusive benefit of the group or some selected individuals rather than as messages to whom it may concern, and, consequently, was encrypted, by necessity or by design, along some rules privy to the relevant addressees.

The purpose of this paper is to review the assumptions behind this epistemological attitude, concerning both language and writing, and to outline a broader, albeit still tentative framework for the semiotic treatment of the visual, graphic data offered by the archaeological record. The following statement by Roy Harris can serve as an incentive to venture on a path that may lead to interesting discoveries: "What is needed – the goal –is [...] clear enough. It must be a semiology which breaks with the old tradition of treating writing systems as indices of cultural progress or cognitive advancement, the tradition which judges writing systems by their 'accuracy' in transcribing the spoken word, the tradition which invariably treats the alphabet, either tacitly or overtly, as the ultimate human achievement in the history of forms of writing. For only then can we feel confident that we have an available semiology of writing which does not merely recycle the old prejudices" (Harris 2000:15).

An evolutionary framework: the cognitive emergence of visual patterns

The perception of differential patterns endowed with some meaning is a vital cognitive adaptation of organisms that have evolved vision. We find indications of the interest of primates for manipulable patterns in a social behavior that has been observed among chimpanzees. Dubbed "leaves grooming" by the researchers who documented and discussed this behavior, it consists of plucking particular leaves from trees and groom them with their mouth or fingers. Some observers have noticed that it is often associated with getting rid of ectoparasites but it has proved to be a more general social behavior in which individuals appear to show a leave to other chimpanzees as an object of particular interest (Wilke et al. 2022; Higgs 2022). All leaves have indeed specific geometric characteristics through both the curve of their contour and the nervure of their surface. Chimpanzees have also been documented to select for consumption some leaves that have therapeutic value, a behavior that is transmitted from mothers to offspring (Newton 1991; Huffman 2001) and is based on the recognition of significant distinct patterns. It can be reasonably assumed that the perception of distinct leaf patterns associated with relevant properties (nutritional or others) is a legacy of the tree-dwelling common ancestor of the primates.

Although comparisons across huge gaps of time and modalities are not scientifically sound, some probes distant from each other (both across species and cultures) may be legitimately considered to be indicative of similar evolutionary pressures, mainly when they point to the cognitive dynamics in a single-family branch such as the primates. The recognition of significant patterns in leaves is of this kind. In this respect and with all due caution, it might be worthy to note that in Romany, the Indo-European language spoken by nomads who originated in Northern India, the word that designates a leaf, *pateran*, also means *sign* (Borrow 1991 [1851]). This is, of course, more generally related to the root that gave the word "pattern" in modern English. These latter remarks are not meant to suggest a form of hypothetical continuum but are nevertheless indicative of the perceptive and cognitive dynamical constraints associated with the production of signs based on differential visual characteristics easily identifiable and manipulable, a step toward abstraction and generalization.

Another source of patterns, mainly when bipedalism became a defining feature of *Homo erectus* who could scan and observe the night sky, is the puzzling diversity of the stars and constellations. Tree-dwellers such as the common ancestors of primates lived in a leafy environment in which attention given to the world above was probably limited to the live-saving detection of flying predators. In addition, like modern apes, they likely were diurnal animals. Once hunters-gatherers roamed the savannah and the steppes, stargazing led inevitably to the identification of patterns of a special kind that were more pregnant as the humans have inherited from their arboreal ancestors a very limited sense of perspective. Consequently, these patterns were bound to appear much closer than they are to the educated modern brains. When the prehistoric night sky was not clouded or blurred by volcanic ashes, the lack of atmospheric pollution undoubtedly made stars and constellations strikingly vivid and proximal. There are still some places in the world such as the Atacama plateau in Northern Chile from which the naked eye can perceive the starry sky with extreme acuity. Making sense of the phenomenal richness of this experience was bound to challenge the nascent cognitive adaptations, even more so since the bright points that are particularly salient during moonless nights are not evenly distributed. Looking for significant patterns necessarily appeared very early in organisms when vision emerged in its many forms across species. We can assume that early humans saw patterns in the sky and strived to find meaning in them. The first step can be expected to have been the iconic identification of objects with which they were familiar in their diurnal environment. Foremost striking are the evocative shapes of the nebulae. There is evidence that the early native populations of the Andes "saw" such darker patterns that looked like mammals and birds, believing for instance that one of these that evokes the outline of a lama was actually the "mother" of all lamas. More abstractly, we can also assume that the perceptive bias that drives us to connect proximal points by lines and create differential geometrical figures that foreground patterns in the sky is an early cognitive adaptation. It is difficult to assess the origin of the names of the constellations -- that is, the grouping of points to form an identifiable pattern – that modern cultures have inherited from literate past civilizations. It is plausible, though, to consider the identification of such patterns as a very early cognitive adaptation because of the unique capacity of these nocturnal "signs" to facilitate orientation on land or sea as a precious, more reliable complement to cues from the landscapes, a kind of natural GPS, so to speak.

It can be expected that the cumulative knowledge acquired from the observation and codification of the night sky became such a precious resource that it was bound to be recorded in one form or another, thus creating vital databases with the means available at the time. This would have been a crucial semiotic step toward the discovered capacity of patterns to refer to or represent relevant aspects of the lifeworld.

Towards an archaeology of writing

The archaeologists who focus on rock art are confronted by abundant painted and engraved geometrical patterns which could be heuristically construed as scripts because of their limited diversity, their relative proportions, and the fact that they often form clusters in which signs appear to be in complementary positions. However, prehistorians have coined the term "scriptoids" to designate these patterns which they tend to consider in isolation as decorative marks or schematized objects and body parts. Even cautious attempts to treat these signs as representing various forms of astronomical computation (e.g., Marshack 1964) or, more generally, systems of notation (e.g., d'Errico 1994) have been met with curiosity and skepticism, and do not seem to have inspired large scale, systematic research programs. In general, mainstream archaeologists claim that these sets of patterns only look like scripts but are not truly so. Their assessment of palaeolithic "abstract signs" as well as, incidentally, "iconic representations" is biased by a set of assumptions they uncritically hold concerning the technology of writing and its history as well as the cognitive capacities of "primitive" humans who populated the earth during the last fifty-thousand years or even much more. As a matter of principle these prehistoric signs are excluded from the emergence and evolution of writing, a technology archaeologists equate with the birth of civilizations which is also the birth of history. From this point of view the expression "prehistoric writing" is an oxymoron. The rationale that is offered for the invention of writing systems is that these devices were created in Egypt, Mesopotamia, and China around 6000 years ago at the most in order to answer the administrative and accounting needs of emerging complex societies. There is obviously a kind of circularity in this argument since societal complexity and writing presuppose each other. In this functionalist, mechanistic approach that construes writing as an administrative tool, created *ab nihilo*, language itself is taken for granted and the reasons for which writing appeared as a parallel system of communication and representation is reduced to an external, basically political, and economic cause. Some archaeologists have early questioned the dominant theory of the invention of writing (e.g., Piette 1905; Petrie 1912) and have retraced the evolution of obviously functional symbolic markings in much deeper time than the few thousands of years that are granted to writing technologies (e.g., Raphael 1947; Forbes and Crowder 1979; Schmandt-Besserat 1992). But retracing over tens of millennia the resilience and evolution of individual marks that could have been either a way of encoding concepts or a way of encoding vocal sounds does not constitute a sufficient ground for assigning a writing status to these marks. It must be demonstrated, in addition, that in a given cultural area these differential marks constitute a semiotic system, that is, a closed set of types whose tokens can be combined according to some syntactic rules in order to convey specific meanings. The primary goal is not to decipher the hypothetical "texts" but to demonstrate whether or not the archaeological record available for a hypothetical "cultural" area exhibits the formal properties of a system that meets the semiotic requirements of a writing system such as iteration. Ultimately, the skepticism that is commonly expressed toward any form of script hypothesis is grounded on fallacious assumptions concerning language itself.

Language is usually perceived by archaeologists from the vantage point of a literate society according to which a language is a stable code which makes it possible to express thought. But this conception of language comes from a state of affairs in which formal spoken languages are anchored in writing systems in spite of blatant discrepancies between spellings and their corresponding oral forms. George Bernard Shaw pointed that out with his celebrated example of what could be an alternate "logical" spelling of "f-i-sh" in English: "gh-o-ti" [gh- like in enough; -o- like in w**o**men; ti like in nation]. We could heuristically fancy a similar sequence composed of figurative drawings. Writing systems have a logic of their own that may or may not be consistent, and are based on *ad hoc* social conventions. Like languages, writing systems do not have a life of their own but live in symbiosis with social groups which can go extinct and precipitate the disappearance of these systems at the same time (Baines et al. 2008). But if these systems were recorded on resilient material, they can be considered as fossils and studied as such like any other paleontological objects according to taphonomy laws and, ultimately, in evolutionary perspective by relating their "skeletons" to each other following cladistic principles. The relationship of a natural or artificial language with its written counterpart is much more complex than the point of view a literate society implies. When we say that a word is pronounced as it is spelled, we actually refer to an arbitrary convention which is time-sensitive as language itself is, but follows its own evolutionary dynamic. Neither spoken language nor its recording in lasting visual marks can escape continuous transformations and re-structuring. As Saussure emphasized in his writings, change is a universal property of spoken languages. Anthropologists who have documented the languages of non-literate cultures have simply recorded the linguistic system of a moment on a long continuous line of language transmission that keeps changing from generation to generation, and often within the same generation since generations overlap. As long as the demography of a population remains within the range that allows its members to stay in close contact, they keep monitoring these changes and keep track of the transformations of their values. They constantly update their language in view of its random changes without being aware of the subtle, cumulative transformations that are constantly going on. But if the demography expands and leads to fissions, the new groups soon use languages which have diverged to a lesser or greater extent. If these groups maintain friendly or hostile relations with each other, and need to keep track of kinship, common myths and ritual which often embody vital information resources, a need for developing some kind of script emerges. As these changes are random and trigger constant re-orderings, languages (or writing systems) that may be related to a common ancestor language (or writing system), new languages and scripts keep emerging. As in all aspects of cultural evolution, transmission with variations, imitation, contagion, protection of information, etc. motivate the constant emergence of scripts. When one considers the mosaic of writing systems that exists in the world or whose existence in the past is documented, there is no reason to suppose that this cultural evolutionary dynamic started suddenly with complex societies.

From the emergence of speech to the craft of scripts

The emergence of articulate speech as an adaptation that enhanced the fitness of hominins is beyond the reach of observation but there seems to be a general consensus based on anatomical and brain capacity data that its earliest forms appeared some two million years ago. Although it is impossible to figure out what kind of languages were spoken by prehistoric populations, there are a few features which can be considered as certain: (i) there is a necessary continuity between these languages and those which are spoken today because there is no absolute beginning in individual languages; (ii) these prehistoric languages kept changing within the groups which were speaking them, and they kept diverging whenever populations branched out; (iii) whenever related populations were separated, even by moderate distances, the "speciation" of their languages had to be dealt with if there was any modicum of interest or advantage attached to the possibility of communicating among groups. One way of controlling linguistic divergence is to rely on agreed upon signs in an ad hoc manner. Whether these visual marks refer to an individual person or landmark, verbal sounds, or concepts, is irrelevant here. A script is not a phonetic code. It is a system of visual differences of patterns that can be mapped onto the differential system of a natural or artificial language. The sharp distinction between so-called ideograms and syllabic or alphabetical systems is a fallacy because most scripts blur the boundaries. The logogrammatic logic, or *rebus* principle, seems to be at the root of most scripts. This is why, in assessing the semiotic status of Pleistocene rock art, figurative and geometric data should not be a priori separated as necessarily distinct, and the possibility that their clustering could form scripts should not be a priori excluded. An article by Sauvet and Wlodarczyk (2008) – probably a translation into English of the authors' earlier piece which appeared in French in 1995 – attempts to uncover the "syntax" of the parietal art of a particular prehistoric cultural area. Typically, they deliberately exclude from their data the geometric signs and they consider only the identifiable representations of the fauna without considering whether bodies are represented whole or in part. They end up by mapping consistent associations between species in various sub-regions of the area considered.

The relationship of writing systems to spoken languages is far more complex full or in than the common-sense view believes. The conceptualization of writing as exclusively the linear representation of spoken language either through syllabic or alphabetic signs is a fallacy. A distinction has been proposed between "semasiography" (the signs are not attached to necessary forms of speech) and lexigraphy (the signs are necessarily attached to forms of speech). For the former, the examples given are petroglyphs, proto-cuneiforms, airport signage, and mathematical notations. For the latter the alphabet is the prime example (e.g., Robinson 2009). But the distinction between these two semiotic modes is very arbitrary. Why should a petroglyph (say a circle with two "arms") not be a syllabic sign, and a letter of the alphabet (say a circle with a vertical "leg") not be a semasiographic sign? Why the letter A which is found in all possible orientations including its earliest occurrences "up-side-down" or even its figurative origin that is the head of a ox, not be a semasiographic sign? The case can be made that all the signs used in all forms of scripts are essentially semasiographic and that, conversely, all semasiographic signs correlates to a lexical or textual segment. It is an illusion to believe that we always apprehend words analytically. The lexical units from which we build meanings are processed as global patterns replete with redundancies. Powell (2009) convincingly shows that jumbling the letters in any word as long as the first and last letters remain in place interferes only minimally with reading: "in what order the letters in a word are the only improatnt tihng...". Powell argues that the purpose, origin, and function of writing are not to represent speech; that writing did not originate in pictures; and that writing systems did not necessarily evolve toward more efficient phonetic representations (Robinson 2009:38). Harris (2000), in his illuminating efforts to rethink writing, points out that a semiological approach implies the following principles: (a) writing is not a mere set of individual marks but a system of differences; (b) the shapes of the marks are irrelevant as long as they can be clearly distinguished from each other; (c) the identity and value of each mark (character) depends on the other marks of the set; (d) the introduction of new marks or the elimination of some existing marks cause a restructuration of the system; (e) the fact that some marks may be observed in the past in different contexts is irrelevant. What counts is the system of marks and their respective differences as they are used at a given moment. The emergence of writing cannot be visualized as a linear history according to which successive improvements would have followed from a one-time invention, It has often been contended with the support of good evidence that the alphabet is no more efficient than other systems which have served their purpose according to their particular logic. It is necessary to approach the question of the archaeology of scripts from a broad disciplinary perspective and an open mind without being constrained by the model of the alphabet considered as the crowning point of an evolution toward progress. Writing systems are ruled by cultural evolutionary dynamics which can be controlled by human agents only to a very limited extent.

Conclusion

In investigating the archaeology of semiotic behavior focused on the earliest forms of potential scripts, there are some basic methodological principles that must be followed: First, it does not make sense to draw conclusion from an open-ended repertory of "scriptoid" patterns gathered from extensive areas across extremely long span of time. Secondly, the contemporariness of closed set of signs must be established. These set may include both figurative and geometrical patterns. Once a corpus meets the criteria of plausibility in view of the taphonomy of the data and the reliability of the dating, its tokens must be calibrated in order to establish a set of distinct types. Then, once sizeable potential "texts" have been transcribed and coded they must be tested with algorithms in order to verify whether they conform to the properties that can be expected from a script. The first goal cannot be the deciphering of rock art data but the demonstration of formal properties determining the logic of collocation of sets of differential signs. Until the latest progress in Artificial Intelligence such as GPT, attempting to complete this task with the recording and computing means that were then available would have been utopian. There is no doubt that the new computing powers that have now become operational can once for all resolve the issue of determining whether the signs, both geometrical and figurative, have been generated by random singular gestures or were instances of systematic, recursive rules of composition that met communicative demands.

Paul Bouissac
University of Toronto, Victoria College
73 Queen's Park Crescent, Toronto ON, Canada M5S 1K7
E-mail: paul.bouissac@utoronto.ca

References

Baines, J., J. Bennet, and S. Houston (eds.) 2008. *The Disappearance of Writing Systems: Perspective on Literacy and Communication.* Equinox Publishing. London.

Bouissac, P. 1994. Art or Script? A Falsifiable Semiotic Hypothesis. *Semiotica* 100 (2/4): 349-367.

Bouissac, P. 2006. Probing Prehistoric Cultures: Data, Dates, and Narratives. *Rock Art Research* 23 (1): 89-96.

Bouissac, P. 2007. The Question of Palaeolithic Scripts. In *Exploring the Mind of Ancient Man.* P.C. Reddy (Ed.). Research India Press. New Delhi.

Bouissac, P. 2008. The Archaeology of Graphic Signs: Evolutionary and Systemic Approaches. In *Pleistocene Palaeoart of the World. Proceedings of XVth UISPP Congress (Lisbon, September 2006).* R.G. Bednarik and D. Hodgston (eds.). British Archaeology Reports, International Series, Vol. 1804 :57-62.

Daniels, P. and W. Bright, (eds.) 1996. *The World's Writing Systems.* Oxford University Press. Oxford.

D'Errico, F. 1994. Notation versus Decoration in the Upper Palaeolithic: A Case-Study from Tossal de la Roca, Alicante, Spain. *Journal of Archaeological Science* 21: 185-200.

DeFrancis, J. 1989. *Visible Speech: The Diverse Oneness of Writing Systems.* The University of Hawaii Press. Honolulu.

Harris, R. 2000. *Rethinking Writing.* Indiana University Press. Bloomington.

Harris, R. 1995. *Signs of Writing.* Routledge. London.

Harris, R. 1986. *The Origin of Writing.* Duckworth. London.

Higgs, E. 2022. Chimpanzees show each other leaves simply to share te experience. IFLscience https://www.iflscience.com/chimpanzees-show-each-other-leaves-simply-to-share-the-experience-66196/

Houston, S., (ed.) 2004. *The First Writing: Script Invention as History and Process.* Cambridge University Press. Cambridge.

Huffman, M. A. 2001. Self-medicative behavior in the African great apes. *BioScience* 51 (8): 651-661.

Marshack, A. 1972. Cognitive Aspects of Upper Paleolithic Engraving, *Current Anthropology* 13 (3-4) (June-October): 445-478.

Newton, P. 1991. The use of medicinal plants by primates: A missing link? *Trends Ecological Evolution* 6 (9): 297-9.

Petrie, W. F. 1912. *The Formation of the Alphabet.* London: Macmillan.

Piette, E. 1905. Les écritures de l'âge glyptique. *L'Anthropologie* 16 (2). 1-11. https://www archive.org/details/anthropologie1619unse/page/n9/mode/2up .

Pope, M. 1999. *The Story of Decipherment: From Egyptian Hieroglyphs to Maya Scripts*, 2nd ed. Thames and Hudson. New York.

Powell, B. B., (2009). *Writing: Theory and History of the Technology of Civilization.* Wiley-Blackwell. Malden.

Rao, P.N., R. Nisha, Y. Mayang, N. Vahia, H. Joglekar, R. Adhikari, and I. Mahadevan 2009. Entropic Evidence for Linguistic Structure in the Indus Script. *Science* 324 (29 May 2009): 1165.

Robinson, A. 2002. *Lost Languages: The Enigma of the World's Undeciphered Scripts.* Mc Graw-Hill. New York.

Robinson, A. 2009. Signs of Meaning. *Science* 324 (3 April): 38-39.

Sauvet, G. and A. Wlodarczyk 2008. Toward a Formal Grammar of the European Palaeolithic Cave Art. *Rock Art Research* 25(2): 165-172.

Sauvet, G. and A. Wlodarczyk 1995. Eléments d'une grammaire formelle de l'art parietal paléolithique. *L'Anthropologie* 99 :193-211.

Schmandt-Besserat, D. 1992. *Before Writing.* University of Texas Press. Austin.

Wilke, C., N. L. Lahiff, K. H. Sabbi, and K. E. Slocombe 2022. Declarative referential gesturing in a wild chimpanzee (*Pantroglodytes)* (November 14, 2022) https://doi.org/10.1073/pnas.2206486119.

16

KEYWORDS: Biofilms – Oxalate – Whewellite – Weddellite – AMS Radiocarbon Dating – Rock Art

A REVIEW OF THE DATING OF OXALATE BIOFILMS ASSOCIATED WITH ROCK ART

Alan Watchman

Abstract: Oxalate minerals in biofilms are often associated with rock art, and are subject to attempts to date that imagery. Here I describe and evaluate various early and recent attempts to determine the age of carbon within oxalate in laminated rock surface coatings. There are issues associated with the identification of the microorganisms, the sources of carbon and the pathways by which carbon is transferred from the environment to a stable oxalate-rich lamination. Caution is therefore required in any attempt to use oxalate minerals to date rock art.

Introduction

Cipriani and Franchi (1958) and Franzini et al. (1984) reported the presence of oxalate minerals in biofilms on rock surfaces in Italy. Later, Del Monte and Sabbioni (1987:114) observed, "the most enigmatic feature of Roman imperial marble monuments exposed to the outside atmosphere is the so-called 'scialbatura', which looks like a superficial film". Publication of the details of the coatings on monuments in Italy led to counter arguments about the origin of the oxalate-rich biofilms (Lazzarini and Salvadori 1989). According to the Italian research, the coatings were either the result of past conservation treatments or formed by the activities of lichen. These conflicting theories were compounded by the discovery in sandstone rock shelters in northern Australia of relatively thick (1-2 mm) oxalate-rich encrustations at sites unsuitable for lichen (no sunlight) and where heritage conservation practices had not been applied (Hughes and Watchman 1983; Watchman 1987).

In 1988, an international conference was held in Milan, Italy to discuss the occurrences, composition and origins of oxalate-rich biofilms on exposed rock surfaces (Alessandrini 1989;

Article received on 15 April 2022
Revised I: 22 April 2022
Revised II: 21 January 2023
Revised III: 2 July 2023
Accepted: 2 July 2023

Watchman 1990a). The conference provided the first opportunity to examine the multiple modes of formation of oxalate biofilms, not only including lichen but also bacteria, fungi and algae. Following the conference, a series of papers progressed research towards developing a method to date rock paintings and engravings associated with oxalate-rich biofilms (Loy et al. 1990; Nelson 1993; Watchman 1990b, 1991; Gillespie 1997). Since those early attempts to use the carbon in oxalate biofilms to date rock surfaces and rock art, the analytical tools and techniques have advanced considerably. The amount of carbon required for AMS ^{14}C dating has been reduced from hundreds of milligrams to micrograms (Russ et al. 1992). Innovations in analytical technology have enabled the identification of minerals in thinly laminated coatings. The chemistry and mineralogy of micro-samples have been facilitated by improvements in non-destructive sample handling and digital data processing of the results of X-ray diffraction (XRD), micro X-ray diffraction general area detector (GADDS), scanning electron microscopy with an energy dispersive spectrometer (SEM-EDS), inductively coupled plasma mass spectrometry (ICP-MS), Fourier transform infrared spectroscopy (FTIR), and Raman spectroscopy applications. Sample collection techniques have progressed from prising off loose encrusted flakes (Loy et al. 1990), to using scalpels (Steelman et al. 2021) and dental burrs using various bits. These tools have been used to grind entire crusts in successive layers (Watchman 1993a; Jones et al. 2017). Another approach was by decomposing the oxalate in laminations using a focused laser (Watchman 1993b, 2000).

As well as on rock surfaces, oxalate minerals occur in plants and the human body. The first report of the presence of calcium oxalate crystals in plants was made in the late 1600s (Leeuwenhoek 1675). Since then, crystals of calcium oxalate have been reported in more than 215 plant families (McNair 1932; Franceschi and Horner 1980). As cited by Richet (1995), Wollaston (1797) and Fourcroy and Vauquelin (1799) identified oxalate mineral accretions in bladder stones.

Since the late 1980s and early 1990s oxalate minerals have been found associated with murals (Rosado et al. 2013) and rock art in Australia (Cole and Watchman 2005; Watchman 1991, 1992, 1993a; Aubert 2012; Jones et al. 2017), Mexico (Watchman et al. 2002; Russ et al. 2017), Texas (Russ et al 1996), South Africa (Mazel and Watchman 1997, 2003), Idaho (Steelman, Rowe et al. 2002, Brazil (Steelman, Rickman et al. 2002), and Montana (Scott et al. 2005).

Attempts have been made to determine the ages of the art by dating the carbon in the oxalate minerals. However, uncertainties regarding the origins of the oxalate minerals have generated concerns about whether the age determinations are reliable. My aim in this paper is to review the issues of the origins, occurrences and ages of oxalate minerals in biofilms associated with rock art.

What is oxalate?

Metallic, crystalline oxalates are widely distributed in rocks, soil, water bodies, plants, and animals. Oxalate compounds constitute a group of relatively rare and scarce carboxylate minerals usually classified as biominerals (Baran 2014). The mono-, di-, and tri-hydrates of calcium oxalate minerals ($Ca(C_2O_4.nH_2O)$), are the most common family of organic minerals in natural environments. Oxalic acid, ethanedioic acid, is the simplest of the dicarboxylic acids and generates a great variety of salts and complexes with all known metallic oxides or bases, and the oxalate anion is a well-known and widely investigated ligand in coordination chemistry. The primary and most stable calcium oxalate mineral is whewellite, $Ca(C_2O_4){\cdot}H_2O$. Weddellite, $Ca(C_2O_4){\cdot}2H_2O$ is subordinate and the rarest is caoxite, $Ca(C_2O_4){\cdot}3H_2O$.

Formation of oxalate biofilms

Relevant to biofilms on rock surfaces and the dating of rock art, calcium oxalate biomineralisation of whewellite and weddellite occurs as a byproduct of mixed microbial communities (Gorbushina 2007), bacteria (Di Bonaventura et al. 1999; Hess et al. 2008; Rusakov et al. 2016), algae (Pueschel 2019), fungi (Gadd et al. 2014), and lichen (Del Monte and Sabbioni 1987; Russ et al. 1996).

A lichen may be described as a symbiotic association between a fungus and a photosynthetic partner, such as green algae or cyanobacteria (Baran 2014). Saxicolous species of lichens occupy rocks as their substrates and are divided into crustose, foliose, and fruticose. Crustose lichens may be subdivided into those living on the surface of the rock (epilithic) and in the interior of the rock (endolithic). Cryptoendolithic forms occupy structural cavities and chasmoendolithic forms inhabit fissures and cracks within rocks, while euendolithic forms actively bore into rocks. The algal or cyanobacterial cells associated with the lichen are photosynthetic and convert atmospheric carbon dioxide into organic carbon compounds such as sugar alcohols and glucose, which are absorbed by lichenised fungal cells (Beazley et al. 2002). The oxalate-rich biofilms found in rockshelters, on cliffs and at many rock art sites are therefore considered biogenic in origin.

Oxalic acid generated from biogenic pathways (Arnott 1995; Friedmann et al. 1972; Zindler-Frank 1976; Jones and Wilson 1986; Pinna 1993) has the potential to create problems with the radiocarbon dating of the carbon in the oxalate salt. The biomineralisation mechanism may consist of an intimate relationship between the oxalic acid-producing thallus of a lichen and the lithological substrate so that the resultant type of insoluble oxalate may contain carbon inherited from the underlying rock (Giordani et al. 2003). For example, on calcareous rocks, such as limestone or dolomite, some carbon might be taken up from the carbonate and incorporated into the calcium oxalate biofilm (Chen et al. 2000). Two approaches are key to understanding the likelihood of this phenomenon: the identity of the microbial community inhabiting the rock surface to determine whether chemical transfer is likely between a lichen and the underlying rock and measuring a series of radiocarbon ages for successive laminations in the biofilm.

Dating of rock art

Oxalate-rich biofilms at rock art sites range in colour depending on the incorporated impurities such as organic matter, micro-charcoal, mineral dust, gypsum and other hydrated salts. The biofilms vary in thickness depending upon the micro-climatic conditions of the habitat for micro-organisms, the age of the encrustation and physical weathering. Biofilms may have been built up in a series of micro-laminations so a micro-stratigraphy develops and in some rock shelters the dusty surfaces formed the background for monochrome and polychrome paintings. However, Del Monte et al. (1987) consider the interface subdividing lichens from the unaltered substrate as extremely irregular, implying oxalate and carbonate interaction (Ariño et al. 1997). Therefore, as Bonazza et al. (2015) suspected, some oxalate patinas cannot be considered as simple laminated deposits on stone, but a transformation of the stone itself. However, Bonazza et al. (2015) counter their own doubts by measuring the carbon isotopic fingerprint of the oxalate salts on two ancient churches on Torcello Island (Venetian Lagoon; δ13C ranging from −22.3‰ to −28.0‰), and attribute the carbon composition of the biofilms as derived almost exclusively from C3 pathway photosynthesis processes. The results obtained demonstrated to them that the calcium oxalate on that monument originated from a biomineralisation process induced by lichen colonisation under specific environmental conditions without any influence of the underlying stone.

Because of its low solubility, the calcium oxalate tends to amass in the thallus of the lichen to form a thin crystalline layer around it (Jackson 1981), and also at the lichen-substrate interface (Ascaso and Galvan1976). Furthermore, after its formation on a rock surface there is no carbon exchange with the substrate (Watchman 1993). Under these ideal conditions, measuring the radiocarbon age of carbon in an oxalate-rich lamination provides a way for estimating the antiquity of a rock painting or engraving.

This approach was first used to determine the ages of oxalate encrustations associated with rock art in Australia (Watchman 1987). The biofilms were observed in rock shelters devoid of direct sunlight, and lichens were dismissed as the potential source of oxalic acid. Instead, fungi were considered as the probable biogenic origin for oxalate formation. Also, at that time, radiocarbon dating using accelerator mass spectrometry (AMS ^{14}C) was in its infancy and grams of pulverised oxalate-rich crusts were combusted into carbon dioxide and converted to graphite (Gove 1992). With refinement in sample preparation and size of the carbon source for ionisation in the spectrometer the quantity of carbon required for measurement of the isotopic activities gradually reduced from grams to milligrams.

Loy et al. (1990) thought they had identified blood proteins in pigments from late Pleistocene art sites in northern Australia, but on re-evaluation, Gillespie (1997: 435) discovered 'the sample measured by Loy et al. (1990) and the new extracts reported by Nelson (1993) could be largely calcium oxalate; it is certainly present as the major organic component in all the rock-skin samples tested and has about the right percentage of carbon.' Furthermore, Gillespie (1997: 436) indicated the permanganate oxidation technique, used in his study, would be a simpler method for obtaining carbon from oxalate alone for AMS dating. He considered it a much more selective approach than total combustion or other extraction by oxygen plasma or focused laser (Russ et al. 1990; Dayton and McDonald 1993). Radiocarbon dating of oxalate biofilms therefore requires an understanding not only of the mechanism of formation of the oxalate minerals, but also the source(s) of carbon, and the possible post-depositional contamination or mobility of carbon between laminations.

In Texas, Russ et al. (1990) demonstrated the direct radiocarbon dating of pictographs using a new technique that overcomes the problem of separating inorganic carbon found in calcite and oxalate coatings from the organic material in the pigments. By using a low-temperature, low-pressure oxygen plasma to selectively oxidise the organic component in the paint they were able to estimate the radiocarbon age of a portion of a pictograph from the Lower Pecos region of southwest Texas to 3,865 ± 100 years BP. The result was consistent with the expected age for the rock art based on archaeological evidence.

Watchman (1993a) made micro-excavations of a laminated crust 2.2 mm thick from a site at Chillagoe, Queensland. The crust contained red and yellow layers of paint sandwiched between dust deposits containing calcium oxalate minerals. A dental burr and a small drill were used to remove successive layers of the laminated crusts to yield multiple powdered samples. Radiocarbon dating of the carbon-bearing oxalate minerals resulted in a conformable series of ages and provided evidence of a 25,000-year-old pictograph. The concordant age estimates for the succession of layers indicated a contemporary atmospheric source of carbon and the lack of contamination from modern sources or from the limestone substrate.

In 1996, fifteen paint samples were collected from parietal art in rock shelters of the uKhahlamba-Drakensberg and eastern Biggarsberg regions of South Africa (Mazel and Watchman 2003). The faded rock paintings with thin mineral biofilms were selected for analysis on the basis of motif and the appropriateness for sample removal. Only partly detached painted flakes of encrusted sandstone were sampled. In the field, it was presumed, from previous research (Mazel and Watchman 1997), that all the encrusted samples contained the carbon-bearing oxalate minerals whewellite and weddellite, and by dating the formation of the biofilms the ages of paintings could be determined indirectly. It was further assumed that the oxalate minerals were the products of microbes that had taken up atmospheric carbon dioxide contemporary with the surface. Lichens were not observed in the dark damp shelters so it was presumed fungi and bacteria contributed to oxalate formation and this was later verified by analysing the stable carbon isotopes. Sunlight was evidently a factor limiting the habitat of ultraviolet-sensitive microorganisms and therefore controlled the distribution of the oxalate-rich encrustations. Radiocarbon ages for oxalate biofilms were obtained after acidification and decomposition using a warm potassium permanganate solution (Gillespie 1997). The results, much older than previously estimated, substantially changed attitudes regarding the antiquity of the parietal art of the region. Acknowledging the limitations of their research Mazel and Watchman (2003: 69) concluded that future investigations should attempt to date specific painted layers, rather than the most readily available pigments and encrustations.

At Jinmium, Northern Territory, Watchman et al. (2000) found the age of oxalate in thin accretions over shallow pecked cupules revealed a much younger age than luminescence dating had led archaeologists to believe (Fullagar et al. 1996; Spooner 1998; Gillespie 1997). Later, Watchman et al. (2004) demonstrated the natural stability of calcium oxalate biofilms over at least 45 ka. This was achieved by measuring consistent and conformable ages of carbon from basal and surface oxalate-rich layers formed on several boulders of fallen slabs of limestone buried beneath sediments at Carpenter's Gap, Western Australia. The oxalate crusts had formed by a similar biogenic process to those found elsewhere in northern Australia (Watchman 2004).

In Brazil, at the Toca do Serrote da Bastiana, Steelman, Rickman et al. (2002) investigated 'calcite' coatings associated with rock paintings and discovered that the mineral accretion also contained whewellite. From their previous experience in Texas (Russ et al. 1996, 1999) the team members realised that the calcium oxalate crusts were ubiquitous as accretions on limestone surfaces (Del Monte and Sabbioni 1987; Scott and Hyder 1993) and were formed from contemporaneous carbon and could be dated (Steelman and Rowe 2002, 2004). Lichen, bacteria and fungi were known to produce oxalate-rich rock crusts (Lazzarini and Salvadori 1989; Di Bonaventura et al. 1999), but the origin of the whewellite at the Brazilian site was not ascertained.

Steelman's team (Steelman, Rowe et al. 2002) used the plasma-chemical extraction method (Russ et al. 1990, 1992) to minimise contamination by oxidising the organic carbon in a sample to leave the carbonate and oxalate minerals unaffected. Calcite and whewellite were found in the accretions covering five motifs, and the carbon in only the oxalate was used for radiocarbon dating after plasma and acid pre-treatment were used to remove organic carbon and the carbonate minerals. The laminated accretions indicated multiple sequential depositions of oxalate, meaning that the radiocarbon determinations for the entire crust sample provided a weighted average of the ages of carbon in the individual layers. The outcome was a much younger age for the rock painting than the age of the archaeological deposits in the floor beneath the painted panel.

In a study of thin sections of rock surface biofilms at the Abrigo de los Oculados on the Iberian Peninsula, Ruiz et al. (2012) observed two calcium oxalate coatings separated by a discontinuity band. They suspected the carbon-bearing layers were probably the result of successive colonisation by lichens or microorganisms, separated by a lapse in time. They did not identify the source of the oxalate, but determined radiocarbon ages for both samples. The results, falling between the middle of the fourth and the first millennium BC, were consistent with the expected chronological range for the iconographic motifs.

Scott et al. (2005) collected a sample of an oxalate accretion overlying a red pigment smear from the Big Log Gulch Pictograph site in the Big Belt Mountains of west-central Montana. It was taken from near an intact (non-flaking) image so as not to damage culturally sensitive rock art. The imagery is characterized by extensive red pigment washes with superimposed images composed of stick-like human figures, zoomorphs, hand-prints, smears, finger lines, mazes, mask-like figures, and geometric designs. The researchers stated that 'calcium oxalate crusts are common as accretions on limestone surfaces. Their source of carbon is assumed to be atmospheric carbon dioxide, meaning that oxalate carbon can be dated using radiocarbon to determine when the oxalate was formed (Beazley et al. 2002).' The researchers did not identify the source of the carbon in the oxalate biofilm, but they measured the radiocarbon age for the carbon in the calcium oxalate accretion overlying a red painting. The result indicated the art was older than 530 cal AD.

Following previous research in Spain (Ruiz et al. 2006; Ruiz López et al. 2009), Ruiz et al. (2012) collected two encrusted rock surface biofilms about 0.3mm thick from Abrigo de los Oculados (Henarejos, Cuenca, Spain). A small overhang of reddish Triassic sandstone formed a small shelter containing a panel of twenty-nine pictographs. The encrusted samples containing calcium oxalate were treated with one millilitre of 1M phosphoric acid (1M = gram-molecular weight of a compound dissolved in 1 litre of water) to remove carbonate and sonicated at room temperature for 30 minutes. Then they were centrifuged for one minute, and the solution removed using a clean Pasteur pipette. The residual solids containing oxalate were rinsed with deionised water and treated with pH 8 phosphate buffer to remove humic acids. The samples were rinsed with deionised water, followed by 1M phosphoric acid, and filtered. The dry materials, essentially containing whewellite and identified using Raman spectra were wrapped in clean aluminium foils, labeled and submitted for AMS radiocarbon analysis.

In addition, two of the biofilms were studied in thin section, and a discontinuity band was observed to separate the oxalate-rich layers. The authors suspected the two layers were probably the result of successive colonisation events by lichens or microorganisms, separated by a time break. Both radiocarbon ages for the oxalate samples indicated the art was painted between 3630-3365 cal BC (2σ) and 910-540 cal BC (2σ); a temporal range consistent with the expected chronology for the iconographic motifs on the Iberian Peninsula.

Smith et al. (2009) used AMS ^{14}C to estimate the age of formation of calcium oxalate biofilms covering archaic engravings at two rock shelter sites in Central Australia (Wanga East and Puritjarra). Constrained by ^{14}C dates of charcoal in sedimentary layers beneath the same engraved slabs the authors demonstrated the rock art is mid-Holocene in age. A similar approach was used to determine the age of paintings in the rock shelters of the Wadeye-Fitzmaurice region of the Northern Territory (Watchman et al. 2010).

In a study of the rock art at the Oxtotitlán Cave, Guerrero, Mexico, Russ et al. (2017) ascertained, using a portable X-ray Fluorescence Spectrometer at the site, that manganese or iron were not present in the black carbon-based pigments. In addition, in the laboratory, they discovered calcium oxalate and calcium sulphate coatings covering the painted rock flakes they had collected. Russ's team presumed the oxalate salts were biogenic in origin, and their ages would correlate with periods of microbial activities on the rock surfaces (Caneva 1993; Russ et al. 2000). However, they were cautious about radiocarbon dating because organic substances can be associated with oxalate formation as a result of the microbial activity (Spades and Russ 2005). Possible contaminants were therefore removed by using the plasma oxidation process prior to dating the carbon in the oxalate salts.

Russ et al. (2017) measured the radiocarbon ages of three oxalate coatings superimposing paintings and two oxalate layers adjacent to the rock art. An attempt to measure the age of the black pigment was unsuccessful because it consisted of asphalt or processed bitumen (lacking radiocarbon because of its geological age). Another dark pigment was identified as a mixture of charcoal and soot and directly radiocarbon dated (1980 ± 190 yr B.P). Carbon in the oxalate layer covering that paint was conformable with its younger stratigraphic position and dated as 1370 ± 30 yr BP. The radiocarbon results of the two oxalate layers, both of which superimposed paint layers, indicated that the paintings were formed before at least 3,195 years ago.

At Ngaut Ngaut, an archaeological site on the Murray River in South Australia, Roberts et al. (2015) investigated the composition of a dark rock coating. Using geological and botanical examination, Raman microscopy, X-ray diffraction, scanning electron microscopy and infrared analyses they found the coating consisted of a mixture of calcite, quartz, gypsum and weddellite. The underlying clastic fossiliferous Mannum Limestone was the likely source of the calcite and quartz whereas gypsum presumably crystallised from ground water. The researchers presumed that the oxalate mineral, weddellite had precipitated from the reaction of calcite with oxalic acid derived from algae. Samples of the dark coating, initially thought to be soot from fires, were not radiocarbon dated and the algae not identified. Subsequent research along the cliffs in the region ascertained that a grey-white oxalate-rich coating over the orange-brown limestone cliffs, presumably resulting from the activities of algae or lichen, began to form at least 15,000 years ago (C. R. Twidale pers. comm.).

In a study of rock art in western Arnhem Land, Australia, Jones et al. (2017) determined the ages of oxalate salts incorporated in thin (< 50 μm) rock surface biofilms associated with the Northern Running Figures (NRFs) style of rock paintings (Lewis 1988; Chaloupka 1993). The NRFs are found in rock shelters of the sandstone escarpment and outlying rock stacks surrounding the floodplains of the East Alligator River. They measured radiocarbon ages for the carbon in oxalate in unlaminated dusty encrustations under and over the painted figures and then also determined the ages of the carbon in the residues. Their samples were obtained by the mechanical grinding of the gritty biofilms and then the bulk powders were treated chemically before dating. Warm sodium hydroxide was used initially to remove 'organic acids and reactive biological components as well as non-acid soluble paint solids.' After rinsing, the samples were subjected to '6M HCl at 60 °C, to remove possible carbonates and to dissolve whewellite and weddellite.' The resulting solutions were centrifuged, the supernate decanted, dried and the carbon converted into graphite targets for dating using AMS ^{14}C (Jones et al. 2017: 85).

Comparing the ages for carbon in oxalate with the residues, seven of nine samples gave older residue ages than the oxalate fractions. Inexplicably, in two samples the residue ages were younger than the oxalate fractions. The authors could not explain why there were noticeable radiocarbon age offsets (approximately 4500 years older and 1770 years younger) between the non-reactive constituents and the calcium oxalate components (Jones et al. 2017, Table 2). However, the authors did not use XRD or FTIR to verify the mineralogical compositions of the two fractions (contrast with Steelman et al. 2021). One likely scenario is for the inclusion of non-reactive dust aerosol particles in the biofilms. Presumably some walls formed at different times during the formation of the rockshelter, so certain parts of rock art panels are much older than others. During dry periods dust was blown into the shelter and settled on the stable rock faces. Those surfaces became habitats for microorganisms (fungi, bacteria) during moist periods. This speculative explanation requires testing to quantify the nature and origins of the inclusions in the biofilms.

Jones et al. (2017: 88) concluded that the NRF style was painted from 9400 cal. BP through to 6000 cal. BP. The authors also demonstrated that the source of carbon in the calcium oxalate biofilms was not related to the carbon compounds in the residue fraction. Furthermore, they showed that the traditional acid-base-acid (ABA) pre-treatment of bulk mineralised biofilms was unlikely to produce correct age estimates for the associated rock art imagery.

Steelman et al. (2021) dated the carbon in oxalate in biofilms associated with Pecos River style paintings at Eagle Cave at Langtry, Texas. They collected partly detached flakes from high on the shelter wall of three Pecos River style anthropomorphic figures associated with thin biofilms. The rock surface coatings under and over a layer of paint consisted mainly of quartz, calcite, gypsum and whewellite. They used individual sterile scalpel blades to scrape successive sub-samples of the outer mineralised layer of oxalate, the paint and the basal biofilm beneath the paint (thickness of 170 to 850 μm for the accretion and paint layers). They washed the painted and background samples using warm (50°C) 1M sodium hydroxide to remove any potential humic acid contamination. The solid samples were then dried prior to plasma oxidation to remove other organic matter. The powdered oxalate samples from the overlying and underlying layers were washed repeatedly using warm 1M phosphoric acid in an ultrasonic water bath to remove calcite. For the outer and underneath oxalate layers the low-temperature plasma oxidation technique was used to remove any organic contamination that might have been included (Steelman and Rowe 2002, 2004; Russ et al. 2017). After the carbonate and organic carbon had been removed, the purified oxalate sample was combusted, graphitised, and dated using AMS ^{14}C.

The procedures adopted for dating the painted samples and oxalate accretions ensured no sample material was lost during the dating process. XRD and FTIR spectroscopy were carried out before and after acid treatment to confirm the complete removal of carbonate minerals and ensure the continuing presence of oxalate minerals (Steelman, Rickman et al. 2002; Russ et al. 2017).

Radiocarbon assays obtained for the overlying accretion layers were younger than the age of the carbon in the paint, and older beneath the paint. The chronological stratigraphy of the two biofilm accretions and the paint layer supported the validity of the tandem approach to dating the rock art. The significant results of the dating study at Eagle Cave arose from the combination of an oxalate minimum age for oxalate overlying pigment, measurement of a direct age for the organic constituents in the paint layer and a maximum age for the underlying oxalate.

In the Kimberley region of Australia, Green et al. (2021) reported the composition and internal laminated structure of mineral accretions collected from sandstone rock shelters associated with rock art. They presented radiocarbon age measurements for carbon in the calcium oxalate fractions as well as from the inert residues of 28 sub-samples from 14 darkly laminated biofilms measuring up to 5 mm in thickness. The oxalate-rich biofilms have formed in rock shelters eroded in orthoquartzite of the King Leopold and Warton Sandstone Formations.

Using microscope imaging of cross-sections of the biofilms they identified alternating light- and dark-coloured layers of varying thickness (typically ~30 to 150 μm) consisting of compacted fine-grained and silty laminations. Well-defined layers were marked by characteristic colour, thickness, grain size, porosity, and mineral composition and apparently correlated across surfaces in well-defined relationships. However, oxalate-rich biofilms directly associated with paintings or engravings were not sampled or dated.

By applying micro-computed tomography (micro-CT) they were able to assess the internal structure and porosity of the micro-laminated biofilms in three dimensions. Often, the horizontal, high-porosity features were laterally continuous in three dimensions and were not disrupted by fissures or otherwise linked to the modern surface, demonstrating the minimal likelihood for the introduction of extraneous carbon into the buried laminations. Some of the observed, infrequent small fissures near the surface did not penetrate to the bottom of the biofilm and were usually mineralised. The discontinuous features were therefore considered unlikely to have contributed younger carbon-bearing contaminants to the sub-surface layers. X-ray diffraction (XRD) analysis of the bulk mineralogy revealed whewellite and gypsum as the major mineral components.

Micro-milling of individual layers in 14 separate biofilms produced sub-sample powders the radiocarbon ages of which indicated deposition of oxalate between 43.1 and 0.2 k years BP. Ages measured on the acid-soluble fractions (representing carbon in oxalate), were in the correct stratigraphic sequence from oldest on the sandstone substrate to youngest at the present surface. In addition, two sub-samples milled from a single layer also returned consistent ages, providing evidence of the reliability of dating the carbon in oxalate.

Identification of the microorganisms

In Texas, Russ et al. (1996) observed the morphology of the pale to reddish brown oxalate-rich biofilm exhibited botryoidal and spherical protuberances, resembling the surface of *Aspicilia calcarea*. The rock surface coating was thin (0.5-1.0 mm). Most of the biofilms consisted of a single layer, although several were observed with distinct continuous stratification. The components were micro-crystalline whewellite, tabular gypsum, quartz, calcite and traces of clay. Apart from the lichen species on the limestone in Texas, no other microorganisms associated with oxalate biofilms at rock art sites have been identified. Presumably, and because the rock surfaces are within the overhanging umbrella of rocks, lichen do not inhabit the rock art panels in rock shelters. It would therefore seem more likely for bacteria and fungi to live on the moist dusty surfaces protected from direct sunlight within rock shelters.

The natural dihydrate form of calcium sulphate, $CaSO4.2H_2O$ (gypsum), was found to be effectively solubilised by both *Aspergillus niger* and *Serpula himantioides* (Gharieb et al. 1998).

When the fungi were grown on malt extract agar medium, modified by the addition of up to 1% (weight/volume) of gypsum, solubilisation activity was evident by the appearance of a clear halo around and under the growing colonies. The halos were found subsequently to enclose concentric rings of newly formed crystalline precipitates of calcium oxalate.

In Macerata Province, Italy, Di Bonaventura et al. (1999) collected aseptic samples of bacterial communities from stone surfaces of two historical buildings, located at L' Aquila (limestone) and Camerino (sandstone). Their aim was to ascertain the production of oxalic acid and other organic acids by incubating the micro-organisms under different physical conditions *in vitro* for seven months. The samples were inoculated into an enriched medium containing glucose and kept at room temperature either in the dark or in the light. High-performance liquid chromatography (HPLC) analyses were carried out periodically to measure the acidic components produced by the living cultures. The researchers characterised and classified the isolated bacterial strains according to Bergey's Manual of Determinative Bacteriology (Buchanan and Gibbons 1989). Several bacteria were isolated from both cultures, among them were species identified as *Alcaligenes* sp., *Actinomyces* sp., *Bacillus* sp., *Flavobacterium* sp., *Micrococcus* sp., and *Nocardia* sp.

Di Bonaventura et al. (1999) found that organic acids were released by incubating the bacterial populations isolated from stone surfaces. Their results gave indirect evidence of the events likely to account for the accumulation of calcium oxalates on a monument's surface. HPLC analyses indicated that all mixed cultures produced oxalic acid in different amounts. Other organic acids, such as lactic, citric, pyruvic, succinic, acetic, and propionic acid were also excreted. After seven months, they observed that the total amount of oxalic acid produced in the dark was higher than in the light. The results demonstrated the production and release of differing amounts of oxalic acid by the microbial populations they examined. Furthermore, the positive correlation at L' Aquila between oxalic acid and the citric, pyruvic, succinic, and acetic acids pointed to an aerobic metabolism of the cultures, possibly related to the Krebs cycle. However, oxalic acid production was also correlated with lactic and propionic acids, so fermentation was also implied. In contrast, when cultures from Camerino were isolated and incubated in light the oxalic acid only correlated significantly with propionic acid, and therefore indicated the lack of involvement of Krebs cycle intermediates. The same cultures, when incubated in the dark, gave good correlations between oxalic acid and the presence of pyruvic, citric, and acetic acids. However, succinic, and lactic acids were not correlated with oxalate.

The very low ionization constant characterising calcium oxalates (whewellite and weddellite), found in oxalate films are not present to the same extent in the calcium salts of other organic acids, and indicate the potential for differential leaching, leading to increasing concentrations of oxalates while the salts of other organic acids are gradually removed. When aerobic or anaerobic metabolism conditions exist and favour the release and accumulation of organic acids then oxalate accumulation is enhanced.

In terrestrial ecosystems, fungi are ubiquitous components of microbial communities (Burford et al. 2003) and oxalates are not the only crystalline precipitates associated with fungal hyphae and lichen thalli. The precipitation of carbonates on fungal hyphae, particularly calcite (CaCO3), has also been reported *in situ* in calcareous soils and calcretes (Kahle 1977; Klappa 1979a, b; Callot et al. 1985a, b; Bruand and Duval 1999). Large amounts of oxalic, citric and gluconic acids are produced by *Penicillium frequentans* in liquid cultures. The acids cause extensive deterioration of clay silicates, as well as micas and feldspars from both sandstone and granite (de la Torre et al. 1993). The oxalate-excreting fungus *Hysterangium crassum* was found to weather clay minerals *in situ* (Cromack et al. 1979).

Later, Hess et al. (2008) identified twenty species of microbes in thirteen samples of oxalate coatings that they had collected from eight sites in the Lower Pecos Region of southwestern Texas. *Bacillus* sp. and *Corynebacterium urealyticum* were the common microbes in the Texas samples, together with the lichen, *Solenspora* sp. Their results, matching similar conclusions drawn from research on Italian stone sculptures (Di Bonaventura et al. 1999), indicated that multiple micro-organic sources of oxalic acid contributed to the production of the oxalate-rich rock coatings. They concluded that the collection of bacteria generated from a single sample to assess oxalate activity was definitely needed.

Larsen et al. (2009) were able to characterise the unique stable carbon isotopic (δ13C) fingerprints of samples of bacteria, fungi and plants using their complex amino acids. Using gas chromatography-combustion-isotope ratio mass spectrometry (GC-C-IRMS), they measured $\delta^{13}C$ of amino acids generated from C3 plants, fungi, and bacteria they had collected and isolated from a boreal forest in interior Alaska, USA. The microorganisms were cultured under amino-acid-free conditions and identified based on DNA sequences. This new approach for the identification of microorganisms may prove invaluable for identifying the sources of oxalate biofilms on rock surfaces associated with rock art.

Biosynthesis of oxalic acid and the formation of oxalates is a property found in a wide variety of free-living and symbiotic fungi (Gadd et al. 2014). Calcium oxalate can be associated with hyphae, as well as strands, cords and rhizomorphs, fruiting bodies, lichen thalli, and mycorrhizal systems in soil, decomposing plant biomass, and rocks as well as in the built environment and rock and mineral-based or mineral-containing cultural heritage.

Discussion

As pointed out by Bednarik (1996, 2002) accurate and reliable measurements of the radiocarbon age of carbon-bearing rock surface coatings depend on knowing the source(s) and history of the carbon analysed (Hedges et al. 1997). A sample containing carbon compounds derived from different sources may not provide a reliable age because a younger component may have contaminated a more ancient constituent (Beck et al. 1998). The different components may be of the same age, but there is no way of knowing their relationship unless each fraction's origin and history is established. One way around this problem with biofilms is to eliminate all contaminants and determine the age of the carbon in the oxalate mineral.

In the early history of the dating of oxalate, Gillespie (1997) recommended the decomposition of warm acidified solutions using permanganate. The method followed pre-treatment of a sample by washing in 2M H_2SO_4 to remove carbonates and other soluble material, rinsed with distilled water, covered in further acid solution, warmed to ~50°C, evacuated to remove carbon dioxide from the air and treated with 0.1M $KMnO_4$ solution. The resulting carbon dioxide was collected, converted to graphite and measured using AMS ^{14}C.

Later, Jones et al. (2017: 85) treated the powders from gritty biofilms with warm sodium hydroxide to remove 'organic acids and reactive biological components as well as non-acid soluble paint solids.' After rinsing with distilled water, the samples were subjected to '6M HCl at 60°C, to remove possible carbonates and to dissolve whewellite and weddellite.' The resulting solutions were centrifuged, the supernate decanted, dried, and combusted in pure oxygen and the carbon converted into graphite targets for radiocarbon dating. In contrast, Steelman et al. (2021) removed carbonates from their samples by using acid treatment and then applied plasma oxidation to remove organic contamination prior to radiocarbon dating the carbon in oxalate.

Green et al. (2021) adopted the method of Jones et al. (2017) and estimated the age of oxalate-rich crusts they examined. The biofilms may indeed be 40,000 years old because considerable time would have been required to deposit dust and oxalate-rich accretions 5mm thick. However, the most troubling issue with Green et al. (2021) and Jones et al. (2017) is the inconsistent relationship between the ages of carbon in the oxalate fractions versus the residues. The authors have not adequately explained the reason why this has occurred.

Green et al. (2021) discuss the radiocarbon ages for the oxalate laminations and their respective residues, but fail to explain why a substantially younger age is obtained for a residue fraction than in both the corresponding acid-soluble fraction and the acid-soluble fraction from the subsequent layer. Green et al. (2021: 10) say, 'the carbon in the residue fraction cannot originate from material deposited on the accretion surface during a hiatus in oxalate deposition between stratigraphically sequenced layers.' In addition, 'The absence of sequenced radiocarbon ages on residue fractions in accretions that do demonstrate stratigraphically consistent ages for the acid-soluble mineral fractions indicate that the residue material may simply not be suitable for radiocarbon dating, potentially demonstrating open-system behaviour and unreliable ages.'

The results and arguments supporting consistent sequences of oxalate ages for the laminated biofilms are worrying. Three of the samples (J030, H739 and J040; Green et al. 2021) with stratigraphically conformable sequences of progressively older oxalate median ages with depths contain residual material the ages of which remains approximately constant throughout the entire encrustation. One alternative explanation is for microorganisms to have formed progressively younger layers of oxalate in a thick deposit of generally homogeneous dust. Another possibility is for fractionation of carbon isotopes either during metabolic processes by the unknown microorganisms or in the aggressive acid pre-treatment of the samples (Jones et al. 2017).

The issue is compounded by the results for H076 where carbon in the residue of the middle micro-unit is 7590 years BP. It is sandwiched between oxalate of the micro-unit above (19,495 years BP) and below (35,905 years BP). How is it possible if, as Green et al. 2021 propose, there has not been any transfer of younger components from the surface into the underlying layers?

Green et al. (2021) cite Dumoulin et al. (2020) for the treatment of oxalate samples used for dating because they too used 6M HCl. Whereas, Green et al. (2021) used stable carbon isotopes (δ 13C values of -8 to -15 ‰) to confirm a microbiological pathway for the origin of the oxalate in their laminated biofilms, but did not identify the microorganisms, Jones et al. 2017 presumed a micro-organic origin. On the other hand, Dumoulin et al. (2020) dated weddellite-rich crusts formed from the urine of the rock hyrax (Prinsloo 2007), not oxalate produced by microorganisms.

One potential issue with such vigorous acid dissolution methods used by Jones et al. (2017) and Green et al. (2021) is the possibly of dissolving carbon from other (non-oxalate) sources. It is noteworthy that the composition of the oxalate-soluble fraction was not monitored in their study in comparison to previous studies (Cole and Watchman 2005; Russ et al. 2017). The integrity of the method used by Green et al. (Prinsloo 2007) has never been tested by repeating the acid leach for additional hours and measuring their radiocarbon ages to see if longer acid dissolution continues to aggregate carbon, possibly changing the fractions and the age determinations obtained from them.

Conclusions

Recent investigations reveal the possibilities of providing age estimates for the substrates and overlying layers of oxalate-rich biofilms associated with rock art. Tightly bracketing carbon in laminations under and over paintings may be the most appropriate way to estimate when they were painted, especially when the paint itself does not contain any suitable dating component.

The challenges facing future researchers are to identify the sources of carbon incorporated into the oxalate minerals as well as understand the pathway by which microorganisms have transferred the carbon from the environment to the biofilm. A further issue is in pre-treating a sample to minimise impurities. Microorganisms that live on the surface of biofilms are removed as part of the pre-treatment process, so do not contribute modern carbon contamination. Studies of cross sections of laminated biofilms will reveal possible fracture fillings and other problems with irregular accumulations of oxalate. This should eliminate the risk that modern oxalate producing microorganisms have influenced the measurement of the age of carbon in an oxalate lamination.

The discordant results of the studies by Jones et al. (2017) and Green et al. (2021) cast doubts about the use of severe acidic pre-treatment of oxalate-rich samples. It would seem preferable to selectively remove possible organic contaminants by low temperature and low pressure plasma, then chemical dissociation of carbonate minerals so as to date only the carbon in oxalate salts by either direct thermal decomposition or oxidation in warm acidified permanganate. By using such procedures, it may be possible to determine the ages of rock art previously considered impossible to date.

Acknowledgements

Dr Graeme Ward provided critical comments on an early draft for which I am grateful.

Dr Alan Watchman
1 Ross Court, Coromandel Valley SA 5051
Email: authoralanwatchman@gmail.com

References

Alessandrini, A. 1989. *The Oxalate Films, Origin and Significance in the Conservation of Works of Art.* Centro Congresso Cariplo, Milan.

Ariño, X., A. Gomez-Bolea and C. Saiz-Jimenez 1997. Lichens on ancient mortars. *International Biodeterioration and Biodegradation* 40: 217-224.

Arnott, H. J. 1995. Calcium oxalate in fungi. In S. R. Khan (ed.), *Calcium oxalate in biological systems.* pp. 73–111. CRC Press, Boca Raton, FL.

Aubert, M. 2012. A review of rock art dating in the Kimberley, Western Australia. *Journal of Archaeological Science* 39(3): 573-577.

Baran, E. J. 2014. Review, Natural oxalates, and their analogous synthetic complexes. *Journal of Coordination Chemistry* 67(23-24): 3734-3768.

Bednarik, R. G. 1996. Only time will tell: a review of the methodology of direct rock art dating. *Archaeometry* 38(1): 1–13.

Bednarik, R. 2002. The dating of rock art, a critique. *Journal of Archaeological Science* 29: 1213–1233.

Beazley, M., R. Rickman, D. Ingram, T. Boutton and J. Russ 2002. Natural abundances of carbon isotopes (^{14}C, ^{13}C) in lichens and calcium oxalate pruina, implications for archaeological and paleoenvironmental studies. *Radiocarbon* 44(3): 675–683.

Beck, W., D. J. Donohue, J. T. Jull, G. Burr, W. S. Broecker, G. Bonani, I. Hajdas and E. Malotki 1998. Ambiguities in Direct Dating of Rock Surfaces Using Radiocarbon Measurements. Science 280 (5372): 2132-2139. DOI: 10.1126/science.280.5372.2132.

Bonazza, A., C. Natali, N. Ghedini, C. Vaccaro and C. Sabbioni 2015. Oxalate Patinas on Stone Monuments in the Venetian Lagoon, Characterization and Origin. *International Journal of Architectural Heritage* 9: 542–552.

Buchanan, R. R, and N. E. Gibbons 1989. *Bergey's manual of determinative bacteriology.* Williams and Wilkins, Baltimore, U. S. A.

Burford, E., M. Fomina, and G. Gadd 2003. Fungal involvement in bioweathering and biotransformation of rocks and minerals. *Mineralogical Magazine* 67(6): 1127-1155. doi:10.1180/0026461036760154.

Bruand, A. and O. Duval 1999. Calcified fungal filaments in the petrocalcic horizon of Eutrochrepts in Beauce, France. *Soil Science Society of America Journal* 63: 164169.

Callot, G., A. Guyon and D. Mousain 1985a. Interrelation entre aiguilles de calcite et hyphes myce´liens. *Agronomie* 5: 209-216.

Callot, G., D. Mousain and C. Plassard 1985b. Concentrations de carbonate de calcium sur les parois des hyphes myce´liens. *Agronomie* 5: 143-150.

Klappa, C.F. 1979a. Lichen stromatolites: criterion for subaeial exposure and mechanism for the formation of laminae calcretes (caliches). *Journal of Sedimentary Petrology* 49: 387-400.

Klappa, C.F. 1979b. Calcified filaments in Quaternary calcretes: organo-mineral interactions in the subaerial vadose environment. *Journal of Sedimentary Petrology* 49: 955-968.

Cromack, K. Jr., P. Solkins, W. C. Graustein, K. Speidel, A. W. Todd, G. Spycher, C. Y. Li and R. L. Todd 1979. Calcium oxalate accumulation and soil weathering in mats of the hypogeous fungus Hysterangium crassum. *Soil Biology and Biochemistry* 11: 463-468.

Caneva, G. 1993. Ecological Approach to the Genesis of Calcium Oxalate Patinas on Stone Monuments. *Aerobiologia* 9(2–3): 149–156.

Chaloupka, G. 1993. *Journey in Time, The 50,000-year Story of the Australian Aboriginal Rock Art of Arnhem Land.* Reed New Holland, Sydney.

Cipriani, C. and L. Franchi 1958. Sulla presenza di whewellite fra le croste di alterazione di monumenti romani. *Bollettino del Servizio geologico d'Italia* 79: 555-556.

Chen, J., H-P. Blume and L. Beyer 2000. Weathering of rocks induced by lichen colonization — a review. *Catena* 39: 121–146

Cole, N. and A. Watchman 2005. AMS dating of rock art in the Laura Region, Cape York Peninsula, Australia, protocols and results of recent research. *Antiquity* 79: 661–678.

Dayton, L. and M. McDonald 1993. The atomic age of cave art. *New Scientist* 137: 34-37.

Del Monte, M. and C. Sabbioni 1987. A Study of the Patina Called 'Scialbatura' on Imperial Roman Marbles. *Studies in Conservation* 32(3): 114-121.

Di Bonaventura, M. P., M. Del Gallo, P. Cacchio, C. Eercole and A. Lepidi 1999. Microbial Formation of Oxalate Films on Monument Surfaces, Bioprotection or Biodeterioration? *Geomicrobiology Journal* 16: 55-64.

Dumoulin, J., M. Lebon, I. Caffy, G. Mauran, A. Nankela, D. Pleurdeau, E. Delqué-Količ, C. Moreau, M.

Perron, M. Sieudat, B. Thellier and L. Beck 2020. Calcium oxalate radiocarbon dating, preliminary tests to date rock art of the decorated open-air caves, Erongo Mountains, Namibia. *Radiocarbon* 62(6): 1551-1562.

De La Torre, M. A., Gomez-Alarcon, G., Vizcaino, C. and M. T. Garcia 1993. Biochemical mechanisms of stone alteration carried out by filamentous fungi living on monuments. *Biogeochemistry* 19: 129-147.

Fourcroy, A. F. and N. L. Vauquelin 1799. Premier mémoire pour servir a l'histoire naturelle, chimique et médicale, de l'urine humaine. *Annales de Chimie* 31: 48-71.

Franceschi, V. R. and H. T. Horner, JR 1980. Calcium Oxalate Crystals in Plants. *Botanical Review* 46 (4): 361-427.

Franzini, M., C. Gratziu and E. Wicks 1984. Patine ad ossalato di calcio su monumenti marmorei. *Societ d'Italiana Mineralogia e Petrografia* 39: 59-70.

Friedmann, E. I., W. C. Roth, J. B. Turner and R. S. McEwen 1972. Calcium oxalate crystals in the aragonite-producing green alga Penicillus and related genera. *Science* 177: 891–893.

Fullagar, R. L. K., D. M. Price, and L. M. Head 1996. Early human occupation of northern Australia, archaeology and thermoluminescence dating of Jinmium rock-shelter, Northern Territory. *Antiquity* 70: 751–73.

Gadd, G. M., J. Bahri-Esfahani, Q. Li, Y. J. Rhee, Z. Wei, M. Fomina and X. Liang 2014. Oxalate production by fungi: significance in geomycology, biodeterioration and bioremediation. *Fungal Biology Reviews* (2014), http://dx.doi.org/10.1016/j.fbr.2014.05.001

Gharieb, M., J. Sayer and G. Gadd 1998. Solubilization of natural gypsum (CaSO4.2H2O) and the formation of calcium oxalate by *Aspergillus niger* and *Serpula himantioides*. *Mycological Research* 102(7): 825-830. doi:10.1017/S0953756297005510

Gillespie, R. 1997. On human blood, rock art and calcium oxalate, further studies on organic carbon content and radiocarbon age of materials relating to Australian rock art. *Antiquity* 71(272): 430–437.

Giordani, P., P. Modenesi and M. Tretiach 2003. Determinant factors for the formation of the calcium oxalate minerals, weddellite and whewellite, on the surface of foliose lichens. *The Lichenologist* 35(3): 255-270.

Gorbushina, A. 2007. Life of the Rocks. *Environmental Microbiology* 9(7): 1613–1631.

Gove, H. E. 1992. The History of AMS, its Advantages over Decay Counting, Applications and Prospects. In Taylor, R. E., A. Long and R. R. Kra (eds), *Radiocarbon After Four Decades*, pp. 7-15. Springer, New York, NY.

Green, H., A. Gleadow, V. A. Levchenko, D. Finch, C. Myers, J. MCGovern, P. Heaney and R. Pickering 2021.

Dating correlated microlayers in oxalate accretions from rock art shelters: New archives of paleoenvironments and human activity. *Science Advances* 7 (33): eabf3632.

Hedges, R., C., Ramsey, G. Van Klinken, P. Pettitt, C. Nielsen-Marsh, A. Etchegoyen, J. O. Fernandez

Niello, M. T. Boschin and A. Llamazares 1997. Methodological Issues in the 14C Dating of Rock Paintings. *Radiocarbon* 40(1): 35-44.

Hess, D., D. J. Coker, J. M. Loutsch and J. Russ 2008. Production of oxalates in vitro by microbes isolated from rock surfaces with prehistoric paints in the lower Pecos region, Texas. *Geoarchaeology* 23(1): 3–11.

Hughes, P. J. and A. L. Watchman 1983. The deterioration, conservation and management of rock art sites in Kakadu

National Park. In D. Gillespie (ed.), *The rock art sites of Kakadu National Park, some preliminary research findings for their conservation and management*, pp. 37–86. Special Publication 10, Australian National Parks and Wildlife Service, Canberra.

JACKSON, D. W. 1981. An SEM study of lichen pruina crystal morphology. *Scanning Electron Microscopy* 3: 279–284.

JONES, D. and M. J. WILSON 1986. Biomineralization in crustose lichens. In B. Leadbeater and H. Riding (eds), *Biomineralization in the lower plants and animals*, pp. 91–105. Oxford University Press, Oxford, UK.

JONES, T., V. LEVCHENKO, P. KING, U. TROITZSCH, D. WESLEY, A. WILLIAMS and A. NAYINGULL 2017. Radiocarbon age constraints for a Pleistocene–Holocene transition rock art style, The Northern Running Figures of the East Alligator River region, western Arnhem Land, Australia. *Journal of Archaeological Science Reports* 11: 80–89.

KAHLE, C. F. 1977. Origin of subaerial Holocene calcareous crusts: role of algae, fungi and sparmicristisation. *Sedimentology* 24: 413-435.

LARSEN, T., D. L. TAYLOR, M. B. LEIGH and D. M. O'BRIEN 2009. Stable isotope fingerprinting: a novel method for identifying plant, fungal, or bacterial origins of amino acids. *Ecology* 90 (12): 3526-3535

LAZZARINI, L. and O. SALVADORI 1989. A Reassessment of the Formation of the Patina Called "Scialbatura." *Studies in Conservation* 34(1): 20-26.

LEEUWENHOEK, A. 1675. Microscopical observations. *Philosophical Transactions Royal Society* 10: 380-385.

LEWIS, D. 1988. *The Rock Paintings of Arnhem Land, Australia*. B.A.R., Oxford

LOY, T. H., R. JONES, D. E. NELSON, B. MEEHAN, J. VOGEL, J. SOUTHON and R. COSGROVE 1990. Accelerator radiocarbon dating of human blood proteins in pigments from Late Pleistocene art sites in Australia. *Antiquity* 64(242): 110–116.

MAZEL, A. and A. L. WATCHMAN 1997. Accelerator radiocarbon dating of Natal Drakensberg paintings, results and implications. *Antiquity* 71: 445-449.

MAZEL, A. D. and A. L. WATCHMAN 2003. Dating the rock paintings in the uKhahlamba-Drakensberg and the Biggarsberg, KwaZulu-Natal, South Africa. *Southern Africa Humanities* 15: 59-73.

MCNAIR, J. B. 1932. The interrelation between substances in plants, essential oils and resins, cyanogen and oxalate. *American Journal Botany* 19: 255-271.

NELSON, D. E. 1993. Second thoughts on a rock-art date. *Antiquity*. 67. 893-895.

PINNA, D. 1993. Fungal physiology and the formation of calcium oxalate films on stone monuments. *Aerobiologia* 9: 157-167.

PRINSLOO, L. C. 2007. Rock hyraces: A cause of San rock art deterioration? *J. Raman Spectrosc.* 38: 496–503.

PUESCHEL, C. M. 2019. Calcium oxalate mineralisation in the algae. *Phycologia* 58(4): 331-350.

RICHET, G. 1995. The chemistry of urinary stones around 1800, a first in clinical chemistry. *Kidney International* 48(3): 876-86.

ROBERTS, A. L., I. CAMPBELL, A. PRING, G. BELL, A. L. WATCHMAN, R. S. POPELKA-FILCOFF, C. E. LENEHAN, C. T.

GIBSON, and N. R. FRANKLIN 2015. A multidisciplinary investigation of a rock coating at Ngaut Ngaut (Devon Downs), South Australia. *Australian Archaeology* 80: 32-39.

Rosado, T., M. Gil, J. Mirão, A. Candeias and A. T. Caldeira 2013. Oxalate biofilm formation in mural paintings due to microorganisms – A comprehensive study. *International Biodeterioration and Biodegradation* 85: 1-7.

Ruiz, J. F., M. Mas, A. Hernanz, M. W. Rowe, K. L. Steelman and J. M. Gavira 2006. First radiocarbon dating of oxalate crusts over Spanish prehistoric rock art. *International Newsletter on Rock Art* 46: 1–5.

Ruiz López, J. F., M. W. Rowe, A. Hernanz Gismero, J. M. Gavira Vallejo, R. Viñas Vallverdú and A. Rubio I Mora 2009. Cronología del arte rupestre postpaleolítico y datación absoluta de pátinas de oxalato cálcico. Primeras experiencias en Castilla — La Mancha (2004– 2007). In J. A. López, R. Martínez and C. Matamoros C. (eds.), *IV Congreso el arte rupestre del arco mediterráneo de la Península Ibérica. 10 años en la Lista del Patrimonio Mundial de la UNESCO, 3, 4 y 5 de diciembre de 2008*, pp. 303–316. Museo de Bellas Artes San Pío V, Valencia, Generalitat Valenciana, Valencia.

Ruiz, J., A. Hernanz, R. A. Armitage, M. W. Rowe, R. Viñas and A. Rubio 2012. Calcium oxalate AMS ^{14}C dating and chronology of post-Palaeolithic rock paintings in the Iberian Peninsula. Two dates from Abrigo de los Oculados (Henarejos, Cuenca, Spain). *Journal of Archaeologic al Science* 39(8): 2655–2667.

Rusakov, A., A. Vlasov, M. Zelenskaya, O. Frank-Kamenetskaya and D. Vlasov 2016. *The crystallization of calcium oxalate hydrates formed by interaction between microorganisms and minerals. Biogenic–abiogenic interactions in natural and anthropogenic systems*. Springer International Publishing. p. 357–377. Berlin.

Russ, J., M. Hyman, H. J. Shafer and M. W. Rowe 1990. Radiocarbon dating of prehistoric rock paintings by selective oxidation of organic carbon. *Nature* 348: 710–711.

Russ, J., M. Hyman and M. W. Rowe 1992. Direct Radiocarbon Dating of Rock Art. *Radiocarbon* 34: 867-872.

Russ, J., R. L. Palma, D. H. Loyd, T. W. Boutton and M. A. Coy 1996. Origin of the Whewellite-Rich Rock Crust in

the Lower Pecos Region of Southwest Texas and Its Significance to Paleoclimate Reconstructions. *Quaternary Research* 46(1): 27-36.

Russ, J., W. D. Kaluarachchi, L. Drummond and H. G. M. Edwards 1999. The Nature of a Whewellite-Rich Rock Crust Associated with Pictographs in Southwestern Texas. *Studies in Conservation* 44: 91–103.

Russ, J., D. Loyd, and T. W. Boutton 2000. A Paleoclimate Reconstruction for Southwest Texas Using Oxalate Residue from Lichens as a Paleoclimate Proxy. *Quaternary International* 67: 29–36.

Russ, J., M. Pohl, C. Von Nagy, K. Steelman, H. Hurst, L. Ashby, P. Schmidt, E. F. Padilla Gutiérrez and M. W. Rowe 2017. Strategies for 14C Dating the Oxtotitlán Cave Paintings, Guerrero, Mexico. *Advances in Archaeological Practice* 5(2): 170-183.

Scott, D. H. and W. D. Hyder 1993. A Study of Some Californian Indian Rock Art Pigments. *Studies in Conservation* 38(3): 155-173.

Scott, S. A., C. M. Davis, K. L. Steelman, M. W. Rowe and T. Guilderson 2005. AMS Dates from Four Late Prehistoric Period Rock Art Sites in West Central Montana. *Plains Anthropologist* 50(193): 57-71.

Smith, M. A., Watchman, A. and J. Ross 2009. Direct Dating Indicates a Mid-Holocene Age for Archaic Rock Engravings in Arid Central Australia. *Geoarchaeology* 24(2): 191–203. DOI:10.1002/gea.20262.

Spades, S. and J. Russ 2005. GC-MS Analysis of Lipids in Prehistoric Rock Paints and Associate Oxalate Coatings from the Lower Pecos Region, Texas. *Archaeometry* 47(1):115–126.

Spooner, N. 1998. Human occupation at Jinmium, northern Australia, 116,000 years ago or much less? *Antiquity* 72(275): 173-178.

Steelman, K. and M. Rowe 2002. Potential for Virtually Nondestructive Radiocarbon and Stable Carbon Isotopic Analyses on Perishable Archaeological Artifacts. *Archaeological Chemistry Chapter* 2: 8-21

Steelman, K. and M. Rowe 2004. Non-destructive plasma-chemical extraction of carbon from organic artefacts. In T. Higham, C. Bronk Ramsey and C. Owen (eds), *Radiocarbon and Archaeology*, pp. 35-42. Proceeding of the 4th International Symposium. Oxford University School of Archaeology Monograph 62, Oxford University Press.

Steelman, K. L., M. W. Rowe, T. W. Boutton, J. R. Southon, C. L. Merrell and R. D. Hill 2002. Stable Isotope and Radiocarbon Analyses of a Black Deposit Associated with Pictographs at Little Lost River, Cave, Idaho. *Journal of Archaeological Science* 29: 1189-1198.

Steelman, K. L., R. Rickman, M. W. Rowe, T. W. Boutton, J. Russ and N. Guidon 2002. AMS radiocarbon ages of an oxalate accretion and rock paintings at Toca do Serrote da Bastiana, Brazil. In K. Jakes (ed.), *Archeological chemistry VI, materials, methods and meaning*. pp. 22–35. ACS Symposium Series.Washington (DC).

Steelman, K. L., C. E. Boyd, and T. Allen 2021. Two independent methods for dating rock art. Age determination of paint and oxalate layers at Eagle Cave, TX. *Journal of Archaeological Science* 126, February 2021, 105315.

Watchman, A. L. 1987. Preliminary determinations of the age and composition of mineral salts on rock art surfaces in the Kakadu National Park. In W. R. Ambrose, and J. M. J. Mummery (eds), *Archaeometry, Further Australasian Studies*, pp. 36-42. Department of Prehistory, Australian National University, Canberra.

Watchman, A. L. 1990a. Rassegna delle croste ricche in ossalato rinvenute en Australie. *Arkos* 9/10" 11-18.

Watchman, A. L. 1990b. A summary of occurrences of oxalate-rich crusts in Australia. *Rock Art Research* 7: 44-50.

Watchman, A. L. 1991. Age and composition of oxalate-rich crusts in the Northern Territory, Australia. *Studies in Conservation* 36: 24-32.

Watchman, A. 1992. Repainting or periodic-painting at Australian Aboriginal sites, evidence from rock surface crusts.

In G. K. Ward (ed), *Retouch, Maintenance and conservation of Aboriginal rock imagery*, pp 26-30. Australian Rock Art Research Association Occasional Publication 5, Melbourne.

Watchman, A. 1993a. Evidence of a 25,000-year-old pictograph in northern Australia. *Geoarchaeology* 8(6): 465-473.

Watchman, A. 1993b. The use of laser technology in rock art dating. *Artefact* 16: 32-76.

Watchman, A. 2000. Micro-excavation and laser extraction methods for dating carbon in silica skins and oxalate

crusts. In G. K. Ward and C. Tuniz (eds), *Advances in dating Australian rock-markings*, pp. 35-39. Occasional AURA Publication 10.

Watchman, A. 2004. Minimum age for a petroglyph on a boulder of significance in Kakadu National Park, Northern Territory, Australia. *Rock Art Research* 21(2): 187-195.

Watchman, A. L., P. Taçon, R. Fullagar and L. Head 2000. Minimum ages for pecked rock markings from Jinmium, northwestern Australia. *Archaeology in Oceania* 35: 1-10.

Watchman, A., M. De La L. Gutiérrez, and M. Hernandez Llosas 2002. Giant murals of Baja California, new regional archaeological perspectives. *Antiquity* 76: 947-948.

Watchman, A. S. O'Connor and R. Jones 2004. Dating Oxalate Minerals 20-45 ka. *Journal of Archaeological Science* 32: 369-374.

Watchman, A. L., G. K. Ward, M. Crocombe and K. Mulvaney 2010. Dating of rock paintings in the Wadeye-Fitzmaurice region, Northern Territory. *Rock Art Research* 27(2): 223-228.

Wollaston, W. H. 1797. On gouty and urinary concretions. *Philosophical Transactions Royal Society* 87: 386—400.

Zindler-Frank, E. 1976. Oxalate biosynthesis in relation to photosynthetic pathways and plant productivity, a survey. *Zeitschrift für Pflanzenphysiologie* 80: 1–13.

17

KEYWORDS: Pictograms – AMS radiocarbon dating – Charcoal pigments – Binder/vehicle pigments – Dominican Republic rock paintings

CHEMICAL ANALYSIS AND THREE RADIOCARBON DATES ON DOMINICAN REPUBLIC ROCK PAINTINGS

Marvin W. Rowe

Abstract: Pictographs occur in the Dominican Republic ascribed to Taínos, inhabiting the island from ~2,000 years ago until post-1492. >400 sites were recorded since mid-1970s and questions abound: The images represent what? Why was it created? Why it's where it is? and What is its' chronology? Little evidence addresses these. With permission, Daniel DuVall collected samples from Cueva del Peñón, Cueva de Vidal, and Cueva de Las Maravillas, all a few km from one another and nearby Cumayasa (SE coast). Ten background specimens were studied. Of five pictographs, three had charcoal pigments, and were radiocarbon dated: 535±80, 690±45 and 1390±85 BP.

Introduction

The objectives of this work were to provide additional ^{14}C dates for the Taino rock paintings and to characterize the pigments used in the pictographs to the extent possible with the chemical techniques available to this study. These objectives have been largely met.

There is substantial rock art documented in the Dominican Republic, most of which is attributed to indigenous, now extinct, Taíno people. The art is speculated to date from 2000 years before present (BP) to the arrival of Columbus about 500 years ago, corresponding with Classic Taíno Culture (Rouse 1992). Few scientific analyses of available materials have been done. Both petroglyphs and pictograms are present and are mostly associated with deep caves with the petroglyphs being found in the partially lighted entrances and the pictograms typically, but not always, found in dark zones. López Belando (2009) and Atiles (2009) suggested various "schools of pictography" based on perceived styles of painting, but these speculations are not based on

Article received: 15 July 2022
Revised I: 11 June 2023
Revised II: 16 June 2023
Accepted: 21 June 2023

scientific evidence and several of these schools are extrapolated from only one or two sites. Relative dating based on super-positioning is not feasible as there is almost never overlapping of motifs. Fray Ramón Pané (1999), during the time of Columbus, wrote of myths and beliefs of the Taíno, but only fragmentary accounts have survived. Gilbert (1995) connected some ethnographic material to rock art and suggested that paintings were associated with shamanistic rituals, creation myths and the Taíno version of the afterworld. Veloz (1976) examined samples from Cueva de las Maravillas and concluded only that kaolin, mica and goethite were present. Two samples from this same cave were analyzed with scanning electron microscopy (see below). Foster et al. (2011) obtained three radiocarbon (^{14}C) dates from the Cueva del Puente, about 50 km from the area of our sampling with rock art in the same apparent style, which fell between 890 ± 40 years BP and 1660 ± 40 years BP.

Experimental Procedures

Sample Collection

Samples of pigments were taken from three sites. Samples V-1 and V-2 are from the same painted panel in Cueva de Vidal (Figure 1). The V-1 motif is slightly darker than V-2, but the difference may be due to diffusion through speleothem deposition on and around V-2. Cueva de Vidal was selected due to its nearly pristine condition, with very little apparent contamination from human visitation and, in fact, its existence has only recently been reported (DuVall 2010). Pictograph sample P-1, thought to be constructed with bat guano, is from a panel in Cueva de Peñón (Figure 2) within the same underground system. The Cueva de Peñón panel is only about 100 m from the Cueva de Vidal area after traversing through some winding tunnels. Color of the pigment here is much lighter brown and appears to be of the same material that is found underfoot,

Figure 1: Panel in Cueva de Vidal. The position of sample V-1 is shown with an arrow.
Photograph by Daniel DuVall

Figure 2: Sample P-1 is from a panel in Cueva de Peñón. Photograph by Daniel DuVall

which was assume to be mostly bat guano. Darker colored motifs there are probably charcoal; but samples were not taken from them due to the lack of sufficient material. These first two sites have been described in detail (DuVall 2010). The third site studied was Cueva de las Maravillas 10 km. Samples M-1 and M-2 were taken from Cueva de las Maravillas, a large cave containing nearly 500 pictograms. Paintings are apparently in the same style as those in Vidal/Peñón, which is to say that many approach one meter in size with heavily applied paint (Figure 3). Compare Figure 3 with the motif from which V-1 was taken (Figure 1). Because Cueva de las Maravillas experienced many years of visitation and in 2002 was fitted with concrete sidewalks and stairs, motion-sensor lighting and an elevator for public visits. Sample M-1 was a crumb of charcoal taken from the small hole indicated by the arrow in Figure 3. Sample M-2 (Figure 4) was taken from a motif about 20 meters from M-1 and was selected for its redder color, perhaps made of bat guano. All samples were taken using stainless steel forceps and wrapping the pigment in aluminum foil.

Optical Microscopy

A Leica Microsystems (Switzerland) Ltd.EZ4 D optical microscope equipped with a 7.1 Mega pixel Leica DC150 digital camera attached to a computer via a USB 2.0 cable was used for microscopic examinations.

Portable X-ray Spectroscopy

A Bruker III-V portable X-ray fluorometer (pXRF) was used to analyze elemental composition of samples. Such hand-held "X-ray guns" have been used numerous times to determine elements involved in rock painting pigments. Newman and Loendorf (2005) were first in the United States

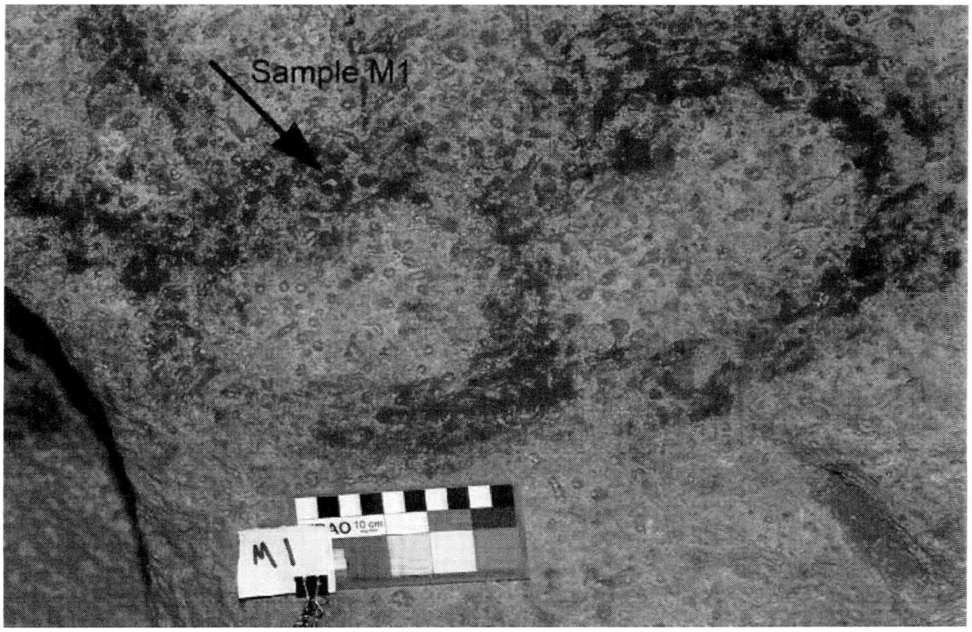

Figure 3: Black motif Sample M-1 in Cueva de las Maravillas. Photograph by Daniel DuVall

Figure 4: Red-brown colored motif location of sample M-2. Photograph by Daniel DuVall.

to report the use of pXRF to study pigmentation of rock paintings. They showed chemically that some green images in Montana and Wyoming were chromium-based, possibly the mineral fushite, and that yellow paint suspected to have been added with a modern repainting indeed contained lead, zinc, arsenic and tin – all pigments used in modern paints. This was followed by pXRF studies of rock art pigments by Rowe et al. (2011) who nondestructively assayed more than 75 pictograph pigments at the Lost Again Shelter (site #03-964) in the Guadalupe Mountains of southern New Mexico and Koenig et al. (2014) who assayed rock painting pigments at eleven rock art sites in the Lower Pecos River Canyonlands, southwest Texas. C. Loendorf (2011) studied pictographs at the Picture Cave and White Rock Shelter at Fort Bliss, TX, concluding that the iron ochre used for coloration included natural arsenic, copper and zinc as well. Le Quellec et al. (2015) then examined a pictograph in Utah purported to be an image of a pterodactyl; the pXRF analyses showed that it was not. Steelman et al. (2021) performed pXRF during rock art documentation at Meyers Spring, Texas (41TE9).

Worldwide, numerous researchers have also applied pXRF to the study of rock art to address research questions (e.g., Beck et al. 2014; Bedford et al. 2018; Dostal and Smith 2015; Huntley 2011, 2012; Huntley et al. 2015; Lins and Prince 2011; Miller et al. 2011; Olivares et al. 2013; O'Regan et al. 2019; Robinson et al. 2015; Roldán et al. 2010; Sepúlveda et al. 2015; Wesley et al. 2014; Zoppi et al. 2002).

Rowe et al. (2011) and Koenig et al. (2014) include experimental details of the procedure used here that need not be repeated. pXRF is useful, especially because we are interested in whether a black pigment is colored by inorganic (manganese) oxides or by a black organic substance, usually charcoal. McPeak et al. (2014) found that black paints used in Oxtotitlán Cave, Guerrero, Mexico, the pigment present is a byproduct of pyrolyzed plant material, most likely a mixture of soot and charcoal. Manganese (Mn) detection is sensitive and easy to determine. Typically, Mn is easily detected in pictographs. There is no pXRF signal for organic materials like charcoal, so they are 'detected' by the absence of potential inorganic elements, e.g., Mn in our case. The method is rapid; because of small sample sizes, 300 second analyses were taken.

Scanning Electron Microscopy

The scanning electron microscope used here was a Model Quanta 400 by FEI Company (USA) at Texas A&M University - Qatar, equipped with elemental chemical capability for qualitative or semi-quantitative analysis. Veloz (1972:1433) used electron microscopy to examine pigment residues collected from a pictogram in La Cueva de Las Maravillas and concluded that they were, "in no way made with charcoal, nor sap from a local mangrove (*Rhizophora mangle*). Nor jaguar (Genipa Americana) although they had been assumed by many to be constituents of the paint." (translated from Spanish by Daniel DuVall, personal communication). The materials found were kaolinite with goethite added for color (Veloz 1972:144). Which of the hundreds of pictograms he sampled is unknown, but it is assumed that it was red.

Results and Discussion

Samples V-1, V-2 and M-1

Samples V-1, V-2 and M-1 were chemically and visually similar to one another. Figures 5 and 6 show optical microscope pictures of the three samples and charcoal is presumed to be black pigment in all these pictographs. There is evidence of discrete charcoal pieces with minor accompanying background rock (limestone, calcium carbonate, $CaCO_3$). pXRF spectra for V-1, V-2 and M-1 showed principally calcium (Ca) with minor/trace iron (Fe), bromine (Br), rubidium (Rb), strontium (Sr),zirconium (Zr), copper (Cu) and zinc (Zn). Of particular note is the absence of Mn peaks, confirming that something else forms the black pigment.

Figure 5: Sample V-2 at 16X magnification. There are suggestions of discrete charcoal pieces with some minor visual evidence for accompanying background rock (limestone, $CaCO_3$). The pXRF spectra for V-1 and V-2 showed principally Ca with minor/trace Fe, Br, Rb, Sr, Zr, Cu and Zn.

Figure 6 shows a microscope photograph of a portion of sample M-1. The black pieces are small and not easy to characterize. The photographs in Figures 5 and 6 suggest that the particles are charcoal. It appears that these three pictographs are pigmented with charcoal, most certainly organic matter, and should be excellent candidates for ^{14}C analysis.

Figure 7 shows a representative pXRF spectrum (for V-1), similar for the three Dominican Republic samples studied here. The principle element measured is calcium (Ca), followed by iron (Fe). These and the other elements indicated are almost certainly components of the rock itself. There is no indication of the use of a mineral pigment here. Organic materials do not have pXRF peaks and so are surmised on the lack of a mineral suited to give the coloration, i.e., the lack of a manganese peak. So, supporting the assignment of charcoal as the black pigment, chemical analysis using scanning electron microscopy (SEM-EDX) also confirmed the lack of Mn, confirming that the black pigment is probably charcoal. Most of the Ca is almost certainly due to the presence of limestone ($CaCO_3$). Calcium oxalate (CaC_2O_4) is often a component of limestone crusts and surfaces as well.

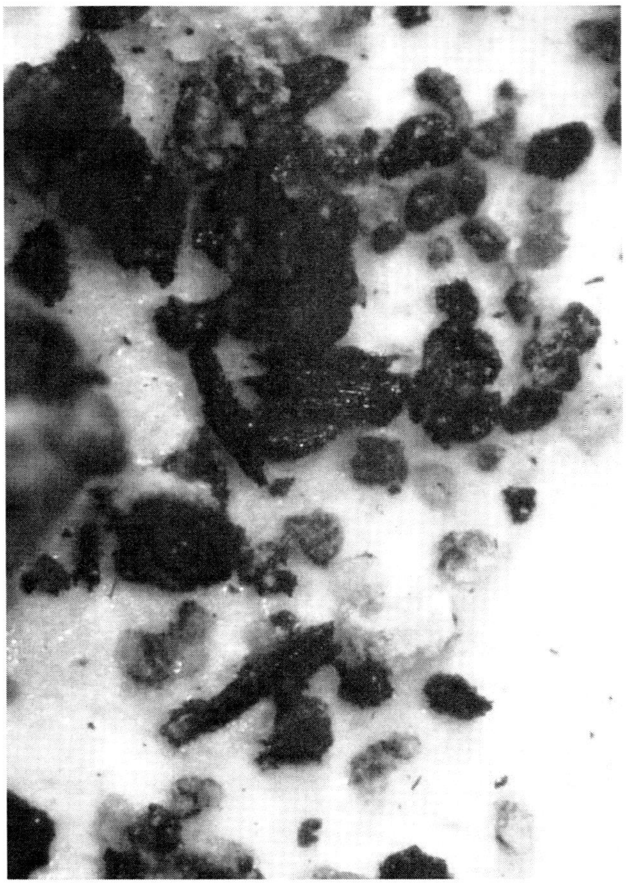

Figure 6: Sample M-1 at X16 magnification. There are what appear to be discrete charcoal pieces intermixed with the white calcium carbonate rock

An SEM-EDX spectrum for the sample M-1 shows elements calcium (Ca), carbon (C), oxygen (O) consistent with limestone (and calcium oxalate), whereas the other elements seen, silicon (Si), iron (Fe), aluminum (Al), potassium (K), copper (Cu), zinc (Zn), bromine (Br), rubidium (Rb), strontium (Sr) and zirconium (Zr) are all consistent with association with silicate rock material. The elements carbon, oxygen, silicon, and aluminum are light (atomic numbers are too low) to register by pXRF. Once again there is no indication of a mineral pigment.

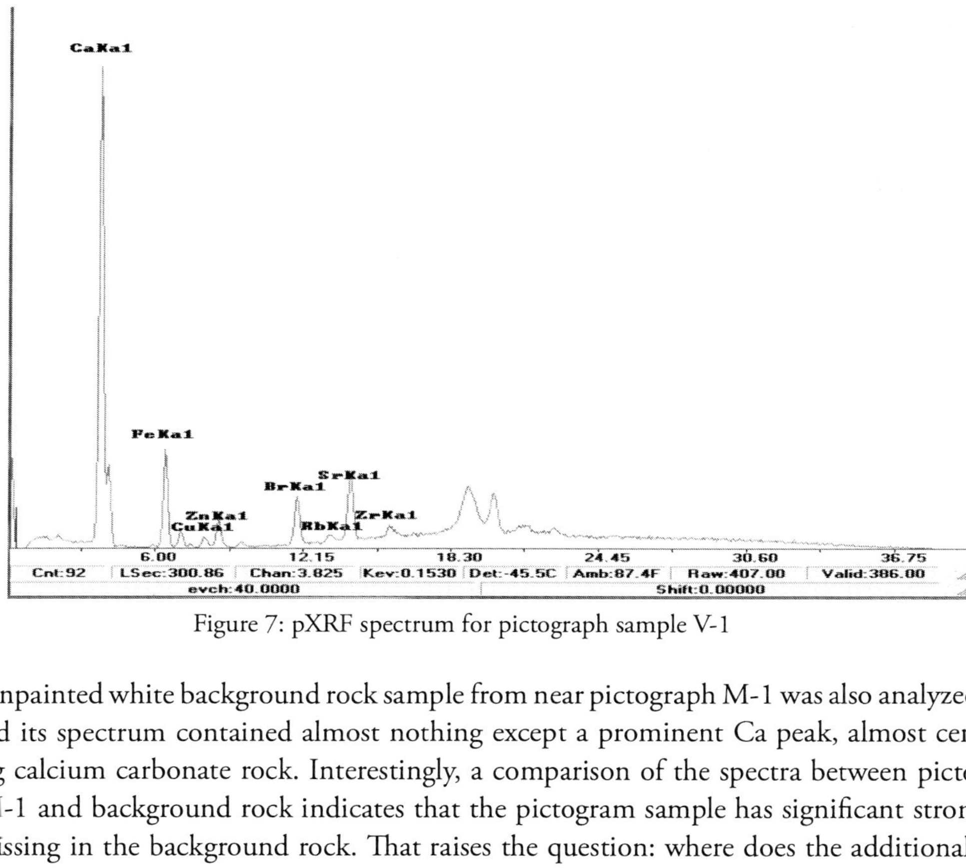

Figure 7: pXRF spectrum for pictograph sample V-1

An unpainted white background rock sample from near pictograph M-1 was also analyzed with pXRF and its spectrum contained almost nothing except a prominent Ca peak, almost certainly indicating calcium carbonate rock. Interestingly, a comparison of the spectra between pictogram sample M-1 and background rock indicates that the pictogram sample has significant strontium, largely missing in the background rock. That raises the question: where does the additional Sr in the paint come from? I'll return to this question later.

Sample M-2

Figure 8 shows a microscope photograph of a portion of sample M-2. It clearly shows the presence of distinct pieces of charcoal. The pXRF spectra of sample M1 and M2 are quite similar. Prominent elements in both are Fe, Sr and Ca. The Fe and Ca are easily enough explained. But there is the mystery of the high Sr. To understand the presence of the Ca peak, background unpainted rock near pictogram sample M-2 was examined. The pXRF spectrum of the M-2 background sample is simple; it contains virtually nothing but Ca, indicative of $CaCO_3$ as expected for limestone. So there is no mystery for the presence of Ca in the pictograph sample M-2; it is just background contamination. The background rock has a small Fe peak, but not large enough to explain the higher Fe in the pictograph.

Another non-pictograph sample was also taken near M-2, M-2 tierra. A microphotograph of the M-2 tierra is shown in Figure 9. Curiously, the 'tierra' sample has the same high Fe and Sr that was observed in the M-1 and M-2 pictograph and M-2 paint sample. Both these paint samples' elemental compositions can now be explained if 'tierra' was incorporated, intentionally or otherwise, in making the paints.

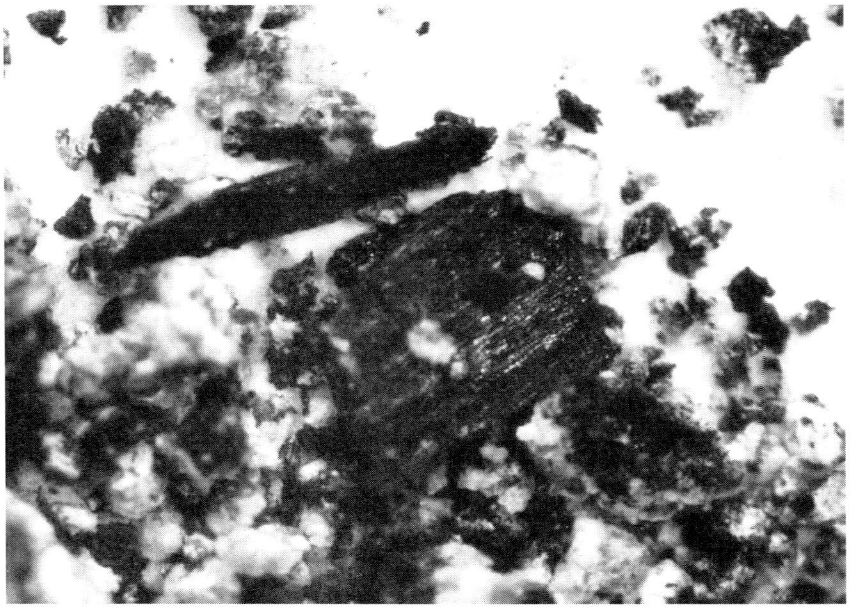

Figure 8: Sample M-2 at 16X magnification. Note that this appears to have easily discerned charcoal particles

Pictograph sample P-1, shown in Figure 10, is suspected to be bat guano. It is a reddish material intermixed with a white material. The most prominent peak in the X-ray fluorescence spectrum is iron, explaining the red color, i.e., iron ocher. The small calcium peak is likely due to calcium carbonate, presumably the white material seen. If this is bat guano, it would not have a clear elemental signature. Since we suspect that this sample was bat guano, it was eliminated as a candidate for ^{14}C dating. Although bat guano is a dateable organic material, it is difficult to assign a measured bat guano ^{14}C date to the painting event. Rather it would date the deposition of the guano, an event not necessarily related to the painting event. Hand held pXRF confirmed background rock contained calcium carbonate.

Figure 9: Sample non-pictograph sample M2 at 16X magnification, "tierra"

Figure 10: Sample P-I shown at 16X magnification. Note that this appears to be a dark conglomerate thought to be bat guano. There were no discrete charcoal particles identified

Radiocarbon Dating of Three Pictograms

Having determined that three of the samples apparently contained charcoal pigments, these (samples V-1, V-2 and M-1) were prepared for ^{14}C dating utilizing the plasma-chemical device located at the Office of Archaeological Studies in Santa Fe, NM (Rowe et al. 2017). The plasma oxidation technique is ideal for dating paintings with a high carbonate ($CaCO_3$) or oxalate (CaC_2O_4) content, because it extracts only organic carbon, leaving the inorganic matrices intact (see reviews by Rowe 2009; Steelman and Rowe 2012; Rowe et al. 2017). That technique alleviates the necessity of removing the carbonates/oxalates with strong acid. Our plasma oxidation apparatus converts organic material (probably charcoal in this case) to CO_2 for accelerator mass spectrometry (AMS) ^{14}C dating. Plasma discharges are produced by RF capacitive coupling with two external copper electrodes. The plasmas used are rarefied (133 Pa) argon and oxygen, partially ionized gases composed of neutral atoms, both negative and positive molecular and atomic ions, and electrons. Temperatures of the oxygen plasmas were <95°C. Active species in the plasma phase allow reactions that normally occur only at high temperatures to proceed rapidly at low temperatures. Oxygen plasmas convert organic matter to carbon dioxide (CO_2), which was frozen by an ethanol/liquid nitrogen slush for AMS ^{14}C dating at the ETH-Zürich MICADAS AMS facility (Fahmi et al. 2013; Ruff et al. 2007; Wacker et al. 2013; Welte et al. 2018). Plasma oxidation has been used to ^{14}C date the organic constituents in over 200 pictographs worldwide.

We maintain pressures of ~10^{-5} to 10^{-4} Pa, and utilize ultra-high purity (UHP, 99.999%) oxygen and argon gases to minimize atmospheric contamination. Sample chambers were cleaned by successive oxygen plasma reactions at 133 Pa oxygen gas until ≤0.5 μg carbon was collected. Oxygen plasma reactions removed any organic material on the inside of the chamber introduced by previous samples or contamination from previous sample removal. Paint charcoal samples were loaded into chambers and evacuated using oil-free vacuum pumps to ~10^{-5} to10^{-4} Pa. Successive argon plasmas were ignited to remove adsorbed CO_2 by surface bombardment of the sample. Argon is an inert gas and reacts by atomic collisions with adsorbed CO_2 that is removed through vacuum pumping. Once a pressure of <10^{-5} to10^{-4} Pa was obtained, it indicated that adsorbed CO_2 was removed (≤0.5 μg carbon).

Samples were then oxidized with oxygen plasmas. Plasma temperatures were ≤95°C. Charcoal in the sample was converted into CO_2 and water during the one-hour exposures. The CO_2 was flame-sealed into a glass tube cooled to liquid nitrogen temperature (-194°C), after the water was removed with a dry ice/ethanol slurry (-58C). Alternatively, we just removed the liquid nitrogen from the stainless-steel collection finger and monitored the pressure rise as the CO_2 was released. Then when the pressure plateaued, i.e., when all CO_2 was released, the valve to the collection tube was closed trapping the water. Sufficient carbon (30 to 100 μg carbon) was sealed into a glass tube that was heat sealed, and sent to the Center for Accelerator Mass Spectrometry (CAMS) at Zürich ETH AMS Laboratory for direct ^{14}C measurement on the CO_2.

Radiocarbon results from three charcoal pigmented pictograms are: Charcoal sample V-1, 1390 years BP; calibrated 435-465, 475-500, 530-780, 785-835, 855-875 AD. Charcoal sample V-2, 690±45 years BP; calibrated 1260-1330, 1355-1395 AD. Charcoal sample M-1, 535±80 years BP; calibrated 1280-1500; 1600-1615, 1505-1510 AD. (Table 1; Figure 11). Calibration used the OxCal computer program version 4.3.2 (Bronk Ramsey 2009, 2015) with IntCal13 curve data from Reimer et al. (2020). Clearly, the painting tradition lasted at least for several centuries.

Table 1: Radiocarbon dates for three pictogram samples from the Dominican Republic

ETH #	*Sample*	*OAS #*	*Age yBP*	*σ yBP*
63120.1.1	V-1	150724b-2	1390	85
65333.1.1	V-2	150812a-1	690	45
63121.1.1	M-1	150731-1	535	80

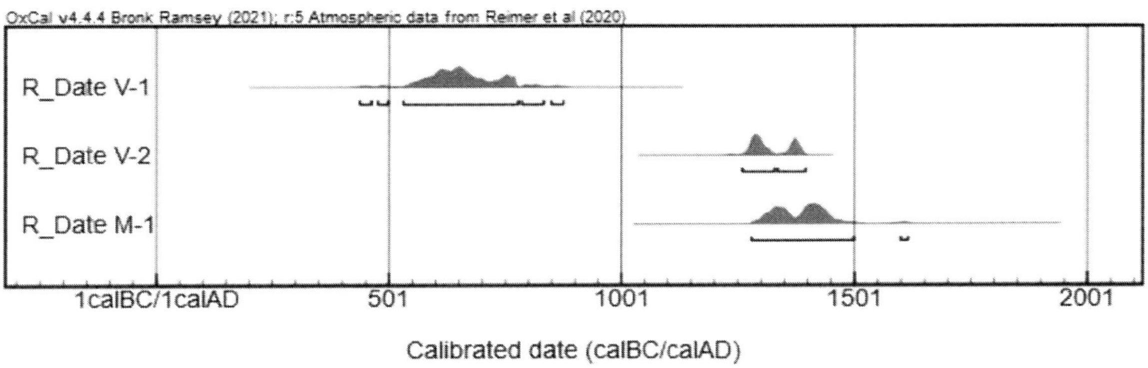

Figure 11: Calibration curves obtained with OxCal 4.3.2 for the three charcoal drawing motifs in two caves in the Dominican Republic (Bronk Ramsey 2009, 2015; Reimer et al. 2020)

Discussion

The prime motivation in examining and dating pigment samples in the Dominican Republic rock paintings was to determine whether this art is of pre-Columbian provenance. Since all of the ages of both Foster et al. (2011)'s and our dated material, except M-1, predate 1492 AD and the arrival of Columbus, this is the case. It is reassuring that the oldest date did not fall outside the window of conceivable human habitation of the island or ca. 4,000 B.C.

It might be supposed that motifs of similar styles, painted or drawn with similar materials and located within apparently coherently composed panels would have been created at the same time, but neither Foster et al. (2011) nor our results support this hypothesis. In La Cueva del Puente, Foster et al.'s two red/brown motifs differ in age by 770 years while one of them nearly matches the age of the nearby black motif which is clearly drawn using a different method and different material. In Foster et al.'s Cueva José María the two dates of two motifs assumed to be concurrent because of similar appearance differed by 1,400 years. In our Cueva de Vidal the two dates of motifs of similar chemical composition, scale and situated at the extremities of the same panel (from our subjective perspective) differ by 700 years.

These panels therefore were obviously not painted by a single artist. Rather, the images were painted a different times spanning almost a millennium. In copiously decorated caves such as we are examining here (José María has close to 1000 pictograms; Peñón/Vidal nearly 400; Cueva del Puente 60) different wall spaces might have been utilized by different family groups to occasionally commemorate something. None of the 1000s of pictograms of which we are aware of in caves in the Dominican Republic ever overlap each other which makes knowing the order in which any of them were painted impossible. Some may *look* older than others but this attests more to differing conditions of preservation within the cave, i.e. speleothem deposition, fungal growth on the pigment, erosion due to cycles of condensation, or exfoliation of the substrate. It is only through direct dating methods that more can be learned about this art.

Conclusion

The objectives of this work, to provide additional ^{14}C dates for the Taino rock paintings and to characterize the pigments used in the pictographs to the extent possible with the chemical techniques available to this study, have been largely met. Three ^{14}C dates are presented and the pigm,nts of thew three dated pictographs were seen to contain charcoal. One other pigment was suspected to be bat guano and would not produce a useful ^{14}C date.

As could have been predicted, the black pigments (samples V-1, V-2 and M-1) that apparently contain charcoal, and certainly organic material of some sort, were good candidates for ^{14}C dating. The ^{14}C dates obtained show a long of use of charcoal in these two caves. The dates are consistent with ages expected. Images of similar styles indicate a substantial range of time of painting (V-1 and V-2).

Acknowledgments

I am grateful for the support of the National Center for Preservation Technology and Training to the Office of Archaeological Studies, Texas A&M University at Qatar, the Qatar Foundation, the Don E. Pierce Endowment for Archaeology and Conservation, and Mark MacKenzie of the Conservation Laboratory of the Museum of New Mexico for support. I very much appreciate Dr. Mohammad Yousef for his assistance with scanning electron microscopy measurements, and J. Royce Cox for assistance on the plasma device as well. Daniel DuVall supplied the samples for this study and assisted in writing the aspects of the paper dealing with general views of Dominican Republic rock art and for providing the specimens used in this study. I thank Domingo Abréu Collado, Head of Speleology for the Department of the Environment of the Dominican Republic for both his permission For Dan DuVall to sample the rock art and for his general assistance and companionship in exploring the caves with Dan DuVall; Alain Gilbert for re-discovering the

Cueva de Péñon and its unique rock art and for sharing it with us; and the Museum of the Dominican Man of Santo Domingo for their support.

Dr Marvin W. Rowe
Research Associate, Office of Archaeological Studies
Center for New Mexico Archaeology
7 Old Cochiti Road, Santa Fe, NM 87507
USA
And Chemistry Professor Emeritus
Texas A&M University
College Station, TX, USA
E-mail: PlasmaC.lab@state.nm.us

References

Atiles Bidó, G. 2009. Rock art studies in the Dominican Republic, in *Rock Art of the Caribbean*, eds. M. H. Hayward, L-G. Atkinson and M. I. Cinquino, University of Alabama Press.

Bronk Ramsey, C. 2009. Bayesian analysis of radiocarbon dates. 2009 *Radiocarbon* 51:337-360. 2015 On-line *OxCal version 4.2.4*

Duvall, D. 2010. Finger fluting and other cave art in Cumayasa, Dominican Republic. *Rock Art Research* 27:137-146.

Duvall, D. 2011. Rock art imagery of the Dominican Republic: an introduction. Editora Búho, Santo Domingo.

Fahrni, S. M., L. Wacker, H.-A. Synal and S. Szidat 2013. Improving a gas ion source for ^{14}C AMS. *Nuclear Instruments and Methods in Physics Research B* 294:320-327.

Fernández, R., M. Tavarez and L. S. Clenis y Domínguez 2013 Presencia del dibujo rupestre en el Boletín del Museo del Hombre Dominicano. Bibliografía comentada. En Rupestreweb, http://www.rupestreweb.info/bibliomuseohrd.html

Foster, J., K. H. McDonald, C. Beeker, and G. Conrad 2011. Let there be light in the dark zone: insights into Taíno Cave paintings in the eastern Dominican Republic. Paper Presented at the 76th Annual Meeting of the Society for American Archaeology, Sacramento, CA.

Gilbert, A. 1995. Arte rupestre et rythologie en République Dominicaine. *Bulletin de la Société Préhistorique de l'Ariège* 117-164

Huntley (neé Ford), J. 2012. Taphonomy or paint recipe: in situ portable x-ray fluorescence spectrometric analysis of two anthropomorphic motifs from the Waronara Plateau, New South Wales. *Australian Archaeology* 75:78-94.

Koenig, c., A. M. Casteñeda, C. E. Boyd, M. W. Rowe and K. L. Steelman 2014. Portable X-ray fluorescence spectroscopy of pictographs: a case study from the Lower Pecos Canyonlands, Texas. *Archaeometry* 54:168-186.

Le Quellec, J.-L., P. Bahn and M. W. Rowe 2015. Death of a pterodactyl. *Antiquity* 89:872-881.

López Belando, A. 2009. Rock art of the Dominican Republic and Caribbean in *Rock Art of the Caribbean,* eds. M. H. hayward, L-G. Atkinson and M. I. Cinquino, University of Alabama Press.

Pané, F. Ramón 1999. *An Account of the Antiquities of the Indians,* translated by Susan C. Griswold. Duke University Press, Durham and London.

Reimer, P. J., W. E. N. Austin, E. Bard, A. Bayliss, P. G. Blackwell, C. Bronk Ramsey, M. Butzin, Hai Cheng, R. L. Edwards, M. Friedrich, P. M. Grootes, T. P. Guilderson, I. Hajdas, T. J. Heaton, A. G. Hogg, K. A. Hughen, B. Kromer, S. W. Manning, R. Muscheler, J. G. Palmer, C. Pearson, J. Van Der Plicht, R. W reimer, D. A. Richards, E. M. Scott, J. R. Southon, C. S.M. Turney, L. Wacker, F. Adolphi, U. Büntgen, M. Capano, S. M. Fahrni, A. Fogtmann-Schulz, R. Friedrich, P. Köhler, S. Kudsk, F. Miyake, J. Olsen, F. Reinig, M. Sakamoto, A. Sookdeo and S. Talamo 2020. The IntCal20 northern hemisphere radiocarbon age calibration curve (0–55 cal kBP). *Radiocarbon* 62(4):725-757. https://doi.org/10.1017/RDC.2020.41

Rouse, I. 1992. *The Taínos.* Yale University Press, New Haven.

Rowe, M. W. 2001. Dating by AMS radiocarbon analysis. In *Handbook of Rock Art Research,* ed. D. Whitley, Chapter 5, pp. 139-166. AltaMira Press, Walnut Creek.

Rowe, M. W. 2005. Dating studies of prehistoric pictographs in North America. In *Discovering North American Rock Art,* eds. L. L. loendorf, C. Chippendale and D. S. Whitley, Chapter 12, pp. 294-319. University of Arizona Press, Tucson.

Rowe, M. W. 2009. Radiocarbon dating of ancient rock paintings. *Analytical Chemistry* 81:1728-1735.

Rowe, M. W., E. Blinman, J. C. Martin, J. R. Cox, M. MacKenzie and L. Wacker 2017. Cold Plasma Oxidation and "Nondestructive" Radiocarbon Sampling. In *Proceedings of the Twenty-year retrospective of National Center for Preservation Technology and Training,* ed. T. Britt, National Center for Preservation Technology and Training, Natchitoches, LA. pp. 64-77. ISBN:electronic format 978-9970440-3-4.

Rowe, M. W., R. Mark, E. Billo, M. Berrier, K. L. Steelman and E. Dillingham 2011. Chemistry as a criterion for selecting pictographs for radiocarbon dating: Lost Again Shelter in the Guadalupe Mountains, southeastern New Mexico. *American Indian Rock Art* 37:37-47.

Ruff, M., L. Wacker, H. W. Gäggeler, M. Suter, H.-A. Synal and S. Szidat 2007. A gas ion source for radiocarbon measurements at 200 kV. *Radiocarbon* 49:307-314.

Steelman, K. L. and M. W. Rowe 2012. Radiocarbon dating of rock paintings: incorporating pictographs into the archaeological record. In *A Companion to Rock Art,* eds. J. mcdonald and P. veth, Chapter 32, pp 565-582. Blackwell Publishing Ltd., Oxford, United Kingdom.

Veloz, M. M. 1976. Análisis de microscópia electrónica de pictografías en las Maravillas, Provincia de San Pedro de Macoris. Anuario Cientifico, Universidad Central del Este, V.1 N.1, San Pedro de Macoris,

Wilson, S.M. (ed.) 1997. *The Indigenous People of the Caribbean,* University Press of Florida, Gainesville.

Wacker, L., S. M. Fahrni, I. Hajdas, M. Molnar, H.-A. Synal, S. Szidat and Y. L. Zhang 2013. A versatile gas interface for routine radiocarbon analysis with a gas ion source. *Nuclear Instruments and Methods in Physics Research B: Nuclear Instruments and Methods in Physics Research B* 294:315-319.

Welte, C., L. Hendriks, L. Wacker, N. Haghipour, T. I. Eglinton, D. Gunter and H-A. Synal 2018. Towards the limits: Analysis of microscale 14C samples using EA-AMS, *Nuclear Instruments and Methods in Physics Research: Beam Interactions with Materials and Atoms* 437:66-74.

18

KEYWORDS: Southeast China – Petroglyph – Microerosion – Age estimates

RECENT SCIENTIFIC RESEARCH AT THE ROCK ART SITES IN THE SOUTHEAST COASTLANDS OF CHINA

JIN ANNI AND CHAO GE

Abstract: A series of petroglyph sites have been discovered along the southeast coastline of China since the last century. Early studies mainly focused on typological and stylistic issues. The IFRAO team's visit to the Jiangjunya site in 2014 was a breakthrough for the development of rock art science in southeast China. Since then, several scientific expeditions were carried out at major sites, and therefore a general understanding of rock art in the area has been preliminarily established.

Introduction

In recent decades, especially during the 3rd National Survey of Cultural Heritage of China from 2007 to 2011, a series of petroglyph sites have been reported within the country's southeast coastlands. The term 'southeast coastlands' generally refers to a vast continental and maritime area covering not only the territory of some littoral regions like Jiangsu, Zhejiang, Fujian and Guangdong but also a part of the East and South China Seas (Figure 1). It contains diverse landforms, including mountains, valleys, basins, plains and deltas. As in the subtropics, the climate in most places is quite warm and humid, e.g., its average temperature ranges between 13°C and 29°C, and the mean precipitation is about 1500 mm yearly. Human activities originated from the area in early Pleistocene, over 1 Ma BP. Since about 10 Ka BP, the local cultures have entered a flourishing phase during which various crucial technologies such as rice farming, wooden building and seafaring occurred and evolved rapidly. The earliest written records about the area can be found in the documents of the 6th century BCE, referring to its original name given by the *Han* people in central China as '*Bai Yue Zhi Di*' (meaning 'the land belonging to a hundred tribes of Yue people'

Article received: 29 November 2022
Revised I: 01 December 2022
Revised II: 012 June 2023
Accepted: 13 June 2023

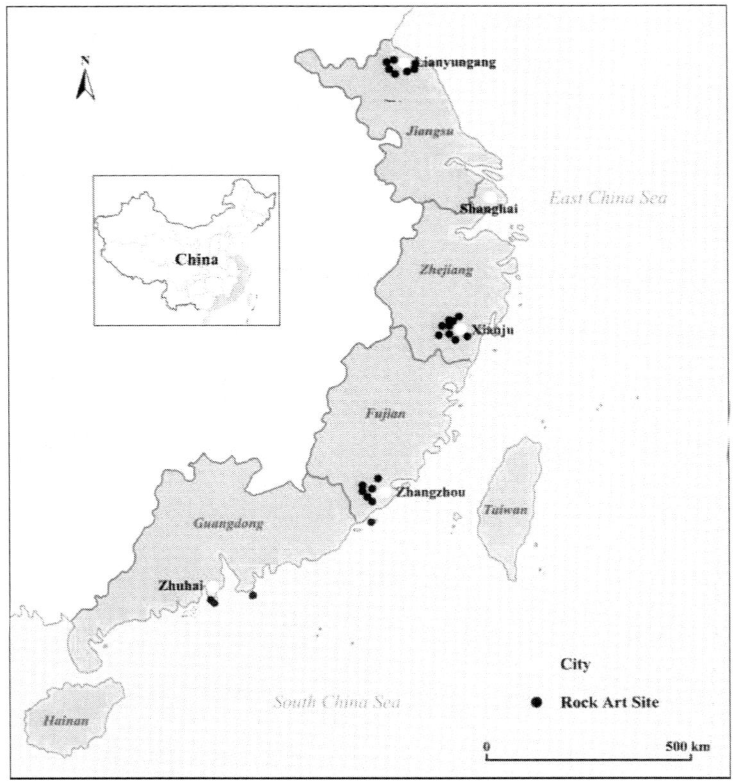

Figure 1: The studied area and the location of rock art sites

in Chinese). It had been gradually brought into the ruling system of the central power since the 2nd century BCE by the unification of the Qin dynasty and the continuous exploration of the successive Han dynasties. For thousands of years, it has played a connecting role between the continental and oceanic civilizations.

The starting point of rock art science in the area

The observation of the southeast rock art originated from Huang Zhongqin's visit in 1915 (Huang, 1935). However, more disciplinary attention occurred relatively late in the 1980s, mainly focusing on the Jiangjunya site in Jiangsu Province and the Xianzitan site in Fujian Province (Li, 1981/1983; Gai, 1983; Chen, 1984; Lin, 1988; Wang, 1991). Since then, researchers have attempted to analyse rock art through stylistic and historical approaches (Di, 1990; Liu, 1992; Ou & Lu, 1994; Zhang, 2009) or just compared them with the finds from adjacent dated archaeological sites (Lin, 1995; Li, 2001; Guo, 2002; Fan, 2007). These seashores have not attracted enough scholarly attention so far, and only very few have realised that the area is an internally connected geo-cultural unit within which the rock art sites share many commonalities.

Strictly speaking, only a few actual scientific works about rock art have been conducted within the area before the participation of the scientific team of IFRAO in 2014, which was an internationally collaborative expedition led by Prof. Robert G. Bednarik. The scientists visited rock art sites in three regions: Henan in central China, Ningxia in the northwest and Jiangsu in the southeast. The team has profitably utilized the country's wealth of rock surfaces suitable for microerosion calibration, especially soundly-dated rock inscriptions, and has managed to secure several calibration curves from quartz and feldspar (Microerosion analysis, known as a specialised dating method for petroglyphs based on field microscopy, was proposed by Robert G. Bednarik in the 1980s and has been applied to a lot of rock art-related scientific activities in various countries around the world. It assumes that precipitation causes weathering of the constituent crystals of the rock and development of micro-wanes on them. So developed micro-wanes on the edge of the fractured crystals can be quantified with high-resolution microscope. Its effectiveness and accuracy highly depended on local calibration curves secured from dated inscriptions until the Universal Calibration Curve was introduced in 2015, making dating feasible even without local calibration data.). However, only the one from an inscription in Mt Deyunshan is reliable. A total of eight age estimates have been secured in the field, all from the Jiangjunya site (Figure 2), varying between E360+60/-90 E5380+380/-530 years BP ('BP' refers to 'before 2014 CE') (Tang et al., 2017). Apart from the dating results, this rock art mission was far more valuable. China's first contact between modern science and rock art was

Figure 2: The IFRAO's scientists and local researchers in fieldwork at the Jiangjunya site in 2014, Jiangsu Province (photo extracted from Tang et al. 2017: 6)

in the 1980s. However, from the authors' perspective, perhaps the year 2014 can be regarded a preferable watershed event opening a whole new era of the rock art research in the country. An integral knowledge system called 'rock art science' including epistemology and methodology has been introduced to the Chinese colleagues for the first time. Four years later, invited by the Rock Art Society of China, Prof. Bednarik visited a petroglyph site with a single motif believed to be a symbol of the sun on Dongmenyu Island, Fujian Province. However, after thorough observation and analysis, natural power has been confirmed the leading cause of its formation (Bednarik, 2019). Most importantly, local participants have shared the precious knowledge to identify natural and artificial rock markings. As the knowledge spreads, many researchers in this country may have to re-evaluate the correctness of their previous claims, and maybe some rock art sites have to face the change of identities.

Recent scientific attempts at the rock art sites in the area (2014-2022)

In the southeast coastlands, the known rock art sites mainly concentrate on a few localities, such as Xianju County of Zhejiang Province, Lianyungang City of Jiangsu Province, Zhangzhou City of Fujian Province, Zhuhai City of Guangdong Province, Gaoxiong City of Taiwan Province, Hongkong and Macau. Cupules (cup-marks), masks, grids, anthropomorphic motifs, canoes, waves and spirals are the most common, in the sense of typology. However, exceptions of single-form dominant sites exist, e.g., the Jiangjunya site in Lianyungang (masks), the Xianzitan site in Zhangzhou (crouching anthropomorphic figures), and the Baojingwan site in Zhuhai (large composite motifs). Since 2014, fieldwork completely following the IFRAO's standards has been conducted at specific sites by the authors of this paper, which aims to report the progress made during the past few years.

Xianju petroglyphs, Taizhou City, Zhejiang Province

Xianju petroglyphs are located in the west of the Taizhou City, Zhejiang Province. Nine site complexes (Songlongshan, Zhongyangkeng, Xiaofangyan, Xitang, Dongping, Yuling, Yangnongdian, Duishangang and Shimengyang) comprising 220 rock art panels have been discovered within a mountainous area since 2002 (Zhang, 2009). The motifs are mainly serpent-like, rake-like, sickle-like and rectangular forms, with which the former two types are the most common. The petroglyphs are characterized by the fluency of their lines and simplicity of style. Two clusters of petroglyphs, Xiaofangyan and Songlongshan, were examined during a direct dating mission by a team of researchers from Nanjing Normal University. Most of the rock surfaces in these two sites contain crystalline quartz that offers opportunities for microerosion analysis where crystals were fractured by rock art production. The scientists have managed to secure a calibration curve on a soundly dated rock inscription Wufubei of 1203 CE and eleven age estimates from petroglyphs, ranging from E1740+590/-580 to E1200+430/-390 years BP ('BP' refers to 'before 2014') (Jin et al., 2016).

Table 1: The microerosion dating results from Xianju petroglyph sites in 2014, calibrated by the 'Wufubei' coefficient (Jin et al. 2016); The coding of micro-wanes consists of location (China Xianju), site (Xiao Fangyan1-5, '1-5' means the 5th motif on the 1st panel), type of crystal (EQ) and date (7/11/2014)

Site	*Motif*	*Micro-wane*	*Age estimate*
Xiaofangyan	'serpent'	China Xianju-Xiao Fangyan1-5-EQ-7/11/2014	E1550+430/-390
	'sickle' 1	China Xianju-Xiao Fangyan2-5-EQ-7/11/2014	E1740+590/-580
	'sickle' 2	China Xianju-Xiao Fangyan3-4-EQ-7/11/2014	E1360+380/-200
	'sickle' 3	China Xianju-Xiao Fangyan4-4-EQ-7/11/2014	E1630
Songlongshan	'square' 1	China Xianju Songlongshan1-1-P5-EQ-7/11/2014	E1310+430/-150
		China Xianju Songlongshan1-2-P4-EQ-7/11/2014	E1310+430/-150
	'square' 2	China Xianju Songlongshan2-1-P4-EQ-7/11/2014	E1240+270/-190
		China Xianju Songlongshan2-2-P4-EQ-7/11/2014	E1360+380/-200
	'square' 3	China Xianju Songlongshan3-1-P4-EQ-7/11/2014	E1220+180/-520
	'rake'	China Xianju Songlongshan4-1-P4-EQ-7/11/2014	E1400+230/-240
	'sickle'	China Xianju Songlongshan5-1-P4-EQ-7/11/2014	E1200+430/-390

Lianyungang petroglyphs, Lianyungang City, Jiangsu Province

The seaside city of Lianyungang was the northernmost locality of rock art concentration within the southeast coastlands. Crust movements forged its dominant landscape consisting of block mountains and alluvial plains during the geological time. Extensive metamorphic strata of Proterozoic exposed during the formation of fold and fracture structures; therefore, gneiss and schist are the most common types of rock around the city, and a tradition of rock art production has existed for thousands of years. Eighteen rock art site complexes distribute along the mountain slopes in the city's eastern suburbs. Cupule is the primary type, in which the ones with steep walls and rough bottoms were probably made with metal tools. However, the Jiangjunya site complex, with many concrete rock art motifs like masks and sun-like motifs (Figure 3), is an exception. In 2018 and 2019, the authors of this paper conducted two expeditions to four of the eighteen site complexes, including the sites of Shipengshan, Xiaoxishan, Shizishan and Jiangjunya. Over 280 rock art motifs (mainly cupules) on nine panels have been studied, providing nine microerosion age estimates between E2020+220/-180 and E920+100/-210 years BP ('BP' refers to 'before 2018'). During the visit to the Xiaoxishan site, the authors discovered an ancient rock inscription engraved in a unique calligraphic style, indicating its creation was no earlier than the 6th century CE. A coefficient secured from the inscription approximates the value of the Universal Calibration Curve (UCC in brief) of microerosion. Then, inspired by this, the two researchers re-calibrated the dating results of the IFRAO's 2014 expedition in the same area. Moreover, another progress worth mentioning: the authors also made the first attempt at dating some standing stones with microerosion analysis and cross-checking with archaeological and historical evidence during the rock art expeditions (Jin & Chao, 2020).

Figure 3: Surveys in 2018 and 2019 in the Lianyungang City, Jiangsu Province: left - a typical cupule group arranged in rose-like circle (photo by Chao Ge); upper right - the authors were using microerosion analysis on a standing stone; lower right - the authors were measuring a cupule and recording its size (photos by Liu Yang)

Table 2: The microerosion dating results from Lianyungang petroglyph sites in 2018 and 2019, calibrated by the UCC (Jin & Chao. 2020)

Site	*Motif*	*Micro-wane*	*Age estimate*
Shipengshan 4	'Grid' 1	China-Shipengshan4-1-EQ-1/11/2018	E2020+220/-180
Xiaoxishan 1	Cupule 17	China-Xiaoxishan1-17a-EQ-2/11/2018	E1170+260/-350
		China-Xiaoxishan1-17b-EQ-2/11/2018	E1210+320/-190
	Cupule 18	China-Xiaoxishan1-18a-EQ-2/11/2018	E920+100/-210
		China-Xiaoxishan1-18b-EQ-2/11/2018	E1070+150/-150
	'Yan Shi Hou San Shi Li' inscription	China-Xiaoxishan1-26-EQ-2/11/2018	E1170+360/-250
Xiaoxishan 2	Cupule 3	China-Xiaoxishan2-3-EQ-2/11/2018	E1410+120/-390
Jiangjunya 2	'Sun' 2	China-Jiangjunya2-S2a-EQ-22/3/2019	E1360+270/-240
		China- Jiangjunya2-S2b-EQ-22/3/2019	E1160+60/-140
Jiangjunya 3	'Mask' 2	China- Jiangjunya3-M2-EQ-22/3/2019	E1550+290/-220

Zhangzhou petroglyphs, Zhangzhou City, Fujian Province

On the southeast margin of the mainland China lies the City of Zhangzhou. Most of its territory consists of mountains and valleys, while the rest are some narrow coastal plains along the shoreline of the East China Sea. Such a natural environment has shaped the cultures for thousands of years. It thus has fostered a dualism between a fishing tradition along the eastern seashore and a mixed economy of agriculture, hunting and gathering in the western hilly lands. Five rock art sites have been reported since the last century. The Xianzitan site is the first discovered and the most well-known for its over fifty crouching anthropomorphic petroglyphs, while the rest four are all recently witnessed cupule sites (Figure 4). In 2019, the authors visited four of them, and the first one was the famous Xianzitan petroglyphs engraved on a vertical cliff of sandstone by the Taixi River. The cliff is a part of the river bank over ten meters high above the water without any places to stand steadily in front of it. The river was very turbulent, even at the end of the rainy season when the authors visited. Practically, observing from an anchored boat or wading across the water was not feasible and even dangerous, so the authors could only observe and record the art with a long-focus camera from a distance of about forty meters at the other side of the river. After that, the scientists went to the other three sites at Hudicun, Sanyangcun and Dahuishan. The petroglyphs are mainly cupules or composite motifs of cupules and grooves. Unfortunately, for the humid climate, rock art surfaces were covered by lichen or dead algae, which means microerosion analysis was not possible.

Figure 4: An overall view of the cliff bearing anthropomorphic petroglyphs at the Xianzitan site, Fujian Province (photo by Chao Ge).

Two years later, in January 2022, the authors visited a village called Zhongteng, located in an adjacent valley to the northwest. The village is known for three of a particular type of traditional earth architecture called '*tulou*', commonly round or rectangular, giant castle-like defensive houses built by the *Hakka*[1]. *Hakka* means 'guest families' in Chinese. It is a Han Chinese ethnic subgroup living in most of the southern regions of China, speaking an ancient dialect of the Chinese language. It is said that their ancestors moved from the Yellow River in central China to the north over one thousand years ago. There have been two controversial theories about the origin of *tulou*: one pointing at the 8th century CE and the other leading to the 14th century CE. Only one of the three *tulou* buildings has a precise date of construction in the late 19th century, while the other two look much older without apparent ages, and the one in the middle with a granite foundation called Yong Ping Lou seems the most primitive. The authors first secured a coefficient almost perfectly matching the UCC from a soundly dated inscription carved on a granite base of a flagpole in front of the newest *tulou* and immediately used it as the calibration curve for two age estimates secured from crushed granite blocks of the foundation of the Yong Ping Lou (Jin & Chao, 2023, in press). This worth-mentioning progress can confirm the effectiveness and correctness of UCC and has revealed the potential of microerosion analysis, perceived as a petroglyph-only method before, in dating historic buildings.

Zhuhai petroglyphs, Zhuhai City, Guangdong Province

The rock art in Zhuhai was found around the Baojingwan Bay of Gaolan Island, about 60 km to the city's southeast. A total of five petroglyph sites scattered near a Neolithic site excavated during 1997-2000. Unfortunately, two of them were vandalised during the construction of a chemical plant in 1994. The Cangbaodong site, regarded as the most important for its magnificent group-connected motifs (Figure 5) on two giant granite cliffs, is the only site accessible nowadays because dense bushes have entirely covered the rest two surviving sites. According to folklore, the rock art at Cangbaodong forms a treasure map carved by pirates in the 19th century CE; however, some experts suggest that it was early human work based on the adjacent to the Neolithic site at the beginning of the Holocene (Li, 2002; Guo, 2002).

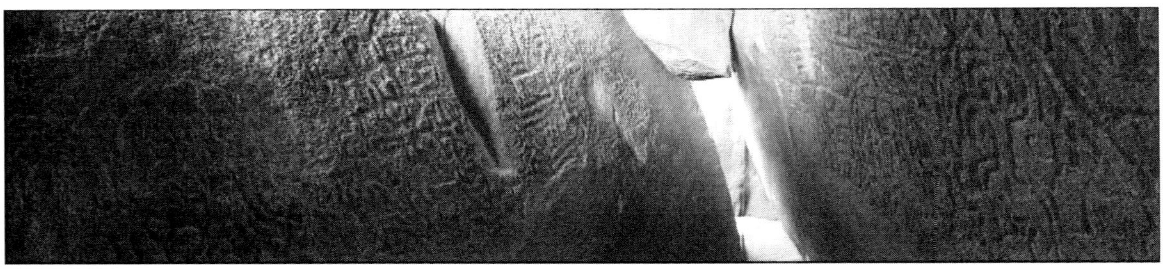

Figure 5: The Baojingwan rock art, Guangdong Province, seeing between two huge granite panels (photo by Chao Ge)

In December 2020, the authors of this paper visited the site for direct dating. After arriving at the site, they realized the positions of rock art motifs on the cliffs were too high to reach (about three meters above the ground). Nevertheless, surprisingly, two brief inscriptions engraved in Chinese, '*jin yi wan*' ('ten thousand golds') and '*mo lao xin*' ('no needs to feel vexed'), were found near the ground. A tiny micro-wane of quartz has been located in the groove of a character and analyzed through a microscope, providing a very late age estimate of E180+60/-30 years BP ('BP' refers to 'before 2020'). Considering that the average annual precipitation of Zhuhai is up to 2000 mm, and the cement of the steep rock surfaces is very loose, the authors suggest that the age of petroglyphs might not be more than one thousand years. According to the authors' rough observation, the petroglyphs and the inscriptions were all severely weathered, while the latter looked slightly better. Therefore, the legend of pirates' treasure seems more convincible, associated with the content of the inscription and the fact that piracy used to be rampant in the coastal waters around Zhuhai in the 19th century CE.

Discussion

Rock art in China's southeast coastlands consists of two major types: cupules and concrete motifs (masks, grids, ships, and waves). The former is higher in quantity but more intensively distributed in Jiangsu and Fujian Provinces, while the latter scatters broadly. A thought-provoking phenomenon is that even if they co-exist in the same area, were usually discovered at different places at different times. For instance, in Lianyungang City, the Jiangjunya site is notable for its numerous and complex mask-like motifs, yet others are all cupule sites. Another example is the petroglyphs in Zhangzhou City where all sites are tiny cupule sites except the Xianzitan site comprising dozens of crouching anthropomorphic motifs. The cupule sites are found countrywide, but their core area is around the Nanyang Basin (a geographical unit in central China). According to the authors' observation, cupule is the dominant type of rock art there (Jin, 2019; Jin & Chao, 2019). Compared with central China, the southeast coastlands have insufficient quantities and types of cupules. As regards the motifs in concrete styles, the connection with the popular types of rock art in the heartland of China can hardly be proved.

A similar conclusion comes from the dating results and technical analysis as well. According to the authors' statistics, in central China, the age estimates of cupules concentrate in the frame of 3280 - 1450 years BP (Jin & Chao, 2019); however, the production of cupules existed in a more delayed period of 1410 - 910 years BP in the southeast. On the other hand, the motifs in concrete styles, which are extremely rare in the central plains of China, occurred along the southeast coastline in the 3rd century CE. Its massive production ceased after the 8th century CE and was still later than cupules. Technically, in the southeast, the proportion of cupules made by metal tools is distinctly higher than in central China, based on the countrywide surveys since 2014 and the results of replication experiments (Jin, 2019; Jin & Chao, 2019/2020/2021). The authors have listed the characteristics of cupules made by tools of different materials (stone/metal) in Table 3 for better understanding.

Table 3: The comparison of cupules made by tools of different materials

Cupule made by stone tools	*Cupule made by metal tools*
shallow/inclined wall/flat and smooth bottom/no distinct marks of impact/the ratio of diameter to depth is no less than three to one	deep/steep wall/rough bottom/distinct marks of impact can be observed sometimes/the ratio of diameter to depth is no more than three to one

From the above, there appears to be two successive cupule production traditions, first within the central plains and then in the southeast coastlands. Such a spread was possibly connected with a continuous migration of ancient *Han* people from the north to the south during the 3rd - 6th century CE to escape nomads' invasion. On the other hand, concrete rock art, especially the crouching anthropomorphic, wave-like, spiral-like and canoe-like ones, compared with central China rock art, seem more local and perhaps even close to some popular styles in the Austronesian traditions. Therefore, considering that cupule sites and concrete rock art sites distribute separately, it is reasonable to assume that in the mid-ancient southeast coastlands, the migrants from the north lived with their clans in compact communities and kept their distance from locals for centuries.

As mentioned above, recent scientific studies on the rock art of southeast China are only the first step to revealing their true story. Still, some basic questions, such as the makers' identities of the complex concrete rock art at the sites of Jiangjunya, Xianzitan and Baojingwan, have not been thoroughly answered, which need further studies to consider. Nevertheless, the future of this regional research seems promising because, from the authors' perspective, our scientific community has underestimated the significance of the IFRAO's pioneering work in 2014. The essence of the 2014 scientific activities is the starting point of a 'scientific revolution' of this country's rock art research. The concept 'scientific revolution' was proposed by T. S. Kuhn in the last century, describing the evolution of science pushed forward by a series of 'paradigm changes' (Kuhn, 1970). Such a transitioning mechanism caused by a growing sense of crisis felt by a small number of members of the scientific community that almost all the methods based on personal experience or self-conscious responses have ceased to function adequately in the explanation of rock art. The paradigm change means a whole new framework of obtaining and verifying knowledge entirely or partially replaces the old ones, just like rock art science has been doing in the discipline. Such a replacement will overwhelmingly reconstruct the basic epistemology, methodology, standards for evaluation, management mechanism, and, most importantly, every community member's cognition. For instance, archaeologists and art historians mainly focus on the styles or types of rock art. However, in the eyes of rock art scientists, rock art production was one of the many events that rock surface has experienced for millions of years. Therefore, their mission is to rebuild the sequence of those taphonomic events. It represents an alternative way to observe the world of rock art. Though the world itself does not change with the paradigm change, from the perspective of the scientists afterwards, they respond to a new world. For the first time, scholars of different backgrounds have been sharing a universal system of terminology and methodology, aiming at puzzle-solving instead of myth-making, based on falsifiability and repeatability, the cornerstones of modern science.

Acknowledgements

We sincerely appreciate the priceless contribution to China's rock art science development made by Prof. Robert G. Bednarik and other international colleagues. Our heartfelt thanks go to Prof. Giriraj Kumar for his warm invitation and professional editing that has significantly improved the paper's quality. The research was supported by the projects FJ2020C030 and 2022M711558.

Dr Jin Anni
School of History, Nanjing University
No. 163, Xianlin Avenue, Qixia District, 210023
Nanjing, Jiangsu Province. China
sagapo330@163.com

Dr Chao Ge (corresponding author)
School of Humanities, Minjiang University
C-519, Fu Wan Lou Building
No. 200, Xiyuangong Road, Minhou County, 350108
Fuzhou, Fujian Province. China
chaogemanu@163.com

References

BEDNARIK, R. G. 2019. Natural or artificial: Fujian rock markings. *Rock Art Research* 36(2): 227-230.

CHEN L. 1984. Analysis of the Jiangjunya rock art (in Chinese). *Journal of Nanjing University of the Arts* (*Nan Jing Yi Shu Xue Yuan Xue Bao*) 20: 24-29.

DI C. 1990. Dating the Xianzitan symbolic engravings (in Chinese). *Southeast Culture* (*Dong Nan Wen Hua*) 77: 118-122.

FAN Z. 2007. The Jiangjunya rock art and the symbolic engravings on the potteries of Dawenkou culture (in Chinese). *Journal of Taishan College* (*Tai Shan Xue Yuan Xue Bao*) 29(1): 18-22.

GAI S. 1983. Discussion on the subject matter of the Jiangjunya rock art in Lianyungang City (in Chinese). *Journal of Xuzhou Normal University* (*Xu Zhou Shi Fan Xue Yuan Xue Bao*) 36: 114-120.

GUO Y. 2002. Two questions about the archaeological site and the rock art site at Baojingwan (in Chinese). *Southern Cultural Relics* (*Nan Fang Wen Wu*) 74: 34-38.

HUANG Z. 1935. The ancient rock inscription at Taixi (in Chinese). *Ling Nan Journal* (*Ling Nan Xue Bao*) 4(2): 1-7.

JIN A. 2019. *Preliminary research of cupules in China* (in Chinese). Nanjing Normal University (PhD Dissertation).

JIN A. and CHAO G. 2019. The 2018 expedition to Fangcheng cupule sites in central China. *Rock Art Research* 36(2): 157-163.

JIN A. and CHAO G. 2020. The 2018 and 2019 rock art expeditions to Lianyungang, east China. *Rock Art Research* 37(1): 74-81.

JIN A. and CHAO G. 2021. The 2018 expedition to Anshan cupule sites, northeast China. *Rock Art Research* 38(1): 3-9.

JIN A. and CHAO G. 2023. A new calibration coefficient for microerosion analysis secured in southeast China. *Rock Art Research* 40(1) (in press).

JIN A., ZHANG J., XIAO B. and TANG H. 2016. Microerosion dating of Xianju petroglyphs, Zhejiang Province, China. *Rock Art Research* 33(1): 3-7.

KUHN, T. S. 1970. *The structure of scientific revolutions* (2nd edition). Chicago: University of Chicago Press.

LI H. 1981. Survey at the Jiangjunya rock art site, Lianyungang (in Chinese). *Relics* (*Wen Wu*) 28: 21-24.

LI H. 1983. The rock art of the Jiangjunya site and early agriculture (in Chinese). *Agricultural Archaeology* (*Nong Ye Kao Gu*) 5: 75-80.

LI S. 2001. Dating of the Baojingwan rock art in Zhuhai (in Chinese). *Southeast Culture* (*Dong Nan Wen Hua*) 151: 65-73.

LIN T. 1988. The Xianzitan rock art site in Hua'an County, Fujian Province (in Chinese). *Archaeology* (*Kao Gu*) 247: 379-380.

LIN T. 1995. Study of the serpent-like rock art of the Caozaishan site in Hua'an County, Fujian Province (in Chinese). *Southeast Culture* (*Dong Nan Wen Hua*) 108: 101-103.

LIU H. 1992. The legend 'Tai Bo Ben Wu' and the Xianzitan rock art (in Chinese). *Journal of Humanities* (*Ren Wen Za Zhi*) 5: 74-78.

OU T. and LU M. 1994. A new interpretation of the Xianzitan rock art (in Chinese). *Archaeology* (*Kao Gu*) 317: 152-158.

TANG H., K. GIRIRAJ, LIU W., XIAO B., YANG H., ZHANG J., LU X., YUE J., LI Y., GAO W. and R. G. BEDNARIK. 2017. The 2014 microerosion dating project in China. *Rock Art Research* 34(1): 40-54.

WANG Z. 1991. Survey at the Xianzitan rock art site in Hua'an County, Fujian Province (in Chinese). *Southeast Culture* (*Dong Nan Wen Hua*) 88: 185-189.

ZHANG X. 2009. Study of the Xianju rock art (in Chinese). *Southeast Culture* (*Dong Nan Wen Hua*) 282: 75-80.

19

KEYWORDS: Phenomenology – Philosophy of science – Rock art

ON THE COMBINATION OF SCIENCE AND PHENOMENOLOGY

LIVIO DOBREZ

Abstract: This article gives an outline of Husserlian phenomenology, then of three philosophies of science (those of Carnap, Popper, and Kuhn). It compares and contrasts these, concluding with comments on my own use of phenomenology and science in the study of rock art.

Introduction

I am discussing science in combination with a particular philosophy because I have found it helpful to use both in writing about rock art. I make no apology for the personal tone I have chosen to adopt, following the example of Popper, who does not scruple to strike a personal note in his writing. Moreover, the personal note, like my topic, is entirely appropriate to the occasion, which is a tribute to Robert G. Bednarik, because it has been through his (forceful) encouragement that I came to a greater focus on science, in addition to an already existing interest in phenomenology. Since my leaning has been theoretical, in what follows I shall focus on the philosophical side of science.

Phenomenology: Husserl

My encounter with phenomenology goes back to postgraduate work, then to a hermeneutics course I ran for many years. Its focus has been Edmund Husserl, the founder of the discipline. Husserl was born in Moravia under the Habsburgs, but chiefly worked in Germany, where he came to be regarded as the country's foremost philosopher. His influence has been widely felt,

Manuscipt received: 7 December 2022
Revised I: 2 February 2023
Revised II:29 April 2023
Revised III: 4 June 2023
Revised IV: 13 June 2023
Accepted: 15 June 2023

and the literature on his work is immense. I intend to concentrate entirely on his earlier *Logical Investigations* (1913/1921 [1900/1901]), though I shall make occasional reference to the late so-called *Lebenswelt* writing, *The Crisis of European Sciences* (1970 [1954]), published after his death.

The *Investigations* puts forward the notion of a foundational rational epistemology which will eventually be spelled out in theoretical detail. In this early context phenomenology is simply a descriptive analysis of the experience of 'understanding', not, after the manner of psychology, as a 'psychic' mechanism but as a logical structure. That equally means not as a matter of individual experience (easily parodied in rock art studies as 'immersion' in another culture) but as non-culture-specific, in short, as universal. Necessary truths cannot be based on individual experience or the merely probable results of psychology. Thus, the law of contradiction (that a proposition cannot be both true and false), the syllogism (premise: all men are mortal; Socrates is a man; therefore—conclusion—Socrates is mortal), the mathematical 2+2=4, are necessarily true. They are true, Husserl argues, even if no one ever thought them. Of course, we may try to doubt them, but in so doing we contradict ourselves, since we continue to apply the rules of logic—without which no coherent communication is possible. Something analogous occurs in the context of everyday perception. We may doubt perception, and in given cases we may be right. But if we doubt systematically, i.e., doubt perception *as such*, we contradict ourselves by acting as if we did *not* doubt. This is the avowedly untenable position of Hume regarding causality, which would have it that my feeling pain when holding a lighted match to my finger is a case of regular coincidence, not—provably— cause and effect (Hume, 1962 [1739]). After which comment, the urbane Hume, reducing the world, and himself, to a series of impressions, smiles in mock despair and suggests sitting down to a meal and good conversation or turning to a game of backgammon. Habit, he says, inevitably drives us to behave against our intellectual scepticism. Thus, the philosophical problem is shifted, unsatisfactorily, to our psychological makeup. At this point there is no epistemological foundation, there are simply regularities that may or may not be there tomorrow. Husserl's reply to this kind of doubt is not Kant's Hume-inspired resorting to an unknowable noumenal reality, coupled with sole knowledge of the phenomenal, i.e., what *appears* to us. Rather Husserl appeals to the apodicticity of perception and of logic. As it happens perception, in the form of the *Lebenswelt*, the reality of the world presupposed in all our acts and thoughts, only takes a prominent role in the *Crisis* of the 1930s. The *Investigations* is much more concerned with the logical structures of understanding, that is, with an epistemology grounded in logic.

This approach involves analysis, from a universalist perspective, of the structures of diverse activities of consciousness, such as thinking, judging, remembering, imagining etc. It views the mind as active, with meaning generated by a mental act which takes linguistic form. Stress on this act, characteristic of philosophies of consciousness, separates Husserl's procedure from psychology. When someone speaks to us, we need not replicate mentally what they are experiencing in order to understand them. That is, we are not interested in the expression as expressed by an individual, which would be matter for psychology, or in the expression as such, which might be matter for linguistics, but in its meaning. Husserl added to this analysis via investigation into the logical structures of Parts and Wholes ('mereology'), and the distinction between 'founding' and 'founded' relations. The reason linguistic meanings function as they do is an objective matter of logic, tied to rules governing combinations, allowing some, precluding others. I can say 'the cat sat on the mat'. I can make statements that are absurd but still meaningful: 'the mat sat on the cat'. But not 'on sat cat mat the the', which is meaningless.

The key concept at this point is that of 'intentionality', which Husserl borrowed from Franz Brentano. Any thought or expression 'intends' an object, or, putting it another way, consciousness is always consciousness of something. So, meaning always intends an object of some sort. The relation of meaning to its object, that is, to meaning's 'intentional object', is at the heart of Husserl's phenomenological analysis. If I say 'the cat sat on the mat' my object is a state of affairs ('sitting') involving an object, the cat. So, the intentional object is simply whatever I am thinking about, talking about, remembering, imagining etc. And if we are listening to someone, we pick up the linguistic meaning but foreground the object of what they say, what meaning refers to, a thing or state of affairs. There are ready examples to illustrate the fact that meaning and intentional object are not the same. 'London' and the French 'Londres' have identical meaning and an identical object, viz the city in question. The expressions 'the victor at Jena' and 'the vanquished at Waterloo' have the same object (Napoleon), but quite different meanings. Knowing that we are all on the autistic spectrum, and with the benefit of a student in my hermeneutics class who worked with autistic children, I have used examples like the following to illustrate the key role played by the intentional object of meaning in phenomenology. An autistic child is asked 'how are you today?' and replies at a loss 'I don't know!' Clearly the meaning of the question has been understood, but its point has eluded the child. I myself knew such a child, high on the spectrum, who was taught to pour tea into a cup. When asked to pour, the child does so, but when the cups run out, continues to pour, this time on the table. Not because the meaning of the request has been misunderstood, but because the point of the exercise has been missed. So, the pouring is without object. The *Investigations* pursues this sort of analysis by means of the distinction between 'meaning-intention' and 'meaning fulfilment'. Full understanding requires an objective correlate of meaning. 'Getting the point' is what ensures apodicticity, grasping an object of thought, language etc. such that it makes no sense to doubt its meaning. The self-evident object is the goal of the kinds of mental acts we are considering, the way, as Husserl used to tell his students, to 'the things themselves ('*die Sachen selbst*'). And analysis of such things is entirely independent of whether they exist or not (we are perfectly able to constitute the intentional object 'unicorn'). Putting it another way, phenomenological description will apply to any logically rigorous judgement. Such a judgement will be scientific in the German sense embracing both *Naturwissenschaft* and *Geisteswissenschaft*, that is, both sciences, in the English sense, and the humanities.

In the hands of Husserl's successors, phenomenology became a varied enterprise. It could be developed away from epistemology and in the direction of ontology, as in Martin Heidegger's work. It could turn to aspects of hermeneutics untouched by Husserl, as with the work of the Polish philosopher, Roman Ingarden. It could take inspiration from the *Lebenswelt* idea and analyse bodiliness, as with that of Maurice Merleau-Ponty. Via Heidegger, it could influence French thinking from Jean-Paul Sartre to Jacques Derrida. Some of these strands of phenomenology, their Husserlian origins by now more or less radically altered, have had impact on rock art studies, the Merleau-Ponty version via Christopher Tilley, the Heideggerian and Derridan via the Julian Thomas take on archaeology.

Philosophy of science: Carnap

What about science, to which I now turn? Archaeology and anthropology (currently involved in rock art studies) have followed the social science desire of approaching their subject with something like the rigour of physics. Of course, on the matter of dating rock art, hard science has had its essential role. In a more general sense, however, Bednarik and others associated with him have been the main proponents of scientific method in rock art studies. In considering scientific theory, I am immediately faced with a difficulty of choice, given that, if there are varieties of phenomenology, there are vastly more varieties of science. To simplify matters, I have opted to focus on three philosophers—Rudolf Carnap, Karl Popper, and Thomas Kuhn—because each represents a different but influential view of science.

Carnap was a German who, like the group in Berlin which included Hans Reichenbach, Carl Hempel and Richard von Mises, joined the Vienna Circle and participated in meetings at which Ludwig Wittgenstein's earlier work was minutely discussed. Key members included Hans Hahn, Otto Neurath and Moritz Schlick. All saw themselves as primarily motivated by current developments in science. Unfortunately, their activities were increasingly taking place in the shadow of Nazism. Eventually, with Schlick assassinated, the group dissolved to reform in a more scattered way outside Germany and Austria, Carnap settling in the United States. The general philosophical leanings of the group, referred to as Logical Positivism (sometimes Logical Empiricism and, in due course, more generally, Analytical philosophy) had an immense influence in anglophone universities, with notable representatives such as Alfred Ayer in the UK and Willard V.O. Quine in the US. An introduction to their ideas may be found in Carnap's *An Introduction to the Philosophy of Science* (1995 [1966]), a publication based on lectures delivered at UCLA. While this represents a somewhat modified position held at a late stage of the author's career it nonetheless provides a reliable account of Vienna Circle views.

Carnap's account begins with observation of everyday facts which leads to the sense of regularities in the world—day followed by night, fire feeling hot etc. In science these regularities are expressed as inductive, ultimately leading to laws which explain and predict. But how does the scientist go from direct observation to indirect knowledge of regularities, i.e. how does induction operate? Whereas deduction, the method used by scientists but more usually associated with philosophy, results in conclusions that are certain (provided the premises are correct), induction cannot attain certain knowledge. The Vienna Circle originally propounded a principle of verification, but it is worth noting that the Carnap of the UCLA lectures puts his emphasis on uncertainty or, at best, confirmation (showing the influence of Popper)—though insisting that confirmation can be strong, according to what he terms 'logical probability'. At the same time, he wants to admit the notion of 'statistical probability', derived from his colleagues Reichenbach and Mises, as a key component of empirical method. Of course, this procedure can never yield more than *probable* probability, though in an infinite series of cases the gap between 'probable' and 'certain' increasingly narrows—without, however, reaching zero. Hyper-aware of Einstein's post-Newtonian revolution, and of Quantum indeterminacy (from which Einstein himself drew back) Carnap abandons nineteenth-century positivist determinism, while accepting, without undue reservations, Humean scepticism. Above all, the current state of science entirely predisposes him to opt for a probabilistic approach to knowledge.

Carnap wants to make the language of science more precise by the use of symbolic logic. Everyday language has to be purified for the purpose ('purification', with its somewhat ominous *1984* connotations, is his term). Formal symbolic language has its specific uses in science, but it is difficult not to see that rewriting language along formal symbolic lines drastically simplifies everyday understanding. How does one express 'Shall I compare thee to a summer's day?' as a symbolic formula? Carnap would no doubt reply that he has no desire to rewrite Shakespeare; it is all a matter of utility. Still, he clearly thinks whatever is expressible in formal terms is of greater significance than what cannot be so expressed. We are close here to the for a time generally accepted line in Analytical philosophy that in order to solve many traditional philosophical problems you merely rephrase them, at which point they turn out to be meaningless and consequently non-problems. I do not think Carnap in the UCLA lectures is exactly promoting such a strategy; he has gone beyond the original heady days of the Vienna Circle. At the same time his antagonism to metaphysics is visceral. Glossing over his own status as a philosopher, he habitually refers to 'philosophers' as the intellectual opposition, reportedly erasing the blackboard, prior to his lecture, of references to Plato or Aristotle left over from the previous class. This should be taken in historical context, however. While the Vienna Circle came about through the immense inspiration generated by Relativity and Quantum, it also represented, as Carnap indicates, a reaction against the legacy of nineteenth-century German Idealism. Such a reaction could lead to the dominance of 'how?' questions over traditionally metaphysical 'why?' questions, indeed to the dogmatic prohibition of all 'why?' questions. It could go as far as regarding the idea of 'matter' as an unjustified metaphysical assumption, not least because modern physics dissolved matter into micro constituents and energy fields. This might, in some minds, raise the issue of philosophical realism: Bertrand Russell reportedly teased Carnap as to whether he thought his own wife actually existed. In fact, Like Russell, Carnap is a realist, indeed in this respect also resembling the late Husserl of the *Lebenswelt* phase which acknowledges the brute fact of observable reality.

What did Carnap think of Husserl? He attended the latter's seminars, but necessarily puts phenomenology in the category of metaphysics, insofar as it relies solely on logic. Of course, Carnap also relies on logic (and indeed Logical Positivism was not called that for nothing), but the positivist element is bound to take an altogether different path. Carnap quotes Schlick as noting that the key to empirical method is the opposition to the notion of a 'synthetic a priori' statement. An analytical statement is a logical one and therefore a priori valid, i.e. independent of experience; a synthetic statement is factual and therefore a posteriori valid, i.e. dependent on experience. But Kant had allowed for the 'synthetic a priori', i.e. factual judgements which precede observation or experience of the world, i.e. which are part of our human structure rather than 'out there', in nature—the famous examples being the perception of space and time. In line with scientific developments, the Logical Positivists located time and space in nature, as an objective fact. They saw the concept of a 'synthetic a priori' as opening the door to speculative metaphysics. At the same time Carnap is highly respectful of Kant in discussing his work. And he had, it seems, good relations with Quine, who queried the fundamental Logical Positivist analytic/synthetic distinction as a dogma of empiricism.

Carnap is an impressive intellectual, and it is evident that his lucid UCLA lectures, addressed to tertiary science students, generated great enthusiasm. At the same time his denial of anything that might be labelled metaphysical is extreme, and not necessarily characteristic of philosophy of science. To my mind it recalls a memorable one-to-one exchange I had at the Australian National University, as a green academic fresh from postgraduate work on Heideggerian ontology and Sartrean existentialism, with the foremost representative of Analytical thought in Australia at the time, Jack Smart. When Smart (who had an entirely attractive habit of being blunt) told me that Sartrean philosophy was rubbish, I was bold enough to ask if he had read it. To which he replied: of course not, since it was rubbish. I myself did not accept Sartre's philosophy, but was surprised at this cavalier dismissal on the basis of circular logic. Carnap's rejection of metaphysics is specifically allied to an equally cavalier attitude to the 'prescientific', or mythic thinking, unfortunately on the basis of total ignorance of anthropology.

Philosophy of science: Popper

If Husserl's methodology is based on logic alone, empiricist methodology gives priority to the objective, not first-person but third-person knowledge. In so doing it replaces the Cartesian mind-body binary with subjective-objective. Logic remains central, though within the empiricist framework. This is so from the Logical Positivists to Popper, whose major work bears the title *The Logic of Scientific Discovery*. Beyond a fundamental, unshakeable allegiance to science, however, Popper's views diverge in every possible way from those of the original Vienna Circle. For Popper, scientific method does not begin with observation (he never ceases to castigate Francis Bacon on this score). There is no raw data (the 'bucket' theory of knowledge); theory (the 'searchlight' approach) comes first. Thus, Popper asks his audiences to 'observe', and when they reply with a puzzled 'observe what?' he has made his point. It is a radical attack on the whole concept of induction (the 'bucket' theory), simply understood as progressing from particular observation to general theory.

Rather, science begins with a problem. Once we have a problem, we seek a solution—by means of a hypothesis. Then we test the hypothesis, but not to verify (Popper does not accept the positivist verification thesis). We test in order to falsify. This according to classical *modus tollens* negative logic. The idea of falsification has great appeal. It is, for a start, in tune with the Humean argument, in my version to the effect that, if I want to verify that the match burns my finger, a thousand instances will not suffice, since the thousand-and-first may not burn. This is a little tendentious: after all, falsification, too, may involve experimental error. Still, it may be more satisfactory than an attempt to prove the hypothesis right. The result of all this is that scientific, like any other knowledge, remains forever conjectural. Its superiority lies entirely in the provision, via falsification, of a critical element. Where even the later Carnap could speak of 'strong' confirmation, Popper will go no further than 'corroboration'. But surely the experiment which confirmed Einstein's general theory of relativity, i.e., that light rays are bent by a gravitational field, suggests otherwise? Though Einstein is Popper's foremost example of scientific modernity, Popper stops short of endorsing any and all experimental results. They are always provisional and should be relentlessly tested for flaws. Science does not reach the truth or, if it does, it cannot know that it has done so. All that remains is a closer approximation to the truth. But can one speak of 'truth' at all in this context? Popper thinks one can, basing himself on Alfred Tarski's rehabilitation of the old correspondence theory of truth as conformity with the facts. It is for this reason that, quite unlike Carnap, he makes light of probabilistic theory, querying, to the (limited) extent possible, the uncertainty built into Quantum. Again his model is Einstein: God does not play dice. In the end Popper's position is more stubbornly realist than that of the Logical Positivists (he repeatedly presses this 'commonsense' view). Like Einstein, he wants an ordered universe governed by ordered laws; and he wants a (quasi-Platonic) criterion of truth as a goal, however remote—equally admitting that truth can neither be demonstrated nor disproved. More precisely, he favours the metaphor of the world as (almost) chaotic (the 'cloud' metaphor), and (almost) ordered (the 'clock' metaphor) with human reality at a mid point between the two poles of chance and determinism. Of course, in the end Carnap too had opted for an element of freedom in human activity, though on non-Popperian grounds.

Popper's views are put forward in *The Logic of Scientific Discovery* (1959 [1934]), and *Objective Knowledge* (1972), and they explain the fact that Popper, a contemporary of the Vienna Circle, was from the start, its greatest critic. Most notably, Popper was willing to take the logic of science to its conclusion, something Carnap does not do. The question becomes: in a situation of maximum conjecture, why rely on any methodology? Is not science itself yet another metaphysics? Popper does not draw back from this conclusion: science is not demonstrably the right path, though he insists that his falsifiability approach makes it a superior metaphysics. Science finally rests on an act of faith, or, as he prefers to say, on trust backed by reason. This makes it a form of secularized religion, a view especially put forward in *The Myth of the Framework* (1994). Willingness to take philosophical logic to its conclusion is part and parcel of Popper's desire, not to conflate but in some manner to reconcile the disparate worlds of the subjective and the objective. Popper outlines his thesis in *Objective Knowledge*, with the notion of three worlds: the world of the physical (world 1), that of consciousness (world 2), and that of objective thought (world 3). The aim is to return scientific knowledge to everyday knowledge, while maintaining what he calls the issue of demarcation, the difference between science and non-science. For Logical Positivism, non-science was strictly non-sense, but Popper allows for a science-oriented rehabilitation of all the old positivist *bêtes noires*: philosophy, understood as including traditional metaphysics, as well as the fought-over 'metaphysical' concepts of e.g., causality and matter. Thus, Popper gives sympathetic treatment to classical philosophies dismissed by positivism, with, e.g., his account of the concept of matter from Parmenides to modern atomic theory. He likewise tries to give weight to mythic thinking, though unfortunately (and, like Carnap, but not to the same extent) with insufficient knowledge of anthropology. Value is assigned to subjective world 2 as indispensable. Husserl's *Logical Investigations* is cited in a neutral context, though apodicticity appears to be a bridge too far.

However, Popper's definition of objectivity (world 3) is certainly odd. It is not understood in the usual ways as testable, quantifiable etc., but as human knowledge fixed in language, or, better, written script. Humans are born with innate dispositions, and at birth are faced with knowledge in preset forms: this constitutes the sphere of objectivity, necessarily including not merely the scientific but also every form of knowledge. The underpinning for this broadening out of scientific epistemology is evolutionary, with special tribute paid to Darwin. Science is viewed as a part of all experiential knowledge and therefore one with life from the beginning (the amoeba to Einstein, as Popper likes to say). However, Popper has his cake while eating it, because at this point evolution itself, from genetics to philosophy, is interpreted as following the Popperian scheme of problem-solving via falsifiability. In the process Popper rewrites human history as the history of science—more specifically as a progress through growth of knowledge. I think Popper's historical knowledge is not very convincingly historical; the teleology is simplistic and somewhat dated (the—especially Germanic—idea of the Greeks, from Thales onwards, as origin of modernity). And the result is a reaffirmation of science as the high point of human knowledge which sits poorly with Popper's insistence on all knowledge as merely conjectural. In spite of this, I think it is possible (provisionally) to accept much of what Popper has to say, with the exception of that ineradicable modern-European obsession with progress. In the event his views gained momentum in the course of the twentieth century, largely supplanting earlier scientific positivism.

Philosophy of science: Kuhn

If Popper is the most impressive twentieth-century philosopher of science, the American scholar, Thomas Kuhn, is more a historian than a thinker. Yet his book, *The Structure of Scientific Revolutions* (1970 [1962]) had an immense impact on thinking about science, and may have been a factor in the decline of Analytical philosophy. Bearing in mind Popper's willingness to allow science as a form of metaphysics, we might say that, just as, for example, the Christian claim to be a 'religion of love' is at best an idealization, so it might be that scientific method too has been idealized by its prominent apologists. Do scientists actually follow the procedures advocated by Carnap or Popper? Perhaps Kuhn is right: the ideal version represents what scientists arguably *ought* to do but in fact do *not* do. Instead of taking scientific thought as a measure of history, as Popper does, Kuhn puts it in historical perspective. The result is a sympathetic but at the same time considerably different view of science.

Kuhn begins with the notion of, at any time, the dominant scientific paradigm whose existence is largely glossed over, though its rules are perfectly evident. While being very far from monolithic, science at any time works by given overriding assumptions. These may remain unconscious; most scientists, if asked, could not readily spell them out: they have no practical need to do so, or even to be overly aware of them. Such assumptions may be found in handbooks, textbooks for student use, and philosophical publications, and are taught as a matter of course. This is what Kuhn terms 'normal' science, science as practised on an everyday basis. It involves not significant discoveries, of which the current scientific world is more likely than not to be intolerant, or which it will ignore in favour of more modest additions to existing paradigmatic structures. The paradigm sets the questions to be asked, and its problems are in the nature of local 'puzzles' within the paradigm. Puzzles are to be understood as limited problems with more or less available solutions. This situation represents the working norm familiar to the average scientist.

Naturally there are anomalies which crop up in any paradigm. These resemble Popper's problems except that they are not generally regarded as problematic. However, at a given stage some of them may begin to loom large. Why is that? Not because current theories are failing, since these continue to provide a context for increasing puzzle-solving and accumulating knowledge within the paradigm—but for many reasons, personal, sociological, political, that is, historical. The most effective reason may simply be a new generation of scientists. At this point a crisis eventuates. Scientists are willing to reconsider anomalies, now seen as contradicting aspects of the paradigm. As with philosophers of science discussed above, Kuhn readily takes the example of Relativity. This theory does not function merely as a limit to existing Newtonian principles: it changes the structure of the Newtonian paradigm. So, crisis can lead to revolution. New problems and solutions now take centre stage and the old normal, with its gradual accumulation of problem-solutions within the old paradigm, is replaced by a new normal with new problems and solutions. Kuhn postulates that paradigm shifts do not take place by the gradual growth of knowledge in the ideal situation suggested by Popper, but may be sudden. The explanation is that of a community psychology, rather than logical progress dominated by individuals. At a time of such change older theorists are unlikely to be converted by logical argument. In some cases, the new will simply have to wait for the old guard to die out. This because the new faith is somewhat in the nature of a conversion, a belief that the new paradigm will take the discipline forward.

I must say that at this point Kuhn describes equally accurately paradigmatic disciplinary shifts I have witnessed in my time as an academic—a period in which formalism in art history, the analytical in philosophy, formalist criticism in literary studies, as well as variants of these in the social sciences, disappeared, to be replaced by theories which flatly contradicted them. Older academics lost influence and the change quickly appeared as perfectly normal. Kuhn describes a scientific revolution in the same terms. At this stage textbooks etc. are revised, so that the revolution itself becomes almost invisible. The change, however radical, is rewritten as part of a single over-arching teleology, in which new premises are accepted and the past is read either as *not* contrary to the new (as in the case of a shift from Newton to Einstein)—or as *totally* contrary (the phlogiston theory), in which case the old theory is dumped.

Overall, this process means that the idealization of scientific progress is just that. You may read the process as growth of knowledge, as Popper does, but this will not be an accurate account of what actually happens. Science moves not by accumulation of knowledge within particular paradigms but by occasional paradigmatic shifts in which old problems are not falsified or new ones, as the Logical Positivists thought, verified. Rather, the old views simply become irrelevant. Does this make Kuhn's account of science relativistic? I think the author's insistence—especially in the 1970 Postscript to the book in response to critics (including Popper)—that this is not the case, should be taken at face value.

Concluding summary

Phenomenology and philosophy of science as discussed above have a common historical origin in the Germanic *Mitteleuropa* of the late nineteenth and early twentieth centuries. On the face of it there are profound differences between the two projects, dramatically highlighted by Carnap and minimized by Popper, though still in the context of a methodological demarcation. At the same time equally profound similarities emerge, notably as regards the stress on logic and universal applicability. Attempting to clarify concepts in rock art studies, it seems to me necessary to bring together scientific and phenomenological universality, and to do so via a biological approach. My response to a largely untheorized situation in rock art studies has been to adopt the realist method of the *Logical Investigations*, applying not the traditionally formalist and historical analysis of art history, nor the historical reconstruction of archaeology, but focussing on reception, i.e., not the intention behind rock art imagery but its reception by the observer. This was a phenomenological, universally valid procedure, provided analysis remained at a level compatible with the biology of seeing. On that basis it was feasible to conduct a logical analysis of rock art (or indeed any) images, via concepts of composition, juxtaposition, association and narrative, and by the identification of image categories: Canonical, Performative, Narrative. In every case the aim was to use perceptual psychology and neurophysiology in ways compatible with phenomenology—a major inspiration being James Gibson's take on visual perception, coloured by his association with Kurt Koffka and consequently Gestalt psychology, itself modelled on phenomenology. The final theoretical justification of my approach being located in the relation of the perceiving human with its ambient world, i.e., the neural/biological in its natural context. That leads to an evolutionary perspective, as, by another route, does Popper's philosophizing about science.

Livio Dobrez
9 Blair St Watson, Canberra, ACT 2602
Australia
E-mail: dobrejliv@gmail.com

References

Carnap, R. 1995 [1966]. *An Introduction to the Philosophy of Science*. M. Gardner (ed.). Dover Publications, New York.

Hume, D. 1962 [1739]. *A Treatise of Human Nature*. Fontana/Collins, London.

Husserl, E. 1913/1921 [1900/1901]. *Logical Investigations*. 2 vols. Trans. J. N. Findlay. Routledge, London/New York.

Husserl, E. 1970 [1954]. *The Crisis of European Sciences and Transcendental Phenomenology: an Introduction to Phenomenological Philosophy*. Trans. D. Carr. Northwestern University Press, Evanston.

Kuhn, T. 1970 [1962]. *The Structure of Scientific Revolutions*. University of Chicago.

Popper, K. 1959 [1934]. *The Logic of Scientific Discovery*. Hutchinson, London.

Popper, K. 1972. *Objective Knowledge: An Evolutionary Approach*. Clarendon, Oxford.

Popper, K. 1994. *The Myth of the Framework: In Defence of Science and Rationality*. M. A. Notturno (ed.). Routledge, London/New York.

20

KEYWORDS: Rock art – Hand stencils and prints – Proprioception – Mirror-neurons

A BIOLOGY-ORIENTED INVESTIGATION OF HAND TRACES IN ROCK ART

PATRICIA DOBREZ

Abstract: The article argues, to my knowledge for the first time, that trace imagery represents a special category in rock art. Focussing on hand stencils and prints, it outlines the affordance logic of trace images, going beyond discussion of their signature quality to their universally-recognizable act-aspect. This is done via a biology-oriented analysis which makes use both of cognitive science (with reference to proprioception) and neuroscience (with reference to mirror-neurons).

Introduction

The (re)discovery of parietal images at Altamira in 1868 and the publication of Sanz de Sautuola's *Breves apuntes sobre algunos objetos prehistóricos de la provincia de Santander* (1880) came in the context of a century of development in historical studies and in the wake of Darwin's 1859 *Origin of Species*. Small wonder that it resulted in an ongoing obsession with origins, including the origins of intentional markings or 'art'. It was a Shock of the Old, amplified in the area of rock art studies by subsequent finds to the near-present—Niaux, 1869; Lascaux 1940; Cosquer 1991; Chauvet 1994. At the same time archaeological work revealed unexpected antiquity in other parts of the world. Candidates for inclusion in the category of the 'earliest' art (or, more broadly, markings; more narrowly, images) are extremely varied and frequently contested: cut/scratch marks on bone or stone, finger flutings, cupules, geometrics, so-called 'naturalistic' figures of animals. My intention for some years of research into rock art has been to propose 'trace' as a possible candidate.

Article received: 7 December 2022
Revised I: 2 February 2023
Revised II:29 April 2023
Revised III: 4 June 2023
Revised IV: 13 June 2023
Accepted: 3 July 2023

The idea is not to supplant previously existing candidates, but to add to the list, and it seems to me there are reasons for it, my idea not being necessarily exclusive of most, perhaps all, others.

Trace is so glaringly an issue in human history and in discussion of rock art that no one has thought of investigating it. It is a phenomenon both self-evident and surprisingly rich in significance once explored. In the simplest terms, a trace is the remaining material evidence of a specific past event. One way of clarifying the notion is suggested by comments made by researchers about Arnhem Land hand stencils. It has been noted (Taçon 1989) that when someone dies, the person's stencil is overlaid with decoration in order to erase or minimize the potency of the image, after the usual indigenous Australian manner of post-mortem rituals aimed at discouraging the ghost of the dead from lingering among the living. However, my interest in this example is not anthropological. Instead, it serves as an illustration of the difference between a trace, in this case of a hand, and a picture of that same hand. Traces have qualities which put them in a different category from other images. I shall elaborate on this in due course. It is already clear that a trace may be of any sort, but my focus in what follows is on hands and feet, and mostly on hands, in rock art. Both leave traces of something that has taken place, and in a way that is distinct from other rock art marks. The Australian National University scholar, Anthony Forge, following the venerable anthropological opposition of nature and nurture, argued that hand stencils belonged to nature rather than to art. Though I disagree with the statement itself (there being nothing 'natural' about a hand stencil), I find it revealing of a desire to separate images of this kind from other images— which is what I have in mind with the concept of trace.

Hand imagery, either in the form of prints or stencils, is found worldwide. It is generally assumed to be very old—even where no imagery is old by world standards (as at Cueva de las Manos, Patagonia). In Australia authorities generally place hands in the early phases of their chronologies. Hands are found in many Palaeolithic European caves (Altamira, Gargas, Cosquer, Chauvet). They have been dated at 65k in Spain, though that result has been very much queried (see Bednarik 2022 for discussion of the issues), and in Sulawesi they are dated to close to 40k, in this case in combination with the earliest figural animal depictions. Interestingly these Asian finds put paid to the originally entirely Eurocentric bias of rock art studies, commented on most pointedly by Bednarik (2017).

However, my argument is less based on dating evidence or on what is generally accepted in rock art studies, with or without reliable dating. Instead, it considers the logic of traces, such as hands and feet, as relevant to the question of antiquity and indeed origin in rock art. It is reasonable to suppose that markings made by chance long preceded intentional ones. Hand prints and footprints, as trace marks, are perfect candidates in this context. A hand print may be made in sand or earth or mud without intention. It is a ready-made image. The same is true for footprints, the reading of which has plausibly been part of hominin experience from that hypothetical beginning. Other markings, for example cut-marks on bone, may be in a similar category, but the hand and foot marks have obvious prominence in the story of rock art. Trace, as a general category, may be understood as the first exogram: it goes before you. With hand and foot prints, we have an image that is an iconic given. It is perhaps easier to see the full significance of trace in the case of footprints, since tracking is a central everyday occupation of known hunter/gatherers, and I have in recent articles been especially concerned with that (P. Dobrez 2015, 2017, 2018, 2022, 2023, Dobrez and Dobrez 2023). There can be no doubt that tracking is one of the oldest activities of our human lineage. It is actually one of those activities whose beginning cannot even be located in human ancestors, as it necessarily shades off into activities engaged in by animals in general, though in different modal ways. The hunter/gatherer phenomenon of 'reading the ground like a book' has been much commented on in various contexts, including the Australian (see especially Strehlow cited P. Dobrez 2023 in press). However, comparable time-depth must be presumed to exist with respect to hands. I am not suggesting that more advanced techniques such as stencilling have been there from the beginning, though they may go back a long way. What is there from the start, with tracking, and the reading of all traces, hand or foot, is the requirement of attention, understood as a particular and everyday activity of the human nervous system. Even when dealing with chance marks of hands or feet we are entitled to assume that these are eye-catching and, in neural terms, attention-grabbing. Potent images, pre-given in this way, will become intentional over time. I do not seek to speculate on this process, only to point out its logic: over time, unintentional traces become intentional marks, and indeed come to be a key component of the rock art imagery repertoire. Nor do I speculate on what might prompt such development, which probably requires both neural and behavioral explanation. Nonetheless, at some point and for a variety of reasons, the hand stencil is added to the hand print, and the foot stencil and, no doubt later, the foot petroglyph, is added to the footprint. So, there is progression from nature to culture, from chance to intentional marking, or to rock art. Surprisingly, so powerful is the original trace impulse that the simplest form of, in particular hand marks, the print, endures to the near-present.

My argument postulates that hand stencils and prints are in a special category of representation. They are distinct in that, whatever else they may be, they cannot be pictures of something, even though they have an iconic quality. Thus, in what follows I exclude consideration of hands that are drawn, painted or engraved. To the extent that the hand image becomes a mimetic likeness it ceases to function as a trace. This is equally true if its making is time-consuming, as with petroglyphs. The trace image must have the quality of immediacy, the elusive indication of trace. This, however, needs to be looked at more closely. A print or stencil is not an inert image but the record of a particular act which remains present in the image, that is, as trace of the act. The trace element has two separable aspects, though these inevitably coexist. I refer to these as 'author-identity' and 'act-identity'. The first of these has been much commented on, usually in an ethnographic context, especially in Australia. It testifies to a particular identity, the maker of the image, necessarily specified via cultural knowledge. Thus, it is said that Australian indigenous people easily recognize stencil hands as being of known individuals (the same is said of feet). This is what I term author-identity. Alternatively, or rather concurrently, the print or stencil records the act as act or as an event that has taken place, that is, it records not merely the maker but the making itself. In this sense the image is self-specifying or self-referential: it registers the immediacy of the action that brought it into being. Since it registers in this uniquely direct manner, it necessarily refers to a single event, which explains why the worked-over image, such as the petroglyph, does not qualify as a trace. I term this second aspect the act-identity of the image, an aspect which has been glossed over in previous discussion of stencils and prints, either because it appears to require no comment, or because commentators have failed to see its significance. In the present context it is this aspect of certain images, distinguishable from cultural knowledge of the sort required for individual identification (author-identity), which is of interest to me.

Act-identity relates to perception of universal, non-culture-specific features. When a hand image receives further decoration, the identity of the author is obliterated to a greater or lesser extent, as is the trace quality. The same is true for patterned hands (hand prints with a superimposed pattern, or a pre-inscribed palm print). Hands involving gestural manipulation retain both author and act identity. (I am referring to the old notion of 'mutilated' hands, partially valid, for example in Australia—the Eora of the Sydney area—and the USA—the Plains Mandan—but now generally discredited). Other features of hand imagery such as placement on the rock surface, size, pigment etc., have no effect on author or act identity. They are simply added cultural factors. Specifically symbolic meanings, also cultural in nature, cannot override the primary meaning of the image, which relates to the act of its making, and can be thought of as a freeze-frame of that original single act. This primary meaning, assuming no subsequent over-painting or alteration, remains accessible to any observer, since it is built into the image: in other words, it will be recognized by anyone, whether familiar with the author and the author's cultural context, or wholly unfamiliar with it.

I have pointed out the fact that trace hands are iconic, a fact that should not be glossed over as self-evident, but needs to be understood as profoundly important, since it qualifies trace imagery of hands (and feet) as the original, made-by-chance iconic image. At the same time, as explained above, the trace image differs from any other mimetic likeness. Hand stencils and prints have the canonical form of the hand without being a mere illustration. It is this distinctive (because direct) likeness that has prompted discussion of the image as a 'signature', an idea that takes one back to stress on author-identity. I certainly accept individual signature as an element of the trace image, but think it is unfortunate that emphasis on it has reduced trace images to their purely deictic meaning: a statement to the effect that 'I am X' or 'X was here'. Instead, I suggest that, following the idea of an act-identity, it makes sense to think of trace images as a statement to the effect that 'X is *doing* this'. Doing, however, envisaged not as the activity of an individual cut off from their environment, but intimately connected with it, and in a strictly bodily way, that is, as doing something to, and in interaction with, the world around it. This point requires further investigation. What I seek to do here, and what has not been done before, is to apply perceptual psychology/cognitive science, combined with my own analysis of trace, to the study of rock art. To begin with, I appeal to stress on the 'ecological', as proposed by James Gibson and others

(Gibson 1979; Neisser 1993). Gibson's concern was mostly with the visual. In what follows, I wish to make particular use of the concept of proprioception, which relates to the experience of one's body, the awareness which makes it possible to drive a car through a gate without having to check the precise width of the space—because the car has been incorporated into the sense of one's body. In the case of print or stencil, once the image has been made it becomes a means of self-recognition on the part of the author, but a recognition that is not simply mental. I think this idea can be grasped with help from the work of various cognitive researchers. In particular I refer to the sense of agency and of body ownership, both part of proprioceptive experience (Bermúdez 1998; Tsakiris et al. 2005, 2007; Knoblich et al. 2006). In general, the sense of one's body and of agency operate together. I know myself in my hand-and-arm action as I make that print, and I equally know I am acting as an agent in the operation. In addition, I am acting within an ecological relationship, affecting that affordant rock surface. (Small wonder that makers of such imagery are more likely than not to regard the rock as more important than the mark placed on it.) It is worth noting, however, that agency and body ownership may be distinguished, as argued by Gallagher (2000, 2005) and demonstrated by experiments based on the rubber-hand or incorporated fake limb illusion (Kalckert and Ehrsson 2012). In the making of prints and stencils the distinctive factor is that the activity has been externalized in an image, that is, in its trace. I suggest the bodily mechanism that comes into play here might be similar to the one involved in one's relation to one's shadow as proposed by Knoblich et al. 2006. Here agency and ownership may be distinguished, as they are in the rubber-hand experiment, and this offers the interesting possibility that if I code my shadow as an externalized body-part (analogous to the rubber hand, or indeed the vehicle I drive through the gate), I may do the same with the hand externalized as a trace image. This certainly begins to explain the complexity of the print or stencilling operation and the deep-time fascination it has had for humans around the world.

There is nonetheless much more to be said on this subject. So far, for a start considering the relation of the image to its maker, I suggest that trace imagery reengages the original act but, because this is now externalized, as no longer the maker's own. Struck by the fact that indigenous people in the Australian Kimberley and Arnhem Land refer to stencils as hand *shadows* (Basedow 1925; Peterson 1972) I also think that the situation may be analogous to that of our shadow, on which we project our body-awareness such that the shadow becomes an incorporated part of ourselves while remaining separate from us. This raises a specific question: which way does the shadow face, that is, away from us, or towards us? Normally the assumption is that it faces away, that is, exactly replicates the body-position. However, it is possible to make a perceptual switch and register it as facing *towards* the body it shadows. There is anecdotal evidence for this, involving such experience as 'fear of one's own shadow'. Applying the perceptual switch to the hand image, we turn from the relation of image to its maker to the relation of image to any subsequent observer. The key point to be made here is that while it is possible to register that hand as going *into* the rock surface, especially via what psychologists have termed semantic intrusion, that is, prior knowledge of the way hand images are made, it is more plausible to consider them as coming *out*, towards the observer. Before I offer experimental support for this statement, I need to raise the parallel with looking at one's palm viewed in a mirror, with its concomitant (dorsal to frontal) switch in which the left hand appears as a facing right hand and a right hand as a facing left one. There is good reason to think of the rock surface supporting a stencil or print as prompting a mirror effect. Various animals have been tested in connection with mirror recognition, with monkeys recognizing themselves as conspecifics, that is, as other monkeys, but only apes and humans recognizing themselves as individuals. These last in fact can perform both operations, the social as well as individual recognition response (Anderson 1994; Gallup 1994; Rochat and Zahavi 2011).

The important element to add here in connection with the response to the hand as mirror-image is that this image is no more static than, as argued above, inert. Experiments in Representational Momentum, initially by Jennifer Freyd, showed that it was possible to measure the extent to which subjects saw movement in a still picture. One experiment (Kelly and Freyd 1987) involved increase/decrease in size of images offered to the viewer. Inevitably increased size in stills registered not as size change but as the image coming *closer* to the viewer (Schiff et al. 1962; Gibson 1979). It is well known experientially that the hand image appears to confront or arrest you, hence its use as a traffic STOP sign. To quote Banggal, a Kimberley custodian 'singing' his stencils:

> *Stop! Stop! Don't trespass*
> *Stop! Listen to us*
> *And this is the hand sign saying stop*
>
> (Ngarjno et al. 2000)

I suggest that the reverse image, as seen in a mirror or in the situation of the shadow, helps explain the element of strangeness or the uncanny in that experience (Rochat and Zahavi 2011), and that something similar occurs with reversed hand imagery, in this case perceived as moving towards the observer. We are now in a position to begin to appreciate the intensity of the response to the hand image, not so much as a mere picture but as a trace, the mark of an act which retains the power of the original activity and indeed communicates it to another person. In line with texts cited above on the phenomenon of proprioception, I also propose that this communication is not merely via the visual. When the hand image appears as encroaching on the observer's personal space or 'looming', the observer registers via a whole-body operation. To fully appreciate this, I appeal to yet another mirror analogy, this time in neuroscience: the work which has been done on mirror-neurons.

This thesis, now widely accepted, postulates that we respond to another person's action through the processing carried out by very particular neural ensembles (Rizzolatti et al. 2001; Rizzolatti and Craighero 2004). In addition to the visual, this response has a motor component, encouraging imitation. I witness X touching her arm and am prompted to do the same. Moreover, I imitate because I have already understood the other's movement. The idea has led to much discussion of mirror-neurons as a substrate for the phenomenon of empathy (Freedberg and Gallese 2007). However, my interest, and the relevance of the argument for the present article, need not go so far. For my purposes, the mirror-neuron thesis proposes a connection between the hand gesture and its imitation. In this context it is critical that the hand should be seen to do something, that is, to move. Hence the emphasis I place on the Freyd experiments of the hand image as forward looming. Mirror-neuron researchers have called their hypothesis 'direct-matching' (Rizzolatti et al.; Urgesi et al. 2006), the process whereby we imitate in a whole-body way by mapping observed movement onto our own motor representation of the act. I suggest this mechanism might operate in the situation of observing a hand image on a rock surface, such as to stimulate the observer's motor system. This ultimately to replicate the print or stencilling act but, equally importantly, to explain still further the fascination of the hand image, ubiquitous in space and time, and, as argued above, a candidate for that *ur*-mark—along with the footprint—the first iconic exogram, no doubt initially made by chance and only over time carried out with specific intent. Experiments show that whereas monkeys respond to transitive hand-object actions (such as imitating a grasping motion), apes and humans also respond to intransitive or non-goal-directed actions (Gallup 1994). This implies that mirror-neurons have great significance for human resonant activities, in particular speech, a view relevant to the position of the motor/hand area of the brain as adjacent to, and working in tandem with, neural areas dedicated to the mouth.

At this point, via the mirror-neuron thesis, hand images may be seen as having a deep-time connection with communication, and in a variety of ways. This conclusion has already been anticipated in the discussion of Representational Momentum and the hand's use as a confrontational sign. As such the hand directly communicates, even if the observer has no cultural information about its specific significance. The hand stops the viewer short, prompting a sense of interest or concern. Whatever else, it is, as noted above, neither inert nor static, and this by virtue of its being a trace of an act. In this way we may postulate a 'matching' of the original making act with a corresponding resonant motor response in the viewer of the stencil or print. The mirror-neuron hypothesis argues that language evolution itself has close relation to the mirror-neural system (Rizzolatti and Arbib 1998; Arbib 2005). This would be via gestural communication, including by means of the mouth, understood as oro-laryngeal gestures, and linked to the adjacent Broca's area. By analogy the hand image speaks for the author in their absence and as a result enables others to communicate both with the author and each other via the hand image. Independently of the mirror-neuron thesis, however, the hand image also has the capacity to be read as a sign in the absence of the maker. This has been proposed, though in a theoretical vacuum: the hand as a sign, through 'digital manipulation'. I think the present article goes well beyond this notion, though it certainly reinforces it. In this context one might envisage studies linking hand images to the origins of written signs, but that is a matter for future research. As I see it, my contribution is primarily to focus on and find surprising depth in the idea of a trace image.

I pointed out earlier in this article that trace has been overlooked and has remained unanalyzed as a key feature of frequently-repeated rock art images. Against this I have argued that trace imagery, for present purposes, hands, is in a very special category. A trace is iconic, but not a picture of something. It has its own engaging logic which I have attempted to trace. To begin with and most importantly it represents the trace of an action. Accordingly, it has both the character of author-identity and act-identity. Author-identity has been implicitly noted in the frequent observation that a hand image functions as a signature of its maker. But I have wanted to go beyond this culture-specific, though itself interesting, aspect of the stencil or print, to the act-identity which is universally recognizable, and, as I try to show, based on biology. I have examined the biological in terms of proprioception, the twin senses of agency and body ownership. Because in the case of hand images, the act of making is externalized in a lasting trace, it is possible to analyse the bodily way in which this affects both the maker, reengaging with the original action, and subsequent observers, able to put the image to further use, either culturally or universally (non-culturally), as a form of communication. In this connection I referred to two analogies, that of the shadow and the mirror, in each case focusing on a perceptual dorsal-to-frontal switch which makes the image intensely resonant by prompting viewer response to it as moving towards the viewer. The issue of motion led to a mirror-neural account of understood and, accordingly, imitated gesture, in turn leading to considerations regarding possible origins of speech in gesture and to gestural sign language, in time, to one possible origin of the written sign. All this in the light of the mirror-neural thesis account of likely substrates for bodily (empathetic) responses, in the present case applied to the hand image. Use of cognitive science as well as neuroscience provided corroborating evidence for my argument from diverse quarters. These are all testable, as indeed I think is much of what I am calling the affordant logic or operational mechanism of trace imagery, something which to my knowledge, and perhaps surprisingly, has not been investigated before. Everything is contained in the phenomenon of trace. Once this has been fully taken in, the rest follows: the fact that the trace, as trace of an act, remains active, that is, prompts a response to perceived motion and in turn prompts motion, ultimately for purpose of communication.

For more detailed discussion of points raised above the reader is referred to P. Dobrez 2013.

Patricia Dobrez
9 Blair St Watson, Canberra, ACT 2602
Australia
dobrezp@gmail.com

References

Anderson, J. R. 1994.The monkey in the mirror: a strange conspecific. In S. T. Parker, W. Mitchell and M. L. Bocca (eds), *Self-Awareness in Animals and Humans: Developmental Perspectives*, pp.315-329. Cambridge University Press, Cambridge.

Arbib, M. A. 2005. From monkey-like action recognition to human language: an evolutionary framework for neurolinguistics. *Behav. Brain Sci.* 28: 105-124.

Basedow, H. 1925. *The Australian Aboriginal.* F. W. Preece and Sons, Adelaide, Australia.

Bednarik, R. G. 2017. *Palaeoart of the Ice Age*. Cambridge Scholars Publishing. Newcastle, UK.

Bednarik, R. G. 2022. The dating of rock art and bone by the uranium-thorium method. *Rock Art Research* 39 (2): 195-204.

Bermudez, J. L. 1998. Ecological perception and the notion of a nonconceptual point of view. In J. L. Bermúdez, A. Marcel and N. Eilan (eds), *The Body and the Self,* pp.153-173. The MIT Press, Cambridge, MA, USA.

Dobrez, P. 2013. The case for hand stencils and prints as proprio-performative. *Arts* 2: 273-327.

Dobrez, P. 2014. Hand traces: technical aspects of positive and negative handmarking in rock art. *Arts* 3: 367-393.

Dobrez, P. 2015. Their proper sphere: situating human feet in rock art. In H. Collado Giraldo and J. J. Garcia Arranz (eds), *Proceedings of the XIX International Rock Art Conference* IFRAO 2015 (Cáceres, Spain), ARKEOS 37 (CD): 259-277.

Dobrez, P. 2017. From tracks to gesture-derived inscription: an Australian genealogy for "tracks and lines" petroglyphs. *Rock Art Research* 34 (2): 149-168.

Dobrez, P. 2018. The body as intelligent tool: the making and reading of trace and trace-derived forms in rock art. *Time and Mind* 11 (1): 41-65.

Dobrez, P. 2022. In Livio Dobrez and Patricia Dobrez. Move! Rock art profile and trace-view images. You Tube ARARA, 14 July 2022, https://www.youtube.com/

Dobrez, P. [In Press] 2023. Rock art profile and plan view narratives, and their combination. *American Indian Rock Art.*

Dobrez, P. and Dobrez, L. (forthcoming) 2023. Negotiating, interpreting and representing the natural world: cognitive aspects of indigenous Australian dreamings. *Rock Art Research.*

Freedberg, D. and Gallese, D. 2007. Motion, emotion and empathy in aesthetic experience. *Trends in Cognitive Science* 11: 197-203.

Gallese, J. J. 1979. *The Ecological Approach to Visual Perception*. Houghlin Mifflin: Boston MA, USA.

Gallagher, S. 2000. Philosophical conceptions of the self: implications for cognitive science. *Trends in Cognitive Science* 4: 14-21.

Gallagher, S. 2005. *How the Body Shapes the Mind.* Clarendon Press, Oxford, UK: 173-178.

Gallup, G. G. Jr. 1994. Self-recognition: research strategies and experimental design. In S.T. Parker, R. W. Mitchell and M. L. Bocca (eds), *Self-Awareness in Animals and Humans: Developmental Perspectives*, Cambridge University Press, Cambridge, UK: pp.35-50.

Kalckert, A. and Ehrsson, H. H. 2012. Moving a rubber hand that feels like your own: A dissociation of ownership and agency. *Frontiers in Human Neuroscience* 6: 1-14.

Kelly, M. H. and Freyd, J. J. 1987. Explorations of representational momentum. *Cognitive Psychology* 19: 369-401.

Knoblich, G., Thornton, I. Grosjean and M., Shiffrar, M. 2006. Integrating perspectives on human body perception. In Knoblich, G., Thornton and M., Shiffrar, M. (eds), *Human Body Perception from the Inside Out*. Oxford University Press, Oxford, UK: 3-8.

Neisser, U. 1993. The self-perceived. In Neisser, U. (ed.), *The Perceived Self: Ecological and Interpersonal Sources of Self-knowledge*. Cambridge University Press, Cambridge, UK: 3-21.

Ngarjno, Ungudman, Banggal and Nyawarra 2000. Gwion Gwion: Dulwan Mamaa. In Doring, J. (ed.), *Secret and Sacred Pathways of the Ngarinyin Aboriginal People of Australia*. Könemann, Köln, Germany.

Peterson, N. 1972. Totemism yesterday: Sentiment and local organization among the Australian Aborigenes. *Man* (new series) 7: 12-32.

Rizzolatti, G. and Arbib, A.1998. Language within our grasp. *Trends Neurosci.* 21: 188-194.

Rizzolatti, G., L. Fogassi and V. Gallese 2001. Neurophysiological mechanisms underlying the understanding and imitation of action. *Nature Reviews Neuroscience* 2: 661-670.

Rizzolatti, G. and L. Craighero 2004. The mirror-neuron system. *Annual Review of Neuroscience* 27: 169-192.

Rochat, P. and D. Zohavi 2011 The uncanny mirror: a re-framing of mirror self-experience. *Consciousness and Cognition* 20: 204-213.

Schiff, W., J.A. Caviness and J.J. Gibson 1962. Persistent fear responses in rhesus monkeys to the optical stimulus of "looming." *Science* 136: 982-983.

Taçon, P. S. C. 1989. From rainbow snakes to "x-ray" fish: The nature of the recent rock painting tradition of western Arnhem Land, Australia. Ph.D. Unpublished Thesis, Australian National University, Canberra, Australia.

Tsakiris, M, P. Haggard, N. Franck., N. Mainy and A. Sirigu 2005. A specific role for efferent information in self-recognition. *Cognition* 96: 215-231.

Tsakiris, M., S. Schütz-Bosbach and S. Gallagher 2007. On agency and body-ownership: phenomenological and neuroscience reflections. *Consciousness and Cognition* 16:645-660.

Urgesi, C., V. Moro, M. Candidi and S. M. Aglioti 2006. Mapping implied body actions in the human motor system. *Journal of Neuroscience* 26: 7942-7949.

21

KEYWORDS: Rock Art Discipline – India – Contribution – Concept – Theory – EIP Project – Replication

INDIA'S CONTRIBUTION TO THE DEVELOPMENT OF ROCK ART DISCIPINE

GIRIRAJ KUMAR

Abstract: Rock art is a global phenomenon and is an important source for understanding the cognitive, intellectual, technical, and cultural development of hominins. A lot of research has been carried out on it throughout the world. However, the IFRAO members, by following the concept and guidelines of IFRAO, are playing a crucial role in developing the Rock Art Discipline by their scientific contributions. This paper presents India's contribution to the development of the Rock Art Discipline in terms of concept and theory.

1. Introduction

Rock art presents the essence of life, which early man depicted on the bare surface of rock in the form of exograms. It depicts his perception of reality in space and time and his code of conduct to behave in relation to the self, with conspecifics, with the physical and living environment, and his understanding of the universe and universal phenomena developed in the light of that perceived reality. It formed the foundation of living a meaningful and blissful life for the authors of rock art. So developed codes of conduct are collectively known as culture. The culture has been lived and transmitted from generation to generation in each environment.

Rock art has been one of the powerful means of such communication created and developed by human beings. It is a global phenomenon. Thus, rock art is an important archaic human creation for communication which has survived the vagaries of time. At some places as in Australia the process of rock art production is continuing even at present, while at other places, like India, some of the forest dwelling communities are somehow associated with rock art sites. Therefore, it is an

Article received:17 August 2022
Revised I:13 January 2023
Revised II: 20 January 2023
Accpted: 21 January 2023

important source for understanding the perceived reality of its authors which can form the basis to comprehend and appreciate the cognitive, intellectual, technological, epistemological and cultural development of early man in each environment through time and space. For that we need scientific study of rock art and the very mindset to do so. That is the future course of rock art research.

For the last two centuries rock art was mainly studied by archaeologists. The focus of archaeology in rock art study has been on observing forms and styles and attempting to determine their antiquity and meaning. Such stylistic constructs were most particularly valued in the creation of chronological sequences. Those of the Upper Palaeolithic cave art of Europe greatly influenced model-building elsewhere. Generations of researchers have modelled their thinking on the now-discredited chronology, and there is strong opposition to reform within the discipline of archaeology (Bednarik 2007: 11). It has badly retarded the development of Rock Art Discipline.

1.1. The birth of IFRAO

The endeavour of rock art science is to understand the cognitive, technological, intellectual, and cultural world of the past and present societies, and ultimately in determining how our species acquired its very concepts of reality. For that the Rock Art Discipline needed freedom from the clutches of archaeology and the focus of rock art scholars and scientists should be on obtaining reliable empirical evidence. To achieve this objective the International Federation of Rock Art Organisations (IFRAO) was established in the first world congress of rock art researchers organised by Australian Rock Art Research Association (AURA) at Darwin in Australia in 1988. IFRAO provided an umbrella to the scholars and scientists to work scientifically to study rock art empirically.

IFRAO was led by very dedicated and resourceful scholars who co-ordinated their strategies so effectively that it caught an antiquated establishment off-guard in some cases. India has been one of the early members of IFRAO. Today, the needed changes in the Rock Art Discipline are far from complete, but it has already become adequately clear that the progress made in the discipline in the last fifteen years of the 20th century exceeds in magnitude that of the previous 200 years (Bednarik 2007: 12). It led the foundation of Rock Art Discipline on solid scientific grounds.

1.2. Nurturing Rock Art Discipline

Within the last few decades, rock art research has adopted numerous new methods, all contributed by scientific disciplines. They include a wide range of physical and chemical analyses of rock art-related materials, such as the identification of inclusions in paint residues and mineral accretions, ranging from fibres to pollen. Much of this work is directed at questions of antiquity, but numerous other issues also attract attention now. For instance, the technology of paints used in rock art, as well as of their application, are being analysed. The nano-stratigraphy of paints and mineral accretions has shown how sequences of rock art can be studied scientifically rather than by archaeological intuition. Numerous approaches are being developed in the ever-crucial question of the age of rock art. Field microscopy of rock art has been developed for several purposes, including microerosion dating, petrography and technological analyses. The discrimination between anthropogenic and non-anthropogenic rock markings, which has been a significant difficulty for archaeologists, has been developed into a fine art. Much the same has been developed for portable art objects, as well as the detection of fakes. Replication studies have been attempted, although they remain still in their infancy. The related subject of production processes of petroglyphs has received some close attention. Of particular importance is the development of taphonomic logic, which is crucial in developing a science of rock art (Bednarik 1994). Rigorously framed statistical approaches are being developed. In all these many new approaches to rock art study, the epistemology applied to the formulation of theories and interpretation of palaeoart has become central.

In this new development, the archaeologist has a role to play in the future development of the discipline as one of the members in a team of several researchers and will no longer be able to dictate the terms of research priorities or the direction of the discipline. Archaeologists, like colleagues from art history, anthropology, ethnography, geography, semiotics, geomorphology, geochemistry, palaeoecology, palaeoenvironmental sciences, nuclear physics, conservation science and so forth, will contribute their diverse talents to this complex discipline if they have the flexibility to collaborate in such ways. However, the agenda will no longer be that rock art is to explain archaeology (Bednarik 2007: 13).

2. India's contribution to the development of Rock Art Discipline

2.1. Initial stage (second half of the twentieth century CE)

Though the first Indian rock art site was 'discovered' by Archibald C. L. Carlleyle in 1886, it was the scientific work in the form of excavations, documentation, and study of rock art of Bhimbetka and in the associated region by V. S. Wakankar in 1970s which laid the foundation of Rock Art Discipline in India (Wakankar 1975, 1978, 2008; Wakankar and Brooks 1976). The Bhimbetka complex of painted rockshelters was discovered by Wakankar in 1957. At that time European cave art was considered as the oldest and superior to the rest of the world. Wakankar believed that rock art of India had its unique narrative features and was as old as that of European rock art. It has been proved by his work at Bhimbetka followed by that of Erwin Neumayer (1983, 1993). However, recent research in central India has established that Indian rock art (early petroglyphs) extends in antiquity to the Lower Palaeolithic and is many times older than European rock art (Bednarik 1993a, Bednarik et al. 2005; Kumar et al. 2005).

Though Wakankar also followed the European model of stylistic classification and study like many scholars in the world, he made some scientific observations such as that the earliest rock paintings of the dynamic dancers and wild herbivores executed in free-flowing fine outlines of green and red colours are concealed under salt accretion which was the result of dry climate. He assigned these rock paintings to Upper Palaeolithic period (Wakankar 1975, 1978, 2008). Such kind of dry climate was followed by the beginning of monsoon climate in the Holocene period.

This change in climate resulted in abundance of vegetable food and wild fauna. The vibrant and thematic Mesolithic art flourished in that congenial environment. Such kind of study of the effect of climatic change on rock art is called as taphonomy of rock art nowadays.

Scientific study of rock art and archaeology of Bhimbetka including excavations during 1970s established that Bhimbetka is a unique Stone Age site in India having continuity of cultural traditions right from Mode-1 (chopper-chopping tool) industry in Lower Palaeolithic age till Historical period up to a few centuries back. This cultural tradition is continued by the *Adivasis* (tribal communities) living in the region. Because of these unique features, the Bhimbetka complex of rock shelters was nominated as the World Heritage Site under natural and human cultural heritage categories by UNESCO in 2003 (Ota 2005: 83–88, 2008).

2.2. *First two decades of 21st century*

2.2.1. The EIP Project

The EIP Project was established in the third AURA Congress, in Alice Springs, Australia, in 2000. EIP is the short form of the high-profile project by RASI and AURA on "Early Indian Petroglyphs: Scientific investigations and dating by International Commission". The primary purpose of the EIP Project was to investigate extraordinary claims from India that imply that the earliest known rock art tradition in the world might have been found in that country. If correct, certain archaic art traditions in India could be several times as old as the oldest previously dated rock art, that of the Upper Palaeolithic of France (dated to about 32,000 years BP in Chauvet Cave up to 2002). The principal Indian sites in question are Auditorium Cave at Bhimbetka (near Bhopal, M. P.), Daraki-Chattan (near Bhanpura, M. P.), and Bajanibhat (a rockshelter near Kotaputli, Rajasthan).

The propositions of an extremely early cultural sophistication in southern Asian rock art are of the utmost importance to world archaeology, to hominid evolution and to profound questions of the origins of culture, cognition, and art-producing human behaviour. Extraordinary claims deserve extraordinary care in their consideration and scientific testing, and it was the purpose of the EIP Project to conduct such testing. This project assembled an international commission to review the claims made concerning Indian early petroglyphs. It used methods such as carbon isotope analysis, optically stimulated luminescence dating, surface luminescence dating, microerosion analysis and archaeological excavation. Palaeomagnetic dating was also tried but could not succeed.

The EIP Project enjoyed the backing and collaboration of several research laboratories in Australia and Greece, and it has substantial support from the Archaeological Survey of India, the Indian Council of Historical Research and the Australia-India Council in Canberra, and also from numerous Indian scholars. This project has been the first of its kind to attempt scientific dating of Indian rock art as well as to provide a comprehensive chronological framework for the Palaeolithic periods of India. It was thus anticipated to result within a very short time in a massive increase in our knowledge of Indian rock art and Pleistocene archaeology.

2.2.1.1. Daraki-Chattan Cave

Daraki-Chattan Cave (DC) in the Chambal basin is of great significance and has been thoroughly studied scientifically under the EIP Project (Fig. 1, 2, 3). Daraki-Chattan is a small, narrow and deep cave in the upper strata of quartzite buttresses of Indragarh hill, which are broken into big blocks by vertical fracturing. With more than 500 cupules on both its vertical walls it is an extraordinary Palaeolithic cupule site in Chambal basin in the Bhanpura-Gandhisagar region, district Mandsaur, Madhya Pradesh (exact location is not given because of protective reasons but the precise GPS coordinates have been recorded; Kumar 1995).

Figure 1: Daraki-Chattan Cave (DC) in quartzite buttresses of Indragarh Hill

Daraki-Chattan Cave was discovered by Ramesh Kumar Pancholi in 1993 (Pancholi 1994: 75) and was scientifically documented and studied by Giriraj Kumar assisted by his son Ram Krishna in 1995 (Kumar 1995), then from 2001 onward under the EIP Project. The study is still continuing. Daraki-Chattan was excavated under the EIP Project from 2002 to 2006 under the direction of Giriraj Kumar. Narayan Vyas, then Deputy Superintending Archaeologist in ASI, Bhopal Circle, was the official representative of ASI and co-director of the excavations. A. Pradhan, P. K. Bhatt and R. K. Pancholi were the other members of the excavation team. Many scholars and scientists from India and abroad visited the site time to time during 2002 to 2009. The area excavated from 2002 to 2006 was 33 square meters. The first tangible findings were presented

Figure 2: Southern face of DC bearing many cupules and showing scars formed due to exfoliation of cupule bearing slabs.

Figure 3: Cupules on the southern wall of the DC.

at the RASI-IFRAO Congress at Agra at the end of November 2004 and have been published in 2005 (Kumar et al. 2002; Kumar et al. 2005, Bednarik et al. 2005), but fieldwork and scientific investigations have continued, and will take several more years to complete (Krishna and Kumar 2010; Krishna and Kumar 2012a, 2012b, 2012c; Kumar and Prajapati (Krishna) 2009; Kumar and Krishna 2014). To make the results of the EIP Project easily accessible a project webpage was established by Robert G. Bednarik at *<http://mc2.vicnet.net.au/home/eip1/web/index.html>*.

2.2.1.1.1. Lower Palaeolithic cupules and linear petroglyphs obtained from the excavations in the Auditorium Cave, Bhimbetka and in the fore front of Daraki-Chattan

2.2.1.1.2. Petroglyphs in the Auditorium Cave

Evidence for one of the oldest forms of rock art in the world comes from Bhimbetka. Here, in Wakankar's trench in Auditorium Cave BHIM III F-24, excavated in 1972, Robert G. Bednarik observed a man-made big, deep cup mark and an engraved meandering line above it on a boulder in 1990 (Fig. 4). It was covered by the uppermost Acheulian stratum that was sealed by a more compact Middle Palaeolithic deposit; hence, there is no chance of later disturbance (Bednarik 1993a: 32, Bednarik 1996) (Fig. 5). Besides, there are nine archaic cupules on the Chief's Rock standing in the centre of Auditorium Cave (Fig. 6).

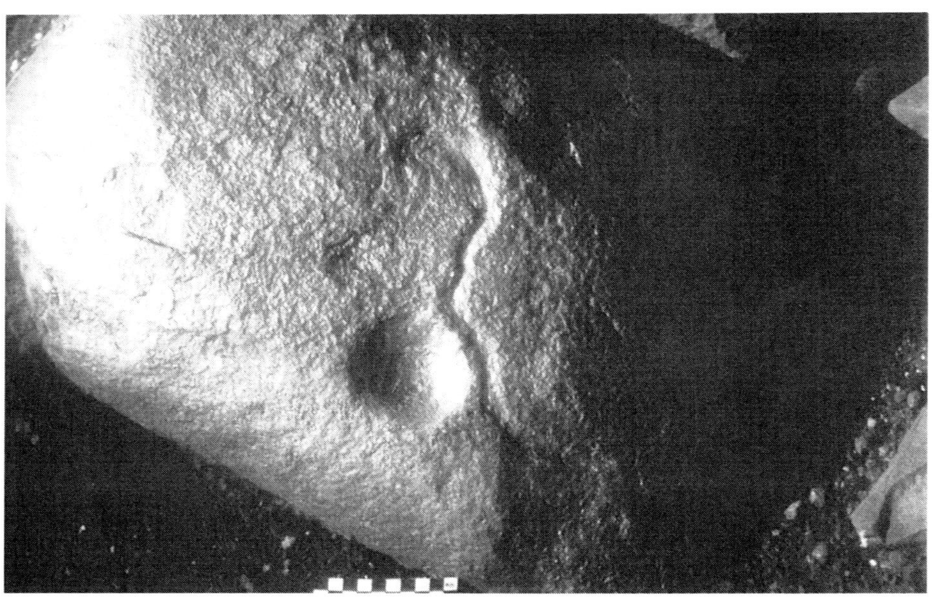

Figure 4: A deep cupule and a meandering line with dark brown patination on a boulder obtained from the Lower Palaeolthic strata in the excavations in the Auditorium Cave, Bhimbetka.
Courtesy Robert G. Bednarik.

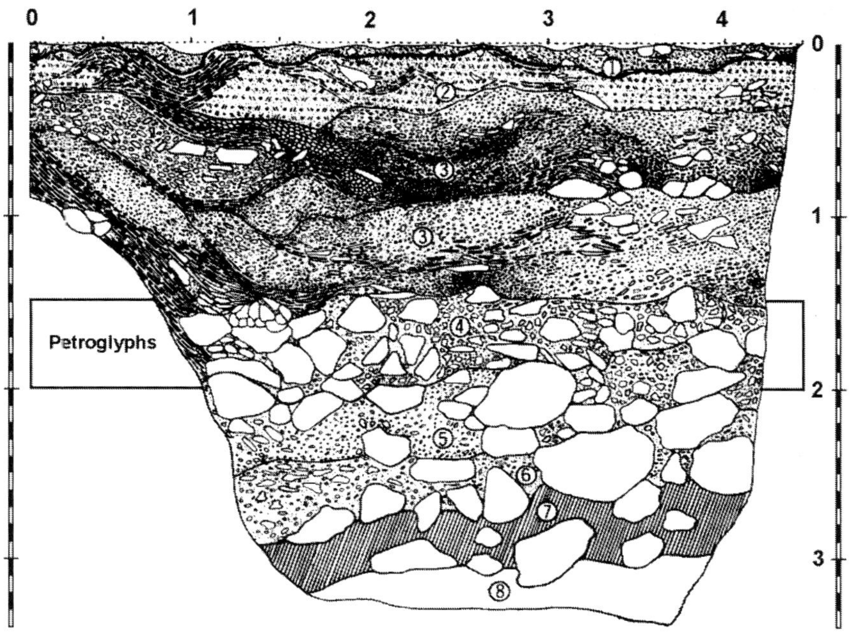

Figure 5: Section map showing the location of the boulder bearing early petroglyphs in the Auditorium Cave. Figure after V. S. Wakankar and Robert G. Bednarik.

Figure 6: Cupules on the Chief's Rock standing in the centre of the Auditorium Rock.

Cupules form most of the oldest surviving rock art known in the world. The oldest cupules found so far in the Americas, Africa, Australia and Europe stretch up to the Mousterian at La Ferrassie in France and to about 50,000 yrs. B.P. in Australia. The cupule found at Bhimbetka in Wakankar's trench appears to be much older, because the Indian Acheulian has been shown, through the thorium-uranium dating method, to be generally beyond the limit of that method, which is around 350,000 yrs B.P. (S. Mishra 1994: 63: Chakravarty and Bednarik 1997: 59). These dates have been pushed back further to 670,000 yrs B.P. by $^{39}Ar/^{40}Ar$ dating of Bori tephra (Mishra et al 1995), >1.2 myr by ESR date from Isampur (Paddayya et al 2002) and to 1.51±07 Ma by $^{26}Al/^{10}Be$ dating of the artefacts at Attarampakkam in Tamil Nadu (Pappu et al. 2011: 1596–1599).

2.2.1.1.3. Petroglyphs in Daraki-Chattan Cave

Daraki-Chattan Cave with more than 500 cupules on its vertical walls is an extraordinary Palaeolithic cupule site. Cupules in Daraki-Chattan cave are circular, oval, elliptical and roughly triangular. In terms of depth, they are broad dish shaped, deep bowl shaped, circular with conical depth, oval or elongated with oblique and conical-receding depth, roughly triangular with roughly triangular depth. The biggest cupule on northern wall measures 54.65 × 51.00 × 16.35 mm and the smallest one 30.30 × 38.60 × 6.00 mm. On the southern wall the dimensions of the biggest and smallest cupules are 55.80 × 64.00 × 15.00 mm and 17.00 × 16.00 × 1.40 mm respectively. Cupules in Daraki-Chattan are patinated and do not show any definite pattern, but pseudo-patterns can be observed in them (Kumar 1995). It is interesting to observe the effect of climate, temperature fluctuations, and the process of exfoliation especially in the front half of the cave. Hence, because of the intense play of these factors a large portion in the first half of the southern wall and a portion in the front of the northern wall bear deep exfoliation scars and are devoid of cupules (Fig. 2). Because of these factors some of the cupules in these parts of the cave are in a different state of weathering, which has not only reduced their size but in some cases even altered their shape also. This process has been going on throughout the life history of the cupules and even prior to their creation. Similarly, some portions of the cave walls and cupules on them have been regularly washed by percolating rainwater every year. The salts carried with sweeping rainwater dries up and gets hard in the following long drier phase of the year. It has been continuously going on for years. The so formed salt layers get peeled off by the play of water or entirely removed with the exfoliating surface of the wall. The cave walls have witnessed many such cycles of deposition and exfoliation of the encrustation on them. This observation explains the very young AMS ^{14}C dates obtained for encrustation on a cupule in DC. Therefore, such kind of observation and understanding of the taphonomic phenomenon are crucial before any conclusion is made from the scientific analyses.

2.2.1.1.4. Observations and study of the excavated material at DC

The excavations at Daraki-Chattan in particular and the EIP Project (Kumar 2000/01; Kumar 2002, 2006; Kumar and Bednarik 2010; Kumar et al 2005, Bednarik et al. 2005; Bednarik and

Kumar 2012; Kumar et al. 2012) in general are endeavouring to secure the first data of Lower and Middle Palaeolithic petroglyphs. The preliminary report of the excavations at Daraki-Chattan provides the unambiguous evidence of exfoliated and stratified petroglyphs, mostly cupules, from archaeological occupation strata of Lower Palaeolithic Age (Fig. 7, 8a, 8b, 9). It endorses the similar evidence from the Auditorium Cave at Bhimbetka. At Daraki-Chattan petroglyphs recovered from the excavations consist of a total of 28 cupules on quartzite slab pieces exfoliated from the cave

Figure 7: Slab pieces bearing cupules obtained from pseudo-layer 3, Acheulian, in the excavation of DC from layer 3 joined together.

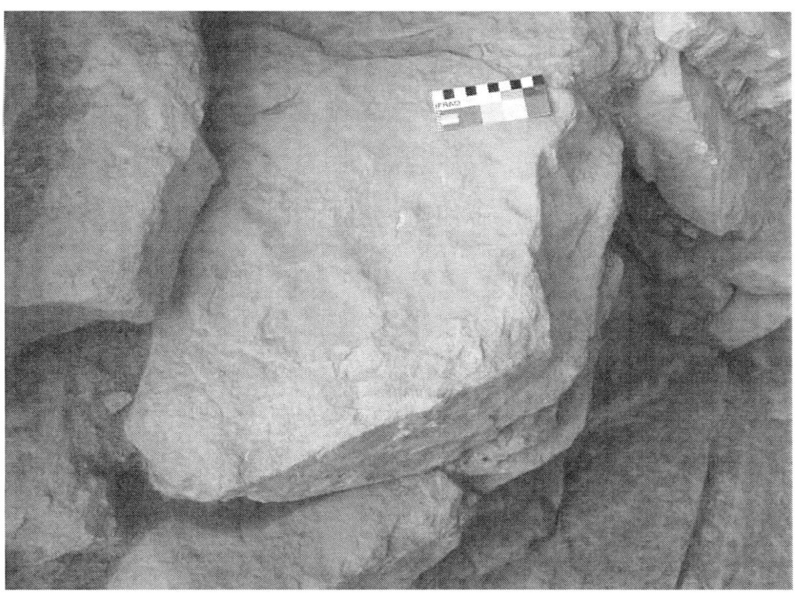

Figure 8a: Slab bearing a highly patinated cupule, broken and lying in the trench obtained from pseudo-layer 5, Lower Palaeolithic, in the excavation of DC.

Figure 8b: Close-up of the same cupule of figure 8a.

Close up of hammerstone. It is with multiple wear facets, one of which is visible above the millimetre scale.

Figure 9: Hammerstone on hard quartzite with multiple wear facets (working heads) obtained from pseudo-layer 4, Acheulian, in the excavation of DC.

wall, and two linear grooves. Besides, ten hammer stones used for producing cupules were also discovered (Fig. 9). The lack of cupules on exfoliation scars on the cave walls implies that the remaining wall cupules are of the ages similar to those in the excavation. The actual age of the cupules must have been much older than that of their archaeological-stratigraphic age, as they must have been exfoliated much later after their production on the cave wall. The same relationship has been suggested for the cupules above ground on the Chief's Rock in the Auditorium Cave at Bhimbetka.

2.2.1.1.5. Global significance

The evidence of Lower Palaeolithic petroglyphs from the Auditorium Cave and Daraki-Chattan Cave shattered the biased conception of the Euro-centric origin of art and culture in Upper Palaeolithic period. It strongly supported the view that rock art is a global phenomenon and non-iconic rock art precedes the iconic art in Pleistocene period. Robert G. Bednarik in his paper on, "The origin of 'Modern Humans' and palaeoart reconsidered" (2008), has presented the long-known early evidences of art-like productions preceding the Upper Palaeolithic by hundreds of millennia.

We have long known about many Acheulian stone beads from Bedford, England and French sites, and recently learned about a proto-sculpture of the Middle Acheulian from Tan-Tan, southern Morocco. The latter is a naturally shaped quartzite enhanced with artificial grooves and haematite paint; the latter is visible in the form of microscopic traces of haematite coating. Even the example of the earliest currently nonfigurative art on a shoulder blade is one of three engravings from Oldisleben, Germany, being of the Micoquian, and there are numerous other examples of palaeoart known preceding the Aurignacian of Europe (Bednarik 2009).

We have a huge numbers of Mode 3 (Middle Palaeolithic) rock art motifs, mostly from Australia (cf. Foley and Lahr 1997) and at least one instance of 18 cupules on the underside of a large limestone slab placed on top of La Ferrassie burial No. 6, the grave of a Neanderthal infant (Fig. 10–13) (Peyrony 1934). In other continents, pre-Upper Palaeolithic rock art and portable palaeoart are much more common (Bednarik 1992, 1993b, 2001, 2002a, 2003, 2005, 2006, 2009; Bednarik et al 2005). But the incidence of Lower Palaeolithic cases remains very rare, and confirmed cases of it are limited to India.

The recent research has shown that our understanding of art origins is rapidly changing. More than any other evidence during the last 100 years, the evidence produced by the EIP Project, especially from the excavations at Daraki-Chattan and Auditorium Caves, has shown that we have misjudged the time depth of palaeoart and human cognition, creative ability and symbolism (Bednarik 2012). Now the time has come to change our mindset (Kumar 2021a). The evidence is so important that it is set to affect not only our concepts of Pleistocene hominin development in southern Asia, but it will influence the way we view cognitive evolution generally. This is an important contribution of India to the Rock Art Discipline in the world.

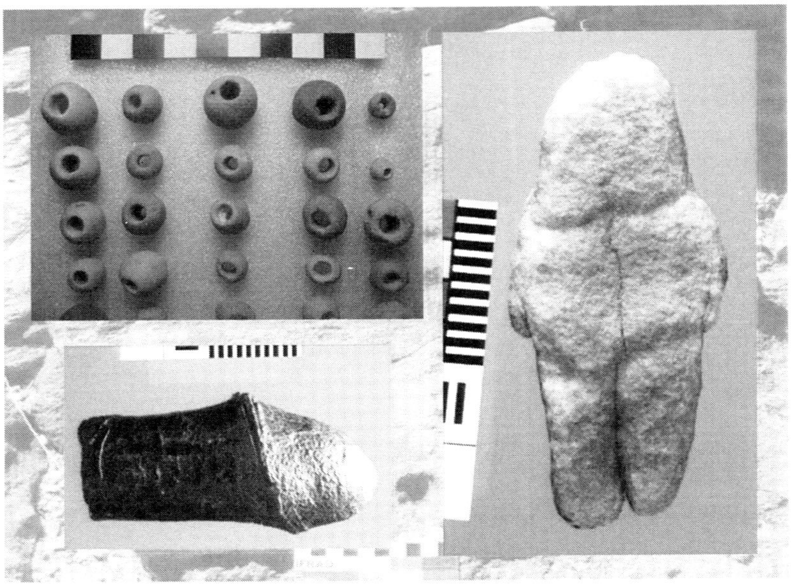

Figure 10: Clockwise from bottom left: Unmodified manuport of a cuttlefish fossil from the late Acheulian of Erfoud, Morocco, resembling a human penis, Acheulian stone beads from Bedford, England and a proto-sculpture of the Middle Acheulian from Tan-Tan, southern Morocco. Courtesy Robert G. Bednarik.

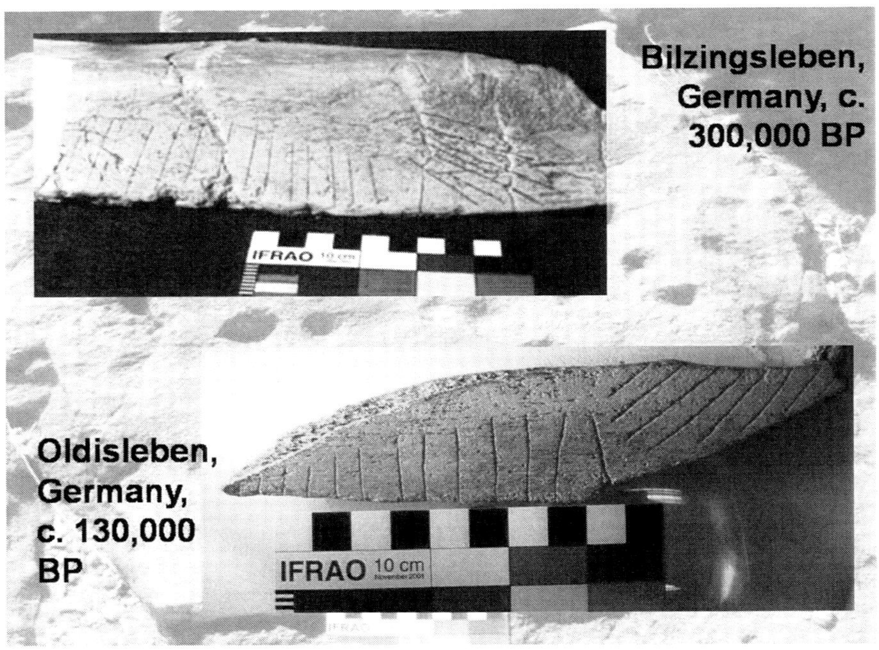

Figure 11: Acheulian and Middle Palaeolithic engraved markings on bone fragments from Bilzingsleben and Oldisleben respectively, Germany. Courtesy Robert G. Bednarik

Figure 12: Middle Palaeolithic cupules from Sandy Creek, Australia.
Courtesy Robert G. Bednarik

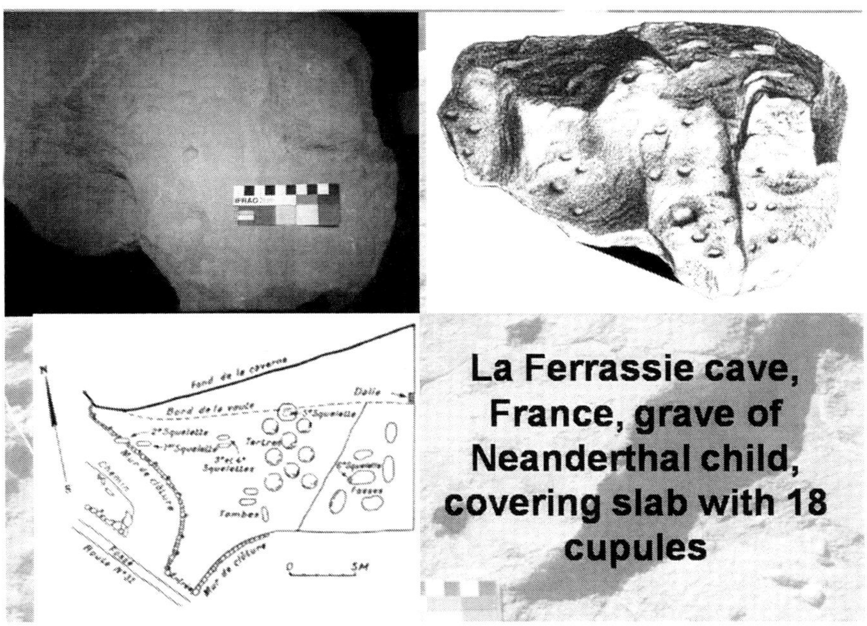

Figure 13: Middle Palaleolithic cupules from La Ferrassie Cave, France.
Courtesy Robert G. Bednarik

2.2.2. Replication of DC cupules

In order to understand the processes of the cupule production in DC myself (Giriraj Kumar) and Ram Krishna (Prajapati) carried out experiments to replicate cupules on the hard quartzite experimental rock, south of Daraki-Chattan (Kumar and Prajapati 2010; Kumar 2010; Krishna and Kumar 2012a, 2012b, 2012c; Kumar and Krishna 2014). It is the continuation of the same bedrock of DC. We observed that it needs nearly 30,000 strokes with concentration and dedication in two days to produce a medium-size cupule of 33.5 × 32.5 × 9.0 mm dimension (Fig. 14). It is incredibly hard to replicate cupules on hard quartzite rock. It required total involvement, precisely focused strokes and commitment. It indicates that cupule production was not a play work, rather it must have been a serious task important in the life of the creators. It was a pioneering replication work to reproduce early petroglyphs of different forms and dimensions in DC, carried out on hard quartzite rock by Indian scholars (Kumar 2010; Kumar and Krishna 2014).

Figure 14: Ram Krishna at work to replicate cupules on hard quartzite bedrock by the southern side of Daraki-Chattan

Big circular cupules, small circular cupules with conical depth and roughly triangular cupules created by direct percussion method were observed in DC. Their replication reflects a steady advancement in technology, skill, precision, intelligence and cognitive development in the order in early human history of the Pleistocene. Such a phenomenon is the result of the social and cultural environment and that of opportunities and encouragement provided by the social groups besides the evolution of skill in different subspecies of *Homo.* The same is the case even at present when we observe the development of juveniles in rural and urban environment in different parts of the world. We can also recall the Industrial Revolution and development of bicycles, motor bikes, cars, aeroplanes, etc from their modest forms in the beginning to the modern advanced forms of the present. The underlying nature of the culture of our ancestors was not significantly different in a qualitative sense from our own. Of course, in the Stone Age, development was a slow process. Different technologies, designs, devices and equipment were developed according to the need of the time to make the tasks comparatively easy and life more comfortable. Thus, cupule production of different forms by early humans appears more related to technological development and cultural evolution deeply embedded in cognitive development in archaic *Homo sapiens.*

2.2.3. Replication of rock paintings of Chaturbhujnath Nala (CBN)

Chaturbhujnath Nala in Chambal valley, abbreviated as CBN, is a magnificent rock art gallery (Kumar 2007a: 21–134, 2022). It is located in the Gandhisagar wildlife sanctuary near Bhanpura in Mandsaur district of Madhya Pradesh. Rock art of Chaturbhujnath nala presents a distinct picture of transition from hunting-food-gathering mode of life to cattle domestication, which started with humpless cattle sometime in the first half of the Holocene period (Kumar 1983, 2007: 21–134, 2022; Kumar and Pradhan 2008: 23–52). In order to understand the cognitive, intellectual, and cultural development of the authors of rock art we undertook the project on replication of rock paintings of Chaturbhujnath Nala (Fig. 15–16) (Kumar 2021b; Kumar et al. 2021; Krishna et al. 2021; Hridayshri et al. 2021a, 2021b; Geetanjali 2021).

Figure 15: Replication of a Mesolithic composition from Chaturbhujnath Nala at a replication site near Bada Mahadev near Bhanpura by applying mineral colour with a palm-twig brush

Figure 16: Pigment obtained from haematite nodule by abrasing the nodule against a quartzite slab with water

We observed that:

1. Obtaining suitable pigment nodules, colour preparation, finding proper material for making the desired brushes to make rock art composition(s) and then its execution by an artist is a tiresome job. Therefore, creation of a rock art composition must have had some specific purpose. To make all the processes enjoyable it must have been a group activity in which different persons were assigned different tasks and all such activities might have been accompanied with some sort of rituals and singing.
2. While replicating the compositions we realised that the figures were made by the mature artists with high level of cognitive development, skills and efficiency to execute and express the experienced reality. The lines and curves of the original rock paintings are very powerful and are capable of communicating information and generating a lot of feelings. We could only replicate them up to an extent after a lot of practice. We missed the crucial curves in the lines and proportion of the figures. It was mostly because we lacked full control on the brush.
3. The chemical analysis of the rock paint compositions and that of the pigment nodules we have been using for replication is essential to really appreciate the knowledge and experience of the artist to use the local resources and his cognitive abilities. It will be materialised in the next phase.

4. We can learn a lot from further scientific and deep study of rock art and the replication of the processes of its production by using multiple methods and material.

3. The conceptual aspects of the scientific study of rock art

As already discussed, rock art needs to be studied as the expression of the essence of life in a holistic way, in its physical and natural ambience. To achieve this goal, we need the scientific study of the essential components of rock art and understanding the processes of rock art production, its survival and damage, viz. preproduction processes, production processes and postproduction processes. The first two stages can be understood up to some extent by replication of rock art and the ethnographical study of the creative traditions of the rock art practicing and/or forest dwelling communities, while the third stage involves pure scientific pursuits of multiple disciplines including taphonomy of the site and rock art. The scientific study of rock art can help us in understanding the roots of humanity, its diverse aspects including strong human emotions and their manifestations at different stages of human development in time and space (Kumar 2023: 205-2011).

The study of the pre-production and production processes involved in rock art creation and the post-production processes the site and rock art have undergone can provide us an insight (of course of limited nature) into the dynamic process of the cultural activities the site has undergone. It can also throw light, up to some extent, on the cognitive, intellectual, technological and cultural development of its authors. However, there is no readymade path to be followed to understand the conceptual ideas and processes involved in the production of rock art. This challenge cannot be met at an individual level. We have to make collective efforts in this direction. It leads us to the conclusion that for the scientific study of rock art we need to incorporate many scientific disciplines and must innovate many new systems to achieve the goal. Besides, it needs a scientific mindset which has to be developed and inculcated with serious efforts. If we could study rock art objectively (which we may not be at present), we might discover how humans developed their ontologies. It will be the most crucial pursuit in a science serving our species because it would illuminate how our species acquired its very concepts of reality and ultimately how man became the dominant species on the planet Earth (Bednarik 2007; Kumar 2021a, 2021b; Kumar et al. 2021). We may obtain answers to some questions and not to others. The latter will give direction to further research in rock art science. Therefore, in order to proceed further in the field of rock art research, we need to adopt the epistemology of rock art science and understand the processes involved in it. This means that our studies need to be based on testable propositions.

4. Concluding remarks

In the light of the above discussion, it is evident that India played a crucial role in the development of scientific study of rock art and its discipline. With a changed mindset India was able to explore the creative and effective communication abilities of early man. Pre-Upper Palaeolithic rock art and portable palaeoart are much more common in continents other than Europe. But the incidence of Lower Palaeolithic cases remains very rare and confirmed cases of it are limited to India. It became possible to demonstrate through the research carried out under the EIP Project, a joint venture of Rock Art Society of India (RASI) and Australian Rock Art Research Association (AURA). It brought a threshold change in the global rock art discipline. Indian pioneering work motivated the scholars in the world to change their mindset to look for early human symbolism much beyond the Upper Palaeolithic cave art of Europe. Similarly, the replication project of DC (Daraki-Chattan Cave) cupules on hard quartzite rock was a pioneering work providing insight into the technology adopted and the processes involved in the production of the cupules of DC. The replication of rock paintings was a different experience at its initial stage. The project needs to be continued in the light of our learnings to understand the role of change in technology and economy brought to the lives of its authors.

In order to understand the rock art at conceptual level, rock art study needs to be focused on understanding the processes involved in its pre-production, production, and post-production levels. However, there is no readymade path to be followed to understand the conceptual ideas and processes involved in the production of rock art. This challenge cannot be met at individual level. We have to make collective efforts in this direction. It leads us to the conclusion that for the scientific study of rock art we need to incorporate many scientific disciplines and must innovate many new systems to achieve goals. Scholars and scientists of different countries can come together in such ventures. Besides, it needs a scientific mindset which has to be developed and inculcated with serious efforts. If we could study rock art objectively (which we may not be at present), we might discover how humans developed their ontologies. It will be the most crucial pursuit in a science serving our species because it would illuminate how our species acquired its very concepts of reality and ultimately how man became the dominant species on the planet Earth (Bednarik 2007, pers. comm. 2021; Kumar 2021a, 2021b). We may obtain answers to some questions and not to others. The latter will give direction to further research in rock art science. Therefore, to proceed further in the field of rock art research, we need to adopt the epistemology of rock art science and understand the processes involved in it. Our studies need to be based on testable propositions.

5. Acknowledgement

I am heartily thankful to all my friends and organisations who helped and supported me in my endeavour of scientific rock art research in India during the last four and half decades.

Prof. Giriraj Kumar
President, Rock Art Society of India (RASI)
Email: girirajrasi.inida@gmail.com

References

Bednarik, R. G. 1992. Palaeoart and archaeological myths. *Cambridge Archaeological Journal* 2(1): 27–43.

Bednarik, R. G. 1993a. Palaeolithic art in India. *Man and Environment* 18 (2): 33–40.

Bednarik, R. G. 1993b. Wonders of Wonderwork Cave. *The Artefact* 16: 61.

Bednarik, R. G. 1994. A taphonomy of palaeoart. *Antiquity* 68: 68–74.

Bednarik, R. G. 1996. The cupules on Chief's Rock, Auditorium Cave, Bhimbetka. *The Artefact* 19: 63–72.

Bednarik, R. G. 2001. The early Indian Petroglyphs Project (EIP). *Rock Art Research* 18(1): 72.

Bednarik, R. G. 2002. An outline of Middle Pleistocene palaeoart. *Purakala* 13(1-2): 39–44.

Bednarik, R. G. 2003. A figurine from the African Acheulian. *Current Anthropology* 44(3): 405–413.

Bednarik, R. G. 2005. Middle Pleistocene beads and symbolism. *Anthropos,* St Augustin. 100(2): 537–552.

Bednarik, R.G. 2006. The Middle Palaeolithic engravings from Oldisleben, Germany. *Anthropologie,* Brno 44(1): 113–121.

Bednarik, R. G. 2007. *Rock Art Science: the scientific study of palaeoart.* Aryan Books International, New Delhi.

Bednarik, R. G. 2008. The origins of 'Modern Humans' and palaeoart reconsidered. In Robert G. Bednarik and Derek Hodgson (Ed*), Pleistocene Palaeoart of the World.* Oxford, England: BAR International Series 1804.

Bednarik, R. G. 2009. Lower and Middle Palaeolithic Palaeoart of the world. Paper presented in Symposium 4: Recent trends in word rock art research, in the IFRAO Congress "Global Rock Art" held at Capivara, Sao Raimundo Nonato, Piaui, Brazil, from 29 June to 3 July 2009.

Bednarik, R. G. 2012. Indian Pleistocene rock art in the global context. In J. Clottes (ed), *Pleistocene Art of the World.* Numero special des Acts du Congress IFRAO, September 2010. Bulletin de la Societe Prehistorique Ariege-Pyrenees. France. pp. 150–151 and in CD 860–878.

Bednarik, R. G., G. Kumar, A. Watchman, and R. G. Roberts 2005. Preliminary results of the EIP Project. *Rock Art research* 22(2): 147–197.

Bednarik, R. G., and G. Kumar 2012. Typological context of the Lower Palaeolithics from Daraki-Chattan Cave, India. In J. Clottes (ed), *Pleistocene Art of the World.* Numero special des Acts du Congress IFRAO, September 2010. Bulletin de la SocietePrehistorique Ariege-Pyrenees. France. pp.154–155 and in CD 895–906.

Chakravarty, K. K. and R. G. Bednarik 1997. *Indian rock art and its global context.* Delhi: Motilal Banarasidas Publishers Pvt Ltd and IGRMS, Bhopal.

Foley, R. and M. M. Lahr 1997.Mode 3 technologies and the evolution of modern humans. *Cambridge Archaeologicl Journal* 7: 3–36.

Geetanjali, R. Krishna, Hridayshri, and G. Kumar 2021. Project on Replication of rock art of Chaturbhujnath Nala in India, Part 2b: Selection of the Chariot Compositions and their study. In the proceedings of the XXVIII Valcamonica Symposium 2021 ROCK-ART, A HUMAN HERITAGE 28-31 October 2021 – Valcamonica (Italy), Symposium, 'Cognitive, Intellectual and Cultural Interface of Rock Art', pp. 149–152.

Hridayshri, Geetanjali, R. Krishna and G. Kumar 2021a. Project on Replication of rock art of Chaturbhujnath Nala in India, Part 3: Pigment selection and their processing for replication of rock painting compositions: A preliminary study. In the proceedings of the XXVIII Valcamonica Symposium 2021 ROCK-ART, A HUMAN HERITAGE 28–31 October 2021 – Valcamonica (Italy), Symposium, 'Cognitive, Intellectual and Cultural Interface of Rock Art', pp. 153–159.

Hridayshri, Geetanjali, R. Krishna and G. Kumar 2021b. Project on Replication of rock art of Chaturbhujnath Nala in India, Part 4: Replication of making brush by using different organic material for producing rock paintings and their ethnological study. In the proceedings of the XXVIII Valcamonica Symposium 2021 ROCK-ART, A HUMAN HERITAGE 28–31 October 2021 – Valcamonica (Italy), Symposium, 'Cognitive, Intellectual and Cultural Interface of Rock Art', pp. 160–164.

Krishna, R, and G. Kumar 2012a. Understanding the creation of small conical cupules in Daraki-Chattan. In J. Clottes (ed), *Pleistocene Art of the World.* Numero special des Acts du Congress IFRAO, September 2010. Bulletin de la Societe Prehistorique Ariege-Pyrenees. France. pp. 216–217 and in CD 1229–1256.

Krishna, R, and G. Kumar 2012b. Replication of early angular cupules on hard quartzite rock at Daraki-Chattan by direct percussion method. *Purakala* 22: 17–28. Agra, India.

Krishna, R, and G. Kumar 2012c. Physico-psychological approach for understanding the significance of Lower Palaeolithic cupules. In J. Clottes (ed), *Pleistocene Art of the World.* Numero special des Acts du Congress IFRAO, September 2010. Bulletin de la SocietePrehistorique Ariege-Pyrenees. France. pp.156–157 and in CD 907–918.

Krishna, R, Hridayshri, Geetanjali and G. Kumar 2021. Project on Replication of rock art of Chaturbhujnath Nala in India, Part 2a: Selection of the Stone Age Compositions and their study. In the proceedings of the XXVIII Valcamonica Symposium 2021 ROCK-ART, A HUMAN HERITAGE 28-31 October 2021 – Valcamonica (Italy), Symposium, 'Cognitive, Intellectual and Cultural Interface of Rock Art', pp. 142–148.

Kumar, G. 1983. *Archaeology of north-western Malwa: Prehistory and Protohistory.* Unpublished Ph.D. Thesis. Ujjain: Vikram University.

Kumar, G. 1995. Daraki-Chattan: A Palaeolithic cupule site in India. *Purakala* 6: 17–28.

Kumar, G. 2002. 2002-EIP Project Report-I, Archaeological excavation and exploration at Daraki-Chattan: A preliminary report. *Purakala* 13(1–2): 5–20.

Kumar, G. 2006. A preliminary report of the excavations at Daraki-Chattan -2006. *Purakala* 16: 51–55.

Kumar, G. 2007. Documentation and preliminary study of the rock art of Chaturbhujnath nala. *Purakala* 17: 21–134.

Kumar, G. 2010. Understanding the creation of early cupules by replication with special reference to Daraki-Chattan in India. In R. Querejazu and R. G. Bednarik (eds), *Mysterious cup marks: proceedings of the First International Cupule Conference,* Cochabamba, Bolivia from 17 to 23 July 2007, pp 59–66. Cochabamba: Sociedad de Investigación del Arte Rupestre de Bolivia (SIARB).

Kumar, G. 2021a. Change of mindset: The need for developing scientific approaches to rock art studies. *Rock Art Research* 38(1): 23–30.

KUMAR G. 2021b. Replication of rock paintings at Chaturbhujnath Nala on Bhanpura plateau in Chambal valley, India, Part 1: The Project Introduction. In the proceedings of the XXVIII Valcamonica Symposium 2021 ROCK-ART, A HUMAN HERITAGE 28-31 October 2021 – Valcamonica (Italy), Symposium, 'Cognitive, Intellectual and Cultural Interface of Rock Art', pp. 137–141.

Kumar, G. 2022. *Chaturbhujnath Nala: A magnificent rock art gallery in India.* Sharada Publishing House.

Kumar, G. 2023. Future direction of rock art research: A pursuit of the epistemology of rock art and the processes involved in it. *Rock Art Research* 40(2): 205-2011.

Kumar, G. and A. Pradhan 2008. Study of the rock art of Chaturbhujnath Nala in Chambal Valley. *Purakala* 18: 23–52.

Kumar, G., R. G. Bednarik, A. Watchman, R.G. Roberts, E. Lawson and C. Patterson 2002. 2002 progress report of the EIP Project. *Rock Art Research* 20 (1): 70–71.

Kumar, G., R. G. Bednarik, A. Watchman, and R. G. Roberts 2005. The EIP Project in 2005: A progress report. *Purakala* 14–15: 13–68.

Kumar, G., and R. G. Bednarik 2010. The difficulties of determining the approximate antiquity of Lower Palaeolithic petroglyphs in India. Paper presented in the Symposium on Dating and Taphonomy, in the in IFRAO-2010 International Conference on Pleistocene Art of the World, Foix, France, from 6 to 11 September 2010.

Kumar, G. and R. Prajapati (Krishna) 2010. Understanding the creation of cupules in Daraki-Chattan, India. *FUMDHAM Mentos* 9: 167–186. Fundaçào Museu do Homen Americano, São Raimundo Noñato, Brazil.

Kumar, G., N. Vyas, R. G. Bednarik, A. Pradhan 2012. Lower Palaeolithic petroglyphs and hammerstones obtained from the excavations at Daraki-Chattan Cave in India. In J. Clottes (Ed), *Pleistocene Art of the World.* Numero special des Acts du Congress IFRAO, September 2010. Bulletin d e la SocietePrehistorique Ariege-pyrenees. France.pp. 152–153 and in CD 879-894.

Kumar, G. and R. Krishna 2014. Understanding the technology of the Daraki-Chattan cupules: The cupule replication project. *Rock Art Research* 31(2): 177–186. Melbourne.

Kumar, G., R Krishna, Hridayshri, and Geetanjali 2021. Replication of rock art of Chaturbhujnath Nala in India, Part 5: Replication of the processes of rock art production and our observations. In the proceedings of the XXVIII Valcamonica Symposium 2021 ROCK-ART, A HUMAN HERITAGE 28–31 October 2021 – Valcamonica (Italy), Symposium, 'Cognitive, Intellectual and Cultural Interface of Rock Art', pp.165–171.

Mishra, S. 1994. The South Asian Lower Palaeolilhic. *Man and Environment* 14(1–2): 57–71.

Mishra, S., T.R. Venkatesan, and B.L.K.Somayajulu 1995.Earliest Acheulian Industry from Peninsular India. *Current Anthropology* 36: 847–851.

Neumayer, E. 1983. *Prehistoric Indian rock paintings,* Delhi: Oxford University Press, pp. 12–13.

Neumayer, E. 1993. *Lines on Stone: The Prehistoric Rock Art of India.* New Delhi: Manohar Publishers and Distributors.

Padayya, K., B.A.B. Blackwell, R. Jhaldiyal, M.D. Petraglia, S. Fervrier, D.A. Chaderton II, J.I.B.

Blickstein, and A. R. Skinner 2002. Recent findings on the Acheulian of the Hunsgi and Baichbal Valleys, Karnataka, with special reference to Isampur Excavation and its dating. *Current Science* 83: 641–647.

Pappu, S., Y. Guanell, A. Kumar, R. Braucher, M. Taib, F. Demory and N. Thouvenys 2011. Early Pleistocene presence of Acheulian Hominins in south India. *Science* 331: 1596–1599.

Peyrony, D. 1934. La Ferrasie (Mousterien, Perigordien, Aurignacien) (in French). *Prehistoire* 3: 1–92.

Ota, S. B. 2005. Declaration of Painted rock shelters of Bhimbetka as world heritage and its management initiatives. *Purakala* 14–15: 83–88.

Ota, S. B. 2008. *World Heritage Series: Bhimbetka.* New Delhi: The Director General, Archaeological Survey of India.

Pancholi, R. K. 1994. Bhanpura kshetra me navin shodha (in Hindi). *Purakala* 5(1–2): 75.

Wakankar, V. S. 1975. Bhimbetka: The Prehistoric Paradise. *Prachya Pratibha* 3(2): 7–29, Fig. 1–11.

Wakankar, V. S. 1978. *The dawn of Indian Art,* Ujjain:Bharti Kala Bhawan, pp. 5–24.

Wakankar, V. S. 2008. Indian Prehistory as revealed by excavations, explorations and rock art study at Bhimbetka and in the adjoining regions. *Purakala* 18: 65–72. Presidential address, Prehistory Section, ISPQS Congress delivered at Jaipur in 1976, published posthumously.

Wakankar, V. S., and Robert, R. R. Brooks 1976. *Stone Age Painting in India.* Bombay: D.B. Taraporewala and Sons.

Study of Palaeoart of the World, Hridayshri, pp. 275-299

22

KEYWORDS: Stone Age Rock Art – Communication Design – Design Fundamentals – Gestalt principles – Replication – Narratives

STONE AGE ROCK ART AND COMMUNICATION DESIGN

HRIDAYSHRI

Abstract: Rock art in India has never been studied by the researchers from a design perspective. The writer observed that the rock art compositions reflect all the design fundamentals like design elements, design principles, and gestalt principles applied individually or simultaneously in the execution of their compositions to build characters, narratives, or themes. It was found that the rock art compositions had been developed intentionally, planned strategically, created as a visual language for an experience of expression and a tool to be understood as visual communication system exhibiting many aspects of authors life. The replication of some compositions from Chaturbhujnath Nala rock paintings helped in understanding the conceptual and technological abilities of the rock art authors, and the processes involved in the creation of these compositions. On the basis of this comprehensive study, an effort has been made to appreciate the rock art from design perspective.

Introduction

V. S. Wakankar, Y. Mathpal, E. Neumayer, G. Kumar, etc.did art appreciation of Indian rock art (Wakankar 1978; Wakankar and Brooks 1976; Neumayer 1983; Mathpal 1984; Kumar 2015a, 2015b, 2022). However, it was never appreciated from design perspective. The author has attempted rock art study from the perspective of communication design for the first time (Hridayshri 2019, 2021).

Design is a plan for arranging elements to accomplish a particular purpose. In this regard, most of the forms and compositions in rock art are good examples of design. Communication

Article received: 10 December 2022
Revised I: 15 February 2023
Revised II: 6 May 2023
Revised III: 19 May 2023
Revised IV: 8 June 2023
Revised V: 28 July 2023
Revised VI: 30 July 2023
Accepted: 31 July 2023

design aims to create compositions that will strategically engage, impact and communicate with the spectator. In order to control the visuals for crafting an effective message, communication designers contemplate the narrative and its developmental aspects, have a strategy for the execution with an approach beforehand. The strategy involved in communicating the desired information through visual design, the terms visual communication and graphic design are largely interchangeable to strategically tell a story to the audience (Dondis 1974, Lester 2011: 45–50, shillington, https://www.shillingtoneducation.com/blog/communication-design/).

While studying rock art, it was observed that the design elements, the design principles and the gestalt principles which we study in design and art at present, had been used from the time human started to execute exogrames thousands of years back. I began my study by analyzing rock art compositions on the basis of the design fundamentals in terms of layout and composition structure, which are as follows:

1. Emphasis, balance, rhythm, scale and proportion, unity, harmony.
2. Line, shape, space and form, colour, value, texture.
3. Information flow, hierarchy, eye movement, concept and narrative.

To create an effective, engaging, and informative composition, these design fundamentals help in connecting the dots to evolve a narrative (Poulin 2011: 19–38). The event chosen for a narrative from the entire story, the characters, and its execution with minimal lines on two-dimensional rock surface can communicate significantly about the cognitive and analytical abilities of the authors of rock art. Just by formulating variations in shapes, stroke's/line's weight, type, their quality, and their joints, colours, and different values of colour can construct varied visual experiences and communicate various aspects of information and character details (Figure 1).

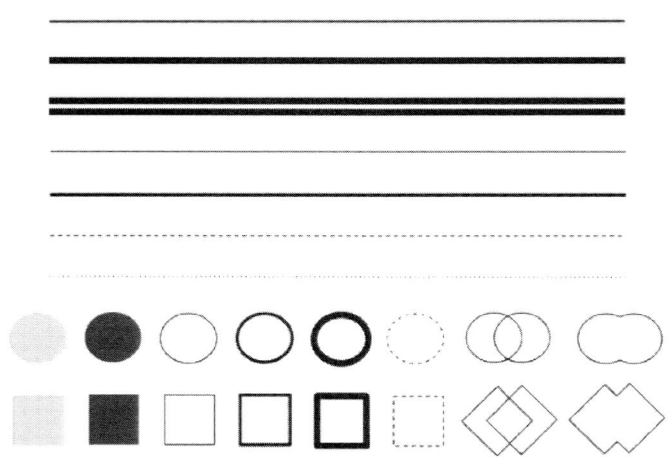

Figure 1: Types of lines and shapes

Gestalt principles describe, "How the human brain perceives elements as a whole." These principles aim to show how complex information can be reduced to simple visual systems. They define how human brain perceives shapes as one unit rather than separate elements, by filling in the blanks to see structures and patterns in order to understand the environment in a better way. There are five basic principles commonly associated with gestalt theory: Similarity, Continuity, Closure, Proximity, Figure and Ground (Chaman: https://www.toptal.com/designers/ui/gestalt-principles-of-design). These principles, as tools and techniques, have been used to bring control on the eye movement in the composition to build visual hierarchy and emphasis. They help in finding focus of the figure or the composition, perceive it cohesively, build different types and layers of information to strengthen or soften the elements and flow of the composition to visually inform on a narrative. It's a language in itself, reflecting the cognitive and conceptual abilities based on the perceived realities and socio-cultural aspects of a larger group.

People seek to remember the past experiences and memories by recording, informing and sharing with others. It visually enhances the communication by capturing our attention and helps us react better. It holds viewers' attention and kindles their vision leading to speculative imagination. The strength of a figure or a narrative resides in the scene chosen to represent and the details around it; leading to visualise the before-and-after-occurrence, tightly holding emotional engagement with the composition.

Throughout the course of research, I discovered a wide variety of compositional themes from the viewpoint of visual communication design. The compositions have definitely incorporated many components of design principles, yet they may have largely one objective as a base or concept for the narrative as following:

1. Conceptual and abstraction
2. Symbolic and Representational
3. Different types of Group Activities
4. Ritualistic
5. Celebration
6. Representation
7. Documentation
8. Informational
9. Exhibition, Experiential or Physical engagement
10. Animated or Character design
11. Technological

Rock art figures are multifaceted and sophisticated, presenting an analytical visual structure for the viewers so that they can comprehend the aspects of communication. The content, format, style, layout, size and scale are integral part of the planning while presenting the idea, context, information flow and narrative (Dondis 1974, Lester 2011).

In the light of my previous two studies (Hridayshri 2019: 15–20, Hridayshri 2021: 21–26) and to understand the process further, Kumar and his team including me carried out the replication of Stone Age rock art compositions of Chaturbhujnath Nala in March-April 2021. During the replication work, I tried to study in depth and understand the Stone Age rock from the perspective of communication design, and tools and techniques by their authors.

Methodology

The present study has been carried out in three stages

Stage 1: Research and review

(a) To support my hypothesis as the first step, I started with rock art study and my review of figures and compositions from the books published in India by eminent rock art scholars. I specifically chose compositions published in the books which have been copied in detail. It helped me study them in depth from the communication design perspective.

(b) After confirming that design elements with design principles have been profusely used in those compositions, I began work for the selected compositions for my comprehensive study.

(c) Then, I visited a few rock art sites, especially Chaturbhujnath Nala and Gandhisagar, to study the compositions in their actual environment so that I could understand the complexities of applying all the design fundamentals and the influence of the environment as an experience while viewing and studying the compositions.

Stage 2: Selection of the rock art compositions

(a) Only Stone Age Mesolithic compositions were selected for study.

(b) The selection was based on the visual clarity to be reviewed and analysed.

(c) Compositions having enough design elements to analyse cohesively to see if together they create a specific or a few visual experiences with emphasis on scale and proportion, variety of textures, different thickness of strokes, eye movement, Information flow, hierarchy, concept and narrative.

(d) Compositions exhibiting interesting concept and context.

(e) Compositions with group activities specially with different size and proportions of the figures.

(f) Figures/compositions with character development created by the strategic use of design elements

(g) Composition which had abstract narrative and concepts for analysis.

(h) Compositions with a variety of themes and context presenting different types of information.

Stage 3: Replication of the rock art compositions in a rockshelter

The replication study was conducted by a team of four scholars in the direction of Prof. G. Kumar in March-April 2021 under a project on *Replication of rock art of Chaturbhujnath Nala in India.* The objectives of the project were to understand the processes, structure and preparatory aspects of rock art. Study of the compositions from photographs and on-site helped me understand how the structure and design elements in the compositions are visually engaging and communicating specific information. Their replication on almost similar rock surface in a rockshelter nearly 28 km in the east of the site helped in understanding the pre-production and production process, the composition design and its relation with the surface, shelter, space, and immediate environment along with several other sociocultural aspects (Kumar 2021, Kumar et al.2021, Krishna et al. 2021; Geetanjali et al. 2021, Hridayshri et al. 2021a, 2021b).

Analytical study

For analytical study I selected rock art compositions from Chambal Valley (Chaturbhujnath Nala, Gandhisagar and Chattaneshwar), Vindhya Hills (Bhimbetka, Lakajoar), and Laterite region of Ratnagiri (Kasheli). On-site study helped me understand the contextual aspects of rock art compositions, while I understood the scientific aspects from the study of the literature.

Figure 2. The intricate design

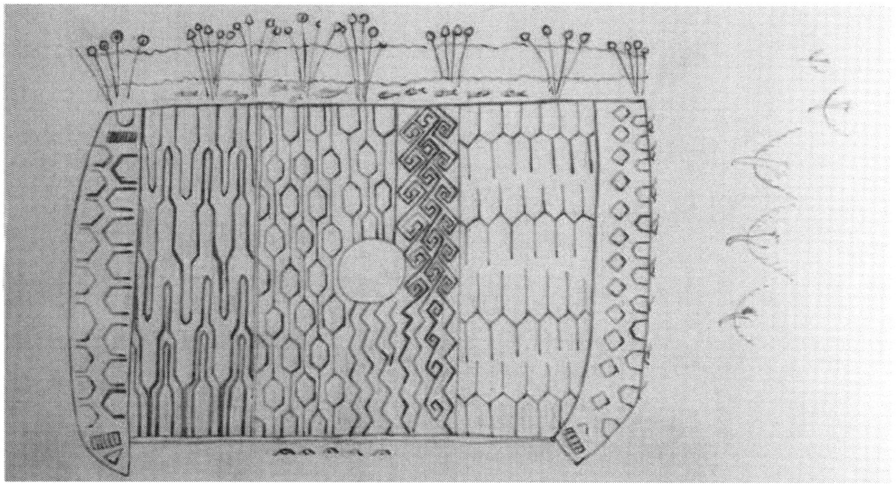

Figure 2: A composition of intricate patterns, the Cosmos! Jaora. Mesolithic (courtesy Erwin Neumayer).

Composition theme: Experiential, abstraction and conceptual information.

This specific composition, called by Erwin Neumyer as the Cosmos (Neumayer 1983, Figure 26e), can be seen as a conceptual representation of a system design (Figure 2). Different design elements have been presented with a variety of patterns and textures. In the main body of the composition there are direction oriented geometric patterns, which make the eyes move up and down. The primary eye movement is vertical from bottom to top and secondary eye movement is horizontal from left to right and right to left because of the fish. At the top, organic plant like line formation gives the eye required break and the grounding stability. Interestingly, all the patterns have visual connectivity with a clear emphasis of the entire drawing towards the central empty space looking like a circle. On the upper side it represents water with fish and vegetation like structure, while flying birds on the left side depicting air environment; all have been depicted co-existing. The types of lines and styles of textures or patters are specific to communicate different information like density, depths, values and motion.

The indicative vegetation, fish and birds in reference to overall drawing with each other are helping to understand the conceptual scale. The geometric composition has an emphasis in the center in the form of an organic circular space, which brings focus to the center. The gestalt law of similarity, proximity, continuity is clearly seen in this composition creating distinctive cluster of environments (Dondis 1974: 30–31; Lester 2011: 45–50; Chaman: https://www.toptal.com/designers/ui/gestalt-principles-of-design), as different areas and their codependent dynamics as part of the composition. The author has managed to achieve so much effectively with just two-dimensional work surface.

Figure 3. The dancers in green

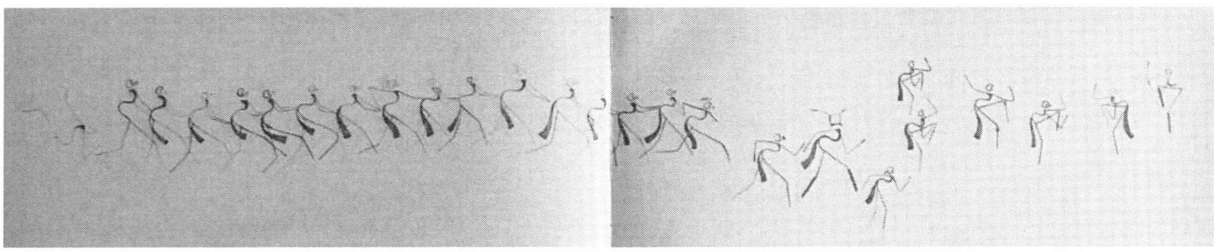

Figure 3a: Composition of a group of dancers, Lakhajoar. Mesolithic (courtesy Erwin Neumayer)

Composition theme: Experiential and celebration group activity information.

This composition of group dancers in green colour from Lakhajoar (Wakankar 1976, Neumayer 1983, Figure 39) is unique due to its self- explanatory line quality (Figure 3a). The lines creating dancing figures are communicating more than just motion and rhythm. The curves of the liner figures are capable of depicting the body form, its structure, agility, rhythm of the dance in coordination with the group, building a mood, especially since the composition is in the green colour. Thin lines have a specific bounce and movement to show the activity of the tall and slender figures. The forms created for the head, costumes and in some cases, headgears are specific along with the position of the dancers adding a directional eye movement to the intended temperament or the celebration of the narrative. The scale of all the figures is tentatively same to have visual harmony depicting planning. Strategically drawn garments with their directional movements attached with the dancer's body are enhancing the rhythm as our eye moves from left to right in the direction of their faces.

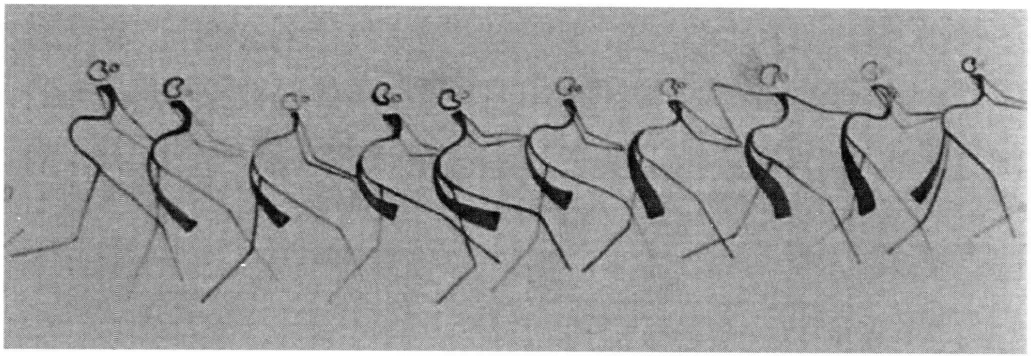

Figure 3b: Close up of figure 3a showing the aspects of semiotics (courtesy Erwin Neumayer).

The interesting aspect of semiotics in this composition is the small circles placed next to the mouth like structure on the dancers while dancing (Figure 3b). The modern designers use this type of signs next to head or mouth to show a thought bubble or speech bubble or a sound bubble. The gestalt law of similarity, proximity, continuity (Dondis 1974: 30-31; Lester 2011: 45–50; Chaman: https://www.toptal.com/designers/ui/gestalt-principles-of-design) are clearly seen in this composition creating a group activity, with their body dynamics as part of the composition.

Figure 4. The hut

Figure 4: A composition of a hut showing three members dining, Lakhajoar. Mesolithic (courtesy Erwin Neumayer)

Composition theme: Experiential and activity information.

The composition from Lakhajoar (Neumayer 1983, Figure 44) represents a hut like structure with its residents, appear to be a private functional space (Figure 4). The composition is experiential, showing details of roof and the floor structure, the space and other details with the dining activity in minimal lines. The variety of lines are representing different information like texture, material with an enclosed spatial environment. Different forms and scale are inter-related to figures with simulating depth, explaining the hierarchy, gender and age group in the perspective. The similarity and scale also show space in perspective with other visual information in the background.

The drawing is a section of the space made with layout showcasing the utility zones. The composition has an emphasis in the center depicted by the activity where large human figures are engaged in dining. The line strokes, textures and forms are creating an anti-clock-wise eye movement, having our attention first to the male figure, then female and then the third small human figure. The arrangement also represents the space utility with the method of storage. The composition has most of the design principles incorporated. The small figure in the female body represents the gestalt law of figure and ground. The structure of hut represents the law of closure and proximity (Dondis 1974: 30–31; Lester 2011: 45–50; Chaman: https://www.toptal.com/designers/ui/gestalt-principles-of-design).

Figure 5. The spectacular elephant

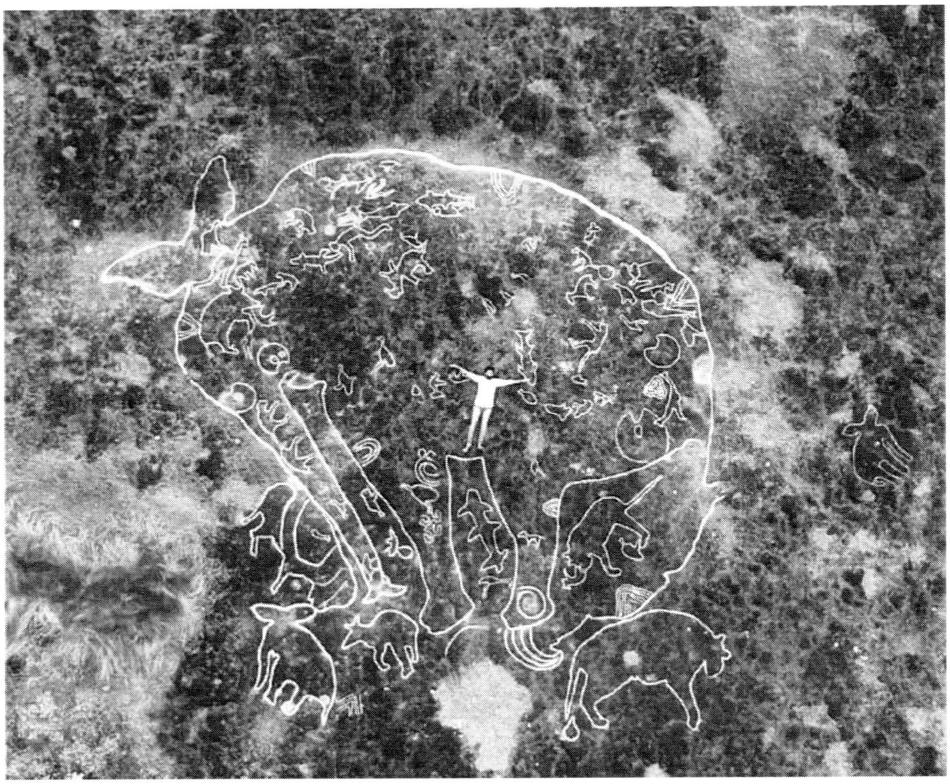

Figure 5: Spectacular giant elephant petroglyph with nearly 70 carvings inside it, Kasheli in Ratnagiri, (Photo by Amar Reddy)

Composition theme: Spatial experience, physical engagement, abstract and conceptual information.

This is a huge composition of an elephant with multiple figures inside and outside created with reductive technique (Figure 5). It has been engraved on flat laterite surface at Kasheli plateau near Ratnagiri, Maharashtra. It is 18 m x 13 m in dimension, almost eight times bigger than a human being (male) of normal size (Garge et al. 2018: 39–47). It can only be seen in totality from the elevated platform from distance. The project of this size demands a vision, conceptualization, brainstorming, doodling, system planning, strategy of its execution from the beginning till the end and then the final execution of the composition. I see zones and visual distribution of the figure in-terms of eye movement. The sheer scale of this composition is enough to make us wonder the cognitive abilities of its author/authors. On the ground one cannot perceive the entire composition as a whole and understand what it is, but can only experience in parts by walking along the lines makes it immediately engaging to trigger an exploratory side in us to make sense. It is a massive spatial experience for interaction and exploration. To create and produce something like this in contemporary scenario design-systems should be in place methodically, it requires a large team, equipment, resources, thorough planning and detailing for execution, but above all it needs solid brain storming on concept and form generation.

This work is an amalgamation of many types and size of figures inside and outside the large elephant, representing a system revolving around the elephant as a principal character. There are many diverse figures, animals, forms in different scale leading brain to subconsciously start looking for visual patters, relations or finding a group system making it visually and physically very engaging as one would have to walk and remember while exploring on this composition, reinforcing the presence of gestalt law here (Dondis 1974: 30-31; Lester 2011: 45–50; Chaman: https://www.toptal.com/designers/ui/gestalt-principles-of-design). Thousands of years back our prehistoric ancestors in Ratnagiri (Garge et al. 2018: 39–47; Lalit 2013:69–72) region in Maharastra have created many such works.

Figure 6. Fierce boar

Composition theme: Experiential and character information.

The figure has a typical boar characteristic with long, blunt snout, big eye and sharp gaze (Figure 6). The boar has petite yet sturdy legs for a stocky body with a thin tail and very fine long unusual horns. To show the strong and defined body, the thick lines have been used as a basic framework which are filled in with geometric intricate patterns in fine lines, giving the boar a majestic yet strong look. This figure as a character has far more emphasized features to make the viewer experience rather than just appreciate a form of boar. In the language of communication design, it is called the character development; where by giving special details to features and body of the figure, we develop a distinctive character. The play of different thickness in lines to communicate physique and frame, the structure of the animal, its strength, holding viewer's eye movement in specific direction to appreciate the entire composition.

Figure 6: Fierce boar, Bhonrawali Hill, Bhimbetka. Mesolithic (Photo by Giriraj Kumar)

The most prominent and distinctive feature is the eye of the boar. The emphasis in the composition is given to the eye, then one can gradually start appreciating rest of the structure and its other characteristics by going along the form with the help of the lines. However, after a while the eye movement carried through the lines would bring you back to the gaze of the boar. In the development of a character, the designer is always clear on emphasizing the strongest feature of the character. Here background and position given to the eye on a solid, dark head with an eyeball in the center creates typical eye gesture expressing fierce gaze as an example of proximity from gestalt principles. The solid background extending and becoming the snout which catches the maximum attention. The angular form of the head and snout, and the line following along through the body creating a bold line in the background as the overall figure has the gestalt law of continuity giving us the impression of an open mouth of the boar, leading the eye movement back to the gaze again (Dondis 1974: 30–31; Lester 2011: 45–50; Chaman: https://www.toptal.com/designers/ui/gestalt-principles-of-design).

Figure 7. A man enjoying his drink

Composition theme: Experiential and narrative.

This composition demonstrates the motion in a static form. The strokes inside the body, indicate the liquid going down (Figure 7). The tilted angles of the composition, body posture and detailing of anatomy; the whole body seems involved in the drinking process, making us comprehend the act, adds to the experience and action as a short narrative. The figure is sitting and slightly tilted taking

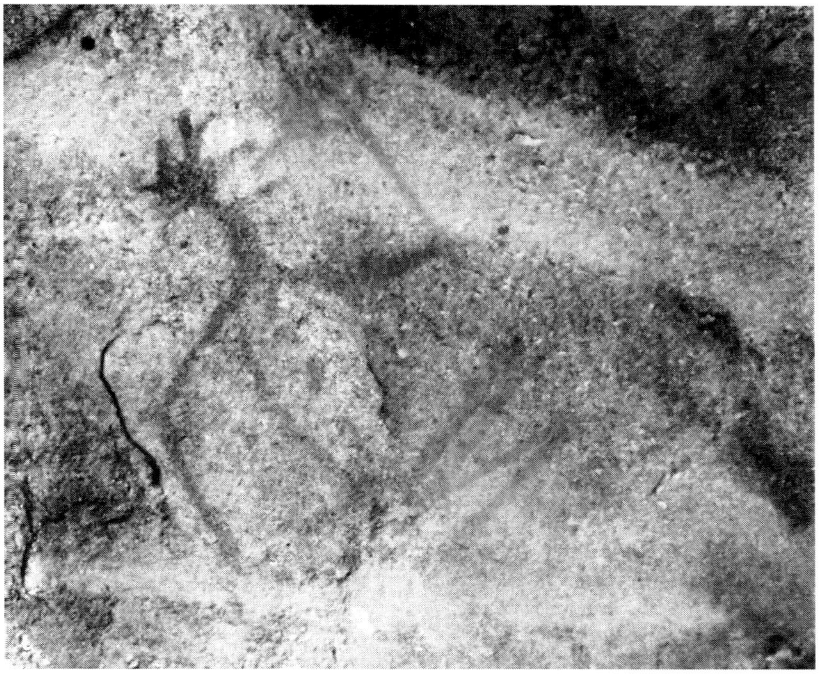

Figure 7: A man enjoying his drink, Bhimbetka. Mesolithic (Photo by Giriraj Kumar).

an arm support backwards while having a drink, which is usually done if having a drink in a relaxed sitting position. The angle of arms in support for the body is seamless despite it being shown with only one line with tilted neck and back, one can see the figure sitting on his hips with support of an arm and his feet. The observations on anatomy and body angles seem well yet presented minimally making this figure very sophisticated. Enjoying the drink from the bottle like container is the theme of the composition, but designer did not stop his imagination here and went further to show the liquid element going down in the body too, making us perceive the act in motion as gestalt law of continuity (Dondis 1974: 30–31; Lester 2011 45–50; Chaman: https://www.toptal.com/designers/ui/gestalt-principles-of-design). The fact that instead of showing the liquid in one line, it has been specifically depicted with broken line that adds to its fluidity and act of swigging.

The headgear and the little skirt of the figure is visually balancing the form and the body structure making the eye movement in circular motion anti-clockwise, giving the composition visual harmony and fluidity.

Figure 8. Tiger attack

Composition theme: Experiential and adventurous narrative.

The tiger attacking composition from Chibbad Nala in Chambal Valley in Bhanpura region is a dynamic composition of an adventurous act either experienced or witnessed by its author (Figure

Figure 8: Tiger attack, Mesolithic, Chibbad Nala. Mesolithic (Photo by Giriraj Kumar).

8). Communication designers when deciding on a frame to represent, they go through a serious of brainstorming and entire narrative to narrow down on the most significant moment which contains the maximum thrill and capacity to build imagination for before and after experience by the viewers. Making a choice of what information will be portrayed in the composition, the details on the figures, layout and other elements which convey to the spectator like a storyteller who narrates a story based on visual reference.

A charged tiger attacking a hunter and grabbing his hand in his mouth, while the fellow archer of the target does not run away in fear, instead shoots an arrow right on the head of the tiger. The size of the tiger is huge, his erect tail and attacking body posture show the force and energy of the act. The composition is shown in an outline style, where the line of animal and attacked archer is merging, depicting a life-threatening scuffle, wrestling as both the fighters appear entwined in one form, like an extension of one another as gestalt law of continuity. The format and position of the figures in the composition is linear, and the direction of the stroke leading to making your eye move from left to right giving momentum to the narrative. Coming back to the tail of the tiger holds the gaze and again it moved from left to right in a continues movement as gestalt law of proximity (Dondis 1974: 30–31; Lester 2011: 45–50; Chaman: https://www.toptal.com/designers/ui/gestalt-principles-of-design).

The overall composition is made with the same thickness of strokes and is visually light giving no immediate emphasis but has equal importance to entire composition, yet the size of animal in proportion to the human figures is largest in occupying visual space in scale. Hence, first we see the tiger and then two human forms.

Figure 9. Ritual Dance

Figure 9a: Ritual Dance, Chattaneshwar, Kota, Chambal Valley. Mesolithic (Photo by Giriraj Kumar).

Figure 9b: Eye copy of Figure 9a, (by Giriraj Kumar)

Composition theme: Ritualistic and group activity information.

Ritualistic dance appears to be the theme, where different elements put together to create metaphorical meaning and experience (Figure 9a, Figure 9b). The rectangular composition is divided in two equal parts by a 'mace' (*gada*) placed almost horizontally in the center. The upper portion consists of two male deer facing right while the lower portion depicts seven adult dancers and two youngsters in a row, all having headgear flap flying towards right. The composition is made in fine lines with same thickness of stroke in dark red colour. Visually one sees the animals first and then the 'mace', followed by the dancing group. The viewing hierarchy has been made by the scale and division in the frame, in-spite of entire composition being made with lines. The linearity of the figures guides the visual eye movement horizontally and vertically. The upper part of the composition with two animals has enough background space to show the openness, whereas the lower part with dancers is dense or crowded. The animal facing right side bring your eye from left to right but as you come down to 'mace' the liner horizontal weapon will bring your eye movement right to left side, following dancers and again the eye moves along with dancer's headgears towards the right side. The eye movement makes the eye travel to the entire composition from left to right, right to left and again left to right and so on. The bottom part of the composition with dancers is visually heavy due to its dense vertical lines giving a base to the composition. Where the gaze might travel everywhere but it will eventually settle at the bottom with dancers.

All the design principles have been applied here thoughtfully to make one appreciate the entire composition without visual disturbance, with focus and strategy to hold the viewer's gaze and make it travel as well (Poulin 2011). By combining the shoulders and arms in their form to show the dancers are holding each other is the example of continuity in gestalt principles. They all appear to be wearing animal skin and headgears facing similar direction showing the gestalt laws of proximity, continuity and similarity which makes one's eye run vertically from their feet to head and then towards the right side due to headgears, appear to be a group. As the law of similarity is in place, it helps us identify the adults and two small figures yet another visual grouping information of different age. Suggesting a community involvement, meant for transmitting the cultural tradition to the younger generation. The extreme left dancer is holding a stout bow and a strong long arrow. (Dondis 1974: 30–31; Lester 2011: 45–50; Chaman: https://www.toptal.com/designers/ui/gestalt-principles-of-design).

The dancers' feet have been made open at an angle, which would make the movement easier in such a group dance. The mase in the composition along with the animals and the dancers, especially at both the ends, make it appear as a ritualistic activity performed collectively.

Figure 10. Dissected reptile

Composition theme: Documented information.

The composition is a line drawing (Figure 10a, Figure 10b) with an attempt to represent a full-scale dissected reptile animal. To fit large scale drawing on the rock surface, author of the

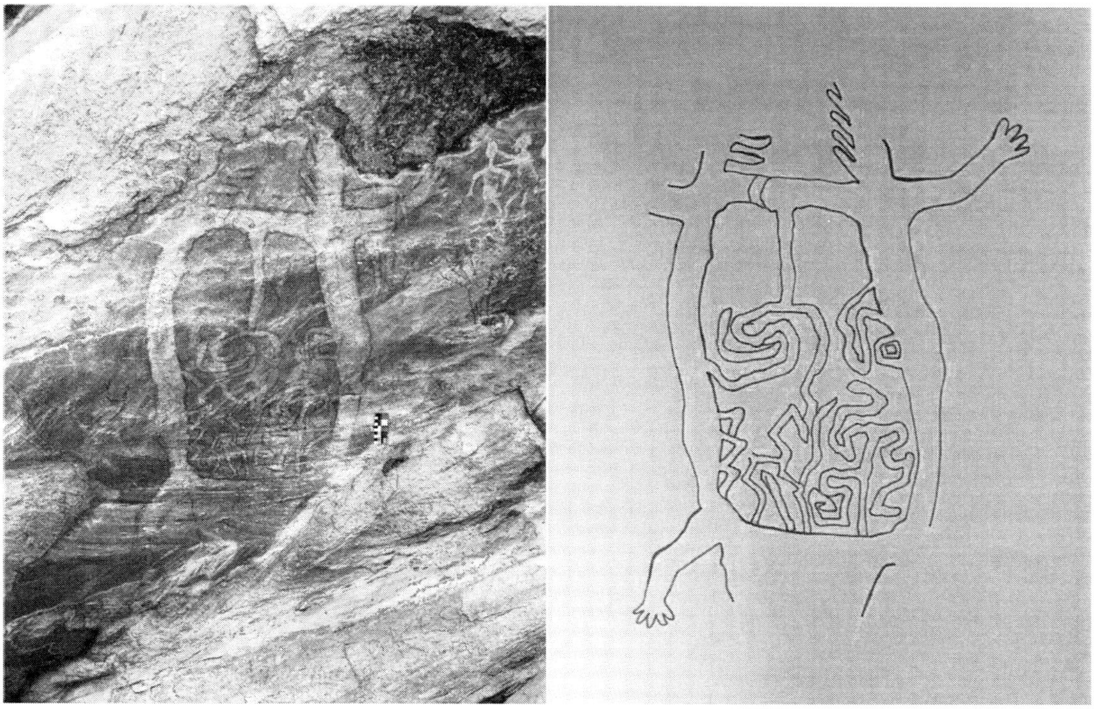

Figure 10a: Dissected reptile, and Figure 10b. its eye copy, Gandhisagar. Mesolithic (by Hridayshri).

composition has utilised the rock formation to its advantage making it appear as if the animal's head and tail partially hidden behind the rock formation, showcasing advance planning to utilize the surface strategically. As the focus was on documenting the dissected part of the animal, the composition is made in line drawing with similar stroke thickness. The dissected animal has white colour filled to make the drawing stand out from the rock surface and to be able to show connections of the organs with the reptile's body representing one system, and to not distracting the viewer from the primary objective of the display. The gestalt law of continuity, similarity, foreground and background is applied here with line consistency to share seriousness of the documented information (Dondis 1974: 30–31; Lester 2011: 45–50; Chaman: https://www.toptal.com/designers/ui/gestalt-principles-of-design).

The organ placement is accurate to represent the digestive system of the reptile. Composition shows the inquisitive nature of its author and an attempt to study, record and document what was perceived or understood from the immediate environment as the site is next to a water body (Kumar et al. 2021a).

Figure 11: Woman in Rhythm, Chaturbhujnath Nala

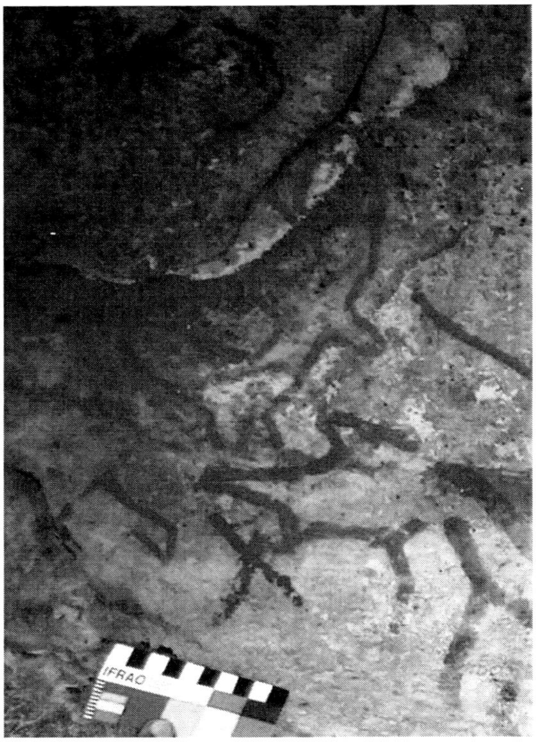

Figure 11: Woman in Rhythm, Chaturbhujnath Nala. Mesolithic

Composition theme: Experiential, conceptual, and abstract.

A female form uniquely represented though abstraction in a rhythmic pose, where the negative space of the lifted arms gives the impression of head of the woman along with her interesting body contours showing a very good example of figure and ground from gestalt principles (Figure 11). Looking at the quality and strategy of the joints used, to create body movement and femineity in the figure appears highly conceptual, depicting gestalt law of proximity and closure (Dondis 1974: 30–31; Lester 2011: 45–50; Chaman: https://www.toptal.com/designers/ui/gestalt-principles-of-design). The author's conceptual understanding of the body structure to exude free spirited, femineity with such grace in a posture is unfathomable to be able to represent with just lines.

During the replication process I found that each stroke, its starting and ending point, each joint of the stroke and even the length of each stroke is crucial to achieve the grace, sophistication and the dynamism of the body. While replicating the figure we just couldn't achieve what the author has managed to create on two-dimensional rock surface. It is an excellent example of design element and design principle working together, while presenting a conceptual figure by the stone age artist-designer. Another unique aspect of this composition is its viewing experience. The spot chosen by its author in the cavity on the roof of the shelter, figure drawn vertically-slightly tilted forward, makes the viewing height as an exceptional exhibiting position, either for one to have a closer look or for a larger group to view from a distance up-to 9.00 m (Kumar G 2015a, 2022; Krishna et al. 2021)

Figure 12. Rhinoceros, upside down

Figure 12a: Rhinoceros, upside down, Chaturbhujnath Nala. Mesolithic
Figure 12b: The author of the article observing the figure in the shelter in the most comfortable position

Composition theme: Spatial experience, narrative, environmental information.

Character design with thin and thick lines. Viewing experience of this composition made me realise that even the Stone Age man was keen on having personal leisurely experience. At first glance this figure appears to be odd one due to its upside-down placement among other figures on the roof of the shelter with viewing of an extremely strenuous neck position. But after careful on-site study, I observed that this particular composition was meant to view while sitting in the shelter at a very comfortable sitting position (Figure 12a, Figure 12b). One can admire the composition for hours while lounging with a good view. It is extremely comfortable to the eyes and neck as we are over looking at an open space from the shelter towards the nala and the greenery of the site with the neck support of the rock under the head. The viewer intuitively includes the landscape with the composition for a simultaneous experience as a narrative. As if we are looking at the majestic rhinoceros on the run in the jungle next to a water body. The use of different line thickness to show the strength, structural and physical details of the animal with the body proportions is clever (Krishna et al. 2021, Kumar G. 2022).

Gestalt law of similarity and proximity is used to share skin thickness details and structural information of the figure (Dondis 1974: 30–31; Lester 2011: 45–50; Chaman: https://www.toptal.com/designers/ui/gestalt-principles-of-design).

Replication of Stone Age rock art of Chaturbhujnath Nala

'Project on Replication of rock art of Chaturbhujnath Nala in India' was to understand the cognitive, technological and cultural development of the early man. The results so obtained can be checked by anyone at any time, hence the method is scientific. Replication of rock paintings of Chaturbhujnath Nala is the first project of its kind in India. It is to understand the pre-production and production processes of the creation of rock art compositions by additive technique. The project was carried out under the direction of Prof. Kumar, thoroughly recorded, and documented all the activities, observations and discussions to understand the objectives of the project. For further advanced study we will need the help of mineralogists, geochemists and physicists for the scientific study of the minerals in the field and in the laboratory.

The team

1. Giriraj Kumar, Professor in rock art science and Indian Culture. Director of the Replication Project.
2. Ram Krishna, an engineer and social scientist. He was also a team member of the DC cupule replication project.
3. Hridayshri, a professional artist and communication designer.
4. Geetanjali, a PG Research Scholar of archaeology and heritage management.

Objectives of the replication project

The objectives of the project were to understand the knowledge and wisdom of the authors of rock art at Chaturbhujnath Nala. Bring understanding on the tools, material and technical specifications used, skills employed, and reasons for selection of the spot and the site for creating specific compositions. The authors' intelligence and cultural impulses working behind the concepts of the compositions as a medium of communication (Kumar 2021).

Pre-Production preparations, processes and planning was adopted to achieve the desired objectives a scientific methodology. Where we studied the existing national and international literature on this subject. For the initial replication study, we selected six Mesolithic Stone Age compositions (Broad Group I) and five chariots from the cattle domestication mode of life and thought process (Broad Group II). The criteria for the selection of the compositions were the uniqueness of the composition and clear visibility, from which one could have the basic understanding of the form, proportions, quality of strokes, brush movement and observe other details. A thorough study of the compositions were carried out along with detailed practice sessions of coping the selected figures, the selection of the replication-site, collection of the material for making brushes, preparation of the brushes to be used, finding the source and collection of the Iron Oxide colour pigments, process to prepare the colour from the pigment nodules, experiment with colour binder, preparation of colour chart and the detail log of the experiences obtained and observations made (Kumar 2021; Kumar et al.2021b; Krishna et al. 2021; Geetanjali et al. 2021; Hridayshri et al. 2021a, 2021b).

Study of the selected compositions

The study of the compositions was made in the RASI studio at Agra and Delhi with the help of enlarged photographs. We also grinded colour pigments to obtain colour and did experiments on making the brushes from different materials along with practicing with both on vertical red stone surfaces.

before visiting the site, and commencing the replication task. Followed by the detailed study on the site to have an exact idea of the location and positioning of the composition. We studied and observed in-depth the strokes and lines of the selected compositions from the photographs and on the site. The point of starting and ending of the strokes, then their merging or joining with the following lines with a systematic follow up to achieve the final result. Quality, movement, thickness, direction and force of the strokes of the composition are communicating various information like gender, tentative age or age group, hierarchy, flow, motion, character, activity intent and the element in the figures of the composition. We also tried to understand the strategy and planning followed by the artist, so that we could replicate it similar to the original figure as far as possible (Krishna et al. 2021; Geetanjali et al. 2021).

Pigment selection and processing for the replication work

Haematite and red ochre were the most popular pigments used in the rock art of Chaturbhujnath Nala (CBN). Most of the early rock paintings in this period have been executed in line drawings in dark red colour, sometimes, with dark brown tone. We did experiment to understand the selection of the pigments used and their processing to obtain colour from them by replication process. Iron oxide pigment nodules were collected from the area near Chaturbhujnath temple in March 2019 and again in April 2021. We observed that darkness of the colour was directly proportionate to the hardness of the pigment nodule and it required hard physical work accordingly (Figure 13). The scientific analysis of the pigments will be followed in the second phase of the project. However, the present experiment throws light on the abilities of the authors of rock art to find the source and collection of the desired pigment nodules, the processes of obtaining colour from them, and their choice of pigments to execute the desired rock art compositions. It indicates the cognitive abilities of the authors of early rock paintings of CBN, and the socio-cultural aspects involved in it (Kumar 2021; Hridayshri et al. 2021a).

The process of making organic brushes for replication work

Understanding the kind of brush used for making the quality lines and strokes of rock paintings is essential to evaluate the knowledge, skill, technology, and cognitive development of the authors of rock art. Our experience of the nature and temperament of the brushes we made by

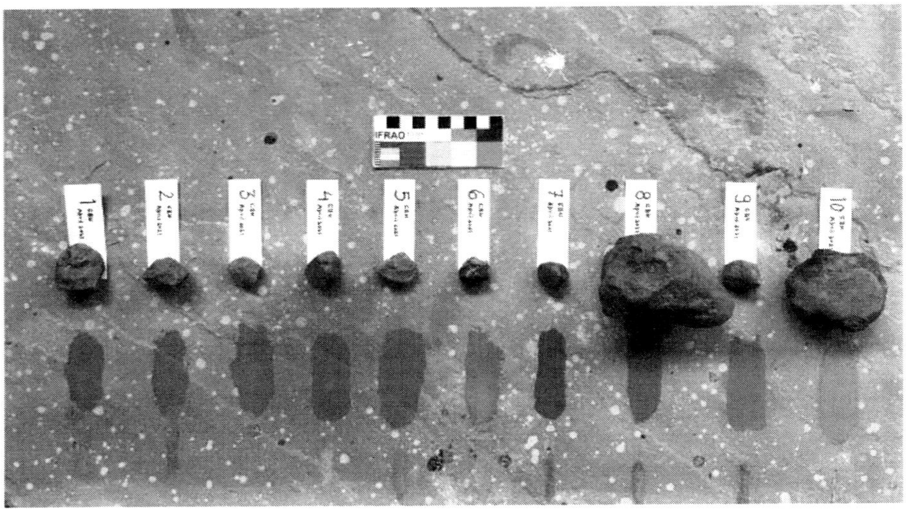

Figure 13: Scale of the pigment hues obtained from the iron oxide nodules by grinding with water and dry-scratching

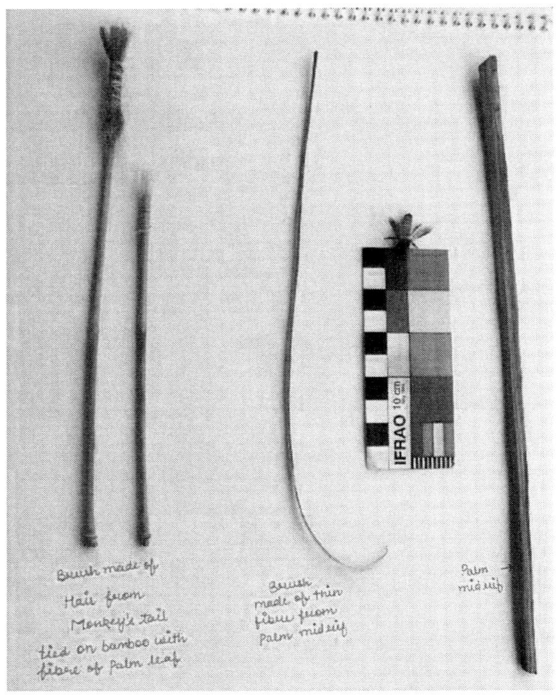

Figure 14: Handmade brush with hair of monkey tail and palm leaf mid-rib fiber

using different organic material while replicating the rock art brought great understanding on the process of execution of rock painting compositions (Figure 14).

We did experiment with many natural and locally available organic materials. Like palm leaf midrib (*Phoenix sylvestris* rachis), bamboo (*Bambusa vulgaris*) branch internodes, and Indian babul (*Acacia nilotica*). Geetanjali also did experiment with brush made of common reed (*Phragmites australis*) in Delhi, prior to the field work. The reed brush absorbs colour and is not suitable for drawing lines and strokes. Out of the materials we used, the midrib fibers of palm leaf were found most suitable for making brush of the needed bristle size from thin to thick (Figure 14). We also did experiments with the brush made of petiole of Dhak (*Butea monosperma*) leaf and hair of a dead langoor tail and squirrel (Hridayshri et al. 2021b).

Replication Process

While replicating the compositions we realised that good quality of brush is as important as the good pigment consistency. Working with natural brushes on the rough rock surface needs very calculated and skilled wrist movement to obtain the desired results (Figure 15a and 15b). The brushes made of different natural material had different temperaments and different pigment holding capacities. With these brushes it is even more difficult to maintain certain thickness of lines especially at curves, angles, arches, circles, starting and ending points of the strokes. For that one needs a lot of experience, planning and skill before putting the brush on the working rock surface. Understanding that the artists who created rock art were matured and skilled enough to deal with the entire process of rock art execution effortlessly (Kumar et al. 2021; Hridayshri et al. 2021b).

Discussion

(a) Painting on rock surface demands micro level of structural planning of the composition, figures and the theme; indicating that their authors were highly skilled, cognitively advance and deeply observant with great conceptual clarity.

(b) The understanding of colour and pigments, brush quality, natural materials, rock surface, painting position and angles, the skills of the author, all are deeply correlated and interdependent to achieve specific and efficient results.

(c) Subjects and inspirations came from the perception of the environment and human interaction with it. The Stone Age authors of rock paintings were cognitively so advanced that they could observe three- dimensional environment, and were able to translate it in a variety of visual themes (compositions) on two-dimensional rock surface in the most powerful and dynamic way.

(d) The environment, context and the position of the composition on the rock surface is an integral part to be emersed in the enhanced physical viewing experience in a particular position.

(e) The replication process brought an observation on the concept of personalized space/corner at the site following the concept of common space, private space or special space.

Figure 15a: Replication in the process close up

Figure 15b: Replicated archers' composition by Hridayshri

(f) Maximum viewing experience largely depends on specific time of the day and climatic conditions thus, indicating that the authors of the rock art compositions were conscious of the environment, activities going around it and experiencing them.

(g) Replicating rock art on different and difficult spot was challenging and physically demanding but once done it was an equally thrilling experience and sharing it with the team. It made us understand an insight on choosing a challenging spot to create, is a demonstration of high level of physical strength and painting skills.

(h) Our replication experience indicates that rock art execution was a group activity where the group was dependent physically, emotionally, and socially. However, it needs further study to authenticate it.

Concluding remarks

The entire study shows that the authors of Stone Age rock art had deep understanding of the nature, rocks, surfaces, pigments, minerals and anatomy of the animals and humans. They lived in harmony with nature and shared their experience and the perceived reality in the form of rock art compositions. Therefore, the design community can learn from these Stone Age design compositions to present their ideas accurately with minimal visual clutter and elements without overloading with unnecessary information. Thus, study of rock art brings direction to our present generation seeking adventure and excitement. Similar philosophical understanding and creative skills are required by the millennial artists and designers to have original ideas and powerful connecting narratives.

The study establishes that the design fundamentals are very much present in the Stone Age rock exogrames and the compositions can be read or interpreted technically from the perspective of design communication for systemic technical study. However further research in the perspective of time, space and systems is required for better understanding of the rock art in terms of communication design.

Acknowledgement

1. Rock Art Society of India, for including me as a team member and its financial support for the replication project.
2. Professor Giriraj Kumar for his mentorship and his valuable guidance during the entire study, on-site discussions, and the replication project. Also providing some of the original photographs for my study and publication.
3. Mr Erwin Neumayer for having figures from his book for my initial study.
4. Dr. Ram Krishna for his unconditional support and valuable discussions during my entire study.

Hridayshri
Artist and Communication designer
Rock Art Society of India
E-mail: hridayshri@gmail.com

References

Dondis, D. A. 1974. *A primer of visual literacy*. Cambridge (paperback edition), Massachusetts, The MIT Press. PP. 21–36.

Garge, T., Kulkarni, B. V., Rhutvij, R. A. and Sudhir, R. 2018. Petroglyphs in Konkan: Historiography, recent discoveries and future endeavours. *Purakala* 27-28: PP. 39–47.

Geetanjali, Krishna, R., Hridayshri, Kumar, G. 2021 (October). Project on Replication of rock art of Chaturbhujnath Nala in India, Part 2b: Selection of the Chariot Compositions and their study *Rock-Art, A Human Heritage,* Proceedings of the XXVIII Valcamonica Symposium, Capo di Ponte (Valcamonica), October 28 to 31, 2021. PP. 147–150.

Hridayshri 2019. Stone Age rock art and communication design: A preliminary study. *Purakala 29:* PP. 15–20.

Hridayshri 2021. Stone Age Rock Art and Communication Design: A Preliminary Study – Part 2 *Purakala 30-31:* PP. 21–26.

Hridayshri, Geetanjali, Krishna, R., Kumar, G. 2021a (October). Project on Replication of rock art of Chaturbhujnath Nala in India, Part 3: Pigment selection and their processing for replication of rock painting compositions. *Rock-Art, A Human Heritage,* Proceedings of the XXVIII Valcamonica Symposium, Capo di Ponte (Valcamonica), October 28 to 31, 2021. PP. 151–157.

Hridayshri, Geetanjali, Krishna, R., Kumar, G. 2021b (October). Project on Replication of rock art of Chaturbhujnath Nala in India, Part 4: Replication of making brush from different organic material for producing rock paintings and their ethnographical study. *Rock-Art, A Human Heritage,* Proceedings of the XXVIII Valcamonica Symposium, Capo di Ponte (Valcamonica), October 28 to 31, 2021. PP. 158–162.

Krishna, R., Hridayshri, Geetanjali, Kumar, G. 2021 (October). Project on Replication of rock art of Chaturbhujnath Nala in India, Part 2a: Selection of the Stone Age Compositions and their study. *Rock-Art, A Human Heritage,* Proceedings of the XXVIII Valcamonica Symposium, Capo di Ponte (Valcamonica), October 28 to 31, 2021. PP. 140–146.

Kumar, G. 2015a. Some unique Stone Age compositions in the rock art of Chambal valley in India. *Purakala* 25: PP. 31–43.

Kumar, G. 2015b. *Rock art of India*. Delhi: Sharada Publication House.

Kumar, G. 2021 (October). Cognitive, technological and cultural interface of rock art. Project on Replication of rock art of Chaturbhujnath Nala in India, Part 1: Project Introduction. *Rock-Art, A Human Heritage,* Proceedings of the XXVIII Valcamonica Symposium, Capo di Ponte (Valcamonica), October 28 to 31, 2021. PP. 135–139.

Kumar, G. 2022. *Chaturbhujnath Nala: A magnificent Rock Art Gallery in India.* Delhi: Sharada Publication House.

Kumar, G., Krishna R., Hridayshri, Singh N., Kumar, A. and Pandey, A. 2021a. Micro-Documentation and comprehensive study of the rock art of magazine rockshelter, Gandhisagar in Chambal Valley, Madhya Pradesh, India. *Purakala 30–31:* PP. 119–148.

KUMAR, G., KRISHNA R., HRIDAYSHRI, and GEETANJALI 2021b (October). Project on Replication of rock art of Chaturbhujnath Nala in India, Part 5: Replication of the processes of rock art production and our observations *Rock-Art, A Human Heritage,* Proceedings of the XXVIII Valcamonica Symposium, Capo di Ponte (Valcamonica), October 28 to 31, 2021. PP. 163–172.

LESTER, P. M. 2011. *Visual communication images with messages*. Boston, USA: Wadsworth Cengage Learning: PP. 45–50.

LALIT, S. 2013. Petroglyphs discoveredon lateritein coastal district Sindhudurga in Maharashtra. *Purakala* 23: PP. 69–72.

MATHPAL, Y. 1984. *Prehistoric rock paintings of Bhimbetka*. New Delhi: Abhinav Publications.

NEUMAYER, E. 1983. *Prehistoric Indian rock paintings.* New Delhi: Oxford University Press,

POULIN, R. 2011. *The language of graphic design.* Massachusetts, USA: Rockport Publishers Inc.: PP. 19–38.

WAKANKAR, V. S. 1978. *The dawn of Indian Art,* Ujjain: Bharti Kala Bhawan.

WAKANKAR, V. S. and ROBERT, R. R. BROOKS. 1976. *Stone Age Painting in India.* Bombay: D.B. Taraporewala and Sons.

CHAMAN, C. https://www.toptal.com/designers/ui/gestalt-principles-of-design.

SHILLINGTON, EDUCATION, https://www.shillingtoneducation.com/blog/communication-design/

23

KEYWORDS: Iconicity – Sound – Elephant Call – Wavy lines – Speech Scroll –Boustrophedon – Gravitational Waves – Sign Language – Empathy

ELEPHANT CALL IN THE ROCK ART OF ALGERIA

AHMED ACHRATI

Abstract: This study presents a new interpretation of curved lines surrounding elephants in the rock art of the Algerian Qsur mountains. By documenting attempts to depict, record, and reproduce sound, this study demonstrates the existence of cross-cultural association between curved lines and the visualization of sound in human imagination. This perception of sound also coincides with the physical manifestation of sound as a wave in nature. This demonstrated pattern of using curved lines to represent sound, coupled with an analysis of elephant behavior and a contextual reading of Algerian art, leads to a plausible hypothesis that the association of curved lines with elephants in this art constitutes a depiction of elephant stress calls, and is the expression of rock artists' empathetic response.

Introduction

At Garet et-Taleb and at Chériha in the Qsur mountains, there is a set of naturally executed engravings (Fig. 1, Fig. 2, and Fig. 3) featuring elephants partially surrounded by a band of wavy lines, referred to in the literature as festoons (*guirlandes*). The leading head of an elephantine procession at Garet et-Taleb (two adult, two juveniles, and a baby) is facing two lions devouring a carcass. While all elephants are drawn in a naturalist style using a fine line (barely visible), only the body and contour of the leading elephant are completely polished smooth. The absence of ears and tusk in this elephant has led some (e.g., Hachid 1992: 109) to describe it as either a bovid or equid, but the context of the scene, as well as the morphology (body, tail, legs, and hooves) resolve this ambiguity. A large-size archer (faded but visible in morning light) can be seen standing in front of the lead elephant. Surrounding this elephant is a band, or festoon, made of two wavy lines running along its back, over the top of its head, descending in front of it, then extending horizontally as

Article received: 9 November 2022
Revised I: 13 November 2023
Revised II: 25 January 2023
Revised III: 1 July 2023
Accepted: 2 July 2023

if to scoop up the archer. The space between the wavy lines is completely smoothed. Beneath the band to the left is an exquisite drawing of two lions devouring something.

About thirty miles as the crow flies east from Garet et-Taleb, a similar scene is found at Chériha. Drawn in deeply incised and smoothed lines, the elephant of Chériha is facing to the right, its tusks curved upward and trunk descending vertically, ending in a horizontal form of *m*. The sex of the elephant is marked in an anatomically incorrect way, resembling a human penal organ. Sheltered between its legs is a baby elephant. Just as at Garet et-Taleb, the top and front of the elephant is surrounded by a band of wavy lines that extend horizontally below an archer in front of it, holding a bow in the left hand and an object (a mallet?) in the right hand. Jumping a two-foot-wide vertical gap in the supporting rock, the wavy lines appear again on the neighboring boulder (Fig. 3).

In both scenes, the wavy lines have been interpreted either as symbols of water, or as signs of potency and hunting magic. For example, M. Hachid said the association of these motifs with an archer *donne à penser que nous avons peut-être là un rituel de chasse qui à chaque fois inclut le même élément, celui des motifs ondulés* ["[this] suggests the idea that we may have here a hunting ritual which every time includes the same element, that of undulated motifs"] (Ibid.). However, close examination of these scenes in the light of available ethnographic, cognitive, and anthropological knowledge suggests that these undulating lines are in fact phonographic depiction of elephant calls.

Figure 1: Elephant and archer seen in the morning glare, Garet at-Taleb. Photo A. Achrati.

Figure 2: Elephants and lions, Garet at-Taleb. Photo A. Achrati.

Figure 3: Disturbed elephants and archer, Chériha. Photo A. Achrati.

Sound and rock art studies

Research into the relationship between sound and rock art has recently gained interest, and many studies have been undertaken to determine the acoustic characteristics of caves, rock shelters, and open sites where art is found (Reznikoff, 2002; 2014; Waller 2012; Díaz-Andreu, Benito, and Lazarich 2014). Employing geological methods and acoustical physics, some researchers have focused on whether echolocation was used by prehistoric populations in the selection and use of rock art sites (Mattioli 2017). Combining anthropology and landscape analysis, others have explored the functions of rock art in both its physical and cultural contexts (Williams 2012). Few researchers have tried to discern pictorial depictions of acoustic events such as music, dancing, and clapping (e.g., Achrati 2012; Achrati 2006; Bovin 2004).

Only a few studies have attempted to specifically identify acoustic depictions in rock, but the results have been mixed. For example, passing reference were made to the effect that signs coming from the mouth of an animal is "a symbolic representation of the animal's voice or soul" (Patterson 1992, 193). Steve Waller investigated possible relationships between thunder myths around the world and rock art motifs found in reverberating locations. He concluded that hoofed animals depicted in reverberant caves are representations of supernatural beings associated with thunder, and that some of the "abstract" strokes and barbed signs are depictions of lightning accompanying the thunderous reverberation (Waller 2012). Therein lies the shortcoming of Waller's study: it is an investigation of visual signs (lightning) rather than acoustic effects (thunder).

More focused on sound are the ethnographic studies of a set of pictograms referred to as "elephants in boxes" in the Western Cap of South Africa, conducted by Anderson Paterson and John Parkington (Paterson and Parkington 2015; Paterson and Parkington 2018; Paterson 2018). As in Fig. 4, these painted images show undulating and crenellated lines surrounding individual elephants and touching their backs, heads, trunks, stomachs, and feet, and connecting them to each other. Paterson and Parkington correctly interpreted these lines as "being depictions of the unique low frequency elephant sound communication system, that happens between members within an elephant family and between elephants within kinship or bond groups over wide areas" (Paterson and Parkington 2015). However, in their interpretation of these images, Paterson and Parkington stressed a shamanistic interpretation, but without the entoptic (visions within the eye) element of this theory, as propounded by Lewi-Williams. These images, according to Lewis-Williams and Dowson, are representations of therianthropes with elephant heads and trunks, and "the surrounding lines are almost certainly entoptic forms" signifying shamanistic visions (Lewis-Williams and Dowson 1989, 138). Agreeing with this entoptic interpretation, Janette Deacon suggested that the lines in these images may also represent clouds, or "lines of potency or magic force" (Deacon 1994, 48; also, Hollmann 2005, 23).

Rejecting the identification of these lines as "entoptic visions seen by shaman/painters while in altered states," Parkington and Paterson argued that the lines are "more likely depictions of elephant

Figure 4: San painting of an elephant family, Ciderberg. Courtesy Andrew Paterson.

sounds" (Parkington and Paterson 2017, 135). But then they characterize these "sound lines" as projections of "somatogenic feelings" and "the shaking of the body," which are an essential part of the healing experience of San shaking dancers. Shamans, they say, "listen to their bodies and read the emergent sensations as manifestations of god and healing power" (Parkington and Paterson 2017, 143 and 136). Thus, the undulating lines became projections of somatic sensations, not the representations of sound–the rumbling of elephants. Parkington and Paterson insist that their explanatory thesis is concerned with sound not as an acoustic event but as an emic phenomenon–an account of the state of mind and body of the shaman. The acoustic element is secondary in this approach, they say (134-135).

The present study argues that rock artists did successfully and intentionally depict sound for no other reason than to record an interesting acoustic event. This is the case in North Africa, where elephants are associated with wavy lines signifying elephant distress calls. This assertion is based on a content analysis of pictorial narratives, supplemented by scientific, anthropological, and ethnographic evidence.

Visual desire and sound

Being optically oriented, humans have always shown a desire to visualize sounds and voices. This desire is well articulated in the Torah/Tanakh (Ex. 19:19 and 20:15), where "Moses spoke, and God answered him by a voice" in which, unlike the audible human voice, "the words of God are seen as light is seen; for we are told that 'all the people saw the Voice'" (JPS Tanakh 1917). For the epiphany of the visible voice, Philo explains, "God wrought on this occasion a miracle of a truly holy kind by bidding an invisible sound to be created in the air more marvelous than all instruments... which giving shape and tension to the air and changing it to flaming fire, sounded forth like the breath through a trumpet an articulate voice so loud that it appeared to be equally audible to the farthest as well as the nearest" (Philo, *On the Decalogue* LCL 320: 22-23; also ; Philo, *On the Migration of Abraham* LCL 261: 158-15).

In modern times, the desire to translate auditory perceptions into visual ones has been attempted by painters, poets, and musicians. The French poet Jean Nicolas Arthur Rimbaud assigned colors to the five vowels in his poem "Voyelles." (Trevor-Roper 1970, 69 and 165). Among modern painters, Wassily Kandinsky was particularly keen on the auditory and the "transmission of color-feeling through the medium of sound" (Kandinsky 1945, 77). Paul Klee also conceived of his paintings in polyphonic terms. As indicated by a recorded note on the back of a watercolor study for his *Orchestras* series, he created a correspondence between forms, colors, and instruments, relating green to the timber of the flute, blue to oboe, horizontal wavy lines to violin, vertical wavy lines for cello, and wavy lines radiating out like stars to trumpet (Ferrier 1998: 20; on visualizing music, see Lochhead 2006). When Rainer Maria Rilke saw some of Paul Klee's works, he wrote: "Even if you hadn't told me he plays the violin, I would have guessed that on many occasions his drawings were transcriptions of music." (*https://en.wikipedia.org/wiki/Paul_Klee*) And in Edward Munch's *Scream*, there is a faint echo of sound in the undulating cloud over the horizon (Munch, 1893, *The Scream*, oil, tempera and pastel on cardboard, 91 x 73 cm, National Gallery of Norway).

Scroll: A graphic shape of sound

Humans invented writing to communicate speech, but the relationship between the acoustic patterns of speech and their logographic or phonetic symbols is conventional rather than natural. Here lies one of paradoxes of the human communication: while speech uses vocal sounds to convey information, it cannot accurately describe sound. Humans are better at imitating sounds than describing them (Lemaitre, Houix, Voisin, Misdariis. *et al.* 2016; Mehrabi, Dixon, and Sandler 2019). Another irony is that while humans acquired an early ability to produce accurate visual likenesses of animals and humans, it took until the industrial age for sound and voice to be successfully recorded and graphically represented. In the meanwhile, many pre-industrial cultures managed to invent ways for graphically depicting sound.

What is interesting about these graphic attempts to circumscribe the invisibility of sound is that they all converge around the curvilinearity of sonic traces. Indeed, different cultures from different continents came upon the idea of using curved signs, scrolls, or banderoles to represent sound, speech, and music.

The earliest use of scrolls to signify speech is recoded in the Mayan writing tradition of Mesoamerica, a logographic script where complete words and ideas are represented by pictures instead of syllables or sounds. In this tradition, a basic convention for denoting speech or song is a scroll or a volute issuing from the mouth of a person. Classic Mayan artists also used images of undulating or jagged lines to signify the powerful rumbling sounds reverberating from the mouths of gods, such as the rain and lightning god Chaak (see Houston, Stuart, and Taube 2006: 163; Colas 2011:15). Animals with scrolls coming from their mouths were also found in stone sculpture, and on painted pottery. To visually represent the echo (acoustic reverberation) in architectural spaces, Classic Mayan artists also used images of detached and scattered speech scrolls.

The convention of symbolizing sound using scrolls and undulating, or jagged lines is also found in Mixtec codices (Fig. 5) (Houston, Stuart, and Taube 2006:163; Colas 2011,15). Conceptually, the Mayan scroll, or volute, seems to have been abstracted from the conch shell, which played a significant role in Mesoamerican cultures. For example, a cross-section view of a conch shell was one of the signature symbols of the Wind God, who played a central role in the creation of humankind in Mexican mythology (Taube 2018: 52; and 144:15; Houston, Stuart, and Taube 2006:13); the conch was also blown particularly to herald battles, ceremonial processions, and sacred rituals.

Figure 5: Talking bird, Codex Fejérváry-Mayer, Pl. 34, archive.org

Shofar and the voice of God

In the Old World, it was the horn that assumed the symbolic functions held by the conch shell in the New World. In Exodus 19, the first account of the revelation portrays the *qol,* or voice of God Himself, as the sound of a great ram's horn, or shofar (Hebrew: *qol shofar gadol*). In Medieval time, this epiphanic visualization of the divine voice was given a pictorial form in various illustration of the Haggadah, the Jewish text which is recited at the Seder during the first and second nights of Passover. For example, in the Sarajevo Haggadah, which originated from mid-fourteenth-century Catalonia, the voice is represented by a horn (The survival of the *Sarajevo Haggadah* is the subject of a 2008 novel, *People of the Book,* by Brooks, Geraldine, New York: Penguin Books, 2008). In the Copenhagen Haggadah (Fig. 6), the depiction of Revelation features a sun containing the text of the First Commandment and two shofars floating mid-heaven, on the sides of a mountain topped by colorful imagery of thundering, lightening, and fiery flames.

Figure 6: Shofar, a symbol of God's voice, Copenhagen Haggadah, 1739, fol. 16b. Reproduced with permission of the Copenhagen Jewish Community.

In the graphic traditions of Medieval Europe, scrolls (banderoles or phylacteries) were used to represent sound, speech, and music. Resembling an unfurled strip of cloth or parchment, speech was represented as scroll floating from the mouth of a person. like a modern-day speech balloon, these floating scrolls often contained the spoken words.

The pictographic traditions of the Eskimo and native American Indians also used voice lines to indicate speech (Fig. 7). For example, to show a person calling and verbally urging his sledge-dogs by means of his voice, a line was drawn, extending from the side of the head – presumably the person's mouth – to the leader dog. Pictographic drawings of the Cheyenne, Arapaho, and Dakota Indians also frequently use lines to indicate the voice (Ibid).

Figure 7: Voice line between lead dog and sled rider. Annual Report of the Board of Regents of the Smithsonian Institution (1895), p. 910, Figure 133.

In recent times, the use of both wavy lines and horns to signify voice is found in the Dongba (Tomba, Tompa or Mo-so), the script of the Naxi, an ethnic group of the Yunnan in southern China. Dongba is another logographic writing system, where pictographic characters are combined in rebus-like puzzles to indicate a new meaning. Developed around the seventh century, Dongba is used today almost solely for decorative and artistic purposes. Dongba frequently uses lines and cow horns to signify sound. Voice, for example, is represented as a curved line emanating from a stylized mouth (Mueggler 2011: 94; Zhou 2013: 86). Snoring is depicted as a person lying on a bed with a trembling line near his mouth (Fig. 8).

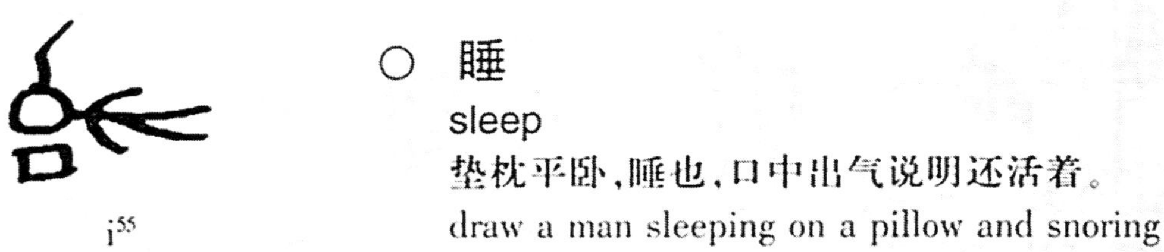

Figure 8: A person sleeping and snoring. He, Pinzheng; Xuan, Naxi Dongba pictoraph dictionary, Qin, p. 75.

It is rather significant that different cultures which had no significant connection or means of communication with each other found graphic expression for sound and speech in curvilinear objects and forms: horns, conch shells, scrolls, and wavy lines. This convergence of logographic patterns leads to the question of whether this association of sound and curvilinear patterns is rooted in the structure of human cognitive processes. A partial answer to this question resides in the phenomenon of synesthesia.

Synesthesia: Sound, sound symbolism, and curvilinearity

In ordinary human experiences, objects and events are perceived at once in a bundled input of multiple sensory modalities (Evans and Treisman 2010). These sensory modalities influence each other, sometimes giving rise to cross-modal associations, or synesthesia (Auracher 2017; Parise 2016; Hanson-Vaux, Crisinel, and Spence 2012; Ramachandran and Hubbard, 2001; Neckar and Bob 2014; Harvey 2013; Grady 2006). In some synesthetic manifestations, words and sounds are perceived as colors, shapes, and movement. This experience of color, shapes and movement does not displace the auditory experience of the synesthete; it only supplements it.

Synesthesia, it should be remembered, is a non-pathological condition, which is experienced by people as "a form of thinking, an imagistic alternative to inner speech, not merely curious sensory anomalies" (Hunt 1989:190). Some researchers have hypothesized the existence of a *neonatal synesthesia*, suggesting that all humans are born with strong cross-modal perception which declines and weakens over a lifetime of most people (Ludwig and Simner 2013).

One of the manifestations of these cross-modal phenomena is sound symbolism, which is a common feature in all spoken languages – though in some more than in others. Sound symbolism occurs when an acoustic constituent of a word (phoneme, syllable, feature, or tone) goes "beyond its linguistic function as a contrastive, non-meaning-bearing unit, to directly express some kind of meaning" (Nuckolls 1999: 228; also, Hinton, Nichols and Ohala, 1994: 4; Hockett 1959; Waugh 1992; Nuckolls 1999; Thompson and Do. 2019; Imai & Kita, 2014; Dingemanse 2012, 655; Blasi, Wichmann, Hammarström, Stadler, *et al.* 2016; Lockwood and Dingemanse 2015; Ohala 1994, Ramachandran and Hubbard 2001; Hunter-Smith 2007; Mompeán-Guillamón and Cifuentes-Férez 2012). In sound symbolism, there is a mapping, or correspondence, that takes place between the form of some words, or ideophones, and the sensory features they depict, which gives these words certain iconicity (a perceived analogy between the form of a sign and its meaning) (Nuckolls 1999; Waugh 1992; Taub 2001; Dingemanse 2012; Dingemanse *et al.*, 2015; Dingemanse 2018; Taitz, Assaneo, Elisei, *et al.* 2018; Perlman, Little, Thompson, *et al.* 2018; Thompson and Do 2019).

Sound symbolism has been subject to extensive linguistic, cognitive, and anthropological studies (Blasi, Wichmann, Hammarström, Stadler, *et al.* 2016; Haynie, Bowern, and LaPalombara 2014; Dingemanse 2012; Sidhu and Paxman 2018; Perlman, Little, Thompson, *et al.* 2018; Peirce, 1902; Sapir 1929; Achrati 2022). Known as the *mil/mal* effect (Sapir, 1929), the earliest sound symbolism studies investigated the properties of vowels and their associations with shape and size. When asked to pair nonwords such as *mil* and *mal* with a small and large shapes, participants generally paired *mil* with the small shape and *mal* with the large shape (Sapir 1929; for a review, see Sidhu and Paxman 2018). Later studies confirmed the association between high and front vowels (e.g., /i/) and small objects; and low and back vowels (e.g., /u/) and large objects across speakers of different languages. Subsequent studies focused on symbolic associations of consonants and vowels. Initially known as the *maluma/takete* effect, these studies were later called the *bouba/kiki* effect in reference to the experiment used by Ramachandran and Hubbard (2001). In these studies, participants were asked to match nonsense words with images of unfamiliar round and angular shapes. These studies confirmed that an auditory pitch can generate cross-modal associations with visual shapes, resulting in high pitch being associated with curvy, rounded shapes rather than angular ones (Evans, citing Wagner, Winner, Cicchetti, & Gardner, 1981; Salgado-montejo et al. 2016).

More pertinent to this investigation are sound symbolism studies that correlated auditory perceptions and visual and motor functions. For example, Salgado-montejo *et al.* (2016), looked at how different sounds (i.e., tones and piano chords) can bias movement. Participants were asked to freely move a computer mouse in response to five different sounds; researchers found that the drawings in response to high-pitches were more jagged and angular, whereas those drawings depicting low-pitched tones or minor chords tended to be rounder in form (Salgado-montejo *et al.* 2016, Fig. 4).

The perceptual tendency for sound to be associated with curvilinear forms and objects is, therefore, well attested in many graphic traditions as well as in sound symbolism. This imitative association between sound and curvilinearity is also indirectly manifested in another way: it is inscribed in some types of writing.

Writing

Humans invented writing to record speech, but writing does not actually capture sounds. Writing is a mnemonic technique for conveying meanings using symbols arbitrarily assigned to the sound units (phonemes or morphemes) of a spoken language. As stated above, the relationship between the acoustic patterns of speech and their logographic or phonetic symbols is conventional rather than natural; letters and symbols do not constitute an acoustic realization of utterances. This is the reason it is possible for a given language to be transcribed in more than one writing system (e.g., Urdu in Hindi and Arabic; Maltese in Arabic and Latin). This is also why in any language, such as English, some letters have a large variety of sound possibilities (Gaur 2000: 36).

There are many language writing systems, and one of the earliest to appear is the Mesopotamian cuneiform, which appeared around 3600 BCE. In this system, logo-phonetic signs stand for words and for syllables which, in combination with other syllabic signs can spell out a word or bound morpheme (Cooper 1996). The subsequent invention of phonetic writing in the Levant in the second millennium BCE gave each constituent sound or phoneme a distinct graphic representation

(Achrati 2007, 154; Hoyland 2001:198-199; Macdonald 2000: 32). Today's writing systems include logographic scripts (e.g., Chinese), phonetic (e.g., English), abjadic (e.g., Arabic), as well as a syllabary system, where the basic unit corresponds to a spoken syllable (e.g., Japanese and Cherokee).

Boustrophedon

Writing is a linear arrangement of graphemes moving in one direction, from left to right, right to left, or up and down. At the early stage of their appearance, many ancient inscriptions were executed in a boustrophedonic form-- a meandering motion where lines, including their letters reverse direction. This, for example, is the case with some Archaic Greek, Latin, and Safaitic inscriptions. As can be seen in boustrophedonic epigraphy, it almost seems that sound has imprinted itself into the observable curvilinearity of the written lines (Fig. 9). Boustrophedonic style is also observed in the meandering motion of childhood handwriting exercises (Cramer 2006: 135).

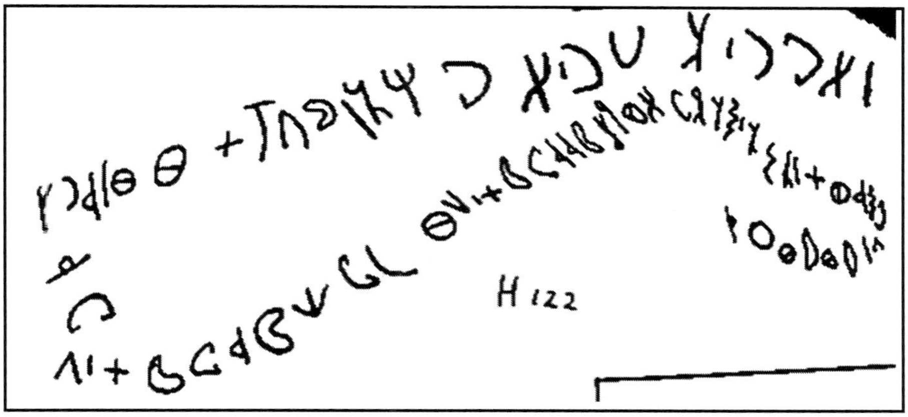

Figure 9: Safaitic writing in boustrophedonic form, Winnett & Harding, 1978.

Stenography

An even clearer example of the tendency of sound to be embedded in curvilinear shapes and graphs appears in stenography. Also known as phonography, shorthand writing is a technique for producing reliable, readable, and speedy transcriptions. As a writing tradition, stenography goes back to Cicero's slave Tiro, who recorded his master' Senate deliberations. A modern example of shorthand writing is the Pitman system, which was developed for the English language by Sir Isaac Pitman (1813–1897).

Most shorthand writings are phonetic systems where, instead of letters, the symbols represent sounds, with words written as they are spoken. Symbols consist of curvilinear strokes, some invoking the Mayan scrolls, others the European banderoles. The intimate relationship between sound and shorthand is confirmed by the comparability of the stenographic symbol and music. As described by Alfred Cramer, the visual resemblance between melody and stenography is as follows: "Exchange an instrument continuously emitting sound for the pen continuously emitting ink, and Romantic melody becomes much like cursive handwriting. It is a continuous stream modulated by rhythmic changes in pitch and intensity as well as consonant and dissonant accompaniment (Cramer 2006: 140, Fig. 3).

So effective and precise is phonography in its representation of the sounds of words that some people thought of it as "a natural method of writing." In fact, in the nineteenth century "stenographers felt so close to capturing the phonetic essence and economy of words that they imagined they would soon transcend ordinary meaning and be able to write down ideas in their pure form" (Cramer 2006: 148). Franz Xaver Gabelsberger (1789–1849) claimed that the written symbols in his system were no longer merely the "signs of the audible sound-form in alphabetic experience," but were also "signs of the spirit that lies latent in the original nature of the linguistic symbol" (Cramer 2006: 148).

Mechanically, the basic principle in many shorthand methods is the use of thick and thin strokes of the pen in various orientations, as well as other basic features of handwriting in recording the sounds of speech (Cramer 2006: 149). In modern stenography, voiced consonants are represented by heavy pen strokes and unvoiced consonants with light strokes, while abrupt consonants are denoted with straight lines, and liquids and nasals with curves. For example, in Pitman shorthand, unvoiced and voiced pairs of sounds (such as /p/ and /b/ or /t/ and /d/) are represented by strokes which differ only in thickness: thin strokes representing "light" sounds such as /p/ and /t/, and thick strokes "heavy" sounds such as /b/ and /d/. To represent vowels, light or heavy dots, dashes, or other special marks are drawn, each in their own position relative to the consonant (Cramer 2006: 149).

Nature, waves, and the physics of sound

Humans did not only want to visualize sound; they also wanted to capture melodies, record them, and retrieve them. Musical notations were created for the representation of melodic tunes played with instruments or sung by the human voice. Humans even created mechanical devices for storing and automatically reproducing music. This technological achievement was first documented in the 9th century, when the Banū Mūsā brothers of Baghdad invented the earliest known mechanical musical instrument, a water-powered organ that played interchangeable cylinders. According to Charles B. Fowler, this "...cylinder with raised pins on the surface remained the basic device to produce and reproduce music mechanically until the second half of the nineteenth century." The Banū Mūsā brothers also invented an automatic flute player, which appears to have been the first programmable machine (Fowler 1967).

It took until the Industrial Revolution in the nineteenth century for humans to be able to visually capture and reproduce sounds. Since then, technological recording of sound has seen stunning progress, moving from acoustic recording (1877-1925), to electrical (1925-1945), to magnetic (1945-1975), to present-day digital.

Robert Hooke's experiments in 1680 showed that running a violin bow along the edge of a plate covered with a powder produces lines and nodal patterns (Fig. 10 and Fig. 11). These patterns were later named the Chladni figures, after the German physicist and musician Ernst Florens Friedrich Chladni (1756–1827), who demonstrated that when resonating, a plate or membrane is divided into regions that vibrate in opposite directions. This causes the granular substance covering the plate to move and concentrate along the nodal lines where the surface is still, indicating regions of maximum and minimum displacement, depending on the medium and the frequency of the vibration.

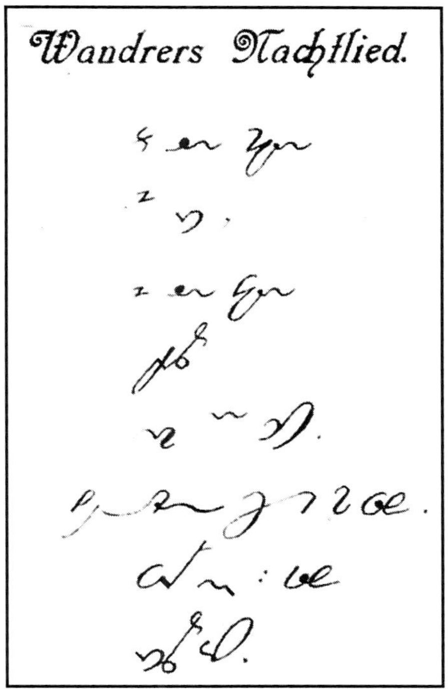

Figure 10: A poem by Goethe in Gablesberger shorthand.

The Chladni effects ("nodal patterns") not only impacted the study of sound; they also contributed to the mathematical solution of the Schrödinger equation for understanding the electron orbital in one-electron atoms in quantum mechanics. Also known as cymatics, these patterns found reception in philosophy as well, giving rise to anthroposophy. Rudolf Steiner, a Swiss educator in the early 20th Century, is the central figure in the history of anthroposophy, and the founder of the School of Spiritual Science in Switzerland which is connected in an anthroposophy (Miller 2016).

Research into the relationship between sound and sight was further advanced in 1807, when Thomas Young (1773-1829), a physician, linguist, and musician, conducted experiments on harmonic sounds and studied the behavior of sound waves (Pesic 2013: 20-21). In one of his

Figure 11: Generation of Chladni's figures. Archive.org.

experiments, Young recorded the graphic imprints of sound this way: he coated a rotating glass cylinder with soot and pushed a pin through a flexible diaphragm; by shouting into the diaphragm, he was able to see the sound waves scratched into the soot.

Perceiving an analogy between the recurrence of Newton's rings and the pitch of musical instrument, Young applied the same physical models and mathematical description of sound to light. He concluded that light is a transverse wave–a wave that vibrates perpendicular to the direction of the path of propagation (Pesic 2013, 16). He demonstrated this by developing the two-slit experiment, another invention that helped develop the study of quantum physics (Pesic 2013: 20).

Further elaboration of Young's experiment in 1854 led Edouard-Léon Scott de Martinville (1817-1879) to finally provide a recording of the visual traces of the voice. An editor and typographer, Léon Scott first conceived of sound recording in 1853 when he came upon a description of the ear while editing a scientific manuscript on human physiology. He then conceived of what he called "the imprudent idea of photographing the word": just as photography could capture fleeting images with lenses modeled on the eye, so it should also be possible that a replica of the ear could capture spoken words. For a visual analysis of sound, he used a vibrating diaphragm and stylus to graphically record sound waves as tracings on sheets of paper. Léon Scott's recording of speech and singing (phonautograms) were recently scanned by audio engineers and digitally converted into audible sound that can be played back (see, e.g., *Au clair de la lune* at https://en.wikipedia.org/wiki/Phonautograph).

Later, Thomas Edison's invention of the phonograph made it possible to record and play back sounds. This retrieval of sound involved the use of phonograph discs, or gramophone records, which served as analog storage of sound. Sound vibration waveforms are recorded as a spiral groove engraved, etched, incised, or impressed into the surface of a rotating cylinder or disc, called a "record". To recreate the sound, the surface is similarly rotated while a playback stylus traces the groove and is therefore vibrated by it.

Following these breakthroughs in the recording and reproduction of sound, efforts shifted to optical recording, or the production of 'graphic sound'. For example, László Moholy-Nagy (1895 –1946), the Hungarian painter, photographer, and professor from the Bauhaus school, thought that the curved grooves on a gramophone which direct the needle of the resonating membrane could be magnified and studied to unlock the relationship between a sound and a gramophone groove. Sounds could then be identified, analyzed, and arranged into musical works. It became possible to synthetically create rich and harmonious sounds simply by making a groove with a proper structure of shape and depth (Robertson 2010: 14). This technique culminated in the optical recording system and sound projection of the early 1930s (Robertson 2010: 15). The manipulation of an optical soundtrack to produce synthetic sound created from images drawn directly onto film or paper that were then played back using a sound system gave rise to what is referred to as "ornamental," "animated sound," "ornamental sound," and "graphic sound."

Gravitational waves: the sound of black holes

When black holes and heavy object collide, it creates undulation in space-time that would spread out across the universe like ripples in the cosmic pond (Cowen 2019: 122). The wavelengths of these events are larger than the massive bodies generating them, and have only a weak impact on matter, which makes their detection difficult. But these wavelengths have several properties in common with sound waves: they alternatively stretch and compress matter—the fabric of space-time. Converting gravitational waves into sound yield rich information about the system that created them. From these waves, the mass and rotation of the source can be determined. What is interesting is that the frequency range of the gravitational waves falls between 10 and 1,000 cycles per second, which is within the audible range (Cowen 2019: 124)

Sound and curves

What the history of the attempts to visualize sounds demonstrates is that human perception and conceptualization of sound is intimately associated with curvilinear objects and forms: scrolls, horns, conch shells, and wavy lines. While the coincidence of the perceptual curvilinearity of sound and its natural manifestation in physics as a wave is a source of wonderment, the question remains of how exactly scrolls, horns, conch shells and wavy lines became symbols of sound. The answer to this question may perhaps be found in gesturing, which underscores the embodied nature of acoustic experiences.

Language, gestures, and iconicity

Gestures and body movements often accompany oral speech and play a role in processing and learning language and other cognitive skills (Goldin-Meadow, Susan, and Brentari 2017). The iconicity of gestures is the basis of sign language. Although the perception of sound is absent in sign language, research on language has shown that the gestural components of signing are produced in the same manual modality as in spoken language: in both languages, the iconicity of a sign relies on the parts of the referent being represented by analogous parts of the linguistic form. The constitution process of iconicity in sign language is described by S. Taub, as follows:

"To create an iconic item, one selects an image to represent, modifies or schematizes that image so that it is representable by the language, and chooses appropriate forms to show or encode each representable part of the image. Moreover, when modifying the image or 'translating' it into linguistic form, one makes sure that the new image preserves the relevant physical structure of the previous stage (Taub 2001: 44)".

For example, to represent an animal in sign language, the signer "draws on both general shape-for-shape iconic devices and the correspondence between animal bodies and the human body." (Goldin-Meadow, Susan, and Brentari 2017: 74). Sometimes an animal's body parts can look significantly different from corresponding human body parts, as is the case of elephants. In such a case, signs for the animal part or action are made using a combined iconic mapping that involves the encoding of a salient body part of the animal and its association metonymically with the concept of the animal itself. Thus, the sign for "elephant" uses a flat hand to show the trunk. Starting near the nose, the hand moves downward and outward to sketch out a path that gives the details of the shape (Taub: 79, fig. 5.10).

Elephant calls, iconic gestures, and signs

The elephant is the descendent of a tapir-like ancestor that lived about fifty-five million years ago. In its course of adaptation, the elephant grew and developed a head with elongated jaws equipped with a pair of tusks (greatly modified teeth) for food and for defense. Over time, the head and jaws became shorter, and the snout combined with the upper lip to become a long, flexible proboscis (Shoshani 1997). Strong and sensitive, the trunk assumed multiple tasks: breathing, drinking, smelling, prehension, and vocalization.

Elephants produce different sounds, but the rumble dominates the elephantine acoustic repertoire. Rumbling is used for communicating over long distances, as well as for greeting, bonding, threatening, soliciting a mate, soothing, or giving reassurance. An elephant may also trumpet when it is excited, lost, angry, playful, or surprised. While most vocalizations are made with the larynx, rumbles originate in the larynx and resonate through the pharyngeal pouch, the nasal passages of the skull, and through the trunk. Some rumbles are produced with the mouth open and others with the mouth closed. Open-mouthed calling is associated with louder, more modulated rumbles. Rumbles vary in modulation and in pitch; in terms of frequencies, they usually range between 8 and 34 Hz depending upon the age, size, and excitement of the elephant. They may be emitted as a soft fluttering whisper or an explosive throaty resonance with high sound pressure levels. In duration, they can vary from less than half a second to almost 12 seconds. By contrast, humans perceive acoustic waves that have frequencies lying between about 20 Hz and 20 kHz. Sound waves above 20 kHz are known as ultrasound and are not audible to humans. Sound waves below 20 Hz are known as infrasound. Different animal species have varying hearing ranges.

Humans can be a threat to elephants, and elephants appear to recognize the level of threat that different human groups in different geographic areas pose (Soltis, *et al.* 2014). The sight, sound and smell of humans elicit vigilant and aggressive responses of elephants, and people who live in proximity of elephants know how dangerous these animals can be. People who share space with elephants have evolved oral traditions about elephant behavior and its dangers. For example, in the oral tradition of Khwe farmers in West Caprivi, detailed information about the interpretations of different elephant sounds is taught, as are ways of avoiding an elephant confrontation. Inhabitants learn to distinguish between an elephant that is grazing, angry, chasing, or intending to kill. When an elephant is under a tree, "you pay respect and face the other way: it will see you but not charge because you are respecting it. The elephant is afraid of us too, we give each other problems" (Moore 2009).

Studies of elephant sounds have shown that elephants reacted differently to different groups of people. They were more excited and aggressive in the presence of olfactory and visual cues of Maasai pastoralists, who are known to kill elephants, and less so in the presence of olfactory and visual cues of Kamba agriculturalists, who pose less of a threat (Soltis, *et al.* 2014; Susan McCarthy 1995; Anthony and Graham 2012).

Sounds of the Qsur Elephants

It is very likely that a description of human interaction with elephants, such as observed among the Massai and Khwe, is the subject of the pictorial narrative at Garet et-Taleb and Chériha. As indicated above, the bull elephant of Chériha is depicted facing an archer in a menacing attitude. The wavy band running over the elephant's back, around its face, and under the archer is most likely a depiction of the elephant's rumbling prompted by the sight of danger. The same can be hypothesized about the band of wavy lines enveloping the lead elephant in Garet et-Taleb and extending towards the lions. Both images portray elephants in a state of excitement prompted by the sight of a threat. Their excitement fills the air with rumbling that emanates from their trunks.

Just as in Taub's description of iconicity (*supra*)— how a visible object is selected, modified, or schematized, then used to encode a particular idea—the elephant trunk, which consists of a ringed or annulated organ, is abstracted as a corrugated band standing for the elephant call. With complete resemblance to the trunk, an anatomical organ of the animal, the band of wavy lines became an iconic sign of sound. Just as the Mayans, the Medieval Europeans, and Dongba people abstracted the curl of the tongue to symbolize sound and speech, so too, the Qsur artists abstracted the elephant trunk to represent elephant rumblings in a state of excitement.

In addition to wavy lines, artists sometimes deliberately relied on features of the supporting rock to highlight the effect of the elephant's call. In Fig. 12, this would be the stream of pecked dots. In fig. 13 where the elephant's feet seem to be caught in spiky traps, wavy lines are added to a well-marked trunk which is deliberately adjoined to a cluster of pecked dots in front of the elephant. Together with the ripples, or corrugation of the trunk, the dots may allude to the sound of the elephant's distress.

Figure 12: Possible elephant's rumble, Mouchgueg. Photo A. Achrati.

Figure 13: Possible elephant in distress, Mouchgueg. Photo A. Achrati.

Conclusion

Just as in sign language, the Qsur and 'Amour artists developed image in a mimetic way, creating an image of sound out of the similitude of the rumbling of an elephant and the corrugated form of its trunk. On the basis of above study, it can be hypothesized that sound and visual image were combined to give a graphic and readable expression of elephant calls in the form of wavy lines that mimic the trunk of the elephant. The directionality of this phonographic pattern also points to the function of elephant call in the presence of danger.

Dr Ahmed Achrati
1936 Wallace Avenue
Silver Spring, MD 20902
USA
E-mail: aachrati@gmail.com

References

Achrati, A. 2022. "Birds, Dream-Flying, Avian Metaphors and Rock Art." *Rock Art Research* 39:2.

Achrati, A. 2012. "Women, music and rock art in Ancient Arabia," *Sahara* 23:160-162.

Achrati, A. 2006. "Music and rock art: A Saharan note," *Rock Art Research* 23(1):71-78.

Achrati, A. 2007 "Arabian rock art: A Thamudic 'informant'," *Rock Art Research* 23(2): 153-64.

Anthony, L., and Graham. S. 2012. *The Elephant Whisperer: My Life with the Herd in the African Wild.* 1st St. Martin's Griffin ed. New York: St. Martin's Griffin.

Auracher, J. 2017. Sound Iconicity of Abstract Concepts: Place of Articulation Is Implicitly Associated with Abstract Concepts of Size and Social Dominance." *PLoS One* 12 (11) (11). doi: http://dx.doi.org/10.1371/journal.pone.0187196.

Blasi, D. E., Søren W., Harald H., Peter F. S., and Morten H. C. 2016. Sound–meaning Association Biases Evidenced across Thousands of Languages. Proceedings of the National Academy of Sciences of the United States of America 113, no. 39: 10818-0823. Accessed August 2, 2020. www.jstor.org/stable/26471840.

Boivin, N..2004. "Rock Art and Rock Music: Petroglyphs of the South Indian Neolithic." *Antiquity* 78 (299): 38–53. https://doi.org/10.1017/S0003598X00092917.

Brooks, G. 2008. *People of the Book: A Novel.* New York: Penguin Books.

Colas P. R. 2011. Writing in Space: Glottographic and Semasiographic Notation at Teotihuacan." *Ancient Mesoamerica* 13–25. https://doi.org/10.1017/S0956536111000046.

Cowen, R. 2019. *Gravity's Century: from Einstein's Eclipse to Images of Black Holes.* Harvard University Press.

Cramer, A. W. 2006. Of Serpentina and Stenography: Shapes of Handwriting in Romantic Melody. Nineteenth Century Music 30 (2) (Fall): 133-165.

Deacon, J. 1998. *Some views on rock paintings in the Cederberg.* Cape Town: National Monuments Council.

Díaz, Andreu, M.; Carlos G. B., María L. 2014. The Sound of Rock Art. The Acoustics of the Rock Art of Southern Andalusia (Spain). *Oxford Journal of Archaeology* 33 (1): 1–18. doi:10.1111/ojoa.12024.

Dingemanse, M. 2012. Advances in the Coss-Linguistic Study of Ideophones. *Language and Linguistics Compass* 6/10: 654–672, 10.1002/lnc3.361

Evans, K. K., and A. Treisman. 2010. Natural Cross-Modal Mappings Between Visual and Auditory Features. *Journal of Vision (Charlottesville, Va.)* 10, no. 1: 6.1–6. https://doi.org/10.1167/10.1.6.

Ferrier, J. -L. 1998. *Paul Klee*. Transl. by M. Imrie. Finest SA/Pierre Terrail Éditions, Paris.

Fowler, C. B. 1967. The Museum of Music: A History of Mechanical Instruments. *Music Educators Journal*, MENC_ The National Association for Music Education, 54 (2): 45–49, doi:10.2307/3391092

Gaur, A. 2000. *Literacy and the Politic of Writing*. Bristol, U.K.; Portland Oregon, USA: Intellect Books

Goldin-Meadow, S., and D. Brentari. 2017. Gesture, Sign, and Language: The Coming of Age of Sign Language and Gesture Studies. *The Behavioral and Brain Sciences* 40: e46–e46. https://doi.org/10.1017/S0140525X15001247.

Grady, J. E. 2005. Image schemas and perception: Refining a definition. In B. Hampe, and J. E. Grady, eds. *From Perception to Meaning Image Schemas in Cognitive Linguistics*, Berlin: Mouton de Gruyter, pp. 35-55.

Hachid, M. 1992, *Les pierres écrites de l'Atlas saharien: el-Hadjra el-Mektouba,* vol. 1, Alger: Enag/Editions.

Hanson-Vaux, G, A-S. Crisinel, C. Spence. 2013 Smelling shapes: crossmodal correspondences between odors and shapes. *Chemical Senses*. Feb;38(2):161-6. https://doi.org/10.1093/chemse/bjs087

Harvey, J. P. 2013. Sensory Perception: Lessons from Synesthesia: Using Synesthesia to Inform the Understanding of Sensory Perception. *The Yale Journal of Biology & Medicine* 86, no. 2: 203–16.

Haynie H, B. C., H. Lapalombara. 2014. Sound symbolism in the languages of Australia. *PLoS One*. Apr 21;9(4):e92852. doi: 10.1371/journal.pone.0092852.

He pin zheng, and Xuan qin. 2004. *Dong ba chang yong zi dian*. Kun ming: Yun nan mei zhu chu ban she. https://archive.org/details/isbn_9787806951682/mode/1up

Hinton L, J. Nichols, JJ. Ohala, editors. 2006. *Sound Symbolism*. Cambridge: Cambridge University Press.

Hockett. C. F. 1959. Animal languages and human language. *Human Biology*, 31(1): 32-39.

Hollmann, J. C. 2005. 'Swift-People': Therianthropes and Bird Symbolism in Hunter-Gatherer Rock-Paintings, Western and Eastern Cape Provinces, South Africa. *Goodwin Series* 9: 21–33.

Houston, S., D. Stuart, and K. Taube. 2006 *The Memory of Bones. Body, Being, and Experience among the Classic Maya*. University of Texas Press, Austin.

Hoyland, R. G. 2001. *Arabia and the Arabs. From the Bronze Age to the Coming of Islam.* London and New York: Routledge

Imai, M. & Kita, S. 2014. The sound symbolism bootstrapping hypothesis for language acquisition and language evolution. *Philosophical transactions of the Royal Society* of London. Series B, Biological sciences, 369(1651), 20130298.

https://doi.org/10.1098/rstb.2013.0298

Jiménez, R, T. and Patrick H. Smith. 2008. Mesoamerican Literacies: Indigenous Writing Systems and Contemporary Possibilities. *Reading Research Quarterly* 43 (1) (Jan): 28-46 https://doi.org/10.1598/RRQ.43.1.3.

Kandinsky, W. 1945. Schematic Plan of Studies and Work of the Institute of Art Culture. In *Wassily Kandisky Memorial.* New York, Solomom R. Guggenheim Foundation.

Lemaitre, G., O. Houix, F. Voisin, N. Misdariis, and P. Susini. 2016. Vocal Imitations of Non-Vocal Sounds. *PloS One* 11, no. 12 (2016): e0168167–e0168167. https://doi.org/10.1371/journal.pone.0168167.

Lewis-Williams, J.D. & Dowson, T.A. 1989. *Images of Power: Understanding Bushman Rock Art.* Johannesburg: Southern Book Publisher

Lewis-Williams, J. D. The Evolution of Theory, Method and Technique in Southern African Rock Art Research. *Journal of Archaeological Method and Theory* 13, no. 4 (2006): 343–77. http://www.jstor.org/stable/20177545.

Lockwood, G., and M. Dingemanse. 2015. Iconicity in the Lab: A Review of Behavioral, Developmental, and Neuroimaging Research into Sound-Symbolism. *Frontiers in Psychology*, vol. 6, 2015, pp. 1246–1246, https://doi.org/10.3389/fpsyg.2015.01246.

Ludwig, Vera U, and Julia Simner. "What Colour Does That Feel? Tactile–visual Mapping and the Development of Cross-Modality." Cortex 49, no. 4 (2013): 1089–99. https://doi.org/10.1016/j.cortex.2012.04.004.

Macdonald, M.C.A., 2004. Ancient North Arabian. In Woodard, Roger D., ed. *The Cambridge Encyclopedia of the World's Ancient Languages.* Cambridge; Cambridge University Press, pp. 488-533.

Maggs, T.M. O'C. & Sealy, J. 1983. Elephants in boxes. *South African Archaeological Society* Goodwin Series 4: 44–48.

Masson, J. Moussaieff (Jeffrey Moussaieff), and Susan McCarthy. 1996. *When Elephants Weep: The Emotional Lives of Animals.* New York: Dell Publishing.

Mattioli, F., A. Farina, E. Armelloni, P. Hameau, M. Díaz-Andreu, 2017. Echoing Landscapes: Echolocation and the Placement of Rock Art in the Central Mediterranean. *Journal of archaeological science* 83: 12–25. https://doi.org/10.1016/j.jas.2017.04.008.

Mehrabi, A., S. Dixon, and M. Sandler. 2019. Vocal Imitation of Percussion Sounds: On the Perceptual Similarity between Imitations and Imitated Sounds. *PLoS One* 14 (7) (07), pp. e0219955–e0219955, https://doi.org/10.1371/journal.pone.0219955.

Mompeán-Guillamón, Pilar and Paula Cifuentes-Férez. 2012. Vowel, Sounds, and Motion. *International Journal of Cognitive Linguistics* 3 (2): 169–.

Moore, L. 2009. Beware the Elephant in the Bush: Myths, Memory and Indigenous Traditional Knowledge in North-Eastern Namibia. *Cultural Geographies* 16 (3) (07): 329-349. doi: http://dx.doi.org/10.1177/1474474009105051.

Mueggler, E. 2011. *The paper road: archive and experience in the botanical exploration of West China and Tibet.* Berkeley, Calif: University of California Press.

Neckar, M., and P. Bob. 2014. Neuroscience of Synesthesia and Cross-Modal Associations. *Reviews in the Neurosciences* 25 (6): 833-840. doi: http://dx.doi.org/10.1515/revneuro-2014-0033.

Nuckolls, J. B. 1999. The Case for Sound Symbolism. *Annual Review of Anthropology* 28: 225-252.

Nuckolls, J. B. 2010. The Sound-Symbolic Expression of Animacy in Amazonian Ecuador. *Diversity* 2 (3): 353-369. doi: http://dx.doi.org/10.3390/d2030353.

Ohala. J.J. 1994. "Sound Symbolis." In L. Hinton, J. Nichols, and J. J. Ohala. *Sound Symbolism.* Cambridge: Cambridge University Press, pp.1-6

Parkington, J., A. Paterson. 2017. Somatogenesis: Vibrations, Undulations and the Possible Depiction of Sound in San Rock Paintings of Elephants in the Western Cape. *The South African Archaeological Bulletin* 72(206): 134-41.

Parise, C. 2016. Crossmodal Correspondences: Standing Issues and Experimental Guidelines. *Multisensory research* 29.1-3: 7–28.

Parkington, J. 2018. Observing and Painting Elephants: San Rock Art of the Cederberg Region South Africa. A Symbiotic, Symbolic and Spiritual Relationship.

https://www.academia.edu/28302518/

Paterson, Andrew., 2018. Elephanthropes of the Cederberg. When Elephants Were People. *The Digging Stick*, 35(3): 1-6.

Patterson, Andrew. 1992. *A Field Guide to Rock Art Symbols of the Greater Southwest.* Boulder: Johnson Books.

Peirce, C. S. 1902. Logic as Semiotic: The Theory of Signs. Reprinted in *Philosophical Writings,* ed. by J. Buchler (1955), 98-119. New York: Dover.

Perlman, M., H. Little, B. Thompson, and R. L. Thompson, 2018. Iconicity in Signed and Spoken Vocabulary: A Comparison Between American Sign Language, British Sign Language, English, and Spanish. *Frontiers in psychology,* 9, 1433.

https://doi.org/10.3389/fpsyg.2018.01433

Pesic, P. 2013. Thomas Young's Musical Optics: Translating Sound into Light. *Osiris* 28, no. 1: 15-39. Accessed June 28, 2020. doi:10.1086/671361.

Philo, *On the Migration of Abraham* LCL 261

https://www.loebclassics.com/view/LCL320/1937/volume.xml

Philo, *On the Decalogue* LCL 320: 22-23

https://www.loebclassics.com/view/LCL320/1937/volume.xml

Ramachandran, V. S., and E. M. Hubbard. 2001. Psychophysical Investigations into the Neural Basis of Synaesthesia. *Proceedings of the Royal Society B: Biological Sciences* 268, no. 1470 (n.d.): 979–983.

Reznikoff, I. 2012. La dimension sonore des grottes paléolithiques et rochers à peintures. In J. Clottes. (dir.), *L'art pléistocène dans le monde / Pleistocene art of the world / Arte pleistoceno en el mundo*, Actes du Congrès IFRAO, Tarascon-sur-Ariège

Hagh-Huglo, B. H. 2010. 'It looks Like Sound!': Drawing a history of 'Animated Music' In the Early Twentieth century. University of Maryland (College Park, Md.). http://hdl.handle.net/1903/10458.

Rock, J. F. The Muan Bpö Ceremony: or the Sacrifice to Heaven as Practiced by the Na-khi. *Monumenta Serica,* Vol. 13 (1948), pp. 1-160.

Salgado-montejo, A., F. Marmolejo-ramos, J. A. Alvarado, J. Arboleda, D. R. Suarez, and C. Spence. 2016. Drawing Sounds: Representing Tones and Chords Spatially. *Experimental Brain Research* 234 (12) (12): 3509-3522. doi: http://dx.doi.org/10.1007/s00221-016-4747-9.

Sapir, E. A Study in Phonetic Symbolism. *Journal of experimental psychology* 12.3 (1929): 225–239.

Seler, E.. 1901-1902. *Codex Fejérváry-Mayer: An Old Mexican Picture Manuscript in the Liverpool Free Public Museums (12014.* Berlin and London. https://archive.org/details/codexfejeyrvayr00sele

Shoshani, J. 1997. It's a Nose! it's a Hand! it's an Elephant's Trunk! *Natural History,* 11, 36-45.

Sidhu, D. M. and M. M. Pexman. 2018. Five Mechanisms of Sound Symbolic Association. *Psychonomic Bulletin & Review* 25 (5) (10): 1619-1643. doi: http://dx.doi.org/10.3758/s13423-017-1361-1.

Smithsonian Institution, 1846. *Smithsonian Institution. Archives, Discoveries in science,* Volume 1895. Washington: Smithsonian Institution Collection. https://library.si.edu/digital-library/book/annualreportofbo1895smit *[Tanakh] : JPS Hebrew-English Tanakh.* Deluxe edition. Philadelphia: Jewish Publication Society, https://www.jewishvirtuallibrary.org/the-tanakh-full-text

Soltis J., L. E. King, I. Douglas-Hamilton, F. Vollrath, A. Savage 2014. African Elephant Alarm Calls Distinguish between Threats from Humans and Bees. *PLoS ONE* 9(2): e89403. https://doi.org/10.1371/journal.pone.0089403

Stoeger-Horwath, A. S., S. Stoeger, H. M. Schwammer, and H. Kratochvil 2007. Call repertoire of infant African elephants: first insights into the early vocal ontogeny. *The Journal of the Acoustical Society of America* vol. 121,6: 3922-31. doi:10.1121/1.2722216

Taitz, A., M. F. Assaneo, N. Elisei, M. Trípodi, L. Cohen, J. D. Sitt, M. A. Trevisan. 2018. The Audiovisual Structure of Onomatopoeias: An Intrusion of Real-World Physics in Lexical Creation. *PLoS One* 13 (3) (03). doi: http://dx.doi.org/10.1371/journal.pone.0193466.

Taub, S. F. 2001. *Language from the Body: Iconicity and Metaphor in American Sign Language,* Cambridge, UK: Cambridge University Press.

Taube, K. A. 2018. *Studies in Ancient Mesoamerican Art and Architecture: Selected Works by Karl Andreas Taube,* Volume1; Precolumbia Mesoweb Press, San Francisco.

Thompson, A. L., and Y. DO. 2019. Defining Iconicity: An Articulation-Based Methodology for Explaining the Phonological Structure of Ideophones. *Glossa* 4(1): 1-40. doi: http://dx.doi.org/10.5334/gjgl.872.

Trevor-Roper, P. 1970. *The world though blunted sight.* Indianapolis and New York: The Bobbs-Merill Company.

Waller, S. J. 2012. Thunderous reverberation and rock art thunderstorm imagery. In J. Clottes. (dir.), *L'art pléistocène dans le monde / Pleistocene art of the world / Arte pleistoceno en el mundo,* Actes du Congrès IFRAO, Tarascon-sur-Ariège, septembre 2010, Symposium « Signes, symboles, mythes et idéologie...

». N° spécial de *Préhistoire, Art et Sociétés, Bulletin de la Société Préhistorique Ariège-Pyrénées*, LXV-LXVI, 2010-2011, CD: p. 1725-1740.

WAUGH, L. R. 1992. Presidential Address: Let's Take The Con Out of Iconicity: Constraints on Iconicity in The Lexicon. *The American Journal of Semiotics*; 9(1): 7-47.

WEISS, R. 2013. Seeing the Sounds: Exceeding the Frame through the Acoustical Sublime in the Revelation at Sinai. *InVisible Culture* (18) (Spring).

WILLIAMS, G. E. 2012. Rock Art and Pre-historic Ritual Behaviour: A Landscape and Acoustic Approach. *Rock Art Research* 29 (1) (05): 35-46.

WINNETT, F. V. AND G. L. HARDING. 1978. *Inscriptions from Fifty Safaitic Cairns.* Toronto; Buffalo; London: Toronto University Press.

ZHOU Z. 2013. Analysis of Dongba Pictographs and Its Application to Pictogram Design. *Higher Education of Social Science,* Vol. 5, No. 2, 2013, pp. 85-88. DOI: 10.3968/j.hess.1927024020130502.2745.

24

KEYWORDS: Tibet – Travertine – Hands and footprints – Uranium-series dating

HAND AND FOOT PRINTS AT QIUSANG IN TIBET: A REVIEW

TANG HUISHENG AND SHARGAN WANGDUE

Abstract: Many imprints of human hands and feet were found on the travertine surface of the gravels at Qiusang Village, Duilongdeqing District, Lhasa City, Tibet. Scholars have obtained several sets of age data ranging from 7,000 years ago to 220,000 years ago after dating based on uranium series, optical luminescence, and ^{14}C dating methods. In particular, the uranium-series dating article published in the journal of *Science* in 2021 is titled "earliest parietal art" in the world. The article caused a sensation around the world. Then arose the questions whether Qiusang's dating of human hand and footprints is credible, and whether it can be regarded as "parietal art" i.e., rock art, which involves the reliability of uranium-series dating, the origin of rock art, as well as the origin of human symbolic thinking, etc.

Introduction

In September 2021, Professor Zhang Dian from the School of Geographical Sciences of Guangzhou University and other related scholars published an article titled "Earliest parietal art: hominin hand and foot traces from the middle Pleistocene ofTibet" in *Science Bulletin*, reporting on the Uranium-series dating of handprints and footprints found in Qiusang Village, Duilongdeqing District, Lhasa City, Tibet. Dating shows that the ancient human hand and footprints are between 169,000 and 226,000 years old, which is considered to be the world's earliest parietal art (Zhang et al. 2021). The discovery was also selected by *Archaeology* as the second place in the "Top Ten World Archaeological Discoveries" in 2021, which caused a great social sensation and public opinion.The article caused a sensation around the world. Then arose the questions whether Qiusang's dating of human hand and footprints is credible, and whether it can be regarded as "parietal art" i.e., rock

Article received: 15 December 2022
Revised I: 6 June 2023
Revised II: 13 June 2023
Revised III: 15 June 2023
Accepted: 16 June 2023

art, which involves the reliability of uranium-series dating, the origin of rock art, as well as the origin of human symbolic thinking, etc.

Foot and Handprints in the Travertine of Qiusang and Their Legends

The remains of ancient human hand and footprints discovered by Professor Zhang Dian are mainly distributed on the travertine at the southwest slope and west foot of Qiusang Hot Spring (Figure 1). The first location is located on the southwest slope of Qiusang Hot Spring, where the hand and footprints of ancient human are believed by local people to be those of Master Tsongkhapa, the founder of the Gelug Sect of Tibetan Buddhism, and they pay homage to him. The remains of ancient human hands and footprints in this area were originally discovered by Professor Zhang Dian in 2002. The second location, at Zadogang at the west foot of Qiusang Hot Spring, is the place for the hand and footprints of ancient humans which was described and studied by Professor Zhang Dian in 2021.

Figure 1: The Qiusang's slope where the "ancient human hand and footprint" remains are located.

The coordinates of the "ancient human hand and footprints" on the southwest hillside of Qiusang Hot Spring are 90°45'40.02" east longitude, 30°0'3.00" north latitude, and 4263 meters above sea level. The site is located about 45 meters southwest of the Qiusang Hot Spring Building complex. The rock with the prints is about 3 meters long and 2 meters wide. There is a small stone platform built later on the upper side of the rock (Figure 2). The remains of "ancient human hand and footprints" are scattered on the rock surface below it, the naked eye observation is very vague, and there seem to be 2-5 traces (Figure 3). The coordinates of the "hand and footprints of ancient human beings" at the foot of the mountain "Zanduogang" are 90°45'3.99" east longitude, 30°0'19.45" north latitude, and 4057 meters above sea level. There are several "hand and footprints of ancient human" distributed on a rock surface about 1 meter square (Figure 4). The surrounding rock faces are also scattered, with a total of about 10, but they are all vague.

Qiusang Hot Spring is recorded in historical resources, which can be traced back to the legends related to Uto Nyingma Yundan Kampot, the ancestor of Tibetan medicine in the 8th century. It is said that Master Yuto Nyingma Yundan Kampot was born in the village of Yutogang at the foot of the mountain west of Qiusang Hot Spring. As a master of Tibetan medicine, Master Uto Nyingma Yundan Kampo not only spent his childhood in the Hot Spring, but also used the Hot Spring to heal the common people when he grew up to be a master of Tibetan medicine. Local people believe that the "ancient human hand and foot prints" at the foot of the mountain "Chaduogang" are the traces left on the rock surface when Master Uto Nyingma Yundan Kampot was playing here as a 6 years old child. In the early 15th century, Master Tsongkhapa, the founder of Gelugpa, came to Qiusang Hot Spring to treat diseases. The locals believe that the footprints on the hillside on the southwest side of Qiusang Hot Spring were left by Master Tsongkhapa.

Figure 2: "Ancient human hand and footprints" at the west foot of Qiusang Hot Spring "Zaduogang"

The Age of Qiusang's Footprints and Handprints

According to Prof. Zhang Dian's analysis, Qiu Sang's ancient hand and foot impressions are patterns on travertine with a thickness of 200-2000 mm, which were just generated by human's feet and hands on the surface of river gravels, which were still soft (pre-lithification). The diagenetic process of travertine from soft to hard generally takes about two years. It can be inferred that the age of travertine hardening is the age of the fingerprints and footprints. Zhang Dian et al. performed uranium-series dating after sampling the cheese-like travertine on the surface of the river gravel with a hand drill. The results show that the ages of the travertine are between 169,000 and 226,000 years ago.

Zhang Dian did research on the remains of the handprints and footprints at the site as early as 2002, and found calcified handprints and footprints belonging to 19 people, including a fire pit. Through photoluminescence dating of quartz crystals deposited in fire pits and hand and foot impressions on the travertine, the age was determined to be between c. 21.7 cal. ka and c. 20.6 cal. Ka (Zhang et al. 2002). For this dating, some scholars at the time believed that the non-weathered quartz debris might be older than the actual age if optical luminescence dating method applied to (David et al. 2006).

In fact, in addition to Zhang Dian, many other scholars have also done dating of the site. For example, Austrian chronologist Meyer and archaeologist Mark and others collected 11 samples from the Qiusang site, using uranium-based dating methods, optical luminescence and carbon 14 dating methods. Several sets of data were obtained from 7.4 to 13,000 years ago (Meye et al. 2017). Judging from the current sets of chronological research data, the ages of the handprints and footprints range from 7,000 years ago to 220,000 years ago. With such a huge age difference, which are more credible?

Due to the antiquity of Zhang Dian's second dating of the Qiusang hand and foot impressions, it involves questions of the origin of rock art, of human art, as well as human symbolic thinking. As soon as the dating was published, it aroused the strong attention of archaeologists, especially rock art researchers. They are strongly concerned, for example, Australian prehistorian Bednarik and others have written articles to discuss the age estimates. Bednarik accepts most of the claims of Zhang Dian et al.., for example, he agrees that the marks on Qiusang travertine are formed by pressing hands and feet into a soft medium, but not by tools; he agrees that these footprints and handprints are deliberate, so they are a form of ancient art; in addition, it is accepted that juveniles made them. Children have been responsible for much rock art production, and specifically for most body part impressions found on soft or formerly soft cave deposits in Europe and Australia. Finally, he agrees with that the markings were made when the travertine was soft and still being precipitated, so they should be of an age matching that of the medium (Bednarik 2008).

But Bednarik disagreed with these authors in just one detail: he questions the basis of their claim that the rock bearing the ichnological traces is of the Middle Pleistocene and in the order of 169 to 226 ka old. The uranium-thorium method they used to arrive at this result has been shown numerous times to provide unreliable Pleistocene age estimates of reprecipitated carbonate deposits. Carbonate speleothems, formed by a similar process, have in all cases yielded significantly more recent radiocarbon ages than the U–Th dates when these were checked (Bednarik 1997(b)). While the ages obtained by the two methods have usually matched reasonably well if they were of the Holocene, the U–Th ages of Late Pleistocene samples increase exponentially with age until they can be many times their actual ages (Bednarik 2022). In the worst of the many cases reported before the Qiusang example, a reprecipitated carbonate film that can only be a few centuries old at most provided a U–Th raw age of 134.6 ka, i.e., hundreds of times its realistic antiquity (Tang et al. 2020). The stochastic distribution of the dates suggests that the distortion is not systematic but seems to be a random function of taphonomic processes distorting the U–Th ratios. Most notably, U is soluble in water and can be readily removed when the deposit is subjected to moisture. This occurs with speleothems frequently and even more so with travertine fully exposed to precipitation. Travertines are not dense crystalline formations like stalagmites; they have varying degrees of porosity which assists the reaction with carbonic acid, reverting to their soluble (bicarbonate) state. In addition to effecting U depletion, moisture may also remove or add detrital Th; there may be a transformation of aragonite to calcite, or components of the support rock may contaminate samples (Bednarik et al. 2022). To reduce the data bias caused by contamination from detrital thorium, Bednarik recommends the use of isochron methods, or core sampling of Qiusang travertine, to compare the apparent ages of different weathering zones. Only then can the extent of the uranium loss be determined.

However, for Qiusang's handprints and footprints, the biggest problem in chronology is not from the inconsistency of various scientific dating, but from the travertine marks themselves. In addition to handprints and footprints, Tibetan letters were also found on the travertine of Qiusang Hot Spring. Although the Tibetan letters are blurred, they are Tibetan letters (Figure 5), especially the Tibetan letters shown in Figure 6. The letter "A" (pronounced "A") is unmistakable (Figure 6). And according to on-site observations, like the footprints and handprints, they were made on soft mud before the travertine diagenetic rock hardened. Judging from the history of the

Figure 3: Tibetan letters on travertine at Qiusang Hot Spring Figure 4 Tibetan letter "A"

earliest Tibetan writings appearing only after the seventh century AD, the Tibetan writings on these travertines are at best more than a thousand years old. If according to Zhangdian's U–Th dating, the petrification age of travertine was the Middle Pleistocene 160,000-200,000 years ago, then these Tibetan characters were also from that time; on the contrary, if the appearance time of Tibetan characters is considered, petrification age of the travertine would be after the 7th century AD, so these human footprints and handprints should also be after the 7th century AD.

From this point of view, the age problem of Qiusang's handprints and footprints need to be confirmed by a more complete dating scheme and more abundant archaeological materials, and the single uranium-thorium method may not be enough to solve the age problem with its conflicts and inconsistency. In addition, other places on the Qinghai-Tibet Plateau, such as Yushu, Jilong, have recently emerged a number of "hand and foot impressions", and the archaeologists should also conduct an investigation and scientific dating of such remains to establish a comparison with the Qiusang site.

Is It "the Earliest Parietal Art"?

The understanding of art can be roughly classified into two types, one of which is Plato's point of view. Plato considered art as a basic need for an individual to imitate what he or she sees. Primitive reality, he argues, is conceptuality, that is, the concept of something that includes the various forms and possible situations of that thing (Plato 1998).

The second perspective derives from the theories of literature and art in the 19th century. These theories hold that art is the artist's expression of his own emotions. This view has given rise to various definitions of art. While these definitions are fanciful, they do nothing to understand prehistoric art. For example, the Norwegian composer Grieg believed that art was actually an excess of desire, which couldn't be expressed in life or through other means, so it was through art. For another example, the Russian novelist Leo Tolstoy believed that art was a human activity, that is, a person consciously transmits his emotional experience to other people through some form of external markers, and other people were affected by these emotional influences and experienced them. French sculptor Auguste Rodin said that his artistic creation was merely "an expression of his dreams" and so on. The so-called "art for art's sake" aesthetic view is based on this recognition that art is regarded as an achievement of human skill whose purpose is to bring aesthetic pleasure rather than utility, and this view is almost useless for our understanding of prehistory, because we know almost nothing about the people who created prehistoric art and their culture (Barn 2004).

However, scholars engaged in prehistoric art research in recent years are more inclined to define prehistoric art as a purely spiritual product or non-utilitarian of human beings, that is, a spatial form that expresses human symbolic thinking. In other words, only non-practical artifacts representing a symbolic system can be defined as works of art (Bednarik 1997). On the issue of the origin of art and religion, the two are often intertwined, thus non-practical forming a confrontation with practical utensils. Anything without a practical function should be a symbolic artwork or religious utensil (Clottes 2007).

Such a definition clarifies the distinction between prehistoric artworks and stone tools, weapons, etc., while avoiding the inconsistencies and ambiguities about definition of art in the 19th century (Bednarik 1997(a); Clottes et al. 2007). Although scholars still refer to them as "arts", in fact more and more scholars stop treating Paleolithic rock art and portable artworks as any art-related objects and are exploring more the cultural connotation it symbolizes and its role in the entire social system (Strathern et al. 1998).

According to this definition, can the human handprints and footprints at the Qiusang site in Tibet be regarded as rock (or parietal) art? Bednarik pointed out that there may be a problem with the Zhangdian report referring to the handprints and footprints at the Qiusang site as "parietal art". "parietal" in anatomy refers to the cavity wall of the bone, borrowed from petroglyph studies to refer to the "cave wall". But the Qiusang site is an open-air place, so it cannot be called "parietal art"(Bednarik et al. 2022). If the two children pressed handprints and footprints purely out of curiosity, this behavior obviously does not have symbolic meaning, so it cannot be recognized as a rock art relic. Anati expressed his agreement with Zhang Dian's dating and the identification of human children's footprints, but doubted his identification as the world's earliest parietal art. Anati thought that the sizes of both hand and footprints are smaller than those of an adult Tibetan of today. The maker may either be an adolescent or a pygmy, an individual having small limbs. According to the article mentioned, the imprints belong to two people. The photo displays the prints of five feet and four hands. All of the footprints seem to relate to a right leg, while three of the handprints belong to the right hand and one to the left hand. The three right hands show the same peculiar position of the thumb. Also, the footprints are likely all to belong to the same individual. The question is, do they indeed belong to two different people, or just to one and the same person? Whatever the case, they do not represent a recurring cultural pattern. Deliberately made Paleolithic handprints are retained to be signatures or acts of presence, related to initiation rites or intertribal agreements. Their presence is documented in the last 70,000 years, at least 100,000 years later than this case. The presence of both hands and feet assembled together in deliberate visual compositions is unusual in Paleolithic graphic representations.

Further, Anati said, according to the photo, both handprints and footprints reveal the deep imprint indicating an effort. At least two of the four handprints show the position of pushing. The evident signs of pressure of the footprints seem to testify the action of pushing aside the block. The superposition of feet and hands indicates successive actions at pushing the block. They appear to be the result of a physical action to move the mud block. The presumed intent of producing a piece of visual art does not seem likely. The term rock art seems to be out of place. To our minds, it may just be the result of the effort of a single individual to move a block of mud. The finding is relevant as a testimony of homo's presence in that area, at that time, but does not seem to illustrate the existence of art in Tibet over 100,000 years before any other place in the world (Anati 2021).

The emergence of art (including religion) is a general phenomenon of human thought and understanding, and a kind of cultural evolution, rather than the sudden emergence of a miracle like a miracle. Qiusang's handprint and footprint era is more than 100,000 years ahead of the era when hand and footprint rock art generally appeared in the world. Its nature as rock art (or cave art) requires careful consideration: why did it appear so early? Why did it become an absolute sound in the time range of hundreds of thousands of years after it appeared? What does it mean to appear alone on the Qinghai-Tibet Plateau above 4,000 meters? and many more.

Pleistocene human footprints discovered around the World

At the beginning of the last century, giant footprints were discovered in Paluxy Riverbed (Glen Rose) near Rose Valley, Texas, USA, along with dinosaur footprints 100 million years ago, which caused a worldwide sensation. Later, after scientific investigation and research, scientists found that the so-called giant footprints actually included three kinds of marks: first, the footprints of metatarsal dinosaurs; secondly, the traces of stones eroded by water flow; The third is the artificially made footprint petroglyphs (Morris et al. 1961; Kuban 1986:57-72; Patton 1990).

However, many fossils of human footprints have indeed been found in geology. The earliest discovered age is the human footprint 3.66 million years ago unearthed near the Olduvai Gorge in Laetoli, northern Tanzania, Africa. First discovered in 1978 by paleontologist Mary Leakey and her team in Laetoli, another set of mysterious footprints was partially unearthed at the nearby site A, but thought to be possibly left by a bear. According to a new study in the journal *Nature*, re-excavation and detailed comparative analysis of the Laetoli site reveal that the footprints were created by early humans, bipedal humans (Leakey 1978).

The oldest footprints in Europe were found in Happisburgh, England, dating back to the early Pleistocene between 1 million and 780,000 years ago Ashton et al. 2014. Near the Roccamonfina volcano in the northern part of Campania, Italy, there is a row of fossil footprints called "Ciampate del Diavolo". One of the best-preserved human footprints ever found in Pleistocene volcanic ash (Avanzini et al. 2004). Although the hydrothermal variability and variable contamination of extensive thermoclastic deposits are already severe, $^{40}Ar/^{39}Ar$ laser probe dating of pure volcanic ash deposits shows that the thermoclastic layers and footprints are dated as about 350,000 years ago (Scaillet et al. 2008).

Ancient human footprints dating back 300,000 to 400,000 years were discovered in the open-air site of Terra Amata in France; 130,000-year-old human footprints were found in Theopetra Cave in Greece. Ancient human footprints (De Lumley et al. 1966). The two footprints found at the site are very complete and appear to be both left feet, with lengths of 150.4 mm and 138.96 mm, respectively. According to modern European standards, these lengths will be consistent with children 2 to 4 years old who are 90 to 100 cm tall (Manolis et al. 2000).

Sites where human footprints have been found in the Late Pleistocene include the Vârtop Cave in Romania, dating from 62,000 years ago; the Grotta del Cavallo in Italy, dating from

44,000 years ago. The first known anatomically modern humans in Europe; a series of cave sites in France such as Lascaux, Niaux, Aldene, Peche Merle, Fontanet, Ariège and Chauvet, Bàsura in Italy and Ojo Guareña (Onac et al. 2005) in Spain (Benazzi et al. 2011; Lockley et al. 2008). There are also human footprints unearthed at the Ságvárian archaeological culture site at Corvintér in Budapest, Eastern Europe, dating from the Last Glacial Maximum between 18,000 and 20,000 years ago (Ringer et al. 2008-2009).

With the exception of Vârtop Cave and Cavallo Cave, all of these sites are less than 30,000 years old and therefore undoubtedly anatomically modern human footprints. Children's footprints appear to be an important part of the Paleolithic cave record. For example, the footprints of a young boy (8 years old, 1.5 m high) were found in Chauvet Cave in southern France, and footprints that may represent children were also found in Neo Cave (Harrington 1999; Pales 1976).

Conclusion

Footprints (including handprints) are commonly recorded objects in ancient documents around the world. *The Biography of Emperor Mu (Mu Tian Zi Zhuan)*, it said that when King Mu of the Zhou dynasty visited the Queen Mother of the West (*Xi Wang Mu*), "The Son of Heaven then tended to ascend to Mount Yan, and he carved his tracks on the stone of Mount Yan ". The book of *The Biography of Mu Tianzi* was unearthed in the tomb of King Wei Xiang during the Western Jin Dynasty (265-317AD), but the book was written and circulated before the Warring States Period. "Tracks" are footprints, and this is a petroglyph theme that was liked to be described in early documents. Another example is *Han Feizi* and other books, which also mentioned the same petroglyph theme: "Zhao Zhu Fu ordered the workers to mount hooks and a ladder to climb Mount Panwu, and carved the giant footprints on it, three feet wide and five feet long, and also carved characters: "Zhu Fu has been here". The same is true abroad: carving footprints on stone is a cultural phenomenon worldwide. According to the Irish legend *The book of Leinster* in the 9th century BC, a pair of footprints of superman in the mythical hero Cu Chulain's epic was carved in a rock, which is probably the earliest written European reference to rock art (Bertuzzo et al. 1998). Outside Europe, throughout the 16th and 17th centuries, several sites of South American petroglyphs are mentioned in the texts of Portuguese and Spanish Jesuit missionaries. In 1549, the Portuguese priest Manuel da Nogrega mentioned the existence of petroglyphs in some of his letters about the Brazilian Indians: "They say that Saint Tome, they call him Zome, pass by here, that's what their ancestors told them. His footprints were printed near a river, I went to see it because I was convinced of the truth, I saw with my own eyes four human footprints with toe marks. "(Nobrega 2004: 47)

Of course, whether this kind of writing can be regarded as the earliest description of rock art is another matter, but we can see that footprints and handprints have not only appeared in rocks since ancient times, but also in written records. Which footprints reflect the natural attributes of human beings, and which ones reflect the symbolic thinking of human beings, we still need to carefully screen and analyze them one by one. The human footprints and handprints in Qiusang are of great significance whether they belong to the archaeological remains that reflect the natural attributes of human beings or the remains of rock art that reflect the symbolic thinking of human beings. As Bednarik pointed out, a proposition of Middle Pleistocene rock art in Tibet is extraordinary, and it requires correspondingly extraordinary evidence and vice versa.

Prof. Tang Huisheng
Archaeological Dept, School of History and Culture
Hebei Normal University, 20 Naerhuandonglu, Shijiazhuang
China
Email:tanghuisheng@163.com,

and

Dr Shargan Wangdue
(Tibet Autonomous Region Cultural Relics Protection Institute)
Lv Hongliang (Sichuan University)

References

Anati, E. 2021. Discussion Forum, *Expression* 37, pp.4–5.

Ashton, N., Lewis, S. G., De Grooter, I., Duffy, S. M., Bates. 2014. Hominin footprints from early pleistocene deposits at Happisburgh, UK. PLoS ONE, 9(2), e88329–1–13.

Avanzini, M., De Anglis, M., Mietto, P., Panarello, A., & Rolandi, G. 2004. Pleistocene human footprints preserved on a zeolite-rich pyroclastic flow (Roccamonfina, Italy). In *International Union of Geological Sciences* (Ed.), 32nd international geological congress (p. 598). Florence: Università di Firenze; Avanzini, M., Mietto, P., Panarello, A., De Angelis, M., & Rolandi, G. 2008. *The devil's trails: Middle Pleistocene human footprints preserved in a volcanoclastic deposit of Southern Italy. Ichnos, 15, 179–189.*

Barn, Paul G. 2004. *Cambridge Illustrated Prehistoric Art History* (Chinese edition), pp.2–3. Shandong Pictorial Publishing House.

Bednarik, R. G. 1997(a). The role of Pleistocene beads in documenting hominid cognition. *Rock Art Research*14(1):27–43.

Bednarik, R. G. 1997(b). Direct dating results from rock art: a global review. *AURA Newsletter* 14(2): 9–12; Bard, E., B. Hamelin, R. G. Fairbanks and A. Zindler 1990. Calibration of the 14C timescale over the past 30,000 years using mass spectrometric U–Th ages from Barbados corals. *Nature* 345: 405–410; Holmgren, K., S. E. Lauritzen and G. Possnert 1994. 230Th/234U and 14C dating of a late Pleistocene stalagmite in Lobatse II cave, Botswana. *Quaternary Science Reviews* 13: 111–119.

Bednarik, R. G. 2008. Children as Pleistocene artists. *Rock Art Research* 25(2): 173–182.

Bednarik, R. G. 2022. The dating of rock art and bone by the uranium–thorium method. *Rock Art Research* 39(2).

Bednarik, R.G., Jin Anni and Chao Ge 2022 The travertine hand and footprints at Quesang, Tibet. *Rock Art Research,* Volume 39(2):215–217.

Benazzi, S., Douka, K., Fornai, C., Bauer, C. C., Kullmer, O., Svoboda, J., Pap, I., Mallegni, F., Bayle, P., Coquerelleo, M., Condemi , S., Ronchitelli, A., Harvati, K., and Weber, G. W. 2011. Early dispersal of modern humans in Europe and implications for Neanderthal behaviour. *Nature*, 479, 525–529.

Bertuzzo, F., C. Prestipino, M.R. Simonassi 1998. *Oltre il segno. Proposta di metodologia e schedatura per le incisioni*. Regione Liguia/Comunita Montana Alta Val Bormida, Millesimo, pp.25–23.

Clottes, J. and David, Lewis-W. 2007. Palaeolithic art and religion. In John R. Hinnells(ed) 2007. *A Handbook of Ancient Religions*.PP. 7-45. Cambridge University Press, New York.

David, D. Z., Matthew, R. Bennett, Hai Cheng, Leibin, W., Haiwei, Z., Sally, C., Reynolds, Shengda Z., Xiaoqing, W., Teng, Li, Tommy, U., Qing, P., Zhifeng, W., Pu Z., Chunru, L., Yafeng, W. , Cong, W., Dongju, Z., R. Lawrence E. 2021 Earliest parietal art: Hominin hand and foot traces from the middle Pleistocene of Tibet. *Science Bulletin* 66 (24): 2506-2515.

David, B. M. Ma Haizhou, P. Jeffery Brantingham, Gao X., David R., Zhang H., John, W. O. 2006. The Late Upper Paleolithic occupation of the northern Tibetan Plateau margin. *Journal of Archaeological Science* 33:1433–1444.

De Lumely, H. 1966. Les fouilles de Terra Amata a Nice. Premiers rèsultats. *Bulletin of the Museum of Anthropology and Prehistory of Monaco*, 13, 29–51.

Harrington, S. P. M. 1999. Human footprints at Chauvet Cave. *Archaeology*, 52(5), www.archaeology.org/9909/newsbriefs/chauvet.html.

Kuban, G. 1986. Elongate Dinosaur Tracks' in: Gillette, David D. and Martin G. Lockley, eds., *Dinosaur Tracks and Traces*, 1989. Cambridge University Press, Cambridge, pp. 57–72.

Leakey, M., 1978. Pliocene footprints at Laetolil, Northern Tanzania. *Antiquity* 52 (205): 133–142.

Lockley, M., Roberts, G., and Kim, J. Y. 2008. In the footprints of our ancestors: An overview of the hominid track record. *Ichnos* 15:106–125.

Manolis, S. K., Aiello, L. C., Henessy, R., and Kyparissi-Apostolika, N. 2000. The middle Paleolithic footprints of Theopetra cave (Thessaly, Greece). In N. Kyparissi-Apostolika (Ed.), Proceedings of the international conference, Theopetra Cave: *12 years of excavation and research, Trikala, 6–7 November 1998, pp. 87–93. Athens:* Greek Ministry of Culture and Institute for Aegean Prehistory.

Meye, M.C., M.S. Aldenderfer, Z. Wang. 2017. Permanent human occupation of the central Tibetan Plateau in the early Holocene, *Science* 355: 64-67.

Morris, H. M. and Johm, C. W. 1961. *The Genesis Flood*, Michigan: Baker Book House, Grand Rapids, pp. 173–175.

Nobrega, M. da, 2004. *Cartas do Brasil e mais escritos. Seleccao de joao Alves das Neves*. Lisbon: Universitaria Editora, p. 47, 60.

Onac, B. P., Viehmann, I., Lundberg, J., Lauritzen, S. E., Stringer, C., and Popita, V. 2005. U–Th ages constraining the Neanderthal footprint at Vârtop Cave, Romania. *Quaternary Science Reviews*, 24, 1151–1157.

Pales, L., 1976. *Les Empreintes de Pieds humaines dans les Cavernes* (Memoir 36, Archives de l'Institut de Paleontologie Humaine (Fondation Albert 1er, Prince de Monaco). Paris: Masson.

Ringer,Á., G. Lengyel 2008–2009. The Upper Palaeolithic site at Budapest Corvinter. *Praehistoria* 9–10: 205–211.

Scaillet, S., G. and Vita-Scaillet, H. 2008. Guillou Oldest human footprints dated by Ar/Ar. *Earth and Planetary Science Letters* 275 (3-4), 15 November: 320–325.

Strathern, A. and M. Strathern 1998. Introduction to *Body decoration in Mount Hagen.* Toronto, University of Toronto Press.

Tang, H., G. Kumar, J. Anni. and R. G. Bednarik 2020. Rock art of Heilongjiang Province, China. *Journal of Archaeological Science* 31:1–8.

Zhang, D., and Li, S. 2002. Optical dating of Tibetan human hand and footprints: An implication for the palaeoenvironment of the last glaciation of the Tibetan Plateau. *Geophysical Research Letters* 29: 1069.

25

KEYWORDS: Squatting Figure rock art – Guangxi – Yunnan – China – Cultural connection

ON THE RELATIONSHIP OF THE SQUATTING-FIGURE-ROCK ART IN GUANGXI AND YUNNAN, CHINA

XIAO BO, CHE JING AND CAO YUJIE

Abstract: The squatting-figure-rock art have been found in both Guangxi and Yunnan provinces, China, and both of which are painted with red pigments. By applying synthetically, the cross–dating and direct dating methods, it was found that the age of the Cangyuan rock art in Yunnan is between 3500 and 2500 years ago, while the age of the Zuojiang Huashan rock art in Guangxi is between 2500 and 1800 years ago. In addition, there are also some similar rock art between the two sites. Through a comparative study of the Squatting-figure-rock art in Guangxi and Yunnan, it was found that there may be a cultural connection between the ethnic groups who painted them.

1. Introduction

'Squatting figure' is an art form that exists widely around the world. The major characteristic of the figure is that both legs are flat and the knees are bent down. Early rock art, pottery, bronzes, and modern art forms including textiles, bark paintings, and paper–cuts all contain a lot of these images. Among them, the squatting figures in the rock art are the most numerous.

Chinese researchers studied squatting figure rock art early and discovered a strong association between these motifs and frogs. Such motifs were formerly known as 'frog figures' in Chinese archaeology. Although some researchers recognized that these images represented human rather than 'frog', they also noticed the relationship between them and frogs. In the article *Research on 'Squatting Figures' in Primitive Art*, Tang Huisheng conducted a comprehensive investigation of squatting figures worldwide, discussing their concept, distribution, connotation, age, and showed a new interpretation of squatting figure rock art in China, with these images comprehensively sorted out (Tang 1996). Subsequently, 'squatting figure' as a professional term was generally accepted by

Article received: 11 October 2022
Revised I: 21 June 2023
Revised II: 25 June 2023
Accepted: 28 June 2023

Chinese academia. However, it should be noted that the authors' standard for the classification of squatting figures was not consistent, and a part of rock art does not have the traits of squatting. In addition, Huang Yaqi also conducted systematic research on squatting figures. She comprehensively sorted out the squatting figures all over the world using study methods from petroglyphs, art, folklore, anthropology, and semiotics. She compared the Zuojiang Huashan rock art extensively with squatting figures, which fully illuminated the cultural significance of this image and elevated the study of Zuojiang Huashan rock art to a new level (Huang 2012). In another article, Huang used the analogy of ethnographic materials to explore the connection between squatting figures and Austronesian (Huang 2014). Recently, some scholars also studied the squatting figure rock art from the viewpoints of semiotics, aesthetics, and scholars also studied the squatting figure rock art

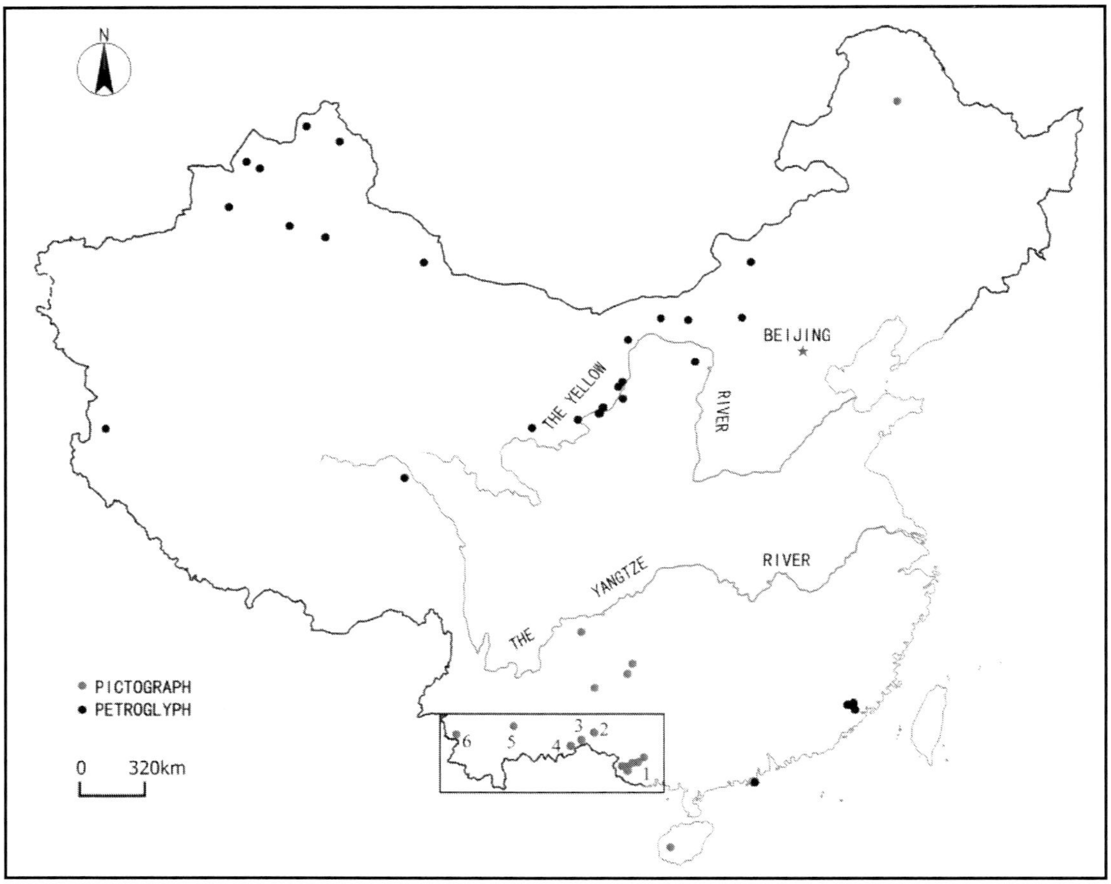

Figure 1: Distribution map of Chinese squatting figure rock art: (1) the Zuojiang Huashan rock art, (2) the Pingshan Rock art in Guangnan, (3) the Yanlashan rock art in Malipo, (4) the Dawangyan rock art in Malipo, (5) the Ta Ke rock art in Yuanjiang, (6) the Cangyuan Rock art. The box represents the research area of this article, by Che Jing

from the viewpoints of semiotics, aesthetics, and sociology. However, a thorough knowledge of their origin and particular evolution is still lacking.

The distribution of the Chinese squatting figure rock art can be divided into three large areas, namely, the southwest area, southeast coastal area, and the northern grassland area, including two kind of producing methods: painting and peaking (Fig. 1). Among them, Guangxi and Yunnan are two areas with more densely distributed squatting figure rock art, and the painting methods are consistent, both of them are having red pigments. In addition, the dating of the Zuojiang Huashan rock art in Guangxi and the Cangyuan rock art in Yunnan are the two most thoroughly studied sites in China. The direct dating methods have been applied to both the sites, and the obtained dates are also relatively reliable. There had been frequent interaction among the populations between the two areas since ancient times, and a large amount of archaeological evidence can be used to confirm this. Therefore, there is a solid foundation to compare the Squatting-figure-rock art in the two places, and a deeper understanding of the cultural exchange between them.

2. The Squatting-figure-rock art in Guangxi

The Squatting-figure-rock art in Guangxi are mainly found in the Zuojiang Huashan rock art. Now let's give a short introduction to it.

2.1. The basic situation of the Zuojiang Huashan rock art

The Zuojiang Huashan rock art is distributed in the riverside areas of Ningming, Longzhou, Jiangzhou, Fusui, Daxin of Chongzuo City, most scholars believe that they are the works of the ancestors of Zhuang People from Warring States to the Eastern Han Dynasty. "Huashan", which is also called "Ba Lai" in the language of the Zhuang ethnic group, meaning a mountain with colorful paintings, and all the mountains that were painted with rock arts on the rock surfaces can be called Huashan. By using scientific methods such as infrared spectroscopy, microelement analysis and XRD, it was found that the Zuojiang Huashan rock art was made with hematite, which is mainly composed of iron oxide (Fe_2O_3). The results of analysis using gas chromatography–mass spectrometer indicate that the adhesive in pigments contains some plant cementing material (plant sap). Kuang Guodun and other researchers found that the surface layer of the rock art pigment is a red film layer mainly composed of hematite, and the calcium oxalate layer which are closely connected, below which is the rock face (calcium carbonate). The calcium oxalate was used as a kind of adhesive (Kuang Guodun 2016). There are nearly 80 rock art sites in the Zuojiang River basin, and almost all of them have squatting figures. Among them, the most famous is the Ningming Huashan rock art, which is also the largest single rock art panel in the world (Fig. 2). Its rock surface is 270 meters high and 350 meters long from north to south. The painted surface is about 170 meters wide, 40 meters high, with an area of about 8,000 square meters. There are still more than 1,900 images that can be identified, and the images can be divided into 110 groups. The rock art is drawn from the foot of the mountain at 2 meters, with the most images in the middle of the 5–20 meters high. The theme of rock art is extremely uniform, and the content is concentrated and basically clear. The most images are *anthropomorphs*, in addition, there are also zoomorphs and artifact images. Anthropomorphs are divided into two kinds, the front-view anthropomorphs and side–view anthropomorphs. The front–view anthropomorphs are generally taller and show a squat style, and side–view anthropomorphs are generally small and usually surrounding an image of tall front-view ones, and some front–view anthropomorphs often with dog images below. The zoomorphs are mainly 'dogs', and a few of them are 'birds'. The artifact images mainly include the bronze drum, sheep–horn bell, ring–head sword, swords with handguard or pommel, flat-stalk dagger etc.

In 2016, the Zuojiang Huashan Rock Art cultural landscape was included in the UNESCO World Cultural Heritage List. The heritage site includes 38 rock art sites in Ningming County, Longzhou County, Jiangzhou District and Fusui County.

Figure 2: Part of the Ningming Huashan rock art (by Zhu Qiuping)

2.2. The age of Zuojiang Huashan rock art

Over the years, researchers have carried out a lot of in-depth research work on Zuojiang Huashan rock art, and have achieved rich results. Based on these achievements, the current consensus of the academic community is that, the age of the Zuojiang Huashan rock art is from the Warring States Period to the Eastern Han Dynasty (475 BC–AD 220). The determination of its age is mainly through mutual verification of cross–dating and direct dating results. The principle of cross–dating is to compare images with diagnostic features to infer the age of rock arts, and the direct dating mainly uses the ^{14}C and the uranium series methods. The research results indicate that there is a high degree of overlap between the ages obtained from cross–dating and those obtained from direct dating.

2.2.1. The Cross–dating methods

The Zuojiang Huashan rock art was first dated based on the archaeological cross–dating methods, by comparing patterns such as sheep–horn bells, ring-head swords, swords with handguard or pommel, flat-stalk dagger and bronze drums to determine the age of the rock arts. However, as the different scholars used different methods to determine the age estimates, the conclusions drawn were also different. Qin Shengmin and others believed that the Zuojiang Huashan rock art should be cultural products from the Spring and Autumn Period (770 BC–476 BC) to the Eastern Han Dynasty (Qin et al. 1987: 138). Wang Kerong and others believed that its age was from the Warring States period (475 BC–221 BC) to the Eastern Han Dynasty (AD 25–AD 220) (Wang et al. 1988: 208).

Among the Zuojiang Huashan rock art, the most important images for dating are the sheep-horn bell images. This kind of images have been found in both Ningming Gaoshan and Ningming Huashan rock arts, one of which is shown in the figure (Fig. 3, No. 1). Scholars generally believe that they are sheep-horn bells hanging on shelves. There are some sheep-horn bells unearthed in Guangxi, and four of them are from Guantong Dalingjiao in Pubei County, are identified as the Warring States Period (475 BC–221 BC) (Fig. 3, No. 2). There is also one unearthed from No.1 of Luobowan Tombs in Gui County could approximately date back to the early Western Han Dynasty (206 BC–AD 25) (Fig. 3, No. 3). The date of the one from Shizhaishan in Jinning County, Yunnan is in the Mid–Western Han Dynasty (206 BC–AD 25). This is the latest sheep–horn bell known till now (Jiang 1984: 66–69). The other sheep–horn bells unearthed from other places are almost all from the early or mid-Western Han Dynasty. It can be concluded that the date of the unearthed bronze sheep–horn bells is from the early Warring States Period to the Mid–Western Han Dynasty. According to this, the date of the Zuojiang Huashan rock art is almost equivalent to this period.

The ring-head sword images are often found in the Zuojiang Huashan rock art, and most of them are worn on the waist of the front–view anthropomorphs (Fig. 4, No. 1). Such images have appeared on the bronze wares of Yue people from the Warring States Period. However, in Guangxi,

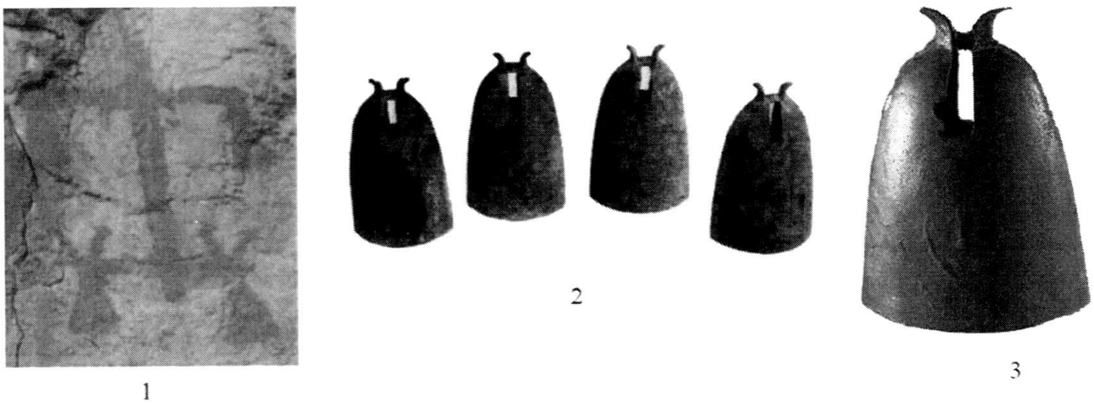

Figure 3: Comparison of images of sheep–horn bells in the Zuojiang Huashan rock art with the unearthed objects in Guangxi: (1) Ningming Gaoshan rock art (by Xiao Bo) (2) Guantong Dalingjiao (after UNESCO 2016: 161) (3) No.1 of Luobowan Tombs (by the Museum of Guangxi Zhuang Autonomous Region)

long ring-head swords are mostly found in the Han Dynasty (206BC–AD220) tombs, but the ring-head is smaller than that in the rock art figures (Fig. 4, Nos 3–5). The ring-head swords in the rock arts have the features of ring-head on the bronze or iron sharpeners in the Warring States Period (Fig. 4, Nos 2, 6 and 7). In conclusion, inferred from the ring-head swords, the earliest date of the Zuojiang Huashan Rock Art should be the Warring States Period (475BC–221BC), and the latest time should be the Eastern Han Dynasty (AD25–AD220).

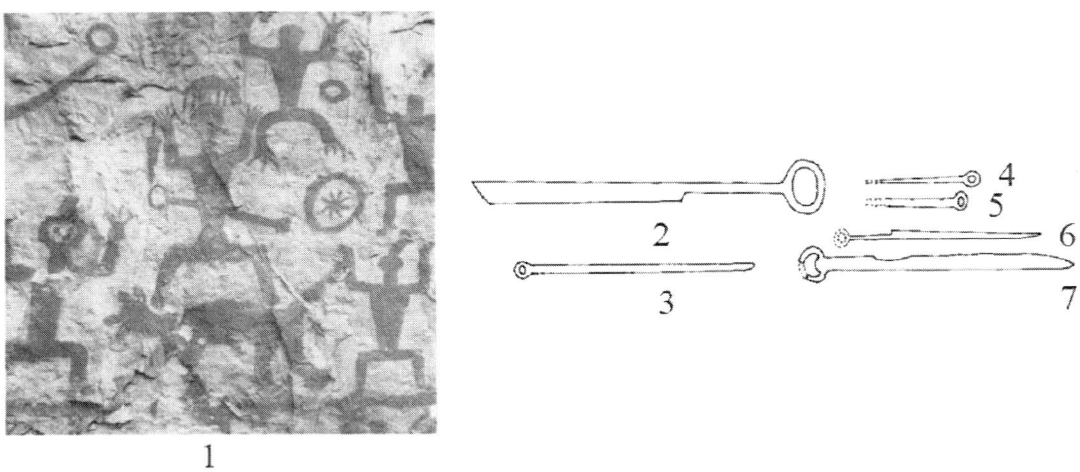

Figure 4: Comparison of images of the ring-head sword on the Zuojiang Huashan Rock Art with the unearthed bronze swords in Guangxi: (1) Zuojiang Huashan Rock Art (by Zhu Qiuping), (2), (6) and (7) the Warring States Yinshanling Tomb in Pingle County (After Qin et al. 1987: 129), (3) the Han Tomb in Hepu county (after Qin et al. 1987: 129), (4) and (5) the Han Tomb in Pingle County (after Qin et al. 1987: 129)

The next cross-dating evidence is the flat-stalk dagger. At present, only one flat-stalk dagger image is found in the Ningming Huashan rock art, which is suspended below the left hand of a front-view anthropomorph, and the dagger is parallel to the forearm of the anthropomorph and slightly longer than the forearm (Fig. 5, No. 2). The flat-stalk dagger has been unearthed in Guangxi (Fig. 5, Nos 3 and 4) and in the tombs of Lijiashan, Yunnan (Fig. 5, No. 5), dating back to the middle and late Warring States period, and some may have been extended to the early Western Han Dynasty. Therefore, it can be inferred that the age of similar rock art figures is roughly equivalent to this. However, the image of the rock art is controversial, and we cannot fully confirm that it is a flat-stalk dagger image. From previous studies, it has been found that the copied image looks very similar to the flat-stalk dagger, but there are still significant differences from the actual image in the rock art (Fig. 5, No. 1). Firstly, the dagger body in the copied image is concave in the middle (Fig. 5, No. 1a), but in the rock art, the 'dagger' body is smooth and without concave; besides, the connection between the 'dagger' body and the hilt is relatively wide, and there are obvious concave marks on the 'dagger' body (Fig. 5, No. 1b), which are not found in the rock art. In addition, we have never seen such a dagger holding method, and the relationship between the image and the position of the anthropomorph's hand makes it difficult to believe that this is a flat-stalk dagger.

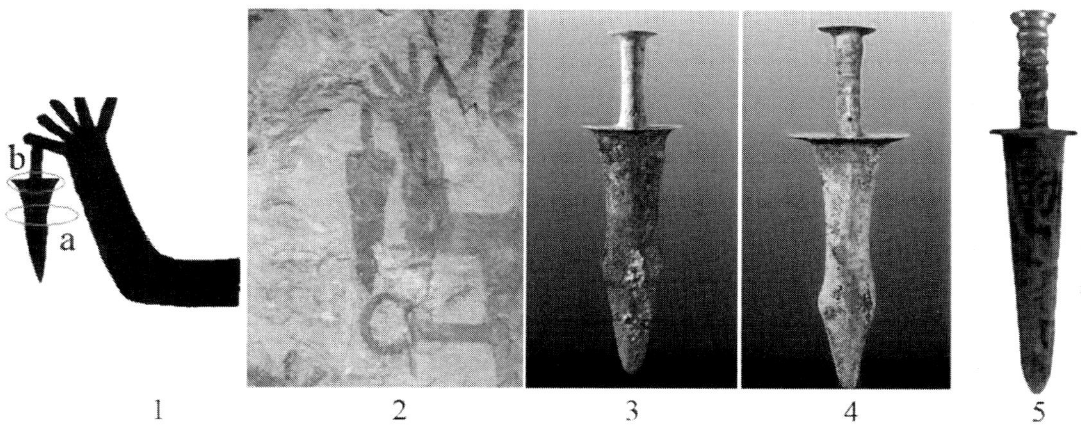

Figure 5: Comparison of images of flat–stalk dagger on the Zuojiang Huashan rock art with the unearthed dagger in Guangxi and Yunnan: (1) the copy of Ningming Huashan rock art (after Qin et al. 1987: 131), (2) the Ningming Huashan rock art (by Zhu Qiuping), (3) and (4) flat–stalk dagger unearthed in Guangxi (UNESCO 2016: 163), (5) flat–stalk dagger unearthed from Lijiashan tomb, Yunnan (Li 1999: 40)

Similarly, there are images of swords with handguard or pommel, which can be found at many rock art sites. Inferred from the long swords unearthed in Guangxi and the bronze wares with images of long swords unearthed in Hunan, the earliest date of the Zuojiang Rock Art is inferred to be the early Warring States Period, and the latest time should be late Western Han Dynasty.

In addition, some scholars also do the cross-dating work by comparing the unearthed bronze drums, as well as the ferry and anthropomorphs, and identified that the date of Zuojiang Huashan rock art was between the Warring States Period and the Han Dynasty. Due to the large age span of ferry boats, anthropomorphs, and bronze drums, the images in rock art of these kinds do not have the significance of cross-dating, it will cause many problems by using these images for dating. However, the approximate age of the Zuojiang Huashan rock art can still be confirmed through cross-dating, and the age of the Zuojiang Huashan rock art is from the Warring States Period to the Eastern Han Dynasty (475BC–AD220).

2.2.2. The direct dating methods

The direct dating methods that used for dating the Zuojiang Huashan rock art are mainly ^{14}C and uranium series. The ^{14}C dating method was carried out for three times, two of which were conducted in 1983, and the other one was in 1985. In 1983, the ^{14}C Laboratory of Archaeology Department of Peking University dated a wood pole that collected at the mouth of the cave on the cliff where Ningming Huashan Rock Art is located. The dating result shows that its age is 2680±80 BP. If considering the growth age of the wood, it is roughly equivalent to the late Spring and Autumn Period or the early Warring States Period. There are rock art figures on both sides at the mouth of the cave where the wood pole was discovered and on the small wall at the junction of the two tributaries. Judged from this situation, the wood pole should be used for tying the ropes to climb up to or down from the cave when they painted the rock art (Qin et al. 1987: 136–137). Therefore, the date of the wood pole can be a reference for inferring the date of rock art. This date is completely trustworthy, but the relationship between wood pole and rock art needs to be further proved. In the same year, the Department of Archaeology in Peking University and other institutions did the ^{14}C dating by analyzing the stalactites overlying and underlying the rock art. According to the test results of two samples, the stalactites underlying the rock art is about 4200 years BP; and the stalactites overlying the rock art is about 1680 years BP (Wang et al. 1988: 208). In 1985, the Dating Laboratory of the Department of Archaeology, Peking University collected nine samples in Ningming Huashan rock art, seven of which are underlying samples, and the other two are overlying samples. According to the date of underlying and overlying stalactites, the drawing date was inferred to be from 2370 BP to 2115 BP. In other words, it was from the Warring States Period till the Western Han Dynasty (475BC–AD25). Nevertheless, taking errors and other factors into account, there are probably some fluctuations in the upper and lower date limit of the rock art. The range of the fluctuations may reach the earliest time limit of the Spring and Autumn Period (770BC–476BC), and the latest time limit of the Eastern Han Dynasty (AD25–AD220) (Yuan et al. 1986: 27–34).

Uranium series dating of the Zuojiang Huashan Rock Art has been mainly carried out for three times. In 2013, at the request of the government of Guangxi Zhuang Autonomous Region, Benjamin Smith and Maxime Aubert from the University of Western Australia and the University of Wollongong collected 12 calcium carbonate samples in direct association with rock art figures at Ningming Huashan Mountain. These 12 samples were sectioned into 24 subsamples, some overlying and others underlying the rock art. It appears that the Ningming Huashan rock art was made within a relatively restricted time of about 1000 years between 1920 BP and 940 BP (Smith and Aubert 2013). In 2014, to determine a precise age on the rock art at Mt. Huashan, Shao Qing–Feng from Key Laboratory of Virtual Geographic Environment, Nanjing Normal University and others collected 56 secondary carbonate layers above and below the paintings, and studied their mineralogy, oxygen, and carbon isotopic compositions and dated by the ^{230}Th/U method. The dating results demonstrate that ages of the rock paintings can be bracketed between 1856 ±16 and 1728±41 yr BP corresponding to the middle to the end of the Eastern Han dynasty (Shao et al. 2017). In addition, in September 2016, Zhao Jianxin from the University of Queensland in Australia and others visited the rock art sites in Ningming, Longzhou, Jiangzhou, Fusui and other places in Chongzuo City, and collected more than 20 secondary carbonate layers. However, due to various reasons, the dating results have not been published.

Based on the results of direct and indirect dating, Zuojiang Huashan rock art was drawn between the Warring States Period and the Eastern Han Dynasty.

3. The Squatting-figure-rock art in Yunnan

The Squatting-figures in rock art in Yunnan are mainly found at Cangyuan, Yuanjiang Ta Ke and Malipo Dawangyan sites. Malipo Yanlashan and Guangnan Pingshan are in Wenshan Zhuang and Miao Autonomous Prefecture, and the last three also called Wenshan Rock Art as a whole.

3.1. The Cangyuan rock art

3.1.1. Basic situation

The Cangyuan rock art is a site where squatting figures are relatively concentrated. It is located in the Cangyuan Wa Nationality Autonomous County of Lincang City, Yunnan Province, and distributed along the Xiaohei River and its tributaries. The Cangyuan rock art is painted with red pigment on limestone cliff surfaces about 2-10m above the ground. There is usually a platform with a capacity of 20–30 people, the space below might have been used for holding ceremonies. By 2017, 17 sites in Cangyuan had been discovered with more than 1200 rock art figures, within an area of nearly 600 m^2 (Wu et al. 2019: 110). The Chemistry Department of Kunming Institute of Technology through chemical analysis of a small piece of painted stone found near the rock art site has proved that the main component of the pigment is iron, therefore assumed that the pigment is haematite (Investigation Team of Yunnan Provincial Institute of History 1966: 15).

There are currently over 1000 recognizable images in the Cangyuan rock art, including anthropomorphs, zoomorphs, objects and geometric symbols. Zoomorphs include images of 'cattle', 'horses', 'sheep', 'pigs', 'dogs', 'birds', 'monkeys', 'snakes' and others. The depicted objects include

Figure 6: Part of the Cangyuan Rock Art (after Editorial Board of Complete Works of Chinese Art Classification 2006: 63.)

purported images of 'bows', 'shields', 'spears', 'pestle' and 'mortars','pole-railing' style 'houses', 'boats', and so forth. Besides, there are also presumed celestial images. Among them, most of the images are anthropomorphs, accounting for more than 70% of the total. All the anthropomorphs are tiny, of which the large ones ranging between 30 and 40 cm high and the small ones are less than 5 cm (Investigation Team of Yunnan Provincial Institute of History 1966: 8) (Fig. 6). Some anthropomorphs are decorated with 'feathers', 'horns' and 'tails', and others have 'male genitals'. According to Wang Ningsheng, these ancient artists painted the rock art by applying haematite pigment with hands, feathers or plant fibres (Wang 1985: 17).

3.1.2. The age of the Cangyuan rock art

Direct dating methods have also been applied to the study of the Cangyuan rock art. In 1981, the Yunnan Provincial Museum sampled the stalactites covering the rock art at Loc. 3 of the Cangyuan rock art site. Later, the samples were ^{14}C dated by the Institute of Vertebrate Palaeontology and Palaeoanthropology, Chinese Academy of Sciences, and the result from the inner layer covering the painting was dated to 3030±70 BP, and the outer layer of the stalactites, to 2300±70 BP (Wu et al.. 2019: 110). In 1984, Hu Yufan and others extracted 216 samples of spores, pollen and diatom fossils from the pigments of the Cangyuan rock art, and compared the sporopollen assemblage with the Blytt–Sernander North-European Postglacial climatic time and forest evolution stratification table. It suggested that the sporopollen assemblage in the Cangyuan rock art was dated to the Subboreal period (5660 to 3710 yrs BP) (Hu et al. 1984: 15). In 2021, Shao Qingfeng and others carried out U–series and AMS ^{14}C dating of the carbonate accretions associated with the rock art figures at eight sites. Among them, 25 samples were overlying the pigments and 14 samples were underlying the pigments. They believed that the combination of all of the reliable U–series dates enable us to constrain the time interval of the main rock art phase to ~3800–2700 yr BP, which is coeval with the regional late Neolithic culture (Shao et al. 2021).

3.2. The Yuanjiang Ta Ke rock art

It is located one kilometer northeast of Ta Ke Village (also known as Longchi Village) in Yuanjiang County, Yunnan Province. Yuanjiang River, a tributary of the Red River, passes through the county. The Yuanjiang River Basin is mostly composed of red sandstone and Silty Shale stratums, and the water is red, hence it is also known as the Red River. The rock art is located at the lower part of the rock face, the images face south, with an altitude of 1532 meters. The total length of the painted surface is 19.5 meters, usually more than 2 meters above the ground, with the highest point reaching 15 meters. The upper part of the rock face extends outward, and there are two layers of platforms in front of the rock wall. Due to forest destruction, the rock mass was exposed and the rock walls broke into blocks. Some images are no longer recognizable due to rock peeling or calcium carbonate cover. There are 94 existing images, including 62 anthropomorphs, 10 zoomorphs, and 22 symbols and other images. The images are dark red, and the anthropomorphs are mostly inverted triangles (Fig. 7). No scientific dating conducted for this rock art site till present. Through comparative studies with the Cangyuan rock art, some scholars believe that its age is earlier, about the middle and late Neolithic (Yang 1986: 38).

1 2

Figure 7: Part of the Yuanjiang Ta Ke rock art (after Chen et al. 2006: 135, 138)

3.3. Wenshan rock arts

The Squatting-figure-rock art in Wenshan are mainly concentrated in three sites, they are the Malipo Dawangyan rock art, Malipo Yanlashan rock art, and Guangnan Pingshan rock art.

3.3.1. The Dawangyan rock art

The Dawangyan rock art site is located at a bend of Chouyang River at the southern end of Yangjiaolao Mountain in the east of Malipo County. The site is about 150 meters above the riverbed on the vertical and steep cliff which is more than 20 meters high and facing south. The rock art is found 3.5 meters above the ground. There are currently 38 recognizable images and can be divided into two groups. The local indigenous Zhuang people refer to 'Dawangyan' as 'Ba Liang', which translates to 'rocks with red pictures' in Chinese. In the 1980s, there was an ancient Zhuang village called "Ba Liang" under Dawangyan, named after its rock art. Images include anthropomorphs, zoomorphs, symbols, etc. Among them, bovines are more distinctive in zoomorphs (Fig. 8, No. 1). There is a Neolithic Xiaohe cave site on the other side of the river. Two shoulder stone tools and fragments of sandy pottery with gray, red, and black colours from 4100 years ago were unearthed in the cave. Archaeologists believe that these potteries have the characteristics of Baiyue culture and were used by the Luoyue people, the ancestors of the Zhuang people. Some scholars believe that the Dawangyan rock art belongs to the same era as the Xiaohe cave site, and the painters of the rock arts should be the ancestors of the Zhuang people (Wang and Jin 2013: 90–92). In addition, the Dawangyan rock art also belong to the Red River basin. From this, it can be seen that there is a close connection between the rock art of Wenshan Prefecture and the Yuanjiang Ta Ke rock art that belong to the same Red River basin.

3.3.2. The Yanlashan rock art

The Yanlashan rock art is located at the northeast end of Moshan Village, about 4 kilometers northwest of Malipo County. The rock art is drawn on a rock wall 1.3 meters above the ground. The rock wall is 2 meters high and 4 meters wide. According to the investigation data of 1987, there are more than 20 images, including 13 anthropomorphs, 4 'snakes', 2 other zoomorphs, and one 'pole-railing' style house (Fig. 8, No. 2). In addition, there are several symbol images and blurred images. The rock mass is severely weathered and peeled off, causing damage to some images. The images are all drawn with red pigments, and judging from the line marks, it might have been drawn with fingers.

3.3.3. The Guangnan Pingshan rock art

The Pingshan rock art is located in the rock shelter about one kilometer east of Huiliangzishang natural village, Pingshan administrative village, and 12 kilometers east of Liancheng Town, Guangnan County. The rock shelter faces southwest, with a height of about 30 meters and a width of about 25 meters. The upper and lower ends protrude, and the middle is concave, forming an

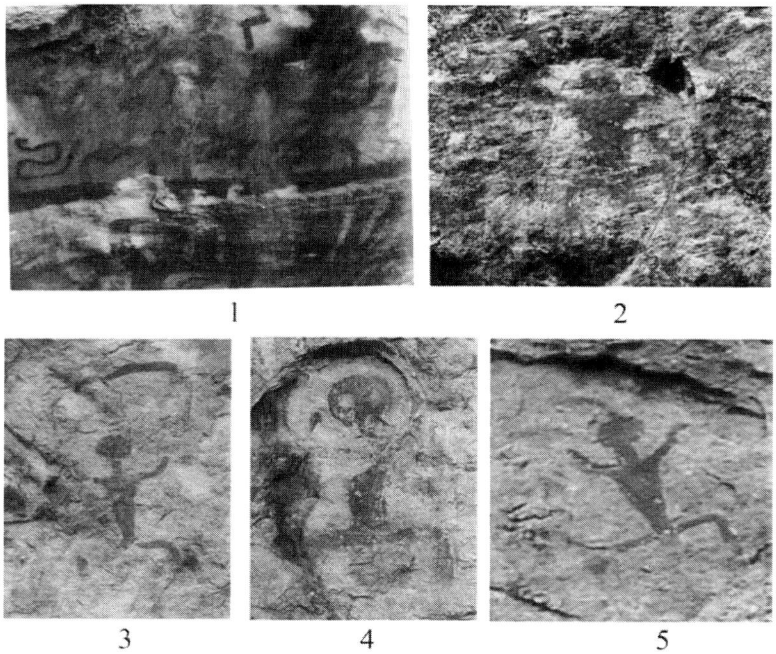

Figure 8: The Wenshan Rock Arts: (1) Malipo Dawangyan rock art, (2) Malipo Yanlashan rock art, (3) – (5) Guangnan Pingshan rock art (after Wang and Jin 2013: 92–125)

inner curved surface. There is a platform, 2.5 meters long and 8 meters wide below the cliff, with a valley about 150 meters deep in front of the platform. The painted area is approximately 1.7 × 4.8 meters; due to weathering, there is a slight peeling of the rock art. The highest point of the image is 3.7 meters, and the lowest point is 2 meters away from the platform. Both are drawn with red pigment, and several squatting figures have been found (Fig. 8, Nos 3–5).

4. The Correlation between Guangxi and Yunnan Squatting-figure-rock art

There are two rock art sites named after "Huashan" in the Zuojiang River rock art in Guangxi, they are Huashan rock art in Ningming and Mianjiang Huashan in Longzhou. As mentioned above, any mountain with rock arts can be called "Huashan", and the local Zhuang language called "Ba Lai". The Dawangyan rock art in Malipo, Yunnan is called "Ba Liang" by local villagers, which also means "a mountain with colorful paintings". Wang Mingfu and others believe that "Ba Liang" and "Ba Lai" belong to the same lineage and both the cultural heritages were created by the ancestors of the Zhuang ethnic group (Wang and Jin 2013: 90). They are the true records of the ecological environment, their adaptation to nature, as well as the creation of civilization of the Zhuang people. In addition, the first site of the Cangyuan rock art, Yunnan Province is called "Pa Dianmu" by the local Dai people, and which also means a mountain with colorful paintings (Lin

1966: 9), We found that the above three rock art sites have similar pronunciations and meanings, indicating a broad cultural connection between them.

In fact, by analyzing the regularities of distribution of rock arts in the aforementioned regions, we can further determine the potential transmission routes of the Squatting-figure-rock art. Wenshan Prefecture in Yunnan is an important distribution area for rock arts, which are mostly located on cliffs near rivers, some of which are also located at the bend of the river. Among the 80 rock art sites in the Zuojiang River area, 72 are distributed on the riverside cliffs, accounting for 90% of the total, and about 80% of the 72 rock art sites are situated round the bend of the river. In addition, there are 8 sites which are away from the river bank from 2.5 to 12 km. And according to Xu Haipeng, *both the rock art sites at and away from the bank of the river had the same geographical locations when they were painted, then the climate change led to the hydrology and geomorphic conditions changed* (Tang 1996: 12). In addition, the Squatting-figure-rock art in Wenshan are all painted with red pigments (Fig. 8, Nos 3–5), and some of them have decorations resembling tails or genitalia (Fig. 8, No. 2). Besides, there are also some bronze drum images. One of the images is particularly noteworthy, with a bronze drum placed in front of a squatting figure, in the shape of a human hitting a drum (Fig. 8, No. 4). This kind of bronze drum images has also been found in the rock art of the Hongyan Cave in Wenshan. The combination of squatting figures and bronze drums is often found in the Zuojiang Huashan rock art (Fig. 2 and Fig.9). This fully demonstrates the possibility of cultural exchange between the rock arts in the aforementioned regions.

Figure 9: Part of the Ningming Huashan Rock art (by Zhu Qiuping)

In addition, Wenshan is an important inhabited area of the Zhuang ethnic group. The unearthed cultural relics show that the Neolithic culture of Wenshan should belong to the same type of culture as Guangxi, and should be the original culture of Luoyue people. The Luo Yue people were ancestors of the Zhuang ethnic group, therefore, the authors of the rock arts in Wenshan were also ancestors of the Zhuang ethnic group. It should be noted that the Squatting-figure-rock art in Cangyuan, Malipo Dawangyan and Zuojiang Huashan all stepping on the ground, and this form of expression is very rare in the rock art of other regions in China, which also demonstrates the widespread cultural exchange in these regions.

In addition, the squatting figures have also been discovered in the unearthed cultural relics in Guangxi and Yunnan, but their sources may be different. A typical squatting figure inscription was found on a late Shang Dynasty bronze You (a kind of wine container in ancient China), unearthed from Wuming, Guangxi (Fig. 10, No. 1). This kind of inscriptions are also found in oracle bone and bronze wares of Shang and Zhou dynasties. Casting inscriptions on bronze wares began to be popular in the late Shang Dynasty and peaked in the Zhou Dynasty (Gao 1996: 41). The squatting figures on the Shang and Zhou bronzes resemble graphic character. They often feature a straight–backed person with a round head and narrow neck, hanging arms, outstretched hands, and half–squatting legs (Fig. 10). Philologists have researched such figures and identified them as '天' (god), also known as '神' (deity) or '帝' (emperor) with supreme status (Tang 1996: 12). In addition, a turtle-like animal is frequently depicted beneath the squatting figure in oracle bone or bronze ware inscriptions. Guo Moruo and Luo Zhenyu interpreted this kind of image as '天黿' (Tianyuan) (Fig. 10, No. 5), namely Xuanyuan and Huangdi, who collectively associated it with ancestor worship (Pang 1993). Besides turtles, there are also various animals that beneath the squatting figure (Fig. 10, Nos 6–10). According to Zou Heng, such combined images ought to represent 'celestial animals' or 'tribal emblems' (Zou 1980). We have noticed that squatting figure with dogs are often found in the Zuojiang Huashan rock art, which should be a continuation of such concepts. There are a lot of inscriptions like that.

Similar images are also found in the Neolithic Times of the Yellow River Basin. The Yangshao Culture (5000 BC–3000 BC), which flourished in the Yellow River Basin, produced painted pottery that included the earliest squatting figures in China (Fig. 12, No. 1). Since then, the squatting figures had spread from the Central Plains to the Gansu–Qinghai region and showed up in great numbers in the Majiayao culture. One of the painted potteries of the Banshan type of the Majiayao culture (2450BC–2150BC) has a squatting figure in the 'X' ray style with a tail (Fig. 12, No. 2). Entering the Bronze Age, the quantity and dispersion of squatting figures further increased. The carriers include pottery, jade, bronze, oracle bone, etc. The squatting figures on the painted pottery are distinctive of Xindian culture. One of them is a double-eared jar from the early Xindian culture (1450BC), which has a squatting figure with a tail painted on both the ear and belly (Fig. 12, No. 3).

Unlike the abstract inscriptions found in Guangxi, the squatting figure in Yunnan is mainly found on bronze weapons and belongs to concrete images. There are 5 bronze weapons unearthed

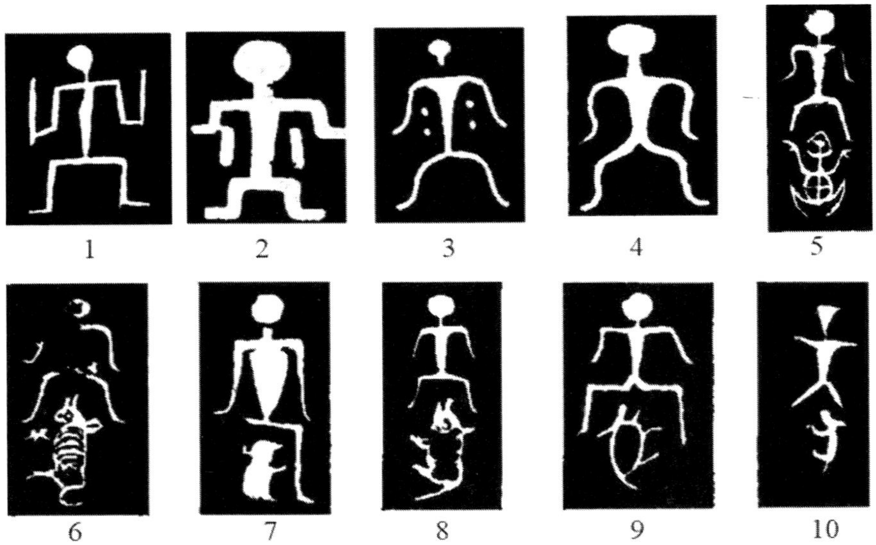

Figure 10: The Squatting Figures in Bronze Inscriptions: (1) Single squatting figure (after Qin et al. 1987: 133), (2) and (3) Single squatting figure (after Hu 1995: 70), (4) Single squatting figure (after Rong 1985: 3), (5) – (10). Squatting figure with beast images (after Zou 1980: 340.)

from Eighttower tomb group, Qujing City, Yunnan province. The weapons include swords, Ge, and pecking (Fig. 11, Nos 1–5). All of them are anthropomorphs shown as three people hands in hands and arms upward, and the squatting figure in the centre is significantly larger than the other two stepping on his feet (Fig. 11, No. 5). Another squatting figure on the bronze Ge unearthed from Yangfutou tomb, Kunming City is similar to the previous images (Fig. 11, No. 6). In the Yangfutou tomb, there is also a bronze cut with two squatting figures arranged up and down on the handle and the head, was skull shape (Fig. 11, No. 7). Similar images have also been found in the Li Jiashan tomb, Jiangchuan District, Yuxi City. A bronze dagger dating from the Warring States Period to the Western Han Dynasty was discovered in the Lijiashan tomb. On both sides of the edge near the blade, there is a figure of a human, raising hands and squatting down (Fig.11, No. 8) (Zhang and Wang 1975: 149-151). Another bronze dagger also comes from the Lijiashan tomb. The dagger stem is cast with four relief human faces, with a snake winding around them, and there is a squatting figure on the upper body of the dagger (Fig. 11, No. 9) (Zhang 2001: 32–36) . 'Snake' figures are also found in the Yanlashan rock art in Malipo. The snakes and squatting figure appear together, indicating that the bronze dagger and the Yanlashan rock art are likely to be a work under the common cultural concepts. Besides, there are many weapons unearthed in Yunnan with such images.

We noticed that unlike the squatting figure unearthed from Guangxi, the squatting figure unearthed in Yunnan belongs to the concrete image. Such images are often visible in the cultural

Figure 11: Squatting figures on the bronze weapons in Yunnan: (1)-(5) Eighttower tomb group (after Zhao and Yang 2020: 63), (6) and (7) Yangfutou tomb (after Zhao and Yang 2020: 62–63), (8) Lijiashan tomb (after Zhang and Wang 1975 : 149) (9) Lijiashan tomb (after Zeng et al. 1995: 8) (1, 8, 9. Bronze–Dagger; 2, 3, 5, 6. Bronze–Ge; 4. Bronze–Peck; 7. Bronze–Cutting)

relics unearthed from the late Chinese New Stone Age to the Han Dynasty. This kind of images can be seen on a massive Jade–cong (Fig. 12, No. 4), which belongs to the Liangzhu Culture (3300BC–2300BC). The upper part of the image shows a sacred human and the lower part shows a sacred animal face motif. The sacred human and animal face motifs combine to create a new image. The sacred human wears a square feather-crown on his head, and his lower limbs are in a squatting position. In addition, the Cernuschi Museum in France has a jade figurine from the Shijiahe culture (2400 BC–1900 BC) in their collection. The jade figurine is squatting sideways, naked, barefoot, with hair draped behind, crown decorations on top, and arms stretched obliquely toward the belly (Fig. 12, No. 5).

Besides, a significant number of squatting figures have also been discovered in the bronze wares of Shang Dynasty. One of these is a middle Shang Dynasty bronze–zun in the shape of double–tiger–eating–man that unearthed from the No. 1 Artifact Pit at the Sanxingdui archaeological site in Guanghan City, Sichuan Province. The upper part of the squatting figure is two tigers with the same head (Fig. 12, No. 6). In another image, the human's head is decorated with double horns, the arms are bent at the elbows and raised, the legs are bent twice, the lower body has male genitals, and the overall shape is squatting (Fig. 12, No. 7).

Squatting figures are increasingly prevalent in bronzes, stone reliefs, portrait stones, tomb murals, and silk paintings from the Warring States Period through the Eastern Han Dynasty (475BC–220AD). In the Warring States Tombs, there is a squatting sacred human motif with long horns on the head and two hands holding 'snakes' (or 'loong'), such as the images engraved on bronze, unearthed from the Warring States Tomb in Gaozhuang, Huaiyin, Jiangsu (Fig. 12, No. 9), and the image on the bronze–qi (Ge) in the Warring States Tombs in Jingmen, Hubei (Fig. 12, No. 10). There is also other squatting figure in the Tomb of Gaozhuang (Fig. 12, No. 8). A squatting figure carved on the north wall of the Han Dynasty stone tomb at Yinan, Shandong. Wang Chongshun and Wang Houyu believe that it depicts the image of 'Chi You' (one of the ancestral deities of China), while Sun Zuoyun believes that it depicts the ancient Fang Xiangshi (Wu) (Fig. 12, No. 12) (*after Zeng et al.* 2009: 223).

In Mawangdui tomb No. 1 of the Han dynasty (ca. 166BC), at the lower part of the 'T' shaped painting on silk, there is a squatting figure which is naked and with upraised arms bent at the elbows. The human is holding the white boundless land, his feet stepping on two huge crossed

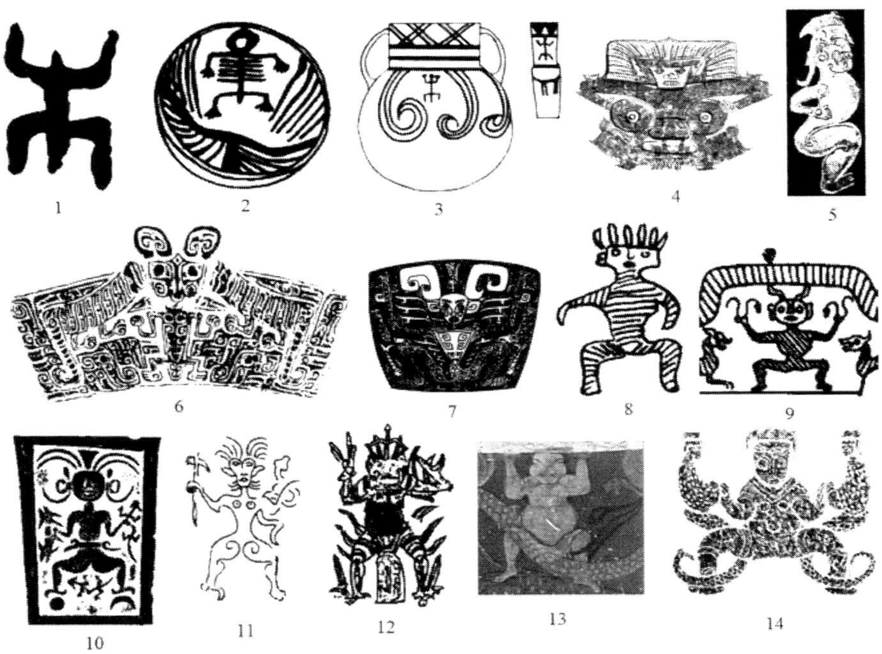

Figure 12. Squatting Figures in excavated cultural relics: (1) Painted pottery of Yangshao Culture (after Tang 1996: Fig. 20); (2) Painted pottery of Banshan type of Majiayao Culture (after Tang 1996: Fig. 22); (3) Round bottom pot with two ears of Xindian Culture (after Tang 1996: Fig. 21); (4) Liangzhu Jade–cong (after Minao 2009 : 54); (5) Jade Figurine of Shijiahe Culture (after Minao 2009: 80); (6) Bronze–zun in the shape of double–tiger–eating–man; (7) Bronze drum of Shang Dynasty (after Tang 1996: Fig. 23); (8) and (9) Bronze of Warring States Tombs in Gaozhuang, Huaiyin (after Zeng et al. 2009: 189, 223); (10) Bronze–Qi of Warring States Tomb in Jingmen, Hubei (after Shanghai Museum 1984:344); (11) Bronze sword of the Eastern Zhou Dynasty collected by Gu Yue Ge; (12) Portrait stone in Yinan, Shandong (after Zeng et al. 2009: 224); (13) Part of 'T'–shaped silk painting from the Han Tomb No.1 at Mawangdui, Changsha (after Hunan Museum and the Institution of Archaeology CASS 1973: fig. 77); (14) The Han dynasty stone relief in Xiao county (Yang 2019: 31).

turtles, and a giant python hovering between the legs (Fig. 12, No. 13). The images on the silk painting, which date to the early Western Han Dynasty, are generally considered to be related to the travel of the soul on its ascent to heaven. A common motif in Han Dynasty tomb art is that Fu Xi and Nv Wa (both are the ancestral gods) appear in couples. One of these images is found on a Han Dynasty stone relief in Xiao county, Anhui Province (Fig. 9, No. 14). In the center is the god "The One", and in the shape of squatting figure. Fu Xi and Nv Wa have human heads and snake bodies, with their tails wrapped around the legs of the god "The One".

5. Conclusion

Through the above discussion, it can be observed that there is a close relationship in the Squatting-figure-rock art in Guangxi and Yunnan. From a geographical point of view, the Cangyuan Rock art in Yunnan is located at the western end, and its age is about 3500–2500 (another statement is about 3800–2700) years, while the Zuojiang Huashan rock art in Guangxi is about 2500–1800 years ago. The time of the Zuojiang Huashan rock art began to draw almost the same time as the Cangyuan rock art painting tradition disappeared. In addition, there are also several rock art sites between the two. Among them, the geographical location of the Wenshan rock art is the closest to that of the Zuojiang Huashan rock art, and has been closely linked since ancient times. In addition, both Wenshan and Zuojiang River basins belong to the Zhuang ethnic settlement areas, therefore, there may be a cultural connection between the rock arts in the two regions. From the perspective of pigments and preservation, the images of the Wenshan rock art are mostly bright red and have a better preservation condition. As for the Zuojiang Huashan Rock Art, some of the images are bright red, and the others are reddish–brown, and its preservation condition is poorer. As for the Yuanjiang Ta Ke rock art, on the one hand, it belongs to the Red River Basin, just like the rock art in Wenshan, and there is the possibility of cultural exchange; on the other hand, the color of Yuanjiang Ta Ke rock art is reddish brown, similar to the Cangyuan rock art, but significantly different from the Wenshan rock art; furthermore, the body of Yuanjiang Ta Ke squatting figure is generally inverted triangular, similar to the Cangyuan rock art but completely different from the rock art of other sites. There are likely to be two rock art systems here, one being the "Cangyuan–Yuanjiang Ta Ke" system, and the other is the "Zuojiang–Wenshan" system. Further in–depth research is needed to determine whether there is a cultural connection between the two systems. In addition, it should be noted that the squatting figures unearthed in Guangxi belong to the bronze ware inscriptions, while the artifacts unearthed in Yunnan belong to concrete shapes. Whether there is a connection between the two rock art systems and the differences between the unearthed squatting figures in Guangxi and Yunnan also needs further thorough study.

6. Acknowledgment

The work presented here was sponsored by Guangxi Minzu University talent introduction research project, 'The Collection and Arrangement of Rock Art Documents in Southeast Asia' (Project Approval

Number: 2020SKQD21); Guangxi Minzu University' research project, The Southwest Rock Art Symbols and the Construction of the Sense of Community for the Chinese Nation', (Project Approval Number: 2021GXMGY0306).

Dr Xiao Bo
Research Center for Nationalities
Guangxi Minzu University
No. 188, Daxue East Road, 530006 Nanning
Guangxi Zhuang Autonomous Region
P. R. China
Email: 2007010576@163.com

Che Jing
College of Ethnology and Sociology
Guangxi Minzu University
No. 188, Daxue East Road, 530006 Nanning
Guangxi Zhuang Autonomous Region
P. R. China
Email: 1228919470@qq.com

Cao Yujie
College of Ethnology and Sociology
Guangxi Minzu University
No. 188, Daxue East Road, 530006 Nanning,
Guangxi Zhuang Autonomous Region
P. R. China
Email: 944278802@qq.com

References

Chen Z., Gai S., Lin Y., Lin Y., Fan W., Wang B., Du F., Li H., Li F., Wu C., Qiu Z., Gao Z., Yang T., Liu S (eds.) 2006. *Complete works of Chinese art classification: Volume 5 of complete works of Chinese rock arts: The second section of southern rock arts.* Liaoning Fine Arts Publishing House, Shenyang.

Hu X. 1995. Deep research on reproductive images in rock arts. *Journal of Kashgar Teachers College* 1: 68–75.

Hu Y., Wu X., Shi P. 1984. Using sporopollen fossils to study ancient cliff paintings. *Fossil* 2: 15.

Huang Y. 2012. Study on the squatting figure rock art of the Zuojiang River. PhD thesis, Minzu University of China, Beijing.

Huang Y. 2014. Study on squatting figure rock art and the spread of Austronesian. *Journal of Southwest Minzu University (Humanities and Social Science)* 9: 38–43.

Hunan Museum and the Institution of Archaeology CASS 1973. *The Han tomb No.1 at Mawangdui, Changsha*. Volume 2, Cultural Relics Publishing House, Beijing.

Jiang T. 1984. Elementary theory of Chime–bells with horn. *Cultural Relics* 5: 66–69.

Kuang G., Liu D., Shu G., Wei L. 2016. Early analysis and research on pigment synthesis and its mechanism of the Zuojiang Huashan rock art, *Chinese Cultural Heritage* 4: 82–85.

Li K. 1999. *A collection of Yunnan ancient art treasures*. Yunnan University Press, Kunming.

LIN S. 1966. Yunnan Cangyuan cliff painting. *Cultural Relics* 2: 7–16+38.

MINAO H (AUTHOR)., CHANG Y., LIU X., WANG, P., LI H. (TRANSLATORS) 2009. *The pattern study of Gods and beasts - the ancient Chinese Gods*. SDX Joint Publishing Company, Beijing.

PANG P. 1993. A probe into the origin of the Yellow Emperor. *Chinese culture: Tradition and modernization* 2: 27–38.

QIN S., QIN C., LU M., YU R. 1987. *Investigation and researches on the cliff paintings in Zuojiang River basin*. Guangxi Nationalities Publishing House, Nanning.

RONG G. 1985. *Compilation of bronze inscriptions*. Zhonghua Book Company, Beijing.

SHAO Q., E. P. BRANCHU., ZHU Q., WANG W., H. VALLADAS, M. FONTUGNE 2017. High precision U/Th dating of the rock paintings at Mt. Huashan, Guangxi, southern China. *Quaternary Research* 88: 1–13.

SHAO Q., WU Y., E. P. BRANCHU., ZHU Q., A. DAPOIGNY, JIANG T. 2021. U–series dating of carbonate accretions reveals late Neolithic age for the rock paintings in Cangyuan, southwestern China. *Quaternary Geochronology* 61: 1–13.

SMITH B. and M. AUBERT 2013. Uranium–series dating of the Huashan rock paintings Guangxi Autonom Guangxi Autonomous Region, China. unpublished.

TANG H. 1996. Research on 'Squatting Figures' in primitive art. *Journal of National Museum of China* 1: 3–18.

UNESCO 2016. *Zuojiang Huashan Rock Art Cultural Landscape*, World Heritage List, Paris.

WANG K., QIU Z., CHEN Y. 1988. *Zuojiang Rock Art in Guangxi Zhuang Autonomous Region*. Cultural Relics Press, Beijing.

WANG M. AND JIN H. 2013. *A Pictorial Collection of the Traditional Art of the Yunnan Zhuang*. Yunnan People's Publishing House, Kunming.

WANG N. 1985. *The rock paintings of Cangyuan County, Yunnan: Their discovery and research*. Cultural Relics Press, Beijing.

WU, Y. and JI, X. 2019. *New thematic study. Rock art in East Asia // Thematic study on rock art in East Asia*, ICOMOS.

XU H. 1988. The geographical environment research on the Zuojiang River rock arts which are not at the riverside. *Guang Xi nationalities research* 1: 88–94.

YANG H. 2019. On the changes and religious significance of "The One" schematism of the Han Dynasty. *Journal of Chinese Antiquity* 1: 29–33.

YANG T. 1986. The Yuanjiang Ta Ke cliff painting in Yunnan. *Cultural Relics* 7: 34–38.

YUAN S., CHEN T. and HU Y. 1986. ^{14}C dating researches on Guangxi Ningming Huashan cliff paintings. *Researches on the Ethnic Groups in Guangxi* 4: 27–34.

ZENG Y., PU C., ZHANG G., ZHA D., LIU T., ZHANG Y., WANG H., QIU X., LI K., HU Z., ZHANG Z. (eds.) 1995. *The Bronze Ware of Lijiashan, Yunnan Province*. Yunnan People's Publishing House, Kunming.

ZHANG X. 2001. Second excavation of Lijiashan ancient tomb group in Jiangchuan County, Yunnan. *Archaeology* 2: 25–40+97-101.

Zhang Z. and Wang D. 1975. Excavation of an ancient cemetery at Li–chia–shan in Chiang–chu'an County, Yunnan Province. *Acta Archaeologica Sinica* 2: 97-156+192-215.

Zhao D. and Yang J. 2020. A preliminary study on the squatting figures on the bronze weapons of Southwestern Yi People. *Cultural Relics* 5: 59–69.

Zheng Z., Li Q., Sun Y., Wang G., Wang J., Chen Y., Zhu H., Wang H., Yin Z., Gu L., Wei Q., Hu B., Zhao H. (eds.) 2009. *Warring States tomb at Gaozhuang, Huaiyin*. Cultural Relics Publishing House, Beijing.

Zou H. 1980. *Collected papers on archaeology of Xia, Shang, and Zhou Dynasties*. Cultural Relics Publishing House, Beijing.

26

KEYWORDS: Ammoglyph - Aeolianite – Pleistocene – Palaeoart – Middle Stone Age – Cape south coast

RESCUING ANCIENT PALAEOART IN COASTAL SOUTH AFRICA

Charles W. Helm, Hayley C. Cawthra, Jan C. De Vynck, Carina J. Z. Helm, Renee Rust and Willo Stear

Abstract. The term 'ammoglyph' was coined to describe patterns created by ancestral humans in unconsolidated sand, which are now evident in rock and are interpretable. The only ammoglyphs described thus far are from South Africa's Cape south coast. The potential for images drawn in sand during the Middle Stone Age to be preserved creates a novel opportunity for the appreciation of palaeoart. Once exposed, ammoglyphs are vulnerable to erosive forces or may be situated in inaccessible locations. We report here on the recovery and curation of two ammoglyph specimens, which enables them to be viewed and studied by palaeoart researchers.

Introduction

Examples of ancient palaeoart are uncommon in the global record. This may be a taphonomic phenomenon, as certain art media deteriorate faster than others, with the result that much ancient palaeoart may no longer be discernible (Bednarik 1994). The record of ancient art is thus biased towards items that endure over time. The identification of sand as a canvas through which palaeoart can be interpreted has thus provided a new avenue for its recognition and appreciation. In describing this form of artistic expression, we coined the term 'ammoglyph' ('ammos' being Greek for 'sand') (Helm et al. 2019, 2020a, 2021).

The concept of ancient palaeoart being created in sand was not new (Hodgson and Helvenston 2007, Morriss Kay 2009). What was new was the appreciation that patterns made in sand could be preserved, and re-exposed in aeolianites and cemented foreshore deposits. Southern Africa has an extensive palaeoart record (Bednarik 2013), and the Cape south coast of South Africa contains

Article received: 19 November 2022
Revised I: 25 November 2022
Accepted: 26 November 2022

a remarkably rich Middle Stone Age archaeological record, in which numerous examples of the emergence of modern human behaviour are apparent (e.g., Brown et al. 2009, 2012; d'Errico et al. 2005; Henshilwood et al. 2011; Marean 2010).

Serendipitously, the Cape south coast, where early modern humans survived and seemingly thrived during the harsh climate of Marine Isotope Stage 6 (Marean 2010), happens to contain some of the world's finest aeolianite exposures. This fortunate combination of circumstances sets the scene for aeolianite palaeosurfaces to record events that transpired on them when they were composed of unconsolidated sand. Consequently, we are able to recognize not only ammoglyphs, but also several hominin tracksites from the Middle Stone Age (Helm et al. 2018, 2020b). The presence of ammoglyphs and numerous other vertebrate ichhnosites on this coastline is explained through a combination of, *inter alia*, high sedimentation rates that promote swift burial of tracks and traces, rapid lithification, and shoreline erosion that re-exposes the trace-fossil-bearing surfaces (Roberts and Cole 2003).

Thus far ammoglyphs have only been reported from the Cape south coast. They typically occur on loose aeolianite slabs that lie close to the high tide mark, often at the foot of coastal cliffs from which they were dislodged from their strata of origin by erosion. Once exposed, ammoglyphs become eroded and may be erased by natural forces of wind and water, and may be pounded and fragmented during high tides and storm surges. Alternatively, they may be covered by metres of beach sand or by landslides, or may slump into the sea. Some of the sites are in remote, hazardous locations with limited opportunities for access by other researchers.

We brought the phenomenon of ammoglyphs to the attention of the palaeoart community through our published findings (Helm et al. 2019, 2020a, 2021). However, we had done nothing to preserve these rocks from their destruction or disappearance. Some have subsequently slumped into the sea or can no longer be located. From our perspective these were among the most important rocks in the world, and we recognized the importance of recovering ammoglyphs whenever this was possible. We describe here two examples of successful recovery efforts, one from the Garden Route National Park and one from the coastline east of Still Bay.

The Garden Route National Park site

The most prominent ammoglyph identified at the Garden Route National Park site comprised 60% of a near-perfect circle (Figure 1), with a central depression and two possible knee impressions that hinted at how it might have been created (Helm et al. 2019, 2020a). Close by were two rocks with possible evidence of foraging behaviour. We reported the significance of the discovery to SANParks (South African National Parks) and to Heritage Western Cape. Fortunately, the site was accessible at low spring tide to 4x4 vehicles. The Blombos Museum of Archaeology in Still Bay offered a safe, reliable repository for curation, exhibition and interpretation. A long-term loan agreement was signed between the museum and SANParks, and permission for recovery of the specimens was granted by Heritage Western Cape. On August 2nd, 2019 the three rocks were successfully recovered by an enthusiastic team, loaded onto a 4 x 4 truck, and safely transported on a mattress to Still Bay, where they were carefully manoeuvred into position in one of the exhibit rooms.

The site east of Still Bay

Compared with the Garden Route National Park site, the site east of Still Bay (Helm et al. 2021) presented substantial challenges. Initially, it comprised two adjacent rocks with large geometric triangular patterns (Figure 2) in the form of linear grooves; one contained a bisecting groove that invited comparison with a purported female fertility motif (Gimbutas 1989; Leroi-Gourhan 1982) that appears in palaeoart in Europe dated to as far back as 37—36 ka (White et al. 2012). The significance of the site was obvious to us. However, during subsequent visits to the site the smaller rock could no longer be located, and we later found evidence that it had been destroyed by tidal forces. We knew that the larger rock awaited a similar fate if we did nothing to preserve it.

Figure 1: The circle ammoglyph as it was found in the Garden Route National Park; scale bar = 10 cm

It lay above the high tide mark at the foot of 30 m high cliffs, in an extremely remote location. We estimated that it weighed around 500 kg. The only possible option for its recovery involved a powerful helicopter with a long-line, a net and a skilled pilot. Members of our research team

Figure 2: The 'geometric' ammoglyph east of Still Bay as it was found; scale bar = 10 cm

received funds from writing a chapter on fossil tracks for a book (the Knysna Basin Project), and chose to donate all these funds to the rescue initiative. This funding enabled the rock rescue by helicopter and the subsequent development of an appropriate museum exhibit.

There were risks to attempting such a rock rescue, including the break-up of the rock in the challenging cliff-side terrain, but we knew that its demise was otherwise inevitable. We received a

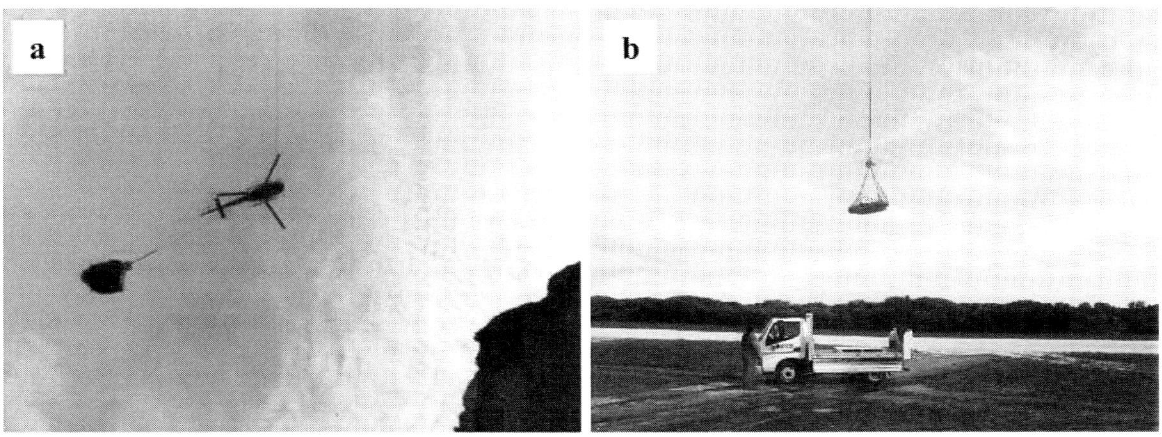

Figure 3: Helicopter rescue of the 'geometric' ammoglyph: (a) lift-off from the cliff-side location (photo credit Richard Webb); (b) gentle drop-off on a pallet on a truck

permit from Heritage Western Cape to proceed, and approval from the landowner. Fortunately, 'Recovery Day' on September 29th, 2022 went smoothly, and our ground crew and the helicopter pilot co-operated superbly. Minutes after being lifted out of the remote location (Figure 3a), the rock was safely placed on a pallet on a truck at the local airfield (Figure 3b). It then began a slow journey to the Blombos Museum of Archaeology, where it was awaited by a team of volunteers ready to carry it into its exhibit space. The operation was filmed by our colleague Richard Webb: https://www.youtube.com/watch?v=L9kvwi_B4TI

Discussion and Conclusions

Establishing the age of these rock specimens is of obvious importance. We have submitted samples for dating through Optically Stimulated Luminescence. Until these results are published, we use stratigraphic correlation to nearby dated sedimentary sequences (Bateman et al. 2011, Roberts et al. 2008) to estimate the ages of the ammoglyphs. Given that in both cases the layer of origin of the specimens appears to be in the lower portion of the cliffs' correlatable stratigraphy, we estimate that the images were registered when the surfaces consisted of unconsolidated sand prior to 130,000 years ago, and clearly during the Middle Stone Age. Bednarik (2013 – p. 7) stated: "there is no doubt a great deal of Pleistocene rock art and mobiliary art in Africa, most of which has not been found or recognised so far". This statement predated the identification of what can be termed 'sand art' in the form of ammoglyphs, which now form an added component of the ancient palaeoart of southern Africa.

It is not surprising that early art thrived on these coastal dunes and beaches. It must have been easier for our ancestors to make grooves in sand using a stick (just as we or our children do on the coast today) than to have to mine and transport ochre to a cave and then get to work engraving an image, as has been described from the same coastline from 77,000 years ago at Blombos Cave (Henshilwood et al. 2002, 2009).

In the cases of the circle ammoglyph and 'geometric' ammoglyph we carefully considered, and were able to exclude, non-anthropogenic origins and more recent anthropogenic activity such as graffiti (Helm et al. 2019, 2021), and have thus been able to attribute them to ancestral human activity. Thus far we have refrained from attempting to ascribe meaning to them.

The plausibility of ammoglyphs cannot be questioned. The relevant question pertains to whether the quality of evidence that we have provided is adequate to withstand critical scrutiny. Further ammoglyphs have been identified, and will be reported on soon. The Blombos Museum of Archaeology now contains all the recovered ammoglyphs (Figure 4), and is accessible to researchers whose input and critique we welcome. We reflect with gratitude that we have not only recognized and described this form of ancient palaeoart, but have managed to secure the safe curation and exhibition of these precious specimens.

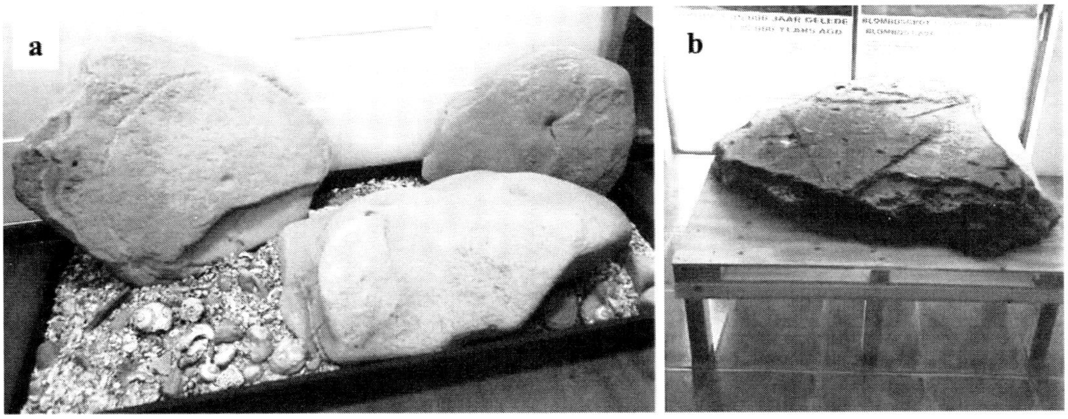

Figure 4: (a)The circle ammoglyph on exhibit in the Blombos Museum of Archaeology, along with two recovered rocks that possibly indicate human foraging; (b) the 'geometric' ammoglyph on exhibit in the Blombos Museum of Archaeology.

Data Availability

Locality data is reposited with the African Centre for Palaeoscience at Nelson Mandela University, Port Elizabeth, South Africa, to be made available to researchers upon request to the corresponding author.

Acknowledgements

We thank SANParks, the Blombos Museum of Archaeology staff and volunteers, Mark Dixon, Linda Helm, Peter Todd, Izak Venter and Richard Webb for their assistance and support.

Charls W. Helm (Corresponding author)
Box 1690
Tumbler Ridge, British Columbia
V0C 2W0
Canada
Email: *helm.c.w@gmail.com*

Hayley Cawthra: *hcawthra@geoscience.org.za*

Jan De Vynck: *jandevynck@vodamail.co.za*

Carina Helm: *helm.carina@gmail.com*

Renee Rust: *rustrenee@gmail.com*

Willo Stear: *willostear@gmail.com*

References

Bateman, M. D., A. S. Carr, A. C. Dunajko, P. J. Holmes, D. L. Roberts, S. J. McLaren, R. I. Bryant, M. E. Marker and C. V. Murray-Wallace 2011. The evolution of coastal barrier systems: a case study of the Middle-Late Pleistocene wilderness barriers, South Africa. *Quaternary Science Reviews* 3: 63–81.

BEDNARIK, R. G. 1994. A taphonomy of palaeoart. *Antiquity* 68(258): 68–74.

BEDNARIK, R. G. 2013. Pleistocene palaeoart of Africa. *Arts* 2: 6–34.

BROWN, K. S., C. W. MAREAN, A. I. R. HERRIES, Z. JACOBS, C. TRIBOLO, D. BRAUN, D. L. ROBERTS, M. C. MEYER and J. BERNATCHEZ 2009. Fire as an engineering tool of early modern humans. *Science* 325: 859–862.

BROWN, K. S., C. W. MAREAN, Z. JACOBS, B. J. SCHOVILLE, S. OESTMO, E. C. FISHER, J. BERNATCHEZ, P. KARKANAS and T. MATTHEWS 2012. An early and enduring advanced technology originating 71,000 years ago in South Africa. *Nature* 491(7425): 590–593.

D'ERRICO, F., C. HENSHILWOOD, M. VANHAEREN and K. VAN NIEKERK 2005. *Nassarius kraussianus* shell beads from Blombos Cave: evidence for symbolic behaviour in the Middle Stone Age. *Journal of Human Evolution* 48: 3–24;

GIMBUTAS, M. 1989. *The language of the Goddess: Unearthing the hidden symbols of Western Civilization*. Thames and Hudson Ltd., New York.

HELM, C. W., R. T. MCCREA, H. C. CAWTHRA, R. M. COWLING, M. G. LOCKLEY, C. W. MAREAN, G. H. H. THESEN, T. PIGEON and S. HATTINGH 2018. A new Pleistocene hominin tracksite from the Cape south coast, South Africa. *Scientific Reports*. Online at: www.nature.com/articles/s41598-018-22059-

HELM, C. W., H. C. CAWTHRA, J. C. DE VYNCK, C. J. HELM, R. RUST and W. STEAR 2019. Patterns in the sand: a Pleistocene hominin signature along the South African coastline? *Proceedings of the Geologists' Association* 130(6): 719–740.

HELM, C. W., H. C. CAWTHRA, J. C. DE VYNCK, C. J. Z. HELM, R. RUST and W. STEAR 2020a. Drawing a line in the sand. *Rock Art Research* 37(1): 95–99.

HELM, C. W., M. G. LOCKLEY, H. C. CAWTHRA, J. C. DE VYNCK, M. G. DIXON, C. J. Z. HELM and G. H. H. THESEN. 2020b. Newly identified hominin trackways from the Cape south coast of South Africa. *South African Journal of Science* 116(9/10), Art. #8156. https://doi.org/10.17159/sajs.2020/8156

HELM, C.W., H. C. CAWTHRA, J. C. DE VYNCK, C. J. Z. HELM, R. RUST, and W. STEAR. 2021. Large geometric patterns from the Middle Stone Age in aeolianites on the Cape south coast, South Africa. *Rock Art Research* 38(1): 10–22.

HENSHILWOOD, C. S., F. D'ERRICO, R. YATES, Z. JACOBS, C. TRIBOLO, G. A. T. DULLER, N. MERCIER, J. C. SEALY, H. VALLADAS, I. WATTS and A. G. WINTLE. 2002. Emergence of modern human behavior: Middle Stone Age engravings from South Africa. *Science* 295: 1278–1280.

HENSHILWOOD, C., F. D'ERRICO and I. WATTS 2009. Engraved ochres from the Middle Stone Age levels at Blombos Cave, South Africa. *Journal of Human Evolution* 57: 27–47.

HENSHILWOOD, C. S., F. D'ERRICO, K. L. VAN NIEKERK, Y. COQUINOT, Z. JACOBS, S.-E. LAURITZEN, M. MENU and R. GARCÍA-MORENO 2011. A 100,000-year-old ochre-processing workshop at Blombos Cave, South Africa. *Science* 334: 219–222.

HODGSON, D. and P. A. HELVENSTON. 2007. The evolution of animal representation: response to Dobrez. *Rock Art Research* 24(1): 116–123.

LEROI-GOURHAN, A. 1982. *The dawn of European art: an Introduction to Palaeolithic cave painting*. Cambridge University Press, Cambridge.

Marean, C. W. 2010. Pinnacle Point Cave 13B (Western Cape Province, South Africa) in context: the Cape floral kingdom, shellfish, and modern human origins. *Journal of Human Evolution* 59(3–4): 425–443.

Morriss-Kay, G. M. 2009. The evolution of human artistic creativity. *Journal of Anatomy* 216(2): 158–176.

Roberts, D. L., M. D. Bateman, C. V. Murray-Wallace, A. S. Carr and P. J. Holmes 2008. Last Interglacial fossil elephant trackways dated by OSL/AAR in coastal aeolianites, Still Bay, South Africa. *Palaeogeography Palaeoclimatology Palaeoecology* 257(3): 261–279.

Roberts, D. and Cole, K. 2003. Vertebrate trackways in Late Cenozoic coastal eolianites, South Africa. *Geological Society of America Abstracts with Programs*, XVI INQUA Congress 70(3), p. 196.

White, R., R. Mensan, R. Bourrillon, C. Cretin, T. F. G. Higham, A. E. Clark, M. L. Sisk, E. Tartar, P. Gardère, P. Goldberg, J. Pelegrin, H. Valladas, N. Tisnérat-Laborde, J. De Sanoit, D. Chambellan and L. Chiotti 2012. Context and dating of Aurignacian vulvar representations from Abri Castanet, France. *Proceedings of the National Academy of Sciences* 109(22): 8450-8455.

Study of Palaeoart of the World, John L. Black & Robin H. Chapple, pp. 367-377

27

KEYWORDS: Murujuga – Burrup Peninsula – Petroglyphs – R G Bednarik – Industry emissions – Ferromanganese coating – Acid rain – Iconoclasm

PETROGLYPHS ON MURUJUGA, WESTERN AUSTRALIA – UNIQUE, ENDANGERED AND DISAPPEARING – THE R.G. BEDNARIK LEGACY FOR HOPE

JOHN L. BLACK AND ROBIN H. CHAPPLE

Abstract: The petroglyphs on Murujuga in northwest Western Australia are unique and Murujuga is regarded by many as the most important prehistoric rock art site in the world. The petroglyphs continue to be endangered and damaged by huge industrial developments and emissions of acid forming gases and nitrogenous compounds. Robert G Bednarik has dedicated his life to documenting the petroglyphs, understanding the chemistry of the ferromanganese rock surface patina and how industrial emissions are destroying the rock art. Most of all, Bednarik has been a towering advocate for removing industry from the area. His efforts and optimism continue today.

Introduction

The petroglyphs on Murujuga (Burrup Peninsula) in northwest Western Australia are unique in the world (Bednarik 2006a; Lorblanchet 2018; Mulvaney 2022). Nowhere else does there remain for all to see today, encapsulated in the rock engravings of Murujuga, potentially 45,000 to 65,000 years of the culture and spiritual beliefs of humankind continuously created through vastly changing environments. The petroglyphs on Murujuga are an unsurpassable tribute to the oldest continuing living culture in the world. They are priceless and irreplaceable. Michel Lorblanchet, the first archaeologist to describe the rock art on Murujuga, recently stated in correspondence '*To my archaeological opinion, Murujuga rock art site is the most important site in the world. ......*

Article received: 4 December 2022
Revised I: 29 November 2022
Revised I: 4 December 2022
Revised II: 4June 2023
Accepted: 5 June 2023

During my life I studied rock art sites in France and in different other countries and I never found sites as important as Murujuga.'

Murujuga is also the site of a huge industrial complex. An iron ore export terminal was established in 1964 and a salt production facility in 1968. Natural gas processing facilities commenced in the early 1980s and were followed by liquefied natural gas production plants in 1995 and 2007. An ammonium fertiliser plant commenced production in 2006 and an ammonium nitrate production facility in 2017. The Australian National Pollution Inventory shows that in 2021-22 the Woodside Energy Limited Burrup gas plants produced annually 9,000 tonnes (t) oxides of nitrogen, 120 t sulphur dioxide and 16,000 t of volatile organic compounds, while the Yara Pilbara fertiliser plants produce another 1,000 t of nitrogen dioxide. The Port of Dampier is one of the busiest bulk-handling ports in the world. During the 2021-2022 were 3,324 vessels entered the port with exports over 160 million t. A single bulk cargo ship burning high-sulphur fuels has been estimated to release 5200 t of sulphur oxides into the atmosphere annually, although since 2021, ships entering Australian ports are to use low sulphur fuel. Nitrogen dioxide and sulphur dioxide form strong nitric and sulphuric acids when mixed with water and air.

There is now undeniable proof the petroglyphs on Murujuga are being degraded by industry and that the outer ferromanganese patina, essential for survival of the petroglyphs, is being dissolved by mineral acids and organic acids from bio-organisms stimulated by the huge nitrogen compound deposition on the rock surfaces (Smith et al. 2022a, Smith et al. 2022b). The fact that we now know the petroglyphs are in such danger of destruction can be traced back to the many earlier activities of Robert Bednarik. Bednarik was one of the first people to realise the extent and significance of the rock art on Murujuga. He recognised the danger industry would pose to the petroglyphs through physical damage and atmospheric emissions. Bednarik made sure he understood the chemistry of the ferromanganese patina and how it would be destroyed by inorganic and organic acids. In addition, Bednarik was an unrelenting advocate for saving the petroglyphs by arguing to governments, industry bosses, academics and others, that industry should not be placed on Murujuga. Bednarik's advocacy was largely responsible for bringing the attention of the public to the plight of the petroglyphs and encouraged the formation of groups such as the Australian Rock Art Research Association for research and Friends of Australian Rock Art to continue public advocacy and protests. The most striking aspect of Bednarik in his efforts to save the Murujuga petroglyphs, is his enormous capacity to read and understand the relevant issues of the day and to communicate these and their possible solutions through prodigious writing to the scientific community and to the public.

Recognition of the significance of Murujuga petroglyphs

Robert was born in Austria in 1944 and became interested in petroglyphs in 1963 when he 'discovered' rock art in limestone caves in Vienna. When industrial development on Murujuga was mooted in the early 1960s, several staff from the Western Australian Museum including Ian

Crawford made a brief visit to the area following their detailed work on Depuch Island. Soon after, other museum staff from the Department of Aboriginal Sites, including Peter Randolph, Vera Novak, John Clarke and Bruce Wright went to Murujuga to start documenting the rock art (Mulvaney 2022). Bednarik recalls that in 1965, he read an Australian newspaper article indicating a lack of archaeological research in northwest Australia. Being an autodidact and enthused by rock art, Bednarik decided to travel to Australia to study the rock art, arriving in Dampier in November 1967 (Bednarik 2006a). He was employed as a Project Manager for a company servicing the mining industry at Dampier (Vinnicombe 2002). Bednarik started photographing and recording petroglyphs on Murujuga, but also spent considerable time studying Aboriginal sites at another Pilbara location undergoing mining development at Mount Tom Price (Bednarik 1977). During these early years, Bednarik worked closely with Traditional Aboriginal Knowledge Holders to better understand the significance and meaning of the rock art motifs. Bednarik's activities complemented those of Enzo Virili, employed by Dampier salt from 1970 to 1974, and Warwick Dix from the Western Australian Museum in documenting petroglyphs on Murujuga (Virili 1977). A description of the Murujuga petroglyphs was presented at the first Australian conference on rock art, held in Canberra in 1974 and sponsored by the Australian Institute of Aboriginal Studies. These discussions in Canberra brought the significance of Murujuga petroglyphs to a wider audience, which resulted in the employment by the Australian Government of the French archaeologist, Michel Lorblanchet, to undertake archaeological studies on Murujuga in 1975-76 and again in 1983-84 (Lorblanchet 1983, 1992, 2018). South African rock art specialist, Patricia Vinnicombe, came to Australia to work with Aboriginal people in the Pilbara region who were still creating pictographs and petroglyphs and could interpret rock art. She was subsequently employed by the Western Australian Department of Aboriginal Sites and the Museum to document petroglyphs on Murujuga in advance of the encroaching industry (Vinnicombe 2002). During this time, she photographed and described many petroglyphs and produced a formal inventory of Murujuga rock art, which include photographs from Bednarik's collection.

Impact of industry on the petroglyphs

Bednarik became fascinated by the outer, thin surface layer of rocks, frequently called the patina, or desert varnish in arid areas of the world. The Murujuga petroglyphs were formed by breaking through the outer brown/red/black patina and removing some of the underlying orange/yellow weathering rind to form a colour and contour contrast. Loss of the patina either through dissolution or flaking destroys the petroglyphs. Bednarik put great effort into understanding the composition of the patina of different types of rocks around the world and speculated on its formation, particularly the influence of environmental pH (Bednarik 1979, 1980). He concluded that the ferromanganese patina found in arid environments would only form under alkaline to neutral environments. Murujuga is a dry desert environment. Bednarik (2002) reported that rainwater at Dampier on Murujuga had a pH around 7.0 with a range of 7.6 to 6.5 in the 1960s prior to industrialisation of the area. Bednarik (2002) commented '*This [ferromanganese] patina is highly susceptible to even minor downward fluctuations in ambient environmental pH, especially in the range from pH 7 to 6*'.

Bednarik (2002) estimated the huge amount of nitrogen dioxide (5,800 t/y) and sulphur oxides (120 t/y) that were being produced by the then existing natural gas treatment facilities on Murujuga. He understood these gases would be deposited on Murujuga rock surfaces and form nitric and sulphuric acids when exposed to water and air. Bednarik (2002) estimated that the amount of acidic forming emissions being produced on Murujuga were greater than for the whole of the Perth metropolitan area. He used basic chemistry to conclude that the nitric and sulphuric acids would dissolve the outer ferromanganese patina and destroy the rock art over time. Bednarik (2002) reports that between early petrochemical industrial development in 1988 and 2001, there was noticeable '*bleaching*' of rock surfaces, which he claimed to confirm through mathematical analysis of colour changes in photographs he had taken over time. Bednarik's (2002) microscopic observations showed the rock surfaces had become '*superficially friable*', with the amorphous silicate skeleton becoming more prominent in the patina as the iron and manganese compounds were dissolved. Bednarik suggested that the rock patina mass may be reduced by <5% to 30% at different places, but emphasised the large variation across rock patina in all measurements.

Bednarik (2007) suggested that because of the very low rainfall on Murujuga, tree canopies can retain large amounts of the dry deposits of nitrogen dioxide and sulphur dioxide because of their many layers of foliage. Rainwater falling through the foliage concentrates these acid forming chemicals beneath the trees. Bednarik (2007) collected the 'through-fall' rain under trees at sites on Burrup Peninsula in 2004 and found it to be highly acidic with pH as low as 3.2. He found complete removal of the rock patina below a tree adjacent to the natural gas facility where the low-pH 3.2 rain was collected (Fig. 1).

Bednarik (1979, 2002) also showed that the patina was completely removed from Murujuga rocks where birds frequently perched. He found that the mean pH was 5.9 across 30 sites on Murujuga where the rock patina had been dissolved by bird droppings.

These conclusions by Bednarik from his early observations that industrial development would physically damage many petroglyphs. His conclusion that a small drop in rock surface pH would dissolve the Murujuga rock patina has proven to be prophetic.

Thousands of rocks with petroglyphs were removed in the early 1980s and 2000s for development and expansion of the natural gas operations (Bednarik 2006b). These rocks were seen by the Western Australian government to be the government's responsibility and directed Ian MacLeod, a corrosion specialist at the Western Australian Museum, to study changes that industry may be having on the rock surface chemistry. MacLeod (2005) found that the pH of rock surfaces near the gas treatment facilities had fallen from near neutral (pH 6.8±0.2) pre-industry to less than 4. MacLeod (2005) stated that: '*the most acidic rock (pH 3.58) … was found down in a gully downwind a few hundred metres from the gas production facility*'.

Figure 1: The photograph from (Bednarik 2007) shows 'bleaching' of patina under a tree near the natural gas treatment facility. Removal of the patina from the rocks extends beyond the tree canopy where water passing through the tree continues down the slope

Critically, MacLeod (2005) showed that, as the rock surface pH falls, there was a logarithmic increase in the dissolution of manganese and iron ions, confirming Bednarik's speculation. Subsequently, theoretical (Black et al. 2017b) and empirical (Smith et al. 2022b) research has confirmed Bednarik's views that the rock surface patina on Murujuga has become lighter and redder in colour and the patina is degrading on rocks with petroglyphs (Fig. 2).

Research within the Murujuga Rock Art Conservation Project at the University of Western Australia has also confirmed that dissolution of manganese from the patina of granophyre and gabbro rocks from Murujuga commences when patina pH falls below 6.10 (5.97-6.22: 95% confidence limits) for granophyre and pH 6.50 (6.01-7.09: 95% confidence limits) for gabbro. Again, these experimental results confirm the proposition by Bednarik (2002) that the critical pH for dissolution of the Murujuga rock surface patina was between pH 6 and pH 7.

Advocacy

Bednarik has been and continues to be a prodigious advocate for the Murujuga petroglyphs. In his writings, he succinctly outlines his concerns about industrial development and its impacts on the rock art, and he almost always provides a potential solution to the issues raised. From his earliest writings, Bednarik realised the importance of research to be undertaken on Murujuga to provide

Figure 2: Left image shows proximity of location to industrial gas flare towers. Red circle in right image highlights area in which the darker rock varnish is starting to break down. A culturally sensitive motif has been blackened out. From Smith et al. (2022b)

empirical evidence for his speculations (Bednarik 1979). He was instrumental in establishing the Australian Rock Art Research Association (AURA) in October 1983. The Association commenced immediately the Journal Rock Art Research, with Robert Bednarik as editor and its first edition appeared in 1984. Bednarik was also responsible for production of the Journal and continues to hold these positions today, with two volumes of the Journal being produced each year. Bednarik writes an Editorial piece for each volume covering many of the perceived issues currently relating to rock art around the world. Bednarik and AURA were responsible for organising the first international academic conference dedicated entirely to the study of prehistoric rock art, held in Darwin during September 1988. The International Federation of Rock Art Organisations was established at this 1988 Darwin Conference. AURA also established a Newsletter in 1986 to cover topics concerning rock art for a wider audience and to outline activities of AURA. This Newsletter continues today covering international rock art issues and is still edited by Bednarik.

Advocacy for research

It was through Bednarik's agitation and publications that the Western Australian government decided in 2002 to establish a four-year research program to determine the processes causing deterioration of the petroglyphs through industrial emissions (Bednarik 2004). The research program was supervised by the Burrup Rock Art Monitoring and Management Committee (BRAMMC) and tenders were given for measuring and modelling of pollutants in the air (Gillett 2008), microbiological studies at Murdoch University (O'Hara 2006) and colour change measurements and gas fumigation studies by CSIRO (Lau et al. 2008). Bednarik (2004) was particularly critical of the colour measurement techniques and fumigation tests to be used by CSIRO. He warned the research would be '*four years of unfocused and purposeless gathering of probably meaningless data*' and '*I predict that the results of this project in 2008 will be inconclusive and unreliable, and that the main finding will be that CSIRO will require further funding to continue the work*'. '*Meanwhile the government expects to continue its destruction of the Dampier rock art, bulldozing many more sites, and permitting the huge petrochemical industries to belch out ever more acidic emissions, at the rate of tens of thousands of tonnes per year.*'

These predictions were proved to be exactly correct. The CSIRO colour measurements continued until 2016, with the claims to 2014 that there were no impacts of industry on the rock art and '*there is no consistent trend for colour change in an increasing or decreasing direction*' (Markley et al. 2015). However, as Bednarik postulated, the results proved to be totally useless because of unsuitable techniques, lack of statistical analysis and false interpretation (Black and Diffey 2016; Black et al. 2017a). The measurements were found to be so unreliable that the results were deemed not to be useful (Data Analysis Australia 2017). In the meantime, the Western Australian government continues to this day to encourage more industrial development on Murujuga (Smith et al. 2022b).

Public advocacy

Bednarik has always been outspoken about the uniqueness of Murujuga rock art and the damage that results from industrial development and emissions (Mulvaney 2022). Partly, as a result of his agitation, a local group of people from the Karratha and Districts Chamber of Commerce led by Gary Slee and including Traditional Elder, Wilfred Hicks, formed the Champions of Burrup Rock Art (COBRA) in the early 1980s to educate the local community and to protest and to lobby the local and state governments to stop further industrial development on Murujuga (Slee 2022). COBRA then morphed in 2006 into a larger national organisation, Friends of Australian Rock Art (FARA), formed by the Australian Greens politician, Robin Chapple, and the organisation's current convenor, Judith Hugo, from 2007. FARA arranged hugely successful protests all around the world with their 'Stand up for the Burrup' campaign to further bring the attention of the world to the plight of Murujuga petroglyphs. FARA continues to protest and make submissions to governments and industry in an endeavour to protect the Murujuga petroglyphs.

Bednarik (2002) had advocated for the non-industrial land on Murujuga to be made into a National Park. The lobbying of Traditional Owners, FARA, AURA, the Western Australian National Trust and Bednarik resulted, in 2007, in the declaration of National Heritage Listing by the Australian government of 44 percent of the Murujuga peninsula and all of the remainder of the Dampier Archipelago. The National Heritage listing resulted in the Australian government, as well as the state government, having power over deciding on the establishment of new industry on Murujuga and the conditions set for industrial operations. Unfortunately, the additional consideration by the Australian government has had little impact on reducing industrial development or emissions on Murujuga.

Bednarik, along with AURA, the National Trust of Western Australia Robin Chapple and Ken Mulvaney, in 2004 were responsible for having Murujuga added to the World Monument Fund's list of the '*100 most-threatened heritage sites*' in the world. Murujuga was the first Australian site to be added to the World Monument Fund list. Despite this listing, the state and Australian governments have allowed industrial development to continue unabated and without meaningful restrictions on emissions into the atmosphere. Both levels of government insist that the petroglyphs and industry can coexist on Murujuga.

Bednarik, in 2011, expressed optimism that changes in the Western Australian and Federal government personnel and attitudes from '*strong leaders*' would bring the required changes in government policies to limit further industrial development (Bednarik 2011). Such optimism, expressed again in 2013 (Bednarik 2013), has not eventuated with further development and high levels of acid forming emissions continuing on Murujuga. Undeterred, Bednarik continues to advocate strongly for preservation of the world unique Murujuga petroglyphs. He wrote in despair that '*despite the declaration of the Murujuga National Park, the industry and the cultural monument to the massacred Yaburara simply cannot coexist, because of the immense acidic pollution by industry. Since the rock art is immovable, it is essential that the industry be relocated*' (Bednarik 2017).

These same sentiments were recently expressed by Mulvaney (2022) '*It cannot be clearer: for the Murujuga petroglyphs to survive, industrial emissions must be eliminated ...... and any future industrial development has to be placed away from the Dampier Archipelago. Industrial representatives and those in government continue with the mantra of coexistence, but what has occurred in the last 50 years proves that 50,000 years of culture heritage can be unhesitatingly erased from existence.*'

Conclusions

Bednarik and many others continue to ask themselves, why do Australian governments persist on placing industrial infrastructure among the petroglyphs of Murujuga and why do they not insist on reducing the permitted levels of emissions from industry to amounts that will not damage the petroglyphs?

Is it, as Ludlam (2021) may suggest in his book '*Full Circle*', the governments are 'Captured States'? Ludlam describes that, in a 'Captured State', the State regulatory agencies operate and legislate in accordance with the private interests instead of the public interests. Or, is the lack of respect for Murujuga petroglyphs, primarily a simple disregard of an ancient and ongoing culture of Australia's original people-iconoclasm?

José Antonio González Zarandona (2020), a world expert in heritage destruction, has characterised this continued damage to the Murujuga petroglyphs as 'landscape iconoclasm', the intentional act to dishonour an entire belief system and supersede Western economic values above Indigenous living spiritual values. He argues that the scarred industrial landscape of Murujuga, bulldozed for decades by industry, intentionally stamps visual confirmation that there are "victors and vanquished" in this landscape. Multinational industry over Aboriginal people, their culture and their heritage.

Landscape iconoclasm is another example of 'othering' described by Edward Said in his 1978 book '*Orientalism*'. Said describes 'othering' as '*disregarding, essentialising, denuding the humanity of another culture, people or geographical region*'. The concept is expanded by Naomi Klien (2019) in her book '*On Fire*'. Klein states that once the 'other' '*has been firmly established, the ground is softened for any transgression: violent expulsion, land theft, occupation and invasion*'. The 'other' simply does not have the same rights as those making the distinction. This description is exactly what has happened on Murujuga, but with a massacre of the population included (Gara 1983). Pursuing justice for the Murujuga petroglyphs and their custodians has been a lifetime pursuit of Robert Bednarik and his great efforts continue.

Acknowledgements

We acknowledge the intergenerational trauma experienced by the Traditional Owners of Murujuga and the adjacent Language Groups. We too, feel their pain from the ongoing senseless destruction of a magnificent culture for the sake of short-term financial gain and natural resource exploitation. We acknowledge also the enormous efforts by many including Traditional Owners, Tim Douglas, Wilfred Hicks and more recently the members of 'Save Our Songlines', Ken Mulvaney, Judith Hugo and FARA members, Gary and Glen Slee, Benjamin Smith and others in their ongoing endeavours to save the Murujuga petroglyphs for future generations. JLB is extremely grateful to the Murujuga Aboriginal Corporation Board and Circle of Elders who, in 2016 and 2017, supported his proposal to raise money from the concerned public to conduct research into understanding the science relating to preservation of the petroglyphs through the Murujuga Rock Art Conservation Project.

Dr John L. Black AM
Warrimoo, New South Wales, Australia
E-mail: jblack@pnc.com.au

Hon Robin H. Chapple
Chapple Research, Derby, Western Australia
E-mail: chappleresearch@iinet.net.au

References

Bednarik, R. G. 1977. A survey of prehistoric sites in the Tom Price region, North Western Australia. *Archaeology and Physical Anthropology in Oceania*, 12: 51-76.

Bednarik, R. G. 1979. The potential of rock patination analysis in Australian archeology - part 1. *The Artefact*, 4: 14-38.

Bednarik, R. G. 1980. The potential of rock patination analysis in Australian archeology - part 2. *The Artefact*, 5: 47-77.

Bednarik, R. G. 2002. The survival of the Murujuga (Burrup) petroglyphs. *Rock Art Research*, 19(1): 29.

Bednarik, R. G. 2004. Recipe for disaster. *AURA Newsletter*, 21 (1): 5-6.

Bednarik, R. G. 2006a. *Australian apocalypse: The story of Australia's greatest cultural monument*. Occasional AURA Publication No. 14. Australian Rock Art Research Association, Melbourne.

Bednarik, R. G. 2006b. *Quantification of the amount of rock art lost at Dampier. Rock Art Research*, 23: 137–140.

Bednarik, R. G. 2007. The science of Dampier rock art - Part 1. *Rock Art Research,* 24 (2): 209-246.

Bednarik, R. G. 2011. The Dampier Campaign. *Rock Art Research,* 28 (1): 27-34.

Bednarik, R. G. 2013. Final victory at Murujuga imminent. *Rock Art Research,* 30 (1): 130-131.

Bednarik, R. G. 2017. Solving the Dampier controversy. *Editorial, Rock Art Research,* 34 (2): 126-129.

Black, J. L. and S. Diffey 2016. *Reanalysis of the colour changes from 2004 to 2014 on Burrup Peninsula rock art sites*, Report submitted to the Western Australian Government, Department of Environment Regulation

Black, J. L., I. Box and S. Diffey 2017a. Inadequacies of research used to monitor change to rock art and regulate industry on Murujuga ('Burrup Peninsula'), Australia. *Rock Art Research,* 34(2): 130-148.

Black, J. L., I. D. MacLeod and B. W. Smith 2017b. Theoretical effects of industrial emissions on colour change at rock art sites on Burrup Peninsula, Western Australia. *Journal of Archaeological Science: Reports*, 12: 457-462.

Data Analysis Australia, J. Henstridge and K. Haskard 2017. *Review of CSIRO report of Burrup Peninsula rock art monitoring*, Department of Environment Regulation, Western Australia. https://www.der.wa.gov.au/images/documents/our-work/consultation/Burrup-Rock-Art/DAA-independent-review-report-May-2017.pdf.

Gara, T. 1983 The Flying Foam massacre: An incident on the northwest frontier, Western Australia. paper presented to the *Archaeology at ANZAAS 1983, 53rd ANZAAS Congress*, Perth, Western Australia.

Gillett, R. 2008 *Burrup Peninsula air pollution study: Report for 2004/2005 and 2007/2008*, Department of Environment and Conservation, Western Australia.

González Zarandona, J. A. 2020. *Murujuga: rock art, heritage, and landscape iconoclasm.* Philadelphia: University of Pennsylvania Press.

Klein, N. 2019. *On Fire: the burning case for a green deal.* Allen Lane part of Penguin Random House, UK.

Lau, D., E. Ramanaidou, S. Furman, A. Hacket, M. Caccetta, M. Wells and B. McDonald 2008. *Burrup Peninsula Aboriginal Petroglyphs: Colour Change and Spectral Mineralogy 2004–2007*, CSIRO. https://www.der.wa.gov.au/images/documents/our-work/programs/Colour_Change_and_Spectral_Mineralogy_2007_report_Sept2008.pdf.

Lorblanchet, M. 1983. Chronology of the rock engravings of Gum Tree Valley and Skew Valley near Dampier, WA. In: M. Smith (ed.), *Archaeology at ANZAAS 1983*. Western Australian Museum, Perth, pp. 39-59.

Lorblanchet, M. 1992. The rock engraving of Gum Tree Valley and Skew Valley, Dampier, Western Australia: chronology and functions of the sites. In: J. McDonald and I.P. Haskovec (eds), *State of the Art: Regional Rock Art Studies in Australia and Melanesia*. AURA Publication, Melbourne, pp. 39-59.

Lorblanchet, M.2018. *Archaeology and petroglyphs of Dampier (Western Australia): An archaeological investigation of Skew Valley and Gum Tree Valley.* Technical Report of the Australian Museum, Number 27. Doi.org/10.3853/j.1835-4211.27.2018.

Ludlam, S. 2021. *Full Circle: a search for the world that comes next.* Black Inc., Schwartz Media, Carlton, Victoria Australia.

MacLeod, I. 2005. Effects of moisture, micronutrient supplies and microbiological activity on the surface pH of rocks in the Burrup Peninsula. *Triennial meeting (14th), The Hague, 12-16 September 2005,* pp. 386-393. James & James, London.

Markley, T., M. Wells, E. Ramanaidou, D. Lau and D. Alexander 2015. Burrup Peninsula aboriginal petroglyphs: Colour changes & spectral mineralogy 2004-2014. CSIRO, Australia. Report EP1410003. https://www.der.wa.gov.au/our-work/programs/36-burrup-rock-art-monitoring-program.

Mulvaney, K.J. 2022. Without them – what then? People, petroglyphs and Murujuga. *In: (Eds. Tacon, P.S.C, May, S.K., Frederick, U.K., McDonald, J. 'Terra Australis 55: Histories of Australian Rock Art'* Chapter 9, p155-172. http://doi.org/10.22459/TA55.2022

O'Hara, G. 2008 *Monitoring of microbial diversity on rock surfaces of the Burrup Peninsula. Monitoring of microbial diversity on rock surfaces of the Burrup Peninsula.* https://web.archive.org/web/20091002135201/http:/www.dsd.wa.gov.au/documents/Microbial_Diversity_on_Rock_Surfaces_-_Sept2008(1).doc.

Said, E.W. 1978. *Orientalism.* Routledge and Kegan Paul Ltd. London.

Slee, G. 2022. *Stompers.* Classic Slee Pty Ltd. Karratha, Western Australia.

Smith, B.W., J.L. Black, S. Hœrlé, M.A. Ferland, S.M. Diffey, J.T. Neumann and T. Geisler 2022a. The impact of Industrial pollution on the rock art of Murujuga, Western Australia. *Rock Art Research* 39: 1-14.

Smith, B.W., J.L. Black, K.J. Mulvaney S. Hœrlé 2022b. Monitoring rock art decay: Archival images of petroglyphs on Murujuga, Western Australia. *Conservation and Management of Archaeological Sites.* Online: DOI: 10.1080/13505033.2022.2131077: https://doi.org/10.1080/13505033.2022.2131077

Vinnicombe, P. 2002. Petroglyphs of the Dampier Archaepilago: Background to development and descriptive analysis. *Rock Art Research,* 19(1): 3-27.

Virili, F.L. 1977. Aboriginal sites and rock art of the Dampier Archipelago. In: P.J. Ucko (ed.) *Form in Indigenous art: Schematisation in the art of Aboriginal Australia and prehistoric Europe*, pp. 439-451.

28

KEYWORDS: Rock Art Heritage – Quantifying – Sustainable development – Standardisation of management parameters – Socio-economic development

QUANTIFYING THE SUSTAINABLE DEVELOPMENT OF ROCK ART HERITAGE

RAM KRISHNA

Abstract: India is one of the three countries in the world having the richest treasures of rock art. However, most of the rock art heritage remains neglected. Even a few of them that have been declared protected by the State and Central Government, are not properly managed in terms of the sustainable development of the heritage site. The author of this paper has studied the problem, and observed that the decision making to manage the site is largely based on individual perception and priorities. The consequences of wrong decisions are fatal and irreversible. In order to meet the challenge, the dynamics of the rock art heritage sites have been understood holistically and standardized the variables to measure and manage the heritage site professionally. Based on the identified critical variables, the stock flow network is developed for modelling and simulation so that future scenarios can be built in real time for efficient and effective conservation and management of the rock art heritage site.

1. Introduction

1.1. Culture

Culture is one of the most important pillars in nation building. Strong cultural roots provide the society and the country, prosperity and strong spirit to meet the challenges coming in the life. Therefore, understanding and conserving the culture is crucial for continuity of our wisdom and traditions for our prosperity for living a meaningful and blissful (*anandmayi*) life (Kumar 2011a, 2011b, 2015).

Article received: 22 December 2022
Revised I: 25 March 2023
Revised II: 10 April 2023
Revised III: 24 May 2023
Revised IV:5 July 2023
Accepted: 30 July 2023

1.2. Importance of Rock Art Heritage

Rock Art is a global phenomenon. and it is the most valuable heritage in the world (Kumar, 2015). It cannot be compared to any other kind of heritage as it is the earliest evidence survived of human evolution and culture. It is the expression of very important aspects of life. It has incomparable and irreplaceable value. Continuously learning from it is important to understand the evolution process, so that we can embrace the process of harmonization with our immediate environment for achieving sustainable and productive development.

1.3. Sustainable Development

According to the Brundtland Commission's definition and a multilateral agreement reached at the UN Conference on Environment and Development in Rio de Janeiro in 1992, sustainable development is defined as a development that satisfies current demands without jeopardising the capacity of future generations to satiate their own needs. In the World Summit on Sustainable Development at Johannesburg, South Africa in 2002 (UNESCO Operational guidelines 2017) the concept of the three pillars of sustainable development—the environmental, social, and economic pillars, was first articulated, they are thought to be "interdependent and mutually reinforcing".

1.4. Sustainable Development of Rock Art Heritage

The road for a UNESCO world historic site's sustainable development is outlined in the UNESCO treaty of 1972. As a result, "Sustainable development" has gained support from the international community. Implementing operational principles within a thoughtful management plan, the protection and conservation of the natural and cultural heritage site make a substantial contribution to sustainable development. (UNESCO Operational guidelines 2017).

The protection of the environment, as well as the social and economic advancements of the local populations, are the main topics. The need to fully contribute as a World Heritage site to sustainable development must be tapped into throughout time (UNESCO Operational Guidelines 2017).

1.5. Sustainable Use of Heritage

World historic properties may support a variety of current and future uses that are ecologically and culturally sustainable and may raise the standard of living in the communities in issue. Additionally, no use diminishes the heritage's Outstanding Universal Value (UNESCO Operational guidelines 2017).

1.6. Protection and Conservation of Rock Art Heritage

The practise of protecting rock art from deterioration caused by the natural factors or human activity is known as conservation (Kumar 2015:168). The protection of the rock art legacy and its biological surroundings from all threats is part of conservation, which is a long-term and comprehensive process. The constant threat of human vandalism, the consequences of climate change, and other natural causes affect rock art. Since we are dealing with the oldest repository of knowledge and wisdom, preservation should be our primary goal (Kumar 2015).

1.7. Rock Art and Tourism

Each year nearly 3.1 million visitors come to the places where the first inhabitants of Europe produced their transcendental rock art (https://www.coe.int/en/web/cultural-routes/prehistoric-rock-art-trails). Tourist as industry provided INR 8.31 lakh crore or 6.3% of the national GDP in 2015 and 37.315 million jobs in India, it is one of the most important means of utilising heritage for economic benefit (www.ibef.org). In case of India, Bhimbetka near Bhopal, Madhya Pradesh, is the only UNESCO world heritage rock art site. It attracted 78,000 visitors in 2019. Hence, tourism based around rock art heritage sites has great potential in in India. Therefore, there is a great potential to bring more major rock art heritage sites in the list of UNESCO world heritage title. It will enhance the global popularity of them and thus will attract maximum visitors both domestically and from all over the world. The UNESCO World Heritage status to a site serves as a marketing tool and a catalyst for socioeconomic growth through tourism. (UNESCO operational guidelines 2017).

1.8. Scope of the study

Above study demonstrates the potential for finding the possibility of developing more rock art heritage sites to tourist attraction and manage it as a resource for sustainable socio-economic development of cultural and natural heritage. Quantification and standardisation will provide the platform to manage the rock art heritage in a better way by the managers.

2. Research gap

Therefore, long term conservation of rock art heritage sites is the most important priority of us as a global community. The management of Altamira, Chauvet, etc limestone cave rock art heritage sites in Europe in close system and Kakkadu National Park in Darwin, Australia in open system and other many examples have already addressed many issues raised in management of rock art heritage sites in a systematic way. Solution is already there with the experiential learning from above cases. But the solutions are subjective and are subject to vary on the basis of many different parameters like Economic state of the country, tourism policy, awareness about rock art, understanding of rock art preservation and tourism development etc. that changes the rationality of decision making and makes it more challenging.

The challenges in rock art conservation are of two kinds, 1. Natural, and 2. Human interference. There is a limit to human capacity to understand the nature and all its dynamics. Hence, challenges posed by natural factors have to be met in the perspective of our awareness and knowledge, especially in managing the environment at micro-level in close environment.

Meeting the challenges of environment protection in open system is relatively easy. However, it is difficult to check the human interference with rock art heritage sites and their environment. It has been depleting the natural environment and damaging the rock art heritage sites for long time. However, the sites have been preserved for thousands of years in their natural setting. So, the solution lies in optimizing the use of resources and keeping the balance in management for the sustainable development of a rock art heritage site and its natural environment. Rock art heritage sites are vulnerable to human interaction more than anything. Multiple factors play role for making optimal decisions. Many issues are not addressed in a sustainable way because of the subjectivity of the management plan.

3. Framework of the study

Decision making - Macro level– outside the heritage premises – Perception of associated Stake holders

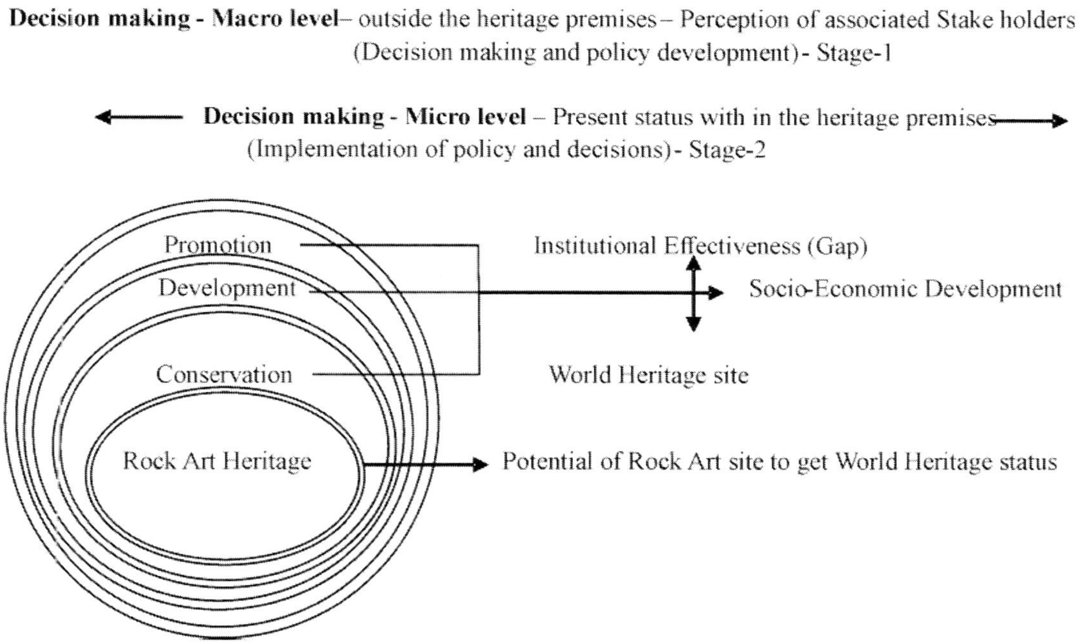

Figure 1: Conceptual Framework of the Decision making in rock art heritage

4. Methodology

Therefore, author has suggested to standardize the inputs needed for the sustainable development. Secondary and primary data analysis is done to identify the parameters. Most of the parameters are sourced from the literature produced by UNESCO. Primary data is collected to check the present status of the parameters of the site. Systems dynamics is applied as approach and causal effect diagram is prepared in phase -1, so all the dynamics can be observed to understand the complexities with holistic understanding, and identified important factors and their priorities. In the phase – 2, CGPA scheme is applied to quantify and standardise the important parameters for sustainable development. In phase – 3, a stock flow network (model) is developed for modelling and simulation of future scenario on the basis of secondary and primary data and a model is presented to be used for helping in decision making for the sustainable development of the rock art heritage sites.

5. Analysis and findings

5.1.1. Phase one: Present status of dynamics of rock art heritage - Causal Loop Diagram and its Analysis

A causal loop diagram is developed to understand the interconnected dynamics of the challenges of sustainable development of a rock art heritage The author has gone through all the experience available in the form of literature to generalise the case. Besides, I personally interviewed most of the stakeholders, some on telephone, to know the present status. On the basis of the literature review, observations made, suggestions received and facts collected in the process, a Causal Loop Diagram is prepared using positive and negative forces considered as reinforcing (R+) and balancing (B-) respectively which is as follows:

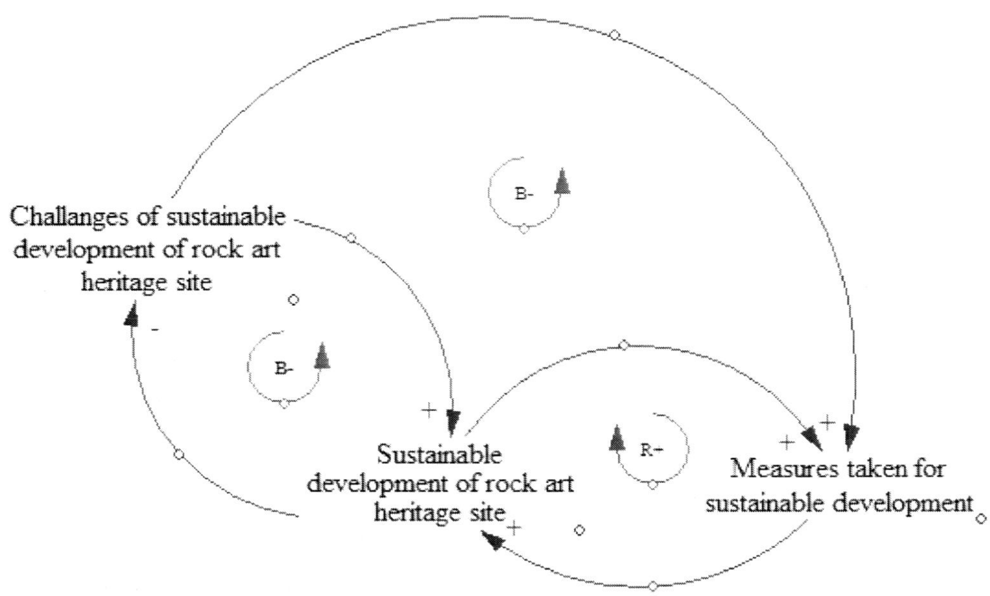

Figure 2: Causal Loop diagram 1 of sustainable development of rock art heritage

Table 1: Description of CLD 1

S. No	*Relationship*			*Nature of Loop*	*Number of Loop*
1.	Sustainable development of rock art heritage (+)	(-)	Challenges of rock art conservation	Balancing	1
		(+)	Measures taken for conservation	Reinforcing	2
		(-) (+)	Challenges of rock art conservation Measures taken for conservation	Balancing	3

Explanation of the above causal loop diagram shows that there are only two dimensions of long terrm survival of rock art heritage. Therefore, the focus should be on reducing the challenges and increasing the measures taken.

In the other loop there are only two challenges, human interaction and weathering effect on site. The natural taphonomic effect of weathering can be minimized, but cannot be stopped completely. Therefore, the emphasis should be on keeping the natural setting of the site intact and minimizing the human interference with it.

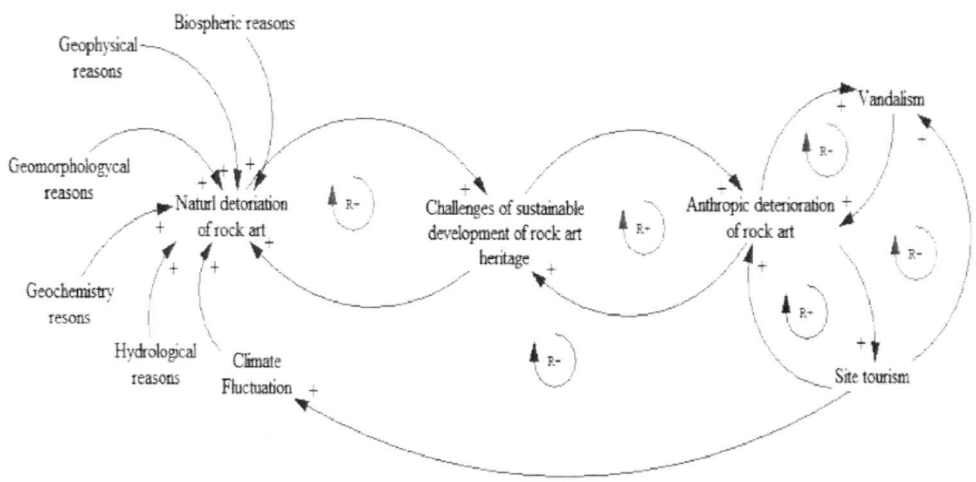

Figure 3: Causal Loop diagram 2, Dynamics of the challenges of sustainable development of rock art heritage

Table 2: Description of CLD 2

S. No	*Relationship*			*Nature of Loop*	*Number of Loop*
1.	Challenges of Sustainable development of rock art heritage (+)	(+)	Natural deterioration of rock art	Reinforcing	4
		(+)	Anthropic deterioration of rock art	Reinforcing	5
	Anthropic deterioration of rock art (+)	(+)	Vandalism	Reinforcing	6
		(+)	Site tourism	Reinforcing	7
		(+) (+)	Site tourism Vandalism	Reinforcing	8
		(+) (+) (+) (+)	Site tourism Climate fluctuation Natural deterioration Challenges of Sustainable development of rock art heritage	Reinforcing	9

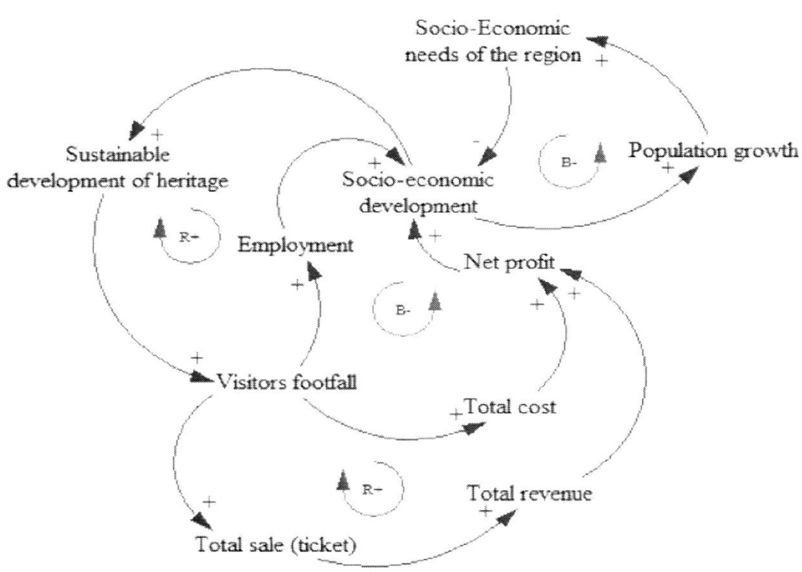

Figure 4: Causal Loop diagram 3, Sustainable development of rock art heritage and its connection with the local community

Table 3: Description of CLD 3

S. No	*Relationship*			***Loop***	***Number of Loop***
1	Visitor foot fall (+)	(+) (+) (+)	Employment Socio-Economic development Sustainable development of heritage	Reinforcing	10
		(+) (-) (-)	Total cost Net profit Socio-Economic development Sustainable development of heritage	Balancing	11
		(+) (+) (+) (+)	Total sale Net profit Socio-Economic development Sustainable development of heritage	Reinforcing	12
2	Socio-Economic needs (+)	(-) (+)	Socio-economic development Population growth	Balancing	13

Explanation: In the above causal loop diagram it is clearly visible that local people have continuous interaction with the heritage site due to economic dependency on the environment around the heritage site. That also increases with the population increase. This creates the need to minimize the pressure on environment. To meet this challenge the first option is to develop the heritage site for tourism and create jobs and employment to local people. So that their concern towards protecting the site and environment is increased rather exploiting it for personal use.

Development of Tourism: With the increase of tourism the number of visitors will increase, which will boost up the socio-economic development that will create the reinforcing loop. But, the increased number of visitors will increase the human interaction with the site, hence the balancing loop is developed increasing the challenges for long term survival of rock art heritage.

It emphasizes that the increased tourist flow directly to the heritage site will damage the site in extreme, and ultimately tourism will be affected, and the whole purpose of long-term survival of heritage will be defeated.

5.1.2. Observations made for long-term survival of rock art heritage

Other than the literature. Researcher has personally visited 10 different protected rock art heritage sites in India further observed and collected the challenges on the practical basis on the site.

Table 4: Observations of challenges made for long-term survival of rock art heritage.

1	Consistent availability of drinking water in deep forest / hill area
2	Consistent availability of electricity water in deep forest / hill area
3	Job security of onsite staff
4	Regularity of salary of onsite staff
5	Short duration of job period of one month if security is provided by Home Guards personals
6	Site location in deep interior area
7	No immediate backup to security in case of any issue to handle
8	Monitoring of big site
9	Lack of awareness of the local people
10	People lacing social character
11	How to behavior at heritage
12	Lack of belongingness of people with heritage
13	Lack of funds
14	Lack of human resource
15	Legal settlements issues of institutions
16	Public Pressure
17	Lack of rock art expertise
18	Lack of personal intention
19	Lack of understanding of developing a heritage site
20	On ground effort to connect people
21	No jobs in rock art discipline
22	Lack of scientific research
23	No interpretation center / Museum
24	Beurocracy is not supportive for project executions (long term decision taking, No concensus on future vision and actions
25	Different structural systems of management of rock art
26	Not a single process is standardised in whole system of rock art heritage
27	Deforestation
28	Door to door awareness campaign is needed
29	Connect youngsters
30	Develop sense of belongingness and pride for individual and country
31	Lack of audio-visual content, short stories, cultural pride
32	Lack of dedicated security personals, insufficient salaries, unsecured future, lack of sufficient number of people
33	Not only protecting the site, the whole ecosystem should be protected that becomes a challenge with big complexes (especially the sites protected by the States).

34	Lack of standardization
35	Lack of archaeological excavations on rock art sites
36	Personal discretion on subject of national interest
37	Need of multidisciplinary approach
38	Development of trained human resource in exploration, documentation, excavation, dating, guides, chronological interpretations, digital marketing and promotion, Short term survival courses using cultural knowledge
39	Branding of Indian rock art heritage
40	Strict laws for misconduct, option for instant penalty
41	Tourism and site development should be close enough but not overlapping
42	Job creation and employment generation to occupy more than 50% of the population living nearby
43	Avoiding lethargy in the execution
44	Holistic decision taking system / approach
45	Deciding roles, deadlines for routine tasks, accountabilities, consequences, transparency.

On the basis of the observations made. Author has identified variable as Starting terminals are as follows: one time investment (amount of money), scientific study (number of standard published papers), unintentional damage; measures taken for conservation, (number of measures); bottlenecks identified are as follows: visitors (Number of visitors), maintenance, monitoring, and feedback; critical points of contact are as follows: maintenance and operational expenses, uncontrolled human interaction with the heritage, number of visitors, connect with site (belongingness).

5.1.3. Analysing dynamics of rock art heritage

As we are right now following the reductionist approach in terms of managing the rock art heritage conservation. But we are in the process of learning that any effort made by human will have its consequences. There are infinite possibilities of consequences of action taken by the conservators. That makes the need to understand the overall dynamics of the environment. Increased awareness will aid the overall decision making from the long-term perspective of sustainable development. Dynamics associated with rock art heritage are already identified (Ram Krishna 2020). It has been already concluded that damage done by natural impact is almost impossible to avoid but the damage can be mitigated or can be managed to minimize the negative impact as the natural forces cannot be blocked, it can only be diverted or channelize (Bednarik 2007. Therefore, we can check the damage done by human interaction for the protection of rock art heritage. It has been established that the major damage was done by human overloading on the heritage site that disturbs and damages the natural or original environment of stability (Bednarik 2007, Kumar 2015). That created the perception to keep visitors or tourists outside the heritage which is convenient to the heritage. It is not a practical approach as the people will find the way to trespass and interfere with the site. It increases vandalism and anti-social activities. Illegal, mining, animal grazing, deforestation, domestic construction, etc. are the outcomes of this factor. It is hard to keep human interaction away from the rock art heritage sites for a long time. Therefore, we have to systemize the human interaction and regulate it rather than unsystematic and unregulated growth of population density and socio-economic needs of the region. In this perspective we can conclude that:

1. Managing human interaction at rock art heritage site is the direction for Sustainable development and long-term conservation of it.
2. Human interaction with the heritage site inevitable.
3. Managing socio-economic pressure on the site including vandalism are the priority.

To mitigate these risks solution has been provided by the experienced scholars is as follows:

1. Instead of opening the complete rock art heritage site to the visitors, only one part of it at a time should be opened with full precautions.
2. Load bearing capacity of the heritage site should be calculated before opening it to the visitors.
3. Elevated pathways be made to channelize the visitors. It will also keep them away from the heritage.
4. Only guided tours are allowed.

However, all these are subjective inputs. Every rock art heritage site is unique in terms of area of the site, number of shelters in the site, climatic conditions, geographic conditions, rock type and rules / regulations / laws, etc. Decision makers of these heritage sites are changed without giving a thought on their experience and abilities. It affects the decision making in a proper and holistic way to meet out the challenges efficiently. That is why, it emphasise the need to measure the parameters and standardize them for the efficient malmanagement of a rock art heritage site.

5.2. Phase 2: Standardisation of sustainable development of rock art heritage

To implement management in order to achieve sustainable development, quantification of rock art heritage parameters is required to measure them. CGPA (Cumulative Grade Point Average) is calculated to quantify the parameters.

5.2.1. A proposed scoring scheme for rating the management of a rock art heritage site

The primary concern of the triple bottom line of sustainable development relates to rock art heritage sites and shows how environmental consciousness is included. The ability of the future generations to meet their own needs is not compromised in order to meet the requirements of the present. It then goes on to apply this business model to the sustainable development of rock art heritage sites, and it suggests the various performance criteria relevant to a department for the sustainable development of a rock art heritage site need to be shortlisted in consultation with the experts and pertinent stakeholders. Scores on the various characteristics can be calculated on a scale from 0 to 100 for the purpose of evaluating the sustainability performance for the management of a rock art heritage site. In order to come up with the CGPA score for management of a site, the weighted average scheme is used (Swami 2021):

The various parameters of performance pertinent to a department need to be shortlisted in consultation with the experts and relevant stakeholders. For example, some parameters could be

- Environmental (Water, Energy, Waste, Emissions, Biodiversity)
- Social (Health, Safety, Social Relations, Training and Education, Diversity, Opportunity, Equity, Community Involvement, Culture Preservation)
- Economic (Employment, Profitability, Demand generation)

The scoring of a site on the various parameters (or sub-parameters) can be measured on a scale from 0 to 10. Further, for each parameter, an importance weight can be assigned signifying its salience in the performance evaluation. For ease of calculation, the weights can be so assigned that they sum up to 100.

Once the above data is collected, the CGPA can be calculated by a multiplicative-summative formula, as given below:

$$CGPA = (w_1 r_1 + w_2 r_2 + \ldots + w_K r_K)/100$$

Here,

w = weight of a parameter (1-100),

r = scoring of a parameter (0-10),

K = total number of parameters

CGPA score thus calculated will be on a scale from 0 to 10 (Swami et al. 2000, 2021).

The score can be used for comparisons of the importance of the three parameters of Environmental, Social and Economic factors. Once the score is calculated, the site managers will know their current status, say, in year 2020. Accordingly, targets can be set for future, say, for years 2025, and 2030. This will also help guide strategies and actions for site managers.

In view of the above discussion, the following key entities can be considered as an initial set affecting the sustainable development of rock art heritage sites:

- International bodies like UNESCO
- Government agencies like Archaeological Survey of India (ASI), Tourism departments, etc.
- Businesses
- NGOs like Rock Art Society of India (RASI)
- Local and indigenous communities
- Academic institutions and Historians
- Society at large

5.3. Phase 3

Rock art heritage sites are very sensitive to decisions. The consequences of a wrong decision cannot be turned back and it also needs a lot of investment to manage as it is usually in deep forest areas and have bigger surface area than any other heritage site. To meet this challenge scenario building of the decisions making and its impact assessment is necessary. That is why the model is proposed.

To comprehend how the rock art legacy system behaves in relation to some of the key system variables, a dynamic model has been built. It will serve as the foundation for understanding the needs of the inputs for formulating policies and conducting tactical and strategic planning.

The structure of the systemic model was developed in order to comprehend how the dynamics of development behave and how they affect the preservation of the heritage of rock art. It makes sense that persons employed from local families would be concerned about the health of our legacy given that both the environment and our heritage are essential to their way of life. Following that, the part of the profit will be reinvested for the region's sustainable growth.

5.3.1. Data Collection

Both primary and secondary data are considered to give practical values in the model as per the requirement of the variables

5.3.2. Model description

This model is developed on adoption of theoretical logic based on BASS model of population adoption (Bass 1994) and modified it for rock art heritage system. Bhimbetka as UNESCO Rock Art World Heritage site has been taken as reference to standardize the behaviour of the system for world heritage sites. Stock, flow, and auxiliary variables, most critical for the development of the model are considered. It can be called as Ram Krishna's Model for sustainable development of a rock art heritage site.

Table 5: Variables of the Model developed for sustainable development of the heritage

Variable Types	*Variables used in the Model*
Stock	Number of visitors, 2. Total sale, 3. Fund for sustainable use as net profit, 4. Operational expenses, 5. Population impact ratio, 6. Economic development of the region
Flow	Rate of visitors growth, 2. Selling, 3. Rate of cost growth, 4. Employment ratio to visitors, 5. Rate of revenue growth, 6. Rate of profit growth, 7. Development
Auxiliary	Promotional effectiveness, 2. Population growth, 2. Contact ratio, 3. Average price per visitor, 4. Unit cost per visitor

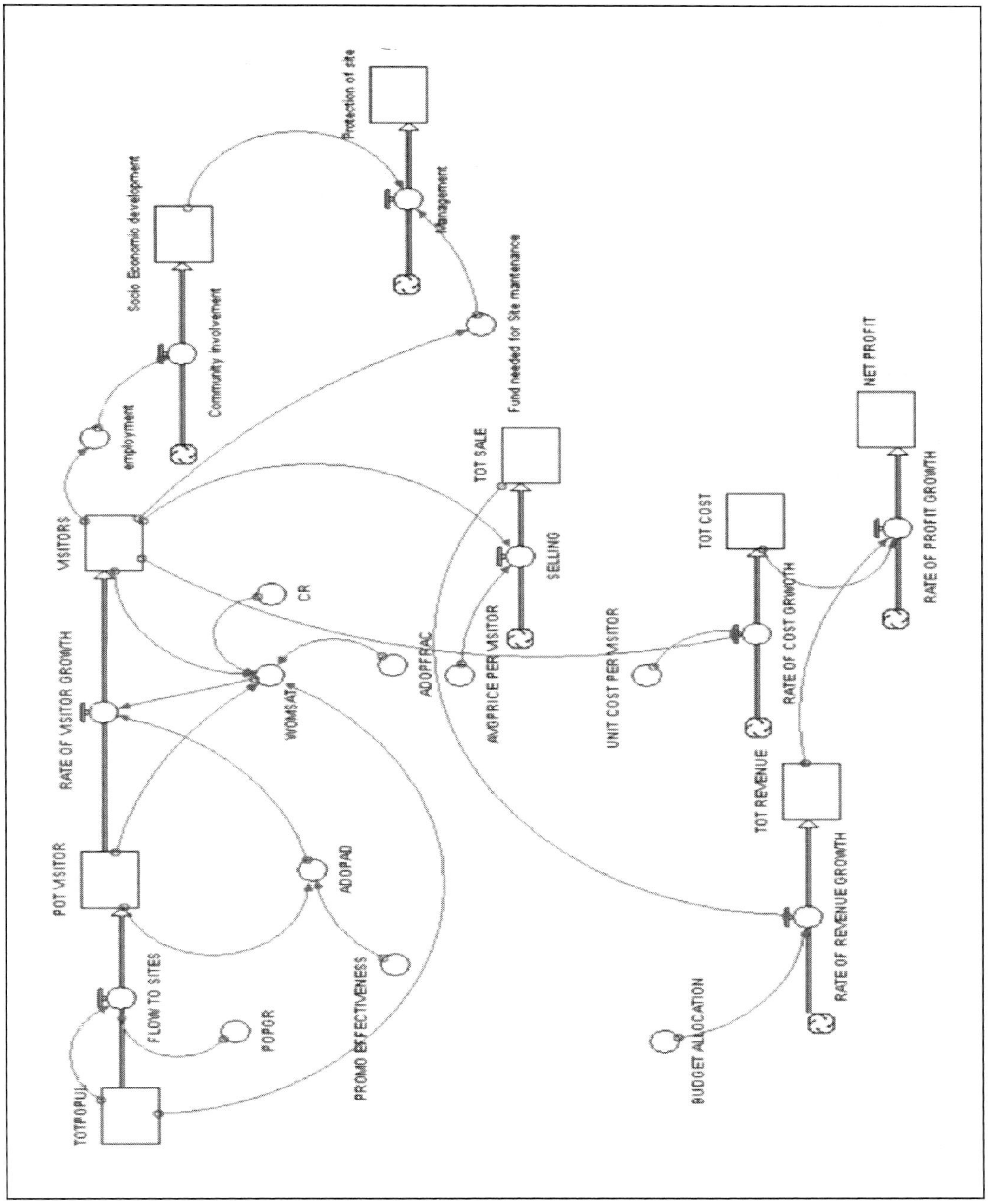

Figure 5: Model for sustainable development of rock art heritage site.

Assumptions of the Model

1. Conservation effort of heritage and environment are made in sufficient and effective manner.
2. Tourist activities are developed at a bearable distance from the rock art heritage site.
3. Rock art used to be a centre of attraction and the tourists are engaged beyond the site premises in other related activities.
4. Benefit sharing with local community people is the critical aspect of the model.
5. Tourism and related industry are the major source of revenue generation and economic development.
6. All the development efforts are followed by green (environment friendly) practices.

5.3.4. Analysis of the Model

It is a model applicable to all the protected rock art heritage sites in India.

1. Present model has emphasized to understand the behaviour of the visitors and the impact of their presence on other variables.
2. Net profit generated at the Heritage site and Socio-Economic development of the region are analysed along with the number of employments that can be produced and its impact on the dependent total population of the region, keeping Bhimbetka as datum for the real time data and model behaviour.
3. Behaviour of the system is over all positive in direction. But magnitude of positive movement is very slow. This magnitude of positive movement will not be sufficient to manage the economic, social and other pressures in proportion to their respective increase.

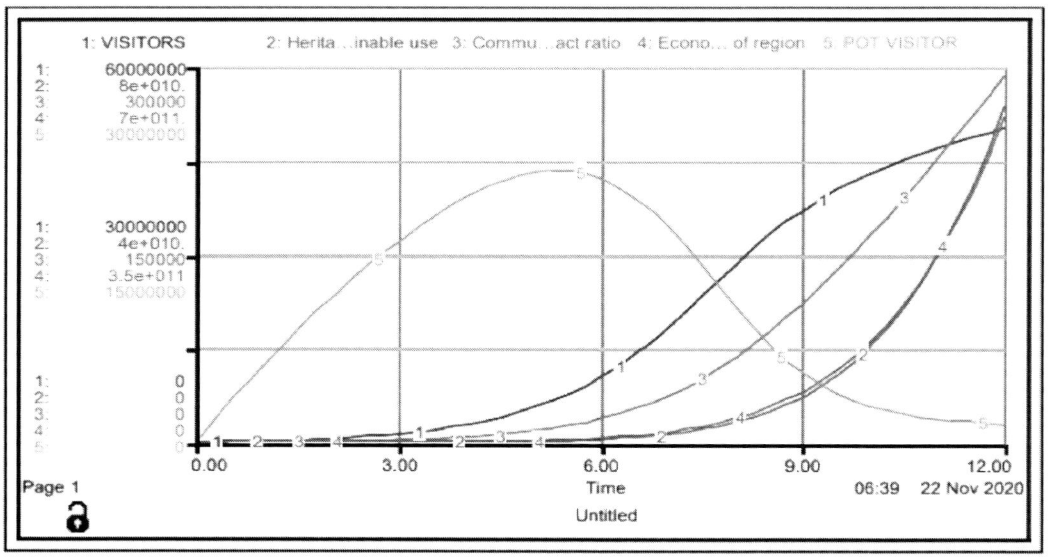

Figure 6: Behaviour of the Model and its variables in 48 years of Time Scale

4. Therefore, external economic triggers are needed to give a new and desired momentum to the system as needed by the policy makers.

5.3.5. Output of the Model

Out of all the variables, five most critical variables are selected in the graph to observe their trend on the long-term timeline of 48 years on the x - axis. The five variables are:

1. Visitors: Number 1.
2. Sustainable find for heritage: Number 2.
3. Community impact ratio: Number 3.
4. Economic development of the region: Number 4.
5. Potential visitors: Number 5.

Model is dependent on the visitors. It can be clearly observed from the graph that as the number of visitors is increased, its impact on community, economic development of the region and fund for sustainable use is increased positively and proportionally throughout the span of graph. The growth rate is very less in the beginning, but with due course of time the growth is exponential. This graph is continuously increasing till the potential visitors are exhausted. Now it is known that putting the limit on the potential visitors will decide the quantum of other variables dependent on them. That will usually depend on the visitor carrying capacity of the roc art heritage site and the target impact on the community people to achieve. It also precisely analyses the gap to manage by other economic activities. That will dependent on the location of site, population of forest dependent community(ies) and some other relevant factors of the site and in the surrounding area.

5.3.6. Sensitivity analysis of the Model

Sensitive analysis has been done to understand the behaviour of the whole system due to variation in the individual variables in it and their impact on the whole model. In this model two critical variables, 1. Promotional effectiveness, and 2. Adoption fraction, have been identified that have high impact on the visitor growth. Therefore, these also have proportional effect on the whole model of sustainable development of protected rock art heritage (Krishna 2021a, 2021b).

5.3.6.1. Sensitivity analysis of promotional effectiveness

In this analysis, values of the promotional effectiveness are fluctuating and the change in behaviour of the model is observed. In this respect two scenarios are observed. The impact on model is observed with the increase and decrease of the value of promotional effectiveness respectively (Krishna 2021a, 2021b).

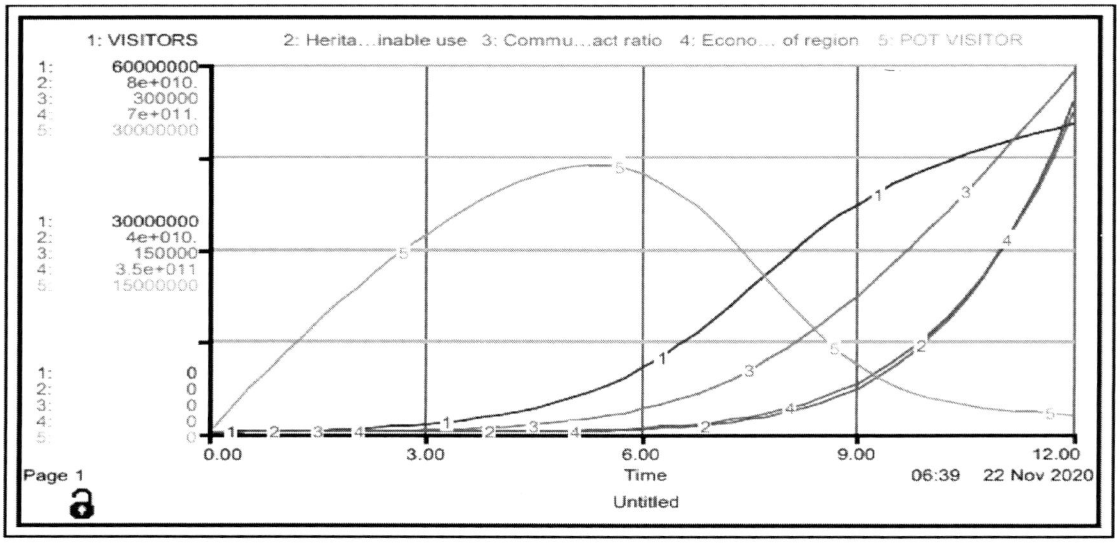

Figure 7: Graph for decreased values of the promotional effectiveness that is 0.0139

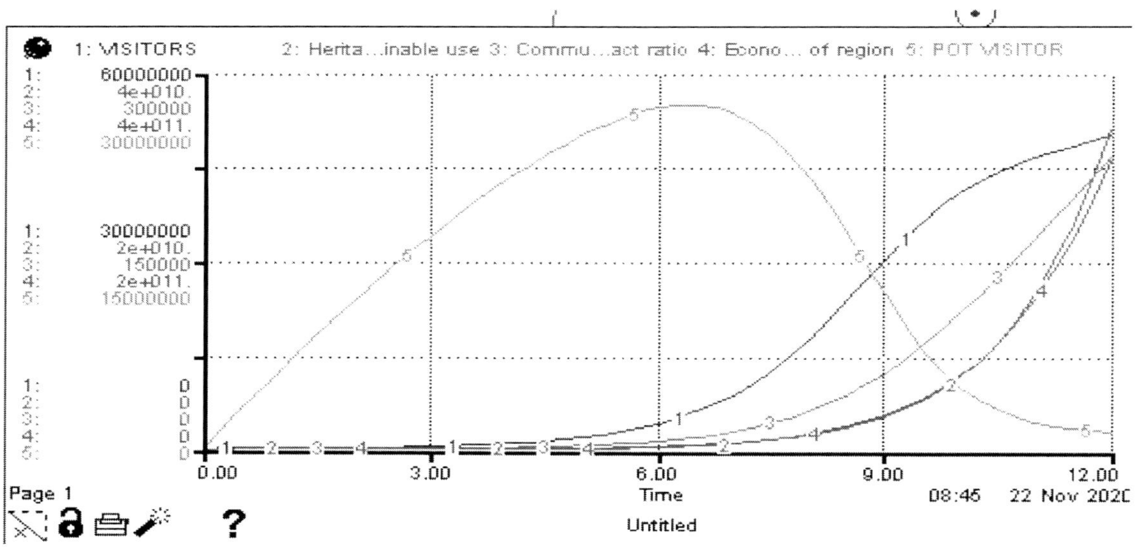

Figure 8: Graph for increased values of promotional effectiveness, that is 0.0739

Output values due to change in promotional effectiveness.

Table 6: Behavioural output of the model with respect to variation in promotional effectiveness

S. No.	*Variables*	*Values at 6th year from start point*		*No. of Visitors*	*Fund generated for sustainable use*
		Present value	0.0439%	289,442	6,488,046.16
1.	Promotional effectiveness	Decreased value	0.139%	92,709	5,178,243.20
		Increased value	0.739%	481659	7,803,616.53

It is clearly visible from the graphs and the values in the table that the behaviour of the model represents an overall decline in the output from present state if the values of promotional effectiveness is decreased and it will increase when the values of promotional effectiveness is increased. That makes the promotional effectiveness as the critical variable to manage the behaviour of the model or the system. Therefore, the promotional effectiveness must be managed with priority before going in decision making for development.

5.3.6.2. Sensitivity analysis of variable adoption fraction

The values of adoption fraction are varied and behaviour of the model output is studied in that perspective (Krishna 2021a, 2021b).

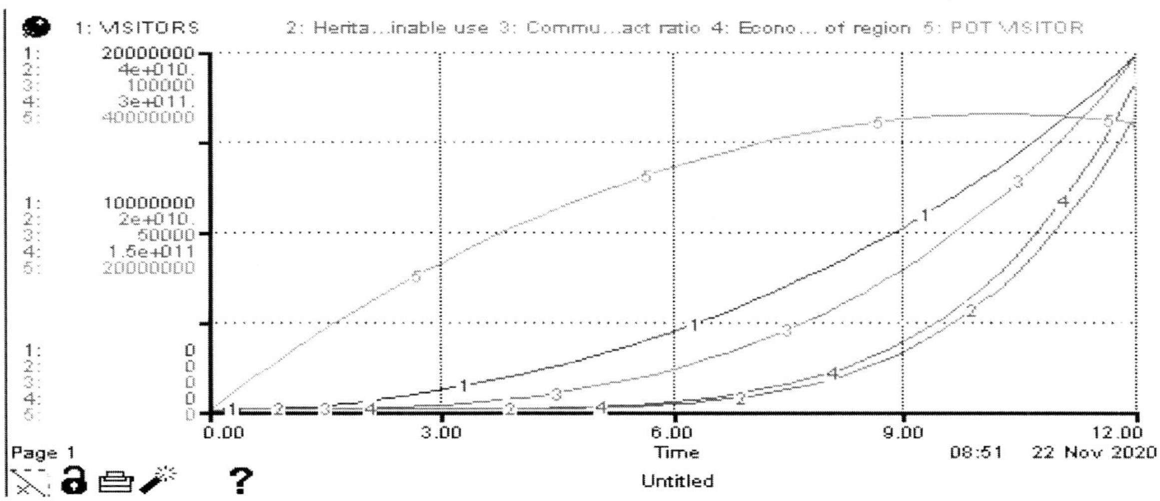

Figure 9: Graph for decreased value of adoption fraction, that is 0.0005

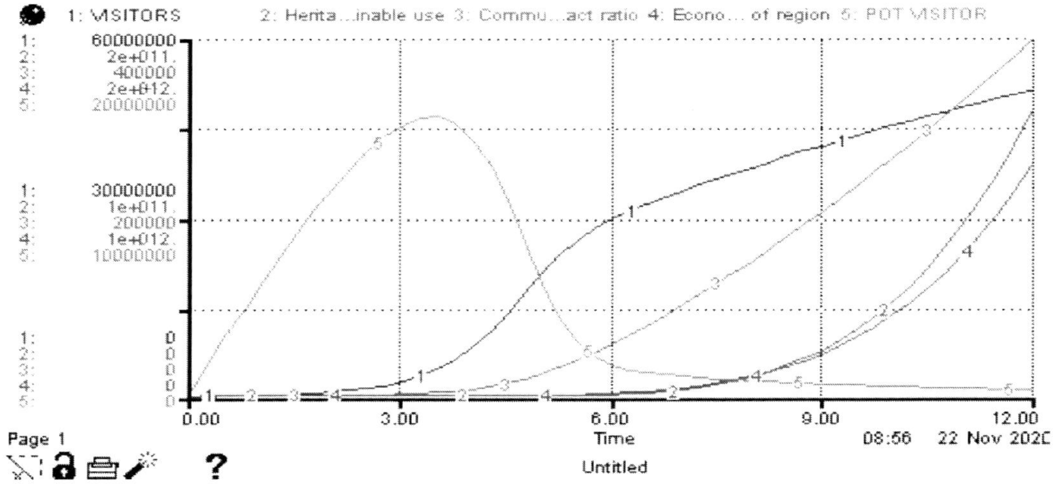

Figure 10: Graph for increased value of adoption fraction, that is 0.45

Table 7: Output of the critical variables of the model values

Variables	*Values at 6th year from initial start*	*values*	*Visitors*	*Fund generated sustainable use*
	Present value	.0015	2,89,442	6,488,046.16
	Decreased value	.0005	2,81,008	6,463,558.97
Adoption fraction	Increased value	.045	3,16,169	6,497,290.09

Behavioural output of the model with respect to variation in adoption fraction.

The study shows that fluctuating the variable adoption-fraction and analysing the system behaviour depicts that it has considerable impact on the output. Decreased value of variable slows decline in funds and increased value of the variable increases the output.

5.3.7. Scenario building for evaluation of the Model

Protection of rock art heritage and community population impact ratio is measured as an important output of the model. Project evaluation and review technique (PERT) is used to evaluate the three different case scenarios of community population impact ratio. Three cases taken viz., 1. most optimistic scenario, 2. most likely scenario, and 3. The pessimistic scenario. The number of visitors being one of the most critical factors in sustainable development and promotion of rock art heritage, the PERT equation is derived and analyzed based on visitors' value in the above discussed three cases.

1. Optimistic scenario (OT)– When the number of visitors reaches to 196,181.15 the value of Community population impact ratio is 15.11% of the community population.
2. Most likely scenario (MLT) – When the number of visitors reaches to 170,961.74, the value of Community population impact ratio is 10.39%.

3. Pessimistic scenario (PT)– When the number of visitors reaches to 168,569.03, the value of Community population impact ratio is 5.66%.

Calculating PERT weighted average equation using the equation [OT +(4 x MLT) + PT]/6. That is equal to [15.11 + (4 x 10.39) +5.66]/6 = 62.33/6= 10.38%.

This result, 10.38 growth percent shows very small deviation from the value of the, 2. Most likely case that is 10.39. That shows more stability in nature and outcome in terms of community impact ratio as a whole system of Bhimbetka rock art heritage site (Krishna 2021a, 2021b).

5.4. Model validation

5.4.1. Experts' validation

The model for sustainable development of protected rock art heritage site developed on the basis of the present research was sent to six eminent experts in the field viz. Prof. V. H. Sonawane, former Head, Department of Archaeology and Dean, Faculty of Arts, M. S. University, Baroda, Dr S. B. Ota, Jt. Director General (former), Archaeological Survey of India and Tagore National Fellow, Dr Giriraj Kumar, Prof. in Rock Art Science and Culture and Secretary General, Rock Art Society of India, Dr Om Prakash Mishra, Cultural Heritage Advisor to the Department of Tourism, Government of Madhya Pradesh, Bhopal, Mr Benny Kurian, Ecotourism and Sustainable Tourism Consultant, Veettal , Pangode, Kerala -682310, and Dr A. Pradhan, Deputy Curator (Exhibition), National Museum, New Delhi. All of them highly appreciated and validated the Model. Some of them also rendered their comments which are given below.

1. Comments by Dr S.B. Ota

(i) One should explain how the revenue generation can be done when the ownership is with forest department whereas the protection is by ASI.

(ii) Interpretation Centre is already on the cards when the land acquisition is completed.

(iii) For the communities living in buffer zone only the development should be planned based on their forest dependency. It is because we will have to retain and preserve the living heritage both tangible and intangible as per the UNESCO declaration of world heritage for Bhimbetka.

2. Comments by Prof. Giriraj Kumar

(i) The model you have developed for the sustainable development of rock art heritage sites appears to be more practical and feasible.

(ii) It will help in formulating the policies by the government for the management of rock art heritage sites.

3. Comments by Mr Benny Kurian

(i) Prior to the development of rock art heritage site, a thorough study of the site and its environment must be carried out in the perspective of culture, landscape, available natural resources, tangible and intangible knowledge of the local community dependent on the forest.

(ii) Responsible Rock Art Tourism (RT) with guided tours is a must for the sustainable development of the rock art heritage sites.

(iii) Participation and Involvement of the forest dependent people of the region in the rock art heritage management is necessary for the sustainable development of the rock art heritage sites.

(iv) Policy framework is required for sustainable conservation of heritage management through forest dependent community participation.

(v) Conduct tourism impact assessment study based on carrying capacity.

(vi) Through the application of the suggested model by Ram Krishna, the rock art heritage site can be protected and conserved without recurring external funding. The site itself can generate required funds for its own conservation and protection through responsible tourism.

(vii) Since the local stakeholders have rights and duties on the rock art heritage in responsible tourism (RT), continuous vigil and monitoring to protect the site from vandalism, weathering etc. would be possible.

4. Comments by Dr Arakhita Pradhan

It is a good attempt to present a Model for the sustainable development of rock art sites. My comments are as follows:

(i) The term "load bearing capacity" may be replaced with "Carrying Capacity"

(ii) The statement regarding, "Enough revenue should be generated" need more clarification as for Centrally protected sites under ASI, the entry fee is uniform for a category of Monument or sites. In a centrally protected monument, the central govt can levy entry fee which is acceptable to all, so how can we generate enough revenue. The expenditure part may be more, if the number of visitors is less. If we allow too much /excess visitors beyond carrying capacity, it will harm the rock art site directly or indirectly.

(iii) We may add, a point of Corporate Funding under CSR for protection of rock art site or for the sustainable development of rock art sites in India."

5.4.2. Event Validity

The model is tested on the data of UNESCO World heritage site Bhimbetka and compared the actual figures with model output.

1. When the visitor growth reached close to 65000, the value of impact on total population of employment is 10%, and
2. Fund generated for sustainable use is increased to INR 14.48 Lakh.

Thus, the output obtained from the model resembles the actual scenario of Management of Bhimbetka. The present research indicates that every rock art site has its own qualities, issues and challenges, still there are some fundamental issues common to all of them such as preservation of the rock art and immediate environment, generating the awareness about the cultural heritage, sustainability of the natural and cultural environment, feeling of connectedness with the heritage site and its environment, sensibilities and accountability for its preservation, etc. Therefore, the researcher has developed this model for sustainable development of rock art heritage. It gives a framework for sustainable development of the site in the perspective of the increase of the socioeconomic development of the region, with the assumption that the proper care has been taken for the conservation and management of the site and cultural environment. This model will help to build a practical scenario to understand the impact of the decisions on the variables and the overall behaviour of the rock art heritage system. Besides, it will also help them to take efficient decisions with respect to time, money and efforts.

6. Conclusion

Based on the present research the researcher has developed a dynamic model for sustainable development of rock art heritage. This model will help in the scenario building for sustainable development of a given rock art heritage site for the coming more than 50 years. It will help the policy makers and the managers to understand the behaviour of the rock art heritage system to take proper decisions for utilisations of the resources and energy in a judicial way for long term. If necessary, the model can be modified in the light of the comments of scholars in future.

Dr Ram Krishna
Joint Secretary, RASI; Assistant Professor in Business Management
Lovely Professional University, Phagwara, Jalandhar, Punjab, India
E-mail: ramkrishna.gem@gmail.com

References

Bednarik, R. G. 2007. *Rock Art Science: the scientific study of palaeoart.* Aryan Books International, New Delhi.

Bednarik, R. G. 2010. Indian Pleistocene rock art in a global context. *L'art pléistocène dans de monde, Actes du Congrès IFRAO, Tarascon-sur-Ariège*, 150–151.

Bednarik, R. G. 1994. Some suggestions for the management of Bhimbetka, with comments by M. N.

Deshpande, K. V. Soundara Rajan, R. C. Agrawal, V. H. Bedekar, G. Kumar and Tej Singh and Author's reply. *Purakala* 5 (1-2): 5–24.

Clottes, J. 2008. Rock art: An endangered heritage worldwide. *Journal of Anthropological Research, 64*(1): 1–18.

Europian Commission 2016. Prehistoric cave gets a makeover in the Ardeche, boosting tourism in the Rhone- Alpes. Europian Commission project. Retrieved from https://ec.europa.eu/regional_policy/en/projects/france/prehistoric-cave-gets-a-makeover-in-the-ardeche-boosting-tourism-in-the-rhone-alpes/

Krishna, R. 2021a. The Dynamics of Sustainable Development and Promotion of Bhimbetka: A UNESCO World Heritage Site. *Purakala* 30-31: 38–45.

Krishna, R. 2021b. Applied systems approach towards sustainable development of protected rock art heritage sites in India. Unpublished Ph. D. dissertation, Department of Management, Faculty of Social Sciences, Dayalbagh Educational Institute, Dayalbagh, Agra.

Kumar, G. 2015. *Rock Art of India.* Delhi: Sharada Publishing house.

Kumar, G. 2011a. Mission rock art: Padmashri Dr V.S. Wakankar memorial lecture. *Purakala* 20-21: 5–22.

Kumar, G. 2011b. Actualisation of rock art sites as monuments of human passion, adventure and creativity.

Rock art in modern Society-I. Kemerovo: Occasional publications of the Siberian Association of Prehistoric Art Researchers.

Kumar, G. 2014. Rock Art. In Dilip Chakrabarti and Makkhan Lal (eds), *History of Ancient India, Vol I:*

Prehistoric Roots, pp. 301-346. New Delhi: Vivekanand International Foundation and Aryan Books International.

Kumar, G 2015. IFRAO Rock art glossary, in *Rock art of India*, pp.161-195. Delhi: Sharda publishing house. *Prehistoric Roots*, pp 301-346. New Delhi: Vivekanand International Foundation and Aryan Books International.

Swami, S., Ghosh, D., and Charu, S. 2020. Sustainability indicators in supply chains. *Encyclopaedia of renewable and sustainable material* 5: 503–511.

Swami, S., Krishna, R., Charu, S., and Bahadur, A. 2021. Concept Paper: Developing standards for the sustainable development of rock art heritage sites: A business management perspective. *Purakala* 30-31: 29-32.

Sterman, J. 2002. Systems dynamics: Systems thinking and modelling for a complex world. PDF dspace.mit.edu/

UNESCO. 2017. *Intergovernmental committee for the protection of world culture and heritage.* Paris: UNESCO.

Undp, 2015. Synthesis of National reports for Rio+20. United Nations Development Programme (UNDP), Retrieved from https://www.undp.org/content/undp/en/home/librarypage/environment-energy/integrating_environmentintodevelopment/synthesis-of-national-reports-for-rio-20.html